THE NEW SOCIOLINGUISTICS READER

Ch. 18
23
21
7 22

The New Sociolinguistics Reader

Edited by

Nikolas Coupland and
Adam Jaworski

palgrave
macmillan

First published 2009 by
PALGRAVE MACMILLAN

Palgrave Macmillan in the UK is an imprint of Macmillan Publishers Limited, registered in England, company number 785998, of Houndmills, Basingstoke, Hampshire RG21 6XS.

Palgrave Macmillan in the US is a division of St Martin's Press LLC, 175 Fifth Avenue, New York, NY 10010.

Palgrave Macmillan is the global academic imprint of the above companies and has companies and representatives throughout the world.

Palgrave® and Macmillan® are registered trademarks in the United States, the United Kingdom, Europe and other countries.

ISBN-13: 978–1–4039–4414–6 hardback
ISBN-10: 1–4039–4414–8 hardback
ISBN-13: 978–1–4039–4415–3 paperback
ISBN-10: 1–4039–4415–6 paperback

This book is printed on paper suitable for recycling and made from fully managed and sustained forest sources. Logging, pulping and manufacturing processes are expected to conform to the environmental regulations of the country of origin.

A catalogue record for this book is available from the British Library.

A catalog record for this book is available from the Library of Congress.

10 9 8 7 6 5 4 3
18 17 16 15 14 13 12

Contents

Acknowledgements   x

1   Social Worlds through Language   ✓   1
    Nikolas Coupland and Adam Jaworski

PART I   LANGUAGE VARIATION

Editors' Introduction to Part I   23

2   Dialect in Society   35
    Walt Wolfram

3   The Social Stratification of (r) in
    New York City Department Stores   49
    William Labov

4   The Social Differentiation of English in Norwich   60
    Peter Trudgill

5   The Transmission Problem in Linguistic Change   66
    William Labov

6   *Be like*: The New Quotative in English   75
    Sali A. Tagliamonte

7   Network Structure and Linguistic Change   92
    James Milroy and Lesley Milroy

8   Demythologizing Sociolinguistics   106
    Deborah Cameron

9   Syntactic Variation and Beyond   119
    Jenny Cheshire

10 Ethnography and the Study of Variation   136
    Penelope Eckert

PART II LANGUAGE, GENDER AND SEXUALITY

Editors' Introduction to Part II 153

11 'Women's Language' or 'Powerless Language'? 159
   William M. O'Barr and Bowman K. Atkins

12 The Relativity of Linguistic Strategies: Rethinking
   Power and Solidarity in Gender and Dominance 168
   Deborah Tannen

13 Fraternity Men: Variation and Discourses of Masculinity 187
   Scott Fabius Kiesling

14 Masculinity Manoeuvres: Critical Discursive
   Psychology and the Analysis of Identity Strategies 201
   Margaret Wetherell and Nigel Edley

15 'Why Be Normal?': Language and Identity
   Practices in a Community of Nerd Girls 215
   Mary Bucholtz

16 Lip Service on the Fantasy Lines 229
   Kira Hall

17 Language and Identity in Drag Queen Performances 250
   Rusty Barrett

PART III STYLE, STYLIZATION AND IDENTITY

Editors' Introduction to Part III 259

18 Language Style as Audience Design 265
   Allan Bell

19 The Process of Communication Accommodation 276
   Howard Giles

20 Crossing, Ethnicity and Code-Switching 287
   Ben Rampton

21 Yorkville Crossing: White Teens, Hip-Hop, and
   African American English 299
   Cecilia Cutler

22 Dialect Style, Social Class and Metacultural
Performance: The Pantomime Dame 311
Nikolas Coupland

23 Refashioning and Performing Identities in Global Hip-Hop 326
Alastair Pennycook

PART IV LANGUAGE ATTITUDES, IDEOLOGIES AND STANCES

Editors' Introduction to Part IV 341

24 Social Class Differences and the Identification of
Sex in Children's Speech 349
John R. Edwards

25 Folk Linguistics 356
Nancy Niedzielski and Dennis R. Preston

26 Language-Ideological Processes 374
Judith T. Irvine and Susan Gal

27 Language Ideology and Spelling Reform: Discourses
of Orthography in the Debate over German 378
Sally Johnson

28 The Production and Reproduction of Language
Ideologies in Practice 390
Alexandra Jaffe

29 Linguistic Resources for Socializing Humanity 405
Elinor Ochs

PART V MULTILINGUALISM, CODE-SWITCHING AND DIGLOSSIA

Editors' Introduction to Part V 425

30 Language, Ethnicity and Racism 435
Joshua A. Fishman

31 Diglossia 447
Charles A. Ferguson

32 Language Change and Sex Roles in a Bilingual Community   457
    Susan Gal

33 Code-switching   473
    Carol Myers-Scotton

34 Bilingual Conversation   490
    Peter Auer

35 Linguistic and Educational Aspects of Tok Pisin   512
    Jeff Siegel

36 Language Rights   526
    Stephen May

37 Sociolinguistic Dimensions of Language Death   541
    Nancy C. Dorian

38 A Sociolinguistics of Globalization   560
    Jan Blommaert

PART VI   LANGUAGE, CULTURE AND INTERACTION

Editors' Introduction to Part VI   575

39 Models of the Interaction of Language and Social Life   583
    Dell Hymes

40 Contextualization Conventions   598
    John J. Gumperz

41 Poetics and Performance as Critical Perspectives
    on Language and Social Life   607
    Richard Bauman and Charles L. Briggs

42 Rules for Ritual Insults   615
    William Labov

43 Humour, Power and Gender in the Workplace   631
    Janet Holmes

44 Social Functions of Small Talk and Gossip   646
    Justine Coupland

45 Greetings in Tourist–Host Encounters   662
    Adam Jaworski

46   Creativity in Sign Languages   680
     Rachel Sutton-Spence

47   Speech Community and Beyond   694
     Ben Rampton

Other Resources for Studying Sociolinguistics   714

Index   729

Acknowledgements

The authors and publishers wish to thank the following for permission to use copyright material:

Richard Bauman and Charles L. Briggs, for material from 'Poetics and performance as critical perspectives on language and social life', *Annual Review of Anthropology*, 19 (1990), pp. 60–61, 72–78, by permission of *Annual Reviews*.

Allan Bell, for material from 'Language style as audience design', in *Sociolinguistics: A Reader and Coursebook*, ed. N. Coupland and A. Jaworski, Palgrave Macmillan (1997), pp. 240–249, by permission of the author.

Mary Bucholtz, for material from 'Why be normal?: Language and identity practices in a community of nerd girls', *Language in Society*, 28(2) (1999), pp. 211–223, table 1, by permission of Cambridge University Press.

Deborah Cameron, for material from 'Demythologizing sociolinguistics: Why language does not reflect society', in *Ideologies of Language*, ed. J. E. Joseph and T. J. Taylor, Routledge (1990), pp. 79–83. Copyright © 1990 by Routledge, by permission of Taylor & Francis Books, UK.

Nancy C. Dorian, for material from *Language Death: The Life Cycle of a Scottish Gaelic Dialect* (1981), pp. 1–8, 98–113, by permission of the University of Pennsylvania Press.

Penelope Eckert, for figure 13.7 from 'The whole woman: Sex and gender differences in variation', *Language Variation and Change*, 1 (1989), pp. 245–267 (included in William Labov, 'The transmission problem in linguistic change'), by permission of Cambridge University Press.

John Edwards, for material from 'Social class differences and the identification of sex in children's speech', *Journal of Child Language*, 6 (1979), pp. 121–127, table 22.1, figure 22.2, by permission of Cambridge University Press.

Joshua A. Fishman, for material from 'Language, ethnicity and racism', in *Georgetown University Round Table on Languages and Linguistics (GURT)*

1977: Linguistics and Anthropology, ed. M. Saville-Troike (1977), pp. 297–309, Copyright © 1977 Georgetown University Press. Reprinted with permission. www.press.georgetown.edu.

Susan Gal, for material from 'Peasant men can't get wives: Language change and roles in a bilingual community', *Language in Society*, 7(1) (1978), pp. 1–16, tables 29.1–29.4, by permission of Cambridge University Press.

John J. Gumperz, for material from 'Contextualization conventions', in *Discourse Strategies* by John J. Gumperz (1982), pp. 130–152, by permission of Cambridge University Press.

Kira Hall, for material from 'Lip service on the fantasy lines', in *Gender Articulated: Language and the Socially Constructed Self*, ed. Kira Hall and Mary Bucholtz, Routledge (1995), pp. 183–216, by permission of Copyright.com.

Dell Hymes, for material from 'Models of the interaction of language and social life', in *Directions in Sociolinguistics: The Ethnography of Communication*, ed. John J. Gumperz and Dell Hymes (1986), pp. 35–71, by permission of Blackwell Publishing.

Judith T. Irvine and Susan Gal, for material from 'Language ideology and linguistic differentiation', in *Regimes of Language: Ideologies, Polities, and Identities*, ed. Paul V. Kroskrity (2000), pp. 35–79. Copyright © 2000 by the School for Advanced Research, Santa Fe, by permission of SAR Press.

William Labov, for material from 'The social stratification of (r) in New York city department stores', in *Sociolinguistic Patterns* by William Labov (1972), pp. 43–54, figs. 2.1, 2.2, tables 2.1, 2.2, by permission of the University of Pennsylvania Press; 'The transmission problem in linguistic change', in *Principles of Linguistic Change: Social Factors* by William Labov (2001), pp. 415–438, by permission of Blackwell Publishing; and 'Rules for Ritual Insults', in *Studies in Social Interaction*, ed. David Sudnow (1972), pp. 297–353. Copyright © 1972 by The Free Press, renewed © 2000 by David Sudnow, by permission of The Free Press, a division of Simon & Schuster Adult Publishing Group.

James Milroy and Lesley Milroy, for material from 'Network structure and linguistic change', in *Linguistic Variation and Change: On the Historical Sociolinguistics of English* by James Milroy (1992), pp. 176–191, by permission of Blackwell Publishing.

William O'Barr and Bowman K. Atkins, for material from 'Women's language' or 'powerless language?', in *Women and Language in Literature and*

Society, ed. McConnell-Ginet et al., Praeger (1980), pp. 93–110, by permission of Greenwood Publishing Group, Inc.

Elinor Ochs, for material from 'Linguistic resources for socializing humanity', in *Rethinking Linguistic Relativity*, ed. John J. Gumperz and Stephen C. Levinson (1996), pp. 407–437, by permission of Cambridge University Press.

Deborah Tannen, for material from 'The relativity of linguistic strategies: Rethinking power and solidarity in gender and dominance', in *Gender and Conversational Interaction*, ed. Deborah Tannen (1993), pp. 165–188, by permission of Oxford University Press.

Peter Trudgill, for material from 'The co-variation of phonological variables with social parameters', in *The Social Differentiation of English in Norwich* by Peter Trudgill (1974), pp. 90–95, tables 14.1–14.3, fig. 14.1, by permission of Cambridge University Press.

Walt Wolfram, for material from 'Dialect in society', in *Handbook of Sociolinguistics*, ed. Florian Coulmas (1997), pp. 107–126, by permission of Blackwell Publishing.

Every effort has been made to trace the copyright holders, but if any have been inadvertently overlooked the publishers will be pleased to make the necessary arrangement at the first opportunity.

CHAPTER 1

Social Worlds through Language

NIKOLAS COUPLAND AND ADAM JAWORSKI

Sociolinguistics is often loosely defined as 'the study of language in society', or 'the study of language in its social contexts'. Simple formulas like these are hard to avoid, and they do have their place, especially when we meet an academic discipline for the first time and when we need to get some perspective on it. What is it all about? What does it do? What are its priorities? 'Studying language in society' is not an unreasonable first attempt at defining what Sociolinguistics is about and what it does, but of course it is more of a slogan than a definition, and it might be misleading. Our own slogan (in the sub-title to this chapter) is a different one – studying 'social worlds through language' – and it might at least have the advantage of opening up a discussion about the status of 'language' and 'society' in Sociolinguistics. Is Sociolinguistics a sort of linguistics (as the word itself seems to imply), and if so, of what sort? Or is it a sort of social science (if that is what we would call the study of 'social worlds'), and in that case what do we mean by 'social' here? But also, we might ask how sensible it is to maintain a distinction between language and society, and whether we actually have to approach Sociolinguistics with this sort of duality in mind. These are some of the issues we will work through in this introductory chapter.

The debate about linguistic versus social priorities has featured in the 50-year history of Sociolinguistics. There have been times when it seemed important to recognize that there were rather distinct treatments of 'language in society' in the field. Such differences related to the diverse disciplinary origins of Sociolinguistics and to its 'founding fathers' (which is, of course, a sociolinguistically note-worthy expression). For example the Sociology of Language (see Joshua Fishman's chapter in Part V of this book) applied sociological models to help us appreciate how different languages were placed in different sorts of multilingual settings. In contrast, some people felt that the term Sociolinguistics should be reserved for analyses of those more small-scale linguistic items, such as accents and dialects (more like some of the studies in Part I), where the technical resources of phonetics and syntactic analysis were needed. Other distinctions recognized that there was a more psychological and subjectively focused 'wing' of Sociolinguistics (see some of the chapters in Part IV); and there was certainly an influential anthropological and culturally focused 'wing' (see Part VI). Because 'language in society' obviously includes the study of how people interact socially, Interactional Sociolinguistics came to be a recognized sub-division, and here we start to see an important overlap between Sociolinguistics and Discourse Analysis (for a comprehensive treatment of Discourse Analysis and its close links with Sociolinguistics, see Jaworski and Coupland 2006).

Although it is still possible to trace these different strands of Sociolinguistics in this way, we have in fact designed this book to reflect what we think is quite a strong *consensus* of opinion in modern Sociolinguistics about the field's priorities and theoretical assumptions, and about how we should deal with the interface between language and society. Although any academic discipline sustains differences of emphasis and approach, and sometimes a good bit of wrangling about priorities, Sociolinguistics has settled around several key principles and orientations that give it a significant degree of unity, despite its extremely broad reach – into vastly different social, cultural and linguistic contexts. Sociolinguistics is now a broad and vibrant interdisciplinary project working *across* the different disciplines that were its origins. We are therefore able to move on from the old debates about the conflicting priorities and 'schools' of Sociolinguistics, and we will use this introductory chapter to highlight some of the key points of agreement. In the different Parts of the Reader, despite the different topics and social issues that they address, it will be possible to see Sociolinguistic converging around very largely the same sets of perspectives. So, for example, Part I deals with the 'variationist' approach to structured differences in accent and dialect usage, and within it we can easily trace a shift from 'classical', descriptive approaches to sociolinguistic variation (in the chapters by William Labov and Peter Trudgill in Part I) through to more critical, interactional and ethnographic perspectives (in chapters by Jenny Cheshire and Penelope Eckert). It is much the same shift as the one we see in Part II between more formal treatments of 'women's language' and 'powerful language' (for example, in William O'Barr and Bowman Atkins's chapter) through to, for example, Mary Bucholtz's and Rusty Barrett's chapters. As we will see below, both these sub-fields and Sociolinguistics generally have incorporated (and have indeed taken the lead in developing) more 'social constructionist' approaches to language, situation and social action. What is shared across the full range of modern Sociolinguistics is, we think, more striking than the differences between different approaches.

We have organized the next sections of this introduction around the concepts of *the linguistic* and *the social*, picking up on the core question that we started with – of how Sociolinguistics makes sense of these fundamental concepts. Our main argument will be that, in contemporary Sociolinguistics, it is actually unhelpful to force these constructs too far apart. We will show how the concept of *social practice* has in many ways dissolved the distinction between 'language' and 'society'. Even so, we will comment on 'the linguistic' and 'the social' in turn, mainly to show the range of phenomena and issues that turn out to be sociolinguistically important in respect of each. In a later section we then consider the theoretical underpinnings of modern Sociolinguistics, exploring what sociolinguists nowadays believe they can achieve through their analyses. After that, we have a section on the research methods that are used in sociolinguistic research, where we overview the main orientations to linguistic and social data. We will continue to make some passing references to later chapters, but not exhaustively. We will introduce the contents and main arguments of the six different Parts of the book in separate short editors' introductions. In a final section of the book we list some further study resources that are currently available to students and researchers.

social practis

'The Linguistic' in Sociolinguistics

What sorts of linguistic phenomena and processes is Sociolinguistics concerned with? We should start with the notion of *diversity*, because, in contrast to many other academic approaches to language, Sociolinguistics is committed to revealing and explaining differences (and indeed different sorts of differences) in how language is used in social life. Everyday references to linguistic diversity might be made using labels and categories such as the following:

> *Yorkshire dialect*
> *the New York City accent*
> *the Hindi language*
> *childish laughter*
> *newspaper editorials*
> *slang*
> *political speeches*
> *small talk*

In each case we are dealing with some supposed 'type of language' which exists in some sort of system of differentiation. (Sociolinguists tend to use the term *variety of language* as a neutral expression to refer to any distinctive way of speaking or writing. So all of the above could be said to be different linguistic varieties, although that doesn't take us very far.)

Michael Halliday (1978) suggested that varieties of language could be organized into two broad sets. The first could be said to show *dialect* variation, in the sense that they mainly reflect 'who the user of language is' (his or her social origins and experience). The second set shows *register* variation, in the sense that they reflect 'what the use of the language is' (what communicative purpose exists and how the language fits into a social context). In these terms, our first four examples could be said to show dialect or 'user' variation, even though we would have to accept a fairly abstract sense of the term 'dialect', because for other purposes we would of course want to establish distinctions between accents and dialects, and between accent/dialect and language. The last four examples would then illustrate register or 'use' variation. A newspaper editorial is, we might argue, linked more to a social context and channel of communication than to a type of user. But we can immediately spot further complications. If we hear something we want to call 'childish laughter', we might well be reacting to a particular use or register of language as much as to a category of language user, and presumably it isn't only 'children' who laugh or speak 'childishly'. Small talk is certainly a particular use (or set of uses) of language (see Justine Coupland's chapter in Part VI), but when we say someone is 'doing small talk', we are probably making some inferences about the speaker's 'type' in some sense or other too. In fact Halliday's main point was that dialect and register are two sides of the same coin. The meaning and significance of any communicative act relates to *both* users *and* uses simultaneously, and to the interaction between them. Very commonly, what is distinctive about a particular variety of language is that it is not only linked to a specific social context but to a specific set of users. Political speeches are rather obviously distinctive both for how they are placed institutionally (they are part of the process of political decision-making) and situationally (they usually happen in government chambers of some sort) *and* for the people who tend to deliver them (they are usually made by people we call 'politicians').

Sociolinguistics has made enormous advances in the analysis of dialect variation (in the more conventional sense of the term dialect) since the days of traditional dialectology (Chambers and Trudgill 1998, and see some of the chapters in Part I), but without losing touch with those early forays into dialect geography. It is conventional to distinguish between *regional* and *social dialects*, where 'social' mainly refers to social class, gender and perhaps age-related varieties of language, as opposed to the familiar idea of dialects being separated across regions or geographical space. Accent then refers to variation only at the level of pronunciation, as opposed to dialect which includes pronunciation differences but also differences at the level of grammar and vocabulary. Varieties we refer to as 'languages' (distinct language codes such as Hindi, English or Spanish) are usually quite distant from each other in their grammatical forms, their vocabularies and in how they build patterns of meaning at the level of discourse, but sometimes they are quite close. To that extent, differences between languages can be very much like differences between dialects, and there is sometimes ambiguity in whether we should refer to a particular variety as a distinct language rather than a dialect. The political implications of this distinction are of course potentially enormous. For example, Stephen May's chapter in Part V comments on defining linguistic varieties as 'dialects' or 'languages' as a 'language rights' issue. Referring to one's way of speaking as 'a language' creates a sense of greater independence and autonomy than is afforded by the term 'dialect'. Likewise, consider the case of 'black' or African American Vernacular English; there is usually a legitimacy around 'using a different language' which can be denied to 'having a different dialect'. Although some languages are certainly subject to heavy social stigmatization (see, for example, Jeff Siegel's chapter in Part V), 'non-standard' dialects of 'standard languages' such as English quite regularly attract social stigma, relative to their 'standard' equivalents (see Nancy Niedzielski and Dennis Preston's chapter in Part IV).

In this (so far rather elementary) discussion of sociolinguistic perspectives on 'the linguistic', we are taking several things for granted. First, we are assuming that speech rather than writing is sociolinguists' main concern. Despite significant research on writing systems and literacies (see Sally Johnson's chapter in Part IV) and sign languages (see Rachel Sutton-Spence's chapter in Part VI), speech has indeed been the main focus in Sociolinguistics, and this can be justified in several important ways. Speech arguably has primacy over writing, in biological, cognitive, historical and developmental terms. Speech comes earliest in human development (for each of us individually, as well as in the evolution of communication) and is deeply coded; competence in writing is afforded high status, but writing is a secondary or overlaid system. Speaking is important to cultural learning and transmission; so is writing, but speaking 'comes first' and it is the primary means by which we are socialized into our families and communities. Speaking is also important in the formulation and expression of people's social identities and relationships (see the following section), and so on. These are some of the conventional justifications for focusing on speech, speaking and spoken interaction or 'talk' in Sociolinguistics. Even so, an important recent development has been to approach analysis in *multi*-modal frameworks, which are sensitive to the interplay between visual and spoken communicative modalities. This wider view is particularly important when we turn to the analysis of cultural rituals and routines as well as in relation to performance events of all sorts. Ultimately, it would be a mistake to restrict the study of 'language' in Sociolinguistics to the study of speech.

Another taken-for-granted assumption in our discussion of varieties of language – and one that has become contentious in contemporary Sociolinguistics – is that it is reasonable to work with *objectified* representations of linguistic varieties, as in the eight labelled examples above. Although there is nothing unusual about expressions like 'Yorkshire dialect' and 'the New York accent' – we find them throughout everyday discourse – there are quite severe limitations to these concepts as analytic categories in Sociolinguistics. One reason is straightforward and based on the problem of describing such categories in a fully coherent way. There is no simple uniformity in how people speak in the northern English county of Yorkshire, and this is immediately apparent when we look into individuals' and social groups' patterns of language use – over time, across genders and ages, across social classes, and so on. Even individual speakers will use 'Yorkshire' speech features variably, for example, in the different social settings they find themselves in and in the different 'registers' that they use. So 'Yorkshire dialect' is clearly an idealized concept. This label has some analytic coherence only if we treat it as a general social *norm* against which more variable and particular ways of speaking can be assessed. The same would be true for 'standard English', which for some speakers in Yorkshire might define an alternative norm. These problems will return in our discussion of 'the social', below.

The objectification of sociolinguistic varieties is troublesome in other ways too; it is not merely the problem that there is always more detectable linguistic variation than can be reflected in the variety label. We have to recognize that labelling as a linguistic activity is fundamentally *ideological*, and this has been the theme of a good deal of research conducted in critical linguistics (for example, Kress 1985). That is, we should ask why some labels come to be used and not others, and whose interests are served by particular ways of referring to social and linguistic categories and not others. This is an important concern in the Sociolinguistics of 'the social', but it applies to reflexive processes of categorizing linguistic varieties too. There is rather little political heat around the category 'Yorkshire dialect', but in other cases there is much more. Just as 'a language' has been said to be 'a dialect with an army and a navy' (see Irvine and Gal's chapter in Part IV), so there are ideological implications in referring to a linguistic variety (an accent or a dialect) as 'standard' versus 'non-standard'. This usage has been conventional in Sociolinguistics for some time and sociolinguists have felt they have been using the terms in a neutral way; that has certainly been their intention. But it is difficult to convince others that 'standard' is not an alternative expression for 'correct'. The politics of 'standard English' have been widely debated (for example, Bex and Watts 1999), but it is only recently that there has been more concerted consideration of the normalizing processes of sociolinguistic analysis. Accepting the importance of ideology critique in Sociolinguistics has been one of the most striking shifts in recent years, and it has led to an upsurge of research interest in how values are attributed to sociolinguistic varieties (see Part IV).

Another problem with the objectification of linguistic variation – the most fundamental problem – is how it reduces our view of language use to a set of static categories, when language use is experienced by users themselves as a complex set of social *processes*. That is, we get a static rather than a dynamic view of how the phenomenon that sociolinguists call 'language variation' is generated in the human activities of speaking and communicating. If we refer to a variety as 'the Hindi language' we treat it as a 'thing', and the 'thing-ness' of such concepts encourages us to view them as social objects, amenable to being described feature by feature in structural terms, either qualitatively (listing their linguistic characteristics) or quantitatively (counting how often particular features are used, when and by whom). For example, we might try to distinguish 'slang' (as an objectified category) from other spoken styles simply by listing the words and phrases that 'are slang' or 'are not slang'. We would then get very little sense of what it *means*, in a social sense, to 'use slang' and of what is achieved in the social world when people engage in this way of speaking. Here we are confronting a basic distinction between linguistic *form* and communicative *function*. There was some very illuminating discussion of form versus function in some early sociolinguistic theorizing (see for example, Dell Hymes's chapter in Part VI, and Hymes 1974), which is still very valuable. Overall, there has been a steady shift away from formalist approaches to sociolinguistic description towards a more integrated approach – understanding how linguistic forms are used *in the context of communicative functions*, and these were Hymes's priorities from the outset.

'Function' is itself a broad concept, and it has become more centrally relevant in Sociolinguistics in a range of different senses. One of them relates to *social meaning*, as we suggested above. While it is possible to describe patterns of difference in language use (for example, asking how 'men's speech' differs from 'women's speech', or asking which languages are used in which social settings in which communities), it is also necessary to explain those patterns in relation to their significance *for speakers and listeners themselves*. Even the phrase 'which languages' might need to be put into scare quotes, because many speakers may not find the notion of using distinct languages particularly apposite or necessary. Bilingual speakers commonly communicate using the resources of 'more than one language' in creative ways, without maintaining a clear separation between codes. Sociolinguistic analysis needs to be 'emic' (explaining meaningful differences) rather than simply 'etic' (describing formal differences and distributions), and an analyst's 'etic' categories may not match speakers' 'emic' understandings. The implications here are considerable, and we will see that 'emic' analysis often requires particular sorts of research methods and orientations to sociolinguistic data.

Another important aspect of a functional perspective is to understand the *indirect* relationship between a linguistic form and social functions. Any particular linguistic form (a feature or a variety) is very unlikely to fulfil, always and only, the same social function. To take an obvious instance, people who use 'the New York City accent' (which we have already said is far too general a description to be used in any technical sense) need not do so in order to 'mark a New York City identity'. Vernacular speech in any given urban environment could, for example, be used to help symbolize an aggressive stance, or to mark a speaker's low status or authority, or for humorous purposes, or to decrease the symbolic distance between the speaker and a similar-sounding listener, and so on. That is, in the 'social' dimension of Sociolinguistics (see below) we need to understand how particular social contexts of language use allow speakers to perform potentially subtle and complex communicative functions. Correspondingly, an adequate linguistic approach has to use concepts that allow us to explain how linguistic forms are socially and contextually embedded.

This necessarily involves drawing on explanatory resources that were originally developed in Discourse Analysis, Conversation Analysis and various interactional approaches in Sociology (see some of the chapters in Part VI). These fields (DA and CA) are nowadays part of the general sociolinguistic programme rather than lying outside it. Every main theme dealt with in this volume benefits from incorporating some interactional/discourse-analytic perspective, whether it is the analysis of sociolinguistic style (for example, Ben Rampton's chapter in Part III), the analysis of language ideologies (for example, Alexandra Jaffe's chapter in Part IV), or the analysis of multilingualism (for example, Jan Blommaert's chapter in Part VI). The theoretical impetus for this has come from research in a variety of traditions, including work on cultural performance (for example, Richard Bauman and Charles Briggs's chapter in Part VI), on sociolinguistic styling and stylization (for example, Coupland 2007; Rampton 1995, 2006) and interactional approaches to language and context (for example, Bucholtz and Hall 2004; Duranti and Goodwin 1992).

In these ways Sociolinguistics has progressively added a *social action* perspective to the *social structure* perspective that dominated at least some parts of the field in earlier decades. 'The linguistic' in Sociolinguistics nowadays needs to account for what speakers, seen as *social actors* or *agents*, are able to achieve (functionally) when they use the *resources* of linguistic diversity. The relationship between structure and action/agency is not, however, one of simple opposition. The sociolinguistic consensus is that we need to keep both structure and agency in the picture. For example, speakers do not come into communicative events without any structured history of sociolinguistic usage, or without a repertoire of sociolinguistic experiences or knowledge of the normative values of sociolinguistic varieties and performances. It is 'structure' in this sense that provides the resources for social action (as Allan Bell notes in his chapter in Part III). This general approach is fully consistent with general theories of language in social practice (Bourdieu 1991; Eckert and McConnell-Ginet 1992), and it is increasingly common for sociolinguistic analysis to be presented as a critical commentary on particular instances of *social practice*. Practice is a more specific concept than action. It suggests regular or routine language activity that has some progressively established social or cultural value. As we will see below, this shift has impacted even more clearly on sociolinguistic approaches to social groups and situations, where the concept of *communities of practice* has been increasingly used.

Finally, in this section, it is important to mention that 'the linguistic' can take either material or more abstract form in Sociolinguistics. In the examples we have considered so far, 'language use' has referred to the observable speech and communicative practices of social actors in particular social situations. It is the sort of data that one can capture through audio- or video-recording, and observation is the mainstream research method in the field (see below). But when we are dealing with ideologies and Discourses – sometimes called 'big D Discourses', in the spirit of Michel Foucault's philosophical and critical theories (for example, Foucault 1977) – we are referring to culturally significant but *latent*, hidden, abstract patterns or 'formations' of 'language'. The idea is that normative cultural understandings of social life are drawn together in ideological Discourses that guide our social actions. Overt language use (the construction of particular spoken or written 'texts') can then be said to be an articulation – or more likely a partial articulation – of a particular Discourse. There are obvious problems of method and interpretation when we treat 'language' this way. But it is also true that an appreciation of 'language in society' does need to go beyond the material 'stuff' of speech and writing. Indeed this principle is already established in the appeals to communicative function and social meaning, where analysis of linguistic form is recognized to be only a first step.

'The Social' in Sociolinguistics

With the concept of social practice we can already see why 'the linguistic' and 'the social' cannot be very clearly separated from each other in Sociolinguistics. Language use is a key element of social practice, but it is practices that generate the meanings that we take to define our social lives. (This is what Elinor Ochs means by 'socializing humanity' in her chapter in Part IV.) To take one example, it might have been possible to approach the sociolinguistic analysis of humorous language in the workplace in a mainly structural way, rather than through the interactional/functional perspective that Janet Holmes adopts (see her chapter in Part VI). Research on this topic might have set up categories of various sorts – types of workplaces, different sorts of social groups, types of humour, lists of 'humorous behaviours' that speakers might use – and then analysed their distributions. But the point about humour is that, as Holmes shows, it is a resource for creating various experiences of workplace interaction. It is humour – and how it figures in, and in opposition to, discourse processes of many other sorts – that gives 'workplace language' its institutional qualities. 'The workplace', and a sense of 'the social' generally, is very much achieved through how language is used – agentively and often creatively by speakers – and through how it is interpreted – by listeners who bring sets of background norms and expectations to bear on their understandings.

For many years, however, some approaches in Sociolinguistics relied on overly simple, structural models of 'society' (see Deborah Cameron's chapter in Part I critiquing early approaches). One of the great achievements of early sociolinguistic research was to establish that intuitively obvious social categories such as social class, gender and age could be reliably correlated with patterns of spoken language use. From a more contemporary perspective, this correlational design is not sufficient in itself. The point is certainly *not* that these correlations are 'meaningless'. After all, they are part of 'what we know' about sociolinguistic diversity, part of our *communicative competence* as language users in particular social environments (again see Dell Hymes in Part VI, also Hymes 1996), and, as above, they may be parts of the normative understandings that we use as resources for social action. But sociolinguists came to recognize the need to work out *which* social categories were most relevant for language users (the 'emic' approach that we mentioned above), *how* they were relevant, and how they came to be so. Rushing too quickly to explanations based on 'etic' demographic taxonomies (such as 'working class' versus 'middle class', 'male' versus 'female', or 'old' versus 'young') came to be thought of as *essentialist* or essentializing. Essentialism is 'the reductive tendency by analysts to designate a particular aspect of a person or group as explanations for their behaviour: the "essence" of what it means, for instance, to be Asian, or Indian, or female' (Mendoza-Denton 2004: 476).

Once again, the key to this shift in contemporary Sociolinguistics is the idea of social action, asking how we create and fill out our 'sociality' (our sense and experience of being social actors in social situations) through our social actions and therefore through our language use. This perspective required a parallel change in how Sociolinguistics theorized *social identity*, which is inevitably a central concept in the field. It was recognized early on that distinctive ways of using language were often associated with people's sense of belonging to a particular social group and of distinguishing themselves from members of other social groups. Using 'Yorkshire dialect' (notwithstanding the complications we considered earlier) might well for many people be a symbolically important practice in presenting themselves (and presenting themselves to themselves as well as to others) as being 'Yorkshire people'. This is the *indexical* function of sociolinguistic diversity – language differences indexing social distinctiveness (see Elinor Ochs' and Judith Irvine and Susan Gal's chapters in Part IV). But indexicality (like identity) is all-too-readily over-simplified.

It has become important to resist the assumption that people's social identities are 'given', inherited 'naturally' from the social structures that they inhabit. That is, someone born in New York City may *or may not* identify in any durable sense with the city – this subjective orientation might not be particularly important in their sense of self (personal identity) or in their ingroup and outgroup alignments (social identity). 'Being a New Yorker' may *or may not* be something that they (a) recognize at all as being important to them; (b) take to 'essentially' define themselves; or (c) regularly (if only intermittently) use in some practical way in their negotiation of social relationships. Even if they do have a durable 'New Yorker' identity, it will inevitably be an identity that (d) competes with many other sorts of social identification, such as 'being American', 'being a woman', 'being a sales representative', and so on, that may be much more salient to them at particular times and particular forms of practice. And there is no reason to suppose that all 'New Yorkers' will use the sociolinguistic resource of 'sounding New York' to the same extent or in the same ways. And finally, we would have to bear in mind that people's identities are not fully within their own control or their own experiences. What we call 'our identity' is often constructed for us, when other people *attribute* social characteristics to us or position us as members of social groups. All in all then, Sociolinguistics now emphasizes the importance of viewing social identities as being *multiple*, *fluid* and *achieved* in social and sociolinguistic activities. Social identification (to use a verbal alternative to the noun 'identity', recasting it as a process or as a project) is achieved in situated *acts of identity* (Le Page and Tabouret-Keller 1985). And it is those acts of identity that need to come under the analytic spotlight.

This is where the concept of *community of practice* that we mentioned earlier comes to the fore (see Eckert and McConnell-Ginet 1992; Eckert 2000; Wenger 1998). Many sociolinguistic studies nowadays set out to understand how very local communities of people, especially those engaged in repeated contact with each other and in activities where people have some commonality of purpose and identity, tend to reinforce sociolinguistic distinctiveness, often in very micro respects. This is an extension of James Milroy and Lesley Milroy's very revealing use of the concept of *social network* (see their chapter in Part I). But whereas Milroy and Milroy took a static view of network structure and a correlational approach to analysing the 'effects' of different measurable sorts of network configuration, community of practice studies try to follow the *emergence* of indexical linguistic forms, and to analyse the use or deployment of such forms in ongoing interaction (see for example, Mary Bucholtz's chapter, and Margaret Wetherell and Nigel Edley's chapter, both in Part II). This is also what distinguishes the community of practice concept from the older idea of *speech community*. The earlier concept tended to be used to refer to any regionally and socially distinctive group, without much attention being paid to the details of how communities gave their members a sense of 'communion' or fellowship. In fact there is still work to be done in refining the term community of practice in this same regard. It is not always clear to what extent and in what ways people said to be engaged in 'shared projects' actually interact with one another, or what subjective sense of belonging they experience, or how we can ascertain that.

In this discussion of social groups, communities and social identification, it is interesting to ask what the status of *the individual* is. Is there scope in Sociolinguistics to study the social worlds of individual people, as well as social processes affecting aggregates of people? The answer is yes. In fact there is growing recognition of the *need* to study single cases, whether this means studying particular social situations and events that are populated by particular individuals or simply studying the sociolinguistic worlds of single individuals. Early variationist research (Labov 1972) showed the importance of studying individuals, even though its strongest contribution was to generalize about group tendencies in language variation and change. The importance of inspecting particular cases lies in the fact that language use is always subject to so many local contingencies, as well as wider social forces, that we inevitably miss some of the explanatory detail when we generalize. Group-level research can't avoid being reductive, even though we of course need to reach for generalizations when we can, as well as for local explanatory detail.

Researching the language use of individuals can be motivated in different ways. While there has been a tendency to focus on 'ordinary people' and 'ordinary language' (sometimes called 'mundane data'), there is also a case for studying the exceptional and even the spectacular in Sociolinguistics. Mundane data is important if we want to show that the social world of language use conforms to some general principles that affect all of us. A good example is how Conversation Analysis has established that there are fundamental patterns of conversational practice, such as the orderly turn-taking patterns that are apparent when people negotiate informal social encounters. We need these generalizations, partly in order to understand why usage differs from the norm in particular social contexts, for example, in Adam Jaworski's analysis of greetings in the context of mass tourism in Part VI. But there is value in studying individuals who may be at the leading edge of social changes, or whose language use has particular prominence or is prototypical of the processes we are interested in. This is why Cecilia Cutler, for example, in her Part III chapter, focuses on shifts in Mike's self-presentational style over time. Appreciating this person's sociolinguistic history under the particular circumstances of his early life, aspirations and networks opens our eyes to what is sociolinguistically possible – and this is another sort of generalization.

So contemporary Sociolinguistics tends to take an open stance on the social. It tries not to presume too much about the influence of social order and structure as these appear to us before we begin our research, and it tends to ask what sense of society or sociality emerges from social practice. It may seem more difficult to adopt this perspective when we are dealing with social identities and social environments that are historically highly structured, and sometimes very aggressively and damagingly so. In terms of social class, for example, we may feel in danger of trivializing the politics of class if we suggest that people 'construct' their experience of class interactionally. Isn't class about social inequality and the distribution of power and authority? The same goes with many aspects of race, age and gender. Aren't people often subordinated to pre-existing social constraints that they cannot resist? Doesn't language use reflect these social arrangements, as opposed to social arrangements being constructed through language use? Here we are dumped back into the most fundamental issue about the relationship between the social and the linguistic.

But to say that social order is at least in part a product of social practice is *not* to depoliticize social conflict or to argue that social constraints do not exist as real phenomena. Rather than that, the perspective presses us to identify those social practices – those material uses of language, those Discourses, those ideologies – through which social oppression is imposed and re-imposed, or resisted and renegotiated. Prejudice and discrimination are not social facts in the sense that they simply exist independently of practice. They are perpetuated in particular acts, and focusing on those acts gives us an opportunity to reassess how people are actually constrained, or not, by these forces. A good example is Ben Rampton's research in London secondary schools (Rampton 2006) where he concludes, from ethnographic research involving audio-recording kids in and around formal teaching sessions, that social class is indeed part of the 'practical consciousness' of young, multi-ethnic British kids. At the same time, the way they use class-weighted speech-styles ('posh' and 'Cockney') suggests that they use these vocal styles to create highly localized identities and relationships, rather than just recycling and recreating a pre-existing class structure through their talk.

It is in the domain of *interpersonal relationships* that Sociolinguistics has most confidently accepted an emergent view of the social. Since the important early research of Howard Giles and Allan Bell in the 1970s and 1980s (see their chapters in Part III), Sociolinguistics has developed dynamic approaches to the negotiation of relationships through linguistic and stylistic choices. For example, one well-established claim is that we are able to 'move closer' to people we are interacting with by adjusting the degree of similarity between our own speech and theirs. The qualities and nuances of our social relationships are therefore partly a matter of how we *design* our language use relative to other people, and how we manipulate interpersonal differences with a degree of *strategic* awareness. We *converge* towards and *diverge* away from other people, and sociolinguistic distance becomes a meaningful metaphor for relational distance (see Jenny Cheshire's chapter in Part I). The social is not only a matter of how society itself is ordered at the macro-level and how we fit into that structure and reproduce it. It is also a matter of how we create local social worlds at the micro-level, and we can see two-party relationships (of the sort that everyday conversation seems designed to serve) as a basic social unit.

But at the other extreme, Sociolinguistics encompasses large-scale processes beyond particular societies or cultures. One set of large-scale processes is usually referred to as *globalization* (see Jan Blommaert's chapter in Part V). For most of its history Sociolinguistics has paid attention to *local* communities, no doubt partly because of its own ideological resistance to 'standard' and 'majority' linguistic varieties and its critical orientation towards the oppressive social forces that tend to coalesce around sources of authority and power. But there is widespread recognition now that local social arrangements – for example, the maintenance of a minority language, or sustaining a sense of pride and belonging in small communities and their sociolinguistic distinctiveness – have to be seen as movements to resist, or alternatively to exploit, the homogenizing tendencies of globalization. That is, *the local* is necessarily defined in relation to *the global*. This is clearly apparent in Alastair Pennycook's chapter on global hip-hop in Part III, but several other chapters in the book illustrate the importance of global interchange and mass media in our understanding of sociolinguistic processes. Our social worlds are reflected back to us through the media, which therefore need to be included as important sources of sociolinguistic data.

Sociolinguistic Approaches to Analysis and Interpretation

If we stand back from the detail of particular sociolinguistic studies of the sort that we have brought together in this book, we might get a sense of what theoretical assumptions and what research philosophies underlie modern forms of sociolinguistic analysis and interpretation. In our view this is a key requirement in getting to grips with contemporary Sociolinguistics. All academic disciplines work within particular philosophical climates, and these change over time, not simply as a matter of intellectual 'fashion' but (we hope) in relation to an evolving perception about what academic research can contribute to our appreciation of how lives are lived. Sociolinguistics was born at a time when the social sciences were still finding their feet but needed, in many people's conceptions, to model themselves on the physical sciences. The term *social science* was used to mark this allegiance, although it has always been uncertain to what extent and in what ways the study of social life is really amenable to principles of 'scientific' research. The study of language has always spanned the humanities and the social sciences, and the humanities have generally avoided attempts to explain language in terms of cause and effect models or through large-scale quantitative surveys, for example.

But there is a clear legacy of 'scientific method' in some sociolinguistic approaches, and in some contemporary research too. Sociolinguists have often found it important to conduct surveys of various sorts and to reach impartial, objective conclusions about how languages and dialects, but also attitudes to language varieties, are distributed and how they might be changing. Survey research has to be based on numbers and there are established principles according to which statistical research must be conducted in order for it to be considered valid and reliable (see the next section). But some of the assumptions behind scientific approaches have proved to be inappropriate for the study of language in society, and probably for social research generally. Our social worlds are probably too complex to be reduced to a set of 'laws' governing 'behaviour', and there are good reasons not to think of language use as a form of 'behaviour' in the first place. The fact that speakers are to some extent reflexively aware of their language use, and the fact that they have agentive and sometime strategic control of their actions (see above), mean that social action is not a 'conditioned response'. We have also considered the problematic status of social categories, and the argument that social categories are not 'given' or pre-ordained as much as constructed through language and discourse themselves.

What we have been calling scientific method is better referred to as a *positivist* philosophy of research, and strong forms of positivism have come under attack in many disciplines, but particularly in the social sciences. Positivism relied on strong structural models of society and the use of controlled experiments as a way of reaching generalizations about the world, including the social world and its 'behaviours'. It had no problems with the concept of *social reality*, and it claimed to be able to study real social phenomena objectively and, often, to be able to predict social behaviour. Objections to positivism were largely based in the argument that human agency complicates the analysis of social structure (again, see above), and modern Sociolinguistics like

The desire to be predictive has no place when agents have strategic control over their actions

other disciplines has to establish a coherent view on the most appropriate relationship between structure and agency. How much should sociolinguistic analysis and interpretation give weight and credence to structures of society and to social patterns and trends, as opposed to exploring how speakers navigate their way into and through social relationships and practices?

A powerful critique of positivism was provided under the heading of *social constructionism*. We briefly mentioned this concept earlier, and there are quite strong undercurrents of constructionism in much of modern Sociolinguistics. This perspective was set out in a famous book by Peter Berger and Thomas Luckmann (1966), sub-titled 'The social construction of reality'. Here is an indicative quotation (where we can again note the gendered references to 'man' and 'men' which were not exceptional in academic writing in the 1960s):

> Man's self-production is always, and of necessity, a social enterprise. Men *together* produce a human environment, with the totality of its socio-cultural and psychological formations ... Social order is a human product. Or, more precisely, an ongoing human production ... Social order is not part of the 'nature of things', and it cannot be derived from the 'laws of nature'. Social order exists *only* as a product of human activity ... The objectivity of the institutional world 'thickens' and 'hardens', not only for children, but (by a mirror effect) for the parents as well. 'There we go again' now becomes 'This is how these things are done'. A world so regarded attains a firmness in consciousness; it becomes real in an ever more massive way and it can no longer be changed so readily. For the children, especially in the early phase of their socialization into it, it becomes *the* world ... To take the most important item of socialization, language appears to the child as inherent in the nature of things, and he cannot grasp the notion of its conventionality. A thing *is* what it is called, and it could not be anything else. (Berger and Luckmann 1966: 51–52)

Notice how Berger and Luckmann (who were not linguists) refer to language as an important means by which people come to construct social reality. In fact there came to be very broad recognition that language played a crucial part in how we orient to social life, and this is referred to as 'the linguistic turn' in the social sciences and beyond. Rather curiously, while some sociolinguists were holding on to a rather positivist concept of their discipline, many more people outside Sociolinguistics were suggesting that we need a constructionist sociolinguistic view of social reality.

There were, however, different versions of the constructionist perspective, some of which can be considered extreme, particularly in their claims about social reality. If language plays a role in the construction of society, perhaps we should dispense with *any* notion of social reality and acknowledge that we live in a world where all we have is discourse. This is not the place to attempt a review, but arguments of this sort are associated with the work of Jacques Derrida, Jean Baudrillard, Jean-François Lyotard and others who may loosely be grouped together as defenders of post-structuralist and post-modern conceptions of language, aesthetics and social life. They generally share a view that social reality is either unattainable or suspect, and they direct their analytic attention to processes of linguistic or semiotic representation, where meanings circulate unattached to any enduring social reality. The question for sociolinguists is whether, in adopting the broad constructionist perspective that is already in the mainstream, they also have to dispense with the notion of social reality. This is a central issue in the sociolinguistic theorizing of language and society.

There is rather little explicit debate about this in Sociolinguistics, although in our view a consensus position is emerging. Sociolinguists do not on the whole commit themselves to a strong anti-realist stance, although they do generally take a constructionist stance, and sometimes an anti-positivist stance. This is an entirely coherent philosophical and theoretical stance and it is one defended by social theorists working under the rubric of *critical realism* (see, for example, Archer 2003) which shares some priorities with Anthony Giddens's *structuration theory* (Giddens 1984) (see also Carter and Sealey 2000 for an argument about realism in Sociolinguistics). Realist theory argues that 'society' (which includes social structures like socio-economic arrangements, and social institutions such as families or schools) *does* have a real existence, independently of how we conceive of it and independently of how we may reshape it by our actions. They point to the fact that it is very different to say (a) that language represents reality, fails to represent it accurately and fully, and colours our assumptions about what social reality is like; versus (b) that language brings society into existence to the extent that there is no social reality beyond discourse. Critical realists are happy with (a) and opposed to (b). They argue that society evolves historically, being continually reshaped by what people do, so that agentive human creativity is a key process. But the history of, for example, social institutions as they really are impacts on us as social beings, and we certainly feel these impacts as social constraints on our actions. But once again, our agentive capacities do not restrict us to conforming to social norms and expectations. Society is indeed socially constructed to some extent, but not wholly and not in the moment of discursive action – we do not simply 'talk society into existence' each time we use language.

This seems to be a theoretical position that most Sociolinguistics can agree with. Sociolinguistics need not relegate society to the realm of the 'purely discursive' and it can respect and comment critically on the power of social structure (including the sorts of social stratification we find in relation to class, age, gender, ethnicity – and all the 'isms') in constraining our actions.

There need be no essentialism in trying to find out 'what society is really like'. Yet Sociolinguistics should contribute important insights in the analysis of how society is progressively reshaped, for individuals in their local circumstances and more broadly for whole societies and cultures over time, in particular acts of meaning-making.

Sociolinguistic Methods

Across the particular chapters of the book several different research techniques and designs will be apparent. What they have in common is a commitment to *empirical* research, by which we simply mean a commitment to developing analyses of actual linguistic data of one sort or another. This might seem to be essential for any linguistic approach, but some traditions of linguistics have relied on researchers' own intuitions about what language is like, rather than on observing language in use. *Observation* generally means 'listening in' and providing a record (audio- or audio-visual) of speech or social interaction, then closely analysing particular aspects of the data gathered, often by transcribing the data with whatever degree of technical detail is necessary for the sorts of analysis being conducted. For example, for the analysis of interactional data, it will often be necessary to transcribe conversations or interviews in ways that go well beyond general, orthographic writing conventions, in order to show details of pausing, overlapping speech, emphasis and other prosodic and paralinguistic features. With multilingual data it is often important to record precise details of switches between languages and of how blended, cross-language forms are realized.

Nonverbal aspects of interaction, such as the spatial alignment of speakers, tone of voice, loudness, intonation, their gestures and other bodily or facial movements, might also need to be captured. All of these can have an important impact on the meanings created and received. For studies of regional and social accents, it is often necessary to subject audio-recorded data to acoustic analysis, because of the limitations of human auditory capacities (although there is also an argument that our analyses should reflect the circumstances under which language is actually encountered by listeners). But in general, these are all typical instances of the empirical sociolinguistic procedures that make for accurate observation.

Alternatively, sociolinguistic data can be *elicited* – generated as responses to questions posed or activities triggered in different formats – via written questionnaires, one-to-one interviews or in focus group discussions. Extreme forms of elicitation take the form of experiments, where informants react to different sorts of stimuli or test-demands. There are important differences between observed and elicited data, most obviously to do with the degree of control that the researcher wants or needs to impose over the research procedures. Observation is a matter of 'take what you get' and analyses are *post hoc* – performed after the event. Eliciting data involves deciding in advance what questions you want informants to answer, or sometimes what words or expressions you want people to produce, for example, in the case of getting them to read aloud lists of words or written texts you have chosen.

Research methods have to be selected in relation to research questions asked, but also in relation to the wider research philosophy and assumptions we are making (see the previous section). Researchers opt for high control over the research process and over the tasks performed by informants, as with some sorts of elicitation procedure, when they assume that there are general tendencies that need to be uncovered, usually across rather large sets of informants. In the study of language attitudes, for example, it is only possible to generalize about broad trends in people's reactions to different ways of speaking (see John Edwards's chapter in Part IV) if we ask all our informants the same questions under specified conditions. If we want to establish differences in the speech-styles of people working in different workplaces, we need to design simple, repeatable questions that will make the results both generalizable and quantifiable (see, for example, William Labov's Chapter 3, in Part I).

On the other hand, a clear majority of the chapters favour more open-ended, observational research methods and smaller-scale data. They sacrifice the ability to generalize about broad tendencies in language use or in social attitudes in favour of helping us understand the intricacies and local complexities of more particular instances, seen 'from the inside'. This is the *ethnographic* research design that has considerable momentum in modern Sociolinguistics. It is important, however, to resist associating *qualitative*, ethnographic sociolinguistic research with research that is 'new' and 'better-informed', and conversely to resist associating *quantitative*, survey-type research with research that is 'old' or 'naïve'. There *is* a tendency for newer research to be conducted qualitatively, but this is because sociolinguists' ambitions for their research have, overall, shifted. More researchers have espoused constructionist principles (although, we suggest, with a realist flavour), and have therefore prioritized agency over structure. As we suggested above, in the wider scheme of things we need to keep structure *and* agency in view, together, and it follows that there are no simple ways of prioritizing one set of sociolinguistic methods over another.

In reading research studies that use different designs, or in designing our own sociolinguistic research, it might be helpful to refer to a simple template of the philosophical and practical assumptions (rather than the 'strengths

and weaknesses' in any straightforward sense) of quantitative and qualitative
sociolinguistic research, as in the following table:

	Sociolinguistic Research	
	Quantitative research designs	Qualitative research designs
Philosophical tradition	more positivist	more constructionist
Research questions asked	where? when?	how? why?
Data samples required	large	small (including single cases)
Approach to data	objective	subjective
Researcher's level of control	high	low
Approach to analysis	testing hypotheses	letting meanings emerge
Basis of interpretation	statistical trends	meanings in context
Researcher's relationship to informants and events	outsider	insider
Where does the main value lie?	in the breadth of generalization	in the depth of contextual detail

REFERENCES

Archer, Margaret. 2003. *Structure, Agency and the Internal Conversation.* Cambridge:
Cambridge University Press.

Berger, Peter and Thomas Luckmann. 1966. *The Social Construction of Reality: A
Treatise in the Sociology of Knowledge.* Garden City, New York: Anchor Books.

Bex, Tony and Richard J. Watts (eds.) 1999. *Standard English: The Widening Debate.*
London and New York: Routledge.

Bucholtz, Mary and Kira Hall. 2004. Theorizing identity in language and sexuality
research. *Language in Society* 33: 469–515.

Bourdieu, Pierre. 1991. *Language and Symbolic Power*. Edited and Introduced by John B. Thompson. Translated by Gino Raymond and Matthew Adamson. Cambridge: Polity.

Carter, Bob and Alison Sealey. 2000. Language, structure and agency: What can realist social theory offer to sociolinguistics? *Journal of Sociolinguistics* 4: 3–20.

Chambers, J. K. and Peter Trudgill. 1998. *Dialectology*. 2nd edition. Cambridge: Cambridge University Press.

Coupland, Nikolas. 2007. *Style: Language Variation and Identity*. Cambridge: Cambridge University Press.

Duranti, Alessandro and Charles Goodwin (eds.) 1992. *Rethinking Context: Language as an Interactive Phenomenon*. Cambridge: Cambridge University Press.

Eckert, Penelope. 2000. *Linguistic Variation as Social Practice*. Malden, Massachusetts: Blackwell Publishers.

Eckert, Penelope and Sally McConnell-Ginet. 1992. Think practically and look locally: Language and gender as community-based practice. *Annual Review of Anthropology* 21: 461–490.

Foucault, Michel. 1977. *Discipline and Punish*. New York: Pantheon.

Giddens, Anthony. 1984. *The Constitution of Society: Outline of the Theory of Structuration*. Berkeley, California: University of California Press.

Halliday, M. A. K. 1978. *Language as Social Semiotic: The Social Interpretation of Language and Meaning*. London: Edward Arnold.

Hymes, Dell. 1974. *Foundations in Sociolinguistics: An Ethnographic Approach*. Philadelphia, Pennsylvania: University of Pennsylvania Press.

Hymes, Dell. 1996. *Ethnography, Linguistics, Narrative Inequality: Toward an Understanding of Voice*. London: Taylor and Francis.

Jaworski, Adam and Nikolas Coupland (eds.) *The Discourse Reader*. London: Routledge.

Kress, Gunther. 1985. *Linguistic Processes in Sociocultural Practice*. Victoria, Australia: Deakin University.

Labov, William. 1972. *Sociolinguistic Patterns*. Philadelphia, Pennsylvania: University of Pennsylvania Press.

Le Page, Robert B. and Andrée Tabouret-Keller. 1985. *Acts of Identity: Creole-based Approaches to Language and Ethnicity*. Cambridge: Cambridge University Press.

Mendoza-Denton, Norma. 2004. Language and identity. In J. K. Chambers, Peter Trudgill and Natalie Schilling-Estes (eds.) *Handbook of Language Variation and Change*. Malden, Massachusetts: Blackwell Publishing. 474–499.

Rampton, Ben. 1995. *Crossing: Language and Ethnicity among Adolescents*. London: Longman. [2nd edition 2005. Manchester: St Jerome Press.]

Rampton, Ben. 2006. *Language in Late Modernity: Interaction in an Urban School*. Cambridge: Cambridge University Press.

Wenger, Etienne. 1998. *Communities of Practice*. Cambridge: Cambridge University Press.

PART I

LANGUAGE VARIATION

Editors' Introduction to Part I

The study of sociolinguistic variation at the level of accent and dialect differences, pioneered in the modern era by William Labov, came to be referred to as *variationist Sociolinguistics*, or just *variationism*. It has sometimes been said that this is the most central tradition of Sociolinguistics, although this narrow view of the discipline is not without its critics (see Cameron, Chapter 8). The Reader presents a view of Sociolinguistics that recognizes the seminal importance of variationist research, but goes well beyond it too. The roots of variationism lie in *traditional dialectology* – a term used to refer to the early geographical surveys of dialect differences. Dialectologists mainly used to study non-mobile, old, rural, male speakers (NORMS), in order to access the most conservative forms of regional speech that could be detected. But the remit of variationism over the last five decades has shifted to the study of systematic patterns of variation within and across social groups defined in terms of region, class (socioeconomic status), age, sex and ethnicity, predominantly in urban settings. So we also find variationism being referred to as 'urban Sociolinguistics'. At one time Labov also referred to it as 'secular Linguistics', possibly suggesting that it was departure from the 'high priesthood' of research into theoretical syntax.

The scene setting chapter by Walt Wolfram (Chapter 2) outlines several key features of *dialect*, a term that refers to any variety of language that is spoken in a distinctive way by an identifiable group of speakers within a language community. Wolfram introduces a number of principles and assumptions underlying the study of dialects. Some forms of dialect variation and change are guided by natural linguistic mechanisms, leading to generalized types of linguistic change in unrelated varieties. For example, the widespread feature of negative concord (or 'double negation') in such English sentences as *They don't do nothing to nobody about nothing* (p. 38) follows the simple structural principle of adding a negative particle to express a negative meaning. Likewise, a systematic phonetic shift in an accent (where 'accent' is an informal way of referring to pronunciation aspects of a dialect) may trigger a chain of related

23

sound changes, simply because sets of sounds need to be kept apart in terms of phonetic space, in order to maintain distinctions of meaning (cf. the sound change referred to as the Northern Cities Shift in Labov, Chapter 5; Eckert, Chapter 10). But dialect differences are primarily of interest because of the *social meanings* that they express.

Variationism has established that accents and dialects vary *systematically* and *inherently*. Dialects differ from each other not just because one dialect has features that another dialect does not, for example, the *-in'* vs. *-ing* realization of the word-final nasal sound in words like *swimming* and *something* (see Trudgill, Chapter 4). Instead, it is often necessary to say that dialects differ in terms of the relative *frequencies* with which variants like these appear in the speech of particular groups of speakers. So the (ing) feature can be treated as a *sociolinguistic variable* that has two alternative variants (the alveolar nasal /n/ and the velar nasal /ŋ/). One of Labov's key contributions was to devise methods for systematically studying the frequencies with which particular variants are used by particular groups of speakers under particular social circumstances. As Wolfram explains, this sort of variation may be regulated by *external* factors – factors external to the linguistic system itself, such as a speaker's membership of a social class that seems to 'favor' one variant over another – but also by *internal* factors, such as a sound occurring in a particular linguistic environment which 'favors' its use.

Classical variationist research is represented in this Part of the Reader in Chapters 3 and 4, by William Labov and Peter Trudgill. The main social dimension involved in these studies is social class, and the related idea of social prestige or status. Different accent/dialect features are stereotypically associated with low-status and high-status speakers. That is, they are *indexical* features, indexing degrees of social status or social stigma. Other things being equal, the speech of high-status, middle-class groups is deemed to be prestigious or 'standard', while that of low-status groups is deemed to be stigmatized or 'non-standard'. Of course, high status and low status are relative terms, and the cultural value or *symbolic capital* of different dialect forms will depend on the value systems subscribed to by different communities and by individual speakers (see Wolfram, Chapter 2, p. 45). For example, Cecilia Cutler (Chapter 21) studies the speech of a white, affluent, male, middle-class teenager from New York adopting dialectal features of African American Vernacular English (AAVE). For him and for members of his peer-group AAVE speech style evokes desirable connotations of participating in the African American street culture epitomized by hip-hop music. If we use the term 'non-standard' to describe AAVE, this is a judgment made from within a value system that views the white, middle-class speech style as a sociolinguistic norm, and this is why we tend to put scare-quotes around the terms 'standard' and 'non-standard'. It is sometimes said that 'non-standard' forms of language have *covert prestige* – positive value attached by a segment of society against mainstream, hegemonic norms and expectations. But once again, there will be many people who value AAVE and other 'non-standard' forms rather overtly.

Wolfram ends his chapter by discussing three types of indexical features, as they were originally discussed in Labov's research: *social stereotypes*, *social markers*, and *social indicators* (see Wolfram, Chapter 2, pp. 46–47; Cheshire, Chapter 7, p. 124). Stereotypes in this specific sense are speech-features that people are aware of and which are therefore likely to be commented on in everyday discussions of language differences. Teachers and parents, for example, are quite likely to comment negatively on kids who do 'G-dropping' (however inadequate that concept is linguistically). Like linguistic stereotypes, markers and indicators are features whose usage distinguishes social groups (mainly social class groups). Markers also show variation *within* the speech of individuals, for example when a speaker 'corrects' his or her usage when speaking formally. With indicators this doesn't happen, because indicators are the variable features that people are least aware of, even though they might still be involved in distinguishing one group's pattern of speech from another. The study of evaluation of dialects, drawing on the broader issue of *language ideology* (see, for example, Irvine and Gal, Chapter 25; Johnson, Chapter 27; Jaffe, Chapter 28), is the domain of perceptual dialectology (see Preston and Niedzielski, Chapter 25).

Labov's department stores study (Chapter 3) was first reported in 1966 and it triggered a wave of quantitative sociolinguistic research. Part of its appeal lies in its neatness and its boundedness – the fact that Labov was able to draw such theoretically rich findings from such a simple technique and such a limited data base. The procedure he used was rapid and anonymous interviewing, simply repeating the same basic request for information to 264 different sales assistants spread across three well-known New York City department stores. A typical request was: *Excuse me, where are the women's shoes?*, because the answer was known in advance to be *On the fourth floor*, a phrase that contained examples of the speech feature Labov was investigating – the now-famous postvocalic /r/. The pattern of /r/ pronunciation in the sales assistants' answers was highly revealing; Labov outlines his methods, findings and interpretations very clearly in the text.

With hindsight, after over fifty years, it is still striking how all the key components of variationist Sociolinguistics are represented in the department stores study:

- a *socially stratified* or ranked community (represented here as the ranked social statuses of the three department stores themselves, and perhaps by implication the social statuses of the assistants that were asked the question);
- a socially sensitive, indexical feature of pronunciation, in this case the variable (r) in words like *fourth* and *floor*, which has two alternative

variants: either an audibly realized [r] sound (which is 'standard' usage in most middle-class USA English speech) or no audible realization at all (which is 'non-standard' in the vernacular speech of some working-class people in the eastern USA);

- a clear pattern of variation in the frequency of its use, showing that the feature had the potential to mark social differences quite regularly; and
- a community where the speech norms are undergoing change; Labov showed that New York City was undergoing a progressive shift toward more use of the 'standard' form of (r).

The study is a classical piece of empirical research in the positivist or 'scientific' tradition. Labov stresses the naturalness of the data he was able to gather and the study's high degree of objectivity. The findings emerge as trends in statistical tables and figures, and in degrees of similarity and difference between different groups of speakers (the assistants in the three different stores). Later sociolinguistic studies have found it important to use rigorous statistical techniques in handling data of this sort, in particular to help decide which numerical differences are significant in a statistical sense and which might have occurred by chance. The investigation proceeds by establishing its hypotheses and its social categories in advance (for example, selecting the three stores in full anticipation of the trends that might emerge) and systematically testing them against the frequency data. There is little commentary on the precise social contexts in which the study was done, except for the purpose of justifying the categories used in the design, and to justify the claims about objectivity. The study is highly elegant and economical – attributes that are considered good qualities in controlled experimentation. It is also important to notice that the study is not designed to tell us anything sociologically novel. The social stratification of the stores was presumed in advance of the investigation, and simply confirmed in the study. What *is* novel is the precise patterning of the linguistic feature, and perhaps particularly the patterning of (r) as between the first and the second occurrences of the word *floor* in Labov's figure 3.2, suggesting a stylistic difference between less and more emphatic contexts. As we saw in the general Introduction, there are radically different types of Sociolinguistics research, and it will be useful to compare Labov's methods in the department-stores study with studies that take a more ethnographic perspective.

The extract (Chapter 4) from Peter Trudgill's Norwich study shows similar emphasis to Labov's study. This is not surprising because the Norwich study is a replication and elaboration of Labov's survey research methods, which was a far more complex and time-consuming design than the department-stores study. (We see some of the results from Labov's large-scale survey research – in Philadelphia – in his Chapter 5.) Trudgill's data come from sociolinguistic interviews, modeled on Labov's procedures. He organized the sample of people being interviewed into five social classes, ranked from 'high' to 'low'. Within each interview, he then set up four sub-conditions, based on different activities that speakers were required to undertake – from speaking casually to reading lists of words. Detailed analysis and counting of how speakers pronounce the (ing) variable allowed Trudgill to produce very consistent numerical patterns, reflecting the social and situational dimensions of his data. The pre-established social class groups and the situation-types are distinguished quite clearly in these numerical patterns.

Trudgill's findings show regular sex differences, with women tending to produce a higher frequency of 'standard' (or, if you like, more 'posh') speech variants than men do. At least from one point of view, speaker sex is an obvious and straightforward social variable, and sociolinguists have often been able to show systematic linguistic variation between males and females. However, as we will see later, in Eckert's chapter (10) and in Parts II and III of the Reader, there is a danger of underestimating the role of perceptual and other subjective social processes in the sociolinguistic analysis of males and females. There is also the danger of over-generalizing about individual speech styles. Individual people, male and female, do *not* necessarily conform in their speech or their other social actions to the norms for males and females, treated as groups. 'Being female' or 'being male' is in any event a more complex social role (gender) than the biological contrast between men and women (sex) implies. All the same, general information about sex-related trends is important. Our reactions to strangers may well be influenced more by our stereotypical views of male and female communication than by people's actual ways of speaking.

One of the fundamental, undisputed principles on which variationist Sociolinguistics, and we might say the whole of Sociolinguistics, is based is that variation and change are universal features of all living languages. Exactly how *linguistic change* happens, and what are the conditions that favor change, are questions at the heart of much empirical work in Sociolinguistics. Labov's chapter on *transmission* overviews several studies, especially concerning the speech of children and teenagers (the latter is based on Eckert's work, which is also reported in Chapter 10). In Chapter 5 he demonstrates how language change is influenced by a combination of several factors, in which age, social class, ethnicity, area of residence, social networks and other demographic factors interact with a complex set of stylistic choices and local meanings attributed to sociolinguistic variants. Labov's text is an extract from his landmark book on the role of social factors in language variation and change. In the extract he explores, first, the mystery of 'directional language change' – the fact that children perpetuate and extend, in their own generation's early speech, the direction of phonetic change that their predecessors began. In the Philadelphia data that Labov refers to, kids were found to have adopted a new, local way of pronouncing short [a] as a tensed variant in highly specific instances (particularly in the word *planet*) and to have developed the Philadelphia-type of tensed realization further than their parents did.

Labov then reviews how kids in the Philadelphia suburb of King of Prussia, where a high degree of social mixing had taken place, came to settle on a shared local pronunciation pattern. An intriguing social pattern emerges whereby kids who have particularly active social networks among their peergroup (those who are mentioned most by their peers) are the ones who come to adopt the fullest range of Philadelphia-sounding accent features. Labov's review of Penelope Eckert's research in Detroit highlights how those groups of kids least aligned with the official values of their high schools – the so-called *burnouts* – are the ones who are leading the most recent stages of the Northern Cities Shift. Labov ends his chapter by outlining five key principles that summarize what his own and his colleagues' research has been able to demonstrate about the social bases of urban linguistic change.

Language is of course changing all around us, and we often become aware of it when we notice that younger people are quite regularly using speechfeatures that older generations are not. This is the observation that underlies the variationist concept of *apparent time*. Although language changes in real time, if we carefully analyse tendencies in the speech of people of different ages we might get a glimpse of how language *was* used in earlier times, in contrast to how it is used 'now'. Older people's speech of course happens 'now' as well, and it would be wrong to assume that, as we grow older, our speech is frozen into the patterns of usage that we first acquired. Even so, the apparent time idea gives sociolinguists one practical if imperfect way of studying language change across the generations, always bearing in mind that it might be blinding us to the sorts of change that we incorporate into our usage as we age individually.

Sali Tagliamonte's chapter (6) summarizes research into the *be like* feature, which is a familiar characteristic of younger people's speech in the USA, Canada, the UK and probably many other parts of the world where English is spoken. The feature remains quite rare in the speech of older people, say those above the age of about 40. *Be like* is a *quotative* expression, a way of introducing quotes and quote-like utterances into your speech, as in *She's sitting there and she's like 'Oh my God!'* (p. 75). The speaker is reporting that someone said, or possibly thought, *'Oh my God!'*. She is quoting what the speaker said or thought. Tagliamonte reports on quite extensive variationist research into *be like* that has established external and internal constraints on its use. It has become the majority way of handling quotative expressions for younger people in Canada, for example, at the expense of more 'standard' devices such as using the word *say* before the quoted utterance. *Be like* is favored in first-person contexts (people quoting their own speech or thoughts) and when people are expressing 'inner dialogue' – things they thought and might have said, but didn't actually express.

Much of the recent research on *be like* is closely modeled on Labov's original methods, updated through the use of statistics. Tagliamonte explains how the statistical technique of multiple regression (made available to socio-linguists in statistical packages such as *Goldvarb*) is able to give us a more complete picture of how different factors or constraints affect overall patterns of usage. Tagliamonte's chapter therefore provides an excellent instance of modern variationist research in the Labovian tradition, as well as shedding light on a highly contemporary aspect of language change. However, in the four remaining chapters in Part I we see progressive steps being taken *away* from classical variationism, with different degrees of acceptance and critique of its fundamental principles. We see this as the evolution of variationist Sociolinguistics toward a much wider, inter-disciplinary sociolinguistic perspective.

James Milroy and Lesley Milroy's chapter (7) takes on the task of explaining linguistic change through the concept of *social networks* that they introduced into Sociolinguistics in their work in Belfast, Northern Ireland. Social networks are important for Sociolinguistics (as Labov acknowledged in his Chapter 5 text) because they help us understand the sorts of pressures that group-membership can exert on speakers. As we have seen, some of the patterns of variation that emerge from sociolinguistic surveys seem rather obvious and self-explanatory. We would have anticipated, for example, that high-status, middle-class speakers would use 'standard' speech forms more frequently; this is part of what we all know about accent variation. On the other hand, status itself doesn't give us a way of explaining why lower-class speakers generally maintain their 'non-standard' vernacular speech, when there would appear to be status benefits in using 'standard' forms. Labov's idea of *covert prestige* (discussed briefly above, and in Wolfram's chapter) takes us some of the way to an answer. 'Non-standard' forms *are* in their own way prestigious, via a local and unacknowledged sort of 'prestige'. But the concept of social networks allows us to be more precise and to escape from the potentially ambiguous notion of prestige.

Within any social group or community, people are linked together in different ways. The 'ties' between them can be stronger or weaker. Strong ties result from high levels of *network density*, where each individual person interacts with all or most other individuals in a network. A second criterion is so-called *network multiplexity*, when individuals relate to others on more than one basis – for example, working and socializing with the same people. As Milroy and Milroy argue, social networks that are both dense and multiplex have strong potential to resist language change and can therefore help us explain how speech forms may remain stable over long periods. They are 'protected', we might say, by the conservative effects of dense and multiplex social networks. On the other hand, weak ties may provide a crucial means by which change – either linguistic or cultural – infiltrates social networks. The Belfast data show the differences in network density that can exist within working-class urban groups. In the Ballymacarrett area of Belfast, the study is able to pick out a significant positive correlation between network structure and the use of certain local forms of speech. But what is most interesting is that this seems to give us a better explanation for linguistic variation than the apparently clear-cut issue of gender differences. In Milroy and Milroy's data, Ballymacarrett males did use more local vernacular speech forms, but this may have been not so much 'because they were males' but because their patterns of association in the community were more dense and multiplex than those of women. In that area of the city, there was relatively low unemployment and men worked and socialized together far more than women did. Their networks may have been an agency for maintaining and focusing local Belfast speech norms.

Network analysis supplements the original variationist account of language change by focusing not so much on which broad demographic groups tend to take the lead in language change (and both adolescents and women in particular have been credited with this role) and more on the local patterns of social relationships that inhibit or allow change. Milroy and Milroy are, however, staunchly in favor of the basic tenets of variationism, including the use of quantitative methods to establish correlations between social and linguistic trends. But reactions to variationism have sometimes been quite fundamentally critical of this approach. Deborah Cameron's chapter (8) is one of the most influential critiques of this sort. Here, Cameron questions the narrowness of social theorizing in early Sociolinguistics and challenges what she labels its *correlational fallacy*. She argues, principally, that statistical trends linking pre-defined social groups to the use of specific sociolinguistic variants do not *explain why* people use language in the ways that they do. Cameron argues that Labov and others are (or were) too ready to accept the belief that language *reflects* society, and that their research is designed on this assumption. Examining how features of pronunciation co-vary with social dimensions like social class, gender or age leaves us unable to explain the symbolic force of such features, and it uncritically accepts that these social categories are the ones that matter. Without recourse to a broader *social theoretical* framework, even the most thorough descriptive account of language variation cannot account for the *social constitution* of linguistic features.

What Cameron urges sociolinguists to take on board, then, is a more socially and politically involved stance. Sociolinguists should acknowledge that language is not an independent organism (a view that Cameron dubs *the organic fallacy*) – an entity that changes, in and of itself. Rather than reflecting society and an individual's position within it, language use is *constitutive of* social differences and identities. Speakers are able to make active and reasoned linguistic choices, while also responding to the combination of social constraints regulating and restricting their verbal repertoires. While variationists have tended to talk about speakers adopting particular norms in their speech, Cameron broadens the scope of inquiry by asking where these norms come from, who imposes them on who(m), and how – through what specific social practices?

These are perspectives that we discussed in the general Introduction to the book, where we traced their origins in the writing of Dell Hymes in particular, and their links to *social constructionism* in general. An example of socially constitutive language usage put forward by Cameron is sexist language. If we treat language use as a form of *social action*, then using sexist language is a form of societal *sexism* because it establishes and perpetuates unfair sexual representations, divisions and inequalities. In recent decades, not least through the work of feminist linguists (and Cameron herself as a leading figure) who advocated a degree of *verbal hygiene* in an attempt to eradicate sexist usage, non-sexist usage has become more widespread. The social norm with regard to language representing and thus *constituting* females and males has undergone change. However, as Cameron argues, this change has not come about 'naturally' or 'organically'. English has not just 'evolved' toward promulgating a less sexist world view. Rather, many of its speakers responded to a socially driven, explicit call for a language reform which has restructured one aspect of their social reality. In fairness, Cameron admits that not all types of linguistic change are motivated by socially and politically driven attempts to change existing norms and conventions. What she unequivocally rejects, however, is the dominant ideology underlying (early) variationist Sociolinguistics that language is a mirror of society, rather than an active ingredient shaping it.

The two remaining chapters in this Part of the Reader, by Jenny Cheshire (9) and Penelope Eckert (10) can perhaps be seen as a methodological response to Cameron's plea for a socially more involved view of language variation and change. Cheshire and Eckert have in fact been leading figures in the further evolution of variationism and in breaking down barriers between variationism and other sociolinguistic approaches. In each case their research has an ethnographic component, responsive to local, 'emic' values for language. They both move on from defining social class, for example, in simple and apparently objective terms. Cheshire divided up her adolescent male speakers (from Reading, England) into groups depending on how closely they stick to the norms of the *vernacular culture*. Some relevant criteria here are skill at fighting, carrying a weapon, participating in minor crimes, dress/hairstyle, and swearing. Cheshire is then able to show that young people's use of some 'non-standard' grammatical features correlates positively with how highly they score on the vernacular culture index. Not surprisingly, the more embedded speakers are in their local, rather anti-social cultural norms, the more 'non-standard' their speech is in certain respects. It may well be true that the people most closely tied to their vernacular culture will be 'working-class'. But Cheshire's study shows us that *degree* of local/subcultural affiliation is itself a factor of some consequence for ways of speaking.

By comparing boys' speech recorded in a local park and recordings of their conversations with their teachers at school, Cheshire is able to demonstrate the boys' stylistic shifts in their use of one salient, 'non-standard' morphological feature – the present tense suffix -*s* with non-third-person singular subjects (for example, *we goes shopping on Saturdays*). However, the pattern is far from simple. The relatively formal context of the school does not merely trigger more use of the 'standard' (zero s, *we go*) form. Acceptance of the school's ethos and a positive relationship with teachers is linked to a decrease of verbal -*s* (convergence with the teachers' consistent use of the 'standard' variant), while rejection of these values is linked to divergence. This application of accommodation theory (see Giles, Chapter 19) to the analysis of variationist data allows Cheshire to demonstrate how local constraints on the communicative resources available to the boys help us to understand the significance of the linguistic choices they make, and how these choices are consistent with the identity positions they wish to project. But what is most distinctive in Cheshire's chapter is her exploratory analysis of grammatical patterns that have specific discourse functions, such as the group of 'discourse-new' markers that she investigates. She shows that variationist research needs to investigate the interface between grammar and discourse, and to be wary of assuming that sociolinguistic variables at the level of grammar are 'equivalent ways of saying the same thing'. She finds interesting patterns in how some young people mark the presence of discursively 'new' (not inferable) items in their talk and calls for more studies of variation in discursive styles and styling (see Part III).

The final chapter in this section by Penelope Eckert (10) has already been flagged up several times. Like Cheshire, Eckert focuses here on adolescent speech, as teenagers are most likely to be at the forefront of linguistic change. Like Cheshire, Eckert orients to her speakers not as members of clearly predefined social class or sex groups but as social actors who hold different degrees of allegiance to one of two dominant friendship groups – *jocks* and *burnouts* – which we can roughly characterize as embracing and rejecting school values, respectively (not unlike Cheshire's vernacular culture index). Eckert added to the conventional variationist methodology of quantifying sociolinguistic features by undertaking a long-term ethnographic investigation of 'Belten

High', a school in one of the suburbs of Detroit, Michigan. It was this participant-observation approach that allowed her to identify the social networks
and internal structures of the groups she was researching. The Belten High
research has been particularly influential, partly because of Eckert's pioneering use of *ethnographic methods* in the study of sociolinguistic variation. It led
the way in showing how ethnographic investigation of a *community of practice*
could provide rich explanatory context around the distribution of sociolinguistic variables (for example, in this case negative concord, vernacular sound
changes). Variation in Belten High was shown to be guided by the speakers'
orientations to the emergent *symbolic value* of particular variants in a local
linguistic marketplace. Variation was a meaningful part of kids' distinct ideologies and lifestyles.

In particular, burnouts' anti-school stance, their desire for autonomy, nurturing of friendship ties, and engagement with the urban lifestyle resulted in
their greater use of 'non-standard' features, in contrast with jocks who are
keen to accept the institutional authority of the school both in their pursuit of academic and extracurricular activities. Friendship relations for jocks
are more competitive and indicative of the corporate lifestyles they are more
likely to pursue in their adult lives. However, contrary to the findings of most
earlier variationist studies which identified women as predominantly 'standard' speakers in contrast to men of the same social background, Eckert identified the 'core' burnout *girls* as leaders in the use of 'non-standard' features (in
contrast to burnout boys and jocks of both sexes), putting them at the forefront of rebelliousness and anti-institutional stances. Language use therefore
provides a set of resources for identity and self-styling by burnouts and jocks,
alongside clothing, makeup, segregation of school territory, drug use, and
so on. Linguistic and social practice are inextricably linked, and we saw in
the general Introduction how modern Sociolinguistics has generally come to
make this assumption and to design and interpret its research accordingly.

CHAPTER 2

Dialect in Society

Walt Wolfram

Introduction

For as long as observations about language have been recorded, the symbolic function of dialect in society has been recognized. Over three thousand years ago, the *sh* versus *s* pronunciation of *shibboleth* in the Hebrew word for 'ear of corn' was used to detect impostors from true allies among the fleeing Ephraimites who attempted to disguise themselves as Gileadites. As indicated in the Biblical account, the social consequences of the dialect difference were quite severe:

> and whenever a survivor of Ephraim said, 'Let me cross over,' the men of Gilead asked him, 'Are you an Ephraimite?' If he replied, 'No,' they said, 'All right, say Shibboleth.' If he said, 'Shibboleth,' because he could not pronounce the word correctly, they seized him and killed him at the fords of the Jordan. (Judges 12: 5–6)

The present-day social consequences of dialect differences may not be quite as gruesome as those described in the account given in the Old Testament, but the diagnostic differentiation of social groups on the basis of dialect remains symbolically just as significant.

The term *dialect* is used here to refer to any regional, social, or ethnic variety of a language. The language differences associated with dialect may occur on any level of language, thus including pronunciation, grammatical, semantic, and language use differences. At first glance, the distinction between 'dialect' and 'language' seems fairly straightforward – dialects are subdivisions of language. However, on closer inspection, the boundary between dialects and languages may become blurry as simple criteria such as structural affinity or mutual intelligibility break down. Thus, many of the so-called dialects of

Source: 'Dialect in Society', by Wolfram, W. in Coulmas, F (ed.) *Handbook of Sociolinguistics* (1997) (Oxford: Blackwell Publishing) pp. 107–26.

Chinese such as Pekingese (Mandarin), Cantonese, and Wu (Shanghai), are mutually unintelligible in their spoken form. By the same token, Swedes and Norwegians are generally able to understand each other although their distinct cultures and literatures warrant their designation as different languages.

In a similar way, the notions of regional, social, and ethnic dialect are not nearly as obvious as we might assume at first glance. Speakers are at the same time affiliated with a number of different groups and their varying memberships may contribute to the variety of language they employ. Speakers located within the same geographical territory may be affiliated with quite different ethnic and/or social groups, and thus end up speaking quite disparate varieties even as they share a subset of regional language peculiarities. While it is certainly convenient to use the term dialect as we do here, to refer to the general notion of a language variety, more precise definition of the term relies on its correlation with the particular parameters of social structure that determine its existence in a given speech community.

Given the apparent inevitability of dialect differences and their widespread social recognition, it is somewhat surprising that the social patterning of these differences has not been accorded more systematic study in the examination of language and/or society. The methodical study of dialects per se did not begin until the latter part of the nineteenth century (Wenker 1877; Gilliéron 1902–1910), and the serious study of dialects in their social context did not begin until the 1960s.

As it has developed over the past several decades, the systematic investigation of dialects in society has challenged some of the established perspectives of both linguistics and dialectology. Linguistics, as it progressed in the second half of the twentieth century, focused on the formal structure of language as an abstract cognitive system, with little attention given to the kinds of variants that were central to the examination of dialect variation. In accordance with more formal descriptive and explanatory goals, the primary data base became native speaker intuitions vis-à-vis actual language usage because of the insight these intuitions could provide to the cognitive processes underlying language. From this perspective, the social context of language was considered outside the purview of an abstract, cognitively based model of language description.

At the same time, dialectology in the twentieth century became more aligned with geography and history as it focused on the distribution of particular variants in geographical space and time. Accordingly, isolated sets of dialectally diagnostic lexical and phonological items collected through the direct elicitation of single instances of forms became primary data (e.g., Kurath and McDavid 1961; Orton, Sanderson, and Widdowson 1978; Carver 1987). The social significance of dialect variants was examined to some extent through the correlation of dialect variants with the background of interview subjects, but it was secondary. For example, in the various surveys of the *Linguistic Atlas of the United States and Canada* (Kurath 1939: 44), subjects were classified according to three different social types in terms of education and social contacts. However, the systematic examination of dialect in society lay beyond the goals of traditional dialectology.

The pioneering investigations of dialect in society by William Labov (1963, 1966, 1972a, b) clearly broke precedent with some of the reified traditions of both linguistics and dialectology in their assumptions, methodology, description, and explanation. For example, the investigation of language in its social context was seen by Labov (1966c) as central to the solution of fundamental problems in linguistic theory and description rather than as a specialized, interdisciplinary subfield combining distinct traditions of inquiry and description. Furthermore, the use of conversational speech data collected through the sociolinguistic interview was based on the assumption that naturally occurring speech reflected the most systematic data for the examination of language variation (Labov 1972c) and on the assumption that the characterization of systematic variation should be integrated into the description of a language. And it was maintained that the description of language change and variation had to appeal to the role of language in its social context in order to achieve its ultimate goal of explanation.

The line of investigation that developed in social dialectology over the past several decades has altered in a significant way our fundamental understanding of the nature of dialect variation in society with respect to both the linguistic and social sides of the sociolinguistic equation.

The Nature of Dialect Variation

According to popular beliefs, dialect patterns are relatively straightforward and simple: All members of one group invariably use one particular dialect form while members of a different group categorically use another one. While this subjective impression is of sociolinguistic import, the objective reality of dialect distribution within society is far more complex and variable than this popular perception. On one level there is an intricate interaction between the systematic patterning of language and social structure; on another level, however, linguistic variation is inherent in the linguistic system, existing apart from the social meaning that may ultimately be assigned to it. In fact, one of the major shortcomings of traditional dialectology as it developed in North America and the United Kingdom over the past half century was its failure to come to grips with the underlying linguistic-systemic principles that guided the organization and direction of much linguistic variation subsumed under the rubric of dialect. The commonly adopted premise in dialectology that 'each word has its own history' (Gilliéron 1902–1910) unfortunately often precluded the extended consideration of the internal linguistic-systemic principles that guide the orderly distribution of language variation. The following sections illustrate a couple of ways in which dialect variation is guided by the internal mechanisms of language systems. From that point, we proceed to show how such variation may distribute itself in society, and the kinds of social meaning that this variation is assigned.

The Internal Motivation of Dialects

Following the 'each word has its own history' edict of traditional dialectology, dialect differences have often been described as if they consisted of unrelated sets of items. Thus various phonetic productions of two different English vowels in assorted dialects of English, such as the /u/ of words such as *boot* and *tube* and the /ɔ:/ of words such as *bought* and *caught,* would be viewed as structurally independent entities because they involve different phonological units within the system. Similarly, the use of the socially diagnostic English reflexive *hisself* versus *himself* in *Kirk liked hisself* and the subject-verb concord pattern *We was down there yesterday* versus *We were down there yesterday* are viewed as socially diagnostic items quite independent of each other since there appears to be no inherent structural relationship between these forms. While the patterned co-occurrence of forms such as these may be noted as a part of an overall dialect profile, their coexistence within a given dialect is viewed as arbitrary from a descriptive-theoretical perspective.

Such a viewpoint seems far too limited in its assessment of the nature of language variation and change that serves as the foundation of dialect differentiation. Furthermore, there is empirical evidence that argues for a set of underlying principles that guide dialect variation, or at least the tendencies of variation, which exist independent of dialect contact and diffusion (Chambers 1993). For example, vernacular dialects of English throughout the world (Wolfram and Fasold 1974; Cheshire 1982; Bailey and Görlach 1983; Trudgill 1990) with no apparent common diffusional source, share the feature of negative concord in sentences such as *They don't do nothing to nobody about nothing.* Such uniformity among vernacular dialects of English suggests that there are underlying, language-internal pressures that guide some types of dialect variation. In the case of negative concord, the predisposition of languages to generalize processes is a natural, internal mechanism that may account for the representation of this process among different, independent, vernacular varieties.

Labov's delineation of vowel rotation alternatives in English (Labov, Yaeger, and Steiner 1972; Labov 1991, 1994) is a prototypical illustration of how dialects shift their vowel systems in orderly and predictable ways which are then assigned social meaning. Given the nature of vowel production, it is convenient to view different vowels as occupying 'phonetic spaces' in a continuum of vowel positions. The notion of phonetic space is important because the shift of one vowel in phonetic space often has an effect on adjacent vowels. As one vowel moves (e.g., becomes higher or more backed in its phonetic position) phonetically closer to or further away from an adjacent vowel, the next vowel may shift its phonetic value to maintain adequate phonetic distance in relation to the vowel that has moved initially. A whole sequence of vowel rotation may thus be set in motion.

The pattern of phonetic rotation in vowels, known as *chain shifting* or the *push-pull chain,* is actively involved in differentiating the current character of long vowels. In the southern vowel shift, the vowel of *bed* takes on a glide, becoming more like *beyd* [bɛɪd]. Meanwhile, the front long vowels (the vowels of *beet* and *late*) are moving downward and somewhat backward, and the back vowels are moving forward.

Systematic Variability

Another dimension that needs to be admitted into the perspective on dialects in society is the systematic nature of variability. One of the important discoveries to emerge from the detailed study of dialects over the past several decades is the fact that dialects are sometimes differentiated not by the discrete or categorical use or nonuse of forms, but by the relative frequency with which different variants of a form occurred. For a number of phonological and grammatical dialect features, it can be shown that dialects are more typically differentiated by the extent to which these features are found rather than the mere absence or presence of particular variants. For example, studies of the alternation of *-in'* [in] and *-ing* [ɪŋ] in words like *swimmin'* or *swimming* show that, while practically all dialects of English show this alternation, different dialects are distinguished by the relative frequency with which we find *-in'* and *-ing* in particular language varieties. Thus we found in a study of speakers representing different social classes in Detroit, Michigan, that the mean use of *in'* ranged from almost 20 percent use for speakers demographically defined as upper middle class to approximately 80 percent usage by speakers designated as lower working class (Shuy, Wolfram, and Riley 1967). It is important to note that *all* of the individual speakers exhibit variability between *-ing* and *-in'.* In the study of variation, frequency levels are computed by first noting all those cases where a form like *in' might have* occurred (namely, an unstressed syllable), followed by a tabulation of the number of cases in which *-in' actually* occurred.

The fact that there is fluctuation between forms such as *- ing* and *in'* does not mean that the fluctuation is random or haphazard. Although we cannot predict which variant might be used in a given utterance, there are factors that can increase or decrease the likelihood that certain variants will occur. These factors are known technically as *constraints on variability.* The constraints are of two major types. First, there are various social or *external* factors which systematically increase or decrease the likelihood that a particular variant will occur. For example, the reference to social class above is an appeal to an external factor, since we can say that a speaker from the lower working class is more likely to use -in' for -ing than are speakers from other classes.

Not all of the systematic effects on variability, however, can be accounted for simply by appealing to various social factors. There are also aspects of the linguistic system itself, known as *internal factors*, that may affect the variability of particular forms apart from social constraints. Particular kinds of linguistic contexts, such as the kinds of surrounding forms or the type of construction in which the form occurs, may also influence the relative frequency with which these forms occur. The systematic effect of linguistic and social factors on the relative frequency of particular forms can best be understood by way of an actual case from phonology. Consider the example of word-final consonant cluster reduction as it affects sound sequences such as *st, nd, ld, kt*, and so forth in various English dialects. The rule of word-final consonant cluster reduction may reduce items such as *west, wind, cold*, and *act* to *wes', win', col'*, and *ac'* respectively. The incidence of reduction is quite variable, but certain linguistic factors systematically favor or inhibit the operation of the reduction process. The linguistic factors or constraints include whether the following word begins with a consonant as opposed to a vowel (more precisely, a nonconsonant), and the way in which the cluster is formed. With respect to the phonological environment that follows the cluster, the likelihood of reduction is increased when the cluster is followed by a word beginning with a consonant. This means that cluster reduction is more frequent in contexts such as *west coast* or *cold cuts* than in contexts like *west end* or *cold apple*. An individual speaker might, for example, reveal consonant cluster reduction in 75 percent of all cases where reduction could take place when the cluster is followed by a word beginning with a consonant (as in *west coast*) but in only 25 percent of all cases where the cluster is followed by a nonconsonant (as in *west end*). The important observation is that reduction may take place in both kinds of linguistic contexts, but it is consistently favored in those contexts where the word following the cluster begins with a consonant.

As mentioned earlier, cluster reduction is also influenced by the way in which the cluster is formed. Clusters that are a part of an inherent word base, such as *wind* or *guest*, are more likely to undergo reduction than clusters that are formed through the addition of an -ed suffix, such as *guessed* (which ends in [st] phonetically – that is, [gest]) and *wined* (which ends in [nd] phonetically – that is, [waind]). Again, reduction takes place in both types of clusters, but it applies more frequently when the cluster is an inherent part of a word rather than the result of the -ed suffix addition. When we compare the relative effects of different linguistic constraints on final consonant cluster reduction, we find that some linguistic factors have a greater influence on variability than others. Thus, in some dialects of English, the influence of the following segment (the consonant versus nonconsonant) is more important than the constraint based on cluster formation type (e.g., non -ed versus -ed clusters).

The Social Distribution of Dialect

In many respects, describing the social distribution of language variation is dependent upon the kinds of group affiliations, interactional relations, and sociocultural ideologies operating within a society. In early studies of dialect in society (e.g., Labov 1966c; Wolfram 1969) it was common for linguists to appropriate a set of predetermined background demographic variables such as region, socioeconomic class, ethnicity, age, and sex, and to show the covariance of linguistic forms with these variables, either in isolation or, more commonly, in intersecting arrays. Later descriptions focused on the nature of communication networks (L. Milroy 1987, and see Chapter 7), the dynamics of situational context (Biber and Finegan 1993), and the projection of social identity (LePage and Tabouret-Keller 1986) in an effort to describe more authentically the social reality of dialect in society. For our purposes here, it is sufficient but critical to recognize that many of the social variables typically appealed to in studies of covariance are abstractions extracted from an intricate, interactive, and multi-dimensional social reality. For example, McConnell-Ginet (1988) and Eckert (1989) point out that dialect differences correlated with gender differences assume a social construction based upon the biological category of sex. But the social construction of gender may be exceedingly complex, as it involves roles and ideologies creating differential ways for men and women to experience life, culture, and society. As Eckert notes, 'there is no apparent reason to believe that there is a simple, constant relation between gender and variation' (Eckert 1989: 247). Similar provisos could be offered for virtually any of the traditional variables examined in the covariation of social and linguistic factors.

The perspective on dialect in society implied in the preceding discussion is an ethnographically informed one, since only such a vantage point can reveal the local kinds of affiliations, interactions, and ideologies that lead to the symbolic functions of dialect within a given community. Our recent studies of Ocracoke, a post-insular island community located 20 miles from the mainland state of North Carolina, reveal how an ethnographic perspective is needed to inform the role of dialect in a community setting (Schilling-Estes and Wolfram 1994; Wolfram and Schilling-Estes 1995). In this post-insular setting, some of the patterns of covariation between linguistic variables and traditional background demographic factors and/or social networks do not match the patterns of covariation that might be expected, based upon traditional sociolinguistic studies. For example, we do not find a unilateral regression pattern between age or socioeconomic class and the loss of traditional island dialect variants. Thus the use of a classic island variable, in which the *ay* diphthong of *high* and *tide* is backed and raised so that it is pronounced close to the *oy* vowel of *boy* or *Boyd*, is often found more frequently among a group of middle-aged, college-educated men who have a fairly wide range of contact outside the local networks than among their older and younger cohorts. Furthermore, the incidence of this island feature does not correlate neatly with the density and multiplicity of the social networks of these middle-aged men. For example, several of the men who use the highest incidence of this traditional island pronunciation are currently married to outsiders and have a fairly wide set of social networks extending well beyond local community members. At the same time, our ethnographic studies showed that these men are part of a highly symbolic, local 'poker game network' which consists of a small, indigenous group of men who meet a couple of times a week to play poker. This group reflects strong, traditional island values, including the projection of island identity through the use of symbolic dialect choices that include the now stereotypical *oy* production in words such as *hoi toide* for 'high tide'. In fact, islanders are often referred to as *hoi toiders,* in reference to this production.

Patterns of Distribution

Quite obviously, not all dialect structures are distributed in the same way within society. Given varying histories of dialect contact, dialect diffusion, and internal dialect change, and the varieties of social meaning ascribed to dialect forms, linguistic variables may align with given social groupings in a variety of ways. The pattern of dialect distribution which most closely matches the popular perception of dialect differences is referred to as *group-exclusive usage,* where one group of speakers uses a form but another group never does. In its ideal interpretation, group-exclusive usage means that *all* members of a particular community of speakers would use the dialect form whereas *no* members of other groups would ever use it. This ideal pattern is rarely, if ever, manifested in dialects. The kinds of social grouping that take place in society are just too complex for this pattern to work out so neatly. In some cases, distinctions between groups exist on a continuum rather than in discrete sets. Furthermore, as we mentioned above, the definition of a social group usually involves a constellation of characteristics rather than a single dimension, thus making the simple correlation of a linguistic form with social structure intricate and multidimensional.

Notwithstanding the qualifications that have to be made when talking about group-exclusive dialect features, there certainly are items that are not shared across groups of speakers. The essential aspect of these dialect forms, however, seems to be the fact that speakers from other groups do *not* use these forms rather than the fact that all the members of a particular group use them. Group-exclusive usage is therefore easier to define negatively than positively. Viewed in this way, there are many dialect features on all levels of language organization that show group-exclusive social distribution.

According to Smith (1985), group-exclusive patterns of dialect distribution may be *saturated* or *unsaturated*. Saturated patterns refer to those that typify the vast majority of speakers within a particular social group or speech community and unsaturated patterns refer to those that are less pervasive, but still group-exclusive. For example, among younger working-class African-Americans, the 'habitual *be*' form with *verb* + *ing* as in *They usually be going to the movies* might be considered a saturated form since the majority of speakers in this group use this form at one time or another. Note that the definition of the group in this case must include at least ethnicity, status, and age. By the same token, speakers of other varieties of English do not typically use this construction. In contrast, the use of the specialized future perfect construction *be done* as in *The chicken be done jumped out the pen* for the same population of working-class African-American speakers might be considered an unsaturated, group-exclusive form, since few, but only speakers of this variety, have been found to use this construction.

Descriptive qualifications such as 'saturated' and 'unsaturated' group-exclusive usage are useful approximate labels, but they have not yet been defined with any rigor. That is, the classification of a form as saturated or unsaturated is not determined on the basis of a specific proportion of speakers sampled within a given population (e.g., more than 75 percent of the speakers in a representative sample use the form in saturated usage and less than 20 percent of the speakers use the form in unsaturated usage). These designations are imprecise and limited, although admittedly convenient as informal characterizations of dialect patterns.

Group-exclusive dialect forms may be taken for granted in one dialect while, at the same time, they are quite obtrusive to speakers from other dialect areas. In American English, speakers from other regions may thus be quick to comment on how strange forms like *youns* 'you pl.', *The house needs painted,* and *gumband* 'rubber band' seem to them when visiting Pittsburgh, Pennsylvania, much to the surprise of the lifetime resident of Pittsburgh who has assumed that these were in common use. With increased interaction across dialect groups, however, speakers may become aware of some of their own group-exclusive usages. As the consciousness about these forms is raised, some of them may take on symbolic significance in identifying people from a given locale or social group. And from these features come the stereotypes of particular regional and ethnic dialects found in popular caricatures. However, it is important to remember that the stereotypical, symbolic caricatures by outsiders, and sometimes even by insiders, are often not linguistically faithful to the actual use of the form by speakers from the particular speech community.

In contrast to group-exclusive forms, *group-preferential* forms are distributed across different groups or communities of speakers, but members of one group simply are more likely to use the form than members of another group. For example, a fine-grained spectrum of color terms (e.g., *mauve, plum,* etc.) is often associated with females in the United States, but there are certainly males who make similar distinctions, and, of course, there are females who do not make such refined color designations. The association of a narrowly defined color spectrum with female speakers is thus statistically based, as more women make these distinctions than men. We refer to this narrowly defined color spectrum as a group-preferential pattern rather than a group-exclusive one. Group-preferential patterns may derive from the nature of the dialect variable or the nature of the social reality that underlies the social variable. For example, as we noted earlier, there are dimensions of group affiliation, interactional relationship, and ideological perspective that make the social construct of gender far more complex than a designation of group membership based solely on biological sex. We would not expect the symbolic effect of a group-preferential pattern to be as socially distinct as a group-exclusive marking, although popular stereotypes of group-preferential dialect patterns sometimes treat them symbolically as if they were group-exclusive. The popular characterization of vernacular dialects of English in their use of *dese, dem,* and *dose* for *these, them,* and *those* is such an instance, where the stereotype of group-exclusive behavior actually betrays a fairly complex pattern which is really group-preferential and also highly variable.

Variable use of socially diagnostic forms may also be distributed in different ways with respect to social variables. For example, given a continuous axis of age, a particular linguistic variable may show continuous unilateral regression between the incidence of a linguistic variant and age, that is, we find a regular slope between decreasing age and the incidence of the variant. For example, the increasing use of post-vocalic *r* for Anglos in the American South (e.g., *bear* for *bea'* or *car* for *ca'*) may show a linear progression in which increasing age is coterminous with the increasing incidence of post-vocalic *r*. This is sometimes referred to as *fine stratification*. Or the pattern may show *sharp* or *gradient stratification*, in which there is an abrupt change in the relative incidence of a feature at some point on a continuous social axis. For example, in the African-American community, there is a sharp decrease in the incidence of subject-verb concord as in *She go to the store* for *She goes to the store* at a midpoint in the social continuum that roughly divides the upper working and lower middle class (Wolfram 1969). Finally, a *curvilinear* pattern might be revealed in the distribution of a socially diagnostic variable, in which the slope of the correlation line between linguistic variation and social variation reverses its direction at some point in the correlation. For example, on the island of Ocracoke, off the coast of North Carolina, the pattern of *ay* backing and raising of items such as *high tide* shows that middle-aged men in the poker game network have a higher incidence of backing and raising than their older and younger cohorts, thus showing a curvilinear pattern of distribution over age.

Stable linguistic variables defined primarily on the standard–nonstandard continuum of English tend to be sharply stratified, whereas linguistic features undergoing change often exhibit fine stratification. This is due in part to the role of social factors in language change within a community. Change tends to start in a given social class and spread from that point to other social classes in a diffuse manner. The kind of correlation that exists between social factors and linguistic variation may thus be a function of both social and linguistic considerations; there is no single pattern that can be applied to this covariation.

The Social Evaluation of Linguistic Features

Although there is no inherent social value associated with the variants of a linguistic variable, it is not surprising that the social values assigned to certain groups in society will be attached to the linguistic forms used by the members of these groups. While this general pattern of social evaluation holds, the correlation of particular linguistic variables with social stratification is not always so direct, as sociolinguistic history molds the diagnostic role of language structures in various ways.

The use of particular language variants may be evaluated as socially prestigious or socially stigmatized. *Socially prestigious* variants are those forms that are positively valued through their association with high status groups as linguistic markers of status, whereas *socially stigmatized* variants carry a stigma through their association with low-status groups. It is essential to understand that stigmatized and prestigious variants do not exist on a single axis in which the alternative to a socially stigmatized variant is a socially prestigious one, or vice versa. The absence of negative concord in sentences such as *She didn't do anything,* for example, in standard varieties of English is not particularly prestigious; it is simply *not* stigmatized. On the other hand, there may be particular patterns of negative formation that carry prestige in some varieties. For example, the choice of single negative marking on the post-verbal indefinite negatives (e.g., *He'll do nothing*) rather than on the auxiliary (e.g., *He won't do anything*) may be considered a prestigious option in some varieties of English, but the alternative marking in the auxiliary is not considered stigmatized.

The discussion of sociolinguistic evaluation up to this point has assumed a particular vantage point about norms of linguistic behavior, namely the perspective of widespread, institutional norms established by higher status groups. These norms are overtly perpetuated by the agents of standardization in society – language academies, teachers, the media, and other authorities responsible for setting the standards of behavior. Community-wide knowledge of these norms is usually acknowledged across a full range of social classes. Linguistic forms that are assigned their social evaluation on the basis of this widespread recognition of social significance are said to carry *overt prestige.* At the same time, however, there may exist another set of norms which relates primarily to solidarity with more locally defined social groups, irrespective of their social status position. When forms are positively valued apart from, or even in opposition to, their social significance for the wider society, they are said to have *covert prestige*. In the case of overt prestige, the social evaluation lies in a unified, widely accepted set of social norms, whereas in the case of covert prestige, the positive social significance lies in the local culture of social relations. Thus it is possible for a socially stigmatized variant in one setting to have covert prestige in another. A youth who adopts vernacular forms in order to maintain solidarity with a group of friends clearly indicates the covert prestige of these features on a local level, even if the same features stigmatize the speaker in a wider, mainstream context such as school. The notion of covert prestige is important in understanding why vernacular speakers do not rush to become standard dialect speakers, even when these speakers may evaluate the social significance of linguistic variation in a way which superficially matches that of their high-status counterparts. Thus widely recognized stigmatized features in English, such as negative concord, nonstandard subject verb agreement, and different irregular verb paradigms, may function at the same time in a positive, covertly prestigious way in terms of local norms.

There are several different ways in which speakers within the sociolinguistic community may react to socially diagnostic variables. Speakers may treat some features as *social stereotypes,* where they comment overtly on their use. In English, items such as *ain't*, 'double negatives', and *'dese, dem,* and *dose'* are classic features of this type on a general level, but particular dialects may have stereotypes on a more local level. Thus the production of *hoi toiders* for *high toiders* has become a stereotype for the island community of Ocracoke, the plural *youns* a stereotype for the city of Pittsburgh, and the use of habitual *be* in *They be doing it* is rapidly becoming a stereotyped form for urban working-class African-American dialects in the United States. Sociolinguistic stereotypes tend to be overly categorical and are often linguistically naive, although they may derive from a basic sociolinguistic reality. For example, the stereotype that working-class speakers *always* use *dese, dem,* and *dose* forms and middle-class speakers *never* do is not supported empirically, although there certainly is a correlation between the relative frequency of the nonstandard variant and social stratification. Furthermore, stereotypes tend to focus on single vocabulary items or selective subsets of items rather than more general phonological and grammatical patterns.

Another type of sociolinguistic role is assumed by the *social marker.* In the case of social markers, variants show clear-cut social stratification, but they do not show the level of conscious awareness found for the social stereotype. Various vowel shifts, such as the Northern Cities Vowel Shift discussed earlier, seem to function as social markers. There is clear-cut social stratification of the linguistic variants, and participants in the community may even recognize this distribution, but the structure does not evoke the kind of strongly evaluated overt commentary that the social stereotype does. Even if participants don't talk about these features in any direct manner, there are still indications that they are aware of their existence. This awareness is often indicated by shifts in the use of variants across different styles of speaking.

The third possible sociolinguistic role is called the *social indicator*. Social indicators are linguistic structures that correlate with social stratification without having an effect on listeners' judgment of social status. Whereas social stereotypes and social markers are sensitive to situational variation, social indicators do not show such sensitivity, as shown by the fact that levels of usage remain constant across formal and informal styles. This suggests that the correlation of socially diagnostic variables with social factors operates on a more unconscious level than it does for social markers or stereotypes.

The social recognition and evaluation of dialects does not relate just to particular dialect variables but to entire dialect communities. Research on *perceptual dialectology* (Preston 1986) shows that overall dialect perception is generated by linguistic differences, popular culture caricatures, and local identification strategies. For example, caricatures of New York City speech make this a highly recognized dialect area for virtually all American English speakers, regardless of their geographical locale. At the same time, the perceptual location of other regional areas may be subjected to a 'proximity factor', in which the more distant the dialect is geographically, the more likely it is to be classified globally.

REFERENCES

Bailey, R. W. and Görlach, M. 1983. *English as a World Language.* Ann Arbor, Michigan: University of Michigan Press.

Biber, D. and Finegan, E. 1993. *Sociolinguistic Perspectives on Register.* New York: Oxford University Press.

Carver, C. M. 1987. *American Regional Dialects: A Word Geography.* Ann Arbor, Michigan: University of Michigan Press.

Chambers, J. 1993. Vernacular roots. Paper presented at NWAV 22, Ottawa, Canada.

Cheshire, J. 1982. *Variation in an English Dialect: A Sociolinguistic Study.* Cambridge: Cambridge University Press.

Eckert, P. 1989. The whole woman: Sex and gender differences in variation. *Language Variation and Change* 1: 245–268.

Gilliéron, J. 1902–1910. *Atlas linguistique de la France,* 13 vols. Paris: Champion.

Kurath, H. and Bloch, B. 1939. *Handbook of the Linguistic Geography of New England.* Providence, Rhodes Island: Brown University Press.

Kurath, H. and McDavid, R. I. Jr. 1961. *The Pronunciation of English in the Atlantic States.* Ann Arbor, Michigan: University of Michigan Press.

Labov, W. 1963. The social motivation of a sound change. *Word* 19: 273–309. [Reprinted in W. Labov, *Sociolinguistic Patterns*, 1–42. Philadelphia, Pennsylvania: University of Pennsylvania Press.]

Labov, W. 1966a. The linguistic variable as a structural unit. *Washington Linguistic Review* 3: 4–22.

Labov, W. 1966b. Hypercorrection by the lower middle class as a factor in sound change. In W. Bright (ed.) *Sociolinguistics.* The Hague: Mouton. 88–101. [Rèvised version in W. Labov. 1972. 122–143.]

Labov, W. 1966c. *The Social Stratification of English in New York City.* Washington, DC: Center for Applied Linguistics.

Labov, W. 1972a. *Sociolinguistic Patterns.* Philadelphia, Pennsylvania: University of Pennsylvania Press.

Labov, W. 1972b. *Language in the Inner City: Studies in the Black English Vernacular.* Philadelphia, Pennsylvania: University of Pennsylvania Press.

Labov, W. 1972c. Some principles of linguistic methodology. *Language in Society* 1: 97–120.

Labov, W. 1991a. The three dialects, of English. In P. Eckert (ed.) *New Ways of Analyzing Sound Change.* New York: Academic Press. 1–44.

Labov, W. 1991b. *Sociolinguistic Patterns.* Philadelphia, Pennsylvania: University of Pennsylvania Press.

Labov, W. 1994. *Principles of Linguistic Change, I: Internal Factors.* Oxford: Blackwell.

Labov, W., Yaeger, M. and Steiner, R. 1972. *A Quantitative Study of Sound Change in Progress.* Philadelphia, Pennsylvania: US Regional Survey. 7.

Le Page, R. B. and Tabouret-Keller, A. 1985. *Acts of Identity: Creole-Based Approaches to Ethnicity and Language.* Cambridge: Cambridge University Press.

McConnell, G. D. 1988. *Dimensions et mesure de la vitalité linguistique* [*Language Vitality: Its Dimensions and Measurement*]. Québec: International Center for Research on Bilingualism.

Milroy, L. 1987. *Language and Social Networks.* 2nd edn. Oxford: Blackwell.

Orton, H., Sanderson; S. and Widdowson, J. (eds.). 1978. *The Linguistic Atlas of England.* London: Croom Helm.

Preston, D. R. 1986. Fifty some – odd categories of language variation. *International Journal of the Sociology of Language* 57: 9–48.

Schilling-Estes, N. and Wolfram, W. 1994. Convergent explanation and alternative reglarization patterns: *Were/weren't* leveling in a vernacular English variety. *Langua Variation and Change* 6: 273–302.

Shuy, R., Wolfram, W. and Riley, W. K. 1967. *Linguistic Correlates of Social Stratification in Detroit Speech.* Michigan State University: Final report, Cooperative research project. 6–1347.

Smith, P. M. 1985. *Language, the Sexes and Society.* New York: Basil Blackwell.

Trudgill, P. 1990. *The Dialects of England.* Oxford Basil: Blackwell.

Wenker, G. 1877. *Das rheinische Platt.* Düsseldorf: n.p.

Wolfram, W. 1969. *A Sociolinguistic Description of Detroit Negro Speech.* Washington, DC: Center for Applied Linguistics.

Wolfram, W. and Fasold, R. W. 1974. *The Study of Social Dialects in the United States.* Englewood Cliffs, New Jersey: Prentice Hall.

Wolfram, W. and Schilling-Estes, N. 1995. Moribund dialect and the endangerment canon. *Language* 71: 696–722.

CHAPTER 3

The Social Stratification of (r) in New York City Department Stores

WILLIAM LABOV

> As this letter is but a jar of the tongue, ... it is the most imperfect of all the consonants.
>
> John Walker, *Principles of English Pronunciation*, 1791

Anyone who begins to study language in its social context immediately encounters the classic methodological problem: the means used to gather the data interfere with the data to be gathered. The primary means of obtaining a large body of reliable data on the speech of one person is the individual tape-recorded interview. Interview speech is formal speech – not by any absolute measure, but by comparison with the vernacular of everyday life. On the whole, the interview is public speech – monitored and controlled in response to the presence of an outside observer. But even within that definition, the investigator may wonder if the responses in a tape-recorded interview are not a special product of the interaction between the interviewer and the subject. One way of controlling for this is to study the subject in his own natural social context – interacting with his family or peer group (Labov, Cohen, Robins, and Lewis 1968). Another way is to observe the public use of language in everyday life apart from any interview situation – to see how people use language in context when there is no explicit observation. This chapter is an account of the systematic use of rapid and anonymous observations in a study of the sociolinguistic structure of the speech community.[1]

Source: 'The Social Stratification of (r) in New York City Department Stores' in Labov, W, (1972) *Sociolinguistic Patterns* (Philadelphia, PA: University of Pennsylvania Press) pp. 43–54, figs. 2.1, 2.2, tables 2.1, 2.2. Also published in 1978 (Oxford: Basil Blackwell).

This chapter deals primarily with the sociolinguistic study of New York City. The main base for that study (Labov 1966) was a secondary random sample of the Lower East Side. But before the systematic study was carried out, there was an extensive series of preliminary investigations. These included 70 individual interviews and a great many anonymous observations in public places. These preliminary studies led to the definition of the major phonological variables which were to be studied, including (r): the presence or absence of consonantal [r] in postvocalic position in *car, card, four, fourth*, etc. This particular variable appeared to be extraordinarily sensitive to any measure of social or stylistic stratification. On the basis of the exploratory interviews, it seemed possible to carry out an empirical test of two general notions: first, that the linguistic variable (r) is a social differentiator in all levels of New York City speech, and second, that rapid and anonymous speech events could be used as the basis for a systematic study of language. The study of (r) in New York City department stores which I will report here was conducted in November 1962 as a test of these ideas.

We can hardly consider the social distribution of language in New York City without encountering the pattern of social stratification which pervades the life of the city. This concept is analysed in some detail in the major study of the Lower East Side; here we may briefly consider the definition given by Bernard Barber: social stratification is the product of social differentiation and social evaluation (1957: 1–3). The use of this term does not imply any specific type of class or caste, but simply that the normal workings of society have produced systematic differences between certain institutions or people, and that these differentiated forms have been ranked in status or prestige by general agreement.

We begin with the general hypothesis suggested by exploratory interviews: *if any two subgroups of New York City speakers are ranked in a scale of social stratification, then they will be ranked in the same order by their differential use of (r).*

It would be easy to test this hypothesis by comparing occupational groups, which are among the most important indexes of social stratification. We could, for example, take a group of lawyers, a group of file clerks, and a group of janitors. But this would hardly go beyond the indications of the exploratory interviews, and such an extreme example of differentiation would not provide a very exacting test of the hypothesis. It should be possible to show that the hypothesis is so general, and the differential use of (r) pervades New York City so thoroughly, that fine social differences will be reflected in the index as well as gross ones.

It therefore seemed best to construct a very severe test by finding a subtle case of stratification within a single occupational group: in this case, the sales people of large department stores in Manhattan. If we select three large department stores, from the top, middle, and bottom of the price and fashion scale, we can expect that the customers will be socially stratified. Would we expect the sales people to show a comparable stratification? Such a position would depend upon two correlations: between the status ranking of the stores and the ranking of parallel jobs in the three stores; and between the jobs and the behavior of the persons who hold those jobs. These are not unreasonable assumptions. C. Wright Mills points out that salesgirls in large department stores tend to borrow prestige from their customers, or at least make an effort in that direction.[2] It appears that a person's own occupation is more closely correlated with his linguistic behavior – for those working actively – than any other single social characteristic. The evidence presented here indicates that the stores are objectively differentiated in a fixed order, and that jobs in these stores are evaluated by employees in that order. Since the product of social differentiation and evaluation, no matter how minor, is social stratification of the employees in the three stores, the hypothesis will predict the following result: salespeople in the highest-ranked store will have the highest values of (r); those in the middle-ranked store will have intermediate values of (r); and those in the lowest-ranked store will show the lowest values. If this result holds true, the hypothesis will have received confirmation in proportion to the severity of the test.

The three stores which were selected are Saks Fifth Avenue, Macy's, and S. Klein. The differential ranking of these stores may be illustrated in many ways. Their locations are one important point:

Highest-ranking: Saks Fifth Avenue
    at 50th St and 5th Ave., near the center of the high fashion shopping district, along with other high-prestige stores such as Bonwit Teller, Henri Bendel, Lord and Taylor

Middle-ranking: Macy's
    Herald Square, 34th St and Sixth Ave., near the garment district, along with Gimbels and Saks-34th St, other middle-range stores in price and prestige.

Lowest-ranking: S. Klein
    Union Square, 14th St and Broadway, not far from the Lower East Side.

The advertising and price policies of the stores are very clearly stratified. Perhaps no other element of class behavior is so sharply differentiated in New York City as that of the newspaper which people read; many surveys have shown that the *Daily News* is the paper read first and foremost by working-class people, while the *New York Times* draws its readership from the middle-class.[3] These two newspapers were examined for the advertising copy in October 24–27,

1962: Saks and Macy's advertised in the *New York Times*, where Kleins was represented only by a very small item; in the *News*, however, Saks does not appear at all, while both Macy's and Kleins are heavy advertisers.

No. of pages of advertising October 24–27, 1962		
	NY Times	Daily News
Saks	2	0
Macy's	2	15
S. Klein	1/4	10

We may also consider the prices of the goods advertised during those four days. Since Saks usually does not list prices, we can only compare prices for all three stores on one item: women's coats. Saks: $90, Macy's: $79.95, Kleins: $23. On four items, we can compare Kleins and Macy's:

	Macy's	S. Klein
dresses	$14.95	$5.00
girls' coats	$16.99	$12.00
stockings	$0.89	$0.45
men's suits	$49.95–$64.95	$26.00–$66.00

The emphasis on prices is also different. Saks either does not mention prices, or buries the figure in small type at the foot of the page. Macy's features the prices in large type, but often adds the slogan, 'You get more than low prices.' Kleins, on the other hand, is often content to let the prices speak for themselves. The form of the prices is also different: Saks gives prices in round figures, such as $120; Macy's always shows a few cents off the dollar: $49.95; Kleins usually prices its goods in round numbers, and adds the retail price which is always much higher, and shown in Macy's style: '$23.00, marked down from $49.95.'

The physical plant of the stores also serves to differentiate them. Saks is the most spacious, especially on the upper floors, with the least amount of goods displayed. Many of the floors are carpeted, and on some of them, a receptionist is stationed to greet the customers. Kleins, at the other extreme, is a maze of annexes, sloping concrete floors, low ceilings; it has the maximum amount of goods displayed at the least possible expense.

The principal stratifying effect upon the employees is the prestige of the store, and the working conditions. Wages do not stratify the employees in the same order. On the contrary, there is every indication that high-prestige stores such as Saks pay lower wages than Macy's.

Saks is a nonunion store, and the general wage structure is not a matter of public record. However, conversations with a number of men and women who have worked in New York department stores, including Saks and Macy's, show general agreement on the direction of the wage differential.[4] Some of the incidents reflect a willingness of sales people to accept much lower wages from the store with greater prestige. The executives of the prestige stores pay a great deal of attention to employee relations, and take many unusual measures to ensure that the sales people feel that they share in the general prestige of the store.[5] One of the Lower East Side informants who worked at Saks was chiefly impressed with the fact that she could buy Saks clothes at a 25 percent discount. A similar concession from a lower-prestige store would have been of little interest to her.

From the point of view of Macy's employees, a job in Kleins is well below the horizon. Working conditions and wages are generally considered to be worse, and the prestige of Kleins is very low indeed. As we will see, the ethnic composition of the store employees reflects these differences quite accurately.

A socioeconomic index which ranked New Yorkers on occupation would show the employees of the three stores at the same level; an income scale would probably find Macy's employees somewhat higher than the others; education is the only objective scale which might differentiate the groups in the same order as the prestige of the stores, though there is no evidence on this point. However, the working conditions of sales jobs in the three stores stratify them in the order: Saks, Macy's, Kleins; the prestige of the stores leads to a social evaluation of these jobs in the same order. Thus the two aspects of social stratification – differentiation and evaluation – are to be seen in the relations of the three stores and their employees.

The normal approach to a survey of department-store employees requires that one enumerate the sales people of each store, draw random samples in each store, make appointments to speak with each employee at home, interview the respondents, then segregate the native New Yorkers, analyse and resample the nonrespondents, and so on. This is an expensive and time-consuming procedure, but for most purposes there is no short cut which will give accurate and reliable results. In this case, a simpler method which relies upon the extreme generality of the linguistic behavior of the subjects was used to gather a very limited type of data. This method is dependent upon the systematic sampling of casual and anonymous speech events. Applied in a poorly defined environment, such a method is open to many biases and it would be difficult to say what population had been studied. In this case, our population is well-defined as the sales people (or more generally, any employee whose speech might be heard by a customer) in three specific stores at a specific time. The result will be a view of the role that speech would play in the over-all social imprint of the employees upon the customer. It is surprising that this simple and economical approach achieves results with a high degree of consistency and regularity, and allows us to test the original hypothesis in a number of subtle ways.

The Method

The application of the study of casual and anonymous speech events to the department-store situation was relatively simple. The interviewer approached the informant in the role of a customer asking for directions to a particular department. The department was one which was located on the fourth floor. When the interviewer asked, 'Excuse me, where are the women's shoes?' the answer would normally be, 'Fourth floor.'

The interviewer then leaned forward and said, 'Excuse me?' He would usu-ally then obtain another utterance, *'Fourth floor,'* spoken in careful style under emphatic stress.[6]

The interviewer would then move along the aisle of the store to a point immediately beyond the informant's view, and make a written note of the data. The following independent variables were included:

the store
floor within the store[7]
sex
age (estimated in units of five years)
occupation (floorwalker, sales, cashier, stockboy)
race
foreign or regional accent, if any

The dependent variable is the use of (r) in four occurrences:

casual: fou_r_th floo_r_
emphatic: *fou_r_th floo_r_*

Thus we have preconsonantal and final position, in both casual and emphatic styles of speech. In addition, all other uses of (r) by the informant were noted, from remarks overheard or contained in the interview. For each plainly con-stricted value of the variable, (r-1) was entered; for unconstricted schwa, lengthened vowel, or no representation, (r-0) was entered. Doubtful cases or partial constriction were symbolized *d* and were not used in the final tabulation.

Also noted were instances of affricates or stops used in the word *fourth* for the final consonant, and any other examples of nonstandard (th) variants used by the speaker.

This method of interviewing was applied in each aisle on the floor as many times as possible before the spacing of the informants became so close that it was noticed that the same question had been asked before. Each floor of the store was investigated in the same way. On the fourth floor, the form of the question was necessarily different:

'Excuse me, what floor is this?'

Following this method, 68 interviews were obtained in Saks, 125 in Macy's, and 71 in Kleins. Total interviewing time for the 264 subjects was approximately 6.5 hours.

At this point, we might consider the nature of these 264 interviews in more general terms. They were speech events which had entirely different social significance for the two participants. As far as the informant was concerned, the exchange was a normal salesman–customer interaction, almost below the level of conscious attention, in which relations of the speakers were so casual and anonymous that they may hardly have been said to have met. This tenuous relationship was the minimum intrusion upon the behavior of the subject; language and the use of language never appeared at all.

From the point of view of the interviewer, the exchange was a systematic elicitation of the exact forms required, in the desired context, the desired order, and with the desired contrast of style.

Overall Stratification of (r)

The results of the study showed clear and consistent stratification of (r) in the three stores. In Figure 3.1, the use of (r) by employees of Saks, Macy's and Kleins is compared by means of a bar graph. Since the data for most informants consist of only four items, we will not use a continuous numerical index for (r), but rather divide all informants into three categories.

all (r-1): those whose records show only (r-1) and no (r-0)
some (r-1): those whose records show at least one (r-1) and one (r-0)
no (r-1): those whose records showed only (r-0)

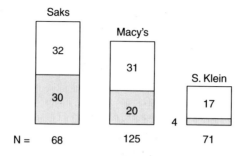

Figure 3.1   Overall stratification of (r) by store

Note: Shaded area = % all (r-l); unshaded area = % some (r-l); % no (r-l) not shown. N = total number of cases.

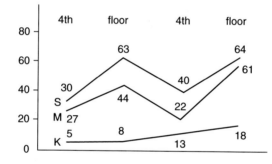

Figure 3.2   Percentage of all (r-l) by store for four positions

Note: (S = Saks, M = Macy's, K = Kleins).

From Figure 3.1 we see that a total of 62 percent of Saks employees, 51 percent of Macy's, and 20 percent of Kleins used all or some (r-1). The stratification is even sharper for the percentages of all (r-1). As the hypothesis predicted, the groups are ranked by their differential use of (r-1) in the same order as their stratification by extralinguistic factors.

Next, we may wish to examine the distribution of (r) in each of the four standard positions. Figure 3.2 shows this type of display, where once again, the stores are differentiated in the same order, and for each position. There is a considerable difference between Macy's and Kleins at each position, but the difference between Macy's and Saks varies. In emphatic pronunciation of the final (r), Macy's employees come very close to the mark set by Saks. It would seem that r-pronunciation is the norm at which a majority of Macy employees aim, yet not the one they use most often. In Saks, we see a shift between casual and emphatic pronunciation, but it is much less marked. In other words, Saks employees have more *security* in a linguistic sense.

The fact that the figures for (r-1) at Kleins are low should not obscure the fact that Kleins employees also participate in the same pattern of stylistic variation of (r) as the other stores. The percentage of r-pronunciation rises at Kleins from 5 to 18 percent as the context becomes more emphatic: a much greater rise in percentage than in the other stores, and a more regular increase as well. It will be important to bear in mind that this attitude – that (r-1) is the most appropriate pronunciation for emphatic speech – is shared by at least some speakers in all three stores.

Table 3.1 shows the data in detail, with the number of instances obtained for each of the four positions of (r), for each store. It may be noted that the number of occurrences in the second pronunciation of *four* is considerably reduced, primarily as a result of some speakers' tendency to answer a second time, 'Fourth.'

Since the numbers in the fourth position are somewhat smaller than the second, it might be suspected that those who use [r] in Saks and Macy's tend to give fuller responses, thus giving rise to a spurious impression of increase in (r) values in those positions. We can check this point by comparing only those who gave a complete response. Their responses can be symbolized by a four-digit number, representing the pronunciation in each of the four positions respectively (see Table 3.2).

Thus we see that the pattern of differential ranking in the use of (r) is preserved in this subgroup of complete responses, and omission of the final 'floor' by some respondents was not a factor in this pattern.

Table 3.1   Detailed distribution of (r) by store and word position

	Saks				Macy's				S. Klein			
	Casual fourth floor		Emphatic fourth floor		Casual fourth floor		Emphatic fourth floor		Casual fourth floor		Emphatic fourth floor	
(r)												
(r-1)	17	31	16	21	33	48	13	31	3	5	6	7
(r-0)	39	18	24	12	81	62	48	20	63	59	40	33
d	4	5	4	4	0	3	1	0	1	1	3	3
No data*	8	14	24	31	11	12	63	74	4	6	22	28
Total no.	68	68	68	68	125	125	125	125	71	71	71	71

Note: *The 'no data' category for Macy's shows relatively high values under the emphatic category. This discrepancy is due to the fact that the procedure for requesting repetition was not standardized in the investigation of the ground floor at Macy's, and values for emphatic response were not regularly obtained. The effects of this loss are checked in Table 3.2, where only complete responses are compared.

Table 3.2 Distribution of (r) for complete responses

(r)		% of total responses in		
		Saks	Macy's	S. Klein
All (r-1)	1 1 1 1	24	22	6
Some (r-1)	0 1 1 1	46	37	12
	0 0 1 1			
	0 1 0 1 etc.			
No (r-1)	0 0 0 0	30/100	41/100	82/100
N =		33	48	34

NOTES

1. I am indebted to Frank Anshen and Marvin Maverick Harris for reference to illuminating replications of this study (Allen 1968; Harris 1968).
2. Mills, C. Wright. 1956. *White Collar*. New York: Oxford University Press. 173. See also p. 243: 'The tendency of white-collar people to borrow status from higher elements is so strong that it has carried over to all social contacts and features of the work-place. Salespeople in department stores…frequently attempt, although often unsuccessfully, to borrow prestige from their contact with customers, and to cash it in among work colleagues as well as friends off the job. In the big city the girl who works on 34th Street cannot successfully claim as much prestige as the one who works on Fifth Avenue or 57th Street.'
3. This statement is fully confirmed by answers to a question on newspaper readership in the Mobilization for Youth Survey of the Lower East Side. The readership of the *Daily News* and *Daily Mirror* (now defunct) on the one hand, and the *New York Times* and *Herald Tribune* (now defunct) on the other hand is almost complementary in distribution by social class.
4. Macy's sales employees are represented by a strong labor union, while Saks is not unionized. One former Macy's employee considered it a matter of common knowledge that Saks wages were lower than Macy's, and that the prestige of the store helped to maintain its nonunion position. Bonuses and other increments are said to enter into the picture. It appears that it is more difficult for a young girl to get a job at Saks than at Macy's. Thus Saks has more leeway in hiring policies, and the tendency of the store officials to select girls who speak in a certain way will play a part in the stratification of language, as well as the adjustment made by the employees to their situation. Both influences converge to produce stratification.
5. A former Macy's employee told me of an incident that occurred shortly before Christmas several years ago. As she was shopping in Lord and Taylor's, she saw the president of the company making the rounds of every aisle and shaking hands with every employee. When she told her fellow employees at Macy's about this scene, the most common remark was, 'How else do you get someone to work for that kind of money?' One can say that not only do the employees of higher-status stores borrow prestige from their employer – it is also deliberately loaned to them.

6. The interviewer in all cases was myself. I was dressed in middle-class style, with jacket, white shirt and tie, and used my normal pronunciation as a college-educated native of New Jersey (r-pronouncing).
7. Notes were also made on the department in which the employee was located, but the numbers for individual departments are not large enough to allow comparison.

REFERENCES

Allen, P. 1968. /r/ Variable in the speech of New Yorkers in Department Stores. Unpublished research paper. SUNY: Stony Brook.

Barber, B. 1957. *Social Stratification*. New York: Harcourt, Brace.

Labov, W. 1966. *The Social Stratification of English in New York City*. Washington, D.C.: Center for Applied Linguistics.

Labov, W., P. Cohen, C. Robins and J. Lewis. 1968. A study of the non-standard English of Negro and Puerto Rican Speakers in New York City. Final Report, Cooperative Research Project 3288, 2 vols. Philadelphia, Pennsylvania: US Regional Survey, 204 N. 35th St Philadelphia 19104.

Walker, J. 1791. *Principles of English Pronunciation*.

CHAPTER 4

The Social Differentiation of English in Norwich

PETER TRUDGILL

Measurement of Co-Variation

One of the chief aims of this work is to investigate the co-variation of phono-logical and sociological variables. In order to measure this type of correlation, a record was first taken of each occurrence of all the variables in the four contextual styles for each informant. Index scores for each informant in each style could then be developed, and, subsequently, the mean index score for each social group calculated. [The following abbreviations are used in this chapter in relation to the social and stylistic stratification of the variable (ng): LWC – lower working-class; MWC – middle working-class; UWC – upper working-class; LMC – lower middle-class; MMC – middle middle-class; WLS – word lists; RPS – reading passages; FS – formal style; CS – casual style – Eds.] By means of these scores we are able: (i) to investigate the nature of the correlation between realisations of phonological variables and social class, social context, and sex; (ii) to discover which variables are subject to social class differentiation and which to stylistic variation; and (iii) to find out which variables are most important in signalling the social context of some linguistic interaction, or the social class of a speaker.

The methods we are using of calculating and portraying individual and group phonological indices were initially developed by Labov (1966). In some respects, however, the present work represents a development of Labov's tech-niques in that use is made of phonological indices for investigating problems

Source: 'The Co-variation of Phonological Variables with Social Parameters', in Trudgill, P. (1974) *The Social Differentiation of English in Norwich,* (Cambridge: Cambridge University Press).

of surface phonemic contrast, and for studying aspects of what is usually termed 'phonological space'.

Let us take as an example the phonological variable (ng), the pronunciation of the suffix -*ing*. This is well known as a variable in many different types of English, and seems likely to provide a good example of social class and stylistic differentiation.

The Variable (ng)

Table 4.1 shows the average (ng) index scores for the five social classes in each of the four contextual styles: Word List Style (WLS), Reading Passage Style (RPS), Formal Speech (FS), and Casual Speech (CS). Tests of significance have not been carried out on this, or on the data for the other variables. As Labov (1970) has said concerning other sociolinguistic data: 'It is immediately obvious to the sophisticated statistician that tests of significance are irrelevant... even if a particular case were below the level of significance, the convergence of so many independent events carries us to a level of confidence which is unknown in most social or psychological research.' Table 4.1 demonstrates that

(i)   the Norwich questionnaire has in fact been successful in eliciting four hierarchically ordered and discrete contextual styles, since, for each class, the scores rise consistently from WLS to CS;

(ii) the social class index has provided a successful basis for the establishment of discrete social classes as these classes are reflected in their linguistic behaviour, since, for each style, the scores rise consistently from MMC to LWC;

(iii) the method of calculating index scores for phonological variables is a successful one and is likely to be useful in the study of Norwich English; and

(iv) the phonological variable (ng) is involved in a considerable amount of social class and contextual variation, with scores ranging over the whole scale from 000 to 100.

The information given in Table 4.1 is more clearly portrayed in Figure 4.1 Index scores, from 000 representing consistent use of [n], to 100 representing consistent use of [ŋ], are plotted along the ordinate. The four contextual styles, from WLS, the most formal, to CS, the most informal, are shown along the abscissa. The lines on the graph connect scores obtained by each of the five social classes in the four contextual styles.

Table 4.1   (ng) Index scores by class and style

	Class	WLS	RPS	FS	CS
I	MMC	000	000	003	028
II	LMC	000	010	015	042
III	UWC	005	015	074	087
IV	MWC	023	044	088	095
V	LWC	029	066	098	100

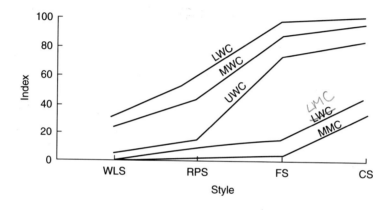

Figure 4.1   Variable (ng) by class and style

The stylistic variation of this variable is portrayed in the consistent down-ward slope of the lines from right to left across the graph, representing an increase in [ŋ] endings as we move from everyday speech to more formal styles. The variable (ng), it can be seen, is a very good indicator of social context, with scores ranging, as we have already noted, from 000 (MMC and LMC in WLS; MMC in RPS) to 100 (LWC in CS). Note that stylistic variation is greatest in the case of the UWC, whose range is from 005 to 087, and whose line on the graph consequently has the steepest gradient. The greater awareness of UWC speakers of the social significance of linguistic variables (shown in Figure 4.1) can be explained by the 'borderline' nature of their social position (see Trudgill 1974, chapter 5). The linguistic insecurity revealed here in the large amount of UWC stylistic variation for (ng) is clearly part of the same tendency.

The social class differentiation of (ng) is, of course, shown on the graph by the clear separation of the lines connecting the scores for each class, and by the hierarchical ordering of these lines, LWC–MMC. The amount of differentiation can be gauged from the spatial separation of the lines on the graph. Thus the greatest amount of differentiation occurs in FS, where the two MC groups appear to have the ability to control (ng) forms to a level nearer that of the more formal styles, whereas the three WC groups have scores which more closely approach their CS level. Note that in CS, which we can assume to be reasonably representative of normal, everyday speech in familiar social environments, the three WC groups show only a small amount of differentiation one from the other, 087–100. This is also true of the two MC groups, 028–042. There is, on the other hand, a very significant difference between the (ng) level of the WC as a whole and that of the MC. This underlines once again the importance of this particular social division in the social structure.

We have shown, then, that the proportion of [n] to [ŋ] suffixes that occurs in speech is a function of the social class of the speaker and of the social context in which he is speaking. Moreover, although (ng) quite clearly differentiates between all five social groups, it is most important in distinguishing MC from WC speakers. UWC speakers have the greatest amount of stylistic variation, and MMC speakers the smallest, although it is instructive to note that even this class uses an average of 28 per cent of forms with [n] in CS.

Sex Differentiation of (ng)

Fischer, in his study of this variable in an American locality (1958), found that males used a higher percentage of [n] forms than females. Generally speaking, this is also the case in Norwich, as Table 4.2 shows. In seventeen cases out of twenty, male scores are greater than or equal to corresponding female scores.[1] We can therefore say that a high (ng) index is typical of male speakers as well as of WC speakers. This link between the linguistic characteristics of WC speakers and male speakers is a common one. Almost all the Norwich variables have the same kind of pattern as that shown in Table 4.2, with women having lower index scores than men. This is a fact which is not, on the face of it, particularly surprising, but one that is at the same time in need of some explanation. There would appear to be two interconnected explanatory factors:

1. Women in our society are more status-conscious than men, generally speaking, and are therefore more aware of the social significance of linguistic variables. There are probably two main reasons for this:

    (i) The social position of women in our society is less secure than that of men, and, generally speaking, subordinate to that of men. It is

Table 4.2 (ng) Indices by class, style and sex

			Style		
Class		WLS	RPS	FS	CS
MMC	M	000	000	004	031
	F	000	000	000	000
LMC	M	000	020	027	017
	F	000	000	003	067
UWC	M	000	018	081	095
	F	011	013	068	077
MWC	M	024	043	091	097
	F	020	046	081	088
LWC	M	066	100	100	100
	F	017	054	097	100

Table 4.3 Sample of ten informants: average scores, word-internal and word-final (t) by style

(t)	WLS	RPS	FS	CS
Word-internal, e.g. *better*	029	052	113	134
Word-final, e.g. *bet*	028	089	151	161

therefore more necessary for women to secure and signal their social status linguistically and in other ways, and they are more aware of the importance of this type of signal.

(ii)   Men in our society can be rated socially by their occupation, their earning power, and perhaps by their other abilities: in other words, by what they *do*. For the most part, however, this is not possible for women, who have generally to be rated on how they *appear*. Since they cannot be rated socially by their occupation, by what other people know about what they do in life, other signals of status, including speech, are correspondingly more important. This last point is perhaps the most important.

2. The second, related, factor is that WC speech, like many other aspects of WC culture, has, in our society, connotations of masculinity, since it is associated with the roughness and toughness supposedly characteristic of WC life, which are, to a certain extent, considered to be desirable masculine attributes. They are not, on the other hand, considered to be desirable feminine characteristics. On the contrary, refinement and sophistication are much preferred.

This discussion is of course necessarily at a rather simple level, but it is clear that we have reflected in these phonological indices part of the value system of our culture as a whole. From the point of view of linguistic theory, this means that, as far as linguistic change 'from below' is concerned, we can expect men to be in the vanguard. Changes 'from above', on the other hand, are more likely to be led by women.[2] The type of sex differentiation shown in Table 4.2 is, in any case, usual. Only a reversal of this pattern, or a large increase in the normal type of male/female differentiation can be considered to be significantly unusual in any way.

NOTES

1. The low score obtained by male LMC speakers in CS requires some comment. The score is clearly unrepresentative, being lower than both the RPS and FS scores and the male MMC score, and is due to the fact that only a very small number of instances of this variable happened to be obtained for this group in CS.
2. Labov's terms 'change from below' and 'change from above' refer respectively to changes from below and above the level of conscious awareness. Usually, however, changes from above involve the downward dissemination of prestige features, i.e. they are social changes 'from above' as well. Changes from below, moreover, very often start among lower class groups (see Trudgill 1972).

REFERENCES

Fischer, J. L. 1958. Social influences on the choice of a linguistic variant. *Word* XIV: 47–56.
Labov, W. 1966. *The Social Stratification of English in New York City*. Washington, D.C.: Center for Applied Linguistics.
Labov, W. 1970. The study of language in its social context. *Studium Generale* XXIII: 30–87.
Trudgill, P. J. 1972. Sex covert prestige and linguistic change in the urban British English of Norwich. *Language in Society* 1: 179–195.
Trudgill, P. J. 1974. *The Social Differentiation of English in Norwich*. Cambridge: Cambridge University Press.

CHAPTER 5

The Transmission Problem in Linguistic Change

WILLIAM LABOV

We can say with some assurance that the diffusion of systematic linguistic change in large cities is promoted by women who combine upward mobility with a consistent rejection of the constraining norms of polite society. The next step in the exploration of the principles of language change is to confront a problem that has not been entered into the agenda of historical linguistics until now.

We can observe that we all speak our mother's vernacular. Granted the many complexities superposed upon this base by later language learning, we necessarily begin with the phonetics, phonology, morphology, and syntax that we acquired from our first caretaker, normally female. The general condition for linguistic change can then be stated in a very simple way: *children must learn to talk differently from their mothers*. Let us refer to this process as *vernacular re-organization*. When and how vernacular re-organization takes place is the first aspect of the transmission problem. The age limitation on this process – the closing off of the critical period – is a recognized research problem that has received much attention from students of second language learning, though work on the acquisition of second dialects is the most relevant to our inquiry into vernacular re-organization. This chapter will consider some recent work on the structural limitations of this process and the social matrix in which it takes place. But the transmission problem has a further aspect that goes beyond any current research. Linguistic changes are not confined to a single generation; they extend across three, four, or more generations of speakers. This is true of most of the changes in the historical record. The general condition for such changes can be re-stated as follows:

> *Children must learn to talk differently from their mothers, and these differences must be in the same direction in each succeeding generation.*

Source: 'The transmission problem in linguistic change' in Labov, W. (2001) *Principles of Linguistic Change: Social Factors* (Oxford: Blackwell Publishing).

How is this possible? This is the core of the *transmission problem*. On the face of it, it is more difficult than any considered so far. To the best of my knowledge, the problem in this form has not been discussed or even recognized in the literature of historical linguistics: yet to understand how any long-range change is possible, we have to have some idea of how such transmission takes place.

Directional Language Change among Philadelphia Children

One of the most remarkable examples of directional transmission at an early age is found in the lexical diffusion of the tensing of short **a** in South Philadelphia. Philadelphia short **a** is tensed categorically only in closed syllables. The 1970s studies showed a low level of tensing in open syllables before /n/ and /l/, with lexical diffusion favoring one word in particular, *planet*. In addition to her studies of the acquisition of stable sociolinguistic variables, Roberts (Roberts and Labov 1995) examined the acquisition of the short **a** tensing pattern. To elicit pronunciation of words that do not occur often in spontaneous speech, she used a picture-naming game, and introduced the word *planet* with a drawing that all adults would name 'planet' without hesitation. On first viewing, the children regularly called it 'a ball'; Roberts corrected them by saying, 'No, it's a planet', and in later repetitions of the game most of the children used that word. In Roberts' pronunciation, *Janet* is tense and *planet* is relatively lax. Despite the fact that they seemed to have learned the word from her, the children's overall pattern was quite different from hers, with a much higher frequency of tensing for *planet*. Table 5.1 shows her results for the children as against the adults recorded between 1974 and 1977.

In the children's speech, the overall level of tensing before intervocalic /n/ has risen from 0.04% to 57%. Furthermore, *planet* has risen from 18% to 93%; the proper name *Janet* also shows tensing at a level of 37%.[1] Thus the children have adopted the adults' arbitrary selection of *planet* as a word to be tensed and developed the change further.

Table 5.1 is a clear and immediate case of directional transmission. How can one account for these children's ability to follow the path of change? They have increased the degree of tensing for a word they hardly knew. One answer might be that their knowledge was greater than it appeared to be in the picture-naming game.[2] But in order to sense the direction of change within the Philadelphia system, they would have to have observed and noted their parents' pronunciation of the word several times, and also observed a series of pronunciations of someone younger than their parents. It seems that accurate inferences about the direction of change can be made on the basis of a very small amount of data.

Table 5.1   Differentiation of *planet* and *Janet* for children and
adults in South Philadelphia

	Adults 18–80, 1974–1977		Children 3–5, 1990	
	n	%	n	%
All NV	256	0.04	250	57
planet	17	18	134	93
Janet	3	0	41	37
hammer	3	0	28	4

Source: Table 1, Roberts and Labov 1995.

Table 5.2   Differentiation of *planet* and *Janet* by younger and
older children in South Philadelphia

	Children 3;2–3;10		Children 3;11–4;11	
	n	%	n	%
All NV	132	52	130	60
planet	60	90	74	96
Janet	29	65	14	10
hammer	14	7	14	0

Source: Table 2, Roberts and Labov 1995.

Table 5.2 shows that this development does depend upon increasing experience. Roberts divided the children into two groups, younger (3;2 to 3;10) and older (3;11 to 4;11). For the older group, tensing of *planet* has advanced even further and is close to 100%, while the tensing of *Janet* has receded to 10%, and *hammer, camera,* etc. remain minimal. Thus children as young as 4 years old are capable of absorbing the direction of change in the community norms, and advancing further in the direction indicated by this vector. It seems probable that they have acquired this information from parents, older siblings, and other slightly older children in the local community. This particular variable does not involve the kind of social factors involved in the stylistic patterning of (ing). The lexical distribution of short **a** words carries no detectable social loading. It is not noticed overtly by community members, is never the topic of social comment, and shows no style shifting. The children's inference on direction of change must be drawn from age distributions alone.

Transmission among Pre-Adolescents in King of Prussia

In most stable communities, the linguistic influence of peers and parents largely coincide. We can best observe their separate influences by locating sites for observation where the influence of parents is clearly distinct from that of the surrounding community. This was the case in Payne's study (1976, 1980) of the acquisition of the Philadelphia dialect in King of Prussia, a new community where half of the parents came from Philadelphia, and half from out of state.[3] Payne studied the progress of 34 out-of-state children in their acquisition of six Philadelphia phonetic variables. These are phonetic outputs governed by simple conditions, like the fronting of /ow/ and /uw/ to [ɛ˃o] and [ɪu] except before liquids. She found that most of the children acquired these patterns within one or two years of residence in Philadelphia. Children who came to King of Prussia before the age of 9 showed more learning of local phonetic rules than those who came afterward, but there were a good range of individual differences. To assess the factors responsible for these differences, Payne recorded for each child the age of arrival in Philadelphia, the number of years under Philadelphia influence, and the number of years under the influence of other dialects. To register social influences, she entered into the matrix the number of peers mentioned by a child in the interview, the number of times the child was mentioned by others, and the number of times that siblings and parents were named. The dependent variable in the study was the number of Philadelphia phonetic variables that were used at a given criterion of consistency, compared to the number by which their parents' dialect differed from the Philadelphia dialect.

Payne reported that the major social variable was age of arrival in the Philadelphia community. While she had expected that the child's place in the local peer group would affect the acquisition of phonetic features, she found no such effect. This result has been regarded as confirming other reports of the importance of the critical age in language learning, and evidence for the primacy of cognitive over social factors in the acquisition of dialect forms. However, a multiple regression re-analysis of Payne's data yields a different result. The most significant independent variable was the number of times that the speaker was mentioned by peers – which is the most sensitive index of the density of the speaker's social network. No significant effect of age, age of arrival, or years spent in Philadelphia appears in any re-configuration of the regression analysis.

Transmission among Adolescents in Detroit

The most systematic data on the linguistic forces that operate among adolescents is provided by Eckert in her study of 'Belten High' in 'Neartown', a suburb of Detroit (1999). She completed a close study of social networks involving several hundred students, through long-term observation in the hallways, courtyards, and environs of the school, personal interviews, and auxiliary studies in a community closer to Detroit, 'Urban City'. Her analysis of the social structure of the high school is published separately as *Jocks and Burnouts* (1989a). It shows these two polar groups as exemplifying the organizing values by which all students classify themselves. Most high schools in the USA are dominated by a group of students who are strongly invested in middle class values, are oriented to college, and in general seek to achieve their goals by conforming to the normative institutions established by adults. These are the Jocks. The other group – known as the Burnouts, Jells, etc. – takes the opposite tack of resistance to adult authority. Burnouts seek to achieve their goals by escaping from adult control, and rely upon local connections and local resources. It is within this intricate social structure that Eckert traces the progress of linguistic change.

As a metropolis of the Inland North, Detroit is fully engaged in the Northern Cities Shift [NCS]. Despite the fact that the city itself is dominated by a large African American population which does not participate in this sound change, the *Atlas of North American English* shows that the remaining whites and the surrounding suburbs are leading exponents of the NCS. Eckert studied the stages of the NCS through impressionistic ratings of the progress of each element.[4] Each variable was categorized in four or five levels; these were then reduced to a single dichotomy, whether the vowel showed an advanced form or not, and the resultant discrete data submitted to a logistic regression analysis.

Eckert's correlations of linguistic and social factors have been published and widely discussed (1986, 1988, 1989b, 1999). Two social oppositions are correlated most strongly with the development of linguistic change: female vs. male and jocks vs. burnouts. Adherence to the jock or burnout ideology is largely predicted by the class status of the students' families. But there is enough social re-organization in the high school that the progress of the linguistic change is linked significantly to the jock/burnout categories, but not to parents' social class. The jock/burnout dimension is best seen as the high school realization of social class, so that the two social dimensions of Figure 5.1 are most comparable to gender and social class in the Philadelphia neighborhoods. Eckert's most striking overall result, shown in Figure 5.1, is that in the course of the Northern Cities Shift class stratification gives way to gender differentiation. The most recent stages in the shift – the backing of /e/ and /ʌ/ – are led by the burnouts and show no significant gender effect. The older, more developed stages – the raising of /æ/, fronting of /o/, and lowering of /oh/ – show the females well ahead (and for females, only, burnouts in advance of jocks (1996)).

The major differentiation is by social activity, not gender. The most advanced speakers are four *brokers* – people who transmit information between jocks, burnouts, and other groups. Next are those engaged in music and theater, a legitimate adult-sponsored jock activity. The lowest values of (æ) are used by the varsity athletes. For all three activities, it is evident that females are ahead of males, yet the major differentiation is not by gender but by social activity. High school girls engaged in varsity athletics show lower forms of (æ) than male brokers or theater people, and one girl athlete has one of the lowest scores of all.

What is particularly significant for the study of language change is the correlation between the local linguistic market place and the advancement

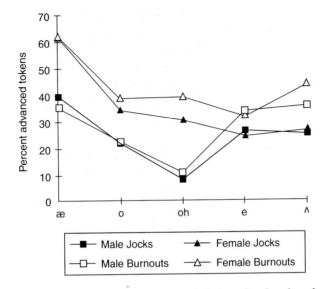

Figure 5.1   Relations of gender and social class in the development of the Northern Cities Shift in Belten High (from Eckert 1989b)

of change. The highest values are shown by brokers, whose status is almost entirely defined by verbal activity, in gossip and negotiation. Almost as prominent is the role of language for the theater and music people. But the status of varsity athletes is in no way involved with the use of language; on the contrary, they stereotypically avoid verbosity.

Today, the raising of (æ) has spread to be a general characteristic of the Belten community; it is certainly not a symbol of working class or nonconformist youth. If the history of (æ) is comparable to the history of (ʌ), we have to project an earlier stage of the variable when it was introduced and led by the working class contingent, just as the backing of (ʌ) is today. How did the transition from one status to the other take place? Our best indication comes from a consideration of the behavior of the majority group at Belten High, the in-betweens.

In Eckert's account, the majority of the Belten population are not defined or do not define themselves as jocks or burnouts. They were commonly referred to as *in-betweens*, sharing characteristics with jocks on the one hand, and with burnouts on the other. They are not bound to avoid or conform to behaviors that are required or forbidden for jocks and burnouts. Eckert quotes one inbetween who dislikes the jock/burnout split and suffers from it:

And I was never a jock and I was never a burnout. I hung around with most, you know, or like there was the jocks and the burnouts who'd sit and give each other dirty looks in the halls, you know... And I just thought that was dumb as could be, you know. So I associated with everybody.... And so that kind of made me feel like a slight outcast you know. Somebody left in between the realms, you know.

For those variables that are led by burnouts, the in-betweens as a whole score slightly lower than the jocks. But the in-betweens can be differentiated by their participation in characteristic burnout activities: smoking in the school courtyard, which jocks categorically avoid, and the activity of cruising the highways and parks close to Detroit. For the more recent stages of the Northern Cities Shift and for the raising of (ay0), these activities are better predictors of linguistic participation than the jock/burnout polarity. This effect appears most strongly in the backing of (e), where in-betweens who use the courtyard have much higher scores than those who do not; in-between boys who cruise are much closer to burnouts than in-betweens who do not.

Eckert's data shows us how the cascade model of the NCS – diffusion from the largest cities to the next largest cities, and so on down – looks from the standpoint of a white suburban population. The leading exponents of the most recent stages of the NCS are those with the strongest connections to Detroit, the burnouts. As the shift progresses, it develops a gender dichotomy; girls, and particularly burnout girls, are the most advanced in the three oldest stages. But in Neartown, as in all other communities in the Inland North, this pattern spreads gradually to encompass the whole community. Neartown does not develop a class dialect that separates working class from middle class, but instead shows a continuum. In the adult community, the most advanced users of the NCS are no longer to be found among the lower and middle working class speakers who were burnouts in their high school days. Fasold's analysis of Detroit in the 1960s showed that women led in the first two stages of the NCS, as they do in Eckert's data. Furthermore, women showed a clear curvilinear pattern, with the lower middle class in advance of the working class and the upper middle class. The Belten High data prefigures this generalization of sound change across the entire speech community. It does not predict the future path of burnout girls, who are now leading in the raising and fronting of (ʌ). If the Detroit suburbs should follow the path of the Philadelphia community, as outlined in the last five chapters, we would expect that the burnout girls would fall behind as they grew older. The adult leaders of linguistic change are most likely to be drawn from the in-betweens who have guarded the connections and social resources that would lead to upward social mobility.

Conversely, we can project the Philadelphia situation back to the high school context of the 1950s. As far as the data carries us, the adult leaders of linguistic change in Philadelphia appear to have been in-betweens in their high school years. While they had connections with the groups who were committed to the rejection of adult norms, they were themselves not committed to this program. They maintained an upwardly mobile path that separated them from lower and middle working class orientation in later years.

Principles of Linguistic Change: Five Steps in the Transmission of Urban Linguistic Change

The principles of linguistic change that are the main topic of this volume (i.e. the source volume for this chapter – eds.) concern the way in which change interacts with and is motivated by features of the social system. These principles do not form a series of distinct findings that can be labeled separately. The central theoretical construction is a view of language socialization: the successive stages of the child's interpretation of linguistic variation. The transmission of linguistic change is inevitably tied to these successive interpretations and re-interpretations. The data presented so far supports the following *Principles of Transmission:*

1. Children begin their language development with the pattern transmitted to them by their female caretakers, and any further changes are built on or added to that pattern.
2. Linguistic variation is transmitted to children as stylistic differentiation on the formal/informal dimension, rather than as social stratification. Formal speech variants are associated by children with instruction and punishment, informal speech with intimacy and fun.
3. At some stage of socialization, dependent on class status, children learn that variants favored in informal speech are associated with lower social status in the wider community.
4. Linguistic changes from below develop first in spontaneous speech at the most informal level. They are unconsciously associated with nonconformity to sociolinguistic norms, and advanced most by youth who resist conformity to adult institutional practices.
5. Linguistic changes are further promoted in the larger community by speakers who have earlier in life adopted symbols of nonconformity without taking other actions that lessen their socioeconomic mobility.

One might call these Principles of *Urban* Transmission because the social patterns described are typical of the social stratification of large cities and the operation of the socioeconomic hierarchy. Most linguistic changes do spread from large cities. In those changes that spread from rural and small town areas (Bailey, Wikle, and Sand 1991), step (4) might take a somewhat different form. The norms that are recognized and resisted by rural speakers are the 'polite' behavior associated with urban patterns. Here the polarity of rural/urban comes into play instead of the social class dimension.

The same reservations must be made in regard to more remote societies and more remote periods of history. The mechanism of stages 1–5 is based on a high degree of social mobility. In those societies where class stratification takes different forms from the more continuous, finely graded system of modern western societies, we must be ready to modify the uniformitarian principle in favor of a more historically specific account of the mechanism of change.

NOTES

1. The contrast of *hammer* and *camera* vs. *Janet* and *planet* is motivated by their phonetic form: the following dark syllable /ər/ has been shown to affect the vowel productions of the first syllable. But there is no reason to expect more tensing in *Janet* than in *planet*: we expect the reverse. Yet *planet* is tensed more than twice as often as *Janet*.
2. One girl, Janell, was recorded at a third session re-playing the picture-naming game. When she saw a card with a planet on it, she said, 'Ball'. Julie said, 'No, you remember that we call that a *planet*'. Janell said, 'Oh, *planet*. E.T. lives on a planet'.
3. The out-of-state parents came from high prestige areas of New York, New England, and the Midwest. The LCV study was designed to give every advantage to parental influence, to assess the relative influence of family and peers on the acquisition of language. King of Prussia was a recently created suburb where half of the residents were Philadelphians, and the other families from out of state had relatively higher prestige jobs than the Philadelphians.
4. Eckert herself discovered the link which completes the circular character of the Northern Cities Shift, the backing of /ʌ/, which is particularly strong in the Detroit area, but had not been noted before by other investigators.

REFERENCES

Bailey, Guy, Tom Wikle, Jan Tillery, and Lori Sand. 1991. The apparent time construct. *Language Variation and Change* 3: 241–264.

Eckert, Penelope. 1986. *The Roles of High School Social Structure in Phonological Change*. Chicago, Illinois: Chicago Linguistic Society.

Eckert, Penelope. 1988. Adolescent social structure and the spread of linguistic change. *Language in Society* 17: 183–208.

Eckert, Penelope. 1989a. *Jocks and Burnouts: Social Categories and Identities in the High School*. New York: Teachers College Press.

Eckert, Penelope. 1989b. The whole woman: Sex and gender differences in variation. *Language Variation and Change* 1: 245–268.

Eckert, Penelope. 1996. Age of a sociolinguistic variable. In Florian Coulmas (ed.) *Handbook of Sociolinguistics*. Oxford: Blackwell.

Eckert, Penelope. 1999. *Linguistic Variation as Social Practice*. Oxford: Blackwell.

Payne, Arvilla. 1976. The acquisition of the phonological system of a second dialect. University of Pennsylvania dissertation.

Payne, Arvilla. 1980. Factors controlling the acquisition of the Philadelphia dialect by out-of-state children. In W. Labov (ed.) *Locating Language in Time and Space*. New York: Academic Press. 143–178.

Roberts, Julie and William Labov. 1995. Learning to talk Philadelphian: Acquisition of short *a* by pre-school children. *Language Variation and Change* 7: 101–112.

CHAPTER 6

Be like: The New Quotative in English

SALI A. TAGLIAMONTE

Introduction

A wide variety of verbs can be used to introduce quoted speech in English, including *say* and *think*, as in (1–2).

1.
    a. I was supposed to be Grumpy but instead I *said*, 'I'm Stinky.' (3/V)
    b. Doctor gives him an empty jar and *says*, 'You bring this back tomorrow.' (2/p)
2.
    a. People will *think*, 'This is a good, like, advantage.'
       I *was thinking*, 'Okay, now we can have our own pictures.' (2/n)
    b. We *thought*, 'Wow, this is really funny.'
    c. Then you *think*, 'He's the original remixer.' (2/z)

Beginning in the early 1980s (Butters 1982: 149) *be like*, shown in (3), appeared on the scene and began to increase and spread.

3.
    a. Even though I have the shirt, I'*m like*, 'I'm going to blend in today.'
       I *was like*, 'But I won't.'
       And we *were like*, 'No you won't.' (2/c)
    b. She's sitting there and she'*s like*, 'Oh my god!'
       She'*s like*, 'That's your boyfriend?'
       And I'*m like*, 'Yeah.'
       She'*s like*, 'Oh, he was a cool one at Lawrence.' (3/T)

75

Since then *be like* has been the subject of many investigations (for example, Blyth, Recktenwald and Wang 1990; Buchstaller 2001, 2006, to appear; Cukor-Avila 2002; D'Arcy 2004; Ferrara and Bell 1995). Among Canadians in their twenties, *be like* has risen from 13% of all quotatives in 1995 (Tagliamonte and Hudson 1999) to 58% of all quotatives in 2002 (Tagliamonte and D'Arcy 2004). Because this change is happening so fast, it provides a unique opportunity to catch language change in action (Labov 2001).

Quantitative Methodology

Language is inherently variable, that is, speakers make choices when they speak. The choice of *be like* is a new development in the English quotative system. The question is how is this happening? A quantitative approach considers the choices people make when there are 'two or more ways of saying the same thing'. Although variants may differ subtly in meaning and distribution, they are viewed as members of the same structured set in the grammar (Wolfram 1993: 195). Moreover, once a large number of choices have been taken into account, the selection of one variant or another can be modeled statistically (Cedergren and Sankoff 1974; Labov 1969).

Why would the analyst want to do this? In essence, the choices speakers make are taken to represent the (underlying) variable grammar as well as the grammar of the speech community to which they belong (Poplack and Tagliamonte 2001: 89). In other words, by tapping into the patterns underlying the use of one form over another, we gain an understanding of the how's and why's of linguistic change.

Principle of Accountability

A foundational concept in the quantitative approach is the 'principle of accountability' (Labov 1972: 72). This principle stipulates that it is necessary to count the number of occurrences of all the relevant forms in the subsystem of grammar that have been targeted for investigation, not simply the variant of interest. In this case, we are interested in the use of *be like* in particular, however we cannot discover how it functions in the grammar without considering it in the context of the quotative system of which it is a part. In other words, the use of *be like* must be reported as a proportion of the total number of contexts where *be like* was used out of the total number of contexts where it could have been used but some other form was used instead.

The essential goal of quantitative analysis of variation is to view the behavior of the dependent variable (in this case choice of quotative verb) as it

distributes across a series of cross cutting independent factors, whether external (social) or internal (grammatical). To gain access to this information, it is
necessary to determine how the choice of, for example, *be like*, is influenced by
different aspects of the contexts in which it occurs (Sankoff 1988: 985). One
of the best tools for analysing this behavior is a computer program that was
specifically designed for modeling the choice process in linguistic behavior,
a type of multiple regression called 'variable rule program' (Sankoff 1988).
The version employed here is *Goldvarb* (Rand and Sankoff 1990; Sankoff,
Tagliamonte and Smith 2005).

Three Lines of Evidence

There are three types of evidence that are available to interpret a multiple
regression analysis using *Goldvarb*. They are: (1) statistical significance (at
the .05 level); (2) constraint ranking; and (3) relative strength (Poplack and
Tagliamonte 2001; Tagliamonte 2002).

In interpreting results, the first question is which factor groups are statistically significant? The program also assigns factor weights to each category
of the factor groups included in the analysis. This measures the probability
of one variant or another in each of the contexts being tested. Constraint
ranking is the hierarchy from more to less of the factor weights of categories
within a factor group. In essence, this constraint ranking or hierarchy is
the 'grammar' underlying the variable surface manifestations (Poplack and
Tagliamonte 2001). An interpretation of the relative strength of each factor
group can be assessed by considering: (1) the 'range' in each factor group,
and (2) the order of selection of factors in the regression analysis. However,
the simplest way to calculate the strength of an effect is to subtract the lowest factor weight from the highest factor weight in the factor group. When
these numbers are compared for each of the factor groups in an analysis,
the one with highest number (that is, range) typically identifies the strongest constraint. The lowest number identifies the weakest constraint, and so
forth.

Patterns of Use

The patterns underlying the use of *be like* can tell us much about its origin,
development and function in the grammar. In this chapter, I will concentrate on the three main patterns that have been studied in the literature. The
first pattern relates to the type of quote. Apparently, *be like* was first used to
introduce hypothetical speech (Romaine and Lange 1991), but has gradually

expanded to introduce all types of quoted dialogue, even direct speech. To test whether this is true and exactly what type of pattern exists, the analyst must categorize quotations into different types. If the quoted material is contained in a sequence of interchanges which advance the story-line or was part of an utterance to which the protagonists responded, it can be considered direct speech. However, if the quoted material is a report of an attitude or a general feeling of the narrator or group of people, it is considered hypothetical speech. For example, in (16) and (17), the final occurrence of the *be like* quotative introduces hypothetical speech. Contrast this with the preceding quotative verbs. These introduce direct speech.

16.
    a. She*'s like* 'Right, you know, we're taking you out.'
      I *was like* 'Ah I don't want to go out. Please no.'
      And they*'re like* 'Come on, go and get dressed.'
      And Sue Parker- Sue Parker's dad makes home brew wine and it's so strong it's absolutely lethal.
      So she brought a bottle of that round and we drank that
      I *was like* 'O.K. I want to go out!' (UK/j)

17.
    a. We're walking around and Season *goes*, 'Oh my God! There he is!'
      I*'m like*, 'There who is?'
      'Well, there's Luigi.'
      I*'m like*, 'Luigi? The guy in the picture, Luigi?'
      And she*'s like*, 'Yeah!'
      And I jumped behind her and I'm looking over her shoulder.
      'See right over there.' [She points]
      She's pointing him out and everything and he seemed to be coming over this way.
      And I*'m like*, 'Oh my God! Oh my God! Oh my God!'
      I was having a heart attack. (CD/a)

The second pattern relates to the grammatical person of the subject. In earlier studies (Blyth et al. 1990; Romaine and Lange 1991) the use of *say* and *go* were reported to be favored for third person subjects, while *be like* was restricted to first person. However, Ferrara and Bell (1995: 279) claimed that *be like* underwent an expansion in function. In their most advanced corpus (*c.* 1994), a change from the previous samples was found: nearly half of all tokens of *be like* were being used with third person subjects. To test this effect in data, the analyst must categorize each quotative verb according to the grammatical person of the subject. For example, the first instance of *be like* in (16) is third person singular. The second is first person singular and the third is third person plural.

The third pattern relates to the sex of the speaker. According to the literature *be like* is used more by females than by males and perceived to be used by more females than males (Buchstaller 2006; Dailey-O'Cain 2000). This difference is also one of the most well-known diagnostics of linguistic change in progress. Ferrara and Bell (1995: 277) argued that as the frequency of *be like* increases and expands into a broader range of contexts it will gradually lose its association with female speakers and spread to males as well.

Explanations

Why does *be* like pattern in these ways? Ferrara and Bell (1995) argued that the patterns underlying the use of *be like* are indications of its ongoing grammaticalization. Grammaticalization refers to the process by which words become part of the grammar of a language (for example, Hopper and Traugott 1993). When this happens the original meaning of word tends to be lost (that is, semantic bleaching) allowing the word to generalize to more and more contexts in the grammar (that is, expansion) and diffuse across the speech community both locally and beyond. Females are traditionally regarded as being at the forefront (for example, Labov 1966/1982; Trudgill 1972) at least with respect to prestige features (Labov 1990). Thus, it makes sense that females would show a higher frequency of *be like*.

Figure 6.1 shows how the patterns underlying the use of *be like* can be interpreted in terms of a generalizing trend from initial to later stages.

According to this model if an analysis finds that *be like* has expanded into third person subjects and is used with direct speech, then we may interpret this as an indication that the variety has reached a later stage in the development of *be like*. Further, if *be like* is found to be used as often by males as females, this too indicates a later development. In this way, patterns of

MEASURE	INITIAL STAGE	LATER STAGE
Sex	Females use more than males	Neutralization of sex difference
Grammatical person	Encode first person	Expansion into third person
Quote type	Used for internal dialogue	Expansion into direct speech

Figure 6.1   Summary of predictions for increasing grammaticalization of *be like* (Ferrara and Bell 1995)

use can be used as measures of developmental change of a linguistic feature within and across varieties.

The case studies that follow track the development of *be like* from 1995–2004. The analyses examine *be like* using the principle of accountability and test the effect of these contextual constraints across time and space: (1) first person grammatical subjects, (2) the type of quoted material, and (3) the speaker's biological sex.

Case Studies

Be like circa 1995–1996

In 1995 and 1996, students in my undergraduate Sociolinguistics course at the University of Ottawa in Ottawa, Canada and the University of York in York, England collected narratives of personal experience of their peers, students between 18 and 28 years of age. Rachel Hudson and I analysed the quotative system in these data (Tagliamonte and Hudson 1999).

Table 6.1 shows the overall distribution of forms.[1]

Not surprisingly, and as noted by all scholars who had examined the quotative system up to that point, *say* is the most frequent form, representing approximately one-third of all quotatives in each variety 31 per cent in British English and 36 per cent in Canadian English. This is consistent with its general semantic function. On the other hand, the distribution of the other forms is quite different between the two corpora. In British English *go*, *be like* and *think* are equally represented (18%) with the *zero* quotative making up most of the remainder (10%). In Canada, however, *go* and the *zero* quotative are

Table 6.1 Overall distribution of quotative verbs, university students

Quotatives	British English 1997		Canadian English 1995	
	%	N	%	N
say	31	209	36	219
go	18	120	22	135
be like	18	120	13	79
think	18	123	4	27
zero	10	66	20	123
Other	4	24	5	29
Total		665		612

robust, 22 per cent and 20 per cent respectively, *think* is negligible (4%). *Be like* represents 18 per cent of the total number of all quotatives in British English and 13 per cent in Canadian English.

Overall distributions such as those reported in Table 6.1, do not reveal the patterns that may underlie the use of these forms, nor their relative strength when all of them are considered simultaneously. Both these perspectives will provide clues as to the competition and reorganization that may be taking place within the quotative system.

Multivariate analysis

To tap into these deeper trends, we performed a multivariate analysis of the contribution of speaker sex, grammatical person and content of the quote to the probability that *be like* will be used as a quotative verb in these data. The results are shown in Table 6.2.

In British English *be like* is favored by females, at 0.67. In Canadian English the same constraint hierarchy is observed for *be like*, that is, females favor, but here the effect is not statistically significant.

Table 6.2 Multivariate analysis of the contribution of internal and external factors to the probability of *be like*, university students

	British English		Canadian English	
	FW	N	FW	N
Quote Type				
Non-lexicalized sound	0.67	39	0.64	17
Internal Dialogue	0.57	194	0.69	75
Direct Speech	0.45	427	0.47	517
Range	22		22	
Grammatical Person				
First	0.56	272	0.60	245
Third	0.43	251	0.41	232
Range	*13*		*19*	
Sex				
Female	0.67	298	[0.54]	382
Male	0.36	367	[0.44]	230
Range	*31*			

Note: Multivariate analysis of the contribution of internal and external factors to the probability of *be like*. Factor weights not selected as significant in square brackets.

The next step is to determine what the internal linguistic conditioning of the quotatives may reveal. The results for grammatical person reveal that *be like* is favored in first person contexts in both British English, 0.56 and Canadian English, 0.60 and in both cases it is statistically significant. Similarly, as far as the type of quote is concerned, *be like* is favored for non-lexicalized sound and internal dialogue and disfavored for direct speech, at 0.45 and 0.47 in both varieties.

This evidence suggests that we have caught these two varieties at an early stage in the development of *be like*. Nevertheless, *be like* has systematic and parallel linguistic patterning in both varieties, which also mirrors patterns of use reported in the United States. The sex effect is more difficult to interpret due to the discrepancy across varieties in the statistical significance of this effect. It could be that the low threshold of *be like* use in Canada prevents this factor from being selected as statistically significant. In fact, females show a preference for *be like* in both contexts. Moreover, *be like* as a female feature is confirmed in perception studies in Canadian and British English (Buchstaller 2006; Dailey-O'Cain 2000). If so, the results for this factor also suggest an early stage interpretation for *be like*.

Be like circa 2002–2003 Toronto, Canada

Let us now move forward in time to 2002–2003. Students in one of my undergraduate research courses at the University of Toronto interviewed members of their own families and social networks, mostly brothers, sisters and close friends. These materials were comparable to the earlier Canadian and British data in terms of speaker age and socio-economic class as well as providing a partial real-time perspective. More important to the building information on *be like* is the fact that this sample includes speakers from the ages of 10 to 19, comprising distinct education levels within the Canadian educational system (primary school, middle school, high school and first-year university). This cross section of the very age groups who are actively engaged in *be like* use permitted Alex D'Arcy and I to tackle the question of how *be like* was changing in apparent time (Tagliamonte and D'Arcy 2004).

Table 6.3 displays the overall distribution of forms in the adolescent age groups.

Focusing first on the inventory of quotatives, we find the same four major verbs – *say, go, think, be like* – and *zero*.[2] Thus, despite innumerable potential quotatives, the well-known frontrunners – *say, go, think, be like* and *zero* – continue to be predominant.

However, by this point in time, *be like* represents a full 58 per cent of the quotative dwarfing both traditional quotatives *say* and *think*. *Think* is particularly

Table 6.3 Overall distribution of quotative verbs, Canadian youth, 9-19 years of age, 2002–2003.

Verb	%	N
be like	58	1198
zero	18	362
say	11	227
go	7	136
think	2	34
Other	5	101
Total		2058

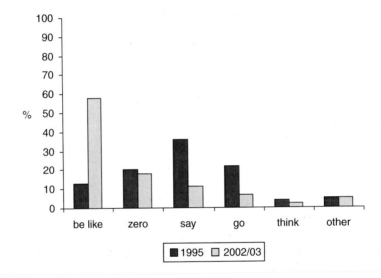

Figure 6.2   Comparison of distribution of quotatives, Canadian youth, 1995 and 2002–2003

scant, accounting for a mere 2 per cent of the data. *Go* is also rare, at 7 per cent. All other quotatives combined represent only 5 per cent of the data. *Be like* has virtually taken over the system.

Figure 6.2 displays a comparison of the overall distribution of quotatives in Canadian English in 1995 and the current data set from 2002–2003.

The perspective of real-time provides a stunning display of linguistic change. In 1995, the frequency of *be like* was only 13 per cent among Canadian 18–28 year olds. In the more recent materials, the overall frequency is 58 per cent. Indeed, a direct comparison with the 17–19 year old speakers in the Toronto English corpus reveals an even higher overall frequency, with *be like* representing 62 per cent of quotative usage. This means that the proportion of *be like* increased by more than four and a half times in seven years! In contrast, *say, go* and *think* all waned in frequency. Indeed, where once scholars consistently reported *say* to be the most frequent form (representing approximately one-third of the quotative system) (Blyth et al. 1990; Ferrara and Bell 1995; Tagliamonte and Hudson 1999), it is no longer, now comprising just 11 per cent of quotative verbs overall. This suggests that *be like* has now moved in on the territory once held by *go, think* and *say* in Canadian English, not simply *go* and *think*, as reported in Tagliamonte and Hudson (1999: 167). *Be like* has encroached into the realms formerly occupied by other quotatives, representing a trajectory of expansion from *go* and *think* into the domain of *say*. The proportion of *zero* and other forms remains constant, suggesting that at least some parts of the system remain unaffected by the encroachment of *be like*.[3]

Be Like across the Speech Community

The next step was to consider *be like* from the perspective of the whole speech community by analysing this feature in the Toronto English Corpus, a 1.5

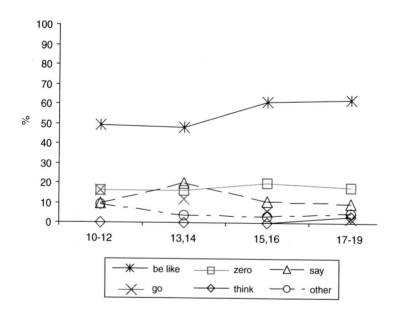

Figure 6.3   Overall distribution of quotatives by age in Canadian youth, 9–19 years of age, 2003–2004

million-word archive comprised of sociolinguistic interviews with 199 speakers, aged 9 to 87. Using these materials, Alex D'Arcy and I were able to track the progression of *be like* within an entire speech community (Tagliamonte and D'Arcy 2007).

Figures 6.3 and 6.4 display the frequency of each of the main quotatives according to speaker age.

This graphic representation of the Toronto speech community reveals a dramatic division in the existing population. *Be like* overshadows all other forms among speakers under age 30. Conversely, *say* is by far the front-runner among those over 40, but in the younger age groups, its use steadily declines. This is where *be like* is supreme. In the middle, among the 30-year-olds, we find a generation in flux where the frequency of *be like* is virtually equal to that of *say*.

To determine whether these Torontonians share the same (variable) grammar for *be like* we tested for the operation of the constraints discussed earlier. Table 6.4 provides a consistent multivariate analysis for each age group for whom *be like* is robust: the 9–14-year-olds, the 15–16-year-olds, the 17–19-year-olds, the 20–29-year-olds and the 30–39-year-olds.

The first line of evidence, statistical significance, confirms that all the constraints are significant. The second line of evidence is constraint ranking.

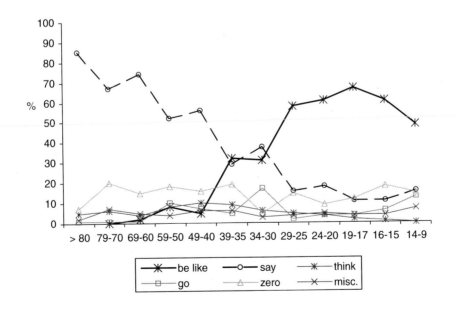

Figure 6.4 Overall distribution of quotatives across age groups in Toronto English, 2002–2003

Here, the hierarchies are entirely as predicted. Internal dialogue consistently favors *be like* over direct speech. The grammatical person constraint is stable with first person subjects favoring *be like* and third persons disfavoring. Finally, females favor *be like* over males, except among the 30-year-olds, where males slightly favor.

The consistency in statistical significance of factors, as well as in the constraint hierarchies for each age group, indicates remarkable stability across the population of *be like* users, suggesting that *be like* is firmly entrenched in their community grammar. Observe also that this form is used well into adulthood (the 30-year-olds), although Figure 6.4 clearly corroborates earlier research heralding that this as an under-40s phenomenon (Ferrara and Bell 1995: 286).

The third line of evidence is strength. Notice that the strength of quotative type differs depending on speaker age. It stands as a clear second ranked constraint for the 9–14 and 15–16 year-olds, with ranges of 22 and 29, respectively. It is also one of the top-ranked constraints among the 30-year-olds. But

Table 6.4   Multivariate analysis of the contribution of internal and external factors to the probability of be like, Canadian English, Toronto, Canada, 2003–2004, 9–39 years of age

	9–14 years 0.63 600		15–16 years 0.85 505		17–19 years 0.82 1992		20–29 years 0.72 1138		30–39 years 0.31 524	
Input total N	FW	N	FW	N	FW	N	FW	N	FW	N
Quote Type										
Thought	**0.70**	50	**0.73**	87	**0.54**	408	**0.55**	265	**0.70**	138
Direct speech	**0.48**	479	**0.44**	351	**0.49**	1443	**0.48**	775	**0.41**	327
Range	22		29		5		7		29	
Grammatical Person										
First	**0.56**	170	**0.55**	163	**0.55**	804	**0.56**	460	**0.51**	232
Third	**0.47**	316	**0.46**	230	**0.45**	905	**0.44**	499	**0.49**	191
Range	9		9		10		12		2	
Sex										
Female	**0.53**	423	**0.55**	340	**0.56**	1518	**0.52**	732	**0.48**	346
Male	**0.44**	177	**0.41**	165	**0.33**	473	**0.47**	406	**0.53**	178
Range	9		14		23		5		5	

among the 17–19-year-olds and the 20–29-year-olds it is very weak. There is little to add about the first versus third person constraint, except to note that it is also quite weak, particularly among the 30-year-olds. Finally, the sex effect peaks in strength among the 17–19-year-olds. Interestingly, among the 30–39-year-olds, it operates in the opposite direction, albeit weakly; males, not females, favor *be like*.

In sum, despite the apparent stability of *be like* in terms of the significance of factors, the detailed evidence from the constraint rankings and their relative strength shows us that there are subtle changes going on in the system.

The next step is to model what the underlying mechanism(s) driving this system might be. The 30-year-olds are likely to have been the first generation of *be like* users. If so, then the speakers in the 20s represent the second generation. These age groups can be positioned in the model as Stage 1 and Stage 2. Labov's (1994, 2001) account of sound change sets the age of stabilization for phonological features at about 17. In these data, not only do the 17–19-year-olds have the highest frequency for *be like*, but they are also the group where the sex effect is strongest. We therefore take them to represent Stage 3.

Figure 6.5 reconfigures the results from Table 6.5, grouping the data into the three age groups that are on the advancing edge of change. What developmental trajectory are they following?

At Stage 1, *be like* favors inner thought. In fact, most studies concur that *be like* entered the quotative system carrying with it this pragmatic correlation. Further evidence to support this comes from the fact that the effect content of the quote is strongest among the 30-year-olds, the early adopters of *be like* in the 1980s. If so, then we would expect the pragmatic constraint to be most salient for them, and it is.

A favoring effect of *be like* with first person has be reported in the literature from the inception of *be like* use, thus it must have been an early correlation as

CONSTRAINTS	STAGE 1 (30-YEAR-OLDS)	STAGE 2 (20-YEAR-OLDS)	STAGE 3 (17–19-YEAR-OLDS)
Quote type	Inner thought favors	Leveling trend visible	Leveling of the content constraint
Grammatical person	First persons favor	First persons favor	First persons continue to favor
Sex	Minimal sex effect	Sex effect still weak, but females take lead	Strong female lead

Figure 6.5 Developmental trajectory for *be like* in the three age groups advancing the change

Table 6.5 Contribution of external and internal factors on the use of *be like* in Toronto English, 17–39 years of age, 2003–2004 re-ordered

	Stage 1 30–39 Years	Stage 2 20–29 Years	Stage 3 17–19 Years
Corrected mean	0.32	0.71	0.81
Total N	453	1137	1842
	FW	FW	FW
Quote Type			
Thought	0.74	0.55	0.54
Direct speech	0.41	0.48	0.49
Range	33	7	5
Grammatical Person			
First	0.52	0.56	0.55
Third	0.48	0.45	0.45
Range	4	11	10
Sex			
Female	0.49	0.52	0.55
Male	0.52	0.48	0.35
Range	3	4	20

well. The evidence in support of this position is that the grammatical person constraint reaches statistical significance for every age group. It too is present from the beginning, although somewhat stronger at Stage 2 and beyond.

When did the sex effect develop? Early studies were inconsistent in their findings for sex (Blyth et al. 1990; Dailey-O'Cain 2000; Ferrara and Bell 1995; Tagliamonte and Hudson 1999). According to Ferrara's and Bell's model, the sex effect is there from the beginning, and gradually neutralized as *be like* expanded in function and diffused in the speech community. Yet in the studies I have reported on here, *be like* appears to do the opposite, developing a correlation with female speakers as it rises in frequency, until this becomes one of the strongest constraints on its use. This is precisely what would be predicted, if, as Labov (2001: 308) suggested, sociolinguistic variation is subsequent to linguistic variation.

In sum the evidence from these building research projects suggests that *be like* has reached what I will refer to as Stage 3 in its developmental trajectory, at least in Canadian English as spoken in Toronto: it is being used for direct speech as much as internal dialogue; however, it continues to be favored with first person subjects and has developed a strong female lead.

Discussion

Putting the research on *be like* in perspective reveals that it has quickly made inroads into the quotative system of contemporary English over the past 20 years or so. The fact that *be like* was actually more frequent in British English (18%) than Canadian English (14%) in 1995–1996 highlights the fact that the spread of this linguistic features does not follow geographic lines of transmission. Yet the same internal linguistic factors seem to be pervasive. In both British and Canadian English, *be like* was highly localized, used for non-lexicalized sound or internal dialogue and for first person subjects. Even at that early stage *be like* was favored in the same contexts as had earlier been reported for in American English.

By 2003–2004, just seven years later, *be like* had risen to be the majority form for all speakers between the ages of 9 and 19 in Canada. The reported internal constraints on *be like* continued to be operational. As in earlier studies, *be like* is favored in first person contexts, a constraint that is maintained in apparent time. The consistency of this effect across major varieties of English – Canadian and British English (Tagliamonte and Hudson 1999) and American English (Blyth et al. 1990; Ferrara and Bell 1995) – and in real time among African Americans in the rural south (Cukor-Avila 2002) suggests that it is a defining feature of *be like*. Similarly, the effect of content of the quote was also operative. However, with this constraint comes evidence for ongoing grammaticalization. Where once *be like* was usually used for inner dialogue or thought – and this is the strongest constraint reported by those who have tested for it (for example, Cukor-Avila 2002; Tagliamonte and Hudson 1999) by the early 2000s there is evidence of *be like* expanding into direct speech (see also D'Arcy 2004). Indeed, 17–19-year-olds in Toronto in 2003–2004 use more *be like* to represent direct speech than any other form. With increasing frequency, speaker sex had become significant, at least for the most advanced speakers. Indeed, the correlation between frequency and sex was confirmed by apparent-time data: the more frequent *be like*, the stronger the effect of sex, corroborating the conjecture that the further *be like* diffuses, 'the more likely it is to differentiate male and female speech' (Tagliamonte and Hudson 1999: 167). Thus, rather than neutralizing, the external constraint of speaker sex becomes more marked increasing in strength as *be like* diffuses further into the quotative system.

It will be interesting to see what the next step in this process will be. Where in the grammar will *be like* expand next? How far and wide into the speech community will it diffuse? Will all varieties change at the same rate and in the same way? Will the adolescents and young adults forego *be like* as they grow older? Only time will tell.

NOTES

1. The 'other' category contained *decide, tell, yell, ask, scream, shout, call, laugh, venture,* and *feel*.
2. There was only a small number of others, including *ask, make, realize, explain*, etc., as well as a smattering of *be just* (N 1/43), and *be* (N 1/49).
3. Of course, these observations rest on the validity of a panel study comparison, namely two corpora from the same sector of the population sampled at two different points in time.

REFERENCES

Blyth, Carl, Jr., Sigrid Recktenwald and Jenny Wang. 1990. I'm like, 'say what?!': A new quotative in American oral narrative. *American Speech* 65: 215–227.

Buchstaller, Isabelle. 2001. An alternative view of like: Its grammaticalisation in conversational American English and beyond. *Edinburgh Working Papers in Applied Linguistics* 11: 21–41.

Buchstaller, Isabelle. 2006. Social stereotypes, personality traits and regional perception displaced: Attitudes towards the 'new' quotatives in the U.K. *Journal of Sociolinguistics* 10: 362–381.

Butters, Ronalds R. 1982. Editor's note [on 'be+like']. *American Speech* 57: 149.

Cedergren, Henrietta J. and David Sankoff. 1974. Variable rules: Performance as a statistical reflection of competence. *Language* 50: 333–355.

Cukor-Avila, Patricia. 2002. *She Ssay, She Go, She be like:* Verbs of quotation over time in African American Vernacular English. *American Speech* 77: 3–31.

Dailey-O'Cain, Jennifer. 2000. The distribution of and attitudes towards focuser *like* and quotative *like*. *Journal of Sociolinguistics* 4: 60–80.

D'Arcy, Alexandra. 2004. Contextualizing St. John's Youth English within the Canadian quotative system. *Journal of English Linguistics* 32: 323–345.

Ferrara, Kathleen and Barbara Bell. 1995. Sociolinguistic variation and discourse function of constructed dialogue introducers: The case of be+like. *American Speech* 70: 265–289.

Hopper, Paul J. and Elizabeth Closs Traugott. 1993. *Grammaticalization*. Cambridge: Cambridge University Press.

Labov, William. 1966/1982. *The Social Stratification of English in New York City.* Washington, D.C.: Center for Applied Linguistics.

Labov, William. 1969. Contraction, deletion, and inherent variability of the English copula. *Language* 45: 715–762.

Labov, William. 1972. *Sociolinguistic Patterns*. Philadelphia, Pennsylvania: University of Pennsylvania Press.

Labov, William. 1990. The intersection of sex and social class in the course of linguistic change. *Language Variation and Change* 2: 205–254.

Labov, William. 2001. *Principles of Linguistic Change. Volume 2: Social Factors*. Oxford: Blackwell Publishing.

Poplack, Shana and Sali A. Tagliamonte. 2001. *African American English in the Diaspora: Tense and Aspect*. Oxford: Blackwell Publishing.

Rand, David and David Sankoff. 1990. *GoldVarb: A Variable Rule Application for the Macintosh*. Montreal: Centre de recherches mathématiques, Université de Montréal.

Romaine, Suzanne and Deborah Lange. 1991. The use of *like* as a marker of reported speech and thought: A case of grammaticalization in progress. *American Speech* 66: 227–279.

Sankoff, David. 1988. Variable rules. In Ulrich Ammon, Norbert Dittmar and Klaus J. Mattheier (eds.) *Sociolinguistics: An International Handbook of the Science of Language and Society. Volume 2*. Berlin: Walter de Gruyter. 984–997.

Sankoff, David, Sali A. Tagliamonte and Eric Smith. 2005. *Goldvarb X*. Department of Linguistics, University of Toronto. http://individual.utoronto.ca/tagliamonte/Goldvarb/GV_index.htm.

Tagliamonte, Sali A. 2002. Comparative sociolinguistics. In Jack Chambers, Peter Trudgill and Natalie Schilling-Estes (eds.) *Handbook of Language Variation and Change*. Oxford: Blackwell Publishing. 729–763.

Tagliamonte, Sali and Alexandra D'Arcy. 2004. *He's like; She's like*: The quotative system in Canadian Youth. *Journal of Sociolinguistics* 8: 493–514.

Tagliamonte, Sali A. and Alexandra D'Arcy. 2007. Frequency and variation in the community grammar: Tracking a new change through the generations. *Language Variation and Change* 19: 1–19.

Tagliamonte, Sali A. and Rachel Hudson. 1999. Be like et al. beyond America: The quotative system in British and Canadian youth. *Journal of Sociolinguistics* 3: 147–172.

Trudgill, Peter. 1972. Sex, covert prestige, and linguistic change in urban British English. *Language in Society* 1: 179–195.

Wolfram, Walt. 1993. Identifying and interpreting variables. In Dennis Preston (ed.) *American Dialect Research*. Amsterdam and Philadelphia: John Benjamins. 193–221.

CHAPTER 7

Network Structure and Linguistic Change

JAMES MILROY AND LESLEY MILROY

[T]he Belfast research design here depends on the idea of norm maintenance, which we have operationalized in terms of *social network,* and within this model we have distinguished between relatively weak and strong network links. In any real community individuals and groups will vary in the relative intensity of ties, and this is what makes it possible to compare them in these terms. But behind this there lies an idealization which predicts that in a community bound by maximally dense and multiplex network ties linguistic change would not take place at all. No such community can actually exist, but the idealization is important, because it also implies that to the extent that relatively weak ties exist in communities (as in fact they do), the conditions will be present for linguistic change to take place. This perception was partly borne out even in the inner-city research. We noted that very few individuals had markedly low network strength scores, and furthermore that these individuals tended to use language much less close to the core Belfast vernacular, with a much lower use of the 'close-tie' variants (such as [ʌ] in words of the (*pull*) class). The idea that *relative strength of network tie* is a powerful predictor of language use is thus implicit in the interpretative model we have used throughout: it predicts, amongst other things, that to the extent that ties are strong, linguistic change will be prevented or impeded, whereas to the extent that they are weak, they will be more open to external influences, and so linguistic change will be facilitated.

Weak ties are much more difficult to investigate empirically than strong ones, and the instinct of the network-based ethnographer is usually to study relatively self-contained small communities that are internally bound by strong

Source: 'Network Structure and Linguistic Change' in Milroy, J (1992) *Linguistic Variation and Change: On the Historical Sociolinguistics of English,* (Oxford: Blackwell Publishing) pp. 176–91.

links and relatively insulated from outside influences. The ethnographic work reported in Cohen (1982), for example, focuses on peripheral areas of the British Isles that have a strong sense of local 'community'. Although we may surmise that urban situations (such as Belfast) are likely to exhibit lower density and multiplexity in personal ties than remote rural ones (and are by the same token also likely to be more open to outside influences), many studies, both urban and rural, have shown that a close-knit network structure functions as a conservative force, resisting pressures for change originating from outside the network; conversely, those speakers whose ties to the localized network are weakest approximate least closely to localized vernacular norms, and are most exposed to external pressures for change (J. Milroy and L. Milroy 1985). This second observation suggests that since strong network structure seems to be implicated in a rather negative way in linguistic change, a closer examination of *weak* network ties might be profitable.

The difficulty in studying weak ties empirically means that the quantitative variable of network (which can be readily applied to close-knit communities) cannot be easily operationalized in situations where the population is socially and/or geographically mobile. The networks of mobile persons tend to be loose-knit; such persons form (relatively weak) ties with very large numbers of others, and these are often open-ended, seldom forming into close-tie clusters. It is therefore difficult, in studying loose-knit situations, to produce direct empirical (quantitative) evidence of the kind usually used to support sociolinguistic theories, and indeed (as we noted above) the speaker-innovator cannot easily be directly observed and located. However, we have argued (J. Milroy and L. Milroy 1985) that the speaker-innovator is a necessary theoretical construct if we are to clarify what is involved in solving the actuation problem. Therefore, as we are again dealing with an idealization here, we use a mode of argumentation that differs from the usual inductive mode favoured by quantitative linguists, and to support the argument we adduce evidence from various sources.

This evidence is of several different kinds. As is the case so often in network analysis, we find that anthropological and sociological studies of small-scale communities (as in Cohen 1982) are illuminating. On the basis of evidence from a number of such studies, Mewett (1982) has observed that *class* differences in small communities begin to emerge over time as the proportion of *multiplex* relationships declines (multiplexity being an important characteristic of a close-knit type of network structure). This observation, in addition to associating social class stratification with the decline of close-knit networks, suggests a framework for linking network studies with large-scale class-based studies in formulating a more coherent multi-level sociolinguistic theory than we have at present. But we have also derived insights from important work by Granovetter (1973, 1982), who has argued that 'weak' and uniplex interpersonal ties, although they may be subjectively perceived as unimportant, are in fact important channels through which innovation and influence flow from one close-knit group to another, linking such groups the wider society. This rather larger-scale aspect of the social function of weak ties has a number of important implications for a socially accountable theory of linguistic change and diffusion, some of which we shall briefly outline.

Granovetter's working definition of 'weak' and 'strong' ties is as follows: 'The strength of a tie is a (probably linear) combination of the amount of time, the emotional intensity, the intimacy (mutual confiding) and the reciprocal services which characterise a tie' (1973: 1361). This is probably sufficient to satisfy most people's feeling of what might be meant by a 'weak' or 'strong' interpersonal tie, and it fits in fairly well with our indicators for measuring network strength in the Belfast inner-city communities. It also fits in with the principles followed in comparing inner-city with outer-city Belfast (see Milroy, J. 1992, chapter 4): broadly speaking, the former is characterized by stronger and the latter by weaker ties. Thus, although *strength of tie* is a continuous variable, for the purpose of exposition Granovetter treats it as if it were discrete, and we need always to bear in mind that we are speaking in relative terms: a tie is 'weak' if it is less strong than the other ties against which it is measured. Granovetter's basic point is that weak ties between groups regularly provide bridges through which information and influence are diffused. Furthermore, these bridges between groups cannot consist of strong ties: the ties *must* be weak (that is, relatively weak when measured against internal ties). Thus, weak ties may or may not function as bridges, but no strong tie can. This is shown in Figure 7.1.

Strong ties, however, are observed as concentrated within groups. Thus, they give rise to a *local* cohesion of the kind that we explored in inner-city Belfast; yet, at the same time, they lead paradoxically to overall fragmentation. Clearly, this perception is potentially very illuminating in accounting for different language states at different times and places at many levels of generality, ranging from the interpersonal situations, through dialect-divergent, bilingual and code-switching communities to the very broadest of language situations, and it throws light on the question of convergence and divergence. The model of strong and weak ties presented graphically in Figure 7.2 can be thought of as an idealized representation of (for example) an urban community which consists of clumps connected by predominantly strong ties, which in turn are connected to other clumps by predominantly weak ties, but it can of course represent other kinds of language situation that we might conceive of.

The important point (from our perspective) that follows from all this is that weak inter-group ties are likely to be critical in transmitting innovations from one group to another, despite the common-sense assumption that *strong* ties fulfil this role. For example, Downes (1984: 155) suggests that the

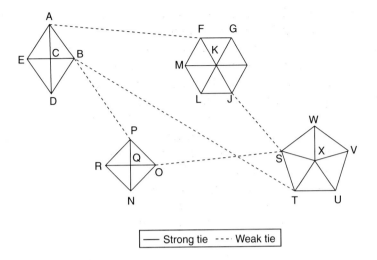

Figure 7.1   **Weak ties as bridges**

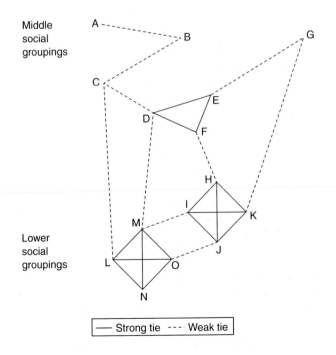

Figure 7.2   Idealized representation of an urban community in which weaker ties are more numerous in middle social groupings and between the groups

network concept is important in developing a theory of linguistic diffusion, but assumes that it is strong ties that will be critical. This assumption seems to be shared by many linguists who have considered the matter; indeed, as we have noticed, Labov (1980: 261) presents a model of the innovator as an individual with strong ties both inside *and* outside a local group. Clearly, this conflicts with the arguments presented here, which predict that to the extent that ties are strong, linguistic change will be impeded, not facilitated.

Granovetter's principle seems at first sight to go against 'common sense', and for this reason we need to expound it a little further. First of all, it is likely that weak ties are much more numerous than strong ties, simply because the time and energy invested in the maintenance of strong ties must place an upper limit on how many it is possible to have, whereas weak ties require little effort. Second, many more individuals can be reached through weak ties than through strong ties; consider for example the bridges set up by participants at academic conferences, which link cohesive groups associated with each institution and through which new ideas and information pass. Conversely, information relayed through strong ties tends not to be innovatory, since persons linked by strong ties tend to share contacts (that is, to belong to overlapping networks). So they may, for example, hear the same rumour several times. This general principle entails that mobile individuals who have contracted many weak ties, but who as a consequence of their mobility occupy a position marginal to some cohesive group, are in a particularly strong position to carry information across social boundaries and to diffuse innovations of all kinds.

In view of the norm-enforcing capacities of groups built up mainly of strong ties, it is easy to see why innovators are likely to be persons weakly linked to the group. Susceptibility to outside influence is likely to increase in inverse proportion to strength of tie with the group. Where groups are loose-knit – that is, linked mainly by weak ties – they are likely to be generally more susceptible to innovation. We might note that this contention is consistent with the principle enunciated by Labov and Kroch that innovating groups are located centrally in the social hierarchy, characterized as upper working or lower-middle class (Kroch 1978; Labov 1980: 254). For it is likely that in British (and probably also North American) society the most close-knit networks are located at the highest and lowest strata, with a majority of socially and geographically mobile speakers (whose networks are relatively loose-knit) falling between these two points.

One apparent difficulty with the proposal that innovators are only marginally linked to the group is in explaining how these peripheral people can successfully diffuse innovations to central members of that group, who are of course resistant to innovation. One part of the answer here is that central members often *do not* accept the innovation: hence, for example, the persistence of regional varieties and minority languages in strong-tie situations (compare here Andersen's (1986) idea of *endocentric* dialect communities). But to the extent that they do accept innovations, two related points are relevant. First, since resistance to innovation is likely to be strong in a norm-conforming group, a large number of persons will have to be exposed to it and adopt it in the early stages for it to spread successfully. Now, in a mobile society, weak ties are likely to be very much more numerous than strong ties (especially in urban communities), and some of them are likely to function as bridges through which innovations flow. Thus, an innovation like the London merger between /ð, θ/ (as in *brother, thin*) and /v, f/ reported in Norwich teenage speech (Trudgill 1986: 54ff.) is likely to be transmitted through a great many weak links between Londoners and Norwich speakers, and Trudgill suggests tourists and football supporters as individuals who might contract such links. Quite simply, before it stands any chance of acceptance by central members of a group, the links through which it is originally transmitted *need* to be numerous (compare Granovetter 1973: 1367). Thus, the existence of numerous weak ties is a necessary condition for innovations to spread: it is the quantity as well as the quality of links between people that is crucial here.

The second point we need to make in explaining the success of marginal members of a group as innovators relates more directly to Labov's view of the innovating personality type. As Granovetter suggests, persons central to a close-knit, norm-enforcing group are likely to find innovation a risky activity (indeed it is probably more in their interests to maintain and enforce norms than to innovate); but adopting an innovation that is already widespread on the fringes of the group is very much less risky. There is of course a time dimension involved, and in this dimension a point may be reached at which central members begin to accept that it is in their own interests to adopt the innovation. Informal observation of cultural and political innovation suggests that this is generally true. As an example we may cite the final adoption of a marginal cult (Christianity) in ancient Rome: it took centuries for this innovation to penetrate to the centre. Central members of a group diminish the risk of potentially deviant activity by adopting (after a lapse of time) an innovation from persons who are already non-peripheral members of the group, rather than by direct importation from marginals, who tend to be perceived as deviant. Thus, we can in this way understand how acceptance – under certain conditions – can be a rational strategy on the part of central members of the group.

Within the network model, therefore, the existence of numerous weak ties is a necessary condition for innovation to be adopted. But there must be additional conditions, and at least one of these is psychosocial: this is that speakers from the receptor community want to identify for some reason with speakers from the donor community. Thus, the Norwich speakers cited by Trudgill in some sense view London vernacular speakers as persons with whom, in Andersen's (1986) terms, they wish to express solidarity. Ultimately, for an innovation to be adopted, it seems that the adopters must believe that some benefit to themselves and/or their groups will come about through the adoption of the innovation. The cost of adopting the innovation in terms of effort will thus be perceived by the adopters as less than the benefit received from adopting it. It also seems that an explanation based on the idea of group identity and solidarity is more satisfactory than one that relies on prestige in a social class dimension (see J. Milroy 1992, chapter 7).

Bearing all these points in mind, it is appropriate now to return to Labov's account of the innovator and compare it with our own. The most general difference is that Labov's account is about a type of person, whereas ours is abstract and structural, focusing on the nature of interpersonal links: it is based on relationships rather than on persons. We might describe Labov's innovator as a person who is sociable and outgoing, and who has many friends both inside and outside the local group. Intuitively, it seems very likely that information of all kinds (including linguistic innovation) can be diffused by such persons, for the reason that they have many contacts. But according to our account, such individuals could not be near the centre of a close-knit group and at the same time have many strong outside ties. More probably, they would have relatively few multiplex links with others, and many of their links would be open-ended and hence low on density; they would have a predominance of weak links, including many that constitute bridges between groups. In class terms such persons would probably be mobile, and their profile would therefore fit in with Labov's view that socially mobile sectors (upper working to lower-middle class) are the ones in which linguistic innovation and change are carried. It seems, however, that this profile is not that of the innovator at all, but that of an *early adopter*, and we shall consider this point fully in the next section.

What we have presented here is an abstract model, supported by the insights of Granovetter, which in effect implies that a community characterized by maximally strong network ties (and hence maximal norm-enforcement) will not permit change to take place within it. Real communities, however, contain varying degrees of internal cohesions and varying degrees of openness to outside influence through weak ties. The speaker-innovator within this model is not a close-tie person, but one who is marginal to more than one (relatively) close-knit group and who therefore forms a bridge between groups across which innovations pass.

Empirical support for our modelling of the speaker-innovator is provided by Rogers and Shoemaker's (1971) studies of about 1500 cases of innovation in many areas of life, including, for example, innovations in agricultural, educational and technological methods. In the present discussion, the most important principle emerging from this work is the distinction between the *innovator* and the *early adopter*. As the innovator has weak links to more than one group and forms a bridge between groups, he or she is, in relation to the close-tie groups, a marginal individual. Rogers and Shoemaker's studies confirm the marginality of innovators and further suggest that innovators are often perceived as underconforming to the point of deviance. If this is correct, the innovator does not resemble Labov's (1980) characterization (an individual who has 'prestige' both inside and outside the local group), but actually seems to have more in common with the famous 'lames' of the Harlem study (Labov 1972). Conversely, Labov's 'innovator' resembles what Rogers and Shoemaker call the 'early adopter'.

Early adopters are relatively central to the group and relatively conforming to the group norms. Once the innovation reaches them, it diffuses to the group as a whole, and at this stage it moves into the middle part of the S-curve structure that is associated with the diffusion of innovations generally. Thus, although linguistic processes are much more complex than many of the other processes that have been studied from this point of view, they share this pattern of diffusion with other kinds of innovation. Later, once the new forms are established in the group, they may diffuse from the centre outwards. At the macro-level, therefore, it is tempting to see these patterns in broad sweeps of cultural and linguistic history (the history of Christianity comes again to mind), but we must leave this speculation aside and return to the matter in hand, because there seems to be no easy way for empirical studies of change in progress to identify in the data the crucial distinction between innovators and early adopters.

However, we should again recall that we are not attempting to describe the characteristics of personality types, but of relations between groups and individuals, and these may vary considerably according to different social and cultural conditions. That is to say that we are not thinking of identifying some individual who lurks around the margins of a group and labelling him or her 'the innovator'. Nor is it a case of 'once an innovator, always an innovator', and it is obviously true that people who are innovative in some ways may not be innovative in others. We are thinking in structural terms, and so we are concerned with the kinds of *relationship between persons* that determine the conditions in which linguistic innovations can be accepted or rejected. Thus, the whole question is relative, just as the definition of the weakness of a tie is relative. What is clear, however, is that if innovations are transmitted across relatively tenuous and marginal links in fleeting encounters that are perceived as unimportant, we are unlikely to observe the actuation of a change. However sophisticated our methods may be, we are much more likely to observe the take-up and diffusion of the innovation by the more socially salient early adopters.

Bearing these difficulties in mind, we now turn to some detailed examples in order to demonstrate how the model developed here affects the interpretation of linguistic variation in speech communities. It is usual to suppose that the diffusion of linguistic change is encouraged by relatively open channels of communication and discouraged by boundaries or weaknesses in lines of communication. In Belfast, however, there are many patterns that are difficult to explain in this apparently common-sense way, and we shall consider two of them here. They are: (1) the social configuration of the spread of /a/-backing from the Protestant east of the city into the Clonard, a West Belfast Catholic community; and (2) the city-wide younger generation consensus on the evaluation of the (*pull*) variable, as against conflicting patterns in the older generation. The backing of /a/ is led by East Belfast males. Figure 7.3 shows this, and it also shows that the movement of back /a/ into West Belfast is not led by Protestant males in the Hammer, as might be expected, but by the younger female group in the Catholic Clonard area. This is the group that exhibits the crossover pattern and reverses the generally expected 'stable norm' patterns. In this group the city-wide female movement *away* from /a/-backing is reversed: the incidence of /a/-backing in the group is higher than in the other older and younger female groups, higher than amongst older females in the same area, and – surprisingly – also higher than amongst their young male counterparts in the Clonard. When measured against other groups, these young women are deviant.

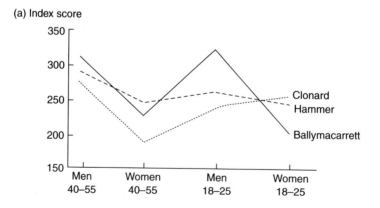

**Figure 7.3   Backing of /a/ in Ballymacarrett, the Clonard
and the Hammer**

The social barriers that inhibit contacts between working-class communities have been well described for many locations throughout the world (examples are cited by L. Milroy 1987), and they were evident in our inner-city fieldwork even *inside* sectarian boundaries. Inter-ethnic conflict in Belfast, however, has had the effect of strengthening the barriers that are present in all such communities (Boal 1978). In fact, the major sectarian boundary in West Belfast is now marked physically by a brick and barbed-wire structure, which is described by the military authorities, apparently without intentional irony, as the 'Peace Line'. The puzzle is that an East Belfast pattern can be carried across these boundaries, evidently by a group of young women whose movements and face-to-face contacts have been constrained from a very early age. [T]here is a long-term shift in the vowel system towards back /a/, and this diffusion pattern from east to west is a continuation of it. That this shift is continuing across the iron barriers (both physical and psychological) that separate the Protestant east and Catholic west, is a fact for which we are obliged to seek a principled explanation.

The most accessible, and possibly the only, explanation is one that takes account of weak ties and the distinction between the marginal innovators and the early adopters. It seems that the Clonard young women are central members of the group, and so they resemble early adopters rather than innovators. This is quite clear from their Network Strength score (as reported by L. Milroy 1987: 204): they all score extremely high on this – much higher than the young Clonard males. Their average score is 4.75 out of a possible maximum of 5.00.

Further personal information about this group points rather clearly to innovation through multiple weak ties. These young women, unlike their male counterparts, were in full employment: they all had regular jobs outside the Clonard community at a rather poor city-centre store. Here they were very likely to be in weak-tie contact with large numbers of people from all over the city, both Catholic and Protestant. Thus, they would be well placed to adopt innovations transmitted by persons peripheral to their core networks, and as a result exposure to innovatory forms would be frequent. Given the large number of service encounters in the store, it becomes possible for the weak-tie encounters with back [a] users to exceed greatly the number of strong-tie encounters with non-back [a] users. Hence the capacity of innovation-bearing weak ties to compete with, and in this case overcome, the innovation-resisting strong ties.

If we have a theoretical perspective such as the one developed here, which explicitly predicts that an innovation will be transmitted through (frequent and numerous) weak ties, we have a solution to the problem of explaining how back [a] can diffuse in this way, and we can present a plausible account of how the innovation can appear to jump across a barrier of brick and barbed wire. If, however, we make the usual assumption that innovations are diffused through strong ties, the pattern is very difficult to explain. Yet, it is only if we make this strong-tie assumption in the first place that [a] diffusion appears to be a puzzle at all.

Whereas back [a] diffusion is mainly a change in a phonetic segment, the change of pattern in the (*pull*) variable is a change of evaluation (or of agreement on norms). This variable is quantified on the basis of a small phono-lexical set consisting of items such as *pull, push, took, shook, foot*, which exhibit vowel alternation between [ʌ] and [u]. Although the [ʌ] variant is recessive, it has very strong affective values and is a very salient marker of casual speech between close acquaintances. But here we wish to point out only one thing – the change in consensus on norms over the generations. Whereas the (*bag*) variable shows consensus across the different groups – old and young, male and female – the (*pull*) variable (shown in Figure 7.4) shows consensus only in the younger generation, where it has become a marker of gender-differentiation. The question is: how can this normative consensus come about in this divided city?

The pattern here is one in which the older groups do not agree on the gender marking in use of the 'in-group' variant [ʌ]. In Ballymacarrett, males favour [ʌ], but in the two West Belfast communities, gender preference is reversed: the [ʌ] variant is favoured by the females. The younger groups,

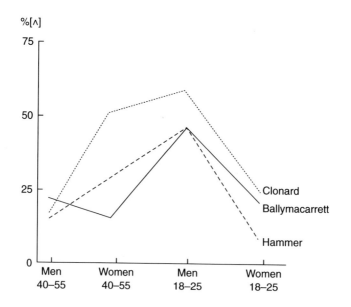

Figure 7.4 Distribution of the (*pull*) variable (percentage of [ʌ] variants are shown) by age, sex and area in inner-city Belfast

however, show the same pattern in all three communities: in all cases [ʌ] preference is stronger among males and weaker among females.

Again the puzzle is to explain how young people living in closed communities, whose outside links are quite tenuous, could reach cross-community consensus on the social value to be attached to the two variants of (*pull*). In their parents' youth there was greater freedom of movement, and people frequently formed friendships across regional and sectarian divisions; however, since the beginning of the civil disorder in 1969, people have been much less able to form strong ties outside their communities. Yet, despite this, the absorption of the (*pull*) variable into the regular socio-linguistic structure of Belfast vernacular has continued unhindered. Again, it is only if we accept that weak ties are the normal channel for the diffusion of innovations that the apparent paradox is resolved.

In these examples, we have selected instances based on extensive quantified information which is very fine-grained and which is fully accountable to the data, but the general pattern here had already become evident from observation of other cases, and the (*pull*) variable can be regarded as testing out a hypothesis that had already been formed. There are many other examples involving different dimensions of variation (including, for example, phonological mergers) that can be observed fairly easily and that appear to show this general pattern of consensus in the inner-city younger generation. Indeed, once you are 'clued in' to the possibilities (especially with regard to gender-differentiation), it is remarkable how readily you can observe the trends in everyday encounters. Perhaps the most dramatic of these trends is the progressive loss of localized lexical items and reduction of phono-lexical variable sets of the (*pull*) type (J. Milroy 1981). Another example is the three-way merger (or apparent merger) of words of the type *fur/fir/fair*, which are very close to being fully merged amongst younger speakers. The few elderly speakers that we studied (around 70 years old in 1975), however, exhibit a three-way differentiation, and middle-aged speakers often have a two-way differentiation. As indications of this greater consensus amongst younger people had already been observed before we started our quantitative analysis, we spoke in terms of 'the rise of an urban vernacular': the first research application in 1975 proposed the hypothesis that we were witnessing in Belfast a fairly early stage in the development of a focused urban vernacular, in which there is a generally observable trend towards greater consensus on norms.

However, we have also emphasized in this chapter the psychosocial barrier of the *sectarian* difference in Belfast, which we might expect to inhibit the trend towards consensus, and from the beginning of our research we naturally wished to discover whether the ethnic difference was consistently and reliably reflected in language. In our pilot research, therefore, we looked at two East Belfast communities, one Catholic and one Protestant (Catholics being a small minority in this part of the city). In our analysis of the tapes, however, we could find no appreciable differences between the two groups: the Catholics spoke with an East Belfast accent (including back varieties of /a/) just as the Protestants did, and their speech was more similar to East Belfast Protestants than it was to West Belfast Catholics. Subsequently, after comparing different communities very fully in our inner-city study, we were able to state, rather cautiously, that 'there is as yet no persuasive evidence to show that the two ethnic groups in Belfast (and Ulster) can be clearly identified by differences in accent' (J. Milroy 1981: 44). Indeed, it seems that those features of differentiation that in the past could have been seized upon as ethnic markers, have been abandoned in favour of greater inner-city agreement on norms of age, sex and contextual style. In general, the Catholic immigrants arrived in the city later than the Protestants and brought from mid and west Ulster a number of features (such as palatalization of initial [k]) that *could* have been used to reinforce differences, but this does not seem to have happened. Both groups seem to be moving in the same direction in the younger generation even though there may be divergent movements in small details; similarly, both groups appear to evaluate variants in much the same way (and this evaluation is often quite divergent from 'standard' evaluations).

REFERENCES

Andersen, H. 1986. Center and periphery: Adoption, diffusion and spread. Paper delivered to the Conference on Historical Dialectology. Poznán, Poland.

Boal, F. W. 1978. Territoriality on the Shankill-Falls divide, Belfast: The perspective from 1976. In D. A. Lanegran and R. Palm (eds.) *An Invitation to Geography*. 2nd edition. New York: McGraw Hill. 58–77.

Cohen, A. (ed.). 1982. *Belonging*. Manchester: Manchester University Press.

Downes, W. 1984. *Language and Society*. Bungay, Suffolk: Fontana.

Granovetter, M. 1973. The strength of weak ties. *American Journal of Sociology* 78: 1360–1380.

Granovetter, M. 1982. The strength of weak ties: A network theory revisited. In P. V. Marsden and N. Lin (eds.) *Social Structure and Network Analysis*. London: Sage.

Kroch, A. 1978. Toward a theory of social dialect variation. *Language in Society* 7: 17–36.

Labov, W. 1972. *Language in the Inner City*. Philadelphia, Pennsylvania: Pennsylvania University Press.

Labov, W. (ed.). 1980. *Locating Language in Time and Space*. New York: Academic Press.

Mewett, P. 1982. Associational categories and the social location of relationships in a lewis crofting community. In A. Cohen (ed.) *Belonging*. Manchester: Manchester University Press. 101–130.

Milroy, J. 1981. *Regional Accents of English: Belfast*. Belfast: Blackstaff.

Milroy, J. 1992. *Linguistic Variation and Change: On the Historical Sociolinguistics of English*. Oxford: Blackwell.

Milroy, J. and L. Milroy. 1985. Linguistic change, social network and speaker innovation. *Journal of Linguistics* 21: 339–384.

Milroy, L. 1987. *Language and Social Networks*. 2nd edition. Oxford: Basil Blackwell.

Rogers, E. M. and F. F. Shoemaker. 1971. *Communication of Innovations* 2nd edition. New York: Free Press.

Trudgill, P. 1986. The apparent time paradigm: Norwich revisited. Paper presented at the 6th Sociolinguistics Symposium, University of Newcastle upon Tyne.

CHAPTER 8

Demythologizing Sociolinguistics

DEBORAH CAMERON

Introduction

A concept of a language involves, and is most often clearly manifest in, acceptance or rejection of what requires explanation about the ways in which languages work. This means that a concept of a language cannot stand isolated in an intellectual no-man's land. It is inevitably part of some more intricate complex of views about how certain verbal activities stand in relation to other human activities, and hence, ultimately, about no man's place in society and in nature. (Harris 1980: 54)

Harris's own work represents an attempt to explore the 'intricate complex of views' that underpin the western tradition of language study. He identifies what he calls a 'language myth' (Harris 1981): a collection of taken-for-granted propositions about the nature and workings of language from which particular questions 'naturally' follow, and lead in turn to particular kinds of solutions. For example, if one accepts the Lockean idea of communication through language as 'telementation', the transference of messages from one mind to another, the obvious question is 'how can this be accomplished?' and the natural solution is to model language as a 'fixed code' located in the mind of every speaker.

Harris's project of 'demythologizing' linguistics consists essentially in making explicit the hidden assumptions which underlie linguists' models, showing

Source: 'Demythologizing Sociolinguistics: Why Language Does Not Reflect Society', by Cameron, D. in Joseph, J. E. and Taylor, T. J. (eds) (1990) (London and New York: Routledge, Taylor & Francis Books) pp. 79–83.

that they are historical constructs (rather than immutable truths given by the nature of language itself) and subjecting them to critical scrutiny. By adopting a different concept of a language, Harris points out, we would inevitably commit ourselves to asking quite different questions and proposing quite other solutions. In Harris's view this is exactly what linguistics ought to do; but I should perhaps add that we do not have to agree with Harris's outright rejection of current linguistic orthodoxy to accept his critical method as a valid and useful tool for reflecting on our practice.

In this chapter, I want to reflect on the practice of Sociolinguistics (by which I mean, more or less, the 'variationist' or 'quantitative' paradigm associated with the work of Labov; whether this is an unreasonably narrow definition of the term 'Sociolinguistics' is a question to which I shall return). In a demythologizing spirit I shall ask what assumptions about language and society underpin work in the quantitative paradigm, why sociolinguists have invested in these assumptions and whether they are useful, or even tenable. I shall argue that if Sociolinguistics is to move forward, or indeed to realize fully its current objectives, it will need to shift its views 'about how certain verbal activities stand in relation to other human activities' a move whose consequences for sociolinguistic methodology and theory may well prove quite radical.

Let me say immediately that I do not wish to deny the value of work in the quantitative paradigm. Indeed, there is an irony in my attempting to demythologize Sociolinguistics, since Sociolinguistics itself was conceived as a demythologizing exercise. The name Labov once gave it – 'secular linguistics' – implies a conscious desire to challenge sacred linguistic dogmas.

The doctrine Labov was most concerned to challenge was that of 'the ideal speaker-hearer in a homogeneous speech community' (I use the familiar Chomskyan formulation, but the central point that linguistics must idealize its object in order to describe it goes back through the structuralist paradigm and to Saussure). Labov debunked this as myth by showing that language is not homogeneous, either at the level of the speech community or the individual grammar. Rather, it possesses 'structured variability'. 'Structured' is important here: it means the variation found in language is not a matter of 'free' or random alterations (which mainstream linguists had recognized but excluded from consideration on the grounds that they were superficial, hence uninteresting, and difficult to model elegantly) but is, on the contrary, systematic and socially conditioned. Labov's work demonstrated that variation could be modeled, and that the analysis of variation provided insight into the mechanism of language change. In other words, he argued convincingly that to accept the myth of the ideal speaker-hearer in the homogeneous speech community was not merely to screen out a few surface irregularities, but rather to miss a fundamental general property of language.

By insisting on the importance of heterogeneity, and developing methods of analysing it, Sociolinguistics clarified questions of real theoretical importance which were not addressed in any principled way by existing paradigms. Like all myths, the myth of idealized homogeneity had foregrounded some things, making them easier to 'see', while rendering other things (like variation and change) impenetrably obscure. Labov's work may with justice be called 'demythologizing' because it pointed this out, and began the task of bringing what was obscure into the light. But the approach he founded is not without myths and blindspots of its own. Quantitative Sociolinguistics has certainly clarified some aspects of language in society. But other aspects remain mysterious, the crucial questions unanswered, or even unasked.

What are these crucial questions? Very briefly, they concern the reasons *why* people behave linguistically as they have been found to do in study after study. Sociolinguistics does not provide us with anything like a satisfactory explanation. The account which is usually given – or, worse, presupposed – in the quantitative paradigm is some version of the proposition that 'language reflects society'. Thus there exist social categories, structures, divisions, attitudes and identities which are marked, encoded or expressed in language use. By correlating patterns of linguistic variation with these social or demographic features, we have given a sufficient account of them. (The account may also be supplemented with crudely functionalist ideas – that speakers 'use' language to express their social identity, for instance – or with a slightly less crude model in terms of group 'norms' at both macro- and micro-levels.)

Two things about this kind of account are particularly problematic. The first problem is its dependence on a naive and simplistic *social* theory. Concepts like 'norm', 'identity', and so on, and sociological models of structures/divisions like class, ethnicity and gender, are used as a 'bottom line' though they stand in need of explication themselves. Secondly, there is the problem of how to *relate* the social to the linguistic (however we conceive the social). The 'language reflects society' account implies that social structures somehow exist before language, which simply 'reflects' or 'expresses' the more fundamental categories of the social. Arguably, however, we need a far more complex model that treats language as *part* of the social, interacting with other modes of behavior and just as important as any of them.

Before I return to these problems in more detail, it is necessary to ask why Sociolinguistics has become caught up in them – why has the quantitative paradigm invested in the whole notion of 'language reflecting society'? This takes us back to the question of what Sociolinguistics is, and how the field has been defined.

'Sociolinguistic and Sociolinguistics': The Rise and Rise of the Quantitative Paradigm

As I pointed out above, to make Sociolinguistics synonymous with the Labovian quantitative is to beg the question. There are other approaches to the study of language in society (such as ethnography of speaking, discourse analysis, sociology of language) which surely have some claim to the title 'Sociolinguistics' so that my definition could be construed as unnecessarily narrow and restricted, not to say biased.

To the criticism of narrowness and bias, however, I would respond by asserting that my definition of Sociolinguistics reflects a historical (and academic-political) reality: over the last fifteen years the quantitative paradigm has so successfully pressed its claims to the central and dominant position in language and society studies, that for most people in the field (and especially most *linguists* in the field) 'Sociolinguistics' does indeed mean primarily if not exclusively 'Labovian quantitative sociolinguistics'. The effect of this shift, for as we shall see it *is* a shift, is to privilege and even to mythologize one kind of approach to linguistic variation.

One can point to any number of textbooks by influential authors in which the primacy of linguistic over social issues is vigorously asserted (Hudson 1980; Trudgill 1978 and 1983). In a rather bizarrely titled introductory essay called 'Sociolinguistics and sociolinguistics', Trudgill puts his notion of what he calls 'sociolinguistics proper' in the following terms: 'All work in this category... is aimed ultimately at improving linguistic theory and at developing our understanding of the nature of language... very definitely *not* 'linguistics as a social science' (1978: 3).

Now there is of course nothing wrong with trying to improve linguistic theory and our understanding of the nature of language; it is also quite true that Sociolinguistics of the sort Trudgill advocates has enabled progress to be made. But one might ask: why this assiduous policing of the disciplinary borders? What is at stake in the emphatic denial of 'linguistics as a social science'? Is Trudgill's stand well motivated in terms of the overall aims of Sociolinguistics, or is it determined by somewhat different considerations?

In my view, what Trudgill says (and he is typical enough) can be interpreted as part of an understandable concern about the academic prestige of Sociolinguistics. Many sociolinguists would like to lay claim to the sort of prestige mainstream linguistics has achieved over the last 25 years; conversely, they would like to distance themselves from the more dubious reputation of contemporary sociology. Academic prestige is dependent on various factors, but one of them is *scientific status*: a prestigious discipline will tend to possess qualities associated with science (however erroneously) such as theoretical

and methodological rigor, 'objectivity', abstraction, and so on. One achievement of the so-called Chomskyan revolution has been to appropriate this sort
of status for linguistics more successfully than previous or alternative paradigms. Little wonder, then, that Sociolinguistics should concentrate on the
'linguistics' to the virtual exclusion of the 'socio'.

The trouble with concentrating on the purely linguistic and eschewing
approaches tainted with the 'social science' tag is that Sociolinguistics, however you try to define it, remains the study of language *in society.*

Linguistic variation cannot be described sensibly without reference to its
social conditioning; and if Sociolinguistics is to progress from description to
explanation (as it must unless it wants to be vulnerable to renewed charges of
'butterfly collecting') it is obviously in need of a theory linking the 'linguistic'
to the 'socio'. Without a satisfactory social theory, therefore, and beyond that a
satisfactory account of the relationship between social and linguistic spheres,
Sociolinguistics is bound to end up stranded in an explanatory void.

Faced with the problem of explaining variation, and in the absence of a
well-thought-out theory of the relation of language and society, sociolinguists
tend to fall back on a number of unsatisfactory positions: they may deny that
anything other than statistical correlation is necessary to explain variation,
they may introduce *ad hoc* social theories of one kind or another, or they may
do both. Let us look more closely at the way these positions are taken up in
practice and at their adequacy or otherwise as explanatory strategies.

Explanation and the Limits of Quantification: The Correlational Fallacy

In the quantitative paradigm, statistical correlations are used to relate frequency scores on linguistic variables to nonlinguistic features both demographic (class, ethnicity, gender, age, locality, group structure) and contextual (topic, setting, level of formality). For instance, it is well known that rising
frequencies of 'prestige' variants like postvocalic [r] in New York City correlate positively with rising social status and rising levels of formality. This kind
of regularity is called a 'sociolinguistic pattern'.

Sociolinguistic patterns are essentially descriptive statements about the distribution of certain variables in the speech community. The question remains
how to explain that distribution. As Brown and Levinson (1987) have noted,
it is commonplace to take correlation as the terminal point of the account.
Thus it could be claimed that my score for the variant [r] is explained by the
fact that I belong to a particular social category say, working-class women of
Italian descent aged 50+ and living in New York City – and am speaking in

a particular context, say a formal interview with a linguistic researcher. The variable (r) acts as what Scherer and Giles (1979) call a 'social marker'. This whole 'explanation' clearly rests on the perception that 'language reflects society': I shall refer to it as the 'correlational fallacy'.

Why is it a fallacy? Because the purported explanation does not in fact explain anything. Someone who subscribes to the sort of account given above has misunderstood what it means to explain something. One does not explain a descriptive generalization (such as 'older working-class female Italian New Yorkers in formal interviews have average (r) scores of n%') by simply stating it all over again. Rather, one is obliged to ask in virtue of what the correlation might hold. Any account which does not go on to take this further step has fallen into the correlational fallacy.

It is precisely at the point where the further step becomes necessary that *ad hoc* social theories are likely to be invoked. A sociolinguist might assert, for instance, that by using n% of (r), older working-class female Italian New Yorkers are expressing their identity as older working-class female Italian New Yorkers; or they are adhering to the norms of their peer group, or possibly (as in the case of a formal interview) the norms of the larger society which dictate a more standardized speech on certain occasions.

There are various difficulties with these suggestions, not all of which can be gone into here in the detail they deserve, but certain problems can at least be sketched in. Take, for example, the notion of speakers expressing a social identity. It is common currency among Sociolinguistics, but a social theorist might pose some awkward questions about it: do people really 'have' such fixed and monolithic social identities which their behavior consistently expresses? Furthermore, is it correct to see language use as expressing an identity which is separate from and prior to language? To put the point a little less obscurely, is it not the case that the way I use language is partly *constitutive* of my social identity? To paraphrase Harold Garfinkel, social actors are not sociolinguistic 'dopes'. The way in which they construct and negotiate identities needs to be examined in some depth before we can say much about the relation of language to identity.

The suggestion that people's use of language reflects groups' norms is a more useful one; it recognizes that human behavior needs to be explained not in terms of invariant causes and effects but in terms of the existence of social meanings, in the light of which people act to reproduce or subvert the order of things. Unfortunately the account of normativity to be found in Sociolinguistics is a curious and extremely deterministic one (a claim which will be illustrated below). There is also the question of where linguistic norms 'come from' and how they 'get into' individual speakers – a problem which becomes all the more acute when, as is often the case, the alleged norms are statistical regularities of such abstraction and complexity that no individual speaker could possibly articulate them either for herself or any other member of the speech community. So once again, the whole issue of norms requires a less *ad hoc* and more sophisticated treatment than it has on the whole received from sociolinguists.

Many of the problems to which I have referred here are also addressed by Suzanne Romaine in an article titled 'The status of sociological models and categories in explaining linguistic variation', which stands as an indictment of the correlational fallacy in Sociolinguistics (Romaine 1984). In her article, Romaine adduces four typical studies in the quantitative paradigm (Gal 1979; Labov 1963; Milroy 1980; Russell 1982) and points out a link between them: they all explain linguistic variation and change in terms of group structure and membership. Tight-knit groups (technically, dense multiplex networks) promote language maintenance whereas looser ties permit linguistic change.

An illustration may make this clearer. Lesley Milroy (1980; see Chapter 7) devised what she called a 'network strength scale' to measure the integration of her Belfast informants into their peer group. Points were scored for such things as having strong ties of kinship in the neighborhood; working at the same place as your neighbors; spending leisure time with workmates; and so on. Individuals scored between 0 and 5 for network strength, and high scores were found to correlate positively with the use of certain vernacular variants. People who were less well integrated for instance because they had been rehoused, were employed outside the neighborhood where they lived or had no work at all – used fewer of these vernacular features. This led Milroy to conclude that people in her survey behaved linguistically as they did because of the normative influence of their peer group. Their sources on linguistic variants were determined by how strong or weak the peer group influence was. Tight-knit groups where people spend a lot of time with each other (and less with anyone else) are efficient norm-enforcing mechanisms – hence the finding that they promote the maintenance of traditional vernacular rather than permitting innovation to creep in.

All this may seem obvious enough, but as Romaine enquires, what kind of an *explanation* is it? The social network is a theoretical construct which cannot therefore 'make' any individual speaker do anything. Yet if we take away the idea of the network's ability to enforce linguistic norms, all we are left with is statistical correlations. Of these, Romaine comments: 'the observed correlations between language and group membership tell us nothing unless fitted into some more general theory' (1984: 37).

What is this 'general theory' to be? Clearly, it needs to engage with the whole issue of how individuals relate to groups and their norms – in Romaine's words, it must make reference to 'rationality, intentionality and the function of social agents and human actors' (1984: 26). Is it then a theory of individual psychology, which seeks to explain how actors make rational decisions in the domain of linguistic behavior? This kind of 'rational choice' line is the one often favored by sociolinguists who do go beyond correlation (cf. Brown and Levinson's explanation (1987) of politeness phenomena in terms of strategies for satisfying universal psychological needs to maintain 'face'). But while an account of individual psychology may be necessary, I think Romaine recognizes it is not sufficient. There is another, neglected area which properly belongs to the study of language in society but which cannot be addressed within the current assumptions of the quantitative paradigm.

Romaine hints at this when she makes the following observation:

> It is legitimate to recognise that an agent's social position and his relations with others may constrain his behavior on a particular occasion in specific ways...People are constrained by the expressive resources available in the language(s) to which they have access and by the conventions which apply to their use. (1984: 37)

This can be interpreted as an argument for social or sociological levels of explanation as well as individual or psychological ones. For what Romaine alludes to here is the fact that speakers 'inherit' a certain system and can only choose from the options it makes available. Social agents are not *free* agents, but this does not mean we have to go back to the notion that they are sociolinguistic automata. Rather, we should ask ourselves such questions as 'what determines "the expressive resources available" in particular languages or to particular groups of speakers? Who or what *produces* "the conventions which apply to their use"? How – that is to say, through what actual, concrete practices is – this done?'

To address such issues seriously requires us to acknowledge that languages are regulated social institutions, and as such may have their own dynamic and become objects of social concern in their own right. With its emphasis on microanalysis and its suspicion of social theory, Sociolinguistics tends to push this kind of perspective into the background. But if we seek to understand people's linguistic behavior and attitudes – and, after all, changes in the linguistic system must at some level be brought about by the behavior and attitudes of actual speakers – an approach to language in society which foregrounds questions like Romaine's is desperately needed. A demythologized Sociolinguistics would incorporate such an approach as a necessary complement to quantification and microanalysis. It would deal with such matters as the production and reproduction of linguistic norms by institutions and socializing practices; how these norms are apprehended, accepted, resisted and subverted by individual actors and what their relation is to the construction of identity.

At this point it is helpful to consider in concrete terms how an approach like this would work and what its advantages might be. I shall therefore turn to a case in point: the changes in linguistic behavior and in certain language systems brought about by the reformist efforts of contemporary feminists. These developments exemplify a kind of linguistic change with which quantitative sociolinguists do not feel at ease, and in relation to which conventional accounts within the 'language reflects society' framework appear particularly lame.

A Case in Point: Sexism in Language

Over the last fifteen years the question of 'sexism in language' has been a hotly contested topic both inside and outside professional linguistic circles. What is at issue is the ways in which certain linguistic subsystems (conventional titles and forms of address, parts of the lexicon and even of grammar, for instance) represent gender. Feminists have pointed out that the tendency of these representations is to reinforce sexual divisions and inequalities. Salient facts about English include, for example, the morphological marking of many female-referring agent nouns (*actress, usherette*); the availability of more sexually pejorative terms for women than men (Lees 1986); the non-reciprocal use of endearment terms from men to women (Wolfson and Manes 1980); and most notoriously, the generic use of masculine pronouns (Bodine 1975).

It should not surprise us that phenomena like these are widely understood as an instance of 'language reflecting society'. 'Society' holds certain beliefs about men and women and their relative status; language has 'evolved' to reflect those beliefs. Feminists have tried to argue that more is going on than passive reflection: sexist linguistic practice is an instance of sexism in its own right and actively reproduces specific beliefs. But nonfeminist sociolinguists have notably failed to take their point.

This becomes particularly evident in discussions of recent changes in English usage – changes which have occurred under pressure from feminist campaigns against sexism in language. For some time, the view of many linguists was that reforming sexist language was an unnecessary, trivial and timewasting objective, since language merely reflected social conditions. If feminists concentrated on removing more fundamental sex inequalities, the language would change of its own accord, automatically reflecting the new nonsexist reality. (This, incidentally, suggests a view of language which might have been supposed to be obsolete in twentieth-century thought, and which we might label 'the organic fallacy': that language is like an organism, with a life of its own, and evolves to meet the needs of its speakers. Exactly how language does this remains a mystery.)

More recently, however, it has become obvious that linguistic reform as proposed by feminists has enjoyed a measure of success. For instance, it is clear that generic masculine pronouns are no longer uniformly used by educated speakers and writers; even such authoritative sources as Quirk *et al.* (1985) acknowledge the existence of alternatives such as singular *they* and *he or she*. What do sociolinguists make of this change in English pronominal usage? Astonishingly, they tell us it has happened 'naturally', as a reflection of the fact that women's social position has radically altered in the last two decades (cf. Cheshire 1984: 33–4 for a statement to this effect).

It is worth pointing out in detail what is wrong with this sort of claim. One immediate flaw in the argument is that it is patently untrue: without campaigns and debates specifically on the issue of sexism *in language*, linguistic usage would not have altered even though other feminist gains (such as equal pay and anti-discrimination legislation) were made. Historically speaking there is certainly a connection between feminist campaigns for equal opportunities and for nonsexist language, but the one has never entailed the other, nor did either just reflect the other. To repeat the crucial point once more: language-using is a social practice in its own right.

It should also be pointed out that a change in linguistic practice is not just a reflection of some more fundamental social change: it is, itself, a social change. Anti-feminists are fond of observing that eliminating generic masculine pronouns does not secure equal pay. Indeed it does not – whoever said it would? Eliminating generic masculine pronouns precisely eliminates generic masculine pronouns. And in so doing it changes the repertoire of social meanings and choices available to social actors. In the words of Trevor Pateman (1980: 15) it 'constitutes a restructuring of at least one aspect of one social relationship'.

Another problem with the 'language reflects society' argument in relation to changes in English usage is that it makes language change a mysterious, abstract process, apparently effected by the agency of no one at all (or perhaps by the language itself – the organic fallacy rides again). This overlooks the protracted struggle which individuals and groups have waged both for and against nonsexist language (and the struggle continues). It ignores, for instance, the activity of every woman who ever fought to put 'Ms' on her cheque book, every publisher, university committee or trade union working party that produced new institutional guidelines on the wording of documents, not to mention every vituperative writer to the newspapers who resisted, denounced or complained about nonsexist language.

The general point here is that there are instances – this is one – where we can locate the specific and concrete steps leading to an observable change in some people's linguistic behavior and in the system itself. We can discover who took those steps and who opposed them. We can refer to a printed debate on the subject, examine the arguments put forward on both sides (and it is interesting that those arguments tended to be about language rather than gender: not 'should women be treated equally' but 'what do words mean and is it right to change them?'). The 'language reflects society' model obscures the mechanisms by which sexist language has become less acceptable, evacuating any notion of agency in language change. Crucially, too, the model glosses over the existence of social conflict and its implications for language use. Here as elsewhere in Sociolinguistics the underlying assumption is of a consensual social formation where speakers acquiesce in the norms of their peer group or their culture, and agree about the social 'needs' which language exists to serve.

It would of course be wrong to claim that all linguistic change is of this kind – organized and politically motivated efforts to alter existing norms and conventions. But some linguistic changes *are* of this kind, and Sociolinguistics should not espouse a concept of language which makes them impossible to account for.

Toward a Demythologized Sociolinguistics

The campaign against sexism in language is one of instance of a type of metalinguistic practice which we might call 'verbal hygiene' (other examples might include Plain English movements or Artificial Language movements; systems regulating the use of obscenity and insults (cf. Garrioch 1987); and, of course, prescriptivism, standardization and associated activities). Such practices are referred to in sociolinguistic work in passing if at all: doubtless it is thought that they are unlikely to advance linguistic theory, and should therefore be left for sociologists to research.

Yet if the arguments put forward above have any force, it may not be so easy to prise apart the concerns of linguistic theory and those of the sociologist. We have seen that sociolinguists make casual but significant use of notions like 'norm' and 'social identity' in order to explain the variation and the attitudes they observe. And I have argued that one of the problems with this is that we are left with no account of where the norms 'come from' and how they 'get into' individual speakers – it is not good enough simply to situate them in some vague and ill-defined 'society', as though society were homogeneous, monolithic and transparent in its workings, and as if individual language users were pre-programmed automata. A detailed investigation of language users' metalinguistic activities – for instance, forms of 'verbal hygiene' – might well tell us a good deal about the production of norms and their apprehension by individuals.

It is striking, for example, that sociolinguists very often refer to the (overt) 'prestige' of standard English and assume this is impressed on speakers by normative instruction carried out mainly in schools; yet I know of no study of how (or even whether) the norms of standard English are inculcated by teachers. Dannequin (1988) has researched this question in France, and the resulting paper is extremely informative – a model of demythologizing.

Metalinguistic activities and beliefs have received, at least in urban Western societies, less attention than they merit. For it is surely a very significant fact about language in these societies that people hold passionate beliefs about it; that it generates social and political conflicts; that practices and movements grow up around it both for and against the status quo. We may consider the well-attested fact that many people, including those with minimal education, read a dictionary for pleasure; that there is a vast market for grammars, usage guides and general interest publications, radio and TV program about the English language; that many large-circulation newspapers and periodicals (such as the *Reader's Digest*) have a regular column on linguistic matters.

Most researchers in the quantitative paradigm are of course well aware of these facts, and more generally of people's keen interest in linguistic minutiae. With some honorable exceptions, though, they tend to treat laypersons' views on usage as manifestations of ignorance to be dispelled, or of crankishness and prejudice to be despised. The axiom that linguistics is 'descriptive not prescriptive', together with the methodological principle that a researcher should influence informants as little as possible, prevent sociolinguists taking folk linguistics seriously. Arguably, though, practices like dictionary reading and writing to the papers on points of usage are striking enough to demand analysis: first, not unnaturally, they demand investigation.

And this is the task I would set for a demythologized Sociolinguistics: to examine the linguistic practices in which members of a culture regularly participate or to whose effects they are exposed. As well as being of interest in itself, this undertaking would help us to make sense of the process noted by Romaine: the constraining of linguistic behavior by the social relations in which speakers are involved and the linguistic resources to which they have access. We might also discover how language change may come about through the efforts of individuals and groups to produce new resources and new social relations. For language is not an organism or a passive reflection, but a social institution, deeply implicated in culture, in society, in political relations at every level. What Sociolinguistics needs is a concept of language in which this point is placed at the center rather than on the margins.

REFERENCES

Bodine, A. 1975. Androcentrism in Prescriptive Grammar. *Language in Society* 4: 129–146.

Brown, P. and S. Levinson. 1987. *Politeness*. Cambridge: Cambridge University Press.

Cheshire, J. 1984. The relationship between language and sex in English. In P. Trudgill (ed.) *Applied Sociolinguistics*. London: Academic Press. 33–49.

Dannequin, C. 1988. Les Enfants Baillonnés [Gagged children]. *Language and Education* 1: 15–31.

Gal, S. 1979. *Language Shift*. New York: Academic Press.

Garrioch, D. 1987. Verbal insults in eighteenth-century Paris. In P. Burke and R. Porter (eds.) *The Social History of Language*. Cambridge: Cambridge University Press.

Harris, R. 1980. *The Language Makers*. London: Duckworth.

Harris, R. 1981. *The Language Myth*. London: Duckworth.

Hudson, R. 1980. *Sociolinguistics*. Cambridge: Cambridge University Press.

Labov, W. 1963. The social motivation of a sound change. *Word* 19: 273–309.

Lees, S. 1986. *Losing Out*. London: Hutchinson.

Milroy, L. 1980. *Language and Social Networks*. Oxford: Blackwell.

Pateman, T. 1980. *Language, Truth and Politics*. Lewes, Sussex: Stroud.

Quirk, R. et al. 1985. *A Comprehensive Grammar of the English Language*. London: Longman.

Romaine, S. 1984. The status of sociological models and categories in explaining linguistic variation. *Linguistische Berichte* 90: 25–38.

Russell, J. 1982. Networks and sociolinguistic variation in an African urban setting. In S. Romaine (ed.) *Sociolinguistic Variation in Speech Communities*. London: Arnold. 125–140.

Scherer, K. and M. Giles. 1979. *Social Markers in Speech*. New York: Academic Press and Cambridge: Cambridge University Press.

Trudgill, P. 1978. Introduction: Sociolinguistics and sociolinguistics. In P. Trudgill (ed.) *Sociolinguistic Patterns in British English*. London: Edward Arnold. 1–18.

Trudgill, P. 1983. *On Dialect*. Oxford: Blackwell.

Wolfson, N. and J. Manes. 1980. Don't 'Dear' Me!. In S. McConnell-Ginet, N. Borker and R. Furman (eds.) *Women and Language in Literature and Society*. New York: Praeger. 79–92.

CHAPTER 9

Syntactic Variation and Beyond

JENNY CHESHIRE

Introduction

Syntactic variation sometimes patterns in similar ways to phonological variation, with the frequencies of specific linguistic variants correlating with the large-scale social variables typically investigated in sociolinguistic research, such as a speaker's social class or gender. It may also pattern with smaller scale, local social factors, again like phonological variation. The following section illustrates this second kind of sociolinguistic variation. It describes how the frequency with which some working-class British adolescent boys use non-standard morphological and syntactic features relates to the boys' participation in their local vernacular culture. We will also consider the linguistic variation from a more dynamic perspective, looking at how some of the boys use the socially symbolic meanings associated with the variable forms to convey their attitudes towards their schoolteachers.

With syntactic variation, these kinds of sociolinguistic patterns and uses are clearest in the case of variables where one variant is prescriptively defined as standard and the other as non-standard, like the nine features described below. In these cases, the standard and non-standard variants can be considered to have the same linguistic function: we will see, for example, that both the presence and absence of verbal -s marks present tense. There are other cases of syntactic variation, however, where the social embedding of the variation is more indirect. Unlike phonological variation, syntactic forms may have discourse functions that are equally well fulfilled by a wide range of linguistic forms, drawn not only from morphology and syntax but also from other components of language. In section Syntactic variation and beyond, I discuss an example

119

of this kind below. It concerns, initially, variation between the different clause structures used to introduce a new entity into the discourse, a function usually considered to fall within the field of information management. We will see that to discover large-scale patterns of variation with social class and gender it was necessary to look beyond syntactic variation and analyse the full range of linguistic phenomena that speakers used to mark new discourse entities.

Variation and Vernacular Culture

In the late 1970s, I carried out a study of morphological and syntactic variation in the speech of adolescent friends, recorded by the method of long-term participant-observation in adventure playgrounds in Reading, England. Their teachers subsequently recorded some of these speakers at school. The study was discussed in detail in Cheshire (1982). Here I briefly describe one aspect of the speech of 13 boys who took part in the research: the relationship between their use of nine non-standard morphological and syntactic variants, and the extent to which the boys participated in the local vernacular culture.[1] The boys were aged between 11 and 16.

Some aspects of the boys' behaviour fitted with the descriptions of delinquent subcultures that were available at that time (by, for example, Willmott 1966). The boys used to meet at the adventure playgrounds at times when they were supposed to be at school, and many of their activities centred around what Miller (1958) referred to as the 'cultural foci' of *trouble, excitement, toughness, fate, autonomy* and *smartness* (in the American English sense of 'outsmarting'). I identified six factors that appeared to be centrally important to the boys' peer group culture, in that they were frequent topics of conversation and were sources of prestige within the friendship groups, and I used these factors to construct a 'vernacular culture index', in the same way that indices of socioeconomic class are commonly constructed.

Four of these factors directly reflected the cultural foci of 'trouble' and 'excitement': three directly, one more indirectly. The three that directly related to these foci were *skill at fighting, carrying a weapon* (such as a knife or a chain) and *participation in minor crime* (such as shop lifting, arson or vandalism). Though related, I treated these as separate indicators of adherence to the local vernacular culture, first because not all the boys took part in all these activities, and second because all did not have the same degree of importance to the boys. For similar reasons, I treated the nature of the job the boys hoped to take when they left school as a separate indicator. This was an important contributing factor to personal identity. Jobs that were acceptable to the peer group reflected 'trouble' and 'excitement', even if only indirectly.

They included, for example, working as a slaughterer in an abattoir, or as a lorry driver, motor mechanic or soldier. Unacceptable jobs were mainly traditionally white-collar jobs involving working in a shop or an office. A fifth indicator was 'style': the extent to which dress and hairstyle were important to the boys. Many writers have stressed the importance of style as a symbolic value within adolescent subcultures (see, for example, Hebdige 1988; and, more recently, Eckert 2001). Finally, a measure of the extent to which the boys swore was included in the index, since this was an important symbol of 'belonging' for the boys (and the girls; see Cheshire 1982). Swearing, of course, is a linguistic feature, but for these speakers it involved only a few words that were not involved in the morphological or syntactic variation analysed here.

The behaviour of each boy was scored separately for each of the six indicators and displayed on a Guttman scale. The coefficient of reproducibility was 0.97, confirming that the data were scalable. I then divided the boys into four groups on the basis of their total score, with group 1 consisting of the boys who, according to the vernacular culture index, conformed most closely to the norms of their vernacular culture, while the boys in group 4 took virtually no part in the vernacular culture. Groups 2 and 3 were intermediate in their adherence to the vernacular culture, with group 2 conforming more closely than group 3.

I analysed the frequency with which each of the four groups of boys used the nine non-standard morphological and syntactic features listed in (1) to (9) below, and illustrated in (1a) to (9b). The examples all come from the playground recordings. Each of the features has a corresponding standard English equivalent, as shown in the invented examples (1b) to (9b). It is important to note that the standard and non-standard forms have the same referential meaning and the same grammatical function; for example, *go* and *goes* in (1) both refer to the same activity and both indicate first person plural and present tense.

(1) verbal -*s*:
(1a) we goes shopping on Saturdays
(1b) we go shopping on Saturdays

(2) *has*
(2a) we has a little fire, keeps us warm
(2b) we have a little fire, keeps us warm

(3) past forms of *be*
(3a) you was outside
(3b) you were outside

(4)   multiple negation
(4a) I'm not going nowhere
(4b) I'm not going anywhere

(5)   *never* with preterite verb forms
(5a) I never done it, it was him
(5b) I didn't do it, it was him

(6)   relative *what*
(6a) there's a knob what you turn
(6b) there's a knob which/that you turn

(7)   auxiliary *do*
(7a) how much do he want for it?
(7b) how much does he want for it?

(8)   past tense of *come*
(8a) I come down here yesterday
(8b) I came down here yesterday

(9)   *ain't* (with all persons, for past *have* and past *be* (auxiliary and copula)
(9a) I ain't got any, I ain't going, she ain't a teacher
(9b) I haven't got any, I'm not going, she isn't a teacher

Table 9.1 shows the frequency with which the groups used the non-standard forms. In Table 9.1, the linguistic features are arranged into three classes, reflecting the extent to which the features correlate with adherence to vernacular culture. Class A contains four features whose frequency is very finely linked to the boys' vernacular culture index. The most sensitive indicator is non-standard verbal -*s*, which occurs very frequently in the speech of the boys in group 1 (those who conform most strongly to the vernacular culture norms) and progressively less frequently in the speech of groups 2, 3 and 4. This linguistic feature, then, functions as a powerful indicator of vernacular loyalty.

The two linguistic features in class B also function as indicators of vernacular loyalty, but they are less sensitive indicators than those in class A. There is significant variation only between speakers in group 1 and group 4: in other words, between the boys who conform most closely to the norms of the vernacular culture and those who conform least closely. This type of sociolinguistic variation is not unusual: Policansky (1980), for example, reports similar variation in the expression of subject-verb concord in Belfast English,

Table 9.1 Adherence to vernacular culture and frequency of non-standard forms

		Group 1	Group 2	Group 3	Group 4
Class A	verbal -s	77.36	54.03	36.57	21.21
	has	66.67	50.00	41.65	(33.33)
	past forms of *be*	90.32	89.74	83.33	75.00
	multiple negation	100.00	85.71	83.33	71.43
Class B	*never* with preterite verb forms	64.71	41.67	45.45	37.50
	relative *what*	92.31	7.69	33.33	0.00
Class C	auxiliary *do*	58.33	37.50	83.33	–
	past *come*	100.00	100.00	100.00	(100.00)
	ain't = have	78.26	64.52	80.00	(100.00)
	ain't = be	58.82	72.22	80.00	(100.00)
	ain't = copula	100.00	76.19	56.52	75.00

Note: Bracketed figures indicate that the number of occurrences of the feature is low and that the indices may not, therefore, be reliable. Following Labov (1970), less than five occurrences was considered too low for reliability.

Table 9.2 Frequency indices for Group B forms in the speech of group 1, groups 2/3, and group 4

	Group 1	Groups 2 and 3	Group 4
never with preterite verb forms	64.71	43.00	37.50
Relative *what*	92.31	18.00	0.00

where there is significant variation only in the speech of individuals at the extreme ends of a social network scale. When groups 2 and 3 are merged, a regular pattern of variation with adherence to the vernacular culture emerges for class B forms, as Table 9.2 shows. These features do function as indicators of vernacular loyalty, then, but they are less sensitive indicators than those in class A, with patterns seen only for broad groupings of speakers.

Features in class C, on the other hand, do not correlate with the vernacular culture index: for the most part, the figures form a completely irregular pattern. Interestingly, each of these linguistic features is involved in other, more complex kinds of sociolinguistic variation, and perhaps this explains why they do not function as straightforward indicators of vernacular loyalty.

Forms of auxiliary *do* are undergoing linguistic change away from an earlier dialect form toward the standard English system, such that the present tense forms of auxiliary and main verb *do* are no longer distinct. Some forms of *ain't* function as a direct marker of a vernacular norm (Cheshire 1982). Non-standard *come* functions as a marker of vernacular loyalty for adolescent girls in these friendship groups, but for boys it is an invariant form: none of the boys ever uses the standard variant *came*, irrespective of the extent to which he conforms to the vernacular culture.

Variation and Style

Only eight of the thirteen boys were recorded at school, since four boys had recently left, and one was so unpopular with his teacher that she refused to spend extra time with him. Jeff and Alec were recorded by their teacher during class discussions where they each had a lot to say. A teacher, talking to two or three of the boys together, made the other school recordings. Again, full details of this part of the research can be found in Cheshire (1982).

Table 9.3 compares the frequency indices of the non-standard variants in the playground recordings and the school recordings, analysing the tokens for all eight speakers together. Those features that are sensitive indicators of vernacular loyalty (class A) all occur less often in the boys' school speech than in their playground speech (although for *was* the difference in frequency is very low). Non-standard *never*, in class B, also occurs less often in the school recordings, although non-standard *what*, another class B form, occurs slightly more often in the school recordings than in the playground. The class C features, similarly, pattern irregularly: non-standard *come* remains invariant while *ain't* as *have* and as copula *be* increases in frequency in the school recordings (non-standard *do* did not occur in the school recordings, and *ain't* as an auxiliary occurred infrequently).

In Labov's (1970) framework, the linguistic variables in class A could be seen as markers, exhibiting both social and stylistic variation. Non-standard *never* might also be considered a marker, in these terms. Within the same framework, non-standard *what* could be considered an indicator, showing social but not stylistic variation. This classification, however, relies on the group frequency figures. Although there are many practical advantages to analysing groups of speakers rather than individual speakers – especially in cases such as this where the school recordings were sometimes short, yielding only small numbers of tokens – it is revealing to compare the linguistic behaviour of individuals. Consider, for example, Table 9.4, which shows the frequency of use of verbal -*s*, a variable that occurred frequently in both sets of recordings.

Table 9.3 Stylistic variation in the frequency of non-standard forms

		playground	*school*
Class A	verbal -s	57.03	31.49
	has	46.43	35.71
	past forms of *be*	91.67	88.57
	multiple negation	90.70	66.67
Class B	*never* with preterite verb forms	49.21	15.38
	relative *what*	50.00	54.66
Class C	Auxiliary *do*	–	–
	past *come*	100.00	100.00
	ain't = *have*	93.02	100.00
	ain't = copula	74.47	77.78

Table 9.4 Non-standard verbal -s in the playground and at school

	playground	*school*
Nobby	81.00	77.78
Tommy	70.83	34.62
Pete	71.43	54.55
Jeff	45.00	0.00
Rob	45.71	33.33
Nicky	57.14	31.75
Benny	31.58	54.17
Alec	38.46	0.00

Table 9.4 reveals some striking individual variation in the use of non-standard verbal -s in the two speech styles. Nobby, a group 1 speaker, uses the non-standard form only slightly less often at school than in the playground, whereas the other group 1 speakers (Tommy and Pete) use the form much less frequently when they are at school. Jeff, a group 2 speaker, does not use the non-standard variant at all in his school recording, although the other group 2 speakers (Rob and Nicky) continue to use the non-standard variant, albeit less frequently than in the playground recordings. Alec, like Jeff, does not use the non-standard form at school; in contrast, Benny's use of the non-standard form increases at school, and by a quite substantial amount.

Some insight into these patterns of individual variation comes from considering the situations in which the school recordings were made. Benny,

Rob and Nobby were recorded together, by their teacher. The teacher was asking them about what they liked to do outside school, and the boys were telling him about a disco that they were trying to organise. The teacher was making valiant efforts to understand what the boys were telling him, but was clearly unfamiliar with the kind of amplifying equipment and the general situation that the boys were discussing. It is relevant that Benny and Nobby both hated school and in the playground recordings they had made many derisory remarks about their teachers. Benny had just returned to school after an absence of a whole term, and Nobby currently attended school only intermittently. Rob, on the other hand, had a strict father and he did not dare to miss school as often as his friends did.

In the circumstances I have just outlined, speech accommodation theory (Giles, Coupland and Coupland 1991; Giles in this volume, Chapter 19) can help us understand the boys' different patterns of use of non-standard verbal -s. The teachers use only standard English variants. Rob knows the teacher, attends school regularly and, we can assume, accepts the constraints of the school situation. As a result, his speech converges toward the teacher's, and he uses fewer non-standard variants than he does outside school. Nobby, on the other hand, hates school and dislikes the teacher. As a result, he asserts his allegiance to the peer group culture rather than to the school, by refusing to acknowledge the situational constraints and to accommodate to the teacher's way of speaking. The frequency with which he uses the non-standard form, therefore, does not change (or rather, changes only slightly). Benny, who has only just returned to school, asserts his independence and hostility to the school by using more non-standard forms than he does usually. This is a very clear example of speech divergence. As we saw in the previous section, Benny is not closely involved in the peer group culture, and this is reflected in his playground speech by a relatively low use of non-standard verbal -s forms. When he wants to assert his independence from the school culture, however, he exploits the resources of the language system and chooses to use the non-standard form more frequently than he does normally.

Speech accommodation theory can also account for the behaviour of the other boys in this small study. Tommy, Pete and Ricky were recorded together, by a teacher that they knew well, and liked. The teacher had taken them on camping and fishing weekend expeditions, with other boys from their class. The conversation that the teacher recorded began with some talk about one of these weekends and then moved on to discuss racing cars and motorbikes, topics that interested both the teacher and the boys. Speech accommodation theory predicts that in this situation the linguistic behaviour of the boys would converge towards that of the teacher (and vice-versa, of course, but we do not have the information needed to comment on the teacher's changing speech patterns). This is precisely what happens – all three boys use the non-standard form less often here than they do in the playground recordings. The fact that they continue to use some non-standard forms, however, still allows them to express their allegiance to the vernacular peer group culture.

Jeff and Alec behave differently from the other boys, as we saw, in using only standard forms in their school recordings. This is especially surprising in the case of Jeff, who as a group 2 member (like Rob and Nicky) conforms quite closely to the norms of the vernacular culture. However, both recordings were made in a classroom discussion with about 20 other students and their teacher, at different times and by different teachers. Both Jeff and Alec participated a great deal in the discussions, partly, perhaps, because their teachers had purposely chosen topics on which they were known to have strong views (smoking and football hooliganism in Jeff's case, and truancy in Alec's case), or because the teacher encouraged them to take part because he knew that their speech was being investigated. It is possible that the overall formality of a public classroom discussion over-rode the option of displaying linguistically the boys' allegiance to the vernacular peer group culture. Alternatively, the fact that no other members of the friendship group were present may have made the boys more susceptible to the pressures of the school norms.

In any event, it is clear that a simple analysis of stylistic variation in terms of the overall formality or informality of the situation cannot fully account for the linguistic variation observed here. It is better to think in terms of situational constraints on exploiting the resources of the linguistic system. Non-standard verbal -*s* is a strong indicator of loyalty to the vernacular culture, and in some cases this symbolic function over-rides other situational constraints on linguistic variation (as in the speech of Nobby and Benny). In other cases (as with Jeff and Alec in a classroom discussion), the situational constraints exclude the possibility of using the form in this way. It is also clear that to understand how speakers exploit sociolinguistic variation we need to look beyond group scores to consider how individual speakers use the resources of their linguistic system to signal a range of different interactional meanings.

Syntactic Variation and Beyond

So far, I have discussed social variation between morphological and syntactic forms in cases where it was straightforward to identify the function of the forms. For example, both non-standard *was* and standard *were* indicated past tense for the verb *be*: no other linguistic forms available to the adolescent speakers could express this grammatical function. We will now consider a less straightforward example of sociolinguistic variation involving syntactic forms. In this case, the analysis began by focusing on two variant syntactic forms used to introduce new information into the discourse. We will see, however, that these were not the only forms that speakers used for this function and that the analysis had to expand to take account of the other linguistic forms serving the same function.

The data come from a research project based on interviews with 14–15 year olds in three English towns: Reading, Hull and Milton Keynes (Cheshire, Kerswill and Williams 1999). In each town we recorded 32 adolescents aged 14–15, of whom 16 attended a school in a middle-class area and 16 attended a school in a more working-class area (with 'class' defined broadly in each case, in terms of the residential area and parents' occupation). In each school, the fieldworker[2] recorded eight female and eight male adolescents. Thus, a total of 96 speakers took part in the project.

Full details of the analysis can be found in Cheshire (2005); here, I give a brief and necessarily simplified account. I was interested initially in the variation between existential *there* constructions such as (10a), taken from one of the interviews, and canonical subject-verb clauses, as in the invented (10b):

(10a) there's a car in the village square . it's parked near the bus shelter
(10b) a car's in the village square . it's parked near the bus shelter

In the interviews the most frequent function of the existential *there* constructions was to introduce a discourse-new item; in other words, a noun phrase referring to an entity that had not been mentioned before and that could not be inferred from something else that had been said. In (10a) and (10b), for example, *a car* is a discourse-new item; neither the adolescent nor the fieldworker had mentioned a car before. Discourse-new items contrast with both discourse-old items and inferable items. *It* in (10a) and (10b) is a discourse-old item, referring to *car*, which has just been mentioned. *The bus shelter*, on the other hand, is an inferable item: the speaker presumably assumes that the fieldworker knows the village square (which is near to the school where the recording was made) and that she can infer that *bus shelter* refers to the shelter that is in the village square (this account of discourse-old and discourse-new items is a simplified version of Prince's 1981 framework). I identified all the clauses where speakers introduced discourse-new items, with the intention of distinguishing those that occurred in an existential *there* construction and those that occurred in a canonical subject-verb construction. It soon became clear, however, that the adolescents used a very wide range of linguistic forms to mark the noun phrases that introduced a discourse-new item, and that these should therefore be included in the analysis alongside the existential *there* constructions and the canonical clause constructions. The forms included other marked clause constructions, such as left dislocation, possessive *have* (*got*) constructions and *it* constructions, as in (11)–(13).

   (11) Hayley: and then who my uncle's married to she comes from Somerset

   (12) AW: so who do you live with then who's in your family?

→   Sally: my mum and my dad and my three sisters and we've got my sister's friend staying with us since Christmas

   (13) Jerry: it's like too many people are going into business

These clause structures all allow speakers to position the discourse-new entities at the end of the clause rather than the beginning, a strategy that helps interlocutors to process the utterance (Prince 1981: 228).

Another way of marking discourse-new items was to use a linguistic form that explicitly creates interspeaker involvement. These forms included pragmatic particles such as *and stuff*, *sort of* and *like*, as in (14). The particles are often considered to signal an assumption of common ground between speaker and hearer, and in this way they can signal that the hearer has to use this shared knowledge to identify a new discourse referent. Other forms that functioned in this way included high rising tones and indefinite *this*, as in (15).

   (14) *Ann Williams has just asked Sam whether he has a job, to which he replied that he has a Saturday job*

       a. AW: where do you work?

→ b. Sam: it's just in a like a fish place

       c. AW: selling fish?

       d. Sam   yeah. World of Water [it's like a

       e. AW: [oh I see selling tropical fish =

       f. Sam: = tropical fish that's the thing

   (15) Linda: my mum and dad started having this conversation

A further strategy used by the adolescents was to utter a noun phrase and then immediately expand it, perhaps because the speaker realised that they had not given enough information for their interlocutor to successfully identify the referent (Clarke and Wilkes-Gibbs 1986: 4). An example of this is given in (16), where *RDC* is expanded to *remedial dance clinic*.

   (16) *Alison has been telling Ann Williams about her activities as a dancer, and mentions that she gets a lot of injuries*

     AW: doesn't that worry you a bit?

     Alison: well I've been going to RDC remedial dance clinic because I thought I had an injury

Non-restrictive relative clauses served a similar function, allowing speakers to add extra information to the noun phrase as the discourse proceeds. Thus in (17) *who's my nan's sister* expands *my aunt Lucy.*

(17) Carol: in my family I've got my mum my dad my nan and then my aunt Lucy who's my nan's sister

I also needed to include in the analysis a range of features that are sometimes considered to be dysfluencies. They included repetition, hesitation, false starts and filled and unfilled pauses. Some researchers suggest that dysfluencies always show that speakers are having difficulty producing their speech (see, for example, Arnold, Wasow, Losogno and Ginstrom 2000: 47), but the difficulty can have many causes including accessing from the mental lexicon a noun that has not been previously mentioned. The fact that the speaker lingers over the production of the noun phrase can function as a clue to the interlocutor, indicating that the speaker is about to produce new information (Geluykens 1992). Repetition used before a discourse-new entity in this way is illustrated in (18).

(18) *Sally is talking about her brother*

Sally: he lives with his with his girlfriend

Finally, there was a miscellaneous group of discourse-new items marked in diverse ways that included explicit efforts at lexical retrieval, as in (19), and multiple strategies, as in (20), where Andrew introduces the discourse-new entity *Australian teenage band* using an existential *there* construction and *like*, with repetition of the construction and a brief pause before the repeat.

(19) AW: and what do you want to be when you leave school?
     Jeff: either a doctor or a computer s.s.scientist well you know make computers programming erm computer programming that's it

(20) Andrew: well there's this . there is like an Australian teenage band at the moment that play that kind of music

There were no consistent patterns of gender of social class variation in the use of any of these different categories of discourse-new markers, nor in any of the individual syntactic constructions, pragmatic particles or dysfluencies that were used to mark discourse-new items. However, in all three towns there was a highly significant gender and social class distribution in the use of 'bare' NPs. An example of a 'bare' NP is *instruction sheets* in (21).

(21) *Sam is talking about his stick insects*

> Sam:　they bred so fast we had to sell them with instruction sheets at the summer fair

As many as 410 discourse-new items (42.27%) were introduced in canonical clauses in this way, without any explicit linguistic marking. Working-class female adolescents used the highest proportion of bare NPs, and middle-class male adolescents the lowest proportion. The effect of gender was particularly striking for the middle-class groups in all three towns, as Figure 9.1 shows. It was weaker, though still significant, for the working-class groups, as seen in Figure 9.2.

The gender distribution can be seen very clearly when the scores for individual speakers are compared. Figure 9.3, for example, shows the percentage of bare NPs used by the middle-class adolescents in Reading. Although there was much individual variation in the use of the different forms that could mark discourse entities as new, with some speakers using, say, more pragmatic particles and others using more syntactic constructions (and others using all the forms mentioned above), every female speaker used bare NPs at least once – mostly more than once – and most used bare NPs more

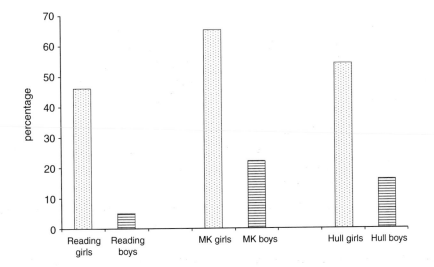

Figure 9.1　Percentage of discourse-new forms that are marked: middle class groups

Notes: Reading chi square value 27.2833, df=1, p< 0.001
MK chi square value 16.1644, df=1, p < 0.001
Hull chi square value 31.1918, df=1, p< 0.001S.

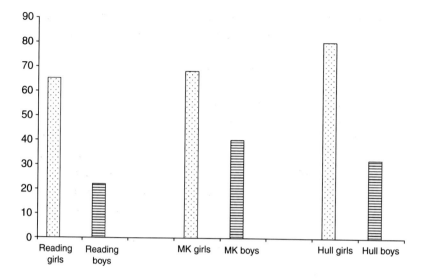

**Figure 9.2   Percentage marked discourse-new forms that
are marked: working class groups**

Notes: Reading chi square value 34.9280, df = 1, p < 0.001
Milton Keynes chi square value 7.8232, df = 1, p < 0.01
Hull chi square value 11.0653, df = 1, p < 0.001.

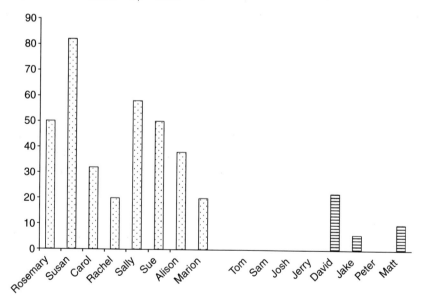

**Figure 9.3   Individual speakers' marking of discourse-new forms:
Reading middle class group**

Note: Dotted bars represent percentage of bare NPs used by girls; striped bars represent percentage of bare NPs used by boys.

frequently than any of the discourse-new markers. In contrast, only three of the middle-class boys used bare NPs, and the frequency with which they used them was uniformly low.

The fact that the same gender and social class patterns occur in three separate regions of England is compelling evidence of a previously unsuspected tendency for male adolescent speakers, especially the middle-class boys, to mark discourse-new items in their talk.

Thus, variation between existential clauses and canonical clauses did not of itself have a role in distinguishing gender or social class groups. However, it did form part of a complex of strategies harnessed by speakers to accomplish a specific discourse function (marking discourse-new entities). When the full complex of forms was taken into account it became possible to see sociolinguistic patterning within the data analysed here.

The next step, of course, is to consider the implications of this kind of social variation and to try to explain why it may exist. It is possible that it relates to historical and cultural factors that have given rise to different discourse styles for working-class and middle-class groups, and for male and female speakers. There is a large research literature suggesting that male speakers are more concerned with the referential content of their talk and female speakers with the affective meaning (see, for example, Holmes 1995), and this may account for the higher frequency with which the boys in our study marked their discourse-new items. In other words, they may have paid more attention than the female speakers to the information status of the entities they introduced into their discourse. There is also a research literature on social class differences that indicates that middle-class speakers may have an independent, speaker-oriented speech style, leading them to make their own opinions and viewpoints explicit, whereas working-class speakers take a more collaborative, addressee-oriented approach to talk, allowing their interlocutors more opportunities to infer meanings and to draw their own conclusions (see, for example, Macaulay 2002). To some extent, this may be the legacy of the more frequent participation of the middle classes in formal public settings where it is necessary to construct explicit meanings.

These interpretations are, of course, open to question: what is important is to note that the social variation that was found in this analysis calls for a different kind of interpretation than the variation discussed in sections variation and vernacular culture and variation and style of the chapter.

Conclusion

Syntax is central to the construction of discourse. This means that when we are analysing sociolinguistic aspects of syntactic variation we need to take account not only of grammatical functions (such as tense marking) but also of discourse functions (such as the marking of new information) that may be fulfilled by lexical, phonetic and other linguistic forms and strategies, as well as syntactic forms. With grammatical functions it is often possible to analyse syntactic variation in terms of a simple alternation of variants, as shown in early sections of this chapter. Even here, however, it is worth considering what we may be overlooking by taking a variationist approach to the analysis. For example, I considered *ain't* as a simple variant of different forms of *be not* and *have not*. It is possible, however, that *ain't* is a more emphatic form of negation than *isn't*, say, or *haven't*, in which case it would be instructive to consider whether individuals who use *ain't* frequently have a different interactional style from speakers who use it more rarely. A similar point can be made about the use of negative concord.

When the syntactic form in which we are interested serves a specific discourse function, we may be forced to look beyond syntax to identify the full range of forms that can be used for the same discourse function. If a broad analysis of this type then uncovers sociolinguistic variation this may suggest that different social groups have different interactional styles. Thus, the analysis of syntactic variation provides us with a range of intriguing and complex perspectives on how speakers use language to create social meanings and social life.

NOTES

1. Perhaps it is necessary to stress that the speech of the girls is not considered here purely for reasons of space, not because it is less interesting or important.
2. The interviewers were Ann Williams and Paul Kerswill. 'AW' in the illustrative extracts that follow stands for Ann Williams, who was the main interviewer. Obviously, the analysis could not have been done without the work of Ann and Paul, and I would like to thank them for this, as well as for their helpful comments on Cheshire (2005).

REFERENCES

Arnold, Jennifer E., Thomas Wasow, Anthony Losogno and Ryan Ginstrom. 2000. Heaviness versus newness: The effects of structural complexity and discourse status on discourse ordering. *Language* 76: 28–55.

Cheshire, Jenny. 1982. *Variation in an English Dialect*. Cambridge: Cambridge University Press.

Cheshire, Jenny. 2005. Syntactic variation and beyond: Gender and social class variation in the use of discourse-new markers. *Journal of Sociolinguistics* 9: 479–509.

Cheshire, Jenny, Ann Gillett, Paul Kerswill and Ann Williams. 1999. The role of adolescents in dialect levelling. Ref. R000236180. Final Report submitted to the Economic and Social Research Council, June 1999.

Clarke, Herbert H. and Donna Wilkes-Gibbs. 1986. Referring as a collaborative process. *Cognition* 22: 1–39.

Eckert, Penelope. 2001. Style and social meaning. In Penelope Eckert and John R. Rickford (eds.) *Style and Sociolinguistic Variation*. Cambridge: Cambridge University Press. 119–126.

Geluykens, Ronald. 1992. *From Discourse Process to Grammatical Construction: On Left Dislocation in English*. Amsterdam/Philadelphia: John Benjamins.

Giles, Howard, Justine Coupland and Nikolas Coupland (eds.) 1991. *Contexts of Accommodation: Developments in Applied Sociolinguistics*. Cambridge: Cambridge University Press.

Hebdige, Dick. 1988. *Subculture: The Meaning of Style*. London: Routledge.

Holmes, Janet. 1995. *Women, Men and Politeness*. Harlow: Longman.

Labov, William. 1970. The study of language in its social context. *Studium Generale* 23: 66–84.

Macaulay, Ronald. 2002. Extremely interesting, very interesting, or only quite interesting? Adverbs and social class. *Journal of Sociolinguistics* 6: 398–417.

Miller, W.B. 1958. Lower class culture as a generating milieu of gang delinquency. *Journal of Social Issues* 14: 5–19.

Policansky, L. 1980. Verb concord variation in Belfast English. Paper delivered to the Sociolinguistics Symposium, Walsall, UK.

Prince, Ellen. 1981. Towards a taxonomy of given-new information. In Peter Cole (ed.) *Radical Pragmatics*. New York: Academic Press. 223–254.

Willmott, P. 1966. *Adolescent Boys of East London*. London: Routledge and Kegan Paul.

CHAPTER 10

Ethnography and the Study of Variation

PENELOPE ECKERT

Why Ethnography?

William Labov's survey study of the English of New York City appeared in 1966, to be followed over the next decade or so by a series of similar studies in other cities. These studies established solid evidence of general patterns of linguistic variation over large urban populations. Most particularly, they showed a regular stratification of features by socioeconomic class, in which the use of local and regional phonological features, and of non-standard grammatical features (such as negative concord) correlates inversely with socioeconomic status. Correlations with gender have been a bit more varied, as overall men tend to use more non-standard forms than women, but women commonly lead men in the use of local and regional phonological features. The stratification of phonological features often represents the progress of sound changes as they spread through the population, making women and the working class leaders in the adoption of innovation. These large-scale correlations form the backbone of the study of variation, and the explanation for these patterns lies in the dynamics of gender and class. In the case both of class and gender, correlations of linguistic usage with broad demographic categories – a continuum in the case of class and an opposition in the case of gender – can provide us with important general patterns, but they cannot provide explanations for those patterns. Class and gender patterns in language and other kinds of behavior exist because people living in different places in the social matrix find themselves in different circumstances, and as a result tend to behave differently. And while survey studies provide information about where people are in that social matrix, they don't get directly at

136

the behavior, or practice, that produces and reproduces that structure. If we want to get at explanations for the patterns we see, we need to get closer to the social practices in which the patterns are created. While surveys provide us with the big picture of variation, we turn to ethnography to get closer to the meaningful activity in which people deploy linguistic resources.

Ethnography differs from survey research in several ways. Survey research attempts to gather equivalent data from a sample of people that are taken to be representative of some wider population. Equivalence is sought through using the same instrument with everyone in the sample – for example, asking the same questions in the same way under the same circumstances. This strict equivalence is not a reasonable goal in research trying to get at natural speech, but the sociolinguistic interview (Labov 1972) is designed to engage speakers in interactions that are as similar as possible and will elicit similar styles. Inasmuch as the same instrument is used across speakers, and inasmuch as sampling techniques determine the choice of interviewees, both the interviewees (or the criteria for selecting interviewees) and the questions are established in advance and remain uniform throughout the study. Ethnography, on the other hand, is a process of discovery, hence it defines and refines both its questions and its selection criteria as it goes along. Thus, while a survey study will begin with its social categories (for example, class, gender) an ethnographic study will go into a community to find out what social categories are salient. While survey research views the world essentially from the top down, ethnographic research views the world from bottom up. The ethnographer engages in a community in order to understand the local – and while the survey researcher seeks out the typical, the ethnographer seeks out the particular.

In what follows, I will illustrate the use of ethnography in the study of variation with my own work in a Detroit-area high school, with the purpose of showing how the methods and the findings of survey research and ethnography complement each other. The discussion will show how the ethnographic approach, time-consuming though it is, provides a very local perspective on adolescent Sociolinguistics that could not be gained by other means. The work took place in Belten High School,[1] one of four high schools that serve Neartown, a suburb lying in the midst of the urban sprawl that emanates from Detroit. The population of Neartown, almost exclusively of European descent, covers the full socioeconomic range from lower working class through upper middle class. Only the wealthy and the very poor are missing from the student population of Belten High.

Why Adolescents and Why in School?

One demographic correlation that I have not so far mentioned, that has surfaced in survey studies, is age. Age-graded studies often show a regular differentiation of linguistic usage by age, with progressively younger age groups leading in the adoption of sound changes in progress and in the use of local and vernacular forms. However, this age differentiation shows one suggestive bump – it is adolescents, not children, who show the most local, the most vernacular, and the most innovative use. Furthermore, there is some evidence that adolescents do not show the same socioeconomic stratification as other age groups. While children's patterns of variation can be predicted by their parents' socioeconomic class, the correlation of adolescents' language with their parents' socioeconomic class is less robust. It is this slight mismatch, and the status of adolescents as linguistic movers and shakers, at least in western industrialized societies, that led me to study the language of adolescents. If adolescents lead in linguistic change, then we need to seek the social dynamics of change among adolescents, not among adults. This means, among other things, understanding what social class means to adolescents.

Socioeconomic class is generally assessed as a composite of adult achievements – educational level, occupation, income, and sometimes value and style of residence – just those aspects of life that adolescents do not yet control. Examining adolescent language in the light of their parents' socioeconomic class, therefore, embodies sociolinguistic assumptions about the relation between parents' class and kids' language that are frequently glossed over. On the one hand, it is possible that the adolescent speaker acquires class-based linguistic patterns from one or both parents. On the other, it is possible that aspects of parents' socioeconomic status influence the adolescents' own orientations to the world which, in turn, affects their patterns of speech. There are no doubt combinations of these factors, for example, in the combination of parental and peer influence found in a stable neighborhood. The neighborhood is determined by the parents' material possibilities, and determines one's earliest and most accessible peers. To the extent that the neighborhood is socially homogeneous, parental influence and peer influence are difficult to separate. But even if the neighborhood is relatively homogeneous, school populations are generally more heterogeneous. And in the US, while elementary schools tend to be neighborhood-based, the system of comprehensive secondary schooling provides extensive contact among a heterogeneous student body. This makes the high school an excellent site for the examination of the relation between the linguistic influence of family and that of peers. The school also offers up a community that is small enough to study up close, yet that is representative of the larger local population in one age group.

School represents the transition from childhood to adulthood, and from parents' socioeconomic status to one's own. The two life stage elements are manifest in high school: kids still live at home, and in neighborhoods shared with some classmates and far from others. Their parents' socioeconomic status determines, to some extent, what they can buy, where they can go, and what they can do. To some extent, it also determines their outlook on the world, and on school; their expectations and their desires. And to the extent that they hang out with other kids from their neighborhood, their friends' backgrounds are likely to have had a similar effect on them, intensifying class-based orientations. What they do in school – what curriculum they follow, what activities they participate in, and what kinds of grades they get – will determine to some extent what they do after they leave school. Thus all high school students are simultaneously coming from and going toward. What they do in high school is a pivot point, and for some it is a continuation of a style of life from home while for others it is a transition to a new style of life.

Belten High

My first day in Belten High, I walked around the halls innumerable times, feeling pretty much like a jerk. At some point, I wandered into the auditorium where something was going on, and got to talking to a student standing at the back of the room. He introduced me to some of his friends, and so it began. [Ethnography involves moving gradually into a community, getting to know people, establishing connections and trust, participating in activities and talking to a lot of people over and over again. It involves observing carefully, following strands of ideas, always backing up and making sure one hasn't moved into a social corner. Dislike is suspended, because everyone becomes important, and everyone becomes interesting. In the end, I spent over two years in Belten High, focusing on one graduating class] The following analysis is based on the tape-recorded speech of 69 people, selected from a larger sample of 200.

As I walked around Belten on that first day, I couldn't help but notice that people looking very different were hanging out in different places. Some boys had long-ish hair, some had short. Some girls wore candy-colored makeup, some wore lots of black eye liner and mascara. Some boys wore chains and studs and Detroit or auto factory jackets, some wore Belten High jackets and letter sweaters. Some boys and girls wore bell-bottomed jeans, some wore straight-legs. Some boys and girls wore black, some wore pastels. Some boys and girls wore dark-colored rock concert Tees, some wore Isod polo shirts. And these different features of adornment clustered into styles – the 'preppy' look of pastel makeup and clothes, the latest fashionable straight-legged jeans, school sports and cheerleading apparel; and the 'urban' look of dark colors, the bell bottoms of the seventies 'freak' era, long hair and metal, and jackets from the city. Finally, the styles clustered in different territories in the school. During classes, one saw the preppy look in the front halls of the school rushing about on school business, and one saw the urban look in the halls around the vocational classrooms and the rear exit. During lunch, the preppy look filled the hall in front of the cafeteria and the sports and student activities offices, while the urban look filled the courtyard that served as a smoking area.

Styles, of course, can be studied empirically. Figure 10.1 is based on several days of observations, in which I noted down every pair of jeans and where it was standing during lunch hour. I gave a value to each of the 800 pairs of jeans I recorded, based on the ratio between the width at the bottom of the leg and the knee: a 4 for wide bells, 3 for flared jeans, 2 for straight-legs, and 1 for the pegged legs that were just coming into fashion. As shown in Figure 10.1, the wider jeans bottoms spent their lunch hour in the courtyard, while the narrower ones spent their lunch hour in the hall in front of the cafeteria, with a gradual narrowing as one moved from the courtyard to the cafeteria entrance. The kids in the courtyard were called (and called themselves) *burnouts*, while those in front of the cafeteria were called *jocks*. These two styles marked the polarized social categories that represented the extremes of school-based identity in Belten High, much as they did in all the predominantly white high schools across the northeast and midwest at the time.

While we tend to think of style as something superficial, it is generally an outward manifestation of a person's deeply held ideologies. And this is certainly true of the jocks and the burnouts. Jocks and burnouts have very different beliefs about their life stage, about their relation to adults, about friendship, and many other things. And because they come together in the school, these differences come to be focused on orientation to that institution.

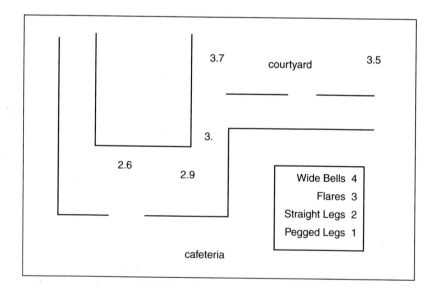

Figure 10.1   Jeans at lunch time

Students spend about six of the best hours of each weekday in school. Some of them remain for several hours after school, engaged in extracurricular activities, and then spend several hours on homework. The school's 'ideal' participant can easily spend eleven or twelve hours a day on school-related activities, making school an intensive full-time enterprise. It is not unknown for particularly zealous students to suffer extreme stress and even breakdowns – not from a rigorous academic program but from the combination of academic and social programs. The school's least enthusiastic participant, on the other hand, can frequently get away with spending just a few hours a day in school, and with the absolute minimum required number of days of attendance. While most of the student body falls between these two extremes, the high school social order is based on the opposition between the two extremes. A division is almost universal in American high schools between students who base their social lives in the school and those who reject the school altogether as a basis of their social lives, orienting themselves more toward the neighborhood and the urban area. The two extremes constitute opposed social categories, which are sufficiently important to commonly have names, which vary not locally, but by region. Not just in Belten High but in the schools around Detroit (and throughout the midwest and much of the east), those who embrace and those who reject the school are called (and call themselves), respectively, *jocks* and *burnouts* (see Eckert 1989 for a more complete ethnographic account of these social categories). The fundamental status of these categories is reflected in the fact that kids who consider themselves neither jocks nor burnouts – the majority of kids in the school – overwhelmingly refer to themselves as 'in-betweens'.

The jocks and the burnouts constitute two distinct communities of practice – that is, they are groups of kids who interact on a regular basis, brought together by a common orientation to school, and engaging in social practices that unfold from, and reproduce, that orientation. The jocks and the burnouts, respectively, constitute middle class and working class cultures, or trajectories, within the adolescent context. While neither category is homogeneous in its class origins, the jocks are predominantly from middle class homes and the burnouts are predominantly from working class homes, as shown in Figure 10.2. The in-betweens fall, true to their characterization, in between.

But as important as where they come from is where they are going. The jocks, heavily engaged in school, intend to continue from high school into college, while most of the burnouts are bound for the local blue and pink collar workplace. The jocks' primary orientation to the school institution provides them access to, and preparation for, college admission and college practices. The burnouts, on the other hand, have little to gain from engaging in such practices, and prefer to focus on the local community and the wider urban area that it is part of, and into whose workplaces they will graduate from school.

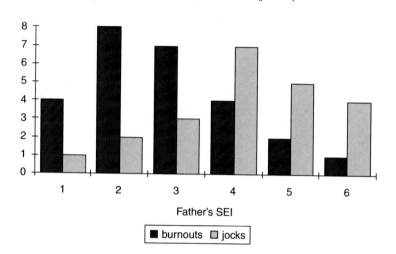

Figure 10.2   Social category affiliation and father's socioeconomic index

Social networks reflect these differing orientations. While jocks empha-size getting to know as many people as possible in school, and particularly those engaged in extracurricular activities, burnouts emphasize getting to know those who have contact with people beyond the school, and who know how to get around outside of school. The jocks admire people who excel in extracurricular activities, while the burnouts admire people who are able to make their way in the urban environment and seek access to the resources of the greater Detroit urban-suburban area. For the adolescent, these resources may include automotive and auto body expertise and supplies, after-school jobs, bars that serve minors, pool halls, parks, parties, excitement, and people who in turn have access to these and to other kinds of urban knowledge and resources. While the jocks pursue their social activities in and around school, the burnouts frequent parks and cruising strips in and around Detroit, and some burnouts pursue friendships with people living closer in to Detroit.

More personal, one might say emotional, differences enter into this differ-ence in orientation. Jocks' focus on school activities leads them to base not only their activities, but their friendships, in the school, and to choose friends who are engaged in the same activities. The burnouts, on the other hand, base their friendships primarily in the neighborhood and place a high value on maintaining old friendship networks. The jocks, engaged in a hierarchical activity scheme, tend to have more competitive relationships – and to not con-fide too much in their friends in order to keep negative information out of the system. The burnouts, on the other hand, view friends as their major support system, sharing problems and placing an emphasis on trust and egalitarianism. Thus the differences between jocks and burnouts go quite deep, and are clearly connected to their anticipated class-based futures. Stuck together in the same institution, the jocks and the burnouts compete to define adolescent norms, and each category sees the other as embodying false values and undermining its own arrangements with the adult establishment. The opposition between jocks and burnouts, therefore, is hostile, and foregrounded in high school discourse. Resources of all kinds are exploited to construct the opposition: clothing and other adornment, territory, substance use, musical tastes, demeanor, and of course language.

Jocks, Burnouts, and Linguistic Variables

Negative Concord

Given the jocks' greater participation in the standard language market through their participation in school, one would expect them to use more standard grammar than the burnouts. And indeed, they do. Figure 10.3 shows the percentage of times that jocks and burnouts use negative concord, or nonstandard negation, as in *I didn't do nothing*. The burnouts' use of negation is far more non-standard than the jocks', and boys use it more than girls overall,

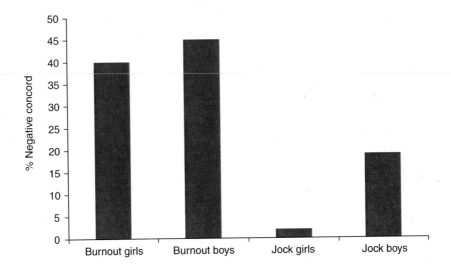

Figure 10.3 Jocks' and burnouts' use of negative concord

but note that this gender difference is far greater among the jocks than among the burnouts (I will return to the gender difference below).

The difference between jock and burnout usage is not a matter of differential knowledge of the forms, since the burnouts uniformly use standard negation at least as often as non-standard. Nonetheless, since negative concord regularly correlates with class, one might ask if this difference is a result of upbringing – if the burnouts' greater use of negative concord is something they learned from working class parents. Indeed, kids' use of negative concord correlates to some extent with their parents' – particularly their mothers' – educational status. But the stronger correlation is with the speaker's own status as a jock or a burnout. Of course, it's easier to get a neat correlation with two categories than with a fine-grained socioeconomic hierarchy, but the fact remains that kids who cross over – that is, working class jocks and upper middle class burnouts show the pattern that reflects their adolescent category rather than their parents' education. Kim, for example, a burnout whose father is a college graduate and whose mother graduated from high school, uses negative concord 65 per cent of the time. And Becky, a jock whose father didn't finish elementary school and whose mother graduated from high school, uses none. Clearly the difference in their usage is not simply a result of what they were exposed to at home. There is also a correlation between patterns of negation across the entire student body (in-betweens as well as jocks and burnouts) and the speaker's own academic involvement, but the stronger correlation is with participation in extracurricular activities, as shown in Figure 10.4. The school activity index is a rough scale of participation in school activities as follows:

1 = no activities
2 = 1–2 activities
3 = 3–8 activities
4 = 9–19 activities
5 = 20 or more

I have referred elsewhere (Eckert 1989) to school extracurricular activities as a corporate enterprise – students participating in such things as student government and other clubs build up careers that play an important role not only in their visibility and status in the school, but also in their dossier for college admission. These activities, then, are a major locus of the standard language market, and appear to be a more meaningful locus of standard language than the classroom as the high school cohorts have appropriated language norms into their own social order.

One might say, then, that patterns of negation are a matter of style. Negative concord is a linguistic stereotype – all speakers recognize it as signaling such

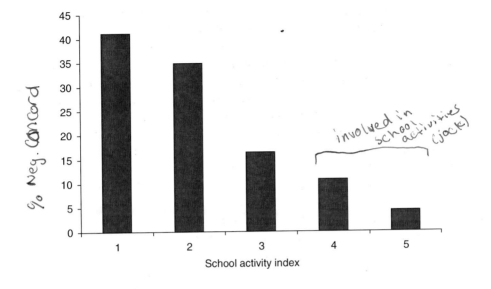

Figure 10.4   Use of negative concord and participation in extracurricular activities across the cohort

things as lower occupational and educational status, and as such it is a prime candidate for signaling an oppositional stance. Small middle class kids, particularly boys, are known to use it to act tough and bad, and kids have been known to use it in the classroom to mock their teachers. If we think of jock and burnout speech as distinct styles, we might see negation as iconic of their opposing stances toward the school, and its place in the standard language market. If the use of negative concord is a stylistic matter, then it must show up in more fine-grained stylistic performances. And indeed it does. Within any social category, there are always differences – and among them differences that mirror the differences on which the categories themselves are based. Judith Irvine and Susan Gal (Irvine and Gal 2000; this volume) call this embedding of a larger opposition *recursivity*, and argue that it is a means of magnifying the differences between the categories. The fact that some jocks are more jocky than others, and some burnouts are more burnouty than others intensifies the distinction between jocks and burnouts, and this shows up in language use as shown in Figure 10.5. Among the jocks, negative concord is such a taboo that almost no girls use it. Among the male jocks, though, there are some who use it. There are two ways a boy becomes a jock – either by playing varsity sports or by participating in student government. Most do both, but there are some who do one or the other. Among the boys whose jock status is based only on participation in student government, there is only a 2.5

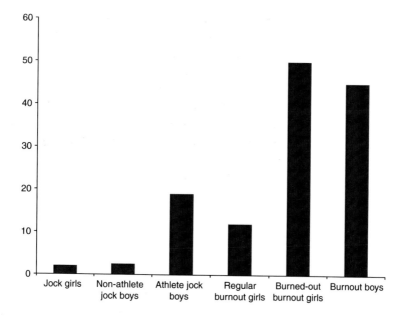

Figure 10.5   Percent use of negative concord by six subcategories of jocks and burnouts

per cent use of negative concord, whereas the athletes use negative concord 19 per cent of the time. This figure is nothing like the burnout boys' 45 per cent, but it is considerably more than their politician peers. The burnout girls show a similar differentiation, between two quite separate groups. Most of the burnout girls fall into two overlapping friendship groups totaling about 35, and think of themselves as the 'main' group of burnout girls. While the main burnout girls have a generally urban and anti-school stance, and like to party, they tend to avoid major trouble with the police. On the other hand, there is a group of ten girls who are often referred to as the 'burned-out burnouts'. They described themselves to me as the 'biggest burnouts', and pride themselves on coming to school stoned on hard drugs, and getting into serious trouble with the police. The burned-out burnout girls wear more extreme clothing and makeup, and refer to the main burnout girls as 'jocks'. The difference in styles shows up in their use of negative concord – the burned-out burnout girls use negative concord 50 per cent of the time – more than the burnout boys' 45 per cent, and much more than the main burnout girls' 13 per cent.

Note that it is the burned-out burnout girls that make the gender difference among burnouts so small. But what does that say about gender differences? Is it reasonable to say that girls or women use more standard grammar than boys or men? Certainly the overall statistics in Belten High, like in adult populations, confirm this generalization. But the question is what do these statistics tell us? Does the correlation between negative concord and male status indicate that negative concord means 'male'? Certainly not. Rather, it indicates that negative concord has some kind of social meaning that is more useful to men in general than to women in general. In the case of Belten High, there are some girls – the burned-out burnout girls – who are constructing a style that calls for the kind of rebelliousness, or anti-institutional stance, associated with negative concord. And the jock girls, who are very protective of what one might call a squeaky-clean image, are clearly backing off from any linguistic indication of rebelliousness.

Urban Vowels

Of course, patterns of negation do not constitute a style in themselves. Linguistic style involves a wide range of choices – from discourse patterns down to phonetics. And while I will not report on discourse patterns here, I will turn to phonetics as an apparently less conscious variable than negation. There are several sound changes in progress in the Detroit suburban area that appear to be traveling from the periphery of Detroit out into the suburbs. These are the latest stages of the Northern Cities Shift, a shift that involves all the mid and low vowels. The three latest changes are the backing of (e) to [ʌ] so that *flesh* sounds more like *flush*, the backing of (uh) to [ɔ] so that *lunch* sounds more like *launch*, and the raising and backing of the nucleus of the diphthong (ay) to [ɔ] so that *fight* sounds more like *foyt*.

If negative concord evokes the normativity of schooling, local sound changes moving out from the urban center evoke urban life and characters. One would expect speakers to adopt these changes readily to the extent that they admire or identify with that life and those characters. The burnouts' urban orientation involves not simply a desire for the physical resources of the city, but an admiration for the independence, knowledge, and street smarts of urban youth. It stands to reason, then, that the burnouts would adopt these changes well before the jocks and indeed, as Figure 10.6 shows, the burnouts lead the jocks in the use of all three urban sound changes.

You will note that while (uh) and (e) do not show any significant gender differentiation, (ay) does: the burnout girls raise the nucleus the most, and the jock girls use it the least – while the jock and burnout boys fall in the middle range. In other words, the girls show greater socially distinctive use of this variable than the boys. And as in the case of negative concord, it is the burned-out burnout girls who are driving the high values.

The jocks and the burnouts (particularly the student council jocks and the burned-out burnouts) represent the extremes of practice in the high school,

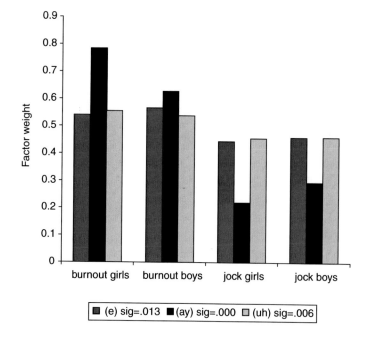

Figure 10.6   Jocks, burnouts, and the use of urban sound changes

and the extremes of linguistic usage. But the practices that distinguish the two extremes are, themselves, salient for the rest of the population of the school. The burnouts are not the only people who are urban-oriented and the jocks are not the only people who participate in school activities. Not only do in-betweens refer to themselves by that term, they also readily place themselves with respect to the two extremes – sometimes in terms of distance between the two, and sometimes in terms of shared features ('I like to party, but I'm also into school'). Figure 10.4 gave one example of how negative concord falls out across the larger school population. Figure 10.7 shows another. Cruising – repeatedly driving a fixed and widely shared route – is a teenage practice that is popular across the country. In the Detroit area, there are a couple of routes along the edge of Detroit that attract high school students from across the suburbs. Driving slowly along these routes thrusts kids into an urban environment, and into contact with others like them. Kids who cruise seek excitement and connections outside the purview of the school, and engagement with the urban milieu. And while the burnouts spend a good deal of time hanging out in the urban area, there are in-betweens who do as well, and the non-school and urban-identified linguistic resources serve as valuable symbolic material for them all. Figure 10.7 represents the speech

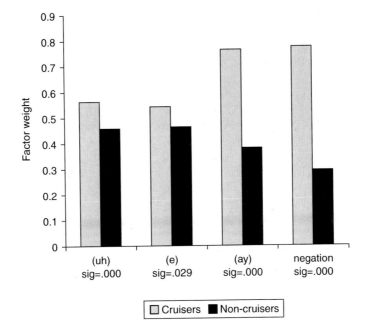

Figure 10.7 Cruising and the use of four variables across the cohort

of the entire sample – jocks, burnouts and in-betweens – correlating all four variables with the practice of urban cruising.

As this figure shows, the correlations of linguistic features with jocks and burnouts are part of a wider connection between linguistic and social practice. Linguistic variables are not simply markers of social categories, but carry kinds of social meaning that are central to these categories, but that are relevant as well to the broader population of the school. Indeed, it is the general central-ity of these meanings that allows the jocks and the burnouts to represent the extremes of the school population. Orientation to the institutions that consti-tute the standard language market – schools and later workplaces – is a funda-mental component of class in our society. Also fundamental, is orientation to the local area. The jocks are institutional beings. They locate their activities, identities, and social networks, in the school institution. The burnouts, on the other hand, locate these in the local area – the Detroit conurbation. This is the early instantiation of the major class difference among adults – the locally based working class and the corporate-based upper middle class. And while school authorities tend to see jocks and burnouts as simply 'good kids' and 'bad kids', their differences reside in very different and strong ideologies about such things as autonomy and friendship, and in very practical considerations about the relation between schooling and the rest of life.

Back to Ethnography

So how does this analysis, based on ethnographic fieldwork, differ from what a survey study of Belten High would have given? If I had gone into the school looking for a sample stratified by socioeconomic class, I might have gotten more jocks in one part of my sample and more burnouts in another, but I would have gotten many in-betweens as well. And while they might have talked about social categories in the course of a sociolinguistic interview, I would not have been able to examine those categories first hand. It was the ethnographic depth of the work in Belten that brought these categories to my attention, that told me the relation between these social categories and class, and that told me what kinds of social practices makes jocks jocks and burnouts burnouts. It was ethnographic work that allowed me to chart out the social networks and to identify the burned-out burnout girls, and to chart the relations among jocks, burnouts, and in-betweens. Being able to identify practices such as cruising, network clusters such as the burned-out burnout girls, and the values that give these social categories and practices meaning requires a continuous presence and close familiarity with the student body.

Of course, once I had done the work in Belten High, I was able to use the categories jock and burnout from the start in a more survey-like technique. I was able to go into other high schools in the Detroit suburbs and find the jocks and burnouts simply by asking the school principal where their territories were, or by asking who was the biggest jock and who was the biggest burnout. After all, the local salience of these categories makes them highly visible. But finding interviewees in this way will close off a good deal of the potential for trust on the part, particularly, of burnouts. In these schools, I found the jocks by seeking out the class president but I found the burnouts by finding their territory and hanging out. And while using this 'quick and dirty' method gave me access to interviewees and allowed me to sample the speech of jocks and burnouts in a matter of weeks, it did not give me the kind of textured information I gained at Belten, and it certainly did not give me access to particular friendship groups or any kind of systematic view of the in-betweens. So while I developed a picture of how jocks and burnouts use variables across the geographic continuum of the suburban area, I was never as sure of the status of my data in the other schools as I was in Belten.

The lack of correlation with parents' socioeconomic class in these data is no doubt partially due to the sample selection. The speaker sample in the study of Belten High is not a random sampling based on parents' socioeconomic factors. Rather, choice of speakers was based on place in social networks and particularly relation to social categories, foregrounding the speakers' own socioeconomically related choices. A sampling that did not focus on the two extreme social categories may well downplay individual social mobility and show a greater correlation between linguistic variables and parents' status. It is just this difference that forms the heart of this research, which was designed to focus on the transitional nature of adolescence, and particularly on the relation between the speaker's construction of identity and linguistic variation.

Language does not exist simply in the abstract, untouched and untouchable; it is used and reproduced in the service of local communities. The sociolinguistic enterprise involves, importantly, the investigation of the local deployment of linguistic resources as they are imbued with social meaning. While we may find that language use patterns with global abstract categories such as class, gender, ethnicity or age, these categories point to, but do not define, the social meanings that speakers associate with linguistic form. Because meaning is made in day-to-day practice, much of it tacitly, the study of social meaning requires access to this practice. Surveys, questionnaires, and experiments all have their place in the study of language in society. But all of them presuppose and test categories and meanings, rather than discover them. Observations and interviews come closer to providing access to kids' meanings, but if used alone they have serious limitations for one must know what to watch for, and what questions to ask. Any or all of these methods, pursued within a context of ongoing ethnography, will bring the researcher close to day-to-day practice. Ethnography requires a considerable time investment, and it requires for many a serious adjustment of attitude, but in the end it yields insights that cannot be obtained by any other means.

NOTE

1. All local names are pseudonyms.

REFERENCES

Eckert, Penelope. 1989. *Jocks and Burnouts: Social Categories and Identity in the High School*. New York: Teachers College Press.

Irvine, Judith T. and Susan Gal. 2000. Language ideology and linguistic differentiation. In Paul V. Kroskrity (ed.) *Regimes of Language: Ideologies, Politics, and Identities*. Santa Fe, New Mexico: SAR Press. 35–83.

Labov, William. 1966. *The Social Stratification of English in New York City*. Washington, D.C.: Center for Applied Linguistics.

Labov, William. 1972. Some principles of linguistic methodology. *Language in Society* 1: 97–120.

PART II
LANGUAGE, GENDER AND SEXUALITY

Editors' Introduction to Part II

Probably no other area of Sociolinguistics has stirred up so much controversy, led to so much (useful) theoretical debate, and generated so many publications (including its own journal – see the Resources section toward the end of the book) as 'language and gender'. The question 'Do men and women speak differently?' was the first question to be asked, and it has captivated researchers and non-specialists for decades. This is why we have decided to include a separate section of the Reader representing some of the early debates, but focusing mainly on current developments in this area. Even so, gender is central to the concerns of several chapters in other parts of the book too (for example, Eckert, Chapter 10; Edwards, Chapter 24; Gal, Chapter 32; Holmes, Chapter 42).

The chapter by O'Barr and Atkins (11) opens this section partly as a record of one of the most influential books in Sociolinguistics – Robin Lakoff's *Language and Woman's Place*, originally published in 1975, which the authors summarize. This development was interesting because Lakoff's work up to that point had been better known for her contribution to formal, theoretical linguistics. Indeed, her methodological approach to the discussion of sex differences in speech was closer to that tradition, drawing data from introspection, intuition and anecdote rather than analysis of 'naturally occurring', audio-recorded talk. In any case, however stereotyped Lakoff's own insights about the features of women's (and by implication – men's) talk may have been, they provided a vision and a template for generations of researchers in this area. Some have set out to 'prove' or 'disprove' the Lakoff hypothesis, as it is sometimes referred to, while others have used it as a reference point for more fine-grained, functional analyses of language use and gender. For example, Lakoff's suggestions that women are 'more polite' and that they have a 'poorer sense of humour' than men are in some ways echoed in Janet Holmes's chapter in Part VI, even though Holmes could not be further from endorsing such categorical views.

Lakoff's aim was to instigate a research program to provide linguistic evidence for the pervasiveness of societal *sexism*, and this aspect of her work has never been disputed. She wanted to discuss an assemblage of linguistic/ discursive features that marked tentativeness or powerlessness, on the basis that, she argued, women were socialized into using such features as part of their subservient role to men. O'Barr and Atkins not only provide a suc- cinct summary of Lakoff's key insights, but they also provide one of the first attempts to empirically test the hypothesis. From their examination of audio-recordings of male and female witnesses in a US court, they concluded that *both* men *and* women used features of Lakoff's 'women's language', even though in their sample more women did so than men. But they also found that such features were also used by individuals of *either* sex whose status was relatively low, in terms of occupations or their roles in trial proceedings (for example, 'ordinary' vs. 'expert' witnesses). So O'Barr and Atkins proposed a shift away from using the label 'women's language' toward the label 'powerless language'.

With hindsight we might say that O'Barr and Atkins's suggestion simply exchanges one troublesome category label for another, but their chapter cer- tainly demonstrates how misleading it can be to associate a specific demo- graphic group of speakers (here, women) with a set of 'typical' linguistic forms (see also our Introduction to Part I). Deborah Tannen's chapter (12) deals with a related complication, that of assigning fixed meanings to spe- cific linguistic features or strategies. Tannen discusses her data in relation to two broad dimensions of interpersonal relations that have surfaced time and time again in Sociolinguistics, *power* and *solidarity*. She demonstrates how each linguistic strategy (including the features that Lakoff discussed, for example, 'being indirect') may accomplish seemingly opposite goals in different contexts. Despite this, early sociolinguistic research on language and sex, no doubt drawing its inspiration from Lakoff, tended to focus on women as a relatively homogeneous group, although effectively it was the speech of white, middle-class, English-speaking women that provided the main point of reference. This methodological *essentializing* of 'sex' was soon to be abandoned, partly in view of researchers' increasing interest in 'men's language', but mainly as dissatisfaction with working with straightforward social categories grew. As more research was done, it was readily apparent that 'males' and 'females' were more sociolinguistically heterogeneous than was previously thought, and that gender and language were linked in more interesting and challenging ways.

Scott Kiesling (Chapter 13) contributes significantly to this debate, drawing on Judith Butler's *performative* view of gender, transplanted into Sociolinguistics mainly be Deborah Cameron, and represented in this Reader in the chapters by, for example, Wetherell and Edley (14), Hall (16), Barrett

(17) and Pennycook (23). This post-modern turn in language and gender studies is sometimes referred to as 'third wave feminist linguistics', the second wave being associated with Lakoff's and Tannen's work, among others. Kiesling and the other authors just mentioned extend the study of gender as an identity position, or role, by examining how the particular biological trait of being male or female is enacted or performed in talk, with respect to the speaker's projected sexuality and his or her power and solidarity relations with other members of same or opposite sex. Kiesling demonstrates how particular versions of 'being a man' are realized through his subjects' ideological positioning and linguistic stance-taking within an all-male group. In his study, white, middle-class, young American university students (members of a fraternity) adopt a dominant, hegemonic version of masculinity based on displaying specific *discursive* moves: categorical differentiation from women, foregrounding heterosexual orientation, claiming authority, and bonding with other men. Through a detailed analysis of one sociolinguistic variable – the realization of (ing), see Part I – in two distinct *activity types* (*meetings* and *social talk*), Kiesling also shows how this sociolinguistic feature is used variably by men as part of their identity construction, to take different interpersonal stances toward one another.

While Kiesling unravels the construction of hegemonic masculinities among American university students, Wetherell and Edley's chapter (14) concentrates on young British men's construction of counter-hegemonic masculine identities. Based on recordings of discussions with 17–18 year-olds in a private school in the UK, the authors examine accounts of antagonistic relations between institutionally and physically dominant 'rugby players' or 'hard lads', and a group of friends marginalized and subordinated by these young men. Here we see how non-rugby-playing students use talk to *contest* the *hegemonic masculinities* of the rugby players by undermining their status as physically violent, macho and 'chauvinistic'. They do so by using insults (for example, 'wanker'), expressly negative evaluations ('mentally weak'), and ironic voicing of their opponents' language, indicating distance from their values, behavior and speaking style. Some individuals also use the term 'wimp' in reference to themselves, although this label undergoes a number of definitional transformations in the course of the discussions, allowing these young men to be seen as different from the rugby players, yet strong both physically and mentally. What this chapter illustrates, then, is how (gender) identities are constructed through talk *relationally* (creating contrasts between self and other) and *dynamically*, through constant re-negotiation of one's own subjectivity and position within the hierarchy of a group. This is especially salient in the case of marginalized individuals, like the young men in Wetherell and Edley's study, who face an *ideological dilemma* in their need to distance themselves from their tormentors, yet claim enough cultural capital to shed their subordinate status.

Chapters 13 and 14 therefore make a clear case that social identity is not a monolithic attribute that a person *has*, but a dynamic, hybrid, multiple and often paradoxical achievement of the linguistic work that a person *does*. The three remaining chapters in this Part of the Reader are equally committed to this constructionist perspective. In Chapter 15, Mary Bucholtz mirrors Wetherell and Edley's research (and Eckert's in Chapter 10) by reporting data from an ethnographic study of a small friendship group of female students in a California high school. This group is described as a *nerd community of practice*, and this phrase aptly encapsulates the girls' identity position and Bucholtz' framework of analysis. This approach to 'community' views groups not in terms of their pre-determined social attributes but as constellations of individuals united in joint action of some sort, and identified by research-ers through ethnographic research (see the discussion of ethnography in Rampton's Chapter 47 and in our general Introduction, as well as Eckert's Chapter 10). Taking on the social identity of a 'nerd' allows young women in Bucholtz's study to contest the hegemonic ideology of femininity while main-taining high levels of intellectual ability and performance.

Among other *social practices* and strategies for self-presentation, nerd girls use a wide range of stylistic resources in their speech: phonological (for example, avoidance of 'colloquial' pronunciation), syntactic (avoidance of 'non-standard' and adherence to 'super-standard' grammar), lexical (avoid-ance of slang and adherence to formal words of Greek and Latin origin), and discursive (heightened reflexivity in language use through punning, parody and neologisms). Bucholtz refers to the stylistic practices that we are calling 'adherence' as *positive* – actively creating a sense of chosen identity – while the others are *negative* practices – actively dissociating the nerd girls from rejected identities. We saw a similar pair of positive and negative practices at work in the Wetherell and Edley chapter, where the marginalized boys laid claims to an identity based on physical and mental strength while rejecting the machismo of the rugby boys.

In Chapter 16, Kira Hall presents an inversion of identity play as it is dis-cussed in the previous two chapters. Hall analyses a series of interviews with telephone sex workers, several women and one man, who describe their prac-tices of creating a vocal guise and hence an identity of a 'perfect woman', to satisfy the fantasies of their male clients. Here we see the appropriation and commodification of hegemonic femininity by relatively marginalized and low paid speakers (sex workers). Apart from being a good example of how language skills and communication practices become increasingly *mar-ketized* and *commodified* in the service industries in globalized, post-industrial economies, this chapter demonstrates some of the top-down practices of instructing employees in the service sector how to use language, for example by creating manuals with *scripts* for interaction. So how is the identity of a 'perfect woman' created? First of all, female sex workers must tap into the common stereotypes of how a perfect woman should sound, and these seem to match the features of submissive and tentative talk as described by Lakoff (see above). Overall, the sex workers' accounts of their professional personas includes the following discursive and stylistic strategies: (1) creating extended narratives (for example, describing self for up to five minutes; creating a mental picture of self in the mind of the customer; creating the 'right' mood; creating the appearance of enjoyment); (2) using 'special' sensuous vocabulary and voice quality (for example, extraordinary adjectives and color terms; 'feminine' names for intimate body parts; whispering); and (3) performing racially stereotyped talk (different clients may think of their 'perfect woman' as black, white, Asian, and so on).

Rusty Barrett's investigation of performances by African American drag queens (AADQs) in Chapter 17 again builds on Judith Butler's view of gender as performative. Barrett demonstrates how AADQs construct their multiple stage personas of sophistication and glamour, as well as their *defiance of racism and homophobia*, by appropriating and mixing a range of different, frequently incongruent speaking styles: exaggerated, stereotyped speech of a 'white woman' (again matching Lakoff's description of 'women's language'), contrasted with swearing and obscenities, and features of African American Vernacular English. On the one hand, this stylistic mélange allows AADQs to claim multiple identity positions with regard to class, gender and sexuality. On the other hand, it creates a disjuncture between the mainstream, hegemonic white, upper class, heterosexual, feminine identity and Afro-American, working class, masculine, gay identity, and is a platform from which racial stereotypes can be ridiculed and resisted.

As we noted in our general Introduction, theorizing *social identity* is a central concern in Sociolinguistics, and gender and sexuality have been key themes in this regard. However, not infrequently, other aspects of personal and group identities may be equally important or foregrounded by social actors, and many chapters in the remaining Parts of the Reader take up the constructionist stance prevalent in language and gender research to examine equally intriguing themes. They include professional identities in broadcasting, policing and business (Chapters 18, 19, 43), social class and ethnic identities (Chapters 20, 21, 22, 44, 45), and many others.

CHAPTER 11

'Women's Language' or 'Powerless Language'?

WILLIAM M. O'BARR AND BOWMAN K. ATKINS

Introduction

The understanding of language and sex in American culture has progressed far beyond Robin Lakoff's influential and provocative essays on 'women's language' written only a few years ago.[1] The rapid development of knowledge in what had been so significantly an ignored and overlooked area owes much to both the development of sociolinguistic interest in general and to the woman's movement in particular. But as a recent review of anthropological studies about women pointed out, this interest has grown so quickly and studies proliferated so fast that there is frequently little or no cross-referencing of mutually supportive studies and equally little attempt to reconcile conflicting interpretations of women's roles. A similar critique of the literature on language and sex would no doubt reveal many of the same problems. But in one sense, these are not problems – they are marks of a rapidly developing field of inquiry, of vitality, and of saliency of the topic.

Our interest in language and sex was sharpened by Lakoff's essays. Indeed, her work was for us – as it was for many others – a jumping off point. But unlike some other studies, ours was not primarily an attempt to understand language and sex differences. Rather, the major goal of our recent research has been the study of language variation in a specific institutional context – the American trial courtroom – and sex-related differences were one of the kinds of variation which current sociolinguistic issues led us to consider. Our interest was further kindled by the discovery that trial practice manuals (how-to-do-it books by successful trial lawyers and law professors) often had special sections on how female witnesses behave differently from males and thus special kinds of treatment they require.

Source: '"Women's language" or "powerless language"?' by O'Barr, W and Atkins, B. K, in McConnell-Ginet et al. (eds) *Women and Language in Literature and Society* (1980) (Praeger/Greenwood Publishing Group) pp. 93–110.

In this paper, we describe our study of how women (and men) talk in court. The research we report here is part of a 30-month study of language variation in trial courtrooms which has included both ethnographic and experimental components. It is the thesis of this study that so-called 'women's language' is in large part a language of powerlessness, a condition that can apply to men as well as women. That a complex of such features should have been called 'women's language' in the first place reflects the generally powerless position of many women in American society, a point recognized but not developed extensively by Lakoff. Careful examination in one institutional setting of the features which were identified as constituting 'women's language' has shown clearly that such features are simply not patterned along sex lines. Moreover, the features do not, in a strict sense, constitute a *style* or *register* since there is not perfect co-variation.

Briefly, what Lakoff had proposed was that women's speech varies from men's in several significant ways. Although she provides no firm listing of the major features of what she terms 'women's language' (hereafter referred to in this paper as WL), we noted the following features, said to occur in high frequency among women, and used these as a baseline for our investigation of sex-related speech patterns in court.

1. *Hedges.* ('It's sort of hot in here'; 'I'd kind of like to go'; 'I guess...'; 'It seems like...'; and so on.)
2. *(Super) polite forms.* ('I'd really appreciate it if...'; 'Would you please open the door, if you don't mind?'; and so on.)
3. *Tag questions.* ('John is here, isn't he?' instead of 'Is John here?'; and so on.)
4. *Speaking in italics.* (Intonational emphasis equivalent to underlining words in written language; emphatic *so* or *very* and so on.)
5. *Empty adjectives.* (*Divine; charming; cute; sweet; adorable; lovely;* and so on.)
6. *Hypercorrect grammar and pronunciation.* (Bookish grammar; more formal enunciation.)
7. *Lack of a sense of humor.* (Women said to be poor joke tellers and to frequently 'miss the point' in jokes told by men.)
8. *Direct quotations.* (Use of direct quotations instead of paraphrases.)
9. *Special lexicon.* (In domains like colors where words like *magenta, chartreuse,* and so on are typically used only by women.)
10. *Question intonation in declarative contexts.* (For example, in response to the question, 'When will dinner be ready?', an answer like 'Around 6 o'clock?', as though seeking approval and asking whether that time will be okay.)

What We Found

During the summer of 1974, we recorded over 150 hours of trials in a North Carolina superior criminal court. Although almost all of the lawyers we observed were males, the sex distribution of witnesses was more nearly equal. On looking for the speech patterns described by Lakoff, we quickly discovered some women who spoke in the described manner. The only major discrepancies between Lakoff's description and our findings were in features which the specific context of the courtroom rendered inappropriate, for example, *tag questions* (because witnesses typically answer rather than ask questions) and *joking* (because there is a little humor in a courtroom, we did not have occasion to observe the specifically female patterns of humor to which she referred).

In addition to our early finding that some women approximate the model described by Lakoff, we also were quick to note that there was considerable variation in the degree to which women exhibited these characteristics. Since our observations were limited to about ten weeks of trials during which we were able to observe a variety of cases in terms of offense (ranging from traffic cases, drug possession, robbery, manslaughter, to rape) and length (from a few hours to almost five days), we believe that our observations cover a reasonably good cross-section of the kinds of trials, and hence witnesses, handled by this type of court. Yet, ten weeks is not enough to produce a very large number of witnesses. Even in a single case a witness may spend several hours testifying. In addition, the court spends much time selecting jurors, hearing summation remarks, giving jury instructions, and handling administrative matters. Thus, when looking at patterns of how different women talk in court, we are in a better position to deal with the range of variation we observed than to attempt any precise frequency counts of persons falling into various categories. Thus, we will concentrate our efforts here on describing the range and complement this with some non-statistical impressions regarding frequency.

Our observations show a continuum of use of the features described by Lakoff.[2] We were initially at a loss to explain why some women should speak more-or-less as Lakoff had described and why others should use only a few of these features. We will deal with our interpretation of these findings later, but first let us examine some points along the continuum from high to low.

A. Mrs. W,[3] a witness in a case involving the death of her neighbor in an automobile accident, is an extreme example of a person speaking WL in her testimony. She used nearly every feature described by Lakoff and certainly all those which are appropriate in the courtroom context. Her speech contains a high frequency of *intensifiers* ('*very* close friends', '*quite* ill', and so on often with intonation emphasis); *hedges* (frequent use of 'you know', 'sort of like', 'maybe just a little bit', 'let's see', and so on); *empty adjectives* ('this *very* kind policeman'); and other similar features. The first example below is typical of her speech and shows the types of intensifiers and hedges she commonly uses.[4] (To understand what her speech *might* be like without these features, example (2) is a rewritten version of her answers with the WL features eliminated.)

(1) L. State whether or not, Mrs. W., you were acquainted with or knew the late Mrs. E. D.

    W. Quite well.

    L. What was the nature of your acquaintance with her?

    W. Well, we were, uh, very close friends. Uh, she was even sort of like a mother to me.

(2) L. State whether or not, Mrs. W., -you were acquainted with or knew the late Mrs. E. D.

    W. Yes, I did.

    L. What was the nature of your acquaintance with her?

    W. We were close friends. She was like a mother to me.

Table 11.1 summarizes the frequency of several features attributed to WL by Lakoff. Calculated as a ratio of WL forms for each answer, this witness's speech contains 1.14 – among the highest incidences we observed.

B. The speech of Mrs. N, a witness in a case involving her father's arrest, shows fewer WL features. Her ratio of features for each answer drops to 0.84. Her testimony contains instances of both WL and a more assertive speech style. Frequently, her speech is punctuated with responses like: 'He, see, he thought it was more-or-less me rather than the police officer.' Yet it also contains many more straightforward and assertive passages than are found in A's speech. In example (3), for instance, Mrs. N is anything but passive. She turns questions back on the lawyer and even interrupts him. Example (4) illustrates the ambivalence of this speaker's style better. Note how she moves quickly to qualify – in WL – an otherwise assertive response.

(3) L. All right. I ask you if your husband hasn't beaten him up in the last week?

    W. Yes, and do you know why?

    L. Well, I ...

    W. Another gun episode.

    L. Another gun episode?

    W. Yessiree.

(4) L. You've had a controversy going with him for a long time, haven't you?

    W. Ask why – I mean not because I'm just his daughter.

C. The speech of Dr. H, a pathologist who testifies as an expert witness, exhibits fewer features of WL than either of the other two women. Her speech contains the lowest incidence of WL features among the female witnesses whose speech we analysed. Dr. H's ratio of WL features is 0.18 for each answer. Her responses tend to be straightforward, with little hesitancy, few hedges, a noticeable lack of intensifiers, and so on. (See Table 11.1.) Typical of her speech is example (5) in which she explains some of her findings in a pathological examination.

(5) L.   And had the heart not been functioning, in other words, had the heart been stopped, there would have been no blood to have come from that region?

    W.   It may leak down depending on the position of the body after death. But the presence of blood in the alveoli indicates that some active respiratory action had to take place.

What all of this shows is the fact that some women speak in the way Lakoff described, employing many features of WL, while others are far away on the continuum of possible and appropriate styles for the courtroom. Before discussing the reasons which may lie behind this variation in the language used by women in court, we first examine an equally interesting finding which emerged from our investigation of male speech in court.

We also found men who exhibit WL characteristics in their courtroom testimony. To illustrate this, we examine the speech of three male witnesses which varies along a continuum of high to low incidence of WL features.

D. Mr. W exhibits many but not all of Lakoff's WL features. Some of those which he does employ, like intensifiers, for example, occur in especially high frequency – among the highest observed among all speakers, whether male or female. His ratio of WL features for each answer is 1.39, actually higher than individual A. Example (6), while an extreme instance of Mr. W's use of WL features, does illustrate the degree to which features attributed to women are in fact present in high frequency in the speech of some men.

(6) L.   And you saw, you observed what?

    W.   Well, after I heard – I can't really, I can't definitely state whether the brakes or the lights came first, but I rotated my head slightly to the right, and looked directly behind Mr. Z., and I saw reflections of lights, and uh, very, very, very instantaneously after that, I heard a very, very loud explosion – from my standpoint of view it would have been an implosion because everything was forced outward, like this, like a grenade thrown into a room. And, uh, it was, it was terrifically loud.

E. Mr. N, more toward the low frequency end of the continuum of male speakers, shows some WL features. His ratio of features for each answer is 0.64, comparable to individual B. Example (7) shows an instance of passages from the testimony of this speaker in which there are few WL features. Example (8), by comparison, shows the same hedging in a way characteristic of WL. His speech falls between the highest and lowest incidences of WL features we observed among males.

(7) L.   After you looked back and saw the back of the ambulance, what did you do?

W.   After I realized that my patient and my attendant were thrown from the vehicle, uh, which I assumed, I radioed in for help to the dispatcher, tell her that we had been in an accident and, uh, my patient and attendant were thrown from the vehicle and I didn't know the extent of their injury at the time, to hurry up and send help.

(8) L.   Did you form any conclusion about what her problem was at the time you were there?

W.   I felt that she had, uh, might have had a sort of heart attack.

F. Officer G, among the males lowest in WL features, virtually lacks all features tabulated in Table 11.1 except for hesitancy and using *sir*. His ratio of WL forms for each answer is .46. Example (9) shows how this speaker handles the lack of certainty in a more authoriatative manner than by beginning his answer with 'I guess…'. His no-nonsense, straightforward manner is illustrated well by example (10), in which a technical answer is given in a style comparable to that of individual C.

(9) L.   Approximately how many times have you testified in court?

W.   It would only have to be a guess, but it's three or four, five, six hundred times. Probably more.

(10) L.   You say that you found blood of group O?

W.   The blood in the vial, in the layman's term, is positive, Rh positive. Technically referred to as a capital r, sub o, little r.

Taken together these findings suggest that the so-called 'women's language' is neither characteristic of all women nor limited only to women. A similar continuum of WL features (high to low) is found among speakers of both sexes. These findings suggest that the sex of a speaker is insufficient to explain incidence of WL features, and that we must look elsewhere for an explanation of this variation.

Once we had realized that WL features were distributed in such a manner, we began to examine the data for other factors which might be associated with a high or low incidence of the features in question. First, we noted that we were able to find *more* women toward the high end of the continuum. Next, we noted that all the women who were aberrant (that is, who used relatively few WL features) had something in common – an unusually high social status. Like Dr. H, they were typically well-educated, professional women of middle-class background. A corresponding pattern was noted among the aberrant men (that is, those high in WL features). Like Mr. W, they tended to be men who held either subordinate, lower-status jobs or were unemployed. Housewives were high in WL features while middle-class males were low in these features. In addition to social status in the society at large, another factor associated with low incidence of WL is previous courtroom experience. Both individuals C and F testify frequently in court as expert witnesses, that is, as witnesses who testify on the basis of their professional expertise. However,

Table 11.1   Frequency distribution of women's language features[a] in the speech of six witnesses in a trial courtroom

	Women			Men		
	A	B	C	D	E	F
Intensifiers[b]	16	0	0	21	2	1
Hedges[c]	19	2	3	2	5	0
Hesitation forms[d]	52	20	13	26	27	11
W asks L questions[e]	2	0	0	0	0	0
Gestures[f]	2	0	0	0	0	0
Polite forms[g]	9	0	2	2	0	1
Sir[h]	2	0	6	32	13	11
Quotes[i]	1	5	0	0	0	0
Total (all powerless forms)	103	27	24	85	47	24
# of Answers in interview	90	32	136	61	73	52
Ratio (# powerless forms for each answer)	1.14	0.84	0.18	1.39	0.64	0.46

Notes: a The particular features chosen for inclusion in this table were selected because of their saliency and frequency of occurrence. Not included here are features of WL which either do not occur in court or ones which we had difficulty operationalizing and coding. *Based on direct examinations only.* b Forms which increase or emphasize the force of assertion such as *very, definitely, very definitely, surely, such a,* and so on. c Forms which reduce the force of assertion allowing for exceptions or avoiding rigid commitments such as *sort of, a little, kind of,* and so on. d Pause fillers such as *uh, um, ah,* and 'meaningless' particles such as *oh, well, let's see, now, so, you see,* and so on. e Use of question intonation in response to lawyer's questions, including rising intonation in normally declarative contexts (for example, 'thirty?, thirty-five?') and questions asked by witness of lawyer like 'Which way do you go ... ?'. f Spoken indications of direction such as *over there,* and so on. g Include *please, thank you,* and so on. Use of *sir* counted separately due to its high frequency. h Assumed to be an indication of more polite speech. i Not typically allowed in court under restrictions on hearsay which restrict the situations under which a witness may tell what someone else said.

Source: Original data.

it should be noted that not all persons who speak with few WL features have had extensive courtroom experience. The point we wish to emphasize is that a powerful position may derive from either social standing in the larger society and/or status accorded by the court. We carefully observed these patterns and found them to hold generally. For some individuals whom we had observed in the courtroom, we analysed their speech in detail in order to tabulate the frequency of the WL features as shown in Table 11.1. A little more about the background of the persons we have described will illustrate the sort of pattern we observed.

A is a married woman, about 55 years old, who is a housewife.

B is married, but younger, about 35 years old. From her testimony, there is no information that she works outside her home.

C is a pathologist in a local hospital. She is 35–40 years old. There is no indication from content of her responses or from the way she was addressed (always *Dr.*) of her marital status. She has testified in court as a pathologist on many occasions.

D is an ambulance attendant, rather inexperienced in his job, at which he has worked for less than 6 months. Age around 30. Marital status unknown.

E is D's supervisor. He drives the ambulance, supervises emergency treatment and gives instructions to D. He has worked at his job longer than D and has had more experience. Age about 30–35; marital status unknown. *F* is an experienced member of the local police force. He has testified in court frequently. Age 35–40; marital status unknown.

'Women's Language' or 'Powerless Language'?

In the previous section, we presented data which indicate that the variation in WL features may be related more to social powerlessness than to sex. We have presented both observational data and some statistics to show that this style is not simply or even primarily a sex-related pattern. We did, however, find it related to sex in that more women tend to be high in WL features while more men tend to be low in these same features. The speech patterns of three men and three women were examined. For each sex, the individuals varied from social statuses with relatively low power to more power (for women: housewife to doctor; for men: subordinate job to one with a high degree of independence of action). Experience may also be an important factor, for those whom we observed speaking with few WL features seemed more comfortable in the courtroom and with the content of their testimony. Associated with increasing shifts in social power and experience were corresponding decreases in frequency of WL features. These six cases were selected for detailed analysis because they were representative of the sorts of women and men who served as witnesses in the trials we observed in 1974. Based on this evidence, we would suggest that the phenomenon described by Lakoff would be better termed *powerless language,* a term which is more descriptive of the particular features involved, of the social status of those who speak in this manner, and one which does not link it unnecessarily to the sex of a speaker.

Further, we would suggest that the tendency for more women to speak powerless language and for men to speak less of it is due, at least in part, to the greater tendency of women to occupy relatively powerless social positions. What we have observed is a reflection in their speech behavior of their social status. Similarly, for men, a greater tendency to use the more powerful variant (which we will term *powerful language*) may be linked to the fact that men much more often tend to occupy relatively powerful positions in society.

NOTES

1. Lakoff, Robin. 1975. *Language and Woman's Place.* New York: Harper and Row.
2. Actually each feature should be treated as a separate continuum since there is not perfect co-variation. For convenience, we discuss the variation as a single continuum of possibilities. However, it should be kept in mind that a high frequency of occurrence of one particular feature may not necessarily be associated with a high frequency of another.
3. Names have been changed and indicated by a letter only in order to preserve the anonymity of witnesses. However, the forms of address used in the court are retained.
4. These examples are taken from both the direct and cross examinations of the witnesses, although Table 11.1 uses data only from direct examinations. Examples were chosen to point out clearly the differences in style. However, it must be noted that the cross examination is potentially a more powerless situation for the witness.

CHAPTER 12

The Relativity of Linguistic Strategies: Rethinking Power and Solidarity in Gender and Dominance

DEBORAH TANNEN

Theoretical Background

Power and Solidarity

Since Brown and Gilman's (1960) introduction of the concept and subsequent elaborations of it, especially those of Friedrich (1972) and Brown and Levinson ([1978] 1987), the dynamics of power and solidarity have been fundamental to sociolinguistic theory. Brown and Gilman based their framework on analysis of the use of pronouns in European languages which have two forms of the second-person pronoun, such as the French *tu* and *vous*. In English the closest parallel is to be found in forms of address: first name versus title-last name. In Brown and Gilman's system, power is associated with nonreciprocal use of pronouns; in English, the parallel would be a situation in which one speaker addresses the other by first name but is addressed by title-last name (for example, doctor and patient, teacher and student, boss and secretary, building resident and elevator operator). Solidarity is associated with reciprocal pronoun use or symmetrical forms of address: both speakers address each other by *tu* or by *vous* (in English, by title-last name or by first name). Power governs asymmetrical relationships where one is subordinate to

Source: 'The Relativity of Linguistic Strategies: Rethinking Power and Solidarity in Gender and Dominance' in Tannen, D (ed) *Gender and Conversational Interaction* (1993) (Oxford: Oxford University Press) pp. 165–88.

another; solidarity governs symmetrical relationships characterized by social equality and similarity.

In my previous work exploring the relationship between power and solidarity as it emerges in conversational discourse (Tannen 1984, 1986), I note that power and solidarity are in paradoxical relation to each other. That is, although power and solidarity, closeness and distance, seem at first to be opposites, each also entails the other. Any show of solidarity necessarily entails power, in that the requirement of similarity and closeness limits freedom and independence. At the same time, any show of power entails solidarity by involving participants in relation to each other. This creates a closeness that can be contrasted with the distance of individuals who have no relation to each other at all.

In Brown and Gilman's paradigm, the key to power is asymmetry, but it is often thought to be formality. This is seen in the following anecdote. I once entitled a lecture 'The Paradox of Power and Solidarity.' The respondent to my talk appeared wearing a three-piece suit and a knapsack on his back. The audience was amused by the association of the suit with power, the knapsack with solidarity. There was something immediately recognizable in this semiotic. Indeed, a professor wearing a knapsack might well mark solidarity with students at, for example, a protest demonstration. And wearing a three-piece suit to the demonstration might mark power by differentiating the wearer from the demonstrators, perhaps even reminding them of his dominant position in the institutional hierarchy. But wearing a three-piece suit to the board meeting of a corporation would mark solidarity with other board members, whereas wearing a knapsack in that setting would connote not solidarity but disrespect, a move in the power dynamic.

The Ambiguity of Linguistic Strategies

As the preceding example shows, the same symbol – a three-piece suit – can signal either power or solidarity, depending on, at least, the setting (e.g., board meeting or student demonstration), the habitual dress style of the individual, and the comparison of his clothing with that worn by others in the interaction. (I say 'his' intentionally; the range of meanings would be quite different if a man's three-piece suit were worn by a woman.) This provides an analogue to the ambiguity of linguistic strategies, which are signals in the semiotic system of language. As I have demonstrated at length in previous books, all linguistic strategies are potentially ambiguous. The power-solidarity dynamic is one fundamental source of ambiguity. What appear as attempts to dominate a conversation (an exercise of power) may actually be intended to establish rapport (an exercise of solidarity). This occurs because (as I have worded it elsewhere) power and solidarity are bought with the same currency: The same linguistic means can be used to create either or both.

This ambiguity can be seen in the following fleeting conversation. Two women were walking together from one building to another in order to attend a meeting. They were joined by a man they both knew who had just exited a third building on his way to the same meeting. One of the women greeted the man and remarked, 'Where's your coat?' The man responded, 'Thanks, Mom.' His response framed the woman's remark as a gambit in a power exchange: a mother tells a child to put on his coat. Yet the woman might have intended the remark as showing friendly concern rather than parental care-taking. Was it power (condescending, on the model of parent to child) or solidarity (friendly, on the model of intimate peers)? Though the man's uptake is clear, the woman's intention in making the remark is not.

The Polysemy of Power and Solidarity

Brown and Gilman are explicit in their assumption that power is associated with asymmetrical relationships in which the power is held by the person in the one-up position. This is stated in their definition: 'One person may be said to have power over another to the degree that he is able to control the behavior of the other. Power is a relationship between at least two persons, and it is nonreciprocal in the sense that both cannot have power in the same area of behavior' (254). I have called attention, however, to the extent to which solidarity in itself can be a form of control. For example, a young woman complained about friends who 'don't let you be different'. If the friend says she has a particular problem and the woman says, 'I don't have that problem', her friend is hurt and accuses her of putting her down, of acting superior. The assumption of similarity requires the friend to have a matching problem (Tannen 1990b).

Furthermore, although Brown and Gilman acknowledge that 'power superiors may be solidary (parents, elder siblings)' and 'power inferiors, similarly, may be as solidary as the old family retainer' (254), most Americans are inclined to assume that solidarity implies closeness, whereas power implies distance. Thus Americans regard the sibling relationship as the ultimate in solidarity: 'sister' or 'brother' can be used metaphorically to indicate closeness and equality. In contrast, it is often assumed that hierarchy precludes closeness: employers and employees cannot 'really' be friends. But being linked in a hierarchy necessarily brings individuals closer. This is an assumption underlying Watanabe's (1993) observation, in comparing American and Japanese group discussions, that whereas the Americans in her study saw themselves as individuals participating in a joint activity, the Japanese saw themselves as members of a group united by hierarchy. When reading Watanabe, I was caught up short by the term 'united'. My inclination had been to assume that hierarchy is distancing, not uniting.

The anthropological literature includes numerous discussions of cultural contexts in which hierarchical relationships are seen as close and mutually, not unilaterally, empowering. For example, Beeman (1986) describes an Iranian interactional pattern he dubs 'getting the lower hand'. Taking the lower-status position enables an Iranian to invoke a protector schema by which the higher-status person is obligated to do things for him or her. Similarly, Yamada (1992) describes the Japanese relationship of *amae*, typified by the parent-child or employer-employee constellation. It binds two individuals in a hierarchical interdependence by which both have power in the form of obligations as well as rights vis-à-vis the other. Finally, Wolfowitz (1991) explains that respect/deference is experienced by Suriname Javanese not as subservience but as an assertion of claims. The Suriname Javanese example is particularly intriguing because it calls into question the association of asymmetry with power and distance. The style Wolfowitz calls respect-politeness is characterized by both social closeness and negative politeness. It is hierarchical insofar as it is directional and unequal; however, the criterion for directionality is not status but age. The prototypical relationship characterized by respect politeness is grandchild-grandparent: a relationship that is both highly unequal and very close. Moreover, according to Wolfowitz, the Javanese assume that familial relations are inherently hierarchical, including age-graded siblings. Equality, in contrast, is associated with formal relationships that are also marked by social distance.

We can display these dynamics as a multidimensional grid of at least [two] (and, potentially and probably, more) intersecting continuua. The closeness/distance dimension can be placed on one axis and the hierarchy/equality one on another. (See Figure 12.1.) Indeed, the intersection of these dimensions – that is, the co-incidence of hierarchy and closeness – may account, at least in part, for what I am calling the ambiguity and polysemy of power and solidarity.

Similarity/Difference

There is one more aspect of the dynamics of power and solidarity that bears discussion before I demonstrate the relativity of linguistic strategies. That is the similarity/difference continuum and its relation to the other dynamics discussed.

For Brown and Gilman solidarity implies sameness, in contrast to power, about which they observe, 'In general terms, the *V* form is linked with

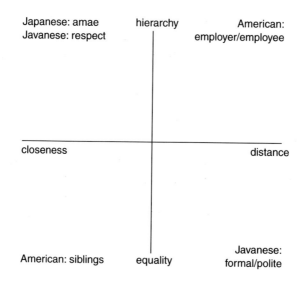

Figure 12.1   The intersecting dimensions of closeness/distance and hierarchy/equality

differences between persons' (256). This is explicit in their definition of 'the solidarity semantic':

> Now we are concerned with a new set of relations which are symmetrical; for example, *attended the same school* or *have the same parents* or *practice the same profession*. If A has the same parents as B, B has the same parents as A. Solidarity is the name we give to the general relationship and solidarity is symmetrical. (257; italics in original)

The similarity/difference continuum calls to mind what I have discussed elsewhere (Tannen 1984, 1986) as the double bind of communication. In some ways, we are all the same. But in other ways we are all different. Communication is a double bind in the sense that anything we say to honor our similarity violates our difference, and anything we say to honor our difference violates our sameness. Thus a complaint can be lodged: 'Don't think I'm different.' ('If you prick me, do I not bleed?' one might protest, like Shylock.) But a complaint can also be lodged: 'Don't think I'm the same.' (Thus, for example, women who have primary responsibility for the care of small children will be effectively excluded from activities or events at which day care is not provided.) Becker (1982: 125) expresses this double bind as 'a matter of continual self-correction between exuberance (i.e., friendliness: you are like me) and deficiency (i.e., respect: you are not me)'. All these formulations elaborate on the tension between similarity and difference, or what Becker and Oka (1974) call 'the cline of person', a semantic dimension they suggest may be the one most basic to language: that is, one deals with the world and the objects and people in it in terms of how close (and I would add, similar) they are to oneself.

As a result of these dynamics, similarity is a threat to hierarchy. This is dramatized in Harold Pinter's play *Mountain Language*. Composed of four brief scenes, the play is set in a political prison in the capital city of an unnamed country that is under dictatorial siege. In the second scene, an old mountain woman is finally allowed to visit her son across a table as a guard stands over them. But whenever she tries to speak to her son, the guard silences her, telling the prisoner to tell his mother that it is forbidden to speak their mountain language in the capital. Then he continues:

GUARD

... And I'll tell you another thing. I've got a wife and three kids. And you're all a pile of shit.
Silence.
PRISONER

I've got a wife and three kids.
GUARD

You've what?
Silence.
You've got what?
Silence.
What did you say to me? You've got what?
Silence.
You've got *what?*
He picks up the telephone and dials one digit.
Sergeant? I'm in the Blue Room...yes...I thought I should report, Sergeant...I think I've got a joker in here.

The Sergeant soon enters and asks, 'What joker?' The stage darkens and the scene ends. The final scene opens on the same setting, with the prisoner bloody and shaking, his mother shocked into speechlessness. The prisoner was beaten for saying, 'I've got a wife and three kids.' This quotidian statement, which would be unremarkable in casual conversation, was insubordinate in the hierarchical context of brutal oppression because the guard had just made the same statement. When the guard said, 'I've got a wife and three kids. And you're a pile of shit', he was claiming, 'I am different from you.' One could further interpret his words to imply, 'I'm human, and you're not. Therefore I have a right to dominate and abuse you.' By repeating the guard's words verbatim, the prisoner was then saying, 'I am the same as you.' By claiming *his* humanity and implicitly denying the guard's assertion that he is 'a pile of shit', the prisoner challenged the guard's right to dominate him. Similarity is antithetical to hierarchy.

The ambiguity of closeness, a spatial metaphor representing similarity or involvement, emerges in a nonverbal aspect of this scene. In the performance I saw, the guard repeated the question 'You've got what?' while moving steadily closer to the prisoner, until he was bending over him, nose to nose. The guard's moving closer was a kinesic/proxemic analogue to the prisoner's statement, but with opposite effect: he was 'closing in'. The guard moved closer and brought his face into contact with the prisoner's not as a sign of affection (which such actions could signify in another context) but as a threat. Closeness, then, can mean aggression rather than affiliation in the context of a hierarchical rather than symmetrical relationship.

The Relativity of Linguistic Strategies

The potential ambiguity of linguistic strategies to mark both power and solidarity in face-to-face interaction has made mischief in language and gender research, wherein it is tempting to assume that whatever women do results from, or creates, their powerlessness and whatever men do results from, or creates, their dominance. But all the linguistic strategies that have been taken by analysts as evidence of dominance can in some circumstances be instruments of affiliation. For the remainder of this chapter I demonstrate the relativity of linguistic strategies by considering each of the following strategies in turn: indirectness, interruption, silence versus volubility, topic raising, and adversativeness, or verbal conflict. All of these strategies have been 'found' by researchers to express or create dominance. I will demonstrate that they are ambiguous or polysemous with regard to dominance or closeness. Once again I am not arguing that these strategies *cannot* be used to create dominance or powerlessness, much less that dominance and powerlessness do not exist. Rather, my purpose is to demonstrate that the 'meaning' of any linguistic strategy can vary, depending at least on context, the conversational styles of participants, and the interaction of participants' styles and strategies. Therefore we will have to study the operation of specific linguistic strategies more closely to understand how dominance and powerlessness are expressed and created in interaction.

Indirectness

Lakoff (1975) identifies two benefits of indirectness: defensiveness and rapport. Defensiveness refers to a speaker's preference not to go on record with an idea in order to be able to disclaim, rescind, or modify it if it does not meet with a positive response. The rapport benefit of indirectness results from the pleasant experience of getting one's way not because one demanded it (power) but because the other person wanted the same thing (solidarity). Many researchers have focused on the defensive or power benefit of indirectness and ignored the payoff in rapport or solidarity.

The claim by O'Barr and Atkins (this volume) that women's language is really powerless language has been particularly influential. In this view women's tendency to be indirect is taken as evidence that women don't feel entitled to make demands. Surely there are cases in which this is true. Yet it can easily be demonstrated that those who feel entitled to make demands may prefer not to, seeking the payoff in rapport. Furthermore, the ability to get one's demands met without expressing them directly can be a sign of power rather than of the lack of it. An example I have used elsewhere (Tannen 1986) is the Greek father who answers, 'If you want, you can go', to his daughter's inquiry about going to a party. Because of the lack of enthusiasm of his response, the Greek daughter understands that her father would prefer she not go and 'chooses' not to go. (A 'real' approval would have been 'Yes, of course, you should go.') I argue that this father did not feel powerless to give his daughter orders. Rather, a communicative system was conventionalized by which he and she could both preserve the appearance, and possibly the belief, that she chose not to go rather than simply obeying his command.

Far from being powerless, this father felt so powerful that he did not need to give his daughter orders; he simply needed to let her know his preference, and she would accommodate to it. By this reasoning, indirectness is a prerogative of the powerful. By the same reasoning, a master who says, 'It's cold in here', may expect a servant to make a move to close a window, but a servant who says the same thing is not likely to see his employer rise to correct the situation and make him more comfortable. Indeed, a Frenchman who was raised in Brittany tells me that his family never gave bald commands to their servants but always communicated orders in indirect and superpolite form. This pattern renders less surprising the finding of Bellinger and Gleason (1982, reported in Gleason 1987) that fathers' speech to their young children had a higher incidence than mothers' of both direct imperatives (such as 'Turn the bolt with the wrench') *and* implied indirect imperatives (for example, 'The wheel is going to fall off').

The use of indirectness can hardly be understood without the cross-cultural perspective. Many Americans find it self-evident that directness is logical and aligned with power whereas indirectness is akin to dishonesty as well as subservience. But for speakers raised in most of the world's cultures, varieties of indirectness are the norm in communication. In Japanese interaction, for example, it is well known that saying 'no' is considered too face-threatening to risk, so negative responses are phrased as positive ones: one never says 'no', but initiates understand from the form of the 'yes' whether it is truly a 'yes' or a polite 'no'. And this applies to men as well as women.

The American association of indirectness with female style is not culturally universal. Keenan (1974) found that in a Malagasy-speaking village on the island of Madagascar, women are direct and men indirect. But this in no way implies that the women are more powerful than men in this society. Quite the contrary, Malagasy men are socially dominant – and their indirect style is more highly valued. Keenan found that women were widely believed to debase the language with their artless directness, whereas men's elaborate indirectness was widely admired. In my own research (Tannen 1981) I compared Greeks and Americans with regard to their tendency to interpret a question as an indirect means of making a request. I found that whereas American women were more likely to take an indirect interpretation of a sample conversation, Greek men were as likely as Greek women, and more likely than American men *or women,* to take an indirect interpretation. Greek men, of course, are not less powerful vis-à-vis women than American men.

Indirectness, then, is not in itself a strategy of subordination. Rather, it can be used by either the powerful or the powerless. The interpretation of a given utterance and the likely response to it depend on the setting, on individuals' status and their relationship to each other, and also on the linguistic conventions that are ritualized in the cultural context.

Interruption

That interruption is a sign of dominance has been as widespread an assumption in research as in conventional wisdom. Most frequently cited is West and Zimmerman's (1983) finding that men dominate women by interrupting them in conversation. Tellingly, however, Deborah James and Sandra Clarke (1993), reviewing research on gender and interruption, do not find a clear pattern of males interrupting females. Especially significant is their discovery that studies comparing amount of interruption in all-female versus all-male conversations find more interruption, not less, in all-female groups. Though initially surprising, this finding reinforces the need to distinguish linguistic strategies by their interactional purpose. Does the overlap show support for

the speaker, or does it contradict or change the topic? I explore this phenomenon in detail elsewhere (Tannen 1989) but I will include a brief summary of
the argument here.

   The phenomenon commonly referred to as 'interruption', but more
properly referred to as 'overlap', is a paradigm case of the ambiguity of
power and solidarity. This is clearly demonstrated with reference to a two
and a half hour dinner table conversation that I have analysed at length
(Tannen 1984). My analysis makes clear that some speakers consider talking along with another a show of enthusiastic participation in the conversation (solidarity, creating connections); others, however, assume that
only one voice should be heard at a time, so for them any overlap is an
interruption (an attempt to wrest the floor, a power play). The result, in
the conversation I analysed, was that enthusiastic listeners who overlapped
cooperatively, talking along to establish rapport, were perceived by overlap-resistant speakers as interrupting. This doubtless contributed to the
impression reported by the overlap-resistant speakers that the cooperative
overlappers had 'dominated' the conversation. Indeed, the tape and transcript also give the impression that the cooperative overlappers had dominated, because the overlap-aversant participants tended to stop speaking as
soon as another voice began.

   It is worth emphasizing the role of balance in determining whether an
overlap becomes an interruption in the negative or power-laden sense. If one
speaker repeatedly overlaps and another repeatedly gives way, the resulting
communication is asymmetrical, and the effect (though not necessarily the
intent) is domination. But if both speakers avoid overlap, or if both speakers
overlap each other and win out equally, there is symmetry and no domination, regardless of speakers' intentions. Importantly, though, and this will
be discussed in the last section under the rubric of adversativeness, the very
engagement in a symmetrical struggle for the floor can be experienced as creating rapport, in the spirit of ritual opposition analogous to sports. Further,
an imbalance can result from differences in the purpose for which overlap
is used. If one speaker tends to talk along in order to show support, and
the other chimes in to take the floor, the floor-taking overlapper will tend to
dominate.

   Thus, to understand whether an overlap is an interruption, one must consider the context (for example, cooperative overlapping is more likely to occur
in casual conversation among friends than in a job interview), the speakers' habitual styles (for example, overlaps are more likely not to be interruptions among those with a style I call 'high-involvement'), and the interaction
of their styles (for example, an interruption is more likely to occur between
speakers whose styles differ with regard to pausing and overlap). This is not to
say that one cannot use interruption to dominate a conversation or a person,

only that it is not self-evident from the observation of overlap that an interruption has occurred, or was intended, or was intended to dominate.

Silence versus Volubility

The excerpt from Pinter's *Mountain Language* dramatizes the assumption that powerful people do the talking and powerless people are silenced. This is the trope that underlies the play's title and its central theme: By outlawing their language, the oppressors silence the mountain people, robbing them of their ability to speak and hence of their humanity. In the same spirit, many scholars (for example, Spender 1980) have claimed that men dominate women by silencing them. There are obviously circumstances in which this is accurate. Coates (1986) notes numerous proverbs that instruct women, like children, to be silent.

Silence alone, however, is not a self-evident sign of powerlessness, nor volubility a self-evident sign of domination. A theme running through Komarovsky's (1962) classic study, *Blue-Collar Marriage*, is that many of the wives interviewed said they talked more than their husbands: 'He's tongue-tied', one woman said (13); 'My husband has a great habit of not talking', said another (162); 'He doesn't say much but he means what he says and the children mind him', said a third (353). Yet there is no question that these husbands are dominant in their marriages, as the last of these quotes indicates.

Indeed, taciturnity itself can be an instrument of power. This is precisely the claim of Sattel (1983), who argues that men use silence to exercise power over women. Sattel illustrates with a scene from Erica Jong's novel *Fear of Flying*, only a brief part of which is presented here. The first line of dialogue is spoken by Isadora, the second by her husband, Bennett. (Spaced dots indicate omitted text; unspaced dots are a form of punctuation included in the original text.)

'Why do you turn on me? What did I do?'
Silence.
'What did I do?'
He looks at her as if her not knowing were another injury.
'Look, let's just go to sleep now. Let's just forget it.'
'Forget what?'
He says nothing.

. . .

'It was something in the movie, wasn't it?'
'What, in the movie?'

'...It was the funeral scene....The little boy looking at his dead mother. Something got you there. That was when you got depressed.'
Silence.
'Well, *wasn't* it?'
Silence.
'Oh come on, Bennett, you're making me *furious*. Please tell me. Please.'

The painful scene continues in this vein until Bennett tries to leave the room and Isadora tries to detain him. The excerpt certainly seems to support Sattel's claim that Bennett's silence subjugates his wife, as the scene ends with her literally lowered to the floor, clinging to his pajama leg. But the reason his silence is an effective weapon is her insistence that he tell her what's wrong. If *she* receded into silence, leaving the room or refusing to talk to him, his silence would be disarmed. The devastation results not from his silence alone but from the combination of his silence and her insistence on talking, in other words, the interaction of their differing styles.

Researchers have counted numbers of words spoken or timed length of talk in order to demonstrate that men talk more than women and thereby dominate interactions. (See James and Drakich [1993] for a summary of research on amount of talk.) Undoubtedly there is truth to this observation in some settings. But the association of volubility with dominance does not hold for all settings and all cultures. Imagine, for example, an interrogation, in which the interrogator does little of the talking but holds all the power.

The relativity of the 'meaning' of taciturnity and volubility is high-lighted in Margaret Mead's (1977) discussion of 'end linkage', a concept developed jointly by Mead, Gregory Bateson, and Geoffrey Gorer. Their claim is that universal and biologically constructed relationships, such as parent-child, are linked to different behaviors in different cultures. One of their paradigm examples is the apportionment of spectatorship and exhibitionism. In middle class American culture, children, who are obviously the weaker party in the constellation, are expected to exhibit while their more powerful parents are spectators; in contrast, in middle- and upper-class British culture, exhibition is associated with the parental role and spectatorship with children, who are expected to be seen and not heard.

Furthermore, volubility and taciturnity, too, can result from style differences rather than speakers' intentions. As I (Tannen 1984, 1985) and others (Scollon and Scollon 1981; Scollon 1985) have discussed at length, there are cultural and subcultural differences in the length of pauses expected between and within speaking turns. In my study of the dinner table conversation, those who expected shorter pauses between conversational turns began to feel an uncomfortable silence ensuing while their longer-pausing friends were simply waiting for what they regarded as the 'normal' end-of-turn pause. The result was that the shorter pausers ended up doing most of the talking, another sign interpreted by their interlocutors as dominating the conversation. But their intentions had been to fill in what to them were potentially uncomfortable silences, that is, to grease the conversational wheels and ensure the success of the conversation. In their view, the taciturn participants were uncooperative, failing to do their part to maintain the conversation.

Thus silence and volubility, too, cannot be taken to 'mean' power or power-lessness, domination or subjugation. Rather, both may imply either power or solidarity, depending on the criteria discussed.

Topic Raising

Shuy (1982) is typical in assuming that the speaker who raises the most top-ics is dominating a conversation. However, in a study I conducted (Tannen 1990a) of videotaped conversations among friends of varying ages recorded by Dorval (1990), it emerged that the speaker who raised the most topics was not always dominant, as judged by other criteria (for example, who took the lead in addressing the investigator when he entered the room). In a twenty-minute conversation between a pair of sixth-grade girls who identified them-selves as best friends, Shannon raised the topic of Julia's relationship with Mary by saying, 'Too bad you and Mary are not good friends anymore.' The conversation proceeded and continued to focus almost exclusively on Julia's troubled relationship with Mary.

Similarly, most of the conversation between two tenth-grade girls was about Nancy, but Sally raised the topic of Nancy's problems. In response to Nancy's question 'Well, what do you want to talk about?' Sally said, 'Your mama. Did you talk to your mama?' The ensuing conversation focuses on happenings involving Nancy's mother and boyfriend. Overall, Sally raised nine topics, Nancy seven. However, all but one of the topics Sally raised were questions focused on Nancy. If raising more topics is a sign of dominance, Sally controlled the conversation when she raised topics, although even this was subject to Nancy's collaboration by picking them up. It may or may not be the case that Sally controlled the con-versation, but the nature of her dominance is surely other than what is normally assumed by that term if the topics she raised were all about Nancy.

Finally, the effect of raising topics may also be an effect of differences in pacing and pausing, as discussed with regard to my study of dinner table conversation. A speaker who thinks the other has no more to say on a given topic may try to contribute to the conversation by raising another topic. But a speaker who was intending to say more and was simply waiting for the appropriate turn-exchange pause will feel that the floor was taken away and the topic aggressively switched. Yet again, the impression of dominance might simply result from style differences.

Adversativeness: Conflict and Verbal Aggression

Research on gender and language has consistently found male speakers to be competitive and more likely to engage in conflict (for example, by arguing, issuing commands, and taking opposing stands) and females to be cooperative and more likely to avoid conflict (for example, by agreeing, supporting, and making suggestions rather than commands). (Maltz and Borker [1982] summarize some of this research.) Ong (1981: 51) argues that 'adversativeness' is universal, but 'conspicuous or expressed adversativeness is a larger element in the lives of males than of females'.

In my analysis of videotapes of male and female friends talking to each other (Tannen 1990a), I have begun to investigate how male adversativeness and female cooperation are played out, complicated, and contradicted in conversational discourse. In analyzing videotapes of friends talking, for example, I found a sixth-grade boy saying to his best friend,

> Seems like, if there's a fight, me and you are automatically in it. And everyone else wants to go against you and everything. It's hard to agree without someone saying something to you.

In contrast, girls of the same age (and also of most other ages whose talk I examined) spent a great deal of time discussing the dangers of anger and contention. In affirming their own friendship, one girl told her friend,

> Me and you <u>never</u> get in fights hardly,

and

> I mean like if I try to talk to you, you'll say, 'Talk to <u>me</u>!' And if you try to talk to me, I'll <u>talk</u> to you.

These examples of gendered styles of interaction are illuminated by the insight that power and solidarity are mutually evocative. As seen in the statement of the sixth-grade boy, opposing other boys in teams entails affiliation within the team. The most dramatic instance of male affiliation resulting from conflict with others is bonding among soldiers, a phenomenon explored by Norman (1990).

By the same token, girls' efforts to support their friends necessarily entail exclusion of or opposition to other girls. This emerges in Hughes's (1988) study of girls playing a street game called foursquare, in which four players occupy one square each and bounce a ball into each other's squares. The object of the game is to eliminate players by hitting the ball into their square in such a way that they fail to hit it back. But this effort to 'get people out' is at odds with the social injunction under which the girls operate, to be 'nice' and not 'mean'. The girls resolved the conflict, and formed 'incipient teams' composed of friends, by claiming that their motivation in eliminating some players was to enable others (their friends) to enter the game, since eliminated players are replaced by awaiting players. In the girls' terms 'getting someone out' was 'nice-mean', because it was reframed as 'getting someone [a friend] in'. This dynamic is also supported by my analysis of the sixth-grade girls' conversation: Most of their talk was devoted to allying themselves with each other in opposition to another girl who was not present. So their cooperation (solidarity) also entails opposition (power).

For boys power entails solidarity not only by opposition to another team, but by opposition to each other. In the videotapes of friends talking, I found that all the conversations between young boys (and none between young girls) had numerous examples of teasing and mock attack. In examining pre-school conversations transcribed and analysed by Corsaro and Rizzo (1990: 34), I was amazed to discover that a fight could initiate rather than preclude friendship. In the following episode, a little boy intrudes on two others and an angry fight ensues. This is the way Corsaro and Rizzo present the dialogue:

Two boys (Richard and Denny) have been playing with a slinky on the stairway leading to the upstairs playhouse in the school. During their play two other boys (Joseph and Martin) enter and stand near the bottom of the stairs.

Denny: Go!
(Martin now runs off, but Joseph remains and he eventually moves halfway up the stairs.)
Joseph: These are big shoes.
Richard: I'll punch him right in the eye.
Joseph: I'll punch you right in the nose.
Denny: I'll punch him with my big fist.
Joseph: I'll- I- I-
Richard: And he'll be bumpety, bumpety and punched out all the way down the stairs.
Joseph: I- I- I'll- I could poke your eyes out with my gun. I have a gun.

Denny: A gun! I'll- I- I- even if-
Richard: I have a gun too.
Denny: And I have guns too and it's bigger than yours and it poo-poo
          down. That's poo-poo.
(All three boys laugh at Denny's reference to poo-poo.)
Richard: Now leave.
Joseph: Un-uh. I gonna tell you to put on- on the gun on your hair and
          the poop will come right out on his face.
Denny: Well.
Richard: Slinky will snap right on your face too.
Denny: And my gun will snap right-

Up until this point I had no difficulty interpreting the interaction: the boys
were engaged in a fight occasioned by Joseph's intrusion into Richard and
Denny's play. But what happened next surprised and, at first, perplexed me.
Corsaro and Rizzo describe it this way:

> At this point a girl (Debbie) enters, says she is Batgirl, and asks if they have
> seen Robin. Joseph says he is Robin, but she says she is looking for a different
> Robin and then runs off. After Debbie leaves, Denny and Richard move into
> the playhouse and Joseph follows. From this point to the end of the episode the
> three boys play together.

At first I was incredulous that so soon after their seemingly hostile encounter,
the boys played amicably together. Finally I came to the conclusion that for
Joseph picking a fight was a way to enter into interaction with the other boys,
and engaging him in the fight was Richard and Denny's way of accepting
him into their interaction – at least after he acquitted himself satisfactorily
in the fight. In this light, I could see that the reference to poo-poo, which
occasioned general laughter, was the beginning of a reframing from fighting
to playing.

Greek conversation provides an example of a cultural style that places more
positive value, for both women and men, on dynamic opposition. Kakava
(1989) replicates Schiffrin's findings by showing how a Greek family enjoy
opposing each other in dinner table conversation. In another study of modern
Greek conversation, Tannen and Kakava (1992) find speakers routinely disagreeing when they actually agree and using diminutive name forms and other
terms of endearment – markers of closeness – precisely when they are opposing each other. These patterns can be seen in the following excerpt from a
conversation that took place in Greece between an older Greek woman and
me. The woman, whom I call Ms. Stella, has just told me that she complained

to the police about a construction crew that illegally continued drilling and pounding through the siesta hours, disturbing her nap:

Deborah: Echete dikio.
Stella: Ego echo dikio. Kopella mou, den xero an echo dikio i den echo dikio. Alla ego yperaspizomai ta symferonta mou kai ta dikaiomata mou.
Deborah: You're right.
Stella: I am right. My dear girl, I don't know if I'm right or I'm not right. But I am watching out for my interests and my rights.

My response to Ms. Stella's complaint is to support her by agreeing. But she disagrees with my agreement by reframing my statement in her own terms rather than simply accepting it by stopping after 'I am right.' She also marks her divergence from my frame with the endearment 'kopella mou' (literally, 'my girl', but idiomatically closer to 'my dear girl').

In another conversation, one which, according to Kakava, is typical of her family's sociable argument, the younger sister has said that she cannot understand why the attractive young woman who is the prime minister Papandreou's girlfriend would have an affair with such an old man. The older sister, Christina, argues that the woman may have felt that in having an affair with the prime minister she was doing something notable. Her sister replied,

Poly megalo timima re Christinaki na pliroseis pantos.
It's a very high price to pay, re Chrissie, anyway.

I use the English diminutive form 'Chrissie' to reflect the Greek diminutive ending -aki, but the particle re cannot really be translated; it is simply a marker of closeness that is typically used when disagreeing, as in the ubiquitously heard expression 'Ochi, re' ('No, re').

REFERENCES

Becker, A. L. 1982. Beyond translation: Esthetics and language description. In Heidi Byrnes (ed.) *Contemporary Perceptions of Language: Interdisciplinary Dimensions. Georgetown University Round Table on Languages and Linguistics 1982.* Washington, D.C.: Georgetown University Press. 129–138.

Becker, A. L. and Oka, I Gusti Ngurah. 1974. Person in Kawi: Exploration of an elementary semantic dimension. *Oceanic Linguistics* 13: 229–255.

Beeman, William O. 1986. *Language, Status, and Power in Iran.* Bloomington, Indiana: Indiana University Press.

Bellinger, David and Jean Berko Gleason. 1982. Sex differences in parental directives to young children. *Sex Roles* 8: 1123–1139.

Brown, Roger and Albert Gilman. 1960. The pronouns of power and solidarity. In Thomas Sebcok (ed.) *Style in Language.* Cambridge, Massachusetts: M.I.T. Press. 253–276.

Brown, Penelope and Stephen Levinson. [1978] 1987. *Politeness: Some universals in Language Usage.* Cambridge: Cambridge University Press.

Coates, Jennifer. 1986. *Women, Men and Language.* London: Longman.

Corsaro, William and Thomas Rizzo. 1990. Disputes in the peer culture of American and Italian nursery school children. In Allen Grimshaw (ed.) *Conflict Talk.* Cambridge: Cambridge University Press. 21–65.

Dorval, Bruce. 1990. (Ed.) *Conversational Coherence and its Development.* Norwood, New Jersey: Ablex.

Friedrich, Paul. 1972. Social context and semantic feature: The Russian pronominal usage. In John J. Gumperz and Dell Hymes (eds.) *Directions in Sociolinguistics.* New York: Holt, Rinehart and Winston. 270–300.

Hughes, Linda A. 1988. 'But that's not *really* mean': Competing in a cooperative mode. *Sex Roles* 19: 669–687.

Kakava, Christina. 1989. Argumentative conversation in a Greek family. Paper presented at the Annual Meeting of the Linguistic Society of America, Washington, D.C.

Keenan, Elinor. 1974. Norm-makers, norm-breakers: Uses of speech by men and women in a Malagasy community. In Richard Bauman and Joel Sherzer (eds.) *Explorations in the Ethnography of Speaking.* Cambridge: Cambridge University Press. 125–143.

Komarovsky, Mirra. 1962. *Blue-Collar Marriage.* New York: Vintage.

Lakoff, Robin. 1975. *Language and Woman's Place.* New York: Harper and Row.

Maltz, Daniel N. and Ruth A. Borker. 1982. A cultural approach to male-female miscommunication. In John J. Gumperz (ed.) *Language and Social Identity.* Cambridge: Cambridge University Press. 196–216.

Mead, Margaret. 1977. End linkage: A tool for cross-cultural analysis. In John Brockman (ed.) *About Bateson.* New York: Dutton. 171–231.

Norman, Michael. 1990. *These Good Men: Friendships Forged from War.* New York: Crown.

Ong, Walter J. 1981. *Fighting for Life: Contest, Sexuality, and Consciousness.* Ithaca, New York: Cornell University Press; Amherst, Massachusetts: University of Massachusetts Press.

Sattel, Jack W. 1983. Men, inexpressiveness, and power. In Barrie Thorne, Cheris Kramarae and Nancy Henley (eds.) *Language, Gender and Society.* Rowley, Massachusetts: Newbury House. 119–124.

Scollon, Ron. 1985. The machine stops: Silence in the metaphor of malfunction. In Deborah Tannen and Muriel Saville-Troike (eds.) *Perspectives on Silence.* Norwood, New Jersey: Ablex. 21–30.

Scollon, Ron and Suzanne B. K. Scollon. 1981. *Narrative, Literacy and Face in Interethnic Communication.* Norwood, New Jersey: Ablex.

Shuy, Roger W. 1982. Topic as the unit of analysis in a criminal law case. In Deborah Tannen (ed.) *Analyzing Discourse: Text and Talk. Georgetown University Round Table on Languages and Linguistics 1981*. Washington, D.C.: Georgetown University Press. 113–126.

Spender, Dale. 1980. *Man Made Language*. London: Routledge and Kegan Paul.

Tannen, Deborah. 1981. Indirectness in discourse: Ethnicity as conversational style. *Discourse Processes* 4: 221–238.

Tannen, Deborah. 1984. *Conversational Style: Analyzing Talk among Friends*. Norwood, New Jersey: Ablex.

Tannen, Deborah. 1985. Silence: Anything but. In Deborah Tannen and Muriel Saville-Troike (eds.) *Perspectives on Silence*. Norwood, New Jersey: Ablex. 93–111.

Tannen, Deborah. 1986. *That's Not What I Meant!: How Conversational Style Makes or Breaks your Relations with Others*. New York: Ballantine.

Tannen, Deborah. 1989. Interpreting interruption in conversation. In Bradley Music, Randolph Graczyk and Caroline Wiltshire (eds.) *Papers from the 25th Annual Regional Meeting of the Chicago Linguistic Society. Part Two: Parasession on Language in Context*. Chicago: Chicago Linguistic Society. 266–287.

Tannen, Deborah. 1990a. Gender differences in conversational coherence: Physical alignment and topical cohesion. In Bruce Dorval (ed.) *Conversational Coherence and its Development*. Norwood, New Jersey: Ablex. 167–206.

Tannen, Deborah. 1990b. *You just don't Understand: Women and Men in Conversation*. New York: Ballantine.

Tannen, Deborah and Christina Kakava. 1992. Power and solidarity in modern Greek conversation: Disagreeing to agree. *Journal of Modern Greek Studies* 10: 12–29.

Watanabe, Suwako. 1993. Cultural Differences in Framing: American and Japanese Group Discussions. In Deborah Tannen (ed.) *Framing in Discourse*. New York and Oxford: Oxford University Press. 176–209.

West, Candace and Don H. Zimmerman. 1983. Small insults: A study of interruptions in cross-sex conversations between unacquainted persons. In Barrie Thorne, Cheris Kramarae and Nancy Henley (eds.) *Language, Gender and Society*. Rowley, Massachusetts: Newbury House. 103–117.

Wolfowitz, Clare. 1991. *Language Style and Social Space: Stylistic Choice in Suriname Javanese*. Urbana and Chicago, Illinois: University of Illinois Press.

Yamada, Haru. 1992. *American and Japanese Business Discourse: A Comparison of Interactional Styles*. Norwood, New Jersey: Ablex.

CHAPTER 13

Fraternity Men: Variation and Discourses of Masculinity

SCOTT FABIUS KIESLING

Introduction

How Do Men Use Language to Be Men?

This question is one that has not been widely addressed in the work on language and gender, and especially in studies of language variation and gender. Two trends prevent the asking of the above question, or at least cause researchers to overlook it. First is a view of language use in society as mechanical and almost functionalist (in the sociological sense): men and women mechanically use certain linguistic forms – variants – because of social pressures on them as men or women. In other words, the question that I began with is turned around so that it is asked in the form, 'Why do men use language in a particular way (which has been determined to be different than the way women use language)?' The second trend is one of focus. A question about gender difference inherently has at least two parts, one focusing on men and masculinity and the other on women and femininity. Questions have normally been (and still usually are) formulated asymmetrically, with a focus on women. For example, we are most likely to hear, 'Why do women use more of the prestige variant than men?'

To be sure, there are exceptions to these trends. For example, men are the focus of Trudgill's (1972) 'covert prestige', but this explanation is still primarily mechanical – men in a certain class position use covert prestige because that's what men do to 'appear tough.' But why do men want to appear this

187

way, especially working-class men? Even in more recent language and gender work in which men and women are conceived as performing gender through language, women remain the focus of attention. In her masterful sociolinguistic study, Eckert (2000: 171–212, this volume) focuses on girls in Belten High as the 'sociolinguistic icons,' and provides a much more detailed discussion of girls' networks than boys', and focuses her explanations on the motivations of the girls much more than the boys. However, this work is one of the best variationist works on gender, and provides the most balance between men and women. In fact, one of Eckert's important points is that differences between genders can be explained partly by competition within genders.

In this chapter I outline some of the ways some men use language to 'be men,' and suggest that an explanation for men's patterns of language use in the US lies in four *discourses of masculinity*. These discourses of masculinity serve to structure the stances the men take in interaction (as men actively desire to follow them and fear transgressing them), and their language in turn helps them to create these stances.

I am only focusing on masculinity in the context of mostly white, middle-class, young men in the US. My approach assumes that discourses of masculinity will likely be different in other places, and therefore lead to different kinds of language use (although I do believe the discourses are widely shared in the US). The same caveat holds for men of other races, ethnicities, classes and ages.

I focus here on the use of a single linguistic variable in the fraternity community, and show how this variable patterns across different speech events and individuals. I first outline the setting and a variation pattern found in the fraternity, then I explain how these patterns are related to stances habitually taken by the different men. Finally, I outline the discourses of masculinity and show how they relate to the stances the men take and the patterns of variation.

Patterns of Variation in the Fraternity

I spent a little over a year in 1993–1994 with a fraternity at a University in Northern Virginia, in the suburbs of Washington, D.C. A fraternity of this kind is an all-male social group, essentially an institutionalized friendship network that also does volunteer work to help the university and the surrounding community.

Much of the fraternity's community and interaction takes place in social situations, both mundane such as 'hanging out' at a member's room, apartment or house, and special social situations such as large parties and other events. But the business of the fraternity (planning parties, philanthropic activities, membership issues and elections, for example) is done in meetings.

Both the socializing situations and the meetings are events in which the men's status and role in the fraternity is important, and both are sites that can be recorded to better understand how language creates the men's identities.

They are, however, different interactions, in that the socializing situations stress the solidarity and togetherness of the fraternity while the meetings often highlight the hierarchical organization and differential status of each member. We would therefore expect language use to be different, as men highlight different aspects of their persona (or even different personae) in these different interactions of their community. To that end, I performed a variation analysis of the men's use in these different social contexts, as well as in recorded ethnographic interviews with me. By examining how individual men approach the same speech activity in different ways, we can understand more about how men use language to 'be men', and why they want to be men in these particular ways.

I examine the variation between [in] and [iŋ] in word final position in words like *ceiling, walking,* and *during*, which I will refer to as the (ING) variable. I will refer to the [in] variant simply as -*in*, and [iŋ], -*ing*. The (ING) variable is perhaps the most studied variable in the English language, because it is variable in all varieties of English and is sensitive to most of the factors Sociolinguistics have considered for any variable. Moreover, the general picture is the same across dialects for the other factors, so that even in places as far apart as Los Angeles, Norwich, and Canberra, men tend to have a higher rate of -*in* than women (see Labov 1989). This regularity and stability is attractive for analyzing language use in the fraternity, where members are not all from the same dialect area. A number of patterns with respect to (ING) tend to repeat themselves over and over again, even if the overall rate of -*in* is quite different. In addition to the pattern of men tending to have higher rates of -*in* than women, working-class speakers are more likely to use -*in* than speakers of middle and upper classes, and -*in* is more common in more 'casual' styles of speech. Finally, -*in* is more common in words that are more verbal, and -*ing* is more common in more nominal words (see Houston 1985).

I coded each token of (ING) as -*in* (a coronal nasal preceded by an untensed vowel) or -*ing* (a velar nasal). Each token was also coded for the independent variables of speaker, activity type, following phonological environment, and grammatical category. Speakers were coded individually. Activity type is similar to the style factor in Labov (1972) and other studies, and to the speech event in the Ethnography of Communication (Hymes this volume); an activity type is defined by the goals, setting and participants in the interactions. (ING) tokens coded as the *meeting* activity type are tokens spoken during the full weekly meetings. A sample of meetings was coded, chosen at random. *Socializing* is less specific than meetings; this activity type takes place at a number of locations and with differing numbers of participants, and is principally defined by the main social purpose of the talk. Tokens for the socializing activity type were exhaustive for each speaker, because this activity type was the most difficult to record, and therefore fewer tokens were available. I also coded *interview* tokens. These interviews were used to understand the fraternity and its ideology, gather information about members, and find out how they see their role in the fraternity. All interviews were not identical in key (in Hymes' sense), because not all were private, and I did not have a close relationship with all interviewees. Interviews were coded for the first 45 minutes, or the complete interview, if shorter. Because of the volume of talk in interviews, they comprise over half of the total tokens.

Finally, I coded the following phonological environment and the word's grammatical category. In addition to grammatical categories outlined by Houston (1985), the marker *fuckin'* was included as a separate category. This word functions as several different grammatical categories, but is almost categorically -*in*.

Tokens were analysed using the Varbrul program (see Paolillo 2001; Sankoff et al. 2005, and Tagliamonte, Chapter 6), which takes into account all the independent variables and creates weightings or probabilities for each individual factor within a factor group (for example, the 'meetings' factor in 'activity type' factor group). In the discussion that follows, if the weighting is over 0.5, then the factor favors -*in*; the closer to 1.0, the stronger the influence in favor of -*in*. If the weighting is under 0.5, then the factor disfavors -*in*; the closer to 0.0, the stronger the effect against -*in*.

The results for the speaker factor group are displayed in Table 13.1 (for details about how this analysis was arrived at, see Kiesling 1998). Varbrul analysis provided information on how to group different individuals with respect to their variable use: one group favors -*in*, but to differing degrees (Speed and Mick), another group disfavors -*in* (Pencil, Hotdog, Saul, Mack and Ram, who may even be considered to be in a group by himself), while the other speakers form a middle group (Pete, Art, Waterson and Tommy) neither strongly favoring nor disfavoring -*in*.

We can thus see from the first analysis that the men are behaving quite differently with respect to this linguistic feature. There is no common 'objective' social factor uniting these groups; all show differences in the length of time they have been members of the fraternity, geographical origin and class (see Kiesling 1998 for details).

However, speaker was not the only language independent variable that affected the use of (ING); activity type was also significant. Socializing highly favored -*in* at 75 percent (0.72 probability), while meetings disfavored -*in* strongly at 47 percent (0.30 probability). Interviews fell in between at 53 percent (0.54 probability). As Labov (1972) eloquently noted, the interaction between style (activity type) and class (speaker) is one of the interesting

Table 13.1 Probabilities and percentages of alveolar (-*in*) application of (ING), for the combined speaker factor group

Speaker	p	%	N
Speed	0.91	80	130/162
Mick	0.63	66	84/128
Pete	0.51	67	179/268
Tommy			
Art			
Waterson			
Pencil	0.33	45	218/486
Hotdog			
Mack			
Saul			
Ram	0.15	22	12/54
Input/total	0.61	57	623/1098

aspects of this variable. Thus it is important to investigate the interaction patterns through a cross tabulation. I thus performed a varbrul analysis in which the speaker and activity type factor groups are combined into one group. A single factor thus consisted of a speaker and an activity type (for example, Saul in Meeting activity type). The weightings are graphed in Figure 13.1.

The weights in Figure 13.1 show a striking interaction. All speakers favor -*in* in the socializing activity type, and no speakers disfavor -*in*. The interview activity type exhibits the largest range of weightings; this is probably due to the fact that the interviewees took widely differences stances toward me, so that some speakers considered the interviews to be more like socializing, and other more like meetings. Speed and Ram were the high (0.97) and low (0.09) outliers, respectively, while the rest of the men split into two groups, one disfavoring -*in* (0.32), another slightly favoring -*in* (0.56).

The meeting shows a further split in speakers: a large group who strongly disfavor -*in*, in a range of 0.09 to 0.16, and two speakers who strongly favor -*in* in meetings: Speed (.078) and Mick (0.60). Note that Waterson's weighting is effectively 1.0; even though his meeting tokens were excluded from the varbrul analysis, I include them because they were 100 percent -*in*. Moreover, Pete and Art (0.21) do not disfavor -*in* to the same degree as the biggest group (0.11). These figures show a clear differentiation among speakers within the meeting activity type, a fact that is more significant when we consider that the meeting is a relatively public activity type, while the interview is not, so that the men have access to models in the meetings, but not in the interview. The varbrul analysis confirms the view that the men tend to use -*in* more alike in

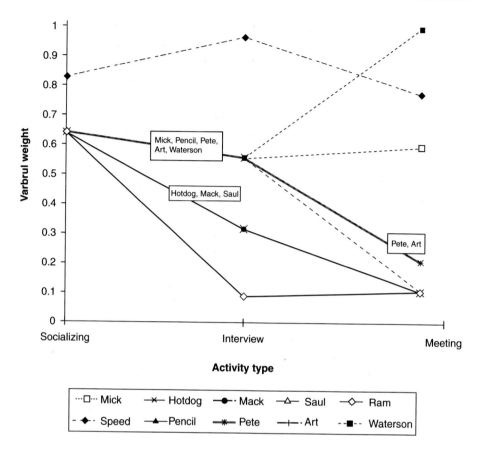

Figure 13.1 Varbrul weightings for cross-tabulation of speakers and activity types, with speakers combined into groups when possible

the socializing activity type than in the meeting activity type. By investigating the differences in how the men talk in meetings, then, we should be able to understand more about the social meaning of this variable for the men.

Men's Stances and Variable Use

Why do the men who use *-in* more in meetings do so? Why do the men who use *-ing* shift in the meetings? The direction of change we expect, based on previous research and our knowledge of the meeting as a more 'formal' activity type, is for the men to use more *-ing* in the meeting. So let us consider two speakers at either end of the spectrum to determine what they are doing differently and how that may help us explain the variation differences.

I will operationalize 'what they are doing differently' through the concept of stance. Stance is the attitude or position a person takes in conversation. Stance comes in two main forms, epistemic stance and interpersonal stance. Epistemic stance is the attitude a speaker is taking toward their talk (for example, are they certain, are they unsure, are they responsible for that talk), while interpersonal stance is the relationships a person is taking to their addressees and overhearers. These two types of stance are of course connected, because by taking an epistemic stance of certainty, for example, one can also take a stance of authority. Following Ochs (1992, this volume), I argue that in conversation, speakers focus their attention primarily on taking an interpersonal stance. Linguistic features are in the service of this stance-taking endeavor, and repeatedly used stances become associated with one person, eventually 'becoming' their identity, or persona. An identity is then a bundle of stances, or a long-term, repeatedly used repertoire of stances.

I turn to an analysis of Speed and Mack's stances in the conversation below, but this discussion will require some background. The only time all members gather to discuss the 'business' sphere of the fraternity, meetings are also the most formally organized activity. The most important aspects of meetings are the participant structure and purpose. The meetings are 'formal' in that there is an explicit rule that one member has the right to the floor at a time (although this rule is often broken), and the president serves as chair. In terms of purpose, the 'business', or organizational, aspects of the fraternity are the topics of meetings, so a member's office and age is more salient than in other speech activities.

We will consider speeches from an election meeting; this type of meeting is exceptional – it takes place twice a year – but it is more useful than other meetings for our purposes. First, both younger and older members speak; in most meetings, only older members speak. More importantly, members overtly evaluate each other's flaws and skills when they argue for and against specific candidates. The goal is to persuade, so the need to speak powerfully is even more important than usual.

The portion of the election meeting we will consider in detail consists of comments on candidates for the office of chapter correspondent. The chapter correspondent communicates with the national fraternity through letters published in the fraternity's national magazine. The position traditionally goes to a younger member, because it is assumed that it requires little experience or knowledge of how the fraternity works. The only duty is writing one or two letters describing the local chapter's activities. We will focus on the discussion period, which takes place after the four candidates have given their speeches and left the room, so that the rest of the members discuss the candidates' strengths and weaknesses.

Speed

Speed's first contribution comes early in the meeting. His statement is short and to the point. (Line numbers represent numbers from the transcript of the full conversation.)

Extract 1
```
82   Mick:    Speed.
83   Speed:   Ri:tchie. I like Ritchie 'cause he's smart
84            and he probably (writes really good) too:.
85            so let him do it dude.
```

Speed at first does not justify his statement. He merely states Ritchie's name. Then he notes that Ritchie is smart and that Ritchie is capable of doing the job. His short statement indicates that for him the choice, based on Ritchie's ability, is simple. It is just a matter of 'letting him do it'. By first only uttering Ritchie's name, Speed implies that members should be swayed by the mere fact that he is for Ritchie. His comment is also less formal in tone, spoken slowly, almost off-hand. Note his use of the discourse particle *dude* in line 85 (*so let him do it dude*). This use of *dude* is derived from an address term that indexes solidarity and casualness (see Kiesling 2005), and is used by several of the men in their speech frequently, even when addressing more than one person. Speed's use of *dude*, especially in conjunction with *let him do it*, implies a casual stance, which contrasts with Ram's formality. The brevity of Speed's statement, his apparent lack of concern with creating a position that highlights his age, and his focus on Ritchie's ability, all foreshadow his later comments, in which he creates a stance that confronts and challenges the hierarchical structural roles other older men index. I do not have space to include this analysis here (but see Kiesling 1997).

Ram

An older brother, Ram, has just finished a year as treasurer, one of the highest offices of the fraternity. He creates a fatherly, 'wise elder' stance through his comment:

Extract 2
```
119   Ram:   um I'd like to endorse Kurt here, surprisingly
120          I mean the kid-
121          I don't want to see him fall into another-
122          and I'm not saying that he would
```

123	Kevin Fierst type thing,
124	I think we need to make him-
125	we need to strongly involve him *now*
126	I think he's pretty serious about it, y'know
127	and with a little guidance I mean he'll do a fine job.

Ram creates a powerful stance by putting himself in the role of a person with age and experience – at the top of the fraternity's hierarchy of membership. He states that he will *endorse* Kurt; those who endorse candidates are elected officials or some other leader. Thus, the use of this word indexes a relationship between subject and object. The verb assumes a context in which a leader is endorsing a candidate. Here Ram uses it to highlight a leadership position for himself.

Ram also refers to Kurt as *the kid*, which implies that Ram is older and more knowledgeable, thus indexing a fatherly stance. Finally, he shows off his knowledge of past members of the fraternity by mentioning a past incident (*Kevin Fierst type thing*) in lines 121–123 (Kevin Fierst was a member who dropped out of school because of substance abuse problems). Ram further creates a fatherly stance through his use of the phrase *with a little guidance*, suggesting that he is qualified to give that guidance because of his position in the fraternity. He also shows concern for Kurt (*I don't want to see him fall into another…Kevin Fierst type thing*), which suggests a fatherly position. Thus, he draws on the part of the fraternity ideology of camaraderie that stresses 'looking out for' another brother. Upon hearing this episode, Pete remarked that he would respect what Ram said because he was among the group of members who were going to be leaders (separate from those who would be 'workers not leaders' and a third group of 'just bodies' who didn't do anything but socialize). But even though he shows 'charity,' Ram does not abandon fraternity ideology in his comments, but in fact reinforces it by putting himself at the top of the hierarchy as a wise, fatherly, elder.

Other *-ing* users create similar kinds of stances as Ram, with variations, as Waterson and Mick, to some extent, create similar stances as Speed. While there are still individual differences, we find that the men using the *-in* forms are more likely to be oppositional (Speed, Mick), casual (Speed, Waterson), or to explicitly build power through solidarity (Waterson, Speed). The men who use more *-ing*, by contrast, put themselves at the top of a formal hierarchy, gaining their authority from their position in the fraternity.

The *-in* form, through its widespread indexicality of casualness (see Campbell-Kibler 2005) is one of the resources Speed, Waterson and Mick use to take these stances, along with other linguistic features. In fact, I argue that these men are primarily taking these stances, and not thinking about the individual meaning of each linguistic feature. The *-ing* users complement the *-in* users' use, and draw on the 'standard' associations connected to the 'correct' way of pronouncing this variable. This 'correctness' helps them connect to qualities associated with people in positions of structural power in society, and use those associations to help create structural power in the fraternity.

We can thus posit an explanation for the men's (ING) use in fairly local terms; that is, by looking at the individual 'personalities' in the fraternity. But can we connect these patterns to larger patterns of men's language use in middle-class white American society? What do these meeting interactions tell us about how men can use language? Does it shed any new light or is it just another (more particular) way of saying 'covert prestige?' In the next section, I argue that these strategies are available to the men because of four discourses of masculinity that men connect to when performing identities through language.

Discourses of Masculinity

My main argument is that through stance-taking, all speakers connect to various cultural discourses of identity in interaction. The stances they wish to take and have available to them normatively are constrained by cultural discourses. The variation patterns researchers have found for men, then, are explained through these patterns, in such a way that the particulars of men's interaction as seen in the above examples are also explained.

Cultural discourses, a notion that owes its genesis to the work of Michel Foucault (see Foucault 1972), are culturally shared ways of thinking, doing, making, evaluating and speaking. (I will distinguish this kind of discourse from the talk normally analysed by linguists by referring to the latter as 'inter-action' or 'talk-in-interaction'). These discourses are similar to *ideologies*, in that they describe unquestioned background assumptions that people of a culture share. However, discourses are more than ideology, even though they encompass it; discourses include social practices, artifacts, processes and even desires. Most importantly, they are not controlled by one person or group, but arise through the social practices, talk, thoughts and desires of those people using them. They are therefore ever-changing and, most importantly, contestable. It is the use of discourses that distinguishes the current trend of feminist research, increasingly referred to as *third-wave feminism*.

Third-wave feminism incorporates a performative view of identity (Butler 1990; Cameron and Kulick 2003), but also adopts the post-structuralist view that gender is composed of cultural discourses. Performances are embed-ded in cultural discourses, and the meaning of performances can only be understood through a decoding of the social semiotic significance of these performances. Many of the analytical categories and dichotomies often seen in gender studies are thus products of cultural discourses themselves, and we must understand how speakers understand and relate to those discourses (which include of course their own performances). Importantly, while there may be one *dominant* cultural discourse, there are always *competing* discourses which people may adopt, refer to and so forth. In the case of discourses of masculinity, *all* men in American society are affected; men who resist or ignore these discourses are nevertheless in a milieu in which their practices are evaluated against the discourses (and this evaluation may be positive *or* negative, depending on the evaluator's stance with respect to the discourses). Cultural discourses are thus a valuable part of a theory of how social practices, structures and beliefs structure language use, and how that language use as a social practice is interpreted.

While gender takes different forms and different importance across cultures, it is a bundle of discourses that in some way help to organize every culture. In most cultures, these discourses are organized by two main archetypes of gender: femininity and masculinity. If we understand this engagement in social practices to be accomplished through performances, then we arrive at a definition of masculinity as *social performances which are semiotically linked (indexed) to men, and not to women, through cultural discourses*. The definition is categorically dichotomous and relational, because that is the way cultural discourses organize gender: feminine performances are categorically opposed to masculine ones, and men are categorically opposed to women. I deliberately make no specific claims about whether properties like sexuality, power and so forth must be connected to men in the definition. Rather, these specifics flow from the surrounding discourses of gender. This view is different, but compatible with, the theoretical perspective on masculinities of Robert Connell, which has dominated masculinities research in the 1990s (see especially Connell 1995).

I have distilled four dominant, or hegemonic, discourses of masculinity from a number of sources: observation in the fraternity, personal experience, analyses of American literature and film, and the now-extensive literature on men and masculinities (see Flood 2006 for a comprehensive bibliography). To the extent that these sources agree on what these cultural discourses are, with the caveat that such discourses are ever-changing, we can find validity by triangulation. The discourses are:

Gender difference: this sees men and women as naturally and categorically different in biology and behavior.

Heterosexism: the definition of masculinity as heterosexual; to be masculine in this discourse is to sexually desire women and not men.

Dominance and power: the identification of masculinity with dominance or authority; to be a man is to be strong, authoritative, and in control, especially when compared to women, and also when compared to other men. There are different kinds of power that can be associated with masculinity, as noted in Kiesling (1997).

Male solidarity and exclusivity: a discourse that takes as given a bond among men. Men are understood to normatively need to do things with groups of other men exclusive of women; women 'get in the way' of the kinds of activities men normatively enjoy.

These are the ways that Americans expect men to perform (or hope that they don't perform). In any man's performance, that performance is thus compared to the dominant cultural discourses of masculinity whether the person doing the comparison supports or resists these discourses.

Explanation Through Discourses

Note that these discourses make any man's performance a balancing act: a 'masculine stance' can connect to dominance and power, but it should also connect to male solidarity, heterosexism and difference. In explaining the patterns in the fraternity, I have argued (Kiesling 1997, 1998, 2003) that men are drawing on different cultural discourses of masculinity. But at a deeper level they are balancing the discourses in different ways.

Speed's casual stance is one which relies more on male solidarity and less on overt dominance (although he is relying on a kind of effortlessness that does index power). His performance is masculine, and persuasive, not because he connects himself with a legitimate power structure, but because of a combination of power and masculine solidarity. When Speed says *Let him do it, dude*, he is at once indexing power through a command that gives permission and an address term (used for the entire meeting audience, not any particular member) that shows a casualness that connects with masculine solidarity.

An important corollary of this argument is that femininity does not include this (kind of) solidarity, nor this kind of power, and we can use this difference to explain the overall gender variation pattern found in many studies (see Labov 1989). In this view, women will not use the *-in* form as much because the stance that Speed is taking does not connect with discourses of femininity; in short, it would not be a successful strategy at a sorority election meeting (and it was, to the extent we can tell, successful for Speed, since Ritchie won the election). This observation allows us to posit that the overall rate of *-in* (or variants with similar social meanings) is higher in men because they sometimes take this more casual, solidarity-focused stance (similar to 'cool solidarity' as outlined in Kiesling 2005). This is not true all of the time (as seen in the rates for the meeting), but it is true enough times that the overall rate of variable use is lower for men than for women.

We can thus add this male-focused explanation to others that focus on women, such as Eckert's (1989) observation that women are more often evaluated based on their moral authority than their accomplishments, making 'proper speech' (which is often connected with morality, especially sexual purity) an important part of femininity. Any explanation for gender patterns should be made thus, because the patterns we find are not created because the members of one gender are acting to differentiate themselves, but because all humans are actors on the social stage, performing and differentiating their gender from what they perceive to be the other.

REFERENCES

Butler, Judith. 1990. *Gender Trouble: Feminism and the Subversion of Identity*. New York: Routledge.

Cameron, Deborah and Don Kulick. 2003. *Language and Sexuality*. Cambridge: Cambridge University Press.

Campbell-Kibler, Kathryn. 2005. Listener perceptions of sociolinguistic variables: The case of (ING). Unpublished PhD dissertation. Standford, California: Stanford University.

Connell, Robert W. 1995. *Masculinities*. Berkeley, California: University of California Press.

Eckert, Penelope. 1989. The whole woman: Sex and gender differences in variation. *Language Variation and Change* 1: 245–267.

Eckert, Penelope. 2000. *Linguistic Variation as Social Practice*. Oxford: Blackwell Publishing.

Flood, Michael. 2006. *The Men's Bibliography*. 15th Edition. Canberra, Australia. URL: http://mensbiblio.xyonline.net/. Accessed October 15, 2006.

Foucault, Michel. 1972. *The Archeology of Knowledge*. London: Tavistock.

Houston, Ann. 1985. Continuity and change in English morphology: The variable (ING). Unpublished Ph.D. dissertation. Philadelphia, Pennsylvania: University of Pennsylvania.

Kiesling, Scott F. 1997. Power and the language of men. In Sally Johnson and Ulrike Meinhof (eds.) *Language and Masculinity*. Oxford: Blackwell Publishing. 65–85.

Kiesling, Scott F. 1998. Variation and men's identity in a fraternity. *Journal of Sociolinguistics* 2: 69–100.

Kiesling, Scott F. 2003. Prestige, cultural models, and other ways of talking about underlying norms and gender. In Janet Holmes and Miriam Meyerhoff (eds.) *The Handbook of Language and Gender*. Oxford: Blackwell Publishing. 509–527.

Kiesling, Scott F. 2005. Dude. *American Speech* 79: 281–305.

Labov, William. 1972. *Sociolinguistic Patterns*. Philadelphia, Pennsylvania: University of Pennsylvania Press.

Labov, William. 1989. The child as linguistic historian. *Language Variation and Change* 1: 85–97.

Ochs, Elinor. 1992. Indexing gender. In Alessandro Duranti and Charles Goodwin. *Rethinking Context: Language as an Interactive Phenomenon.* Cambridge: Cambridge University Press. 335–358.

Paolillo, John. 2001. *Analyzing Linguistic Variation : Statistical Models and Methods.* Stanford, California: Center for the Study of Language and Information.

Sankoff, David, Sali Tagliamonte, Eric Smith. 2005. Goldvarb X: A Variable Rule Application for Macintosh and Windows. Department of Linguistics, University of Toronto. http://individual.utoronto.ca/tagliamonte/Goldvarb/GV_index.htm. Accessed October 15, 2006.

Trudgill, Peter. 1972. Sex, covert prestige and linguistic change in the urban British English of Norwich. *Language in Society* 1: 179–195.

CHAPTER 14

Masculinity Manoeuvres: Critical Discursive Psychology and the Analysis of Identity Strategies

MARGARET WETHERELL AND NIGEL EDLEY

Introduction

In this chapter we want to return to a particular historical moment (the mid-1990s) and to the identity struggles of a group of young white middle-class men as they negotiate their place within regimes of hegemonic masculinity. We first researched and wrote about this group of young men some ten years ago (Edley and Wetherell 1997). Our aim in turning back to this work is to argue for a particular 'take' on gender, discourse and identity. We want to highlight the benefits of approaches to discourse and gender which incorporate both fine-grain micro analysis and more macro-cultural perspectives. Our work is within the broad tradition of discursive psychology (cf. Edwards and Potter 1992; Potter and Wetherell 1987) but unlike forms of discursive psychology which follow conversation analysis (for example, Edwards 2006; Potter 2000, 2005) we seek to combine the study of discourse in action with analyses of the broader social context (Edley and Wetherell in press; Wetherell 1998, 2007; Wetherell and Edley 1998, 1999). Indeed, we believe that it is impossible to make sense of gender identities as these appear in the flow of everyday life without this dual focus.

In common with many other discursive and sociolinguistic approaches, our research adopts a broadly constructionist frame. In other words, feminine and masculine identities are seen as historically and culturally specific, as accomplished and performed rather than generated by – or an automatic expression of – some fixed and essential nature. Gender is flexible. We assume that identities are both 'given' and actively produced (Billig 1991). That is, women and men will work with the historical and cultural resources available for making sense of Self. Individuals are limited by these resources but also able, as agents, to customise them, play with them, negotiate, re-combine, create anew and substantially change collective flows of meaning-making. Practice is open and transforming while always in relation to the sometimes apparently unassailable quality of past practice and the already taken-for-granted. As Connell (1987) notes, some configurations of masculinity and femininity are more 'culturally exalted' than others (some gender regimes are hegemonic) and the effects of these power relations can be traced in what identities are constructed and how interactions, relationships and institutions are managed.

Constructionist approaches see the social actor as 'unfinished'. The performative is emphasised as well as the emergence of identities through reiteration (Butler 1990). Increasingly, constructionist perspectives try to pay attention to complex interactions with the biological and with the embodied. Identities are seen as plural and complex. There are multiple possibilities for identification and a sense of Self is articulated at the intersections of relevant social categorisations – not just a man, for example, but also white, middle-class, young and British (Brah and Phoenix 2004; Frosh et al. 2002). In our analyses we try to pay attention to the ways in which identities vary in their chronology and durability from the speaking positions of the interactional moment, emergent in a fleeting conversation, to the idiosyncratic subject positions an individual might configure over time as their own 'personal order' and personal narrative canon, to the cultural slots or locations recognised, admired or despised by large and small 'communities of practice'. We assume that active subjects compress together and work on these different orders in the moment. We study identity then as an assemblage of intertwining patternings.

Much of this is now very familiar and a comforting orthodoxy for discourse scholars. Indeed, social constructionist approaches got their impetus from the 'turn to discourse' across the social sciences. These approaches developed out of and in tandem with post-structuralist and other macro-discourse theories. Constructionism established discourse (talk and texts) as the raw material for empirical work and qualitative research and led to an explosion of language based research on gender (for an up-to-date account of the field of discourse and identity see Benwell and Stokoe 2006 and for a review of recent language based work on gender see Speer 2005). In common with others (Billig 1987; Edwards and Potter 1992), our own work over the years has tried to shift the unit of analysis in qualitative studies. We argued that attention should no longer be focused on the self-contained and bounded individual but on the practices which construct identities. Analysts should examine talk and conversation, self-accounting and self-presentation in interviews, in relatively natural social settings and in everyday mundane social interaction. We, and others, focused on social practices which we described as psycho-discursive (Wetherell and Edley 1999). Psycho-discursive practices are those regularities within the practical discursive realm which construct psychological states. They are the regular procedures through which people build self-descriptions, tell stories about their emotional lives, construct memories and recollections, perform attributions, formulate their life histories, and so on. We suggest that such procedures produce a psychology and infuse subjectivity – they come to be inhabited as well as deployed in talk and social interaction.

Jockeying for Position

Having now set the broad theoretical scene, let us return to the young men and to the specifics of their identity work. The material we analysed came from a series of tape-recorded group discussions conducted over a nine-month period between 1992 and 1993. These discussions were held on a weekly basis with small groups of 17–18 year old white young men from a Midlands based, single sex, independent school and they were designed to cover a wide range of different topics, including sexuality and relationships, images of men in popular culture and feminism and social change (see Edley and Wetherell 1997, for details of the method). The collection of discursive material was informed by a reflexive ethnography conducted by Nigel Edley drawing on his own experiences of a similar educational context.

As the research developed it rapidly became apparent that one of the main concerns for the young men themselves and one of the main topics of their conversation was the relations between several somewhat antagonistic groups making up the community of the sixth form, centered on daily interactions in their common room. Our participants represented the situation as a conflict between what they called the 'hard lads', the most powerful group, made up primarily of the school's rugby players and other groupings forced as they saw it out to the peripheries. A key part of the domination of the 'hard lads' was physical. During break-times, for instance, they would take over the common room with boisterous games. Generally speaking, these games, like that of rugby, served to underline the participants' abilities to give and take physical punishment. The status of the rugby lads was further supported and sustained by certain formal structures within the school. For example, its 'honours' system recognised sporting achievement in a much more explicit way than academic success, with each member of the school's rugby (and cricket) team being entitled to wear a distinctively coloured blazer, which clearly elevated them above the black-blazered majority. Furthermore, the rugby players were heavily over-represented in terms of positions of authority within the student body – such as head boy, house captains and prefects. These positions provided their incumbents not only with institutional power, but also with the kudos of having been personally selected by the school's head teachers.

The majority of the participants in our research came not from this dominant group but from a network of friends who defined themselves as 'diametrically opposed' to the rugby players. The antipathy felt towards the hard lads appeared to be a very real part of this group's day-to-day school life. 'We hate their guts', declared one, speaking on behalf of his friends. 'They're a complete bunch of wankers', remarked another in a later interview. Not only did these young men see themselves as different to the rugby players, but they also saw themselves as superior. 'You need to realise' one explained 'that we are not the hard lads and we probably enjoy being slightly different and doing different things'.

This battle in the school common room echoed a wider debate in popular culture. In the late 1980s and early 1990s attention was becoming focused on the figure of the 'new man'. Rutherford (1988) was one of the first to suggest that dominant conceptions of masculinity were shifting, beginning to exemplify a tension between two dominant images or subject positions: 'new man' and what he called 'retributive man'. Retributive man represented a more traditional form of masculine identity. He was the (major) breadwinner of the family and the principal source of authority within the home: tough, competitive and emotionally inarticulate. In contrast, new man was represented as the ideal partner for the modern, liberated, heterosexual woman ('Germaine Greer's soul mate' – *The Independent on Sunday*, 14 April 1991).

Our analysis, then, concentrated upon the efforts of the young men we studied to construct alternative or counter-hegemonic identities for themselves. It became clear that there were no neat distinctions between the hegemonic and counter-hegemonic – rather strategies and routines are more frequently hybrid and often derive their energy and power from their hybridity. Our analysis also suggested that the pressure for challenging and changing the ways of being and understanding masculinity may come as much from within communities of men as without. Overall, in support of Connell's (1987, 1995) groundbreaking work, our analysis demonstrated the ways in which masculinity is contested, not a given, or a fixed entity but plural, argued over and constantly shifting over time – in such a way as to maintain what Connell describes as the 'patriarchal dividend' most men still enjoy in relation to most women.

Defined by Difference: Constructing Self and Other

We turn now to the detail of the discursive picture in the common room. Post-structuralist theorists have pointed out that all concepts are *relational*; defined, that is, by contrast with other concepts (Derrida 1973). For identity, Edward Said (1978), among others, has suggested the importance of 'otherness' for defining Self. Those who are not 'us' define who 'we' are. We noted the beginnings of this kind of 'categorical struggle' in the comments of the non-rugby playing young men about their 'hard lad' peers. How did this play out in practice? Consider Extracts 1 and 2. (Note the young men have been given pseudonyms; Nigel Edley is the interviewer.)

Extract 1
AARON: With our group I think it'd be fair to say it would be the easiest group to join. Whereas to be in the rugby group would be hard (.) I mean if you want to or not (.) I mean I wouldn't but you'd have to (.) it's all very chauvinistic and male and all that stuff (.) to get in there you'd have to like be 'ard and get kicked about a bit
(C 3)

Extract 2
NEIL: [...] whereas they'd probably see themselves as <u>men</u> and I'd probably see myself as a <u>person</u> rather than a man (.) well I am a man (.) I don't know
(B 1)

Aaron's comment begins to open up an ideological dilemma (Billig et al. 1988) which more clearly surfaces in Neil's puzzling over his status. The dilemma is this: if the 'hard group' are male, where male is defined through participation in chauvinistic activities and capacity for taking physical punishment, then where does that leave Neil, Aaron and their friends? As Neil says, are they men or just people? How can he be simultaneously a man and yet not a man? One solution to this dilemma might be to side with the feminist critique of traditional macho masculinity and to abandon claims to traditional masculinity for themselves. Aaron, as we saw, uses a term from the feminist lexicon – 'chauvinistic' and in Extracts 3 and 4 there are further indications of the young men's familiarity with aspects of this critique.

Extract 3
NATHAN: And I do think that they do define masculinity by (.) which women they've been out with and <u>shagged</u> [making a quote-marks sign]
(B 1)

Extract 4

PHIL: Yeah (.) er I think if you had to erm (.) if you were listening to election speeches by all these groups of people the rugby sporting group would be you know (.) 'We'll turn the common room into a football pitch and we'll have free beer' and like this and 'It'll be really great and you'll have a really (.) and there'll be girlies (.) beer and girlies and rugby' and things like that you know (C 2)

In these extracts, the talk seems to be simply about the rugby players. And yet, we can see the two speakers are simultaneously constructing their own identities. When Nathan uses the word 'shagged', for example, he is careful to signal that this is *not* part of his vocabulary at this moment. Rather, like Phil's talk of 'beer and girlies and rugby', it is constructed as referencing a lexicon which belongs to another type of man: the *macho* man. So, if the macho man is Other, where does this leave Nathan and Phil? In producing a critical discourse of the rugby players as male chauvinists, presumably one possibility would be to assume an alternative subject position like the 'new man' identified by Rutherford and others and available in contemporary popular culture of the day.

For Aaron and his friends, the identity or subject position of the 'new man' could represent an important cultural resource, allowing them not only to distinguish themselves from the rugby players, but also to challenge the basis of their power. For within its terms, the rugby players become objects of derision rather than admiration; their macho games appearing stupid rather than cool, pathetic rather than hard. But the situation is not quite that simple. In their new 'new man' guise, the young men, of course, are vulnerable to the gaze back from the macho lads. Identity, as noted, is relational and one very familiar taunt they become exposed to in the common room is that they are 'wimps'. One response is to accept this identity of the 'wimp' and re-work it. Consider Extract 5.

Extract 5

NIGEL: Okay there was something you said Neil that just interested me there (.) you said erm that you described yourself as a erm pacifist (.) wimp (1.0) do you <u>really</u> see yourself as [a] wimp

NEIL: Oh <u>yeah</u> (1.0) yeah because (2.0) I've got this theory that em (1.0) I'm ss (.) I don't do anything (.) I'm scared of getting hurt (.) I mean I suppose everybody is but er (1.0) <u>yeah</u> I do I mean er if a wimp (1.0) a wimp (2.0) if a wimp's somebody who'll <u>back</u> down from a <u>fight</u> or won't get into them (.) and is seen as being (.) you know (.) physically less able (.) then that's fine (.) I'm happy with that

KEITH: There's nothing wrong with being a wimp is there? [laughter] It stops you getting beaten up [laughing]
(B 4)

The hesitations here perhaps suggest the care with which this identity needs to be worked. Indeed three turns later on in this conversation, Neil has another go at it, producing another version of himself – one which sees him disowning the identity of the wimp.

Extract 6

NEIL: Actually (.) just thinking like that I think you know a wimp is probably not just physically (.) I think people who are mentally weak as well (.) and I don't think I'm mentally weak as in I can't stand up for myself verbally or you know (.) or perhaps a wimp's someone's who's timid and shy as well (.) but yeah I mean if you ask somebody they'd probably say some Emo Phillips [a stand-up comedian who adopts the persona of a weak, ineffectual man] type character (.) someone you know like that

[material omitted]

I mean we probably strike a balance between you know (.) talking about what they talk (.) talking about what (.) you know probably we'd class as the other people's talk because I mean they talk about all sorts of you know (.) there's this lad Kelner who'll talk about nuclear physics or something you know spiel on for hours and the other lot'll talk about how did United do at the weekend and did you see that gorgeous bit of tot or whatever (1.0) so I think we probably (.) you know we talk about some interesting things including some bits in the middle

(B 4)

Neil's new definition of the wimp is centered on a distinction between two kinds of strength (or weakness): namely, physical and mental. Under this new definition, the wimp appears as someone who has neither of these attributes. Neil, on the other hand, lays claim to mental toughness. In other words, the wimp is constructed as another kind of Other, a second reference point from which Neil can differentiate himself. Like Jason and the Argonauts, Neil and his friends can be seen carefully navigating a course for themselves between the Scylla of the macho man and the Charybdis of the wimp. Not as obsessed about sport as the hard lads, or about nuclear physics like the wimps, Neil and his friends are betwixt and between, a diluted mix of both.

There would appear to be an element of *complicity* here between Neil and the hard lads (cf. Connell 1995). He may not have the physical strength of the rugby players, but at least he has got *some* kind of strength. In a sense, therefore, the credibility of Neil's identity is dependent here upon some level of proximity to or correspondence with those of the macho men. In the following extract we see Neil drawing upon the very same distinction between physical and mental strength in order to undermine the position of the rugby lads.

Extract 7

NEIL: I mean you could probably draw a list up (.) of what the qualities that make you eligible for [the hard group] (.) I mean (.) you've probably got to be attractive (.) handsome (.) good at sport (.) physically strong and I'd probably say mentally <u>weak</u> to go along with them [laughter] but I mean you've got to be (.) probably pretty sheepish follow the herd to do that whereas I doubt if one of them would stand out and say something against their whole group whereas one of us lot wouldn't think twice about it

(B 1)

Here we see Neil constructing a kind of identi-kit portrait of the typical rugby player. At first the list seems pretty complimentary, but then comes the sting in the tail. For all their bulging biceps, the rugby players are said to lack mental strength. They are portrayed as unthinking conformists, incapable, or even scared, perhaps, of doing their own thing. In this way a *categorical* difference is established between the identity of the speaker (and his friends) and the hard lads. No longer are they pale versions of the same thing. Instead a rough kind of equality is struck: both groups are represented as being strong, albeit in different ways. This attempt to undermine the position of the rugby players is extended further in Extracts 8 and 9 where, yet again, the same conceptual distinction is used. In both instances the young men are taking part in a broader conversation about the role of violence in men's lives.

Extract 8

KEITH: No but I think it's because like for some of us it would take a bit of working up before (.) but for them they're always ready to give some (.) I suppose you're right (.) but it's not so much that if they did start anything it's just that it's always the outwards show of muscle

NEIL: It's like a show of weakness I think (.) that you have to resort to that (.) so that's probably what stops me having a go at one of them

NATHAN: I don't like to use physical violence not just because sometimes I might like lose or whatever but like sometimes I have in the past like (.) lost control and I don't like doing that

(B 2)

Extract 9

NEIL: There's a few people (.) a few you know perhaps in September I've thought you know 'I've about had enough of this (.) I'm gonna go and smack this kid' but I (.) you know I've only (.) I've only started (.) I've only had a brief fight with one person since September you know I (.) I've got quite a lot of self-control because I could probably name about ten people who I've you know been extremely tempted or less than that (.) but you know there's a few people

I really would like to go and er smack because they really do get on my nerves and I don't (.) I don't bother <u>them</u> but they bother <u>me</u> (**NIGEL**: Hm m) and er (.) I think sometimes it'll come to a point where I may have to do that (.) but it's not something that I'd be proud of (.) I mean I'm more proud of the fact that I've been restrained I think than letting go

(B 4)

As with Extract 7, a key difference between the participants and the rugby players is said to be the latter's lack of mental toughness (in this case 'control' or strength of character). Moreover, the hard lads' outward displays of physical aggression are constructed by Neil as being evidence of their lack of character. Unlike him, they lack the mental discipline or sophistication to deal with difficult situations in civilised ways. As soon as the rugby players are provoked they have to resort to violence. In contrast, Neil, Nathan and, arguably, Keith pride themselves upon being able to 'restrain' themselves.

Yet perhaps the most significant feature of these extracts is the way in which each speaker manages to construct himself as *capable* of physical aggression. It is not that they cannot engage in displays of macho violence, it is just that they all have the self-discipline to control such outbursts. Keith argues that he and his friends just require 'a bit of working up' before they resort to violence. So while they claim to have slightly longer fuses, the implication is that that when they 'go off', the result is just as spectacular. Similarly, Neil portrays himself as teetering on the brink of 'smacking' some of the hard lads. It is not that he cannot do it; it is just that he does not want to. Nathan's account is also constructed upon a supposed distaste of physical violence. Yet, in many ways, his argument is even stronger. For unlike the others, he claims to have actually lost control of himself in the past. The main virtue of this account is that, in claiming a history of physical violence, Nathan heads off the assumption that his current pacifism hides a cowardly streak. However, of all these tales of self-containment, probably the most colourful appears in Extract 10 below.

Extract 10

AARON: I'm fairly quick thinking on my feet so I can usually talk my way (.) talk myself out of doing anything more than anything else

PAUL: You tend to size up the situation you just think (.) there's no point in getting into a fight you're gonna lose is there?

AARON: No (.) I mean (.) a lot of situations [inaudible] the first option that really presents is <u>hit</u> them and then the rest of them are self control measures (1.0) think quick on your feet (.) talk your way out of this (1.0) so I've got (.) I have to talk my way out of it so that I'm not seen as the loser (**NIGEL**: Right) I don't mind a draw but I can't be a loser so I have to talk my way out of it so I look good to myself (.) otherwise I get very aggressive

NIGEL: Okay, so erm (.) there has to be some sort of showdown which can be verbal?

AARON: Yeah (.) I mean (.) as I say I'm a fairly quick talker (.) so I'm (.) with regard to other people I think

NIGEL: Can you think of an episode where that's been the case?

AARON: Not recently (.) not really (.) erm (.) well (.) perhaps with Tommy Ladham on the football field (1.0) he's a (.) he's very aggressive but not very intelligent (**NIGEL:** Hmm) I'm not saying I'm intelligent (2.0) so there was a situation (.) well it was a dodgy tackle (.) I mean both of us just went for the ball as hard as possible and there wasn't really (.) and he got all on his high horse (.) 'If you do that again I'll take your <u>shins</u> away' (.) and erm (.) you know (.) the aggression bar went straight up on me (.) I was thinking to myself and erm (.) I mean I totally outworded the lad (.) because I'm quick at thinking on my feet (1.0) I can just quickly reel off something (.) blah blah blah blah and he just (.) walked off

(C 7)

Reminiscent of a scene from the film *Cyrano de Bergerac*, Aaron describes a battle between brawn and brains. And just as in the story, the hero defeats his enemy with a mixture of guile and wit. It is a victory of mind over muscle, of mental control over violent physical action. Looking back over the last three extracts it is possible to detect a certain 'turning of the tables' taking place. In differentiating themselves from the rugby players, Aaron, Neil and the other members of the friendship group have not really distanced themselves from the traditional definition of masculinity at all. Indeed, they have represented themselves as out-doing the rugby players at pretty much their own game. Across all of the extracts, the result, then, is a set of hybrid identity positions – mixing elements of critique of traditional masculinities with subtle claims to key elements of those very masculinities.

Conclusions

In this chapter we have looked at the construction of masculine identities within a specific cultural and institutional setting. The institutional practices of the school in which the research was conducted both privileged and, to a certain extent, produced a particular version of masculinity. The hard lads or sporty boys were its main representatives (both symbolically and literally). As a consequence, school life for them tended to be relatively straight-forward. For the remainder, however, whose voices we examined above, life was much more difficult. They were the ones who are most alienated by the dominant cultural order. As John Shotter argues,

> It is in the very nature of the phenomenology of power that those [...] who have it [are] the least aware of it. [T]o have power is to find no resistance to the realisation of one's desires. [I]t is those without power who find at every turn resistances to the realization of their desires. (1993: 40; see also Billig 1991, chapter 4)

We have tried to demonstrate the active and highly creative rhetorical work involved in formulating identity under these circumstances. As discursive psychologists would anticipate, our analysis did not reveal the existence of stable or consistent selves, but a good deal of variation in the ways in which the participants talked about their own gender identities. This picture of rhetorical selves and the constant negotiation of Self in talk vindicate the broadly social constructionist perspective on gender outlined in our introduction.

Second, we have tried to illustrate in this chapter the value of a form of analysis which combines an interest in patterns of discourse in situ with attention to the social context. Although broad sweep analyses of cultural types such as the 'new man' and the 'retributive man' found in cultural studies are useful, cultural theory does not convey the lived texture of identity negotiations and historical shifts and their instantiation in everyday discursive practices. As we have argued elsewhere (cf. Wetherell 1998), conversation analysis and forms of discursive psychology which restrict researchers to the interactional details of the talk alone on a turn-by-turn basis similarly are inadequate for understanding the patterning of gender. The feminist ethnomethodologist, Dorothy Smith (1990), puts it well when she argues for investigations which focus instead on how objectified social relations enter into people's situated activities. Our approach attempts to emphasise *both* the situated and the objectified.

More particularly, we take from post-structuralism and macro-discourse analyses an interest in what Michael Shapiro (1992) calls 'institutions of intelligibility' or the 'background' structures of intelligibility which organise talk. It is clear that every live conversation – such as the ones presented above – represents a victory for certain institutionalised forms of intelligibility at the expense of others. Conversations are a product of the lines of force which shape the economies of the said and unsaid. But, in common with forms of more micro discourse analysis, we also maintain that social activities are partly self-organising – their intelligible character emerges as people manage their joint conduct, collaborate, recognise and constitute their circumstances as something accountable and recognisable. Social interaction is indexical – what things mean, how they work is fluid and open; the meanings, what actually is happening, and any closure around this, has to be achieved over and over again. The data above demonstrate how each action is context renewing and context creating as participants inter-subjectively worked out how to go on with each other as part of the 'long conversation' (Maybin 2006) which made up the culture of their common room.

The final point we wish to stress is that when looked at in this way, identity strategies appear complex, contradictory and multiple. In terms of ideological practice, they are messy and inevitably hybrid. On the one hand, the young men interviewed built a critique of a form of masculinity, a form which certainly requires critical examination. In Connell's terminology, the dominant position of the rugby players, the hegemonic group, was challenged by a subordinated or marginalised group – a cultural struggle was thus vividly reproduced in talk. Yet, in this case, there was also complicity. New identities were built in dialogue with the identities which were to be challenged and superseded. The development of an adequate feminist politics around masculinity depends on taking these patterns in the mobilisation of meaning into account, both in terms of the content of the identities being formulated here by young, white, middle-class men and the process of discursive change which seems entailed. For an adequate discursive psychology of masculinity, it seems necessary to be able to work closely with text and talk, to examine its design, as well as interpreting the place of those designs in terms of more global social contexts.

Transcription Notation

The following transcription notation is a simplified version of that developed by Gail Jefferson (see Atkinson and Heritage [1984] for a more comprehensive account).

(.)	Short pause of less than 1 second
(1.0)	Timed pause (in seconds)
[...]	Material deliberately omitted
[text]	Clarificatory information
text	Word(s) emphasised

Acknowledgements

The research reported in this chapter was funded by the Economic and Social Research Council (Grant No. R000233129), the Open University and the

Nottingham Trent University. Our most important debt, however, is to the young men who took part in this study. Needless to say, without their kindness, co-operation and openness and their willingness to submit their discourse to critical commentary such work as this would never get done.

REFERENCES

Atkinson, J. Maxwell and John C. Heritage (eds.). 1984. *Structures of Social Action: Studies in Conversation Analysis*. Cambridge: Cambridge University Press.

Benwell, Bethan and Elizabeth Stokoe. 2006. *Discourse and Identity*. Edinburgh: Edinburgh University Press.

Billig, Michael. 1987. *Arguing and Thinking: A Rhetorical Approach to Social Psychology*. Cambridge: Cambridge University Press.

Billig, Michael. 1991. *Ideology and Opinions: Studies in Rhetorical Psychology*. London: Sage.

Billig, Michael, Susan Condor, Derek Edwards, Mike Gane, David J. Middleton and Alan Radley. 1988. *Ideological Dilemmas: A Social Psychology of Everyday Thinking*. London: Sage.

Brah, Avtar and Ann Phoenix. 2004. Ain't I a woman?: Revisiting intersectionality. *Journal of International Women Studies* 5: 75–86.

Butler, Judith. 1990. *Gender Trouble: Feminism and the Subversion of Identity*. London: Routledge.

Connell, Robert W. 1987. *Gender and Power*. Cambridge: Polity

Connell, Robert W. 1995. *Masculinities*. Cambridge: Polity.

Derrida, Jacques. 1973. *Speech and Phenomena and Other Essays on Husserl's Theory of Signs*. Evanston: Northwestern University Press.

Edley, Nigel and Margaret Wetherell. 1997. 'Jockeying for position': The construction of masculine identities. *Discourse and Society* 8: 203–217.

Edley, Nigel and Margaret Wetherell. in press. Discursive psychology and the study of gender: A contested space. In Lia Litosseliti, Helen Saunston, Kate Segall and Jane Sunderland (eds.) *Gender and Language: Theoretical and Methodological Approaches*. Basingstoke: Palgrave Macmillan.

Edwards, Derek. 2006. Discourse, cognition and social practices: The rich surface of language and social interaction. *Discourse Studies* 8: 41–49.

Edwards, Derek and Jonathan Potter. 1992. *Discursive Psychology*. London: Sage.

Frosh, Stephen, Ann Phoenix and Rob Pattman. 2002. *Young Masculinities*. Basingstoke: Palgrave Macmillan.

Maybin, Janet. 2006. *Children's Voices: Talk, Knowledge and Identity*. Basingstoke: Palgrave Macmillan.

Potter, Jonathan. 2000. Post cognitivist psychology. *Theory and Psychology* 10: 31–37.

Potter, Jonathan. 2005. Making psychology relevant. *Discourse and Society* 16: 739–747.

Rutherford, Jonathan. 1988. Who's that man? In Rowena Chapman and Jonathan Rutherford (eds.) *Male Order: Unwrapping Masculinity*. London: Lawrence and Wishart. 21–67.

Potter, Jonathan and Margaret Wetherell. 1987. *Discourse and Social Psychology: Beyond Attitudes and Behaviour*. London: Sage.

Said, Edward. 1978. *Orientalism*. Harmondsworth: Penguin.

Shapiro, M. (1992) *Reading the Postmodern Polity*, Minneapolis, Minnesota: University of Minnesota Press.

Shotter, Michael J. 1993. *The Cultural Politics of Everyday Life*. Milton, Keynes: Open University Press.

Smith, Dorothy E. 1990. *Texts, Facts, and Femininity: Exploring the Relations of Ruling*. London: Routledge.

Speer, Susan. 2005. *Gender Talk: Feminism, Discourse and Conversation Analysis*. London: Routledge.

Wetherell, Margaret. 1998. Positioning and interpretative repertoires: Conversation analysis and post-structuralism in dialogue. *Discourse and Society* 9: 387–412.

Wetherell, Margaret. 2007. A step too far?: Discursive psychology, linguistic ethnography and questions of identity. *Journal of Sociolinguistics* 11, 5: 661–681.

Wetherell, Margaret and Nigel Edley. 1998. Gender practices: Steps in the analysis of men and masculinities. In Karen Henwood, Christine Griffin and Ann Phoenix (eds.) *Standpoints and Differences: Essays in the Practice of Feminist Psychology*. London: Sage.

Wetherell, Margaret and Nigel Edley. 1999. Negotiating hegemonic masculinity: Imaginary positions and psycho-discursive practices. *Feminism and Psychology* 9: 335–356.

CHAPTER 15

'Why be Normal?': Language and Identity Practices in a Community of Nerd Girls

MARY BUCHOLTZ

Eckert (1989a; also Chapter 10, this volume) offers an account of the social organization of a typical suburban US high school. She found that students' social worlds and identities were defined by two polar opposites: the Jocks (overachieving students who oriented to middle-class values) and the Burnouts (underachieving students who were bound for work, rather than college, at the end of their high-school careers). Yet the dichotomy that separated these students also united them in what can be understood as a single community of practice, since the ultimate goal of members of both groups was to be *cool*. The difference lay in how each group defined coolness.

Not all high-school students, however, share the Jocks' and Burnouts' pre-occupation with coolness. A third group, the nerds, defines itself largely in opposition to 'cool' students – whether Jocks, Burnouts, or any other social identity. Nerds stand as the antithesis of all these groups, a situation that Eckert succinctly captures in her observation, 'If a Jock is the opposite of a Burnout, a nerd is the opposite of both' (1989a: 48). But despite the structural signifi-cance of the nerd in the organization of youth identities, few researchers have examined its implications, and those who have tried have fallen far short of the mark in their analyses. Thus the sociologist David Kinney, in a rare study of nerds (1993), argues that, in order to succeed socially, nerds must undergo a process of 'recovery of identity' that involves broadening one's friendship

Source: 'Why be normal?: Language and identity practices in a community of nerd girls', by Bucholtz, M. in *Language in Society*, 28(2) (1999) (Cambridge: Cambridge University Press) pp. 211–23, table 1.

network, participating in extracurricular activities, and heterosexual dating:
In short, they must become Jocks. Another scholarly treatment (Tolone and
Tieman 1990) investigates the drug use of nerds in an article subtitled 'Are
loners deviant?' – in other words, are nerds really Burnouts?

What both studies overlook is that being a nerd is not about being a failed
Burnout or an inadequate Jock. It is about rejecting both Jockness and
Burnoutness, and all the other forms of coolness that youth identities take.
Although previous researchers maintain that nerd identity is invalid or deficient, in fact nerds, like Jocks and Burnouts, to a great extent consciously
choose and display their identities through language and other social practices. And where other scholars tend to equate nerdiness with social death,
I propose that nerds in US high schools are not socially isolated misfits, but
competent members of a distinctive and oppositionally defined community of
practice. Nerdiness is an especially valuable resource for girls in the gendered
world of the US high school.

Elsewhere (Bucholtz 1998) I describe the social identity of the nerd and
detail the phonological, syntactic, lexical, and discourse practices through
which nerd identity is linguistically indexed. Here I propose a framework
for the classification of such practices. These linguistic indices are of two
kinds: *negative identity practices* are those that individuals employ to distance
themselves from a rejected identity, while *positive identity practices* are those
in which individuals engage in order actively to construct a chosen identity.
In other words, negative identity practices define what their users are *not*,
and hence emphasize identity as an intergroup phenomenon; positive identity practices define what their users *are*, and thus emphasize the intragroup
aspects of social identity. The linguistic identity practices of nerds in the
present study are shown in Table 15.1.

The negative identity practices listed here work to disassociate nerds from
non-nerds, and especially from cool teenagers. Each of these practices, which
mark nerdy teenagers as avowedly uncool, constitutes a refusal to engage in
the pursuit of coolness that consumes other students. Meanwhile, all the positive identity practices listed contribute to the speaker's construction of an
intelligent self – a primary value of nerd identity. These linguistic practices
also have non-linguistic counterparts in positive and negative identity practices of other kinds (see below).

But linguistic practices can often reveal important social information that
is not available from the examination of other community practices alone. For
example, Eckert and McConnell-Ginet (1995) apply the theory of the community of practice to Eckert's study of Jocks and Burnouts. Linguistic analysis
revealed that the two groups were participating at different rates in the Northern
Cities Vowel Shift, with the most innovative vowels being those used by the
'Burned-Out Burnout girls', the most extreme adherents to this social identity. Eckert and McConnell-Ginet's finding runs counter to the sociolinguistic

Table 15.1   Linguistic identity practices of nerds at Bay City High School

Linguistic level	Negative identity practices	Positive identity practices
Phonology	Lesser fronting of (uw) and (ow)[a]	
Phonology	Resistance to colloquial phonological processes such as vowel reduction, consonant-cluster simplification, and contraction	Employment of superstandard and hypercorrect phonological forms (e.g. spelling pronunciations)
Syntax	Avoidance of nonstandard syntactic forms	Adherence to standard and superstandard syntactic forms
Lexicon	Avoidance of current slang	Employment of lexical items associated with the formal register (e.g. Greco-Latinate forms)
Discourse		Orientation to language form (e.g. punning, parody, word coinage)

Note: a In Bucholtz (1998) I offer a fuller discussion of the phonological and syntactic patterns of nerds. The present article focuses primarily on lexicon and on discursive identity practices. The variables (uw) and (ow) are part of a vowel shift that is characteristic of California teenagers (Hinton et al. 1987; Luthin 1987). It is stereotypically associated with trendy and cool youth identities.

tenet that 'in stable variables, women use fewer non-standard variants than men of the same social class and age under the same circumstances' (Chambers 1995: 112).[1] The researchers argue that the vowels employed by the Burned-Out Burnout girls are resources through which they construct their identities as tough and streetwise; unlike the boys, who can display their toughness through physical confrontations, female Burnouts must index their identities semiotically, because fighting is viewed as inappropriate for girls. Thus Burnout girls and boys share an orientation toward toughness in their community of practice, but the practice of toughness is achieved in different ways by each gender. By viewing language as equivalent to other social practices like fighting, Eckert and McConnell-Ginet are able to explain the ethnographic meaning of the Burnout girls' vowel systems, and to show how, as symbolic capital (Bourdieu 1978), language can acquire the empowering authority of physical force itself.

Nerds, of course, attain empowerment in very different ways than either Burnouts or Jocks. One of the primary ways they differ from these other, more trend-conscious groups is through the high value they place on individuality. Compared to both Jocks and Burnouts – who must toe the subcultural line in dress, language, friendship choices, and other social practices – nerds are somewhat less constrained by peer-group sanctions.

For girls, nerd identity also offers an alternative to the pressures of hegemonic femininity – an ideological construct that is at best incompatible with, and at worst hostile to, female intellectual ability. Nerd girls' conscious opposition to this ideology is evident in every aspect of their lives, from language to hexis to other aspects of self-presentation. Where cool girls aim for either cuteness or sophistication in their personal style, nerd girls aim for silliness. Cool girls play soccer or basketball; nerd girls play badminton. Cool girls read fashion magazines; nerd girls read novels. Cool girls wear tight T-shirts, and either very tight or very baggy jeans; nerd girls wear shirts and jeans that are neither tight nor extremely baggy. Cool girls wear pastels or dark tones; nerd girls wear bright primary colors. But these practices are specific to individuals; they are engaged in by particular nerd girls, not all of them.

The community of practice model accommodates the individuality that is paramount in the nerd social identity, without overlooking the strong community ties that unify the nerd girls in this study. The community of practice also allows us to look at nerd girls in the same way that Eckert and McConnell-Ginet (1995) view the Burnout girls: as speakers *and* social actors, as individuals *and* members of communities, and as both resisting and responding to cultural ideologies of gender.

Identity Practices in a Local Nerd Community

To illustrate the value of the community of practice framework, I will focus on a single social group that displays the nerd social identity. Nerds at the high school in my study constitute a single community insofar as they engage in shared practices, but this identity is divided into particular social groups whose members associate primarily with one another, and these groups form their own communities of practice. In communities of practice, unlike speech communities, the boundaries are determined not externally by linguists, but internally through ethnographically specific social meanings of language use. As suggested above, ethnographic methods therefore become crucial to the investigation of communities of practice (see Chapter 10).

The ethnographic fieldwork from which the data are taken was carried out during the 1994–1995 academic year at a California high school that I call Bay City High. The social group of nerd girls that is the focus of this discussion is a small, cohesive friendship group that comprises four central members – Fred, Bob, Kate, and Loden – and two peripheral members, Carrie and Ada. (Ada does not appear in the data that follow.) All the girls are European American except Ada, who is Asian American. The same group also formed a club, which I will call the Random Reigns Supreme Club.[2]

Random Reigns Supreme is more properly described as an anti-club, which is in keeping with the counter-hegemonic orientation of nerd identity. It was created by members in order to celebrate their own preferences, from Sesame Street to cows to Mr. Salty the pretzel man. Members emphasize the 'randomness' of the club's structure. It is not organized around shared preferences; instead, any individual's preferences can be part of the club's de facto charter, and all six members are co-presidents. This structure contrasts with the corporate focus and hierarchical structure of most school clubs, which bring together people who are otherwise unconnected to perform a shared activity (Eckert 1989a). The Random Reigns Supreme Club centers around members' daily practices, not specialized activities. It has no goals, no ongoing projects, and no official meetings. Nevertheless, members proudly take their place among the corporate clubs in the pages of the school's yearbook. The girls' insistence on being photographed for the yearbook has a subversive quality: The photo publicly documents the existence of this otherwise little-recognized friendship group, and demands its institutional legitimacy on par with the French Club, the Backpacking Club, and other activity-based organizations. Like their yearbook photograph, the language used by the girls not only marks their nerd identity but also expresses their separation from outsiders. As shown by the following examples (taken from a single interaction), the details of interaction are important and contested resources in defining a shared oppositional nerd identity within the club's community of practice.

Positive Identity Practices

As indicated above, many positive identity practices in which nerds engage contribute to the display of intelligence. The community value placed on intelligence is reflected in non-linguistic identity practices oriented to the world of school, books, and knowledge. This orientation is amply illustrated in the following.[3]

(1) 1 Carrie: Where where do those seeds come from?
     2 ⟨points to her bagel⟩
     3 ⟨laughter⟩
     4 Bob: [Poppies.   ]
     5 Fred: [Sesame plants.]
     6 Carrie: {But what do they look like?} ⟨high pitch⟩
     7 Fred: I have no idea. hh
     8 Bob: Sesame:.
     9 Carrie: [Is anybody– h]
    10 Fred: Ask me (.) [tomorrow.   ]
    11   I'll look it up for you. h
    12 Carrie: h Is anybody here knowledgeable about (.)
    13   the seeds on top of bagels?/
    14 Fred: /Sesame.
    15 Bob: They're sesame?

16   They're not sunfl– ?
17   No,
18   of course they're not sunflower.
19 Loden: Yeah,
20   [What kind of seeds are–   ]
21 Carrie: [Because sunflower are those whopping ones?]
22 Bob: [Yeah.
23   Yeah.
24   I know.   ]
25 ⟨laughter⟩

Carrie's question in line 1 creates the conditions for intellectual display. Although the humor of the question is acknowledged through laughter (line 2), it receives immediate, serious uptake from two participants, Bob and Fred (lines 4–5). Carrie's subsequent question (line 6), however, forces an admission of ignorance from Fred (line 7).

Because knowledge is symbolic capital within the nerd community of practice, Fred's admission results in some loss of face. She recovers from this (minor) social setback by invoking the authority of a reference book (*I'll look it up for you*, line 11). In this way Fred can safely assure her interlocutor that, although she does not yet know the answer, she soon will. She is also able to one-up Bob, who has misidentified the bagel seeds (line 4) and continues to show some skepticism about Fred's classification of them (*Sesame:*, line 8). Fred tracks this indirect challenge for five lines, through her own turn and Carrie's next question; rather than continuing to participate in the series of adjacency pairs that Carrie has initiated (lines 12–13), she responds to Bob (line 14). Fred thus succeeds in displaying both actual knowledge, about the type of seeds under discussion, and potential knowledge, about the appearance of sesame plants.

Claims to knowledge are, however, often disputed in this community of practice. After Bob provides an incorrect answer to Carrie and receives a correction from Fred, she continues to exhibit doubt about Fred's knowledge (line 15). She offers a second incorrect identification of the seeds in line 16, but this time she interrupts herself and self-corrects (lines 17–18), in an effort to prevent further other-correction. She does not succeed, however; and when Carrie explains why Bob is mistaken, the latter overlaps with her, offering three quick acknowledgments that are designed to cut off Carrie's turn (lines 22–24).

This passage shows several deviations from the preference organization of repair in conversation (Schegloff et al. 1977), according to which self-initiation and self-repair are preferred over initiation and repair by another. Bob twice initiates dispreferred repairs of Fred's turns (lines 8, 15), and she even begins to carry out the repair itself in line 16. When Bob initiates a repair of her own utterance through self-interruption in the same line, Carrie performs the repair despite Bob's efforts to prevent her from doing so (lines 21–24). The frequent apparent violations of repair organization suggest that, in this community of practice, self-repair is preferred only by the speaker; the listener's positive face (the desire to be viewed as intelligent) wars against and often overrides consideration of the speaker's negative face (the desire not to be viewed as unintelligent).

Bob's loss of face in Extract 1 leads her, in Extract 2, to initiate a new conversational direction:

(2)	26	Bob:	They come from trees.
	27		They have big trees and they just
	28		[ra:in down seeds]
	29		[⟨laughter⟩]
	30	Carrie:	[No they don't.]
	31		Uh uh.
	32		Why would little tiny seeds [come from–]
	33	Fred:	[{into baskets.}] ⟨smiling quality⟩
	34		Ye:p,
	35		[({I've been there.})] ⟨smiling quality⟩
	36	Carrie:	[No:.]
	37	Loden:	[No:.]
	38	Bob:	[[Little tiny <u>leaves</u> come from trees,]]
	39	Fred:	[[And the whole culture's built <u>around</u> it,]]
	40		like in: some countries,
	41		All they do is like the women come out and they have ba(h)skets on
	42		th(h)eir h(h)eads and they st(h)and under a [tree,]

Bob jokingly provides an authoritative answer to Carrie's question (lines 26–28) and thereby skillfully shifts attention from her own lack of knowledge to Carrie's. Fred eagerly joins in with the parody of scientific discourse, amplifying on the theme while supplying invented anthropological details that invoke the didactic style of a typical high-school classroom or public television documentary (33–35, 39–42). Such teasing episodes are frequent in this friendship group. But more importantly, this exchange is a collaborative performance of nerd identity: The participants collude in sustaining the frame of an intellectual debate, even as laughter keys the talk as play. Nerd identities are here jointly constructed and displayed.

In Extract 3, Carrie – who up to this point has mostly provided opportunities for others to display their nerd identities, rather than participating herself (but see below) – shifts the topic, which she sustains for the rest of the interaction:

(3) 43 Carrie: [My–]
    44   You sound like my crusty king,
    45   I'm writing this (·) poem because I have to like incorporate these
    46   words into a poem, and it's all about–
    47 ⟨interruption, lines omitted⟩
    48 Fred: So what about this king?

Carrie's discussion of a class assignment returns to a central value of nerdiness: school. The topic is sustained for 56 lines and 26 turns; and although it is interrupted immediately after Carrie introduces it (line 47), Fred prompts her to return to the subject several minutes later (line 48). Carrie's enthusiastic description of her poem – and the eager participation of others in this topic – is rare among students with cool social identities, but it is quite common among nerds, for whom academic pursuits are a central resource for identity practices.

At the same time, however, Carrie's selection of subject matter for her poem, with its mildly scatological – or at least 'gross' theme (line 80) – is playfully subversive of school values and emphatically counter to traditional feminine topics, as Extract 4 illustrates:

(4) 49 Carrie: He's like (·) has this (·) castle,
    50   (xxx: Is he xxx king?)
    51 Carrie: No–
    52   Yeah,
    53   he is.
    54 Loden: hh
    55 Carrie: He has this–
    56   {He has this castle right?
    57   except it's all crusty,}
    58   ⟨rustling of lunch bag, clanging of aluminum can⟩
    59 (Fred: Uh huh.)
    60 Carrie: And so he lives on a boat [in the moat.]
    61 Bob: [A crusty–   ]
    62 ⟨Fred crushes her aluminum can⟩
    63 Kate: Who:a!
    64 ⟨quiet laughter⟩
    65 Bob: Is it really [crusty?]
    66 Carrie: [He's–]
    67   And so like the– like because– the people are trying to convince
    68   him that like he should stay in the castle and he's all,

69		{'No, it's crusty!'} ⟨high pitch, tensed vocal cords⟩
70		[⟨laughter⟩]
71	Carrie:	[{'I'm in the moat!'}] ⟨high pitch, quiet⟩
72		right,
73	Bob:	What's wrong with [crusty castles?]
74	Carrie:	[And so–]
75		Well,
76		Would [you want to live]=
77	Kate:	[Crusty (castles).]
78	Carrie:	=in a castle full of crust?
79		{[iəi]} ⟨noise of disgust and disapproval⟩
80	Kate:	[How gross.]
81	Bob:	[I mi:ght.]
82	Carrie:	Huh?

Bob here enters into the unfeminine spirit of Carrie's narrative, even outdoing Carrie with her repeated insistence on her own immunity from 'gross' subjects like crustiness (lines 73, 81). A competitive tone is also evident in the multiple challenges she issues to Carrie throughout the latter's narrative (lines 65, 73). As questions, these challenges echo Carrie's earlier questions (lines 1, 6, 12–13); but whereas Carrie's appeared to be genuine information-seeking questions. Bob's are not Carrie's recognition of this fact is shown by her failure to respond at all to the first question, and by her answering the second question with an equally challenging question of her own (*Would you want to live in a castle full of crust?*, lines 76, 78). Bob's face-threatening response (*I mi:ght*, line 81) perpetuates the jocular-combative tone. In Extract 5, however, this combativeness becomes not a shared resource for joint identity construction, but a marker of social division. The positive identity practices that dominate in the earlier part of the interaction are replaced by negative identity practices, as community members experience a threat not only to their face but also to their identities.

Negative Identity Practices

Example 5 is a continuation of Bob's face-threatening questions to Carrie. This final series of questions is unified through a shared template (*like* + ADJ + *crust*); their syntactic similarity emphasizes that they are designed as a series, and it thus produces an effect of unremitting interrogation.

(5)	83	Bob:	What kind of crust?
	84		Like,

85   bread crust?
86   Carrie: Like
87   Bob: Like [eye crust?   ]
88   Carrie: [crusty crust.]
89   Like {boo:tsy} ⟨high pitch, tensed vocal cords⟩
90   crust.
91   ⟨laughter⟩
92   Bob: Oh.
93   Well,
94   Maybe if it's bootsy,
95   I don't know.
96   Fred: {Boot[sy!   ]} ⟨falsetto, sing-song⟩
97   Kate: [⟨coughs⟩]
98   ⟨laughter⟩

These questions display Bob's nerd identity through her use of puns on the word *crust* (lines 85, 87). Punning, as a discourse practice that orients to linguistic form, is characteristic of nerds' discourse style (see Table 15.1). Carrie's refusal (line 88) to participate in Bob's punning thus constitutes a negative identity practice – one which, moreover, indexes a rejection of nerd identity as it has been constructed through preceding interactional practices. The refusal is made more evident by her exploitation (lines 86, 88–90) of Bob's syntactic template. By conforming to the syntactic form of Bob's turn, while failing to conform to the discourse practice of punning, Carrie separates herself from Bob at a point when the latter is fully engaged in nerdy identity practices.

This analysis is confirmed by Carrie's choice of upgraded adjective in line 89. *Bootsy* is a slang term with a negative evaluative sense; it is not used by other members of the Random Reigns Supreme Club. The introduction of youth slang into a group that explicitly rejects such linguistic forms is part of a strongly negative identity practice, and the reactions of Carrie's interlocutors are correspondingly negative: Bob's response (lines 92–95) jokingly concedes the point, while underscoring that Carrie has violated the rules of nerdy argument by appealing to the authority of cool youth culture. Fred's mocking repetition of the term (line 96) demonstrates that the use of slang is itself worthy of comment. With Carrie's narrative entirely derailed – it never becomes clear how it is connected to the earlier discussion – she soon afterward moves away from the group.

The complex interaction presented above reveals Carrie's peripheral status in this community of practice. As a non-core member, she moves between friendship groups – in fact, the interaction occurred when Carrie approached the core group in the middle of lunch period. Carrie's social flexibility has made her a cultural and linguistic broker for the Random Reigns Supreme Club, whose members become aware of current youth slang in large part through contact with her. Hence many slang terms that circulate widely in the 'cool' groups are labeled by club members as 'Carrie words'.

Yet Carrie also demonstrates her ability and willingness to participate in the group's positive identity practices. She does so most obviously by engaging in sound play in recounting her poem (*crusty king*, line 44; *a boat in the moat*, line 60). More significant, though, is the subtle shift in her speech practices at the beginning of the interaction. Thus Carrie's question *Is anybody here knowledgeable about* (·) *the seeds on top of bagels?* (lines 12–13) draws on the formal register through her choice of the word *knowledgeable*. Among nerds, this register projects a speaker's persona as smart and highly educated. But the use of the formal register is strategic, not a mechanical result of membership in a particular social category. This point is supported by the fact that Carrie employs the nerd identity practice only after she asks two related questions in colloquial register (lines 1, 6). Her unwillingness to overlap her turn with Fred's (lines 9, 10) further suggests that the question is a performance of nerdiness, not just a manifestation of it; she does not produce her utterance until she is assured of an attentive audience. That is, Carrie is simultaneously displaying and commenting on nerd practice – showing her awareness of nerdy linguistic forms, and announcing her willingness to enter a nerdy interactional space by carefully gauging her utterance to match the group's practices. Thus Carrie's performance of nerdiness places her within the community of practice; but her use of slang, as the other members are quick to let her know, moves her outside it. Such adjustments at interactional boundaries may reflect adjustments at community boundaries.

Conclusion

Because all the participants in the above exchange are middle-class European American girls from the same California city, the traditional sociolinguistic perspective would classify them unproblematically as members of the same speech community. Such an analysis would overlook the details of greatest interest to language and gender researchers: the performances of identity, and the struggles over it, which are achieved through language. However, by viewing the interaction as the product of a community of practice, we can avoid this problem, as well as others associated with the speech community model.

The ethnographic method brings into view the social meanings with which participants invest their practices. These meanings emerge on the ground in local contexts; thus what it means to display academic knowledge, or to use slang, depends not on fixed identity categories but on where one is standing.

Nor do participants necessarily agree on the meanings of their actions; ner-diness, like all identities, is a contested domain in which speakers struggle both over control of shared values, via positive identity practices (Who's bet-ter at being a nerd?), and over control of identity itself, via negative identity practices (Who counts as a nerd?). Such conflicts reveal the heterogeneity of membership in the community of practice – its constitution through the work of central and peripheral members alike. In this project, the interactional choices of specific individuals matter. Thus Carrie's identity is on display – and at risk – in a way that Loden's, for example, is not. These actions must be seen as choices, not as the outputs of interactional algorithms. While some practices reproduce the existing local social structure (as does Carrie's use of the formal register), others undermine it (e.g. her use of slang). Likewise, some nerdy practices (such as being good students) comply with the larger social order, while others (such as rejecting femininity) resist it. Linguistic practices, moreover, have no special status in this process. Instead, they work in conjunction with other social practices to produce meanings and identi-ties. Bob's interactional work to distance herself from hegemonic femininity, for instance, is part of her overall participation in anti-feminine practices and her non-participation in feminine practices, as evidenced also by her physical self-presentation.

For sociolinguists, the community of practice represents an improvement over the speech community in that it addresses itself to both the social and the linguistic aspects of the discipline. As a well-grounded framework with currency in a number of fields, practice theory in general, in particular the community of practice, revitalizes social theory within Sociolinguistics. What is more, it does so at a sufficiently general level to accommodate multiple dimensions of social analysis – including both structure and agency, both ideology and identity, both norms and interactions. The community of prac-tice also provides an avenue for a more complete sociolinguistic investigation of identity. Although introduced for gender-based research, the community of practice has never been restricted to the analysis of a single element of identity. Indeed, it lends itself to the simultaneous investigation of multiple aspects of the self, from those at the macro level – like gender, ethnicity, and class – to micro-identities like Jocks, Burnouts, or nerds. The framework also allows for the study of interaction between levels of identity. The concepts of positive and negative identity practices, as proposed in this article, are intended as one way to develop the potential of the community of practice in this arena.

In addition to its benefits for social analysis, the community of practice offers an integrated approach to linguistic analysis. By understanding all socially meaningful language use as practices tied to various communities, the model enables researchers to provide more complete linguistic descriptions – along with social explanations – of particular social groups. Moreover, the community of practice provides a way to bring qualitative and quantitative research closer together. Because both kinds of linguistic data emerge from practice, both can be included in a single analysis. This richly contextualized approach to both language and society is one of the great strengths of the community of practice as a sociolinguistic framework.

The community of practice, having revolutionized the field of language and gender almost as soon as it was first proposed, enables researchers of socially situated language use to view language within the context of social practice. Perhaps the most valuable feature is that the community of practice admits a range of social and linguistic phenomena that are not analysed in other theoretical models. Local identities, and the linguistic practices that produce them, become visible to sociolinguistic analysis as the purposeful choices of agentive individuals, operating within (and alongside and outside) the constraints of the social structure. To describe and explain such complexity must be the next step not only for language and gender scholars, but for all sociolinguists concerned with the linguistic construction of the social world.

Acknowledgement

My thanks to Janet Holmes, Chris Holcomb, Stephanie Stanbro, and members of the Ethnography/Theory Group at Texas A&M University for comments on and discussion of the ideas in this article.

NOTES

1. Eckert (1989b) calls this simple formulation into question; see also Labov (1990, and Chapter 5) for a response.
2. Though this is not its actual name, it preserves the flavor of the original. All other names are pseudonyms chosen by the speakers.
3. Transcription conventions are as follows:

.	end of intonation unit; falling intonation
,	end of intonation unit; fall-rise intonation
?	end of intonation unit; rising intonation
–	self-interruption
:	length
underline	emphatic stress or increased amplitude
(.)	pause of 0.5 seconds or less
(n.n)	pause of greater than 0.5 seconds, measured by a stopwatch
h	exhalation (e.g. laughter, sigh); each token marks one pulse
( )	uncertain transcription
⟨ ⟩	transcriber comment; nonvocal noise

{ }   stretch of talk over which a transcriber comment applies
[ ]   overlap beginning and end
/   latching (no pause between speaker turns)
=   no pause between intonation units

The transcript emphasizes sequential organization in order to highlight speakers' orientation to one another. It excludes phonological detail that is necessary for a complete analysis of nerd identity performance.

REFERENCES

Bourdieu, Pierre. 1978. *Outline of a Theory of Practice.* Cambridge and New York: Cambridge University Press.

Bucholtz, Mary. 1998. Geek the girl: Language, femininity, and female nerds. In Natasha Warner et al. (eds.) *Gender and Belief Systems: Proceedings of the Fourth Berkeley Women and Language Conference.* Berkeley, California: Berkeley Women and Language Group. 119–131.

Chambers, J. K. 1995. *Sociolinguistic Theory.* Oxford: Blackwell.

Eckert, Penelope. 1989a. *Jocks and Burnouts: Social Categories and Identity in the High School.* New York: Teachers College Press.

Eckert, Penelope. 1989b. The whole woman: Sex and gender differences in variation. *Language Variation and Change* 1: 245–267.

Eckert and McConnell-Ginet. 1995. Constructing meaning, constructing selves: Snapshots of language, gender, and class from Belten High. In Kira Hall and Mary Bucholtz (eds.) *Gender Articulated: Language and the Socially Constructed Self.* London: Routledge. 459–507.

Hinton, Leanne, et al. 1987. It's not just the Valley Girls: A study of California English. *Berkeley Linguistics Society* 13: 117–128.

Kinney, David A. 1993. From nerds to normals: The recovery of identity among adolescents from middle school to high school. *Sociology of Education* 66: 21–40.

Labov, William. 1990. The intersection of sex and social class in the course of linguistic change. *Language Variation and Change* 2: 205–254.

Schegloff, Emanuel, Gail Jefferson and Harvey Sacks. 1977. The preference for self-correction in the organization of repair in conversation. *Language* 53: 361–382.

Tolone, W. L. and C. R. Tieman. 1990. Drugs, delinquency and nerds: Are loners deviant? *Journal of Drug Education* 20: 153–162.

CHAPTER 16

Lip Service on the Fantasy Lines

KIRA HALL

When the deregulation of the telephone industry co-occurred with a number of technological advances in telecommunications in the early 1980s, American society witnessed the birth of a new medium for linguistic exchange – the 900 number. On the fantasy lines, which generate annual revenues of more than $45 million in California alone, women's language is bought, sold, and custom-tailored to secure caller satisfaction. This high-tech mode of linguistic exchange complicates traditional notions of power in language, because the women working within the industry consciously produce a language stereotypically associated with women's powerlessness in order to gain economic power and social flexibility. In this chapter, I refer to research I conducted among five women-owned fantasy-line companies in San Francisco in order to argue for a more multidimensional definition of linguistic power, one that not only devotes serious attention to the role of sexuality in conversational exchange but also recognizes individual variability with respect to women's conversational consent.

The linguistic identification of women's language as 'powerless' and men's language as 'powerful' has its origins in early readings of the work of Robin Lakoff (1975), who argued in *Language and Woman's Place* that sex differences in language use both reflect and reinforce the unequal status of women and men in our society. After identifying an array of linguistic features ideologically associated with women's speech in American English – among them lexical items associated with women's work; 'empty' adjectives such as *divine, charming,* and *cute,* tag questions in place of declaratives; hedges such

Source: 'Lip service on the fantasy lines', by Hall, K, in Hall, K. and Bucholtz, M (eds.) *Gender Articulated: Language and the Socially Constructed Self* (1995) (New York: Routledge) pp. 183–216.

as *sort of*, *kind of*, and *I guess*, intensifiers such as *so* and *very*; and hypercorrect, polite linguistic forms – Lakoff suggested that the association of indirect speech with women's language and direct speech with men's language is the linguistic reflection of a larger cultural power imbalance between the sexes. Her treatise, packaged beneath the unapologetically feminist photograph of a woman with bandaged mouth, has inspired two decades of heated debate among subsequent language and gender theorists.

In this chapter, I address the superficial conflict in the use of submissive speech for reasons of power. The adult-message industry has enjoyed considerable financial success during the past decade, grossing well over $3 billion since its national debut in 1983. As fear of the AIDS epidemic and the accompanying interest in safe sex spreads throughout the culture at large, the demand for women's vocal merchandise promises to expand into the next millennium. The growing success of this discursive medium in the marketplace calls for a new interpretation of the place of women's language in contemporary society. Its easy marketability as a sexual commodity and the profits it reaps for the women who employ it suggest that the study of cross-sex linguistic exchange must acknowledge the more subversive aspects of conversational consent.

Fantasy and the Telephone

The telephone, as a medium that excludes the visual, allows for the creation of fantasy in a way that face-to-face interaction cannot. In the absence of a visual link, the speaker is able to maintain a certain anonymity that can potentially allow for a less self-conscious and, in the appropriate circumstances, more imaginative presentation. On the 900-lines, where the sense of anonymity is of course heightened by the fact that the two interactants have never met, callers must construct their conversational partner visually. Once they have created such a representation, they have already entered into a fantasy world of sorts, and the construction of any additional representations is facilitated by this entry.

The advent of telephone deregulation in the United States and the increasing availability of the mobile telephone have prompted telecommunication theorists like Frederick Williams (1985: 191) to argue that the telephone is shifting 'from a "home" or "business" based communications link to an individual, personal based one'. This shift is nowhere more apparent than in the advertising strategies of the telephone industry itself, which regularly appeals to the personal, private, and expressive contact that it affords. With just one thirty-second AT&T telephone call, clients can find a long-lost friend, pacify a weeping mother, or 'reach out and touch' that special someone. Perhaps it is not so strange after all to see advertisement after advertisement on late Saturday-night television for 'romance lines', 'friendship lines', 'party lines', 'psychic lines', 'teenage date lines', 'therapy lines', and 'confession lines'.

For fantasy to be effective, it must somehow parallel reality, and if its intended audience is the culture at large, it must necessarily prey on certain cultural perceptions of what the ideal reality is. To sell to a male market, women's prerecorded messages and live conversational exchange must cater to hegemonic male perceptions of the ideal woman. The training manual for operators of 970-LIVE, a male-owned fantasy-line service based in New York City, instructs female employees to 'create different characters' and to 'start with one that resembles the ideal woman' – as if this is a universal, unproblematic concept. To train women to fulfill this ideal, the manual gives additional details on how to open and maintain conversations while preserving 'professionalism':

Create different characters:
Start with one that resembles the ideal woman. Move on to bimbo, nymphomaniac, mistress, slave, transvestite, lesbian, foreigner, or virgin. If the caller wants to speak to someone else, don't waste time being insulted. Be someone else. You should be creative enough to fulfill *anyone's* fantasy.

To start a conversation:
'What's on your mind?' 'What would you like to talk about?' 'What do you do for fun?' 'What are you doing right now?'
Remember: Never initiate sex. Let the caller start phone intimacy.

Ways to keep callers interested:
Tell them crazy fantasies: Jell-O, honey, travel, ice cream, lesbian love, orgies. If conversation stays clean, tell them an interesting story: movies, TV, books, etc. Make it sound like it really happened. *Insist* that it happened.

Professionalism:
Do not talk to *anyone* besides a caller when taking a call. Always be bubbly, sexy, interesting, and interested in each individual caller. Remember, *you* are not your character on the phone.

[Reprinted in *Harper's Magazine*, December 1990, 26–27.]

What makes the ideal woman from a verbal point of view is reminiscent of Pamela Fishman's (1978) definition of *maintenance work*: encouraging men to develop their topics by asking questions (*What's on* your *mind! What would you like to talk about! What do you do for fun!*), showing assent (*Always be bubbly, sexy, interesting and interested in each individual caller*), and listening (*Don't talk to* anyone *besides a caller when taking a call*). Because the conversation will be meaningless unless it in some way approximates the male caller's under-standing of reality, what becomes critically important to its success is for it to 'sound like it really happened' – for the woman to *'insist* that it happened'. This realization, coupled with the fact that many clients may be calling the lines in response to the increasing threat of AIDS, has even led some compan-ies to practice 'safe phone-sex'. The number 1–900-HOT-LIPS, for instance, which advertises as a 'steamy safe-sex fantasy number', has all of its fantasy-line operators 'carry' – in the verbal sense, that is – condoms and spermacides to their vocal sexual encounters. The suggestion that an interactant might need to practice safe sex over the telephone wires is of course ludicrous; by overtly referencing this practice in its advertisement, however, the message service suggests that there is a very real physicality to the medium and simul-taneously alludes to its inherently 'safe' nature.

The Prerecorded Message

The language promoted in the trainer's manual is precisely the kind of lan-guage sold by the prerecorded services – language that, through extensive detail and supportive hearer-directed comments, presents a certain reality. The two-minute prerecorded message reproduced below in (1) is played daily on a national fantasy line that advertises as 'girls, girls, girls'. The speaker is unquestionably the perfect woman: she loves to shop, she wears feminine clothes, she likes to look at herself in the mirror, and she lies in bed half the day fulfilling male fantasies.[1]

(1)   oo::f:: – i'm so .((in breathy voice)) ex<u>ci</u>ted. – i just got a <u>hot</u> new job. (0.8) well, – ((in slight Southern accent)) i've been bored lately..hh – i live in a small town and my husband travels a lot, (0.5) i have lots of time on my hands. – .hhh of course, i've always managed to stay busy. (0.4) lots of girl-friends, you know, – ((whispered)) i love to <u>shop,</u> – i ((laugh)) ^<u>pract</u>^ically live at the mall it seems, but still-.hhhh (2.0) <u>anyway.</u> – this friend told me about this job i can do at <u>home.</u> – all i need is a <u>phone.</u> – and a lusty imagination. ((laugh)) yeah, you've got it – .hh i'm doing <u>h::ot</u> sexy phone calls these days. (0.5) i <u>really</u> get into it <u>too.</u> – .hhh i love that sexy hot fel-lows from all over the country call me and enjoy my ((whispered)) voice and my fantasies. (0.4) i like to <u>dress</u> the part too. – i went to my favorite lingerie ((in hoarse, breathy voice)) store, – victoria's secret? – and bought <u>s::atin</u> bikinis, <u>l::acy</u> thong underwear, – a tight black corset – and fishnet stockings, (1.0) ((in lower voice)) and a <u>dangerous</u> pair of <u>red</u> ((whispered)) <u>spiked heels.</u> ((smack)) – <u>umh</u>mm:::: .hhh – <u>then.</u> when i'm in a dominant

mode? .hh i have this leather g-string and bra and thigh-high boots. – ooh
<u>baby</u>. ((giggle)) (0.5) when i dress up and look in the mirror, ((slower,
breathy voice)) i – get – so – <u>crazy</u> .hhhhh i just can't wait for that first
ca::ll. (0.6) <u>then,</u> – i assemble all my favorite little (0.3) <u>toys</u> all around me,
(0.4) lie back on my big bed with s::<u>at</u>in sheets .hhhh (1.0) and live out my
fantasies with some my<u>ster</u>ious stranger .hhhhhhh oo:::::h <u>hear</u>ing those
voices. .hh – those excited whispers and moans, ((in breathy voice)) u::h,
it gets me so- .hhhh – well, – you know. (2.0) then (0.5) i just go <u>wi::ld</u>, – i
have <u>so</u> many great <u>idea::s</u>. – they come fa::st and furious, (in hoarse voice))
oo::h, i can't get enough. -.hh each call makes me hotter, – i just keep going,
<u>over</u> and <u>over</u>, ((gasping)) ^<u>o:h</u>^ – .hhh <u>yea:h b</u>aby do it a<u>gain</u> – ^oo^:::f,
.hhhhhhh – <u>well.</u> (2.0) i <u>love</u> my workday – ^but^ – by the time I put in a
few hours on the phone? – i'm so re<u>la:xed</u> hh, – and when my husband gets
home ((smack)) – <u>oo</u>::h – he gets the treatment – he lo:ves it. – .hh but (1.0)
shhh. ((whispered)) don't tell. – it's <u>our</u> secret.

In the absence of a visual link, this ideal is created solely through language (as
the speaker herself says, 'All I need is a phone and a lusty imagination'). She
begins by constructing a visual image of herself with words popularly thought
of as feminine: *girlfriends, lusty, lacy, lingerie, satin,* and *secret.* Her voice is
dynamic, moving from high-pitched, gasping expressions of pleasure to low-
pitched, breathy-voice innuendoes. Although this is unidirectional discourse,
she makes it quite clear that she would be an admirable conversational partner
in any female–male dyad – she 'just can't wait for that first call' so that she can
respond supportively to all those 'voices' and 'excited whispers'. Additionally,
she sets up her monologue so as to establish an exclusive intimacy with her
absentee partner, referring to their conversational relationship as a passionate
'secret' that should be kept from her husband.

Particularly telling is what happens at the end of this fantasy, when the
speaker's verbal creativity comes to represent the sex act itself: *I have so many
great ideas. They come fast and furious – ooh, I can't get enough.* An equation of
the spoken word with the sex act is a common element in such messages, a
fitting metaphorical strategy given the nature of the exchange. Often in the
beginning of the fantasy scenario, the speaker will be reading a book at a
library, selling encyclopedias door to door, or taking a literature course at the
local college. By the end of the scenario, swayed by the voice and intellect of
the suitor in question (who is often identified with the caller so as to bring him
directly into the fantasy), she has discarded her books, her encyclopedias, and
her academic pretensions for the bedroom.

In the fantasy reproduced below, for example, the speaker projects the persona of a young college student who is obsessed with her English professor.

Having established the power imbalance inherent to this scenario – she, the eager coed; he, the aloof, self-involved intellectual – the student develops a preoccupation with her professor's voice, describing how it repeatedly 'penetrates' her during lecture:

(2) ^hi. – my name's vicky^, – and i <u>guess</u> i'm in <u>deep</u> trouble in one of my <u>class</u>es at college. (1.5) ((whispered)) it's my english professor. – he's got me <u>cra::zy</u>, (0.5) and i think i'm losing my <u>mi:nd,</u> – he's really (0.4) not handsome or anything, – it's the way he talks, (1.0) his voice gets deep inside me where it counts, – turns me to jelly, (1.5) i sit at the front of the class, – and i just can't seem – to keep ^still^, (1.5) i remember the first day, i wore jeans and a sweater. (0.5) and my long blond hair up in a bun. (0.6) i felt pretty studious, – but the moment i started <u>listen</u>ing to him, i knew i was gonna <u>change</u> – all – <u>that.</u> (2.0) and the next session, i showed up in the <u>short</u>est mini-skirt i could find. (0.5) ^i'm real tan^ ((in breathy voice)) and in <u>real</u> good shape. (0.5) and i <u>knew</u> i looked pretty good in that mini-skirt. – i wore a silk blouse that ((slowly)) <u>should</u> have had his eyes riveted on me, – instead – he hardly ^<u>no</u>^ticed, (1.0) ^o:::h^ i was getting so ^<u>cra::</u>^zy. (2.0) well – after a few weeks, – the weather changed and it got <u>real</u> hot, – so i started wearing shorts and this <u>great</u> little halter top, (1.5) i know i looked okay, because guys in the class were stumbling over themselves to sit next to me. – but my professor – there he was, just a few feet away, and hardly a ^<u>glance</u>^. (1.0) and still i go back to my dorm room and lay in my bed, and dream about that voice, ((in breathy voice)) <u>all</u> of me reponds to it, (2.0) ((sigh)) hhhhh it's as if he's penetrated me, ((slowly)) <u>reached</u> the <u>depths</u> of my <u>soul</u> and <u>won't</u> let go. (1.0) i dream about the moment – when we'll be alone, – maybe it'll be after class, (1.5) maybe it'll be a chance meeting at a coffee shop or something, but when that moment comes, (0.5) i know i'm going to tell him what he <u>does</u> to me, – and i don't think he'll be surprised, – because i ^<u>think</u>^ he already knows.

The speaker begins the fantasy by establishing that she is attracted to this particular professor not because of his physical appearance but because of the 'way he talks': *His voice gets deep inside me where it counts, turns me to jelly*. After several unsuccessful attempts to impress the professor by relaxing her studious stance and gendering herself with the appropriate apparel, the speaker goes back to her dorm room so that she can at the very least 'dream about that voice'. She concludes the fantasy by exclaiming, rather emphatically, that she becomes powerless before the sound of it: *All of me responds to it, it's as if he's penetrated me, reached the depths of my soul and won't let go*. Although in this particular text it is the speaker, not the hearer, who is the owner of the fantasy, the one-sided nature of the created exchange (that is, even though the coed talks incessantly in the hopes of attracting her professor's attention, he fails to offer her any individualized verbal acknowledgment) parallels the real-life interaction between operator and client. The caller, unable to respond to the emotional desires of a prerecorded voice, easily assumes the role of the coed's nonresponsive superior.

As this scenario nicely illustrates, the reality presented on the message line presents an interactive inequality between the sexes, portraying men as dominant (penetrating, powerful, intellectual) and women as submissive (penetrated, powerless, emotional). To have a successful conversation, the fantasy-line recording must affirm this inequality, for it is essential to the frame of male pornographic discourse. Rosalind Coward (1986), with reference to visual pornography, argues that although images of women are never inherently pornographic, they necessarily become so when placed within a 'regime of representations' (i.e., a set of codes with conventionally accepted meanings) that identify them as pornographic for the viewer. The captions and texts that surround such images identify them explicitly as figures for male enjoyment, affirming the differential female-as-object versus male-as-subject. In vocal pornography, because there is no visual link, this differential must be created through voice and word alone. The fantasy-line operator has been assisted, of course, by the many advertisements in adult magazines that have already situated her within this frame, but she must still actively assume a submissive position in the conversation. In the telephone advertisement below, for example, offered by a message service as a 'free phone-job sample', the speaker sells the number by highlighting this very inequality:

(3)   ((in quick, low, breathy voice)) baby I want you to listen closely, – dial 1–900–884–6804 <u>now</u> for <u>hard</u> love, – for <u>tough</u> love, – for girls who <u>need</u> <u>men</u> to <u>take</u> contro::l. – dial 1–900–884–6804, – for women who aren't afraid to say what they <u>rea</u>::lly want, – for girls who need <u>powerful</u> men to open their deep desires, dial 1–900–884–6804, and go all the way. (0.5) <u>deep</u> into the secret places for a fantasy experience that just goes <u>on</u> and <u>on</u> and <u>on,</u> – dial 1–900–884–6804, and get a girl who wants to give <u>you</u> the ultimate pleasure, 1–900–884–6804, ((quickly)) just half a dollar a minute, forty the first. (0.5) <u>now</u> I can tell <u>you</u> everything, now i can give you everything you want, <u>all</u> you desire, i can do it now, i <u>want</u> to, i <u>have</u> to, ((giggle)) dial 1–900–884–6804.

In a low, breathy voice, the operator explains that the women who work at this particular company will provide the 'love' (which is here overtly sexualized with the modifiers *hard* and *tough*) if the caller provides the 'control'. They are women who need 'powerful men to open their deep desires' – who not only *want* to submit and give their callers 'the ultimate pleasure' but *'have* to' do so.

Certain types of work structures, particularly those that involve women in typically feminine jobs, require female employees to perform emotional labor for their bosses. As Catherine Lutz (1986, 1990) and other anthropologists have pointed out, such divisions follow from the way emotion has been constructed along gender lines within Western society, so that men are expected to be rational and women emotional – a construction that has effects on women's language and on societal perceptions of what women's language should be. What is noteworthy with respect to the present discussion is the way in which fantasy-line operators consciously appropriate ideologies of emotional language and sexual language (which are not always entirely distinguishable) in order to intensify the perceived power imbalance. As one fantasy-line operator explained, 'My job is kind of a three-conversation trinity – one part prostitute, one part priest, and one part therapist.'

Interviews with San Francisco Fantasy-Line Operators

The eleven women and one man interviewed for this study, all residing in the San Francisco Bay Area and working for services that advertise to a heterosexual male market, were aware of the recent feminist controversy over pornography and were highly reflective of their position within this debate. Each of them had reinterpreted this debate within the vocal sphere, perceiving their position in the linguistic exchange as a powerful one. Their positive attitude may have much to do with the fact that in San Francisco, many of the adult-message services are women-owned and -operated, with a large percentage of employees identifying themselves as feminists and participating actively in organizations such as COYOTE, Cal-Pep, and COP – political action groups established for the purpose of securing rights for women in the sex industry. For these individuals, many of whom are freelance artists, fashion designers, graduate students, and writers, work on the telephone brings economic independence and social freedom. To them, the real prostitutes in our society are the women who dress in expensive business suits in the financial district, work fifty hours a week, and make sixty-five cents to a man's dollar. They understand the adult-message industry as primarily a creative medium, viewing themselves as fantasy tellers who have embraced a form of discourse that has been largely ignored by the women of this sexually repressed society. Moreover, they feel a certain power in having access into men's minds and find that it empowers them in their everyday cross-sex interactions.

Before embarking on this study in 1991, I informed the San Francisco Sex Information Hotline of my project and asked for assistance in locating phone-sex workers who might be interested in being interviewed. Over the next few months I spoke with twelve people, including nine 'call-doers' (as fantasy makers, are sometimes called), two managers, and a woman who is co-owner of one of the oldest phone-sex companies in the United States (K. G. Fox). Most of the interviews were conducted anonymously by phone because many of the participants did not wish to have their names publicized. Approximately half of the interviewees allowed me to record our interviews over the telephone. The race, age, sex, and sexual-orientation backgrounds of the operators I spoke with were roughly equivalent to those of employees working for women-owned and -operated services in San Francisco. Six of the employees I interviewed were heterosexual, three bisexual, and three lesbian; eight were European American, two Latino, one African American, and one Asian American. The employees who granted me interviews ranged in age from twenty-three to forty-six; they were generally from middle-class backgrounds, college-educated, and supportive of the industry. Many of these women had sought employment with women-owned services in reaction to the poor treatment they had received from various men-owned services in the city, among them the financially successful Yellowphone.

At the beginning of each interview I explained that I was writing an article on the phone-sex industry from the point of view of its labor force; only at the end of the interview did I disclose my particular interest in language use. The female participants all believed that both the antipornography feminism of Dworkin, Jeffreys, and MacKinnon and the pro-freedom feminism of Bright prioritize an issue that most of the women in this country – because they suffer from serious economic and social oppression – do not have the privilege of debating. The most important issue to the women I interviewed is not whether pornography is oppressive or whether women's sexuality is repressed but, rather, how they, as a group, can mobilize for a better work environment so that the job they have chosen will be as nonoppressive as possible. They spoke of the need for a sex workers' union, for health-care benefits, and for approval from people working outside the industry. Each of them chose her or his line of work initially for the economic freedom and social flexibility it offered. Like the fantasy-line operators quoted in excerpts (4) through (6) below – who variously identify themselves as *militant feminist, humanist,* and *feminist most definitely* – they regard the issue of sexual oppression as comparatively unimportant to the other types of economic and social oppression they have suffered.

(4)   Yes, in one word, the reason I got involved in this work is Reaganomics. It doesn't filter down to people like me. I'm an artist. I refuse to deal with

corporate America. I'm an honest person. I have integrity. I work hard. There's no place in corporate America for me.... About a year and a half ago when the economy really started to go sour, I started thinking, well, I'm going to have to get a part-time job. I looked around at part-time jobs and it was like, you want me to dress in $300 outfits when you're paying me six bucks an hour? Excuse me, but I don't think so. And I saw an ad in the *Bay Guardian* for a fantasy maker, and I thought about it for months, because I had an attitude that it was really weird and I was concerned that I would end up really hating men, and finally it got down to, well, you can go downtown and spend a lot of money on clothes, or you can check this out.

(5)   I moved out here a couple of years ago from Ohio, and one of the main reasons I moved out here is so I could still be as strange as I am and do a job. I have piercing – body piercing, facial piercing – and I have tattoos, and I'm an insurance adjuster. And I wanted to come out here and get the piercings, and I'd been having to wear make up over the [tattoo] ring on my finger, and that kind of thing. And I thought, well, god, San Francisco! If I can't get away with it there, then where can I? Well, I couldn't get away with it here either – not in the financial district. So I started watching *SF Weekly* and the newspapers, and I originally went to a company called [deleted]. And they told me it was a chat line and there'd be a few fantasy calls and not to be surprised by that. And oh boy, I was like, yeah, this is great money, I love it! And so I said sure. And that's basically how I got into it.

(6)   For me, I can work at home, I can make my own hours. If I want to take off and go on vacation on last minute's notice and be gone for a month, I can do that and know that my job is there. And I like that flexibility and I like the idea of not really having a boss to answer to. In some ways, it's powerful and in some ways it's definitely not. [We're] people who are sort of marginalized, [there's a lot] that we don't have access to- like health care. It's like forget it, you get sick and you don't have insurance. We don't have any kind of union. I think it would be great if we could have some kind of sex workers' union. So it's a mixed bag, but I guess for me, in light of what the options would be for me to make a living at this point in time, it seems like the best thing I can do for myself. Definitely one of the best compared to the options I see out there, I'm pretty damn lucky with what I'm doing. Because I've tried to have a few sort of semi-straight normal jobs and I didn't cut it very well. I don't deal very well with authority, especially if I feel like the person is not treating me with the respect that I deserve, and that I'm not getting paid what I deserve for the quality of work that I'm putting out- like I have to dress a certain way that I'm uncomfortable in.

All three women have balanced the patriarchal oppression found in corporate America against the patriarchal oppression in a capitalist enterprise like pornography and have opted for the latter (although they made it quite clear that the women-owned services treat them much more kindly than those owned by men, especially with respect to advertising technique).

The first of these women entered the industry for economic security in a reaction to 'Reaganomics', but the other two did so primarily for social flexibility. When the final operator speaks of the phone-sex industry as a *mixed bag*, she is not referring in any way to the sexual subordination that such a job might require of her but, rather, to the subordination required by a society that has marginalized her line of work: she has no benefits, no sex workers' union, no societal support.

Because the income of these women is entirely dependent upon verbal ability, they are very conscious of the type of language they produce and often explain specific linguistic qualities that make their language marketable. The features that make the prerecorded message persuasive are the same features that these operators choose to emphasize in their live-conversation exchanges: those that have been defined by linguists working in the area of language and gender as powerless. They explained that they make frequent use of feminine lexical items, incorporate intensifiers into their conversation whenever possible, regularly interrupt their narrative with questions and supportive comments, and adopt a dynamic intonation pattern.

One operator, a thirty-three-year-old European American heterosexual who calls herself Rachel, pointed out that 'to be a really good fantasy maker, you've got to have big tits in your voice'. She clarified this comment by explaining that she creates sexy language through lexical choice, employing 'words which are very feminine':

(7)   I can describe myself now so that it lasts for about five minutes, by using lots of adjectives, spending a lot of time describing the shape of my tits. And that's both – it's not just wasting time, because they need to build up a mental picture in their minds about what you look like, and also it allows me to use words that are very feminine. I always wear peach, or apricot, or black lace- or charcoal-colored lace, not just black. I'll talk about how my hair feels, how curly it is. Yeah, I probably use more feminine words. Sometimes they'll ask me, 'What do you call it [female genitalia]?' And I'll say, well my favorite is the *snuggery*. ... And then they crack up, because it's such a feminine, funny word.

Rachel initiates conversation on the fantasy lines by creating a feminine image of herself through soft words like *curly* and *snuggery* together with nonbasic color terms such as *peach, apricot,* and even *charcoal* instead of black – a creation markedly reminiscent of Lakoff's [1975: 8] early assertion that women are thought to use 'far more precise discriminations in naming colors' than men. Another operator, a European American self-identified butch bisexual whom I will call Sheila, defines what makes her language marketable as an intonational phenomenon. When she explains that she 'talks in a loping tone of voice' with a 'feminine, lilting quality', she alludes to a vocal pattern identified by Sally McConnell-Ginet (1978) almost two decades ago as characteristic of women's speech:

(8)   I feel like definitely the timbre of my voice has a lot to do with it. I don't know, the ability to sound like, I hate to say it, feminine and kind of that lilting quality, and to sound like you're really enjoying it, like you're turned on and you're having a good time. I think that has a lot to do with it because they're always telling me, 'Oh yes, you have such a great voice! God, I love listening to your voice!' I think that's a big part of it, it's just the sound of the person's voice. Some people will tell you that they really like detail and lots of description, and so I can provide that too. But I think so much of it is the way that you say things, more than what you're actually saying. That's kind of funny, you know- sort of an inviting tone of voice.

A third operator, Samantha, a manager of a San Francisco company established in 1990 by a woman and her male-to-female transsexual partner, emphasizes the maintenance work she uses to engage her male callers in a more collaborative exchange, mentioning that she tries to draw out shy callers with supportive questions and comments ('I stop a lot to say things like, 'Oh, do you like that?' You know, that kind of thing. I try to get them to talk as much as I can, because some of these people would sit here and not say one word. And if I get one of those, from time to time I say, 'Hello? Are you still there?''). K. G. Fox alludes to the importance of maintaining this conversational attentiveness when she explains, 'You got to be in the moment, you got to pay attention, you got to keep it fresh. It's a performance and you have to stay in time with your audience. After all, it's really a one-person show.' To make the fantasy effective, then, these fantasy makers consciously cater to their clients by producing a language that adheres to a popular male perception of what women's speech should be: flowery, inviting, and supportive.

Even though an attentive and nurturing discursive style seems to be the primary posture adopted by the women I interviewed, many of them additionally explained how they embellish this style by incorporating more individualized linguistic stereotypes of womanhood, particularly those of age and race. Samantha, for instance, makes her voice sound 'sexy' by performing four different characters: (1) herself, whom she calls Samantha; (2) a girl with a high-pitched eighteen-year-old voice who fulfills the 'beach bunny' stereotype; (3) a woman with a demure Asian accent whom she calls Keesha; and (4) a dominating 'older woman' with an Eastern European accent whom she calls Thela. That these performances serve to approximate linguistic stereotypes rather than reflect any particular linguistic reality is underscored by Sheila in her discussion below; she identifies the irony in the fact that European American women are more successful at performing a Black identity on the phone lines than African American women are:

(9) Most of the guys who call are white, definitely, and for them talking to someone of a different race is exotic and a fetish, you know. So it's really weird. They have this stereotypical idea of how, like, a Black woman should sound and what she's gonna be like. So frequently, we'd have women who were actually Black and we'd hook them up, and they wouldn't believe the woman, that she was Black, because she didn't <u>sound</u> like that stereotype. So conversely, what we had to do- I remember there was this one woman who did calls and she had this sort of Black persona that she would do, which was like the total stereotype. I mean, it really bugged me when I would hear her do it. And the guys loved it. They <u>really</u> thought that this is what a Black woman was!

Sheila's irritation with her colleague's performance points to the restrictive nature of the discourse; operators must vocalize stereotypes that cater to the racist assumptions of their clients. Because the vast majority of male callers request European American women, Sheila explains that operators must also know how to sound 'white' on the telephone. That women of color are often more successful than white women at doing so is underscored by the remarks of a second manager I interviewed, who acknowledged that 'the best white woman we ever had here was Black'. On the fantasy lines, we have the somewhat unusual situation of speakers' being able to perform others' ethnicities more 'successfully' than their own. This fact not only points to the strength of stereotyping in the realm of fantasy but also demonstrates the inseparability of race and gender in the public reception of an identity.

This inseparability is particularly evident in the phone-line performances of Andy, a thirty-three-year-old Mexican American bisexual who poses as a female heterosexual before his male callers. As with the women interviewed for this study, Andy finds that his conversations are well received when he projects a cultural stereotype of vocal femininity: not only is he attentive to the desires of his unsuspecting caller, but he also projects a 'soft and quiet' voice.

(10)   Believe it or not, it's important to them that you're basically in the same mood as they are, that you're enjoying it too. So if you can sound like you <u>are,</u> then that's the better, that's <u>always</u> the better. And the other thing I've found over the years is it's better to sound soft and quiet than loud and noisy...if you're a woman. ... [It's] better to sound ((whispered)) soft, you know, softer. ((in natural voice)) You know, like whispering, rather than ((in loud voice)) OH HO HO HO, ((in natural voice)) really <u>loud,</u> you know, and <u>screaming.</u> 'Cause basically you're in their ear. And physically that's a very strange thing also. Because with the phone, you know, you <u>are</u> in somebody's ear.

To convince callers of his womanhood, Andy style-shifts into a higher pitch, moving the phone away from his mouth so as to soften the perceived intensity of his voice. This discursive shifting, characterized by the performance of the vocal and verbal garb associated with the other sex, might more appropriately be referred to as *cross-expressing*.

The parallel between such an undertaking and the more visual activity of cross-dressing becomes especially apparent in the excerpt below, when Andy performs a European American woman whom he calls Emily:

(11)   So here, I'll give you the voice, okay? Hold on. (4.0) ((in high pitch, soft whisper)) Hello. (2.0) Hello? (2.0) How are <u>you?</u> (1.5) This is <u>Emily.</u> ((in natural voice)) See? It's more – it's more nostrily. I higher the phone – I lift the phone up. Right now I'm just talking regular but I do have the phone lifted up higher. ...And then I lower my vocals (3.0) ((inhales, then in slow, high, breathy voice)) Hello::. Hi::. ((gasps)) Oh <u>yes</u>! (0.5) I'm <u>so</u> horny right ^<u>no</u>^:w. ... ((in natural voice)) It's funny how I've actually taped myself and then played it back, and it's actually <u>two separate</u> voices.

Andy's use of the term *the voice* for his female persona is telling. On the phone-sex lines, person and voice are indistinguishable, with the latter coming to substitute for the former. He begins the conversation by tailoring it to his interactant's state of mind (*Hello. Hello? How are you?*), even before offering up his own name. The phone receiver itself becomes an extension of his vocal apparatus, as he moves it away from his mouth and simultaneously lowers his voice so as to achieve the varied pitch range he associates with European American women's speech.

But female heterosexuality is one of the few constants in Andy's cast of phone-sex characters. He presents himself variously as Asian, Mexican,

African American, and Southern, catering to the desires of individual callers. As with his performance of women's language, he garnishes his speech with features hegemonically associated with particular ethnic groups.

(12)   And then when I put the other little things into it, like – if I want an Oriental, then I have to put a little – you know, then I have to think Oriental sort of ((laughs)) and then it comes out a little bit different. Well it's- for example, okay- (1.0) ((in alternating high and low pitch)) hull^o^::. ^hi^i:::, ^how are^ you::? This is Fong ^Su^u:. ((in natural voice)) See? Then you give them like- I think like I'm ((laughs)) at a Chinese res- taurant, and I'm listening to the waitress-you know, take my order or something. And then the Hispanic is more like ((clears throat, in high breathy voice)) He:llo::::, this is *Ésta* es *Amelia, cómo estás?* (.hhhhh) o:::h *lo siento bien,* (1.0) *rica.* ((in natural voice)) Then I think I'm like watching Spanish dancers or Mexican dancers- you know, with their big dresses? ((sings)) da:: dadada da:: dadada- the *mariachis.* (1.5) And then the Black is a little bit- you know, on and on it goes. [My Black name is] Winona- Winona. Like from the Jeffersons? No, I mean- not the Jeffersons, it was uh- the one guy, Jay-Jay? I can't remember the show name, but anyways the sister was named Winona or Wilona or something like that. And then there's the Southern sound, you know, and then like I say, there's a British sound and a French sound. For the Southern woman I'll use, like, Belle, ((laughs)) something Belle, ((laughs)) Oh, I play right up to it sometimes. ... You <u>def</u>initely have to use ((in slow Southern accent, with elongated vowels)) a Sou:::thern a::ccent. ((laughs, in natural voice)) Abso<u>lute</u>ly, that has to come through. Shining. So that's a real concen- trator, I have to really- you know, be really quiet.

Andy models his Asian persona on a submissive waitress, adopting a quiet voice that serves to highlight the inequality between himself and his conver- sational master; his voice, perhaps in attempted imitation of a tonal language, moves back and forth between two distinct pitches. His Mexican voice, in contrast, which he models on a flamboyant Spanish dancer, is more overtly sexual; with breathy inhalation and emphatic pronunciation, he manages to eroticize a number of very common Spanish expressions. Because the success of the interaction depends on the middle-class white male caller's ability to recognize the fantasy frame, the operator's language tends to recall dominant instead of localized gender and race ideologies – ones often deemed highly offensive by the group to whom they are ascribed.

    Yet the fantasy maker, while admitting the often degrading nature of such an enterprise, nevertheless views her employment of this language as power- ful and identifies her position in the conversational exchange as superior. The operators who participated in the study reported that they are completely in control of each conversation: they initiate and dominate the conversational exchange; they are creators of the fantasy story line and scenario; they can decide what kind of fantasies they will entertain; and they can terminate the conversation with a simple flick of the index finger. Indeed, Natalie Rhys (1993), a phone-sex worker in San Francisco who recently wrote about her experiences in the book *Call Me Mistress: Memoirs of a Phone Sex Performer*, comments that the real victims in the exchange are the customers, who feed their time, energy, and money into a noncaring enterprise that exploits them: 'To the workers, pornography is a job no more exciting than any other job. To the owners and managers, it's a business. Both feel superior to the customers. If this attitude seems calloused, consider that it's difficult to have much respect for someone when the only contact you have with him is when you're exploiting his neediness. You might have compassion for him, but not respect' (119).

In accordance with this outlook, most of the women I spoke with described their work first and foremost as artistic. Sheila calls herself a *telephone fantasy artist*. Rachel, whose self-definition is reproduced below, describes what she does for a living as *auditory improvisational theater on the theme of eros*:

(13)   I'm a good storyteller. A lot of what I do is wasted on most of these peo-
       ple. They're not bright enough to know some of the words I use. And
       then about every fifteenth call is one that makes it worthwhile. Because
       it's someone who will go, 'God, you're really good at this! You really
       use language well! This is fun! I was expecting this to be really weird,
       but you're cool!' I have a large vocabulary. I read a lot and I'll use other
       words. I don't own a television. I think that's a big part of my greater
       command of language than the average human being. And since I've
       gotten into this, I've also decided that if I'm going to be a storyteller, I'm
       going to study more about storytelling. I've listened to Garrison Keillor
       for years, and in the last year or so, I've taped him several times and lis-
       tened for the devices that he's using to be a more effective storyteller.

This particular operator has written erotica for a number of years and identifies herself primarily as a *good storyteller*. She explains that she actively incorporates storytelling techniques into her own fantasy creations, imitating
Garrison Keillor of *Prairie Home Companion*, as well as a number of other
well-known storytellers. She and the other fantasy makers would often jokingly refer to themselves as *phone whores* and their switchboard operators as
phone pimps, but they did not perceive the conversational exchange as representative of any particular asymmetrical sexual reality. Like the woman in
this excerpt, who mentions her 'large vocabulary' and her 'greater command

of language than the average human being', the operators interviewed felt that they were so superior linguistically to the average man who called the service that male power was just not an issue. The only exchanges they did perceive as asymmetrical, and in which they consequently did not like to participate, were those domination calls where the male caller overtly restricted their freedom of expression by limiting their feedback to a subservient *yes sir* and *no sir*. Many of the women refused to take these calls altogether, although one operator did say that these low verbal expectations did at least allow her to get a lot of dishes done.

Still, the same fantasy operators would readily admit that they had to subdue their own creativity in order to please a comparatively uncreative audience. The fantasy maker above who considers herself a storyteller, for instance, explained that her linguistic creativity makes her less popular than some of the other fantasy operators because she often refuses to adopt the expected 'stupid, pregnant, and dumb' voice:

(14)　If I'm in a surly mood and I get a call from a guy who sounds like he just let go of his jackhammer and graduated with a 1.2 average, you know. I have a hard time with those guys. I mean, they need love too, but jesus! Dumb people bug me.... It's hard to realize that you're a lot smarter than whoever it is you're dealing with, and number one, if you're really bright then you won't let them know it, and number two, if they do figure it out, then you're in trouble, because they don't like it, especially if it's a man. I mean, that's just the way it is. Girls are supposed to be stupid and pregnant, or just dumb, so that the testosterone type can get out there and conquer the world for you, or whatever it is that they do.... I'm approaching this from the angle that I want to be a better storyteller, I want to increase my linguistic abilities. But that isn't what the average customer wants.

Another operator similarly explained that she had to 'be constantly walking that line' between embracing a sexuality for herself and catering to customer expectations of her sexuality. Interesting in her interview, reproduced in excerpt (15), is that she describes her clients' perception of women's language as a submissive sexual position:

(15)　I wonder if it really is women's language or is it mostly that we're repeating what it is that the men want to hear and want to believe that women like and think. I think it's more what's in their heads. You know, scenarios where I'm being mildly submissive, even though they don't call it that, and they're like calling me a slut and a horny little bitch. ... It's a total turn off, I never think of myself that way. And that definitely goes through their heads. ... So having to sometimes sort of like repeat their ideas back to them because it's what they want to hear can be a drag. So sometimes it's more my idea than my language and sometimes it's there and it's what they're reading out of these stupid magazines, you know, that they really want to believe women are like. ... It's interesting to be constantly walking that line where you're trying to make sure they're happy and please them and get them off and at the same time- you know, for me, I want to do my best not to perpetuate all the bullshit that goes on in their minds. It is a difficult task sometimes. It's a challenge to come up with ways that you can still turn them on without perpetuating all the bullshit about women that they believe.

She realizes that the male fantasy of female sexuality is so firmly rooted within our culture that even though she tries not to perpetuate it, there is little she can do to dispel it. Her feeling is also shared by Andy. He states that being a man has given him more liberty to speak against such degradation, yet he also recognizes the negative influence such attitudes have had on him as an individual:

(16)   What I think has bothered me over the years more than anything about it has been the degradation of women that I've had to kind of feel because of the way [men] <u>think</u> and <u>feel</u> towards women – a lot of them. You know, there is a lot of degradation involved and basically it filters over to <u>you</u> if you're not careful, and you could yourself either feel degraded or degrade others. [I think I notice this] more than the girls, because the girls are interested, I think, in just <u>pleasing</u>, you know, and trying to do the best they could on the call, whereas I feel that I'm beyond doing good on the call.

Both Sheila and Andy speculated that for the male callers this interactive fantasy was in some sense very real, evidenced by the dismay of those callers who for some reason came to suspect that the voice on the telephone was not the beautiful young blonde it presented itself to be. It seems that although these employees are aware of and wish to break away from the negative stereotypes about women's language and sexuality, they are restrained by their clients' expectations of the interaction, and they must therefore try to strike a balance between employing a creative discourse and a stereotypical one.

Conclusion

What exists on the adult-message lines is a kind of style shifting that is based primarily on gender and secondarily on variables of age, class, geography, and race. When on the telephone, the fantasy-line operators in this study, whether Asian American, African American, European American, or Latino, switch into a definable conversational style that they all associate with 'women's language'. Bourdieu (1977) might argue that these women, as 'agents continuously subjected to the sanctions of the linguistic market', have learned this style through a series of positive and negative reinforcements:

> Situations in which linguistic productions are explicitly sanctioned and evaluated, such as examinations or interviews, draw our attention to the existence of mechanisms determining the price of discourse which operate in every linguistic interaction (e.g., the doctor-pateint or lawyer-client relation) and more generally in all social relations. It follows that agents continuously subjected to the sanctions of the linguistic market, functioning as a system of positive or negative reinforcements, acquire durable dispositions which are the basis of their perception and appreciation of the state of the linguistic market and consequently of their strategies for expression. (654)

According to Bourdieu, speakers develop their strategies for expression through their experiences within the linguistic market, a notion that he refers to elsewhere as *habitus*. In their interactional histories (e.g., at school, in the family), the female fantasy-line operators have received positive reinforcement for this particular style of discourse and are now, through additional reinforcement within the workplace, selling it back to the culture at large for a high price. Like examinations and interviews, fantasy-line conversations are situations in which linguistic production is explicitly sanctioned and evaluated. If the operator fails to produce the appropriate discursive style (one that is feminine, inviting, and supportive), she will lose her clients and therefore her economic stability. But for such a style to be so overtly reinforced within this particular medium of discourse, the same reinforcement must exist within the larger public, so that women at a very early age begin to, in the words of Bourdieu, 'acquire durable dispositions' toward this particular strategy of expression.

The question then follows: How can current definitions of linguistic power account for the fact that on the fantasy lines, speech that has been traditionally thought of as 'powerless' suddenly becomes a very powerful sexual commodity? Many of the authors represented in this volume have followed Penelope Eckert and Sally McConnell-Ginet (1992) in arguing that discussions of gender should be located within particular communities of practice. By studying the local meanings attached to interactions, researchers will develop a more flexible understanding of gender – an understanding that allows for variability of meaning within and among communities. These San Francisco-based fantasy-line operators challenge theories that have categorized women's language as powerless and men's language as powerful. Within the context of the adult-message industry, women have learned that manipulating the female conversational stereotype can in fact be powerful, and sometimes even enjoyable. It potentially brings them tens of thousands of dollars; it allows them to support themselves without having to participate in a patriarchal business structure; it lets them exercise sexual power without fear of bodily harm or judicial retribution. Clearly, there is another dimension to power besides the dichotomy of oppressor-oppressed. To say that all women are powerless in sexual interaction, as MacKinnon does, or to say that all women are powerless when they assume a role traditionally thought of as subordinate in a conversation, denies real women's experience of their situation. The women quoted in this chapter view the success of their exchange in terms of how creative they can be in fulfilling a fantasy. Although they recognize that they often have to perpetuate the girly-magazine stereotype of women to maintain a clientele, they consider the men who require this stereotype so unimaginative that to attribute any power to them in the conversational exchange is ludicrous. This somewhat ironic state of affairs indicates that any theory of linguistic power in cross-sex interaction must allow for a variety of influences with respect to individual consent.

NOTES

1. The transcription conventions used in this chapter are adapted from those developed by Gail Jefferson:

h	an *h* indicates an exhalation (the more *h*'s, the longer the exhalation)
.h	an *h* with a period preceding it indicates an inhalation (the more *h*'s, the longer the inhalation)
(0.4)	indicates length of pause within and between utterances, timed in tenths of a second
a - a	a hyphen with spaces before and after indicates a short pause, less than 0.2 seconds
sa-	a hyphen immediately following a letter indicates an abrupt cutoff in speaking
(( ))	double parentheses enclose nonverbal movements and extralinguistic commentary
(text)	single parentheses enclose words that are not clearly audible (i.e., best guesses)
[ ]	brackets enclose words added to clarify the meaning of the text
<u>text</u>	underlining indicates syllabic stress
CAPS	upper case indicates louder or shouted talk
:	a colon indicates a lengthening of a sound (the more colons, the longer the sound)
.	a period indicates falling intonation
,	a comma indicates continuing intonation
?	a question mark indicates rising intonation at the end of a syllable or word
^ a ^	rising arrows indicate a higher pitch for enclosed word(s) or syllable(s)
...	deletion of some portion of the original text

REFERENCES

Bourdieu, Pierre. 1977. The economics of linguistic exchanges. *Social Science Information* 16: 645–668.

Coward, Rosalind. 1986. Porn: What's in it for women? *New Statesman.* 13 June.

Eckert, Penelope and Sally McConnell-Ginet. 1992. Think practically and look locally: Language and gender as community-based practice. *Annual Review of Anthropology* 21: 461–490.

Fishman, Pamela. 1978. Interaction: The work that women do. *Social Problems* 25: 397–406.

Hochschild, Arlie Russell. 1983. *The Managed Heart: Commercialization of Human Feeling.* Berkeley, California: University of California Press.

Lakoff, Robin. 1975. *Language and Woman's Place.* New York: Harper and Row.

Lutz, Catherine. 1986. Emotion, thought, and estrangement: Emotion as a cultural category. *Cultural Anthropology* 1: 287–309.

Lutz, Catherine. 1990. Engendered emotion: Gender, power and the rhetoric of emotional control in American discourse. In Lila Abu-Lughod and Catherine Lutz (eds.) *Language and the Politics of Emotion.* Cambridge: Cambridge University Press. 69–91.

MacKinnon, Catherine. 1987. *Feminism Unmodified: Discourses on Life and Law.* Cambridge: Harvard University Press.

McConnell-Ginet, Sally. 1978. Intonation in a man's world. *Signs* 3: 541–559.

Rhys, Natalie. 1993. *Call Me Mistress: Memoirs of a Phone Sex Performer.* Novato, California: Miwok Press.

Williams, Frederick. 1985. Technology and communication. In Thomas W. Benson (ed.) *Speech Communication in the 20th Century.* Carbondale, Colorado: Southern Illinois University Press. 184–195.

CHAPTER 17

Language and Identity in Drag Queen Performances

RUSTY BARRETT

Drag Queens

This chapter examines language variation in performances by African American drag queens (AADQs) in gay bars in Texas, focusing on a style of speaking AADQs refer to as speaking like a 'white woman'. It is typically assumed that the use of a particular language variety implies a desire to identify with the social group associated with that variety (Labov 1972; LePage and Tabouret-Keller 1985). However, AADQs do not identify themselves with whites or with women, despite using the 'white woman' style. Drag queens are gay men who dress and, in certain respects, behave in ways that are typically associated with women. Drag queens should not be confused with other transgender groups such as transsexuals or transvestites. Transsexuals are individuals who feel that their gender identity does not correspond to their biological sex. Transsexuals often pursue sex-reassignment surgery so that their physical bodies will correspond to their gender identity. Also, transsexuality is independent from sexual identity, as transsexuals do not share any particular sexual orientation. For example, a transsexual who is biologically male and sexually attracted to women may undergo surgery to become a lesbian. Drag queens differ from male-to-female transsexuals in that they do not identify themselves as women but as men who adopt feminine gender characteristics for the sake of performance. Drag queens are also distinct from other types of transvestites or 'cross-dressers' (individuals who dress in clothing associated with the opposite gender). The majority of transvestites are heterosexual men who wear women's clothing (often only in private).

Gender Performativity and Indexicality

In our everyday experience we rarely question what exactly makes an individual's speech recognizable as male or female. Two concepts that are important for understanding social behavior related to gender are indexicality and performativity. *Indexicality* refers to indirect social meanings associated with particular linguistic signs (words, pronunciations, or syntactic constructions). Indexical meanings must be distinguished from referential meanings of the 'real-world' concept corresponding to a given sign. The terms *have sexual relations with* and *shag* share referential meaning because they correspond to the same physical act. However, the two terms have very different indexical meanings because they are associated with different social contexts (including the identity of speakers). The idea of Bill Clinton saying 'I did not *shag that woman*' (as opposed to *have sexual relations*) is humorous because the indexical meanings associated with *shag* are inappropriate for a speaker whose identity is president of the United States speaking in a public context.

The term *performativity* (Austin 1962) refers to the ability of language to make a change that extends beyond language. A statement like *The sky is blue* is primarily descriptive and does not change our understanding of the sky or the quality of being blue. A statement like *I now pronounce you man and wife* is performative because it may make an actual change in the world. When this statement is uttered in the proper context, two individuals are recognized as being married to one another. For an utterance to succeed as a performative (to be *felicitous*), listeners must recognize it as the repetition of an utterance that has previously succeeded in making a particular change in the world. The identity of the speaker and the context in which an utterance is made are also important for making a performative successful. If the statement *I now pronounce you man and wife* is preceded by the statement *By the power invested in me by the state of inebriation* and occurs in the context of friends drinking excessively, we would not consider the two individuals to actually be legally married because the social context of the utterance would not be appropriate for this particular performative.

The ways in which speakers manipulate indexical meanings may also be considered a performative use of language. Because particular linguistic signs index specific social contexts and speaker identities, the use of a given sign may performatively assert the social background of a speaker or the social context in which an interaction occurs. Upon hearing the phrase *once upon a time*, for example, most listeners recognize that the speaker intends to index the genre of the fairy tale. Such uses of indexical meanings are performative because they create a social context for interpreting language. Listeners will accept that they are about to hear a fairy tale just as they accept that a marriage has occurred when they hear *I now pronounce you man and wife*.

Judith Butler (1990) has argued that social behaviors associated with gender are performative because they are based on a series of repetitions (or citations) associated with appropriate 'masculine' or 'feminine' behavior in specific contexts. Interpretations of social behavior depend upon recognition of a sign as a citation of previous instances in which that sign has successfully entailed a given indexical meaning. Because such repetitions depend upon the personal experiences of individual listeners, indexical meanings may be specific to a given community. Thus, the social behaviors that index masculinity and femininity differ widely across cultures. The American joke 'I'm not sure if he's gay or just British' conveys that the indexical meanings associated with masculinity in Britain may not be felicitous to Americans (who base judgments of sexual orientation on a different set of performative citations). Among AADQs, the use of highly standard and feminized English, an exaggerated stereotype of Lakoff's (1975) 'woman's language', is referred to as 'speaking like a white woman'. The indexical association between hyperstandard English and 'white women' is a local indexical meaning in that it is specific to AADQs. The ability to control the 'white woman' style of speaking is considered crucial to a successful AADQ performance. For example, a producer of AADQ performances in my research told one drag queen that she should just 'keep her mouth shut' because she was not a 'white woman'. Among AADQs, the use of 'white woman' speech is considered a marker of social class (rather than race or gender) and successful use of 'white woman' speech indexes skill in presenting one's self as sophisticated and glamorous, traits that are considered vital to a successful AADQ performance. AADQs do not, however, simply appropriate a 'white woman' style of speaking. Rather, they alternate between the 'white woman' style and other varieties to index a multi-faceted identity. In addition, AADQs often juxtapose contradictory ways of speaking to produce political critiques of the racism and homophobia that they confront in their daily lives.

The 'White Woman' Style as Used by AADQs

AADQs mix the use of the 'white woman' style with stereotyped forms of gay male speech and forms of African American Vernacular English (AAVE). The combination of these three speaking styles is the generally 'unmarked' norm for AADQ speech. The example below is taken from RuPaul's speech at a 1993 rally for gay and lesbian rights in Washington, D.C. In this example, she begins speaking in the 'white woman' style, but also includes features of gay male speech (such as the use of 'baby' and 'Miss Thing') and African American English (such as the use of the 'call-response' routine in lines 7 and 8).

Extract 1

1 You know people ask me all the time
2 Where I see myself in ten years
3 And I say I see myself in the White House, baby!
4 Miss Thing goes to Washington
5 Can you see it? Wha- we gonna paint the mother pink, OK?
6 We put one president in the White House, I figure you can do it again.
7 Everybody say love! [audience responds, 'love!']
8 Everybody say love! [audience responds again, 'love!']
9 Now drive that down Pennsylvania Avenue!

In many of their performances, AADQs use alternations between speaking styles to draw on the indexical associations between speaking styles and social contexts. In Extract 2, the speaker performs a series of sales pitches for the different types of 'rat traps' used in various neighborhoods in a city in Texas. In the first few lines, associated with a small mousetrap, the speaker uses the 'white woman' style. The speaker repeatedly uses final rising intonation in the phrases in the first few sentences (lines 1–3 and 5–6). This rising intonation is characteristic of the 'white woman' style and reflects stereotypes of young, upper-class women's speech in the United States. The speech style indexes the upper-class white neighborhood where the 'rat trap' would be used. In lines 7 and 8, she stops using the 'white woman' style, ending the series of phrases with final high intonations. The use of the term 'mother fucker' clearly differentiates the two styles, as obscenities are not part of the upper-class white woman style. In the remainder of the routine, the AADQ switches into African American English, using multiple negation (line 10), reducing word-final consonants (for example, [don] for 'don't'; [fu:ʔ] for 'food', lines 10 and 14, respectively).

Extract 2

1 OK! What we're gonna talk about is, um, rat traps, um.
   [holds up mouse trap]
2 This is a rat trap from \<name of upper-class white neighborhood>.
3 It's made by BMW. It's real compact.
4 It's, thank you. [audience cheers].
5 It's really good. It's very convenient and there's insurance on it.
6 And this is from \<name of upper-class white neighborhood>.
7 OK, now for \<name of housing project>
   [holds up large rat trap]
8 This rat trap is made by Cadillac. It's a big mother fucker.
   [holds up gun]

 9 Now for <name of inner city area>
10 You just don't need no rat trap.
11 Cause those mother fuckers look like dogs out there.
12 Shit!
13 I put in a piece of cheese, the mother fucker told me,
14 'Next time put in some dog food.'

In the following extract, the AADQ makes explicit reference to the absence of obscenities in the 'white woman' style of speaking. Although the entire sequence is spoken in the 'white woman' style, the speaker says that she is not supposed to use obscenities (line 2–3), but continues to use obscenities (line 4) despite explicitly stating that it is not proper behavior. In the final line, she plays on the polysemy of being 'always on her knees' (either in prayer or in performing fellatio) in order to highlight the disjuncture between the performed identity as an upper-class 'white woman' and her 'actual' identity as a working-class African American gay man.

Extract 3

1 Are you ready to see some muscles? [audience yells] ... Some dick?
2 Excuse me I'm not supposed to say that.
3 ... words like that in the microphone.
4 Like shit, fuck, and all that, you know?
5 I am a Christian woman.
6 I go to church.
7 I'm *always* on my knees.

In the final example, an AADQ mocks white stereotypes about African American men by using the white woman style of speaking. In this example, performed in a gay bar with a predominantly African American audience, the AADQ acts out a confrontation between a wealthy white woman and an African American man. Although laughing at fears of rape is clearly misogynistic, the performance is primarily a response to the myth of the African American rapist. As Angela Davis (1983) has noted, false rape charges have historically served as excuses for the murder (lynching) of African American men. The myth of the African American rapist is founded upon the stereotype that African American men are all sexually desirous of white women and will use violence to feed this desire. This stereotype is particularly ridiculous for the gay men and drag queens in the bar, who in all likelihood have no desires for any woman (white or otherwise) but must still deal with the ramifications of the myth of the

African American rapist, including unfounded fears of violence on the part of whites.

Extract 4

1 I'm a rich white woman in <name of wealthy neighborhood>
2 And you're going to try to come after me, OK?
3 And I want you to just...
4 I'm going to be running, OK?
5 And I'm gonna fall down, OK? OK?
6 And I'm just gonna... look at you...
7 And you don't do anything
8 You hold the gun...
9 Goddamn – he got practice. [audience laughter]
10 I can tell you're experienced. [He holds the gun, but so that it faces down, not as if he were aiming it]
11 OK hold it.
12 You know you know how to hold it, don't play it off...
13 Hold that guy... Shit... Goddamn...
14 [Female audience member] Hold that gun!
15 That's right fish! Hold that gun! Shit!
16 OK now, y'all, I'm fish y'all, white fish witch!
17 And I'm gonna be running cause three Black men with big dicks chasing me!
18 [Points to audience member] He's the leader, OK?
19 Now you know I gotta fall, I want y'all to say, 'Fall bitch!'
20 [Audience] Fall bitch! [She falls, then rises, makes gasping sounds, alternating with 'bum-biddy-bum' imitations of the music used in suspense scenes in film]
21 Now show me the gun! [The audience member holds up the gun and the drag queen performs an exaggerated faint]

In this example, the AADQ begins by using the white woman style (lines 1–8), with hyperstandard forms such as the repeated use of 'going to' (as opposed to 'gonna'). She then switches into forms more typical of AAE (for example, 'he got practice'), stepping out of character in working to get the audience member to hold the gun properly. She instructs the audience member not to do anything, but just to hold the gun. The man with the gun is basically passive throughout the exchange and the 'white woman' faints primarily based on fear founded in racism. The performance continues by addressing a corollary to the myth of the African American rapist, the myth that African American women are highly promiscuous. In the final part of the performance, the AADQ performs the character of an African American woman, speaking primarily in AAE. In contrast to the white woman, the African American woman tells the man that he doesn't need the gun and that she will give in willingly because she can tell from the size of his feet that he is well endowed.

Extract 4 (continued)

22 Now this black fish…
23 Black men's running after her…
24 I ain't no boy! Fuck y'all! Fuck y'all mother fuckers! [she looks at the gun]
25 You don't have to use that baby, I see them size feet.
26 Come on! Come on!

In this example, the white woman style is used to produce a political critique of racist stereotypes associated with the myth of the African American rapist. The performance touches on a number of stereotypes associated with the myth, including the fragility of white women, the supposed promiscuity of African American women and stereotypes of the sexual prowess and endowment of African American men. Here, the linguistic variety of the dominant group is used to mark white fear and insecurity. Although AADQs often claim that the white woman style is crucial for successfully conveying sophistication, here the white woman style is used to laugh at white women's fear of violence.

Conclusion

The use of the white woman style by AADQs demonstrates the performative nature of gendered speech patterns. Viewing linguistic markers of gender as indexical signs that performatively assert particular gender identities provides insight into the ways in which gendered speech may be appropriated and used in unexpected contexts. AADQs appropriate the linguistic citations that index a gendered identity, without claiming affiliation with actual white women. The white woman style may also be used as a form of symbolic resistance to racist stereotypes, as in the last example. The use of the 'white woman' style as a form of resistance suggests that the appropriation of a dominant hegemonic variety need not represent collaboration or affiliation with the dominant group, but may actually serve to undermine the hegemony of the dominant variety.

REFERENCES

Austin, J. L. 1962. *How to Do Things with Words*. Cambridge, Massachusetts.: Harvard University Press.

Butler, Judith. 1990. *Gender Trouble: Feminism and Subversion of Identity*. New York: Routledge.

Davis, Angela. 1983. *Women, Race and Class*. New York: Random House.

Labov, William. 1972. *Sociolinguistic Patterns*. Philadelphia, Pennsylvania.: University of Pennsylvania Press.

Lakoff, Robin. 1975. *Language and Woman's Place*. New York: Harper and Row.

LePage, Robert B. and Andrée Tabouret-Keller. 1985. *Acts of Identity: Creole-based Approaches to Language and Ethnicity*. Cambridge: Cambridge University Press.

PART III

STYLE, STYLIZATION
AND IDENTITY

Editors' Introduction to Part III

The concept of *style* has already surfaced in several chapters in earlier sections of the volume – for example in Jenny Cheshire's and Penelope Eckert's chapters in Part I and in Rusty Barrett's chapter in Part II. William Labov used the idea of style in his variationist survey research, where it became conventional to study 'the effects of the social situation' on patterns of speech, analysed quantitatively. If we look back at Peter Trudgill's chapter (4) in Part I, we see tabulated statistical information that summarizes how the speech patterns of particular social class groups shift when speakers are performing different tasks in a sociolinguistic interview, such as speaking casually versus reading a written passage of text. Labov referred to this as *stylistic stratification* – the hierarchical effect that we can derive from looking at language variation across situations in this way. Style was thought of as 'intrapersonal' variation – the way that the language use of any single individual is itself variable rather than consistent.

But as Sociolinguistics came to be more sensitive in its analysis of how language is socially contextualized, as it became more interested in social meaning, and as it invested more heavily in ethnographic methods (see Eckert, Chapter 10), so style needed to be approached in more sophisticated ways. In this part of the book we use the term style as a short-hand way of referring to sociolinguistic research on the social contextualization of linguistic variation – how speakers use the resources of language variation to create social meanings. These meanings relate to how a speaker projects his or her own persona or identity, but also to how a speaker projects an image of a relationship between her/himself and another person. So we are talking about style with respect to *personal and relational identities*.

The two earliest and most distinctive theoretical approaches to the sociolinguistic analysis of style after Labov's foundational research were those of Allan Bell, with his *audience design* model (Chapter 18), and Howard Giles, with his *speech accommodation* model (Chapter 19). These two approaches have many features in common, principally in that each is concerned with how speakers are able to adapt aspects of their own speech in relation to the speech of an addressee. Bell's central insight is that speakers design their speech 'for their audiences', and when they do this they stylistically manipulate the degree to which their speech resembles that of their interlocutors. Bell's first, influential study was an investigation of newsreaders' speech, when he observed that the same set of broadcasters produced measurably different frequencies of particular sociolinguistic variants, especially intervocalic /t/ voicing, when they were broadcasting to more local and more national audiences in New Zealand. Whereas Labov's account of style-shifting was based on the notion that speakers become more aware of their own speech under specific conditions, Bell argues that a different principle must be at work in his radio data – specifically that broadcasters must be sensitive to the variable sociolinguistic norms of different social groups. In his chapter Bell then refers to some other studies, such as Nikolas Coupland's investigation of the speech of a travel agency assistant's speech to different client groups, where similar audience design effects are apparent. There is a significant constructionist aspect to Bell's theory, particularly when he appeals to the idea of *initiative style*, which is when a speaker initiates a change in the apparent social situation through a change in speech style. That is, style does not only 'respond' to changes in the audience dimension of social situations; it constructs different qualities of the social situation and of social relationships.

Even though it clearly has its roots in variationist research, the audience design model is therefore not restricted to the 'society determines language' model that underlay early variationism. The same is true for Giles's speech accommodation theory, which was developed in the Social Psychology of Language rather than in Sociolinguistics itself. Howard Giles can be credited more than anyone else with bringing the study of linguistic diversity into Social Psychology, and for advancing our understanding of *social identity* and *intergroup relations*. The intergroup perspective starts with the view that people often act socially in their capacity as members of social groups, as opposed to acting as individuals, and this insight runs through some key aspects of accommodation theory. In Chapter 19 Giles takes an extended look at relationships between police officers and members of the public, and at how relationships between these groups are mediated by language and communication. Interactions between police and the public can show different degrees of *convergence* and *divergence*, for example in 'traffic stop' encounters. Giles models the relational and practical consequences of convergence and divergence in these encounters, by way of illustrating more general processes of speech and communicative accommodation.

The accommodation model can be applied to many different facets of communicative action, including accent and dialect variation. Indeed,

Coupland's travel agency study (as summarized in Bell's chapter 18) was conceived within an accommodation theory framework. Accommodation theory is constructivist in the sense that it assumes that speakers have a degree of agentive control over the relationships that they can construct communicatively. It tries to specify these processes in the argument that speakers are often motivated to 'make communication more effective' and to 'gain social approval', and that they can go some way to achieving these goals through convergent accommodative acts; also that they can achieve the opposite effects via divergence. Even so, both audience design and accommodation theory have generally been researched quantitatively and quasi-experimentally (see our discussion of different research methods in the general Introduction), in study designs that operate with fixed social categories and look for statistical correlations of various sorts. While they have established some important generalizations – not least that speakers very generally *do* adapt their language in relation to audiences and that this is what we can call a 'pro-social' adaptive process – they have not generally explored the emergent meanings of style in particular social settings. Later research, including all four of the remaining chapters in Part II, complement the first two by using qualitative, ethnographic methods.

Ben Rampton's research has broken new ground in the sociolinguistic analysis of language and social context. We have included Rampton's study of *crossing* in this Part of the book (Chapter 20), mainly because it explains Rampton's use of the term *stylization*, which has become an important concept broadening stylistic analysis. Even so, Rampton's research deals with cross-language as well as (conventionally defined) stylistic processes, and therefore also makes an important contribution to the Sociolinguistics of multilingualism (see Part V). Rampton frames his research as Interactional Sociolinguistics or Sociolinguistic Discourse Analysis. His work contributes to our understanding of language in relation to cultural continuity and change, and in those ways it is also highly relevant to the contents of Part VI.

Rampton works with interactional data revealed through radio-microphone recordings of kids in multi-racial settings in British secondary schools. In this chapter he is particularly interested in the role of sociolinguistic *crossing* – kids using speech styles, sometimes in fragmentary ways, that are most commonly associated with members of ethnic groups *other than* their own (at least, in the sense that we might usually expect this to be the case). Crossing is therefore a process of 'styling the other' in one's own speech. Rampton identifies *stylized Asian English* as a style used by some kids at transitional moments of interaction to destabilize social and ethnic arrangements. Stylized Asian English appears to be a form of 'heretical discourse' (p. 296) that is sometimes able to lead participants to question orthodox assumptions about social and ethnic group membership. It plays with ethnicity and might be one of the means by which inter-ethnic relations come to be renegotiated. Rampton presents crossing as a form of *multiple voicing*, and draws on the theoretical work of Mikhail Bakhtin to help explain the social consequences of creatively deploying 'other people's voices'. There are connections to be made here to the analysis of quotative expressions (Chapter 6), but also to performative explanations of discourses of masculinity (Chapter 13), of nerd girl identity (Chapter 15) and of drag queens (Chapter 17). Indeed the concept of *cultural performance* surfaces in relation to all of these and many later chapters, where the work of Richard Bauman and Charles Briggs (see Chapter 41, in Part VI) is particularly helpful in providing theoretical depth.

Cecilia Cutler's chapter (21) and Nikolas Coupland's chapter (22) both work with the concepts of stylistic creativity, voicing and performance. Cutler traces how one white, middle-class, New York-based youth, Mike, moves into, and later out from, a self-presentational style associated with hip-hop culture and black ethnicity. Hip-hop is clearly a cultural style more than an ethnic ('Black') style, and the use of African American Vernacular (AAV) speech features is only one part of its constitution. As with Eckert's jocks and burn-outs, dress and demeanor are as much part of the performance as language is. Hip-hop is a transnational style (see Alastair Pennycook's Chapter 23), promoted through rap music and its associated visual and expressive motifs. Even so, it is the linguistic aspects of Mike's self-presentation that Cutler mainly focuses on, for example how he incorporates AAV grammar and lexis into his speech at salient moments, and quite consistently so at one stage of his life. Mike's case is a particularly clear and engaging one in the study of sociolinguistic crossing, but Cutler also raises important questions about the durability of stylistic projections of this sort (was Mike's engagement with hip-hop only ephemeral?) and about their cultural impact (how do different groups of people react to this sort of appropriation of cultural styles and voices?).

Coupland's study is located in the politics of social class in Britain and specifically in local experiences and historical conflicts around class in the South Wales Valleys. But the fact that this study focuses on brash and fictive invocations and voicings of social class – in the performance of a 'pantomime Dame' in the context of a low-budget theatrical performance – might make us ask whether we should read social significance into 'performed data'. Bauman and Briggs's perspectives are helpful here (again see Chapter 41) in the way they emphasize the role of performance as a routinely important resource in the articulation of cultural difference. They argue that 'culture' in many senses *only* exists *in its performance*, and that some sorts of performance are able to highlight cultural values particularly clearly. Performance is often *met-acultural*. It exposes cultural forms and values to public scrutiny, and opens them up for reappraisal. This is Coupland's line in the interpretation of the pantomime Dame's use of local vernacular (South Wales) sociolinguistic features, in stark contrast to her voicing of 'posh' and (in this context) 'English' features. Coupland argues that, even in a single continuous data extract, the Dame is able to recreate old cultural, class-based antagonisms that are very familiar to audiences in the Valleys. The Dame's heavily stylized voicings are performed for local humorous effect. But they arguably have much wider resonances, bringing historical cultural experiences into the moment of performance.

Finally in Part III, Alastair Pennycook's chapter (23) widens the analysis of style onto a global stage. As in the Cutler analysis, we are dealing with the appropriation and recontextualization of hip-hop, a popular cultural style, but now in its musical as well as its linguistic forms. Rather than deal with a single case, Pennycook comments on how hip-hop styles *flow* across *global* spaces, and how they are then embedded and *localized* in different sociolinguistic settings. So we are dealing here with the global agenda for Sociolinguistics that Jan Blommaert writes about (in Chapter 38). Identities are central to Pennycook's interpretation, as they have been in all chapters in this Part of the book, whether we mean relational identities (Chapters 18 and 19), ethnic identities (Chapters 20 and 21) or social class identities (Chapter 22). But Pennycook opens a perspective on socio-cultural identities that cannot easily be labeled, and this too has been the tenor of some of the earlier chapters' arguments. What might appear to be the recycling of a known social class or ethnic identity turns out to be a multi-layered, creative semiotic act, which ends up challenging as much as confirming our understanding of those categories.

Pennycook presents instances of Hawaiian and other Pacific Islands hip-hop styles that have mutually influenced each other as well as borrowed from USA-sourced styles, and of French-based as well as English-based hip-hop networks. Among many others mentioned are Asian (for example, Hong Kong and Korean) performers and genres, whose interconnections blur conventional cultural and indeed linguistic categories. The authority of a 'world language' such as English is, Pennycook argues, challenged in densely transcultural and specifically localized hip-hop performances which, for example, play with rhyming and scripting conventions. To understand globalized restylings of hip-hop we need more elaborate theories of performance and performativity. Pennycook endorses Judith Butler's *post-modernist* ideas about the performative dimension of language, which he argues can be characterized as repeated acts of stylization 'that congeal over time to produce the appearance of substance' (p. 336). This interpretive stance is the one we referred to in the general Introduction as being 'anti-realist', and we suggested it was a more extreme constructivist stance than is generally adopted in the sociolinguistic mainstream. At the same time, the stylistic processes that Pennycook is dealing with here are themselves among the most creative and *detraditionalizing* ones that Sociolinguistics has encountered, and it is always necessary to match one's line of interpretation to what the data show.

CHAPTER 18

Language Style as Audience Design

ALLAN BELL

What is Style?

Language style is one of the most challenging aspects of sociolinguistic variation. The basic principle of language style is that an individual speaker does not always talk in the same way on all occasions. Style means that speakers have alternatives or choices – a *'that* way' which could have been chosen instead of a *'this* way'. Speakers talk in different ways in different situations, and these different ways of speaking can carry different social meanings.

Style constitutes one whole dimension of linguistic variation – the range of variation within the speech of an individual speaker. It intersects with what William Labov has called the 'social' dimension of variation – differences between the speech of different speakers. In sum, style involves the ways in which the same speakers talk differently on different occasions rather than the ways in which different speakers talk differently from each other.

Style in Sociolinguistics

We can distinguish two main approaches to the study of style in Sociolinguistics. The first, associated with Dell Hymes, encompasses the many ways in which individual speakers can express themselves differently in different situations. This recognizes that style can operate on the full range of linguistic levels – in the phonology or sound system of a language, in its syntax or grammar, in its semantics or the lexicon, and in the wider patterns of speaking across

Source: 'Language Style as Audience Design', by Bell, A. in Coupland, N. and Jaworski, A. (eds) Sociolinguistics: A Reader and Coursebook (1997) (Basingstoke: Palgrave Macmillan) pp. 240–9.

whole discourses and conversations. So style may be expressed in different forms of address, in the use of tag questions such as *isn't it,* in different ways of asking a question, in choosing one word over another, as well as in the ways that different vowels and consonants are pronounced. On the social side, Hymes has proposed a wide range of factors that may affect the way an individual talks, including audience, purpose, topic, mode, channel and genre (see Chapter 39).

The second approach to style in Sociolinguistics is much more strictly defined on both the social and linguistic dimensions. Labov pioneered in his 1966 New York City study a means of eliciting different styles of speech from people within a single interview. In his recorded interviews, as well as conversing with his informants, he had them carry out a series of language tasks, each of which was designed to focus more and more of the speaker's attention on to their speech. When the speaker talked to someone else rather than the interviewer, or discussed topics which got them particularly involved, they were likely to be paying the least attention to their speech, and Labov called this 'casual' speech. When the speaker was answering questions in typical interview fashion, they would be paying rather more attention to their speech and so produced 'careful' style. When they read aloud a brief passage of a story, they would give still more attention to their pronunciation. Reading out a list of isolated words focused more attention again, and reading a set of minimal pairs – words which differ only by a single sound such as *reader* and *raider* – would make the speaker pay the maximum amount of attention to their speech.

On the social side, therefore, this represents what we might call a minimalist approach, compared with what we might call the 'maximalist' view of the more ethnographic work. Labov has also usually worked with micro aspects of linguistic structure – specific sounds which can alternate as two or more variants of one linguistic 'variable', such as the choice between a 'standard' *-ing* pronunciation and a 'non-standard' *-in'* pronunciation in words such as *leaving* and *building* (see Chapters 4 and 13). These are classed as different ways of saying the same thing, and analyses of such sociolinguistic variables have produced findings which, when graphed, have become classics of the sociolinguistic literature.

Peter Trudgill studied the (ng) variable, and Figure 4.1 on p. 62 of this volume from his work on Norwich English is typical of a social class by style graph. Five social groups are distinguished, ranging from the Lower Working Class to the Upper Middle Class, using four different styles. The pattern of the lines of this graph shows two things. First, as we move from the middle-class groups to the working-class groups the use of the *-in'* variant increases and, conversely, the use of the prestigious *-ing* variant decreases. Secondly, the rise of the lines from word lists to casual speech shows that each group style shifts towards less -*in'* and more -*ing* with each attention-increasing task in the interview. So all four classes use most -*in'* in casual speech, less in careful speech, still less in the reading passage, and least of all in the word lists.

Labov's techniques for eliciting styles have been used in countless studies in many languages and countries since 1966, and in many cases a similar kind of gradient of style-shifting has been found. However, some of the subsequent research has had different findings, and some researchers have questioned whether these styles really apply outside the confines of the sociolinguistic interview. Many have also questioned whether attention to speech is the factor which is operating here. Some have found that attention could be directed to producing all levels of linguistic alternatives, not just the more prestigious forms such as -*ing* rather than -*in'*. Isn't it also possible for speakers to attend to their speech and rather consciously sound *more* non-standard?

Audience Design

One critique and development of earlier sociolinguistic approaches to style was the Audience Design framework outlined in Bell (1984). I proposed that style shift occurs primarily in response to the speaker's audience rather than to amount of attention or other factors. This approach grew out of one particular study on style. While researching the language of radio news in New Zealand, I came across an unanticipated situation which proved to be tailored to locating and explaining style shift (Bell 1991). The organization of the New Zealand public broadcasting system at the time meant that two of the radio stations being studied both originated centrally in the same suite of studios. The same individual newsreaders could be heard reading news bulletins on both of these networks. Station YA was 'National Radio', the prestige service of New Zealand's public corporation radio. It had an audience with higher social status than the audience for station ZB, which was one of a network of local community stations.

Figure 18.1 shows the percentage of intervocalic /t/ voicing for four newsreaders recorded on both these stations. When it occurs between two vowels, usually voiceless /t/ can be pronounced like a voiced /d/, making words such as *writer* and *latter* sound like *rider* and *ladder*. The six newsreaders shifted on average 20 per cent between YA and ZB. Single newsreaders heard on two different stations showed a remarkable and consistent ability to make considerable style shifts to suit the audience. These switches between stations were at times very rapid: at off-peak hours a single newsreader might alternate between YA and ZB news with as little as ten minutes between bulletins on the different stations.

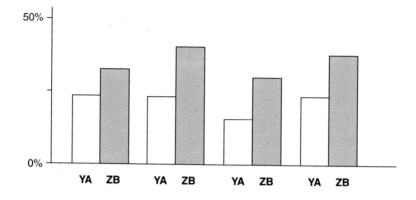

Figure 18.1   Percentage of intervocalic /t/ voicing by four newscasters on two New Zealand radio stations, YA and ZB (from Bell 1984: 162)

What could be the cause of these shifts? There is after all just one individual speaker producing two divergent styles. The institution is the same in both cases. The topic mix of the news is similar (in some cases, even the actual scripted news stories are the same). The studio setting is the same. And there is no reason to suppose that the amount of attention paid to speech is being systematically varied. Of all the factors we might suggest as possible influences on news style, only the audience correlated with these shifts.

Looking beyond this particular study, it seemed clear that the same regularities which were amplified in the media context are also operating in face-to-face communication. In mass communication, a broadcaster's individual style is routinely subordinated to a shared station style whose character can only be explained in terms of its target audience. When we look at ordinary conversation, we can also see the important effect that an audience has on a speaker's style, although the impact is less obvious than for broadcasters. In particular, we know that mass communicators are under considerable pressure to win the approval of their audience in order to maintain their audience size or market share. In ordinary conversation the urge to gain the approval of one's audience is similar in kind although less in degree.

The audience design framework was developed to account for these patterns in face-to-face as well as mass communication. The main points can be summarized like this:

1. *Style is what an individual speaker does with a language in relation to other people.* The basic tenet of audience design is that style is oriented to people rather than to mechanisms such as attention. Style is essentially a social thing. It marks interpersonal and intergroup relations. It is interactive – and active.

Although audience design and its hypotheses are based on evidence behind this proposition, this is really a premise rather than a hypothesis. Our view of style is ultimately derived from our view of the nature of human persons. Behind audience design there lies a strong and quite general claim that the character of (intra-speaker) style shift derives at a deep level from the nature of (inter-speaker) language differences between people.

2. Style derives its meaning from the association of linguistic features with particular social groups. The social evaluation of a group is transferred to the linguistic features that are associated with that group. The link between differences in the language of different groups ('social' variation in Labov's terms) and within the language of individual speakers (stylistic variation) is made by society's evaluation of the group's language (Figure 18.2). Sociolinguists have noted this at least since Ferguson and Gumperz (1960). Evaluation of a linguistic variable and style shift of that variable are reciprocal, as Labov (1972) demonstrated in identifying these 'marker' variables. Evaluation is always associated with style shift, and style shift with evaluation. Those few variables which do not show style shift (indicators) are also not evaluated in the speech community. Stylistic meaning therefore has what we can call a normative basis. A particular style is *normally* associated with a particular group or situation, and therefore carries with it the flavor of those associations.

3. Speakers design their style primarily for and in response to their audience. This is the heart of audience design. Style shift occurs primarily in response to a change in the speaker's audience. Audience design is generally manifested

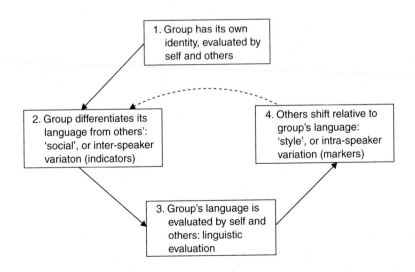

Figure 18.2 The derivation of style from inter-speaker variation

in a speaker shifting their style to be more like that of the person they are is talking to – this is 'convergence' in the terms of the Speech/Communication Accommodation Theory developed by Giles and associates (see Chapter 19). Response is the primary mode of style shift. Style is a responsive phenomenon, but it is actively so, not passive.

This can be seen in a study of the speech of a travel agent carried out by Coupland (1984). Coupland recorded an assistant in a travel agency in conversation with a wide social range of clients. He quantified the assistant's level for the intervocalic (t) voicing variable when speaking to different groups of clients, and compared that with the levels the clients use in their own speech. Figure 18.3 shows how the travel assistant accommodates towards the clients' own levels of (t) voicing, shifting to more (t) voicing for lower-class clients who use more voicing themselves, and to less (t) voicing with higher-class clients. In this style shift she goes on average at least halfway to meet her clients.

4. *Audience design applies to all codes and levels of a language repertoire, monolingual and multilingual.* Audience design does not refer only to quantitative

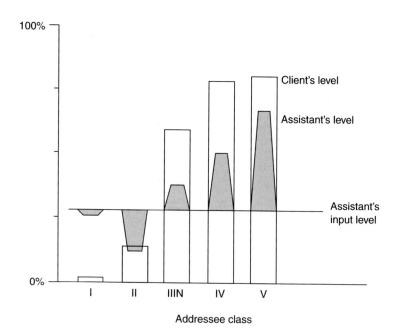

Figure 18.3   Travel assistant's convergence on intervocalic (t) voicing variable to five occupational classes of clients

Note: Input level taken as assistant's speech to own class, IIIN (derived from Coupland 1984: Figure 4).

style shift of individual sociolinguistic variables such as (ng). Within a single language, it involves features such as choice of personal pronouns or address terms (Ervin-Tripp 1972) and politeness strategies (Brown and Levinson 1987), as well as quantitative style-shifting. Audience design also applies to all codes and repertoires within a speech community, including the switch from one complete language to another in bilingual situations. It has long been recognized that the processes which make a monolingual shift styles are the same as those which make a bilingual switch languages. Where a monolingual speaker of English will make quantitative shifts on a number of linguistic variables when talking to a stranger rather than to a family member, a bilingual speaker in parts of Scotland, for example, will shift from talking Gaelic to a family member into English to address a stranger.

5. *Variation on the style dimension within the speech of a single speaker derives from and echoes the variation which exists between speakers on the 'social' dimension.* This style axiom (Bell 1984: 151) claims that the inter-relation between intra-speaker style shift and inter-speaker dialect differences is a derivation. The axiom refers both to the historical origins of styles, and to the present basis on which styles carry social meaning. That is, distinct styles originated in past differences in the language of different groups. And styles carry a particular social meaning now in the present because of their association with the language of particular groups.

The style axiom encapsulates the often-noted fact that the same linguistic variables operate simultaneously on both social and stylistic dimensions, so that for one isolated variable it may be difficult to distinguish a 'casual salesman from a careful pipefitter' (Labov 1972: 240). It also reflects the quantitative relationship of the social and stylistic dimensions: the maximum style shift on graphs such as Figure 4.1 in Chapter 4 (i.e. Trudgill's (ng)) is usually less than the maximum difference between social groups. On Trudgill's graph, the greatest style shift is by the Upper Working Class and is about 80 per cent, while the maximum difference between the different classes is some 95 per cent in style B.

6. *Speakers show a fine-grained ability to design their style for a range of different addressees, and to a lesser degree for other audience members.* These are the classic findings of Giles's accommodation model (e.g. Giles and Powesland 1975; see Chapter 19). In its essence, speech accommodation theory proposed that speakers accommodate their speech style to their hearers in order to win approval. Although the theory was extensively expanded and revised during the 1980s, its principal insight has been that speakers respond primarily to their audience in designing their talk. As well as changing the way they talk when addressing different people, there is good evidence that speakers can make even finer shifts to cater to a range of different people within their audience.

Not all audience members are equally important. We can distinguish and rank their roles according to whether or not they are known, ratified or addressed by the speaker. We can picture them as occupying concentric circles, each one more distant from the speaker (Figure 18.4). The main character in the audience is the second person, the *addressee*, who is known, ratified and addressed. Among the other, third persons who may be present, the *auditors* are known and ratified interlocutors within the group. Third parties whom the speaker knows to be there, but who are not ratified as part of the group, are *overhearers*. And other parties whose presence the speaker does not even know about are *eavesdroppers*.

Speakers are able to subtly adjust their style when a stranger joins a group and becomes an 'auditor' – present in the group but not directly addressed. They even respond to the presence of an overhearer who is within earshot but is not part of the speaker's conversational circle. In a bilingual community in Hungary, for instance, the arrival of a monolingual German speaker at an Hungarian-speaking inn can be enough to make the conversation switch into German (Gal 1979). The switch between different languages is a much more obvious manifestation of overhearer design than the quantitative style shifts within the same language by a monolingual speaker, but the process is basically the same.

7. Style shifts according to topic or setting derive their meaning and direction of shift from the underlying association of topics or settings with typical audience members. This tentative hypothesis suggests that when speakers shift their style because of a change of topic, this is an echo of the kind of shift that occurs when a

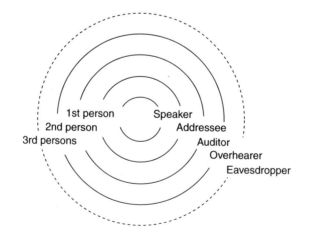

Figure 18.4   Persons and roles in the speech situation

speaker style shifts in response to the kind of addressee a particular topic is associated with. It implies that we talk about education in a style that echoes how we talk to a teacher, or about work in a style that echoes how we talk to the boss. Thus Coupland's study mentioned above also found that the travel agent shifted her style significantly between work-related topics and other topics.

8. *As well as the 'responsive' dimension of style, there is the 'initiative' dimension.* Here the style shift itself *initiates* a change in the situation rather than *resulting* from such a change.

Sociolinguists have drawn attention to this distinction at least since Blom and Gumperz (1972). In responsive style shift, there is a regular association between language and social situation. The entry of outsiders to a local group, for example, triggers a switch from local dialect to standard speech. These situational shifts reflect the speech community's norms of what is appropriate speech for certain audiences. Initiative style trades on such regular associations, infusing the flavour of one setting into a different context. Here language becomes an independent variable which itself shapes the situation. So we find bilingual speakers who switch out of their usual home language into the prestige language of the wider community in order to clinch an argument with a family member. In initiative style shift, the individual speaker makes creative use of language resources often from beyond the immediate speech community, such as distant dialects, or stretches those resources in novel directions. Literary examples of this kind of 'stylization' (Bakhtin 1981) are well known in the use that J. R. R. Tolkien and James Joyce, for example, have made of other dialects or languages to create their own unique voices.

9. *Initiative style shifts are in essence 'referee design', by which the linguistic features associated with a group can be used to express identification with that group.* Initiative style shifts derive their force and their direction of shift from their underlying association with kinds of persons or groups. They focus on an absent reference group rather than the present addressee, for example by adopting a non-native accent. Referees are third persons who are not physically present at an interaction but who are so salient for a speaker that they influence style even in their absence. Initiative style shift is essentially a redefinition by the speaker of their own identity in relation to their audience. So in many New Zealand television commercials, non-New Zealand accents are used in order to call up desirable associations with aristocracy through use of British Received Pronunciation, or with the streetwise wheeler-dealer through imitation of Cockney (Bell 1992). Trudgill's study of the accents of pop singers shows how British singers have adopted features of American English in order to associate with the prestige of American popular music. They have also been known to adopt British working-class features in singing music (such as punk) which is associated with the values of that class.

Conclusion

The study of style has had a chequered career in Sociolinguistics. In 1972 Labov wrote that 'the most immediate problem to be solved in the attack on sociolinguistic structure is the quantification of the dimension of style'. However, in the intervening years there has been much less study of stylistic variation than of variation between different groups of speakers. Style is attracting more interest again, and as the American scholars Rickford and McNair-Knox have written (1994: 52): 'With respect to theory development, stylistic variation seems to offer more potential for the integration of past findings and the establishment of productive research agendas than virtually any other area in sociolinguistics.'

Style research seems to be taking two directions. One of these is manifested in the work of Finegan and Biber (1994), whose 'multi-dimensional' approach developed as an alternative to the one I have taken above. The other direction responds to criticisms of both attention and audience factors as inadequate to account for the pervasiveness of initiative style and for the fact that language is not just a reflection of social structure. Recent critical social theorizing stresses that language is not independent of society. The linguistic and the social are not two cleanly separate dimensions, and language constitutes social reality as well as reflecting it. Identity may be revealed and expressed by language on its own, as for instance when we can tell what kind of person a speaker is just from hearing them on the radio, with no other clues to their character. This approach promises new insights into the nature of sociolinguistic style (Coupland 1997; also Chapter 22, this volume).

REFERENCES

Bakhtin, M. M. 1981. *The Dialogic Imagination*. Austin, Texas: University of Texas Press.

Bell, A. 1984. Language style as audience design. *Language in Society* 13: 145–204.

Bell, A. 1991. Audience accommodation in the mass media. In H. Giles, N. Coupland and J. Coupland (eds.) *Contexts of Accommodation – Developments in Applied Sociolinguistics*. Cambridge: Cambridge University Press. 69–102.

Bell, A. (1992) 'Hit and Miss: Referee Design in the Dialects of New Zealand Television Advertisements', *Language and Communication*, **12**(3–4), pp. 327–40.

Blom, J-P. and J. J. Gumperz. 1972. Social meaning in linguistic structure: Code-switching in Norway. In J. J. Gumperz and D. Hymes, D. (eds.) *Directions in Sociolinguistics*. New York: Holt, Rinehart and Winston. 407–434.

Brown, P. and S. C. Levinson. 1987 [1978]. *Politeness: Some Universals in Language Usage*. 2nd edition. Cambridge: Cambridge University Press.

Coupland, N. 1984. Accommodation at work: Some phonological data and their implications. *International Journal of the Sociology of Language* 46: 49–70.

Coupland, N. 1997. Language, context and the relational self: Re-theorising dialect style in sociolinguistics. In P. Eckert and J. Rickford (eds.) *Style and Sociolinguistic Variation*. Cambridge: Cambridge University Press. 185–210.

Dorian, N. C. 1981. *Language Death: The Life Cycle of a Scottish Gaelic Dialect*. Philadelphia, PA: University of Pennsylvania Press.

Ervin-Tripp, S. M. (1972) 'On Sociolinguistic Rules: Alternation and Co-occurrence', in Gumperz, J. J. and Hymes, D. (eds) *Directions in Sociolinguistics*. New York: Holt, Rinehart & Winston. 213–250.

Ferguson, C. A. and J. J. Gumperz (eds.). 1960. Linguistic diversity in South Asia. *International Journal of American Linguistics* 26(3), part 3. Bloomington, Indiana: Indiana University Press.

Finegan, E. and D. Biber. 1994. Register and social dialect variation: An integrated approach. In D. Biber and E. Finegan (eds.) *Sociolinguistic Perspectives on Register*. Oxford: Oxford University Press. 315–347.

Gal, S. 1979. *Language Shift: Social Determinants of Linguistic Change in Bilingual Austria*. New York: Academic Press.

Giles, H. and P. F. Powesland. 1975. *Speech Style and Social Evaluation*. London: Academic Press.

Labov, W. 1972. *Sociolinguistic Patterns*. Philadelphia, Pennsylvania: University of Pennsylvania Press.

Rickford, J. R. and F. McNair-Knox. 1994. Addressee- and topic-influenced style shift: A quantitative sociolinguistic study. In D. Biber and E. Finegan (eds.) *Sociolinguistic Perspectives on Register*. Oxford: Oxford University Press. 235–276.

CHAPTER 19

The Process of Communication Accommodation

HOWARD GILES

We can talk of 'intergroup' communication when people orient to others based more on their group-based (social) identities, such as being gay or a member of an ethnic minority or a student, than on their distinctive individual (personal) identities. Intergroup research, which is one of the general perspectives adopted in accommodation theory, has addressed countless different social contexts, with police-civilian interactions being a recent interest. Reasons for this development include a degree of unease about community-police relationships, and recognition that better relationships are likely to lead to more productive policing. Civilians encounter police officers in many different circumstances, for example when a victim of crime calls for assistance, or when s/he witnesses a crime. But the most frequent situation, at least in the USA, is on a traffic stop – when a driver is pulled over by a police officer.

This is an event which can involve a great deal of uncertainty and anxiety for *both* parties, and one where group-level identities are highly salient. People will sometimes be unaware of why they have been stopped; they will be anxious about how the police officer is construing them in group terms, perhaps as a 'criminal' of some sort. The police officer will bring different assumptions to the encounter, for example, knowing that these situations can be deadly and that, whatever the local circumstances, the driver may indeed have committed a serious crime. It is perhaps not surprising that many people feel apprehensive in the presence of police officers even when they are not directly interacting (for example, entering a restaurant where a group of officers are on their lunch break), let alone being stopped for a potential violation. But we can take the traffic stop instance as an illustrative instance from time to time in this chapter – as an event where the processes of *accommodation*, when people adapt aspects of their communication styles relative to one another, are visible and consequential. Consider a traffic stop where an older, male, white police officer engages three young female African American students for allegedly running a stop sign (failing to stop at the sign). Think of the variety of social dimensions involved in this situation: gender, culture and ethnicity, social and occupational status, age, and so forth. How are the different personal and social identities negotiated during this interaction? Who changes his or her communicative style to accommodate whom? What are the outcomes of such accommodating behaviors on the relationship between the interactants?

These are the kinds of questions that communication accommodation theory (CAT) addresses. The theory had its origins in Britain of the late 1960s when I was intrigued by why my own English accent so readily changed to sound more urban Welsh (Cardiff, in this case) when attending a soccer match, shifting markedly when I was at a rugby match towards a more general South Walian variety, shifting when at university in North Wales with many English friends towards Received Pronunciation, and, yet again, when talking to locals outside the university setting, towards the local North Walian variety. Should I have been ashamed for being so sociolinguistically inconsistent? Was I a sociolinguistic automaton, when most of my peers told me that they interacted in essentially consistent ways with everyone they encountered, valuing the sense of personal integrity that this implied?

But we now know that this claim of sociolinguistic consistency is simply false, and that we all are, to varying degrees, sociolinguistic chameleons, but strategically and often usefully so. In most instances, it is desirable – even necessary – to converge, to adjust our language patterns towards those of our conversational partners, whether (in group terms) we see them as senior academics or dangerous criminals. What's more, my own experiences were not only of convergence. Visiting certain pubs in North Wales, I encountered situations when a room full of patrons would switch from English into Welsh when my English-speaking friends and I entered. Rightly or wrongly, we took this switching – communicative divergence – to indicate local people's intentional dissociation from us. These and related sociolinguistic and socio-psychological processes needed systematic investigation, and from the early 1970s onwards, the study of accent and dialect shifting, under the rubric of speech accommodation theory, established itself as a research theme in Sociolinguistics.

At the time, conceptual and theoretical approaches to speech style variation in Sociolinguistics – as with other forms of linguistic change – were rooted in normative explanations, on the assumption that certain kinds of speech patterns were demanded in certain kinds of contexts (for example, more hushed tones while talking in a church, more raucous conversation allowable at a football game, and so on). Within Social Psychology, my own discipline, the role of language and communication (some notable exceptions notwithstanding) was considered to be of only peripheral interest. So accommodation theory was born out of the desire to put, if you like, some socio-psychological meat on the bones of sociolinguistic processes, and to develop a linguistic focus in Social Psychology. In due course the theory evolved to take into account a whole gamut of verbal and nonverbal, linguistic and paralinguistic, and broadly discursive processes of communicative adaptation. In that way the theory came to be referred to as communication accommodation theory (CAT), reflecting the fact that its reach extended well beyond local speech (for example, accent) phenomena.

Over the years, with input from colleagues such as Nik Coupland and Cindy Gallois, CAT has undergone a series of elaborations and refinements, and empirical studies have been undertaken in many parts of the world, involving different languages and an array of distinctive methods (see Giles and Ogay 2006 for a flavor of these). CAT has been invoked in studying many different social group relations and in a range of applied contexts – health clinics, law courts, dysfunctional family settings, organizations, new media, to name but a few. The theory spawned other satellite models, including ethnolinguistic identity theory (Giles and Johnson 1987), the communicative predicament model of aging (Ryan, Giles, Bartolucci, and Henwood 1986), and the intergroup model of second language learning (Giles and Byrne 1982). Its impact has been not only as one of the major frameworks in the social psychology of language and communication, but also as a stimulus to cross-disciplinary research.

Convergence: The Foundation of CAT

CAT articulates the motivations driving people's verbal and nonverbal communication adjustments in interactions, together with the personal and social consequences of these changes (see Gallois, Ogay, and Giles 2006 for a detailed history of CAT's development). Accommodation – as a process – refers to how interactants adjust their communication so as to either diminish or enhance social and communicative differences between them. Such shifts can be complete switches of language in a multilingual setting or stylistic shifts within the resources of a single language, as in word choices. The theory has devoted significant attention to examining how and why we converge or diverge from each other. For example, a teenager may attempt to 'fit in with' members of a popular peer group by acquiring (or converging to) their style of talking, phrases, specific mannerisms, and dress style. Such newly acquired speech characteristics can sometimes be provocatively exploited by imposing them on older family members for predictably intended effects – perhaps bewilderment, consternation or annoyance – because they constitute divergence from the older adult norms.

Convergence is the most- researched CAT strategy, and the concept of accommodation is sometimes taken to be synonymous with convergence. Accommodation theorists, however, prefer a more subtle approach in that we think of *both* convergence and divergence as accommodative processes. As above, convergence happens when interactants' communication styles become more similar to another, perhaps in terms of choice of slang, obscenities, grammatical structures, volume, pitch, hand movements, and so on. When the features involved connote positive social value (for example, a fast speech rate, which in many contexts is associated with competence, while a slow one with incompetence), convergence can be termed 'upward' or 'downward'. Upward convergence is when an individual approximates another's more formal or more prestigious communicative style, and downward convergence refers to approximating another person's more colloquial, informal and/or nonstandard style. In its formative years, the essence of CAT lay in social psychological research on 'similarity attraction' – the generalization that we tend to be attracted to people who behave in similar ways to ourselves and that we can evoke favorable evaluations in people we converge towards (see AhYun 2002).

Convergence may, therefore, reflect people's basic desire to signal attraction to and/or glean social approval from others. But accommodative acts may involve certain costs for the speaker, in terms of identity change and expended effort, so such behavior may be initiated only if potential rewards are available. If one can accept the premise that people find social approval and respect from others rewarding, it would not seem unreasonable to suppose that there may be a general tendency or 'set' to converge toward others in most situations. This sort of accommodation can be regarded as an attempt on the part of a speaker to modify or disguise his or her persona in order to make it more acceptable to people being addressed. The speaker's rationale, of which they may not necessarily be consciously aware, has been represented schematically in the following manner:

> Consider a dyad consisting of speakers A and B, and let us assume that A wishes to gain B's approval. A then
> 1. samples B's communicative actions
>   (i)   draws inferences as to the personality and social characteristics of B (or at least the characteristics which B wishes to project)
>   (ii) assumes that B values and approves of such characteristics
>   (iii) assumes that B will approve of A to the extent that A displays similar characteristics
> 2. chooses from their communicative repertoire patterns which project characteristics of which B is assumed to approve.

The effect of this decision process is that A produces speech similar – or at least more similar than their so-called normal speech would be – to the speech of B. The fact that this sort of convergence occurs is substantiated by a good deal of empirical research. For instance, people with higher affiliative needs reciprocate the positive verbal and nonverbal signals of their partners more than those with lower needs, and measurably increased liking for the converger follows as a consequence. In a study conducted in Quebec, we had an audio-taped French-Canadian speaker provide a message to English-dominant Canadian listeners in either French (no convergence), a mixture of French and English (partial convergence), or English (full convergence). The speaker was perceived more favorably in terms of considerateness and in his effort to bridge cultural gaps, the more he converged towards his English listeners. Moreover, when listeners were given the opportunity to record a message back to the speaker, those who were spoken to by him in English converged reciprocally the most (that is, spoke in French). Partners in the partial convergence condition displayed less accommodation and those who were not converged to at all converged back the least.

Non-Accommodation

The Canadian research makes it clear that people do not resonate to *non-accommodative* others. This can signal, other things being equal, that a non-converger does not need a listener's approval or respect, and this is a perception that does not enhance self-esteem. In fact non-accommodation can lead to personal derogation of the non-accommodator. But attributions play an important role in the evaluative and interpretive processes here, and there may be extenuating circumstances for a lack of convergence. For instance, if a listener knows that the speaker doesn't have the language repertoire to produce convergence, then its absence can be discounted. Yet, if we are talking about someone not having learned a particular language in a multilingual setting, how long that gap in competence has existed can itself be relationally significant. Not acquiring the language of a co-existing group for many years (and especially when educational or social opportunities for learning are available) can be deemed inexcusable.

Going back to our opening police scenario, an officer who appears to adopt a non-accommodative stance towards the driver will probably be deemed not only impolite, aggressive, and authoritarian; s/he might also trigger an uncooperative and potentially aggressive response from the driver. The officer must also be wary of being too accommodative, as it could encourage complacency. External attributions are again potentially available, for example, if the driver believes that the officer 'is only doing his or her job' (and is nothing personal).

Attributions of this sort will of course be linked to how police officers as a social group are perceived, so the perceived quality of police work and the general quality of police-citizen relationships are at stake. These chains of communication strategy and social consequence can be discussed in communication skills training, where officers can be sensitized to communication issues of this sort.

An important element in the approval-seeking process is social power. Interviewees, for example, will be inclined to converge more towards their interviewers than vice-versa; newly arrived immigrants more towards the host community than the converse; salespersons more than clients; and those in inferior rather than superior or dominant status positions. In a study involving Chinese- and Anglo-Australians interacting, it was found that speakers did not converge on the basis of their different ethnicities. Rather, their occupational roles (which often carry significant prestige and power implications) determined accommodation; students converged towards their instructors more than vice-versa, for example. Returning to our traffic stop scenario, the officer clearly has the most power as he or she has available the resources to inflict a significant penalty on the driver and maybe her passengers. In other words, the driver is under more pressure to converge than the officer. However, if the driver does converge, members of her group (quite possibly passengers in the car) who overhear her might perceive her as a social 'traitor' (in group terms) and hence construe her derogatorily. On reflection, though, passengers may ultimately see the more positive side of her strategy for all concerned, and especially so if she accounts for her actions to the group as they leave the scene. The general point is, though, that there are different and possibly conflicting pressures to accommodate on all parties in this sort of episode. Police officers yearn for voluntary compliance and we have shown, in a number of studies in different parts of the world, that officers who are perceived as accommodating – that is, those who listen to others, take their circumstances into account, and explain clearly – are trusted, and that this in turn yields compliance with requests and directives (see Hajek et al. 2006). In a data set we have recently analysed (with Travis Dixon and Terri Schell) of actual videotaped traffic stops in Cincinnati, where officers' and drivers' communications were extensively coded, mutual convergence by both parties was predictive of satisfying outcomes.

The Social Functions and Consequences of Accommodation

Accommodative acts occur for a variety of other reasons too, and incur a range of different effects. People can converge to underscore common social identities, to convey empathy, and to develop bonds with others. As above, one effect of convergence is that it allows the sender to be perceived as more similar to the receiver than would otherwise have been the case. This is fascinating also from the perspective of the so-called 'self-expansion model' that claims that interpersonal closeness is a function of how much cognitive overlap can exist between two people. It can be argued that convergence is a communicative step in expanding one's personal terrain into the self-construct of the receiver, thereby increasing mutual positive regard. Such acts of enhancing communicative similarity, especially in initial encounters where interpersonal uncertainty is high, can also make speakers seem more socially predictable. If someone seems more similar to you, with more communicative 'overlap', you can more readily anticipate and appreciate their responses and values; anxiety can be lowered, and relational satisfaction increased. Indeed, our research around the Pacific Rim on successful aging points to the importance of elderly people having stable climates of accommodating others around them – both younger and older – as these can facilitate self-esteem and even reported life satisfaction (for example, Ota et al. 2007). Relatedly, we have data from China showing that when older people perceive young family members as being non-accommodating, this can lead them to report depression more than those who felt they had accommodating youth in their family networks.

Convergence may also be a device by which speakers make themselves better understood and can be an important component of communicative competence. The more the speaker reflects the listener's own mode of communication, the more easily their message might be understood. In this case, interactants attend to their interlocutor's knowledge of, or sophistication about, a particular topic being talked about (also called the 'interpretability strategy'). So taking the perspective of another, their emotive states and inclinations and their conversational needs (such as accommodating their desire to talk about certain topics or themes) increases comprehension, coherence, as well as communication and relational satisfaction. Indeed there are data showing that increased communicative effectiveness between members of a dyad increases interpersonal attraction anyway. It could be suggested that in certain interactions the emphasis is on increasing comprehensibility or appealing to others' conversational needs, while in still others it may be on causing the sender to be perceived more favorably – and, of course, all could be the case. Since all these processes promote interpersonal attraction, it may not be worthwhile for our purposes here to disentangle them. Suffice it to say that different situations have their own goals and related outcomes, and often convergence – enacted at an optimal level and optimal rate – can have social advantages. For instance, physicians may opt for lay terminology rather than medical jargon to increase their patients' comprehension of the medical advice provided and, interestingly enough, this has been found to have positive effects on the latter's reported compliance to following recommended treatment regimes. Furthermore, accommodatively and empathically taking another's distressed state into account can have the benefit of allowing the recipient to reappraise their situation in ways that benefit their emotional states.

As suggested above, convergence can miscarry and be seen as inappropriate. My teenage son has admonished me for using terms and pronunciation patterns *owned*, it seems, by his generation rather than mine, simultaneously pointing out that those were 'last week's words' anyway! A colleague of mine habitually adopted what I regarded as a phoney British voice whenever we were together. I took this to be a put-down, either of me personally, and/or those of my cultural heritage. I later found out from his spouse that he never knew that he made these style-shifts, was apparently quite fond of me, and that these sociolinguistic gymnastics were a reflection, somehow, of his affection. All this emphasizes the subjective complexities of the accommodative process. An important feature of CAT is that people converge, not so much towards people's actual communicative styles in any physical or objective sense, but towards the styles they *believe* them to be using. An illustration might be using traces of an ethnic dialect with a known immigrant who, in actuality (and in ways you do not discern), has linguistically assimilated. In such cases, subjective convergence is translated into, and can be measured by, objective divergence. In addition, people can accommodate to where others expect (or would wish) them to be. This might occur in romantic situations where males take on more macho stances (for example, deeper pitch) while females might incline towards sounding more feminine (for example, softer tones) – tactics called 'speech complementarity', because each style complements rather than matches the other.

Such subjective moves are based on social stereotypes and can therefore be problematic when people 'over-accommodate' certain others. In this vein, much work on intergenerational talk has shown how, due to unfavorable stereotypes that people often hold of those who are older, young people can patronize elderly people by slowing down for them and using overly simple language. For those elders who are socially and cognitively active, such messages (even if constructed due to positive and nurturing motives) risk recipients construing them as being condescending and demeaning. Others who might be frail and dependent seem to appreciate this speech style and do not attribute it with any such patronizing meanings. In this way, accommodative dilemmas can result, to the extent that it is not entirely clear to us what the real conversational needs and social identities of the recipients of our messages are. It is in fact all too easy not to appreciate another's lack of understanding and 'under-accommodate' them – a stance that is often attributed as insensitive and egotistic. Indeed, in our police scenario, imagine if the officer did not explain the reason for the traffic stop and a citation that followed from it, or ask for the driver's view of the transgression and account of the event, or if the officer used excessively ingroup police terminology. That under-accommodating stance could instill further aggravation, with local and possibly wider implications.

Divergence

CAT research has also shed light on why people sometimes choose to *accentuate* communicative differences between themselves and others. As we saw, 'maintenance' is a situation where people do not accommodate and retain their own style or that of their own social group, for instance, by not switching languages when they have the capability of so doing. Moving along the social differentiation continuum, people can more positively *diverge* from others by adopting a contrasting language, dialect, lexical style speech rate, gestures, and so on. Drawing upon social identity theory, CAT has argued that the more a person psychologically invests in or affiliates with a valued ingroup (religious, political, whatever), the more they will want to accentuate that positive identity by communicatively divergent means. (Different intergroup contexts for accommodation are discussed by Harwood and Giles 2005.) This will be evident where the communicative dimensions diverged upon are salient components of social identities, for example, a switch to Greek where that language is a source of pride for Greek-Australians, or when the relevant outgroup has threatened some aspect of their social livelihood, and particularly by illegitimate means. In a study conducted in Hong Kong one year before its handover to the People's Republic of China, respondents who identified strongly with Hong Kong evaluated more favorably their ingroup members who, by using Cantonese, diverged from Mandarin-speaking Chinese people than did respondents who identified themselves with mainland China.

Divergence and non-accommodation can be endorsed as a positive means of maintaining or even accentuating one's social identity. Returning for the last time to a particular version of our police scenario, the driver may well decide – and especially in a context where ethnic profiling is considered commonplace – to emphasize her African-American youth identity. In general, recipients who perceive divergence directed at them will tend to see the speaker in a negative light, other extenuated circumstances notwithstanding. The speaker will appear unfriendly, incompetent, impolite, and, perhaps even belligerent or hostile (as in a situation where an African-American child adopts African-American Vernacular English with a European-American teacher). This need not actually be the intent behind the act, which the speaker might intuitively feel is merely a matter of indexing loyalty towards the ingroup, without any specific intergroup significance. With sufficient numbers of a group frequently engaging in language divergences in an array of public situations (such as in the resurrection of an ethnic minority language or even the widespread creation of a youth code), this can change the whole tenor of the communication and linguistic landscape through street signs, newspapers, TV channels, or on the Internet. Indeed such individual actions can mobilize social movements whereby whole languages and codes are institutionalized and/or revitalized (see Marlow and Giles 2006).

All in all, it appears that satisfying communication requires a delicate balance between convergence – broadly to demonstrate willingness to communicate – and divergence – broadly to incur a healthy sense of group identity. Furthermore, calibrating the amount of perceived non-, under-, and over-accommodation one receives can be an important ingredient in continuing or withdrawing from an interaction and making decisions about anticipated future ones. CAT, therefore, appeals to and captures the evolving histories, politics, and changing priorities of the cultures in which interactions that draw on accommodative moves are embedded (see Giles et al. 2007 for a recent formulation of the theory's propositional structure). Although the theory has not always been sufficiently explicit in its linguistic/discursive detail – it emerged after all from another discipline – its potential for helping us understand sociolinguistic phenomena, processes, and contexts has already been established and will undoubtedly be exploited further.

Acknowledgement

The author wishes to express sincere gratitude for the Editors' feedback on an earlier version of this chapter.

REFERENCES

AhYun, K. 2002. Similarity and attraction. In M. Allen, R. W. Preiss, B. M. Gayle and N. A. Burrell (eds.) *Interpersonal Communication Research: Advances through Meta-analysis*. Mahwah, New Jersey: Erlbaum. 145–167.

Ryan, E.B., H. Giles, G. Bartolucci and K. Henwood. 1986. Psycholinguistic and social psychological components of communication by and with older adults. *Language and Communication* 6: 1–22.

Gallois, C., T. Ogay and H. Giles. 2006. Communication accommodation theory: A look back and a look ahead. In W. Gudykunst (ed.) *Theorizing about Intercultural Communication*. Thousand Oaks, CA: Sage. 121–148.

Giles, H. and J. L. Byrne. 1982. An intergroup model of second language acquisition. *Journal of Multilingual and Multicultural Development* 3: 17–40.

Giles, H. and P. Johnson. 1987. Ethnolinguistic identity theory: A social psychological approach to language maintenance. *International Journal of the Sociology of Language* 68: 69–99.

Giles, H. and T. Ogay. 2006. Communication accommodation theory. In B. Whalen and W. Samter (eds.) *Explaining Communication: Contemporary Theories and Exemplars*. Mahwah, New Jersey: Erlbaum. 293–310.

Giles, H., M. Willemyns, C. Gallois and M. C. Anderson. 2007. Accommodating a new frontier: The context of law enforcement. In K. Fiedler (ed.) *Social Communication*. New York: Psychology Press. 129–162.

Hajek, C., V. Barker, H. Giles, J. Louw, L. Pecchioni, S. Makoni and P. Myers. 2006. Communication dynamics of police-civilian encounters: American and African interethnic data. *Journal of Intercultural Communication Research* 35: 161–182.

Ota, H., H. Giles and L. Somera. 2007. Beliefs about intra- and intergenerational communication in Japan, the Philippines, and the United States: Implications for older adults' subjective well-being. *Communication Studies* 58: 173–188.

Marlow, M. and H. Giles. 2006. From the roots to the shoots: A Hawaiian case study of language revitalization and modes of communication. *Communication Yearbook* 30: 343–385.

CHAPTER 20

Crossing, Ethnicity and Code-Switching

BEN RAMPTON

In this chapter, I shall first give an account of *language crossing*, a verbal practice that was not very widely recognised in Sociolinguistics until the mid- to late 1990s (cf. Rampton 1995/2005). Then I shall consider some general implications of crossing for our understanding of ethnic processes, and for the ways in which we conceptualise and conduct research on bilingual code-switching.

Language Crossing: A Preliminary Definition and Some Examples

The term 'language crossing' (or 'code-crossing') refers to the use of a language which isn't generally thought to 'belong' to the speaker. Language crossing involves a sense of movement across quite sharply felt social or ethnic boundaries, and it raises issues of legitimacy that participants need to reckon with in the course of their encounter. In the multiethnic adolescent friendship groups where I studied it (Rampton 2005),[1] crossing was very much a part of everyday talk and activity, but it occurred at moments when the constraints of ordinary social order were relaxed and normal social relations couldn't be

Source: A longer version of this chapter was originally published in Auer, P. (ed.) *Code-switching in Conversation: Language, Interaction and Identity*, (1998) (London: Routledge) pp. 290–317, and also appeared in *Working Papers in Urban Language and Literacies* 5, at http://www.kcl.ac.uk/ldc. The research reported here was generously supported by the Economic and Social Research Council (Grant no 00232390), the Leverhulme Trust, and the British Association for Applied Linguistics.

taken for granted. Here are some examples:

Extract 1[2]

Participants: Ray [13 years old, male, of Anglo/African-Caribbean descent; wearing radio-mike], Ian [12, male, Anglo descent], Hanif [12, male, Bangladeshi descent], others.
Setting: 1984. Coming out of lessons into the playground at break. Ian and Ray are best friends. Stevie Wonder is a singer whose song 'I just called to say I love you' was very famous. Ray has a bad foot – cf. line 17.

```
 1 Ray:     IA::N::
 2 Hanif:   (          )
 3 Ian:     ((from afar)) RAY THE COO:L RAY THE COO:L
 4 Hanif:   yeh Stevie Wonder YAAA ((laughs loudly))
 5 Ray:          ⌈it's worser than that
 6 Ian:     ((singing)): ⌊I just called to say
 7 Hanif:   ha (let's) sing (him) a song
 8 Ian:     I hate you
 9 Hanif:   ((loud laughs))
10 Anon :   ((coming up))( )are you running for the school (.)
11 Ray:     huh
12 Anon :   are ⌈you running for the school=
13 Ray:         ⌊no
14 Anon :   =⌈I am
15 Ian:      ⌊he couldnt run for th- he couldn't ⌈run for the school
16 Ray:                                          ⌊SHUT UP =
17 Ray:     =I couldn- I don wan-⌈I can't run anyway
18 Hanif:                        ⌊right we're wasting our ⌈time=
19 Ian:                                                   ⌊I did=
20 Hanif:   =⌈come on       (we're) wasting our time=
21 Ian:      ⌊you come last ( )
22 Hanif:   =⌈[mʌmʌmʌ:]
23 Anon:     ⌊I came second
24 Ian:     ((singing)) I just called to say ⌈I got      ⌈a big=
25 Ray:                                       ⌊I hate you ⌊
26 Ian:     =[lʊɬɑ:]
            ((Punjabi for 'willy'))
27 Hanif and others: ((loud laughter))
28 Ray:     ((continuing Ian's song)) so's Ian Hinks (1.5)
29          ((Ray laughs)) no you haven't you got a tiny one (.)
30          you've only got (a arse)
```

In this extract, Ian directs some Punjabi abuse at his good friend Ray, and among other things, the formulaic use of song helps to ensure that it is understood as ritual and jocular, not personal and serious (cf. for example, Goodwin and Goodwin 1987). When he starts out in lines 6 and 8, he seems to be identifying himself with the first person expressed in the song, but when he repeats it in lines 24 and 26, it looks as though he's putting the words in Ray's mouth rather than claiming the 'I' for himself – certainly, Ray's retaliation in line 28 suggests that it's him that has been attributed the item in Punjabi, not Ian. Whatever, Ian comes off best in their brief exchange of ritual abuse: Ian's [luɬɑ:] upstages Ray's effort to preempt him in line 25; it is Ian who wins an enthusiastic response from third parties in line 27; and in lines 29 and 30, Ray evidently judges his own immediate retort (line 28) as itself rather weak.

The second example of language crossing involves Creole:

Extract 2

Participants: Asif [15, male, Pakistani descent, wearing the radio-microphone], Alan [15, male, Anglo descent], Ms Jameson [25+, female, Anglo descent], and in the background, Mr Chambers [25+, male, Anglo descent].

Setting: 1987. Asif and Alan are in detention for Ms Jameson, who was herself a little late for it. She is explaining why she didn't arrive on time, and now she wants to go and fetch her lunch.

```
 1 Ms J:  I had to to and see the headmaster
 2 Asif:  why
 3 Ms J:  (            ) (.) none of your business
 4 Alan:  a- about us   (           )
 5 Ms J:  ((p.)) no        I'll be ⌈back
 6 Asif:                           ⌊((f.)) hey how can you see the=
 7         = headmaster when he was in dinner (.)
 8 Ms J:  ((quietly)) that's precisely why I didn't see him
 9 Asif:  what (.)
10 Ms J:  I'll be back in a second with my lunch ⌈(        )
11 Asif:                                         ⌊((ff.)) NO [ɪ]=
12         = ((f.)) dat's sad man (.) (I'll b      ) =
13         = I ⌈had to miss my play right I've gotta go
14 Alan:      ⌊(            with mine            )
15         (2.5) ((Ms J must now have left the room))
16 Asif:  ((Creole influenced)) ((f.)) l::unch (.) you don't need no= [l::ʌntʃ]
17         = lunch ⌈not'n grow anyway ((laughs))
                   ⌊[natʔn gɹəʊ]
18 Alan:           ⌊((laughs))
19 Asif:  have you eat your lunch Alan
```

Lines 1–9 involve a verbal tussle in which Asif and Alan use questions to undermine the positions that Ms Jameson stakes out in what she says. Asif's question in line 2 treats the account she gives of her late arrival as inadequate; she
rebuts his inquiry as illegitimate in line 3 but this is then undermined by Alan
in lines 4 and 5; and then in lines 6–8, Ms Jameson is delayed in the departure
she announced in line 5 by a question that upgrades the query over her initial
excuse into an explicit challenge. All this time, she has been locked into the
interaction by the adjacency structures set up by the boys' questions, but at line
10, she breaks out of this pattern, ignores Asif's line 9 repair initiation, again
announces her departure and leaves without saying anything more. With the
exchange structure now disrupted and Ms Jameson apparently paying no attention to him, Asif launches into what Goffman (1971: 152–153) calls 'afterburn' –
dissident remarks about another person's unjust or offensive conduct produced
just after they've left the scene – and in this display of resilience, Asif uses some
Creole/Black English. Admittedly, it can sometimes be hard trying to distinguish Creole from the local multiracial vernacular, and in line 12, Asif's stopped
TH in 'dat's sad man' is ambiguous (see below). But in lines 16 and 17, he uses a
characteristically Creole unrounded front open vowel in 'not' (cf. Sebba 1993:
153–154), and the stretched L in his first 'lunch' maybe connects with a black
speech feature noted by Hewitt in South London (1986: 134).

The last example of crossing also relates to a breach of conduct, though
here the putative offender is a younger pupil and the language used is a variety I've called stylised Asian English (SAE):

Extract 3

Participants and setting: At the start of the school year, Mohan [15 years,
male, Indian descent, wearing radio-microphone], Jagdish [15, male,
Indian descent] and Sukhbir [15, male, Indian descent] are in the bicycle
sheds looking at bicycles at the start of the new academic year. Some new
pupils run past them.

1 Sukh: STOP RUNNING AROUND YOU GAYS (.)
2 Sukh: ⌈((*laughs*))
3 Moh: ⌊EH (.) THIS IS NOT MIDD(LE SCHOOL) no more (1.0)
          [aɪ   dɪs   ɪz n̪et̪ʰ mɪd̪   nəʊmɔː]
4   this is a respective (2.0)
          [dɪs ɪz ə ɹəspektɪv]
5 Boy: (school)
6 Moh: school (.) yes (.) took the words out my mouth (4.5)

In this extract, Mohan is claiming that the norms of conduct appropriate to
secondary pupils during breaktime have been broken. In line 1, Sukhbir uses
his normal vernacular for what Goffman calls a 'prime'. This occurs when a

person potentially offends someone else by for example, flouting some convention, and the prime is designed to get the (putative) offender to provide a remedy by desisting, apologising and/or giving an explanation (Goffman 1971: 154ff, 109–114). But in this case, there's no remedy forthcoming. In line 3, the literal meaning of Mohan's utterance simply reminds the (disappearing) addressee that old rules of conduct no longer apply, but the switch to stylised Asian English makes a symbolic proclamation about the transgression's relation to a wider social order. SAE was stereotypically associated with limited linguistic and cultural competence (Rampton 2005: Section 2.3, Chs 3, 6) and in switching away from his normal voice to SAE, Mohan implicitly explains the transgression by imputing diminished control and responsibility to the offender.

Crossing and the Interactional Destabilisation of Ethnicity

Two things seem to run through all three of these examples (as well as many more). First, the speakers each moved outside the language varieties they normally used, and they briefly adopted codes which they didn't have full and easy access to. Admittedly, there were important differences in the extent to which they incorporated these other varieties into their habitual speech. But acts of this kind were frequently commented on (with varying degrees of both enthusiasm and disapproval), and more generally, inhibitions about the use of both Creole and SAE were evident in the fact that white and Punjabi youngsters generally avoided Creole in the company of black peers, while white and black peers hardly ever used SAE to target Punjabis. Second, these appropriations of another variety occurred in moments and activities when 'the world of daily life known in common with others and with others taken for granted' was problematised or partially suspended (Garfinkel 1984: 35). In Extract 1, crossing occurred as a form of ritual abuse, which works by suspending normal considerations of truth and falsity. In Extracts 2 and 3, crossing occurred at moments when there was a heightened sense that decorum had been disrupted. And elsewhere, crossing occurred in games and in the context of performance art, where there is an agreed relaxation of routine interaction's rules and constraints (Rampton 2005: Sections 6.7, 7.2; Sutton-Smith 1982).

These points have implications for our understanding of how these kids construed and handled ethnic difference.[3] First, the fact that crossing generally occurred in moments when the easy flow of normal social interaction was disrupted or suspended suggests that when a person did switch into someone else's language, the speaker was never actually claiming that he or she was 'really' black or Asian – it didn't finally imply that the crosser could move unproblematically in and out of the friends' heritage language in any new kind of open bicultural code-switching. Second, crossing's occurrence in the unsettled margins of interactional and institutional space implied that in the social structures which were dominant and which adolescents finally treated as *normal*, the boundaries round ethnicity were relatively fixed.

Even so, these boundaries weren't inviolable, and quite plainly, adolescents didn't submit reverentially to absolutist ideas about ethnicity being fixed at birth or during the early years of socialisation. Language crossing cannot be seen as a runaway deconstruction of ethnicity, emptying it of all meaning, but ethnicity's influence wasn't left unquestioned, invisibly and incontrovertibly pervading common sense. Crossing was an established interactional practice that foregrounded inherited ethnicity itself, and in doing so, it at least partially destabilised it. In Bourdieu's terms, crossing can be seen as a form of 'heretical discourse' which broke the doxic authority of the idea that ethnically, you are what you're born and brought up (1977: 168–70; 1990: 129). As such, crossing warrants close attention in sociological discussion of the emergence of 'new ethnicities of the margins', hybrid ethnicities 'predicated on difference and diversity' (Hall 1988).

So in the peer group where I studied it, language crossing seemed to be poised at the juncture of two competing notions of group belonging. On the one hand, crossing was a significant practice in the negotiation of an emergent sense of multiethnic youth community, so that when, for example, youngsters of Indian and Pakistani descents talked about white friends who spoke Punjabi, they said 'these two are one of us' and 'he's been in our sort of community, been our friend long time'. But at the same time, this sense of multiracial adolescent community was itself fragile, set around by 'ethnic absolutism', a powerful common sense in which Creole was Caribbean and Punjabi Punjabi, and it seemed to be this tension that generated the feeling of anomaly in language crossing, pressing it into the liminal margins of everyday interactional practice. Interpreted in this way, language crossing represents a cultural dynamic that merits close attention in Sociolinguistics, and indeed, there are potentially strong links with bilingual code-switching as a major sociolinguistic topic. Even so, if we want to treat crossing as a form of code-switching, it may be necessary to revise and elaborate some of the standard accounts.

Crossing and Research on Code-Switching

In the past, studies of code-switching have tended to focus on the conduct of groups in which the use of two or more languages is a routine expectation, either because people have grown up with a multilingual inheritance, or because they have moved into areas or institutions where the use of additional languages is an unremarked necessity. Because of this emphasis on languages which are unexceptional within the ingroup, code-switching research has often provided a rather restricted notion of how people use language to negotiate ethnicity, tending to focus only on variation in the salience and cultural contents of ethnic categories, not on ethnic *recategorisation*, on the exploration or adoption of alternative or competing ethnicities. In a great deal of code-switching research, participants are seen as having a rather limited choice in how they can use language to position themselves ethnically: either (a) they can maintain and/or embrace and cultivate the ethnicity they have inherited (by switching back and forwards), or (b) they can deemphasise or abandon it, so that ethnicity drops from the repertoire of identities available and meaningful to them (by not switching). The study of language crossing throws light on a further option: (c) exploring other people's ethnicities, embracing them and/or creating new ones (cf. Rampton 2005: Section 11.6).

So in the first instance, crossing invites code-switching research to expand its horizons on ethnic self-positioning. Beyond this, it allows us to elaborate on one of the fundamental frameworks in code-switching research – Gumperz's distinction between 'situational' and 'metaphorical' code-switching (Blom and Gumperz 1972). The distinction between situational and metaphorical code-switching has been much debated, but my own inclination is to see

- situational code-switching as a relatively routine 'contextualisation cue', in which speakers introduce (and recipients accept) a new but fairly familiar and accessible definition of the situation. In contrast,
- metaphorical code-switching denies the recipient an easy footing for subsequent interaction. Like figurative language generally, it involves a violation of co-occurrence expectations which makes it difficult for recipients to end their search for meaning in the relatively neat solutions normally achieved with ordinary discourse. Instead, it requires them to run through a much more extensive set of possible inferences, and it provides the recipient with no simple answer to the question 'What next?' (Auer 1988)

Admittedly, it can be hard using the situational-metaphorical dichotomy to classify empirical instances of code-switching, but this is in fact no more than you would expect. As research on 'dead' and 'sleeping' metaphor makes plain (for example, Leech 1969), the distinction between the literal and the figurative, between the ordinary and the exceptional, is highly variable and often ambiguous, and this becomes clear if we return to language crossing.

As already indicated, crossing frequently contradicted the 'world of daily life known in common with others and with others taken for granted' and this links it first and foremost with metaphorical code-switching. But the line between the ordinary and the exceptional was actually often rather blurred, especially with crossing into Creole. When youngsters made use of stylised Asian English, it was fairly easy to distinguish the speaker's 'real self' from the voice they were using (see below), but this could be harder when Creole was used, and here crossing looked much more towards the fusion of speaker and voice into a new identity capable of holding an uncontested place in everyday reality. A range of factors affected the extent to which crossers were able to project Creole as an authentic expression of their identity in acts of serious self-positioning – who the speaker and recipients were, what their relationship was, the degree of their involvement with black culture, the particular occasion, the specific contours of the character being claimed and so forth (see Hewitt 1986: Ch. 5; Rampton 2005: Chs 5, 8, 9). In some exchanges, Creole only occurred in actions that were offered and taken as joking, while in others, the same acts might be taken for real. But what was clear was that social reality and the speaker's position within this were the focus for some degree of interactional renegotiation.

In fact, the contrast between Asian English and Creole allows us to use Bakhtin's notion of 'double-voicing' as a way of elaborating the different forms that 'metaphorical' code-switching can take.

Double-voicing is a term that Bakhtin uses to describe the effect on any utterance of a plurality of often competing languages, discourses and voices. With double-voicing, speakers use someone else's discourse (or language) for their own purposes, 'inserting a new semantic intention into a discourse which already has...an intention of its own. Such a discourse...must be seen as belonging to someone else. In one discourse, two semantic intentions appear, two voices' (Bakhtin 1984: 189). In fact, there are several kinds of double-voicing, and one of these is described as 'uni-directional'. With uni-directional double-voicing, the speaker uses someone else's discourse 'in the direction of its own particular intentions' (1984: 193). Speakers themselves go along with the momentum of the second voice, though it generally retains an element of otherness, which makes the appropriation conditional and introduces some reservation into the speaker's use of it. But at the same time, the boundary between the speaker and the voice they are adopting can diminish, to the extent that there is a 'fusion of voices'. When that happens, discourse ceases to be double-voiced, and instead becomes 'direct, unmediated discourse' (1984: 199).

Double-voicing in Creole generally seemed to be uni-directional. Creole was much more extensively integrated into multiracial peer group recreation than either stylised Asian English or Punjabi, and it was used much more by members of ethnic outgroups. Creole symbolised an excitement and an excellence in youth culture that many adolescents aspired to, and it was even referred to as 'future language'. For a great deal of the time, there was certainly some reservation in the way Creole was used by whites and Asians, and this was most noticeable in the way that they generally avoided it in the presence of black peers. Even so, crossers tended to use Creole to lend emphasis to evaluations that synchronised with the identities they maintained in their ordinary speech, and in line with this, as Hewitt underlines, their Creole was often hard to disentangle from their local multiracial vernacular (Hewitt 1986: 148, 151). In Bakhtin's terms, crossing in Creole came close to the point where uni-directional double-voicing shifted over into direct unmediated discourse, and for an instance of this, see Example 2 above.

The opposite of uni-directional double-voicing is 'vari-directional' double-voicing, in which the speaker 'again speaks in someone else's discourse, but...introduces into that discourse a semantic intention directly opposed to the original one'. In vari-directional double-voicing, the two voices are much more clearly demarcated, and they are not only distant but also opposed (Bakhtin 1984: 193). This often seemed to be the case with stylised Asian English. From interviews and other evidence, it was clear that Asian English stood for a stage of historical transition that most adolescents felt they were leaving behind, and in one way or another, it consistently symbolised distance from the main currents of adolescent life. In line with this, stylised Asian English was often used as what Goffman calls a 'say-for' (1974: 535) – a voice not being claimed as part of the speaker's own identity but one that was relevant to the identity of the person being addressed or targeted (see Extract 3).

So when crossing is situated in the larger sociolinguistic literature, first it invites us to extend code-switching research to cross-ethnic switching into outgroup languages, and second, it allows a systematic elaboration of the classic notion of 'metaphorical' switching', drawing on Bakhtin's account of 'double-voicing'. There is one more significant implication, and this concerns the kinds of data that code-switching research focuses on.

Beyond Conversation

The Sociolinguistics of code-switching has always been strongly opposed to perspectives that treat multilingualism as odd or deficient. To counter these views, research has often very successfully demonstrated the integrity of language mixing and switching by examining them for their grammatical systematicity and pragmatic coherence, and as part of this, it has often stressed that switching and mixing are routine practices in everyday conversation. Language crossing, however, doesn't fit so easily with this prevailing ethos, since in crossing, anomaly, incongruity and contradiction are central issues. Instead, if we want to do justice to practices like the ones I have described in this chapter, the governing notion of conversation needs to be a broad one, encompassing play, ritualisation, and the interruption and suspension of

routine reality production and maintenance. Indeed, it is particularly important not to conceptualise conversation as a genre distinct from stylisation
and artful performance. As Bauman and Briggs stress, 'performances are not
simply artful uses of language that stand apart both from day-to-day life', and
more than that,

> performances move the use of heterogeneous stylistic resources, context-
> sensitive meanings, and conflicting ideologies into a reflexive arena where they
> can be examined critically... Performance... provides a frame that invites crit-
> ical reflection on communicative processes. (Bauman and Briggs 1990: 60)

This certainly applied to language crossing. In the first instance, crossing
was often set off from ordinary talk with only the lightest change of 'key'
(Goffman 1974: Ch. 3), arising spontaneously, for example, in the vicinity
of minor transgressions. And second, as I argued above, crossing also posed
a 'heretical' challenge to dominant notions of ethnolinguistic identity and
inheritance.

In fact, if Sociolinguistics is to engage properly with the politics of language choice, and to understand the ways in which code-switching might dis-
rupt common sense realities and initiate alternatives, it will also need to look
closely at genres which are quite far removed from everyday talk. According
to Bourdieu, if they are to be effective, challenges to dominant ways of seeing
the world need to operate in more than local conversation:

> Heretical discourse must not only help to sever the adherence to the world of
> common sense by publicly proclaiming a break with the ordinary order, it must
> also produce a new common sense and integrate within it the previously tacit
> and repressed practices and experiences of an entire group, *investing them with
> the legitimacy conferred by public expression and collective recognition.* (Bourdieu
> 1990: 129; emphases added)

There is now a substantial body of studies which show received ethnic categories
being questioned and changed within local communities, and in all of these,
newly emergent interethnic sensibilities gain crucial sustenance from artful
public performances, particularly in popular music.[4] Of course, code-switching
performances to a large public need not lend their support only to new mixed
communities – they can just as easily endorse race stratification and promote
narrow and exclusive notions of ethnicity, impacting on local practice in all
sorts of complex and unpredictable ways. Even so, code-switching research
can't afford to overlook all these media representations and their interaction
with everyday practice, because in the end, an exclusive dedication to conversation as the only empirical terrain could produce an analytic parochialism

ill-tuned to the diaspora multilingualisms currently emerging in urban areas at the intersection of global and local. With its eyes glued *only* to the properties of talk, research might end up waving an antiquated banner of holistic coherence at precisely the moment when the crucial values became transition and hybridity. Perhaps that is an overstatement, but at the very least, if academic research seeks to fulfill its potential as a way of helping to de-stigmatise vernacular practices, it needs to reckon with the forms of public legitimation and abuse that are most readily recognised by the people it is studying. Conversation is important, but it is not the only thing that people listen to.

NOTES

1. My project used the methods of ethnographic and interactional Sociolinguistics, and it involved two years of fieldwork focused on one neighbourhood of the South Midlands, with 23 eleven to thirteen year olds of Indian, Pakistani, African Caribbean and Anglo descent in 1984, and approximately 64 fourteen to sixteen year olds in 1987. Methods of data-collection included radio-microphone recording, participant observation, interviewing and retrospective participant commentary on extracts of recorded interaction. My analyses of crossing were based on about 68 incidents of Punjabi crossing, about 160 exchanges involving stylised Indian English, and more than 250 episodes where a Creole influence was clearly detectable.

2. In the ensuing extracts, transcription conventions include

[ ]	IPA phonetic transcription (revised to 1979)
ˈ	high stress
ˌ	low stress
/	low rise
[	overlapping turns
=	two utterances closely connected without a noticeable overlap, or different parts of the single speaker's turn
p.	piano/quietly
pp.	very quietly
f.	forte/loudly
ff.	very loudly
CAPS	shouted speech
:	lengthened sound
(.)	short pause
((*text*))	'stage directions', or comments
( )	speech inaudible
(text)	speech hard to discern, analyst's guess
bold	instance of crossing of central interest in discussion

3. It is worth stressing that in addition to my analysis of episodes like the ones in Examples 1–3, my interpretation of these youngsters' perspective on ethnicity and race drew on a good deal of ethnography. Without that background familiarity, it would be very easy to misinterpret the significance of crossing.

4. For references to popular music in Britain involving cross-ethnic code-switching between Creole, local vernacular English, Black American Vernacular, and/or Punjabi, see the longer version of this chapter (note 1). Also, Rampton 2005: Part IV on crossing in popular music in Southmead, as well as Rampton 2006: Ch 3 for a detailed sociolinguistic analysis of humming and singing.

REFERENCES

Auer, P. 1988. A conversation analytic approach to code-switching and transfer. In M. Heller (ed.) *Code-switching: Anthropological and Sociolinguistic* Perspectives. Berlin Mouton de Gruyter. 187–213.

Bakhtin, M. 1984. *Problems in Dostoevsky's Poetics*. Minneapolis: University of Minnesota Press.

Bauman, R and C. L. Briggs. 1990. Poetics and performance as critical perspectives on language and social life. *Annual Review of Anthropology* 19: 59–88.

Blom J-P. and J. J. Gumperz. 1972. Social meaning in linguistic structure: Code-switching in Norway. In J. J. Gumperz and D. Hymes (eds) *Directions in Sociolinguistics*. New York: Holt, Rinehart and Winston. 407–434.

Bourdieu, P. 1977. *Outline of a Theory of Practice* Cambridge: Cambridge University Press.

Bourdieu, P. 1990. *Language and Symbolic Power*. Cambridge: Polity.

Garfinkel, H. 1984 [1967]. *Studies in Ethnomethodology*. Cambridge: Polity.

Goffman, E. 1971. *Relations in Public*. London: Allen Lane.

Goffman, E. 1974. *Frame Analysis*. Harmondsworth: Penguin.

Goodwin, M. and C. Goodwin. 1987. Children's arguing. In S. Philips, S. Steele and C. Tanz (eds.) *Language, Gender and Sex in Comparative Perspective*. Cambridge: Cambridge University Press. 200–248.

Hall, S. 1988. New ethnicities. *ICA Documents* 7: 27–31.

Hewitt, R. 1986. *White Talk Black Talk*. Cambridge: Cambridge University Press.

Leech, G. 1969. *A Linguistic Guide to English* Poetry. London: Longman.

Rampton, B. 1995. *Crossing: Language and Ethnicity among Adolescents*. London: Longman. [2nd edition 2005. Manchester: St Jerome Press.]

Rampton, B. 2006. *Language in Late Modernity: Interaction in an Urban School*. Cambridge: Cambridge University Press.

Sebba, M. 1993. *London Jamaican: A Case Study in Language Interaction*. London: Longman.

Sutton-Smith, B. 1982. A performance theory of peer relations. In K. Borman (ed.) *The Social Life of Children in a Changing* Society. Norwood, New Jersey.: Ablex 65–77.

CHAPTER 21

Yorkville Crossing: White Teens, Hip-Hop, and African American English

CECILIA CUTLER

Introduction

Recent work on language styles and stylization looks at how individuals play with language resources to construct distinctive configurations of the self. In a departure from traditional sociolinguistic approaches that attempt to establish the systematic nature of dialects and language varieties and map these on to social categories, many researchers now focus on the 'constructed' nature of identity, the agency of the speaker, and the use of language as a semiotic device to signal stances, alignments, and other modes of self presentation. This study explores how a white teenager employed stylistic elements of African American Vernacular English (AAVE) in order to project a Hip-Hop identity but also an urban, streetwise, gangster persona that differed significantly from what his upbringing might lead one to expect. White Hip-Hoppers such as this young man target a particular style that is commonly used by rap artists and young, urban African Americans which I call Hip-Hop Speech Style (HHSS). Unlike dialects which characterize the speech of cultural groups and registers which are tied to situations and activities, language styles are rooted in the speech of individuals. In stylizing their speech, individuals may draw on elements from dialects and registers, but they are using these elements alongside a range of other semiotic devices such as fashion and gestures to signal individual distinctiveness (Irvine 2001).

In the mid-1990s, there was a marked trend in cities as well as suburban areas of the United States for adolescents and teenagers of European-American heritage to the adopt fashions, gestures, and speech styles that were associated with urban African American youth. This trend has continued to the present such that Hip-Hop now represents a more mainstream identity for young people than it once did. Significantly, Hip-Hop culture and the consumption of rap music in particular have played a mediating role in this process, allowing any young person, no matter what his or her background is, to experience a commodified version of urban black American youth culture with little or no actual face-to-face contact with young African Americans.

The current chapter builds on a study done of a 13-year-old girl named Carla who grew up in a black neighborhood in Camden, New Jersey. The author (Hatala 1976) claimed that Carla had acquired African American Vernacular English (AAVE), but her professor, William Labov, reanalysed the data and found that Carla had only acquired a subset of pronunciation features and none of the grammatical, sentence level features of AAVE (Labov 1980). Hatala's research and Labov's reanalysis raised questions about whether and to what extent outsiders can acquire or learn a second dialect, especially the grammatical patterns associated with it.

In this chapter, we examine the speech of 'Mike', a white 16-year-old boy who, like Carla, uses a number of AAVE features. On a personal level there were some important social differences between Mike and Carla: Carla grew up in an overwhelmingly working-class African American neighborhood in Camden, New Jersey, whereas Mike lived in one of the wealthiest neighborhoods in New York City, attended an exclusive private high school, and associated with a primarily white peer group. Carla's friends were mainly African American and her adoption of AAVE features may have reflected an effort to adapt to her environment, but Mike's linguistic behavior begs another explanation.

According to Rose, whites are 'fascinated by [black culture's] differences, drawn in by mainstream social constructions [of black culture] ... as a forbidden narrative, [and] a symbol of rebellion' (1994: 5). In this line of interpretation, the adoption of HHSS is an attempt by young middle class whites like Mike to take part in the complex prestige of African American youth culture. In what follows, I shall elaborate on this, referring to Mike's case in order to discuss the role of Hip-Hop culture in young whites' motivations to adopt HHSS.

Mike's Background

Like many young people who are drawn to Hip-Hop, Mike began showing signs of his affiliation at about the time he hit puberty (age 13). He started wearing exceedingly oversized jeans, designer sneakers, and listening to rap music. Mike became part of a growing cohort of white, well-to-do teenagers dubbed 'prep school gangsters' (Sales 1996). At around the same time he began to change the way he spoke, which initially appeared to be a form of crossing as described by Rampton (1995, Chapter 20).

At first, Mike's linguistic efforts to employ this language were rather fleeting and tentative, but eventually his casual linguistic style began to reflect notable influence from AAVE phonology and Hip-Hop slang. One incident in particular marks an early attempt at imitating Hip-Hop speech style (HHSS). During a phone call with his best friend, Mike made a quick conversational repair to a highly recognized AAVE vernacular form shown in Extract 1.

Extract 1

Mike (age 13; 1993): I gotta ask, I mean *aks* [æks] my mom.

Hewitt (1986) showed that in Britain some white adolescents from primarily white neighborhoods pass through a phase in which they display a cultural allegiance with blacks. Mike behaved in a similar fashion, voicing frequent criticism of groups he viewed as anti-African American (including Jewish- and Korean-Americans), and even accusing his mother of racism when she affectionately referred to one of his African American childhood friends as 'el negrito' (his mother is from Spain). He tried to hide the fact that he lived in an expensive neighborhood in Manhattan by giving out his older brother's Brooklyn phone number to friends and acquaintances.

Mike's projection of a Hip-Hop identity drew on stereotyped conceptions of gangs and African American urban street culture. Discussing formative sociolinguistic studies of AAVE, Morgan criticizes their simplistic depiction of vernacular black culture and language as 'male, adolescent, insular, and trifling' (1994: 328), and indeed a comparable reductionism seems to be at work in the way that many white male teens interpret Hip-Hop culture. Mike's claims of authenticity took the form of activities he and others associated with urban black and Latino youth: he adopted a 'tag' name which he scrawled on the walls of banks and expensive apartment buildings near his house, he began experimenting with drugs, he joined a gang, and he had frequent run-ins with the police. At the end of his first year of high school (when he was 14), a 'friend' (in his words) pushed him through a glass door, cutting through several tendons and a nerve in each wrist. Following surgery and several weeks of recovery, he went out to Central Park against the doctor's orders where some rival gang members – most of them also white – held him down and broke his arms with baseball bats. His mother hoped that these experiences would scare him into changing his behavior but this was not played out immediately. Mike continued to see the same friends and was ejected from the private school he had been attending since kindergarten.

In many ways the position of Hip-Hop in American youth culture has shifted since Mike entered adolescence in the mid-1990s. It appeared that Mike was drawn to Hip-Hop, especially gangster rap, precisely because it seemed off-limits and represented such a contrast to his own rather protected upbringing. Today, Hip-Hop is one of the predominant musical genres played on music video channels and has become more accepted by mainstream culture and the media – something Cornyetz refers to as the 'massification of rap and hip hop style' (1994: 114). In this vein, Cornyetz argues that 'rap has entered a stage characterized by the "sanitization" of Hip-Hop subculture as it makes its appearance in mass culture' (1994: 133n.). But gangster rap's assault on middle-class sensibilities seems to continue unabated. Hornby writes in the New Yorker that not even the 'sonic ferocity' of punk rock music prepares one for the 'sordid, self-mythologizing' nature of gangster rap, a genre that centers on the urban, black gang lifestyle (2001: 167).

In line with the appeal of gangster rap among white male teenagers, Mike's linguistic and social behavior revealed an essentialized conception of young African American males. The lengths that he went to in order to live out some sort of authentic gang experience are probably not very typical, yet his case can provide useful insight into why many white adolescent males are drawn to Hip-Hop as well as their language attitudes. Subsequent interviews with young people I have conducted since 1997 reveal distinct ideologies. Some young whites view their use of HHSS and involvement in Hip-Hop as a form of symbolic political alignment with African Americans and other oppressed or disadvantaged groups. For others, using HHSS symbolizes individual alienation and can mark the speaker as an outsider (where Hip-Hop is not a mainstream youth style). Increasingly, however, it has become the dominant form of youth culture, meaning that young people are now often drawn to it by a desire to fit in (cf. Bucholtz 2001) rather than to reject mainstream identities.

One additional interpretation for the appeal of Hip-Hop culture among white adolescent males may be found in essentialized perceptions of black masculinity. Bucholtz writes, '[w]hite male adolescents position black masculinity, in contrast to white masculinity, as physically powerful and locally dominant' (1998: 1). This view is shaped by racist ideologies that link black masculinity to 'hyper-physicality, hyper-sexuality and physical strength' (Bucholtz 1999: 444), and the white male adolescent fixation with Hip-Hop may represent a desire to project a more masculine identity (cf. Cornyetz 1994).

Mike's Speech

A number of sociolinguists have noted the relative ease with which outsiders can acquire superficial phonological and lexical features of another language variety as opposed to syntax (Labov 1972, 1980; Labov and Harris 1986; Ash and Myhill 1986). In line with this, most of the AAVE-like elements in Mike's speech were indeed phonological, most notably in his tendency toward postvocalic /r/-lessness (*car* as 'cah') and the monophthongization of the /ay/ diphthong (*rhyme* becomes 'rahm'), although he also displayed awareness of syntactic features like habitual *be*.

With regard to /r/-lessness (henceforth /r/-Ø), Labov showed that black speakers differed from whites particularly when a word ending in /r/ is followed by a word beginning with a vowel (as in *four o'clock*): white /r/-less New Yorkers pronounce an /r/ when it is followed by a vowel, but for many in the African American speech community, /r/ becomes a glide or disappears in this position (1972:13). No-one in Mike's family was /r/-less. He wasn't either before the age of 13. However, by the age of 16 his speech showed considerable /r/-Ø (see Table 21.1). This extended to cases where /r/ was followed by a vowel at a word boundary (her age) as shown in Extract 2. Mike's rate of /r/-Ø in this latter environment was 33 percent.

Extract 2

Mike (age 16; 1996): Yo, she still looks *her age* [hə eɪdʒ]

Table 21.1 shows the distribution of /r/-Ø in Mike's speech as compared to the casual speech of Dr. Dre, the African American rap artist and producer recorded from an interview broadcast on the BBC in 2000. Although not identical, the data show that Mike patterns closely to Dr. Dre with regard to postvocalic preconsonantal /r/-Ø (VrC) and approaches Dr. Dre's rate of /r/-Ø when followed by a vowel at a word boundary (Vr##V).

A second pattern found in Mike's speech is the tendency to monophthongize the /ay/ diphthong. The second element of the diphthong or double vowel, the vowel /y/, is reduced or deleted and the first element, /a/, is optionally lengthened, resulting in the pronunciation [ta:m] for *time* and [ra:m] for *rhyme*. Monophthongization is described as a regional marker throughout the

Table 21.1   */R/-Ø in Mike's Speech*

Speaker	VrC	N=	Vr##V	N=
Dr. Dre	77%	142	79%	24
Mike	62%	250	33%	18

American South and the Outer Banks that has been shared by European and African Americans for at least the past 100 years (Anderson 1999). It is also found in the speech of African Americans in northern cities like Detroit and New York, but not at all in the speech of whites from those areas.

For this study, I looked only at monophthongal /ay/ in open syllables or syllables with voiced coda consonants. Anderson (1999) reports that African Americans in Detroit monophthongize /ay/ roughly 76–83 percent in open syllables and syllables with voiced coda consonants. Mike's rate of monophthongization which was 50 percent (N=88) approaches the African Americans in Anderson's data.

Mike also displayed knowledge of AAVE syntactic patterns such as habitual *be* – the use of *be* in its finite form. Habitual *be* is classified as an aspectual marker. Just as tense markers indicate *when* the action takes place, aspectual markers indicate *how* the action takes place. Habitual *be* usually indicates action that is repetitive or habitual as opposed to momentary. A sentence such as 'Keysha be trippin'' indicates that Keysha is always or usually tripping (acting funny). Recent research on habitual *be* suggests that its use is on the rise among young African Americans (Rickford 1999). Morgan (1993) writes that habitual *be* has become a marker of identity for young African Americans and Josey (1999) suggests it might be part of black teenagers' efforts not to sound white.

The use of habitual *be* as a full copula with noun phrases has been identified as one of the defining features of HHSS (Alim 2004; Morgan 2001). Rap artists have reinforced the use of habitual *be* with noun phrases as in Extract 3 below and similar tokens are easy to come across in the speech of deejays and in rap music lyrics on commercial rap radio stations in New York City like Hot 97 (cited in Alim 2004: 398).

Extract 3
New York's Busta Rhymes: This beat **be** the beat for the street.

Although awareness of habitual *be* is quite high among whites, they do not tend to use it very much in their reproductions or performances of AAVE. Preston (1992) reports no instances of habitual *be* use among white college students who were asked to 'talk black' on tape, and Ash and Myhill (1986) make no mention of its use by whites living in African American neighborhoods. Nor does it come up in any of the discussions about Carla, the 13-year-old white girl who grew up in an African American neighborhood. Mike used habitual *be* very sporadically and I was only able to capture a very small number of tokens on tape, one of which appears in Extract 4.

Extract 4
Mike (age 16; 1996): You know sometimes how they **be** wise asses, 'Oh, you have money and ya doin' that shit' ((click)).

Grammar and segmental phonology do not, of course, provide the only – or even the strongest – indication that Mike was orienting to HHSS in his speech. Although his repertoire also included a more standard speech style, he could employ HHSS prosodic features such as vowel lengthening, syllable contraction and expansion, stress and rhythm. Measuring and quantifying such features is difficult, since, as Baugh (1983) points out, they are common to most English dialects. However, as a rule, informal AAVE shows a tendency to contract the initial syllable and expand the second syllable in polysyllabic words with second-syllable stress (for example, 'fraid' for *afraid*). The second syllable variably undergoes vowel lengthening and/or receives greater stress than it would in more formal conversation. Examples of this from Mike's speech are his pronunciation of words like *suppose* as [spoːz], and *confusion* [kəˈfjuːʒn] His realization of *confusion* also contains a completely nasalized vowel in the first syllable, a feature of AAVE cited in Rickford (1999).

Lastly, an alignment with Hip-Hop showed up in the Hip-Hop terms that Mike used in his everyday speech. The study of lexical usage is not really quantifiable, but it can show how speakers employ particular expressions contextually. Some of these terms fall into the category of formulaic expressions while others such as *What up?* and its variants *Wassup?*, and *'ssup?* fall under the category of greetings. A very commonly used 'context-dependent substitute noun' in HHSS is *the shit* which can substitute for any other noun because its meaning depends entirely on the context (Alim 2004). Then there is a series of emphatic terms that come from current Hip-Hop slang like *hell yeah*, or *hells yeah*, *true that*, *for real*, and *word* (cf. Smitherman 1998). Generally, these expressions indicate strong agreement with what was said in the previous turn.

One other group of expressions such as *brother*, *bro*, *nigga*, *kid*, *b*, and *girl* can be termed forms of address. We can see a couple of these in Extract 5 below where Mike and his friends are playing strip poker. Mike is losing and he is complaining that his friends haven't had to take off as many layers of clothing as he has. Hip-Hop terms appear in bold face type. Mike refers to others (all of whom are white) in the room directly and indirectly as *niggas* in lines 10, 19, 21, 23 and 24.

Extract 5

Mike (age 16, and four friends playing strip poker; 1996)[1]

1 B-Boy: **Yo**, you like my shorts, huh?
2 Gus: ⌊Fuck you.
3 Mike: I'm done with you.
4 Katie: ⌊Three more rounds!
5 Mike: I got the ((wi …))

```
 6 ((high pitched inaudible speech, laughing))
 7 Mike:    Get yuh pants down!
 8 Mary:            ⌊We're on the same side!
 9 Katie:   ((son..))
10 Mike:    NIGGA, look at these NIGGAS.
11 Mary:           ⌊Yo, he's got like
12 Mike:    Chill
13 Mary:    ⌊-he's got like...
14 Mike:    Chill!
15 Mary:    [-he's got like...
16 Mike:    Chill!
17 Mary:              He's got like a bathing suit on! ((laughs))
18 Mike:                   ⌊Shut the fuck up! Look at these
19          NIGGAS over here.
20 Gus:     I got phat fuckin shorts on, kid!
21 Mike:          ⌊These NIGGAS's got shoes on.
22 Mary:    He's got a BATHING suit on!
23 Mike:                 ⌊This NIGGA'S got shorts
24          on. He's got a hat on. Yo, y'all NIGGAS have
25          like ten times more clothes than me ON, yo!
26 Mary:    Girls rule. What can I tell you?!
27 Gus:             ⌊Diablo, kid!
```

The excerpt above also shows how terms like *chill* function pragmatically as
a way for the speaker to get attention and/or gain the floor. We can see Mike
employing this expression repeatedly (and unsuccessfully) in lines 12, 14,
and 16 as he gets increasingly agitated. Then in line 18, he gains the floor
by ordering Mary to 'shut up' and makes his point by listing all the items of
clothing that the other boys are wearing.

One very intriguing usage that appears in the previous example is the use
of the word *nigga* by white Hip-Hoppers to refer to themselves and their white
friends (as well as others). Smitherman writes that forms like *nigga* reinforce
blackness 'since, whether used positively, generically, or negatively (and all
three nuances are possible), it can only refer to people of African descent'
(1998: 218). Clearly this definition needs to be expanded in light of the way
whites use the term. The positive and generic uses of *nigga* have become ubiquitous among many young urban African Americans in recent years. Alim
(2004: 399) describes how Tupac Shakur codifies the positive meaning by creating the following acronym: **N**ever **I**gnorant **G**etting **G**oals **A**ccomplished.

But it is important to recall that traditionally in the U.S. this word has
also had drastically different meanings and pragmatic functions depending on the racial identity of the speaker and his or her relationship to the

addressee. African Americans generally use the /r/-less variant, whether positive, neutral, or negative. Whites (in rhotic dialect areas) traditionally employ an /r/-full realization, [nɪgər], in addressing or talking about blacks in a highly pejorative and racist way. On the basis of this negative interpretation of the word alone, many teachers regardless of their ethnic background are often extremely offended and baffled by the ingroup use of this term by their African American students, even though it is the /r/-less variant. I would also add that many African American middle-class parents have a similar response. The widespread use of *nigga* among African Americans appears to have de-sensitized non-African Americans to its use and led to its ubiquity as a racially generic ingroup form of address, especially among male teenagers.

One of my original research questions when I began studying Mike's behavior was how white middle-class young people pick up features of HHSS given that their residential and educational environments are predominately white. Young people who live in New York City clearly have more opportunities to observe a variety of linguistic forms firsthand in subways, on street corners, in parks, night clubs, and so on than their suburban counterparts. Mike spent a great deal of time chilling or hanging out on the street with his friends – something that allowed for some measure of contact with African American and Latino kids. Some of his regular social activities, tagging, playing pool, drinking beer on the street with friends and going out to clubs on the weekends brought him into contact and sometimes conflict with kids from other neighborhoods and ethnic or social groups and may have helped him pick up features of HHSS, AAVE, and other New York City vernacular features he would not have otherwise been exposed to.

My initial research also points to a range of other potential sources for linguistic contact. Beyond the more and less direct face-to-face encounters, access to HHSS is also electronically mediated. As already mentioned, the Internet is an increasingly important source for Hip-Hop terms and expressions, and young people can turn to a host of on-line dictionaries and chat lines to improve their Hip-Hop vocabulary. For Mike and many others, though, popular music was particularly important. He was an avid consumer of rap music and spent a fair amount of time watching rap-oriented television programming. Rap fans regularly consult lyric sheets in CD cases, as well as on the Internet allowing them to learn the latest slang expressions even though they have no routine face-to-face contact with urban African American teenagers. Young people also regularly write rap lyrics using Hip-Hop orthography (cf. Olivo 2001) and post them on the Internet for others to read.

Mike's case suggests that it may be easier to draw on phonological and lexical features of another language variety such as AAVE than grammatical features, confirming the findings of Labov (1980) and Ash and Myhill (1986). Yet it is important to remember that stylization is not about systematic imitation of another group's language patterns, nor is it generally reflective of a desire to pass for a member of the imitated group. The speaker only needs to employ certain widely recognized speech markers in order for his target audience to understand the intended cultural reference. HHSS offers an array of linguistic resources for expressing identities rooted in some degree of affiliation with Hip-Hop culture, but speakers may use them differently and combine them with other sorts of speech markers in order to express their individuality.

Conclusion

Mike's early experimentation with AAVE at age 13–14 reflected an active identification with African Americans. But after changing schools at age 15 he began expressing resentment toward his African American peers, complaining that they 'always hang together' and 'separate themselves', and by 16 he seemed to see himself in opposition to the black community. Nevertheless, he continued to use AAVE phonology and hip-hop expressions throughout his teenage years and as a college student as a way to signal his on-going participation in hip-hop as the dominant consumption-based youth culture.

One important sociolinguistic question that emerges from this research is what happens to the speech patterns of individuals as they age. Adolescence is a volatile period when young people are coming to terms with where they come from and who they want to be. This case study suggests that young people become more selective in their use of HHSS as they enter college even while maintaining an affiliation with Hip-Hop. They tend to reduce or eliminate their use of HHSS phonology and morphosyntax when social norms demand more formal speech, but may continue to use particular lexical items and expressions like 'yo' and 'keepin' it real' around their peers. I have been able to observe Mike for several years since I first wrote about him in 1996 when he was 16 up to his early twenties and his behavior seems to bear out these generalizations. Many college-age male Hip-Hoppers also retain Hip-Hop dress patterns, that is, oversize pants and shirts, closely shorn hair, and so on though they may tone down these elements by wearing baggy but slightly more dressy pants and shirts (in short, replacing the 'ghetto' look with a more 'preppy' look).

White appropriation of black cultural forms is certainly not a new phenomenon, and the language, the music and fashions of black culture have long provided a rich source of inspiration for whites and others in the US and around the world (see Pennycook, Chapter 33). Indeed, there is little that the case study of a single individual can say about the general development of new trends in this relationship. Even so, a case like Mike's can usefully remind us that in spite of its reductive oversimplification of the sources that it targets, the adolescent construction of 'style' can involve tense negotiations of the relationship between self and other. Styling like Mike's may not match the standards of authenticity laid out in traditional Sociolinguistics, but both personally and socially, its origins are complex, its consequences can be serious, and although its representativeness can't be stated systematically, it is not an isolated instance.

NOTE

1. Transcription Conventions:
(( ))	speech inaudible; stage directions; nonverbal utterances
[	overlapping with previous turn
CAPITALS	loud or emphatic enunciation
Bold	instance usage or content relevant to discussion.
-	false start

REFERENCES

Alim, H. Samy. 2004. Hip Hop Nation Language. In Edward Finnegan and John R. Rickford (eds.) *Language in the USA: Themes for the Twenty-first Century*. Cambridge: Cambridge University Press. 387–411.

Anderson, Bridget. 1999. /ai / Monophthongization among African American Detroiters: Another case of dialect leveling? Paper presented at New Ways of Analyzing Variation conference. Toronto.

Ash, Sharon and John Myhill. 1986. Linguistic correlates of inter-ethnic contact. In David Sankoff (ed.) *Diversity and Diachrony*. Amsterdam/Philadelphia: John Benjamins. 33–44.

Baugh, John. 1983. *Black Street Speech: Its History, Structure, and Survival*. Austin, Texas: University of Texas Press.

BBC Tim Westwood Interview with Dr. Dre, Eminem, and Mailman. 2000. http://www.bbc.co.uk/radio1/westwood/.

Bucholtz, Mary. 1998. Geek the Girl: Language, femininity, and female nerds. In Natasha Warner, Ashlee Bailey and Monica Corston-Oliver (eds.) *Gender and Belief Systems: Proceedings of the Fourth Berkeley Women and Language Conference*. Berkeley, California: Berkeley Women and Language Group. 119–131.

Bucholtz, Mary. 1999. You da man: Narrating the racial other in the production of white masculinity. *Journal of Sociolinguistics* 3: 443–460.

Bucholtz, Mary. 2001. The Whiteness of Nerds: Superstandard English and racial markedness. *Journal of Linguistic Anthropology* 11: 84–100.

Cornyetz, Nina. 1994. Hip hop and racial desire in contemporary Japan. *Social Text* 4: 113–139.

Hatala, Eileen. 1976. Environmental effects on white students in black schools. Unpublished MA thesis. Philadelphia, Pennsylvania: University of Pennsylvania.

Hewitt, Roger. 1986. *White Talk Black Talk: Inter-racial Friendship and Communication amongst Adolescents*. Cambridge: Cambridge University Press.

Hornby, Nick. 2001. Pop Quiz: What does the new top ten list mean? *The New Yorker*. 27 August. 166–168.

Irvine, Judith. 2001. Style as distinctiveness. In Penelope Eckert and John R. Rickford (eds.) *Style and Sociolinguistic Variation*. Cambridge: Cambridge University Press. 21–43.

Josey, Meredith. 1999. That be all right now!: Be2 variation in an Atlantan African American community Ph.D. Unpublished Qualifying Paper, New York University.

Labov, William, and Wendell A. Harris. 1986. De facto segregation of black and white vernaculars. In David Sankoff (ed.) *Diversity and Diachrony*. Amsterdam/Philadelphia: John Benjamins. 1–24.

Labov, William. 1972. *Language in the Inner City*. Philadelphia, Pennsylvania: University of Pennsylvania Press.

Labov, William. 1980. Is there a creole speech community? In Albert Valdman and Arnold Highfield (eds.) *Theoretical Orientations in Creole Studies*. New York: Academic Press. 369–388.

Morgan, Marcyliena. 1993. Hip hop Hooray! The linguistic production of identity. Presented at Annual Meeting of the American Anthropological Association, Washington, D. C.

Morgan, Marcyliena. 1994. Theories and politics in African American English. *Annual Review of Anthropology* 23: 325–345.

Morgan, Marcyliena. 2001. Reading dialect and grammatical shout–outs in hip hop. Paper presented at the Linguistic Society of America Convention. Washington, D.C. January.

Olivo, Warren. 2001. Phat Lines: Spelling conventions in rap music. *Written Language and Literacy* 4: 67–85.

Preston, Dennis R. 1992. Talking black and talking white: A study in variety imitation. In Joan H. Hall, Nick Doane and Dick Ringler (eds.) *Old English and New: Studies in Language and Linguistics in Honor of Frederic G. Cassidy*. New York: Garland. 327–355.

Rampton, Ben. 1995. *Crossing: Language and Ethnicity Among Adolescents*. New York: Longman.

Rickford, John. 1999. *African American Vernacular English*. Oxford: Blackwell.

Rose, Tricia. 1994. *Black Noise: Rap Music and Black Culture in Contemporary America*. Hanover, New Hampshire: Wesleyan University Press.

Sales, Nancy J. 1996. Teenage gangland. *New York Magazine*, 16 December. 29: 32–39.

Smitherman, Geneva. 1998. Word from the hood: The lexicon of African-American Vernacular English. In Salikoko S. Mufwene, John R. Rickford, Guy Bailey and John Baugh (eds.) *African American English*. New York: Routledge. 203–225.

CHAPTER 22

Dialect Style, Social Class and Metacultural Performance: The Pantomime Dame

NIKOLAS COUPLAND

Dialect, Social Class and Hegemony

Demonstrating the statistical association between dialect variation and social class was a dominant concern of early variationist Sociolinguistics (see Part I of this volume). Dialect, but more typically that part of dialect that is commonly called 'accent', has repeatedly been shown to co-vary with indices of social class in Western Anglophone societies, particularly in urban settings. But what is social class? And how do accent and dialect function in relation to it?

Rampton interprets social class as 'the lived dominance and subordination of particular classes ... written into the whole body of practices and expectations experienced by the individual' (2006: 229; see also this volume). This replaces the variationist view of social class as a layered or stratified structure of society with a view of social class as a structuring of experience. It replaces the view of language as a set of indexical forms (such as accent features), whose use might correlate with social class categories, with a view of language as a social practice that might bring experiences of social class into people's lives. In Rampton's view, if social class matters in people's lives (and *without* subscribing to the view that it inevitably and always *does*), it ought to be possible to see and hear 'dominance and subordination' happening in social interaction. This is a very different matter from observing that people assigned to 'middle class' versus 'working class' groups (perhaps on the basis of their jobs, where they live, or how much they earn) have different accents, graded on a scale between 'standard' and 'non-standard'. The fact that class-related distributions of linguistic features exist is an important background consideration. But there is no political 'bite', or much explanatory value, in those patterns themselves. So we also need to work out what particular meanings are made when 'standard' and 'non-standard' accents are part of discursive practice, and there is no reason to believe that such meanings will be the same at different times and places, and in different local contexts of talk.

These are some of the reasons for adopting an interactional, critical and constructionist approach to dialect (and accent) in use, and this perspective has come to be associated with the unassuming label of sociolinguistic *style*. In William Labov's original conception, style or stylistic variation referred to how people speak differently across different social situations – again see Part I. It was therefore possible to conceive of language varying in two basic dimensions – a 'social' dimension, where speech variants patterned with some sociological dimension such as social class, and a 'stylistic' dimension, where the same variants patterned with different situational factors, such as speaking in 'formal' versus 'informal' situations. But critical stylistic research has collapsed this distinction. A perspective on 'dialect styling' (Coupland 2007) assumes that accent and dialect are a semiotic resource (among many other parallel resources) for constructing personal identities, relational configurations and group-level associations. Analyses trace the different pragmatic and other social effects created through these acts of identity. Stylistic operations around accent and dialect are therefore the basic means by which people express class-relevant distinctiveness and relations in their talk. From a styling viewpoint, the 'social dimension of language variation' that Labov refers to is merely a statistical abstraction based on observing many instances of stylistic/discursive practice, rather than anything theoretically distinct from styling in discourse.

Social class has its basis in social realities to do with authority, control, poverty and life chances. But meanings linked to social class are also created in discourse, and discursive action can have material consequences. If we define social class, as Rampton does, as a matter of dominance and subordination at the level of social groups, then class is a matter of hegemony. This is 'the legitimation of the cultural authority of the dominant group, an authority that plays a significant role in social reproduction', and 'the deep saturation of the consciousness of a society' (Woolard 1985: 739). Woolard aligns hegemony with Pierre Bourdieu's (1991) concept of 'symbolic domination', which works not so much by people submitting to dominant norms or, on the other hand, freely adopting them, and more by dominant values and dispositions being tacitly naturalised.

Following this chain of associations, social class can therefore be seen as a fundamentally ideological process through which the cultural authority of dominant groups seeps into people's consciousness, who, under particular circumstances, may accept is as 'the way things are'. The link to dialect is that, in Bourdieu's argument, 'standard' language forms are largely accepted as being 'correct' and 'authoritative'; they have high capital value in the linguistic marketplace, and this serves the interests of dominant groups who define what is and what is not 'standard' and 'correct'.

Linguistic Usage, Performance and Stylisation

There is evidence that standard accents of English continue to have high capital value, at least in Britain. In an online survey we conducted in association with the BBC, more than 5,000 people made assessments of the 'prestige' and 'attractiveness' of 34 accent-types that are regularly heard in Britain (Coupland and Bishop 2007). The results very largely confirmed those of smaller-scale research of a similar sort conducted over 30 years earlier, but with some interesting particular trends. The accent labelled 'standard English' was strongly favoured, for both prestige and attractiveness, while some urban vernacular accents, with Birmingham-accented English being the most extreme case, were quite heavily downgraded.

Of course, it is difficult to assess what social significance these patterns of decontextualised judgements have beyond the online task itself. The findings are consistent with the idea that, when they are asked to comment explicitly on linguistic variation, British people can draw on sets of internalised assumptions about accents that generate the highly regular patterns of judgement of the sort we found. People can and do recycle ideological discourses about British accents – which, on the evidence of this particular study, do seem to be 'saturated' throughout the population of respondents – working in favour of 'standard' voices. They do suggest that there is a high level of agreement about the market values of British accent varieties. But where, precisely, is the dominance or the subordination?

At the level of speech itself, it would obviously be wrong to suggest that simply using a 'non-standard' accent somehow entails, or lays a speaker open to, subordination. Accent often remains 'below the radar'. Often, and perhaps usually, accent doesn't stand out as salient feature in the constitution of speech events. Within groups of people who broadly share a pattern of pronunciation, accent is just 'how we speak', and it is interesting that in the Coupland and Bishop survey we found that a voice-type that we labelled 'an accent similar to my own' also attracted an extremely positive profile, even amongst speakers who must have had distinctive regional and social accents, relative to 'standard' speakers. Accent can become salient in social contexts where some sort of contrast is involved, for example, when people with different accents interact, or when accent is somehow foregrounded within the speech event. But even when accent is salient, social class meanings are not the only possible meaning that can be constructed, and not all class-related meanings amount to subordination.

If we take a constructionist stance on language and social class, and if we adopt the strong reading of class as cultural hegemony, we need to find evidence of subordination taking place – social class being brought into existence as '*lived* dominance and subordination', as Rampton suggests. And this sort of evidence is much harder to find. Rampton says that in his own data, collected among multi-ethnic kids in British schools, he actually sees little evidence of 'damage being done', even though the voicing of social class is fairly common. Care is needed, all the same, partly because it is not obvious what counts as dominance and subordination in practice. If we accept that impositional authority is often disguised as rationality, and that power often masquerades as solidarity, then we might miss the evidence we are seeking.

Also, in the discussion above, we have so far failed to take into account acts of *resistance* to class hegemony, and the concept of hegemony itself underplays the dialectic nature of ideology and the existence of competing discourses. Social class, for example, is unlikely to fully 'saturate' a society, to the extent that it becomes entirely invisible and therefore a matter of dogma. In circumstances where there *is lived* dominance and subordination, and where these processes *are* to some extent visible and objectifiable, there is likely to be an opportunity to challenge hegemonic assumptions, and particular resources for doing this. This sort of objectification and resistance is also within the domain of discourse. When people 'use dialect', including speaking through 'non-standard' and 'standard' accents, there is no reason to believe they do so, always and only, in the service of, or in compliance with, a dominant ideology. The meanings and values that are constructed, and the degrees of compliance or resistance that are achieved, are a function of how speech varieties are *contextualised*.

If we talk of *performing* accents rather than 'using' them, it becomes easier to see their creative potential, which includes their potential to transform and resist dominant social values. The concept of performance has been used in many different ways in Sociolinguistics, but I am using it here, broadly following Erving Goffman's (1981) dramaturgical perspective on social interaction, to imply that speakers often maintain a degree of critical distance from their own speech. That in turn means that speaking has a metalinguistic or metapragmatic dimension, because speakers are, to some extent, reflexively aware of their own styling operations can perceive alternatives for themselves. Even though an accent is a deeply coded facet of communicative practice, and part of what Boudieu calls the *habitus* (an ingrained communicative disposition laid down during socialisation), people certainly retain a degree of freedom and control over their own strategic operations through accent. Within limits, a speaker opts to use particular features or styles in preference to alternatives, anticipating that his or her performance will have particular sorts of impact on listeners and on the social situation. Performance is not always a matter of acting counter-normatively. People often opt to perform their speech, and themselves, in conformity with custom or with normative constraints, but this is not to say that the production format is any less one of performance.

We can then envisage different intensities of performance, from more mundane acts of performance to more spectacular ones. There is a broad category of events that we can call *high performance events*. They are distinguished by involving high levels of *focusing*, in different regards (Bauman 1992; Coupland 2007: 147–148). For example, the performance becomes the focal point of audience attention, and audiences are 'gathered' to witness it. Audiences are particularly attentive to performers' use of language and other meaningful actions and they expect them to have special significance – and often, significance beyond what is most immediately discernible. Reflexivity is heightened, because audiences can assume that a high performance event will have been designed or put on, here and now, with specific targeted values and outcomes. High performance events are typically institutionalised events, involving conventional technologies of performance, such as stages, curtains, a sequence of scenes, publicised *dramatis personae* lists and time schedules. But 'ordinary communication' can sometimes assume qualities of high performance, minus these trappings. Bauman and Briggs (1990; this volume) argue that performances of this sort play a key role in making culture visible, analysable and transportable. Performance is part of culture, but it also exposes culture – it is *metacultural*.

In terms of accent, high performance often involves not only styling but *stylisation*, which, following Bakhtin (1986) and critical commentaries by Rampton and others, I take to be a potentially subversive form of multi-voiced utterance. Accent is a productive resource for stylisation because speakers can perform other people's accents/voices. In Ben Rampton's concept (this volume) they can *cross* into sociolinguistic practices most commonly associated with others. Stylisation is a metaphorical construction that brings meanings and values from outside the current context of talk into play, and recontextualises them. It tends towards hyperbole, with clear and often 'over-drawn' or cartoon-like representations of characters and social types, selected from known repertoires. But stylisation is also ambiguous and has an 'as if' quality. Even though the immediate social and cultural referents of stylised performances may be easy enough to retrieve, the purpose of the performance and its characterisations may not be so obvious – it will need to be inferred. High performance stylisation can be parodic and destabilising; in extreme forms it defines whole performance genres such as burlesque and carnival, as analysed by Bakhtin (and see Rampton 2006: 346ff. on 'the grotesque').

Pulling these ideas together, we can see that accent stylisation has a part to play in metacultural performances, reflexively designed and staged in ways that make reference to wider ideological relations and histories. In places where class and cultural hegemony has left a significant social impact, dialect stylisation might have a role to play in highlighting hegemonic relations, opening them up to scrutiny, and implicitly suggesting different social ordering principles. This is what, I want to suggest, is happening in the pantomime Dame data, below.

South Wales, Cultural Hegemony and Industrialisation

Social inequality takes different forms in different historical and spatial environments. In Wales, the historical experience of social class has been strongest and most bitter in the Valleys, the upland areas between the south Wales coastal belt and rural mid-Wales, spreading across most of the breadth of the country between rural south-west Wales and rural Gwent. The Valleys were rapidly industrialised, particularly centring on deep mining for coal – the steam coal that fuelled the enormous expansion of British, European and other countries' transport and industrial processing from the 1840s, reaching a production peak of 56 million tons in 1913. The Valleys were a zone of extreme exploitation, controlled by mine owners mainly from outside the area. Socialist consciousness gelled in the middle years of the twentieth century in Wales, with the National Union of Mineworkers being formed in 1944 after decades of unrest and conflict, including the Depression, the 1926 general strike and the 1927 hunger march.

The South Wales coalfield fostered a collectivist, radical socialist ideology, galvanised by a series of mining disasters, illness, oppressive working conditions and environmental degradation, and positively expressed through the self-improvement programmes of the Miners' Institutes, choirs, bands, chapel-going and rugby. As Jones (1992: 340) suggests, the association of mining with at least one coherent version of Welshness retains a powerful resonance in post-industrial Wales. Socialist resistance to oppression became part of the national consciousness, and 'Wales versus England' took on a powerful class-based resonance, overlaid on centuries of cross-national antagonisms. Social class and, for many, a sense of national identity became closely intertwined, to the extent that it was possible to feel one's Welsh identity as an opposition to privilege and capitalist assertion, whose source was 'naturally' in England.

A programme of pit closures began in the 1950s, leading to the decimation of deep mining communities in the 1980s and the total elimination of deep mining as a commercial venture today. This is widely understood to have been Margaret Thatcher's personal project of retribution against socialist and union-based challenges to her right-wing Conservative government. The de-industrialisation of the Valleys has been one of the most rapid and aggressive social changes ever seen in Britain, generating massive social deprivation which is very much in evidence in the first decade of the twenty-first century. We therefore have a recent history of social class conflict in the South Wales Valleys that fully lives up to the rubric of 'the lived dominance and subordination of particular classes', but that also foregrounds resistance. The work-based practices and the community and family structures that constituted social class experience in the Valleys have now largely disappeared, impacting particularly strongly on men, and leaving damaging levels of male unemployment, general poverty and acute health problems. How the material and symbolic voids will be filled remains an open question. But what part might language play in the contemporary climate?

The Stylisation of Valleys and Posh English Voices in Pantomime

After the rapid influx of workers into the Valleys in the early industrial period, from other parts of Wales and well beyond, Valleys speech settled into being one of the most clearly recognised and, some studies suggest (Garrett, Coupland and Williams 2003), stigmatised English varieties in Wales. More research is needed. But there are undoubtedly strong indexical associations between Valleys voice and a historical sense of place – and a sense of *class* within that history. Lynda Mugglestone (2003) has suggested that, in Britain generally, 'standard' or 'received' English pronunciation has taken on more negative associations, which she sums up as a shift from 'proper' to 'posh'. But in the linguistic ideologies of the Valleys (and of most of Wales), 'posh English speech' has historically defined the axis of political *and national* antagonisms, and Valleys people have never succumbed to the sociolinguistic ideology of 'proper' English. Posh speech is not Welsh speech.

It is in high performance speech events that we most clearly see these symbolic but historically real antagonisms being played out and reworked. *Extract 1*, below, is from a Christmas pantomime, *Aladdin*, performed in late December 2001 at a theatre in a small Valleys town. The show was toured around other theatres across south Wales, although its cultural roots are firmly Valleys. For example, the pantomime is produced by, and stars, a well-known local radio and television performer, Owen Money, who plays the character Wishy Washy. Owen Money is an influential apologist for Valleys speech and cultural values in his radio, TV and live shows in Wales, and he is prominent in the Valleys community in other ways too; he is, for example, director of Merthyr Tydfil football club.

The British phenomenon of pantomime is not easy to explain to people unfamiliar with the genre. Drawing on the traditions of the Italian Commedia dell' Arte, but also on the British Music Hall, it is a generally low budget, burlesque form of music, comedy and drama, performed with a live orchestra, although some productions in major cities can be expensively staged, and the format is on the whole apparently lucrative. 'Pantos' are at present gaining in popularity (Lipton 2007). They run at very many theatres through England and Wales over the winter months, being thought of as Christmas entertainment but not thematically linked to Christmas itself. Pantomimes are often said to be entertainment for children, although family groups make up most audiences. Each pantomime theme is a variation on one of a small number of traditional narratives, with roots in folk tales, often orientalised. Each theme mingles ethnic and temporal dimensions with abandon, and the blurring of social categories in the genre is a key part of its destabilising, carnivalesque potential. The performance of *Aladdin* that I refer to here, like the animated Disney film of that title, builds its plot around an Arabian Nights magic lamp and a magic genie. But the performance also uses stage sets including 'Old Peking', and the Wishy Washy character's name refers to his menial job in a Chinese laundry.

Pantomime plots always involve magic, intrigue, royalty, peasantry and a love-quest. Typically, a noble and honourable prince, the 'Principal Boy', conventionally played by a female, dressed in a tunic and high boots, falls in love with a beautiful girl, the 'Principal Girl', from a poor family. The Principal Girl has either large, ugly, vain sisters or a large, ugly, vain mother, referred to as a Dame – these females are conventionally played by males. The Dame character is named The Widow Twankey in the Aladdin panto. Characters are starkly drawn and heavily stylised. Young love triumphs and royalist grandeur is subverted.

The semiotic constitution of pantomime is bricolage, intermixing light popular songs and comedy routines, exorbitant colours and costumes, and with vernacular, self-consciously 'common' values set against regal pomp and transparently evil figureheads. The interactional format involves a good deal of audience participation and in-group humour. Hackneyed and formulaic plots are interspersed with disrespectful humour on topics of local or contemporary interest. Conventional teases appeal to children (and others) in the audience, who have to shout warnings to the heroine princess, for example, when an evil emperor approaches, or to help the audience's friend (in this case Wishy Washy) to develop his quest (for example to find the magic lamp).

The extract below is the pantomime Dame/Widow Twankey's first entrance in the Valleys performance, close to the beginning of the show after the opening song performed by the full cast and live orchestra. The Dame's entrance is a tone-setting moment for the whole pantomime. She is the mother of

Aladdin, the hero, and she returns regularly through the pantomime, mainly to add the most burlesque dimension of humour on the periphery of the plot. Next to Wishy Washy, she is affectively closest of all the characters to the audience. Pompous, vain and mildly salacious, she is nevertheless funny and warm-hearted. Her transparent personal deficiencies leave her open to be liked, despite them.

Extract 1: Aladdin – Widow Twankey's entrance
(The Dame enters, waving, to the music of '*There is nothing like a dame*')
Line
1 hello everyone
2 (Audience: hello)
3 hello boys and girls
4 (Audience: hello)
5 hello mums and dads
6 (Audience: hello)
7 grans and grandads brothers and sisters aunts and uncles
8 and all you lovely people back home ooh hoo
9 hey (.) now I've met (.) all of you
10 it's time for <u>you</u> to meet (drum roll) <u>all</u> (.) <u>of</u> (.) (cymbal crashes) <u>me</u>
11 (Audience: small laugh)
12 and there's a lot of <u>me</u> (.) to <u>meet</u> (chuckles)
13 now my name is (.) the <u>Wid</u>ow <u>T-wankey</u>
14 and do know what (.) I've been a widow now (.) for <u>twenty-five years</u> (sobs)
15 (Audience: o:h)
16 yes (.) ever since my <u>poor husband died</u>
17 oh what a <u>man</u> he was (.) he was <u>gorgeous</u> he was
18 do you know (.) he was the <u>tallest man</u> (.) in <u>all</u> of Peking
19 and he always <u>had</u> (.) a <u>runny nose</u> (chuckles)
20 hey (.) do you know what we <u>called</u> him?
21 '<u>Lanky Twankey</u> with a <u>Manky Hanky</u>'
22 (Audience: laugh)
23 hey (.) and guess what (.) I've still got his manky hanky to this <u>very day</u>
24 look look at that ugh
25 (Audience: o:h laughs)
26 hey (to orchestra) look <u>after</u> that for me will you?
27 you look like a <u>bunch</u> of <u>snobs</u>
28 (Audience: laugh)
29 anyway (.) I can't stand around here <u>gossiping</u> all day
30 <u>I</u> have got a <u>laundry</u> to run
31 ooh (.) and I've got to find my <u>two</u> naughty boys (.) A<u>ladd</u>in (.) and
32 <u>Wishy Washy</u>

32 so (.) I'll see you lot later <u>on</u> is <u>it</u>?
33 (Audience: ye:s)
34 (to camera) I'll see <u>you</u> later on (.) bye for now (.) tarra (.) bye bye

If we start with the assumption that high performance events can have a metacultural function, how might metacultural awareness and critique work through this Valleys pantomime? Thematically, the conventional pantomime narrative – royalist authority being subverted and the ennoblement of the oppressed – has a particular resonance in local Valleys history. It is easy to map South Wales's socialist past and its recurrent reservations about royalty onto the plot of Aladdin. Nor does this sort of connection have to be inferred for the first time in each context of performance. I noted above that pantomime conventionally intersperses local community themes into its fictional plot-lines. It routinely articulates its own contextualisation, for example, when performers break out of their character roles and refer to the theatre setting, the audience and their own performances. Pantomime is always richly framed in the 'meta' dimension, and the issue is not whether there is metacultural reach, but how far that reach extends. The Wishy Washy character in this performance of Aladdin, as I noted above, is fully recognisable as a local media celebrity, and pantomimes generally have only a thin characterological membrane through which audiences see and appreciate (especially in more expensive productions) 'real celebrities', such as popular singers or comedians. Beyond these individual cases, heavy stylisation ensures that pantomime characters fall into easily recognisable types, with the main dichotomy being between a category of 'good, deserving, beautiful, disenfranchised' characters and a category of 'evil, scheming, ugly, oppressive' characters. A further contrast is between characters who are 'authentic' and those who are 'inauthentic', and this last quality opens up the possibility of some characters being 'inauthentic' but not 'evil'.

In the Dame character, we have someone who is conventionally good but scheming, and *both* authentic *and* inauthentic. She is vain and opinionated, but ultimately warm-heated. In fact her character dramatises a politics of authenticity, and it does this, in the Valleys case, partly through visual means and partly through indexicalities of dialect. The most striking socio-phonetic contrast in the extract is between the Dame's aspirationally posh, mock-Received Pronunciation (RP) voice at the opening of the extract, and the broad vernacular Valleys voice which she otherwise uses. The principal variable speech features that carry this contrast are listed in Table 22.1, where the first-listed variant in square brackets in each case is the 'standard', RP-like variant. Italicised lexical forms are items appearing in the transcript.

Table 22.1 Phonological variables for Valleys English

(ou) –	[əʊ], [ɔʊ], [oː]	(*hello, home, nose; widow* has only the diphthong options)
(ei) –	[ei], [eː]	(*name, later,* but not *hey, day, anyway,* which again have only the diphthongal variant)
(ʌ) –	[ʌ], [ə]	(*brothers, lovely, bunch*)
(ai) –	[ai], [ɔɪ]	(*died, time, find, bye*)
(iw) –	[juː], [jɪw], [ɪw]	(*you,* where the 'local' variant has a prominent first element of the glide, contrasting with the RP-type glide to prominent /uː/)
(ɔː) –	[ɔː], [ʊə]	(*poor*)
(a) –	[æ], [a]	(*grans, grandads, back, Twankey, man, had, Lanky, manky, hanky, stand, Aladdin*)
(h) –	[h], [Ø]	(*hello, home, hey, husband, hanky, he*)
(ng) –	[ŋ], [n]	(*gossiping*)

Lines 1–8 show centralised onset of (ou) in all three tokens of *hello* and in *home*, contrasting with monophthongal [oː] which occurs later, for example, in the word *nose*. In fact [əʊ] is more posh than 'standard', since it indexes a 'middle-class' identity that is not regularly part of the Valleys sociolinguistic ecosystem. We also have fully audible [h] in all cases in these opening lines. The RP voice resonates most strongly at line 8 in the utterance *all you lovely people back home,* where *you, lovely, back* and *home* have significant RP, non-local tokens. These features apparently out-group the Dame relative to the Valleys context in which the performance is geographically and ideologically situated. The Dame's garish, extravagantly multi-coloured dress, plus of course the transparent trans-gendering of her performance, work together to index her inauthenticity, and her phonetic performance of posh as part of this construction creates the inference (unless it is there already) that posh speech *is* inauthentic.

Aitch-less *hey* at the beginning of line 9 and the Valleys-type schwa realisation of the first syllable of *brothers* (in place of the RP wedge vowel) mark a strong shift from posh into Valleys vernacular. The abrupt stylistic shift indexes a cracked or unsustainable posh self-presentation, a chink in the Dame's dialectal armour of posh, which is thereby confirmed to be as suspect as her dress-sense. After line 8, all tokens of (iw) have the Valleys local form, including *you* in lines 9 and 10 (this second instance said with contrastive stress). Note how the discourse itself signals this stance shift when, despite having done conventional greeting, the Dame says it's time for the audience to meet her – and presumably then, her *real* self. The quip that 'there's a lot of me to meet' (line 12, acknowledging that she is a big 'woman') shifts her self-presentation back into the realm of the authentic, and her accompanying laughter implies that she shares the audience's reaction to her visible persona.

The Dame's self- introduction at line 13 pronounces the word *name* with the local vernacular form [e:], although *Widow T-wankey*, when she mentions the name itself, reverts to an RP pronunciation ([æ] for short (a) in the first syllable of *Twankey*). This single utterance again achieves a neat splitting of personas, between the introducing voice (*my name is*) and the introduced voice (*Twankey*), once again pointing up the Dame's capacity for inauthentic and more authentic alternative self-presentations. The sequence setting up the *manky hanky* word play (meaning 'disgusting handkerchief') is performed in a fully formed local vernacular. All three vowels in the stressed syllables of *poor husband died* (line 16) are local Valleys variants. Aitchless *he* on the three occasions in line 17, stressed-syllable schwa in *runny* and monophthongal *nose* in line 19, are prominent.

The Dame's Valleys vernacular style is realised in the grammar and vocabulary too. We have reduplicative *he was* at the end of line 17, the word *manky* (meaning 'disgusting'), the invariant tag *is it?* at line 31 (which, more usually in its negative form *isn't it?* is a strong stereotype of Welsh English), and colloquial *tarra* for 'good bye' at line 34. In further referential aspects of the discourse too, we find personal claims being counter-pointed (and confirmed to have been mock) by later claims. The Dame's feigned grief at being widowed (lines 14 and 16) is subverted by the joke at the husband's expense (line 21) and by laughter interspersed into expressions of apparent grief. The disrespectful word play, *bunch of snobs* (*snobs* evoking 'snot' or nose effluent, visually rendered by the bright green stain on the handkerchief) addressed to the orchestra, builds an allegiance *against* the posh persona she has been affecting. *Snobs* is a direct reference to the politics of both posh and authenticity. The orchestra members are dressed in evening suits and, for present purposes, they embody upper class and hegemonic stances, of the sort that the Dame has herself fleetingly claimed then set aside in acts of self-subversion.

Metacultural Performance and Cultural Practice

It could be argued that pantomimes, and performance events generally, provide data that is irrelevant for Sociolinguistics. The identity potential of accent and dialect has sometimes been said to be activated in the 'real' language of 'real' speech communities, which should therefore take priority. Variationist Sociolinguistics has usually tried to access the untrammelled vernacular, and Widow Twankey's speech (and the speech of all performers in staged performances) can be said to be 'unnatural', precisely because it is 'staged'.

There are several counter-arguments. One is that the ideal of naturalism has been over-played in Sociolinguistics, and that notions of 'natural data' and 'authentic language' are themselves quite fundamentally compromised. Speaking, as I suggested earlier, always entails a 'meta' element and therefore a degree of performativity and the option to self-present strategically. A sense of authenticity is undoubtedly a powerful and important quality of social and personal existence, and to some extent we see that being played out even in the pantomime data. The Widow Twankey's self-*in*validations, in her subversion of posh, also facilitate a contrasting sense of self-validation, indexed through vernacular speech style. Accent and dialect *do* have the potential to evoke a sense of 'who we really are', not least by evoking a contrastive sense of 'who we definitely are not'. But identity is not easily corralled and it is best seen as a work-in-progress – a matter of negotiation or aspiration among shifting considerations and contexts. Identity lies in the domain of social action more than in the domain of social being.

Once we concede that social and cultural identities are projects entertained in discourse, then performance emerges as the 'most natural' place to witness the social construction of identity, and authenticity emerges as one of the qualities of identity that are up for discursive construction. This need not be the cynical perspective that it appears to be, because socially constructed authenticities are experienced as real authenticities. Like social identities, culture itself remains something of an empty set until it is activated, until it is brought into meaningful existence in social action. When that action is organised into specific performance genres that have some acknowledged metacultural focus, then culturally defining meanings can become clearer, but also less dogmatic and less inevitable. They are meanings that, as performers and audiences, we can wither play along with (as we typically do) or withhold from.

When we play along, we can do this in different communicative frames, perhaps in full engaged and celebratory mode or, alternatively, with degrees of agnosticism, irony or even knowing self-deception. How the pantomime audience at the Valleys performance of Aladdin frames its engagement with the Widow Twankey is difficult to assess from the performance data itself. But notice how they *do* play along, and how audience members have a legitimate and indeed a necessary voice as co-performers in panto. There are moments, even in the brief single extract we have considered, when the Dame positively invites very specific responses from the audience. The audience responds audibly to her initial greetings, but not with any great enthusiasm or commitment (see lines 2, 4 and 6). Then the audience has a more pre-figured turn at line 15, when they deliver a formulaic *o:h* in response to the Dame's phoney lament about being a widow; their actions are therefore part of the process of invalidation. Emotional empathy and co-performance happen most obviously at lines 22, 25 and 28. The first two of these are when the audience is suitably disgusted by the *manky hanky* – a glowingly (green) iconic thing – and the second is when the audience aligns with the Dame's *bunch of snobs* insult. The audience laughs along with the Dame's comment to the orchestra, and to some extent they therefore share her stance on snobbery and are drawn into specific anti-snobbish, dialect-indexed values. The interaction creates a space for joint participation and fills that space with a vernacular Valleys style of speech and an ideological alignment against 'posh'.

So this reflexive and stylised public performance is able to focus and put on display important parts of a local vernacular culture. It can play out and dramatise intergroup social class antagonisms that have had, and are still having, real material consequences for Valleys people. But this is still panto-mime – a cultural form that keeps asserting the inauthenticity of its imme-diate references. The Dame's stylised voices, filtered through the inherent extravagances and dissonances of the pantomime genre, come with that 'as if' framing. Do these performances matter? To the extent that, for some people, they do, we might speculate that audiences coming together to laugh their way through stylised accounts of good and evil, of authentic and inauthentic, of us and them, of vernacular and posh, and of Wales and England invite newer rather than older interpretations of what it means to live in the post-industrial Valleys. The old antagonisms are there, on stage; they can be performed. At least in stylised versions, the Valleys can achieve some symbolic retribution, and begin to move on.

REFERENCES

Bauman, Richard. 1992. Performance. In Richard Bauman (ed.) *Folklore, Cultural Performances, and Popular Entertainments*. New York: Oxford University Press. 41–49.

Bauman, Richard and Charles Briggs. 1990. Poetics and performance as critical perspectives on language and social life. *Annual Review of Anthropology* 19: 59–88.

Bourdieu, P. 1991. *Language and Symbolic Power*. Cambridge: Polity Press.

Coupland, Nikolas. 2007. *Style: Language Variation and Identity*. Cambridge: Cambridge University Press.

Coupland, Nikolas and Hywel Bishop. 2007. Ideologised values for British accents. *Journal of Sociolinguistics* 11: 74–93.

Garrett, Peter, Nikolas Coupland and Angie Williams. 2003. *Investigating Language Attitudes: Social Meanings of Dialect, Ethnicity and Performance*. Cardiff: University of Wales Press.

Goffman, Erving. 1981. *Forms of Talk*. Philadelphia, Pennsylvania: University of Pennsylvania Press.

Jones, R. Merfyn. 1992. Beyond identity?: The reconstruction of the Welsh. *Journal of British Studies* 31: 330–357.

Lipton, Martina. 2007. Celebrity versus tradition: 'Branding' in modern British pantomime. *New Theatre Quarterly* 23: 136–151.

Mugglestone, Lynda. 2003. *Talking Proper: The Rise of Accent as Social Symbol*. Oxford: Oxford University Press.

Rampton, Ben. 2006. *Language in Late Modernity: Interaction in an Urban School*. Cambridge: Cambridge University Press.

Woolard, Kathryn A. 1985. Language variation and cultural hegemony: Toward an integration of sociolinguistic and social theory. *American Ethnologist* 12: 738–748.

CHAPTER 23

Refashioning and Performing Identities in Global Hip-Hop

ALASTAIR PENNYCOOK

Introduction: A Global, Postindustrial Signifying Practice

The global spread of a domain of popular culture such as rap/hip-hop presents particular challenges to a Sociolinguistics that has often assumed that languages are spoken by members of communities to which identity is closely tied. As Williams (1992) and Cameron (1995, 1997, this volume) have observed, Sociolinguistics has operated all too often with fixed and static categories of class, gender and identity membership as if these were transparent givens onto which language can be mapped. Cameron argues that a more critical account suggests that 'language is one of the things that *constitutes* my identity as a particular kind of subject' (1995: 16). A growing body of work in Sociolinguistics, however, has started to open up far more fluid ways of thinking about language, identity and belonging. Rampton's (1995) notion of 'crossing', for example (see Rampton, Chapter 20) – ways in which members of certain groups use forms of speech from other groups – or 'styling the Other' – 'ways in which people use language and dialect in discursive practice to appropriate, explore, reproduce or challenge influential images and stereotypes of groups that they *don't* themselves belong to (straight-forwardly) belong to' (1999: 421) – shifts the focus away from a 'linguistics of community', to a 'linguistics of contact' (cf Pratt 1992), 'looking instead at the intricate ways in which people use language to index social group affiliations in situations where the acceptability and legitimacy of their doing so is open to question, incontrovertibly guaranteed neither by ties of inheritance, ingroup socialisation, nor by any other language ideology' (Rampton 1999: 422).

A focus on the 'kaleidoscopic, ludic, open flavor' of language use in popular culture, furthermore, profoundly challenges the methods of mainstream Sociolinguistics 'by transgressing fundamental ideas of "speakerhood"' (Hill 1999: 550–551). And yet, although such sociolinguistic work may focus on contact rather than community, it still often remains tied to localized contexts. What it has not yet found an easy way of dealing with is the mixing that comes about as a result of transcultural global flows. As Hill (1999: 543) goes on to suggest, popular cultural styles move 'outward through mass-media tokens of styling that are exploited in youth-oriented marketing, and turning up in surprising places both in geographical and social space as well as in the space of genre and register'. Thus, we need to get beyond the localized concept of 'speech community' or 'field site', located as they are in modernist concepts of identity and location, and instead 'attack the problem of the precise situatedness of such phenomena in the flow of meaning with macroanalytic theoretical tools'.

In this paper, therefore, I want to open up questions of flow, fluidity, performance and performativity as ways of thinking about language, globalization and popular culture. While not ignoring the many detrimental effects of globalization on economies and ecologies across the world – increased exploitation of workers, forced migration, global 'wars' to serve particular interests, destruction of the environment – I am interested centrally here in the cultural implications of globalization, and in particular the notion of transcultural flows. Critiquing static definitions of cultural identity in ethnography, Clifford (1997: 24) argues that rather than using localizing strategies by which people are considered to exist culturally in a specific location, a more useful image is one of *travel*, with its emphasis on movement, encounter and change, for 'once the representational challenge is seen to be the portrayal and understanding of local/global historical encounters, co-productions, dominations, and resistances, then one needs to focus on hybrid, cosmopolitan experiences as much as on rooted, native ones'. From this point of view, locality is produced, not given, a result of particular ways of constructing identity, 'a phenomenological property of social life, a structure of feeling that is produced by particular forms of intentional activity and that yields particular sorts of material effects' (Appadurai 1996: 182).

As Appadurai (2001: 5) notes, 'We are functioning in a world fundamentally characterized by objects in motion. These objects include ideas and ideologies, people and goods, images and messages, technologies and techniques. This is a world of flows'. Central to Appadurai's argument is an understanding that rather than globalization being 'the story of cultural homogenization' (1996: 11), it is better conceived as a 'deeply historical, uneven and even *localizing* process. Globalization does not necessarily or even frequently imply homogenization or Americanization', since 'different societies appropriate the materials of modernity differently' (17). Connell and Gibson (2003) look at music in terms of 'fluidity', which refers to the movement and flows of music across time and space, and 'fixity', which refers to ways in which music is about location, tradition and cultural expression. As they argue, a focus on fluidity and fixity takes us beyond the static dialectic of the global and the local, or the rather trite 'glocal', reflecting 'more dynamic ways of describing and understanding processes that move across, while becoming embedded in, the materiality of localities and social relations' (17).

Unlike Phillipson (1999: 274), therefore, who views the global spread of English as indelibly linked to 'an uncritical endorsement of capitalism, its science and technology, a modernisation ideology, monolingualism as a norm, ideological globalization and internationalization, transnationalization, the Americanization and homogenization of world culture, linguistic, culture and media imperialism', I am interested here in the ways in which transcultural flows and global Englishes produce new forms of identification, new ways of indexing the local and the global, new, fluid ways of articulating what it means to be 'from somewhere'. Thus, while we of course have to view popular music within unequal patterns of commodification and distribution, we can also look at hip-hop in terms of fluidity and fixity, as 'a global, postindustrial signifying practice, giving new parameters of meaning to otherwise locally or nationally diverse identities' (Levy 2001: 134).

While hip-hop is only one site amongst many forms of popular culture that we might explore here (comics, clothing or clubbing are amongst many other possibilities), it is one of particular interest for a number of reasons: It has become a global subculture that has been taken up and localized in many diverse parts of the world; as a multimodal cultural formation which includes MC-ing (rapping), break dancing, graffiti, and DJ-ing, it presents a diverse set of practices of which language is only a part; and yet the highly skilled oral performance of MC-ing /rap nevertheless makes this aspect of hip-hop culture of great interest to those interested in issues of language. Responding to challenges that hip-hop is on the one hand indelibly tied to African American culture and, on the other, nothing but a reflection of the imperialism of US media, Mitchell (2001: 1–2) argues that 'Hip-hop and rap cannot be viewed simply as an expression of African-American culture; it has become a vehicle for global youth affiliations and a tool for reworking local identity all over the world', or what Potter (1995: 10) calls 'a transnational, global artform capable of mobilizing diverse disenfranchised groups'. Thus, there is 'now scarcely a country in the world that does not feature some form or mutation of rap music, from the venerable and sophisticated hip-hop and rap scenes of France, to the 'swa-rap' of Tanzania and Surinamese rap of Holland' (Krims 2000: 5).

While talking of flows, however, we also need to address the question of direction: are transcultural flows only one-way flows, from the centre (particularly the United States) to the periphery? As Pennay (2001: 128) comments in his discussion of rap in Germany, 'Regrettably, the flow of new ideas and stylistic innovations in popular music is nearly always from the English-speaking market, and not to it'. Critiquing the 'romantic Afro-Atlanticism' (17) of Gilroy's (1993) notion of the Black Atlantic, Perry (2004) argues that although African American culture is exported globally, 'Black Americans as a community do not consume imported music from other cultures in large numbers' and thus ultimately the 'postcolonial Afro-Atlantic hip hop community is ... a fantastic aspiration rather than a reality' (19). There is another side to this question, however: While it may well be the case that the global hip-hop scene has little effect on the dominant US scene, and the mutual influences of the Black Atlantic may appear overdrawn, at least from a US perspective, we can nevertheless discern a range of alternative circles of flow.

Hawaiian hip-hoppers such as Sudden Rush, for example, who 'have borrowed hip hop as a counter-hegemonic transcript that challenges tourism and Western imperialism' (Akindes 2001: 95), have been influenced not only by US rap but also by other Pacific Islander and Aotearoa-New Zealand hip-hop that constitutes a 'Pacific Island hip-hop diaspora' and a 'pan-Pacific hip-hop network that has bypassed the borders and restrictions of the popular music distribution industry' (Mitchell 2001: 31). Alongside English, one of the most influential circles of flow is the French, linking the vibrant music scenes in Paris and Marseille in France, Dakar, Abidjan, and Libreville in West Africa, and Montreal in Quebec. And like many urban popular cultures, French language rap is also mixed with many other languages and influences; thus the urban French rap scene is infused with Caribbean and North African languages and cultures; in Quebec, as Sarkar and Allan (in press) show, citing the Haitian-background Impossible from hip-hop group Muzion, 'Le style montréalais' (the Montreal style) is 'un mélange culturel' and 'un mélange des langues' (a mixture of cultures and languages): 'l'anglais, créole, pis le français, mais un français quand même québécois' (English, Haitian Creole, then French, but all the same Quebec French). And in Libreville, Gabon, rappers use 'relexified French' including 'borrowings from Gabonese languages, languages of migration, and English (standard and non-standard, but especially slang)' as well as *verlan*[1] and 'Libreville popular speech and neologisms' (Auzanneau 2002: 116), so that they are 'inserted into large networks of communication that confer on them a plurality of identities' using a wide 'diversity of languages with their variants, along with their functioning as markers of identity (of being Gabonese, African, or an urbanite)' (120).

Across East/Southeast Asia, numerous cross-influences and collaborations are also emerging, mixing English and local languages. Thus Hong Kong DJ Tommy's compilation, 'Respect for Da Chopstick Hip Hop' – the title itself, typical of the global/ local interplay of external (Respect/ Da) and regional (Chopstick Hip Hop) referents – features MC Yan from Hong Kong, K-One, MC Ill and Jaguar from Japan, and Meta and Joosuc from Korea, with tracks sung in English, Cantonese, Japanese and Korean. Popular Malaysian rappers Too Phat, meanwhile, feature Promoe of Loop Troop (Sweden), Vandal of SMC (Canada), Freestyle (Brooklyn, New York) and Weapon X from Melbourne, Australia on their collaborative track, 6 MCs (360°): 'From sea to sea, country to country/ 6 MC's bring the delicacies/ It's a meeting of the minds to ease the turmoil/ 360 degrees around the earth's soil'.

Elsewhere on this CD, Too Phat operate both with a global vision of themselves as rappers:

'Hip hop be connectin' Kuala Lumpur with LB
Hip hop be rockin' up towns laced wit' LV
Ain't necessary to roll in ice rimmed M3's and be blingin'
Hip hop be bringin' together emcees'

(Just a lil' bit featuring Warren G)

as well as a much more localized set of images of early morning prayer and Malaysian food:

'If I die tonight, what would I do on my last day
I know I'd wake early in the morn' for crack of dawn's last pray
Then probably go for breakfast like I used to do
Fried Kuey teow FAM and roti canai at Ruja's with my boo'

(If I die tonight featuring Liyana)[2]

and 'rap Melayu' lyrics (Malay with a spattering of English) from Joe Flizzow in Ala Canggung (do you wanna have a party?):

'Ya!!! Kau tertarik degan liriks, baut lu terbalik
Mr Malique, Joe Flizzow dan T-Bone spit it menarik'

(You are attracted to the lyrics, they make you feel
good Mr Malique, Joe Flizzow and
T-Bone spit it cool)

These are some of the circuits of language use, play and invention that are the new language communities, subcultural empires that identify across national and linguistic boundaries, that borrow, shift, mix and remake language in a new state of flow and flux.

Flows, Fixities, Englishes

English is used and imagined in relation to other languages in parts of East and Southeast Asia in intricate ways.[3] Given the dominance of English globally, and more particularly in domains such as popular music, it is hardly surprising that English is both the medium through which a new genre may enter a region and the medium of choice for artists hoping to reach a wider audience. English-language popular music carries both images of modernity and possibilities of economic success. Nevertheless, while English (or other metropolitan languages such as French) is often the language through which a form of popular music enters a local music scene, it is common in many contexts to see the growth of hip-hop in local languages, the localization of English, and then a composite interplay between local, regional and global flows of language and culture, 'a linguistically, socially, and politically dynamic process which results in complex modes of indigenization and syncreticism' (Mitchell 2003: 14–15).

In Holland, for example, a local 'Nederhop' movement of Dutch language rap developed principally by white Dutch youth contrasts with a more English-language orientation by non-white youth of predominantly Surinamese background (Krims 2000; Wermuth 2001). In Tanzania, the initial adoption of African-American idioms, from clothes and names, to language and musical style, eventually transformed into the 'swarap' movement where 'Swahili became the more powerful language choice within the hip hop scene because of a desire among youth to build a national hip hop culture that promoted local rather than foreign values, ideas and language' (Perullo and Fenn 2003: 33). While Tanzanian hip-hoppers continue to adopt and adapt American styles and lyrics into their music and identity, the meanings of these appropriations change as they are reembedded in local urban contexts with different cultural references, social concerns and musical styles.

A 'world Englishes' perspective on the localization of English around the world typically divides the world into three circles, inner, outer and expanding, with English seen as having local norms in the first two circles, but external norms in the vast expanding circle (Kachru and Nelson 1996). From this point of view, English 'will probably never be used within the Japanese community and form part of the speaker's identity repertoire. There will not be a distinctly local model of English, established and recognizable as Japanese English, reflecting the Japanese culture and language' (Yano 2001: 127). Thus, while Too Phat's outer circle lyrics (above) can be accorded the status of a distinct variety, and the language users may be accorded the status of ('functional' rather than 'genetic') native speakers of this variety, Japan's expanding circle status forecloses such possibilities. Yet this focus on nationally constructed local models of English, able to reflect a national culture and language, surely misses the point that English is used, whether in Australia, Malaysia or Japan, in multiple ways in a complex, transgressive series of identifications. Indeed, the use of these national labels,[4] and the assumption that they somehow identify linguistic and cultural behaviors, is highly problematic, and goes against the more complex vision of language use expressed by many hip-hop artists.

When Condry (2001) speaks of the Japanese hip-hop scene as part of 'an emerging global popular culture' (222), it is clear that such locally emerging scenes are neither mere reflections of a global culture nor nationally bound local appropriations, but rather participants in a much more dynamic flow of linguistic and cultural influences.[5] And talking of dynamic flows, here is Japanese MC Zeebra (The Rhyme Animal), playing with different rhymes in katakana (the script used generally for borrowed words in Japanese) (dynamic, titanic), and producing a final mixed rhyme with the Japanese dai (big) and panic (daipanikku – big panic – to rhyme with dainamikku – dynamic).

Lyrics	Transliteration	Translation
のっけからダイナミック	*nokkekara*	From the very begin-
まるでタイタニック	***dainamikku***	ning, it was dynamic,
想像を超える大パニック	*marude **taitanikku***	just like Titanic, and an
	souzouwo koeru dai	unimaginable big panic.
	panikku	

Other artists present different ways of embedding English in Japanese (or Japanese in English). In the following lyrics, for example, DJ Tonk (Move On) uses the English word 'listen', written in katakana (rissun), followed by 2 (meaning 'to'); and 'our blues moonlight' (in katakana: buruusu muunraito) is juxtaposed with the traditional-sounding Japanese (in kanji) 'under the moonlight' (tsukiakari no shita). Here, then, we have the old and the new, English and Japanese, contrasted, mixed and combined in a way that makes them hard to disentangle.

Lyrics	Transliteration	Translation
リッスン２俺達の	***rissun*** two *oretachino*	Listen to our blues moon-
ブルースムーンラ	***buruusu muunraito***	light under the moonlight.
イト月明かりの下	*tsukiakari no shita*	

The popular Japanese group Rip Slyme's CD Tokyo Classic (Pennycook 2003) presents various other ways in which English is interwoven with Japanese. In the first example, from the track, 'Bring Your Style', one line of African American-influenced rap – with its indexical 'yo' – is juxtaposed with a line of Japanese, albeit Japanese which contains a constructed word – freaky side – in katakana.

Lyrics	Transliteration	Translation
Yo Bringing That,	*Yo Bringing that,*	Yo Bringing That, Yo
Yo Bring Your Style	*Yo Bring your style*	Bring Your Style
人類最後のフリーキーサイド	*Jinrui saigo no*	The last freaky side
	furikiisaido	of the human race

Rip Slyme's use of English, however, is not limited to such indexical pointing to African-American English. The track 'By the way', which uses the English chorus 'By the Way Five Guy's Name (x3), Five Guy's Name is Rip Slyme 5' (By the Way, Tokyo Classic) throughout, is somewhat different. From the register of the phrase 'by the way[6]' to the pronunciation of 'five guy's name' (with its four or more syllables) and the syntax of the sentence (five guy/ possessive particle/ name/ topic particle/ Rip Slyme 5) all suggest Japanese-influenced English. Thus while the lyrics are in English and perform the activity not uncommon to rap of self reference (announcing the name of the crew), they also locate themselves phonologically and syntactically as Japanese performances in English. In a third example, a line from the track 'Tokyo Classic', they mix English and Japanese in more complex ways. By naming Kinshichoo (a suburb of Tokyo) and by doing so in kanji, Rip Slyme locate their Japaneseness explicitly, yet at the same time they use the English word for Japanese, seeming in the same instant to refashion their identity from the outside. This Japanese identity is then both 'freaky' and 'double', the latter a recently coined term to describe people of mixed origin. English and Japanese flow across the boundaries of identity, becoming both fixed (Rip Slyme 5, from Kinshichoo) and fluid (Yo, double, Japanese), producing new possibilities of what it means to be Japanese, to use English, to participate globally, to be local.

Lyrics	Transliteration	Translation
錦糸町出 Freaky	*Kinshichoo de freaky*	Freaky mixed
ダブルの Japanese	*daburu no Japanese*	Japanese from
'Tokyo Classic'		Kinshichoo

Perhaps what emerges here above all is the sense that English and Japanese become so intertwined, and meaning is so dependent on the mixture of the codes, that the very separability of English and Japanese becomes an impossibility; the very notion of whether English is being used to represent Japanese culture can simply no longer be asked.

Bilingual Korean MC Tasha, who like Ilmari of Rip Slyme, has a mixed cultural and linguistic familial background, interweaves English and Korean in a more complex flow. From the opening of 'Memories... (Smiling Tears)' from Tasha Hip-Hop Album, for example, she builds a mixture of English and Korean around the Chinese idiom (commonly used in Korea): 七顚八起 (chil jeon pahl gi) meaning: If I'm knocked seven times, I come back on my eighth (or something like 'no pain, no gain').

Lyrics	Transliteration	Translation
Yo if I fall two times I come back on my third 절대로포기않지 and that's my word	*Jeol dae roh poh gi ahnchi*	I never give up
If I fall five times I come harder on my sixth 조금만더가면돼포기않지난아직	*Joh geum mahn deo gah myeon dwae poh gihi ahn chi nahn ah jik*	I'm not far from the goal, I haven't given up yet
If I'm knocked 7 times I come back on my eighth 칠전팔기내인생끝까지가볼래	*Chil jeon pahl gi nae in saeng gyeut ggah gi bohl lae*	Even if I fail seven times, I will try again; I will keep trying until the end of my life
Now knowledge of self thru the pain in this world 난절대로포기않지 and that's my word	*Nahn jeol dae roh poh gi ahn chi*	I never give up

In this example, then, Tasha uses a well-known Korean idiom and embellishes it in the two languages, each phrase working with the other to develop the meaning. Elsewhere, from the track Meditation, Tasha combines English and Korean differently. Unlike the lyrics above, where English and Korean complement each other – the lyrics in English and Korean reinforce the meaning – here she moves from English to Korean across both meaning and sound: 'Rainy day' is echoed immediately in *Naerinae*, also meaning rain, with the same ryhme – day, *Naerinae, igosae, smyeodeunae, goeenae* – repeated through the rest. The common rap feature of repeated rhymes within a sentence is here reproduced across languages.

Lyrics	Transliteration	Translation
Rainy day 내리네 이곳에 스며드네 내 작은 방바닥에 고이네	*Naerinae igosae smyeodeunae nae jahggeun bahng bah dahg aeh goeenae*	Rainy day, raining, soaking and gathering on the floor of my small room

What Tasha achieves here is a mixture of Korean and English that combines the different flows, sounds and meanings of English and Korean. As Krims points out, the 'rhythmic styles of MCing, or "flows," are among the central aspects of rap production and reception, and any discussion of rap genres that takes musical poetics seriously demands a vocabulary of flow' (Krims 2000: 48). It is one thing, however, to master the flow of one language (and there has been much debate over whether some languages are better oriented towards rap flows than others), but it is quite another skill to 'flow-switch' as Tasha does here. By artfully integrating the flows of English and Korean rap styles in a bilingual performance, she presents English and Korean in new relationships that take us out of the realm of codeswiching, bilingualism, or choices between English and Korean as separate languages, and into a newly imagined space of global translingualism.

Performing Language

'Central to hip hop culture', argues Walcott (1999: 102), 'is the idea of performance or rather acts of performativity'. Performance has often been dismissed in language studies, either as the largely irrelevant domain of real language use (in a Chomskyan competence/ performance divide), or as the play of non-serious etiolations in speech act theory. And yet, as Bauman and Briggs argue, 'performances are not simply artful uses of language that stand apart both from day-to-day life and from larger questions of meaning, as Kantian aesthetics would suggest. Performance rather provides a frame that invites critical reflection on communicative processes' (1996: 60; see also this volume). In this view, then, verbal performances put language on display, making language available to scrutiny. The code and flow mixing of Tasha and Rip Slyme, for example, make visible the possibility of English being intermingled with Korean and Japanese, thus raising questions about the monolingual fallacies that underlie many assumptions about language, pedagogy and identity.

According to Dimitriadis, the notion of performance suggests that 'texts – whether symbol systems or lived experiences – are always in performance. They contain no essential or inherent meaning but are always given meaning by people, in particular times and in particular places' (2001: 11). If we extend this insight to incorporate the use of particular languages, which are then seen as always in performance, as given meaning only by people, in particular times and in particular places, it is possible to start to think of language use not so much as expressive of a prior identity based in a language/ community commonality, but rather as a performance that brings forth possible identities. As I suggested at the beginning of this chapter, new ways of thinking about language and identity stress the importance of the production or performance of identity in the doing. The notion of performativity (see Pennycook 2007), drawing on the work of Butler (1990), opens up ways of thinking about language use and identity that avoid foundationalist categories, suggesting that identities are formed in the linguistic performance rather than pregiven, and that language use is an act of identity that calls that language into being.

As Butler suggested in her work on the performativity of gender (1990: 25), 'gender proves to be performative – that is, constituting the identity it is purported to be. In this sense, gender is always a doing, though not a doing by a subject who might be said to preexist the deed'. Performativity, then, following Butler, can be understood as the way in which we perform acts of identity as an ongoing series of social and cultural performances rather than as the expression of a prior identity. As she goes on to argue: 'Gender is the repeated stylization of the body, a set of repeated acts within a highly rigid regulatory frame that congeal over time to produce the appearance of substance, of a natural sort of being' (1990: 33). Taking this up within studies of language and gender, Cameron suggests that 'Whereas sociolinguistics traditionally assumes that people talk the way they do because of who they (already) are, the postmodernist approach suggests that people are who they are because of (among other things) the way they talk' (1997: 49). The question for language and gender studies, then, is not how men and women talk differently, as if males and females preexisted their language use as given categories of identity, but rather how to do gender with words.

As Kandiah (1998: 100) points out, most approaches to the new Englishes miss the point that these Englishes 'fundamentally involve a radical act of semiotic reconstruction and reconstitution which of itself confers native userhood on the subjects involved in the act'. The crucial point here, then, is that it is not so much whether or not one is born in a particular type of community but rather what one does with the language. At the point of semiotic reconstruction, rappers create blends of languages that cannot be predefined as first, second or foreign languages, and cannot be deemed to be representing or not representing preexisting cultures. It is in the performance that the identity is created. The notion of performativity, then, can take us beyond views of language and identity that tie them to location and origins, and instead opens up possibilities for seeing how languages, identities and futures are constantly being refashioned. In both the claims that hip-hop is a language itself (an assertion made by a number of hip-hop artists), a form of communication that transcends assumed divisions between languages, and the mixing of English with other languages, we can see the performative possibilities of a constantly shifting range of identifications.

From this point of view, 'history, tradition and identity are all performances, all the result of invested actors who position themselves vis-à-vis others in a complex and unfolding reality not of their own making' (Dimitriadis 2001: 11). The importance of this observation in terms of understanding transcultural flows and global Englishes is that it opens up ways in which English is used to perform, invent and (re)fashion identities across borders. Thus in performing their acts of semiotic reconstruction, it is no longer useful to ask whether Rip Slyme are using Japanese English to express Japanese culture and identity as if these neatly preexisted the performance, or whether Too Phat are native speakers of a nativized variety of English, as if such nationally constructed codes predefine their use, or whether Tasha's bilinguality is atypical because Korea is not a bilingual country, as if national language policy precludes alternative possibilities. When we talk of global English use, we are talking of the performance of new identities. Just as Hopper (1998: 171) argues that grammar is an emergent consequence, not a precondition, of communication, and that 'language is not a circumscribed object but a confederation of available and overlapping social experiences', thus echoing Butler and Cameron in their arguments that identities are produced in language rather than pregiven, so we can see in these hip-hop identity performances the production of newly imagined linguistic and cultural identities that transcend the boundaries of language, community and nation as commonly conceived.

NOTES

1. *Verlan*, as Doran (2004) explains, 'is a kind of linguistic *bricolage* marked by the multilingualism and multiculturalism present in the communities where it is spoken, which include immigrants from North Africa, West Africa, Asia and the Caribbean. Given the marginal status of these communities vis-à-vis elite Parisian culture, Verlan can be viewed as an alternative code which stands both literally and figuratively outside the hegemonic norms of Parisian culture and language' (94).
2. While the local references here pull this in to the Malaysian context, the song itself is nevertheless an intertextual reference to 2Pac's 'If I die 2Nite'.
3. Data used in this article draw on research from an Australian Research Council (ARC)-funded project, Postoccidental Englishes and Rap. Different versions of this paper can be found in Pennycook (2003, 2007).
4. When I use these labels here, this is only intended as a pragmatic terminology to refer to certain ways of cutting up local scenes. As this paper argues more broadly, such labels make little sense in the global context of this paper.
5. As a Japanese 'Nip Hop' website puts it, 'Hip-hop is a culture without a nation. Hip-hop culture is international. Each country has its own spin on hip-hop. Japan has one of the most intense hip-hop cultures in the world...Japanese Hip-Hop has its own culture, but a culture that has many similar aspects of Hip-Hop around the world. These aspects include the DJ, MC, dancers and urban artists (taggers, spray paint art)'.
6. This feels like a translation of the Japanese *tokorode*, a phrase whose register differs somewhat from the English 'by the way'.

DISCOGRAPHY

DJ Tommy. 2001. *Respect for Da Chopstick Hip Hop.* Warner Music Hong Kong.
DJ Tonk. 2004. *Move On.* Featuring Mili, K-On. Funai Entertainment, Japan.
Rip Slyme. 2002. *Tokyo Classic* Warner Music Japan.
Tasha. Nd. *Hiphop Album.* Gemini Bobos Entertainment, Korea.
Too Phat. 2003. *360°.* Positive Tone/ EMI Malaysia.
Zeebra. 1998. *The Rhyme Animal.* Polystar: Japan.

REFERENCES

Akindes, Fay Yokomizo. 2001. Sudden rush: *Na Mele Paleoleo* (Hawaiian Rap) as liberatory discourse. *Discourse* 23, 1: 82–98.
Appadurai, Arjun. 1996. *Modernity at Large: Cultural Dimensions of Globalization.* Minneapolis, MN: University of Minnesota Press.
Appadurai, Arjun. 2001. Grassroots globalization and the research imagination. In Arjun Appadurai (ed.) *Globalization.* Durham: Duke University Press. 1–21.
Auzanneau, M. 2002. Rap in Libreville, Gabon: An urban sociolinguistic space. In A-P. Durand (ed.) *Black, Blanc, Beur: Rap music and Hip-Hop Culture in the Francophone World.* Lanham, MD: The Scarecrow Press. 106–123.
Bauman, Richard and Charles Briggs. 1996. Poetics and performance as critical perspectives on language and social life. *Annual Review of Anthropology* 19: 59–88.
Butler, Judith. 1990. *Gender Trouble: Feminism and the Subversion of Identity.* London: Routledge.
Cameron, Deborah. 1995. *Verbal Hygiene.* London: Routledge.
Cameron, Deborah. 1997. Performing gender identity: Young men's talk and the construction of heterosexual masculinity. In Sally Johnson and Ulrike H. Meinhof (eds.) *Language and Masculinity.* Oxford: Blackwell. 47–64.
Clifford, J. 1997. *Routes: Travel and Translation in the Late Twentieth Century.* Cambridge, MA: Harvard University Press.
Condry, Ian. 2001. A history of Japanese Hip-Hop: Street dance, club scene, pop market. In T. Mitchell (ed.) *Global Noise: Rap and Hip-Hop Outside the USA.* Middletown, CT: Wesleyan University Press. 222–247.
Connell, John and Chris Gibson. 2003. *Sound Tracks: Popular Music, Identity and Place.* London: Routledge.
Dimitriadis, Greg. 2001. *Performing Identity/ Performing Culture.* New York: Peter Lang.
Doran, M. 2004. Negotiating between *Bourge* and *Racaille:* Verlan as youth identity practice in suburban Paris. In Aneta Pavlenko and Adrian Blackledge (eds.) *Negotiation of Identities in Multilingual Contexts.* Clevedon: Multilingual Matters. 93–124.
Gilroy, Paul. 1993. *The Black Atlantic: Modernity and Double Consciousness.* Cambridge, MA: Harvard University Press.
Hill, Jane. 1999. Styling locally, styling globally: What does it mean? *Journal of Sociolinguistics,* 3, 4: 542–556.
Hopper, Paul. 1998. Emergent grammar. In M. Tomasello (ed.) *The New Psychology of Language.* Mahwah, NJ: Lawrence Erlbaum. 155–175.
Kachru, Braj and Cecil Nelson. 1996. World Englishes. In Sandra McKay and Nancy Hornberger (eds.) *Sociolinguistics in Language Teaching.* Cambridge: Cambridge University Press. 71–102.

Kandiah, Thiru. 1998. Epiphanies of the deathless native users' manifold avatars: A post-colonial perspective on the native speaker. In Rajendra Singh (ed.) *The Native Speaker: Multilingual Perspectives*. New Delhi: Sage Publications. 79–110.

Krims, A. 2000. *Rap Music and the Poetics of Identity*. Cambridge: Cambridge University Press.

Levy, Claire. 2001. Rap in Bulgaria: Between fashion and reality. In Tony Mitchell (ed.) *Global Noise: Rap and Hip-Hop Outside the USA*. Middletown, CT: Wesleyan University Press. 134–148.

Mitchell, Tony. 2001. Introduction: Another root – hip-hop outside the USA. In Tony Mitchell (ed.) *Global Noise: Rap and Hip-Hop Outside the USA*. Middletown, CT: Wesleyan University Press. 1–38.

Mitchell, Tony. 2003. Doin' damage in my native language: The use of 'resistance vernaculars' in hip hop in France, Italy, and Aotearoa/ New Zealand. In H. Berger and M. Carroll (eds.) *Global Pop, Local Language*. Jackson, MS: University Press of Mississippi. 3–17.

Niphop http://www.gijigaijin.dreamstation.com/Introduction.html Last accessed 21 June 2004

Pennay, Mark. 2001. Rap in Germany: The birth of a genre. In Tony Mitchell (ed.) *Global Noise: Rap and Hip-Hop Outside the USA*. Middletown, CT: Wesleyan University Press. 111–133.

Pennycook, Alastair. 2003. Global Englishes, Rip Slyme, and performativity. *Journal of Sociolinguistics*, 7, 4: 513–533

Pennycook, Alastair. 2007. *Global Englishes and Transcultural Flows*. London: Routledge.

Perry, I. 2004. *Prophets of the Hood: Politics and Poetics in Hip hop*. Durham, NC: Duke University Press.

Perullo, A. and J. Fenn. 2003. Language ideologies, choices, and practices in East African hip hop. In H. Berger and M. Carroll (eds.) *Global Pop, Local Language*. Jackson, MS: University Press of Mississippi. 19–51.

Phillipson, Robert. 1999. Voice in global English: Unheard chords in Crystal loud and clear. Review of D. Crystal, *English as a Global Language*, Cambridge: Cambridge University Press. *Applied Linguistics* 20, 2: 265–276.

Potter, R. 1995. *Spectacular Vernaculars: Hip-hop and the Politics of Postmodernism*. Albany, NY: State University of New York Press.

Pratt, Mary Louise. 1992 *Imperial Eyes: Travel Writing and Transculturation*. London: Routledge.

Rampton, Ben. 1995. *Crossing: Language and Ethnicity among Adolescents*. London: Longman.

Rampton, Ben. 1999. Styling the Other: Introduction. *Journal of Sociolinguistics* 3, 4: 421–427.

Sarkar, M. and D. Allen. 2007. Hybrid identities in Quebec Hip-Hop: Language, territory, and ethnicity in the mix. *Journal of Language, Identity and Education* 6, 2: 117–130.

Walcott, Rinaldo. 1999. Performing the (Black) postmodern: Rap as incitement for cultural criticism. In Cameron McCarthy, Glenn Hudak, Shawn Miklaucic, and Paula Saukko (eds.) *Sound Identities: Popular Music and the Cultural Politics of Education*. New York: Peter Lang. 97–118.

Wermuth, Mir. 2001. Rap in the low countries: Global dichotomies on a national scale. In Tony Mitchell (ed.) *Global Noise: Rap and Hip-Hop Outside the USA*. Middletown, CT: Wesleyan University Press. 149–170.

Williams, Glyn. 1992. *Sociolinguistics: A Sociological Critique*. London: Routledge.

Yano, Yasukata. 2001. World Englishes in 2000 and beyond. *World Englishes* 20, 2: 119–131.

PART IV

LANGUAGE ATTITUDES, IDEOLOGIES AND STANCES

Editors' Introduction to Part IV

For the most part, the readings we have encountered in earlier Parts of this book have dealt with sociolinguistic differences at the level of usage or practice. As we said in the general Introduction, Sociolinguistics takes linguistic diversity to be its main concern, and the authors' of many chapters have set out to establish how, where and when language use differs, for example between members of different social class groups, gender groups or regional groups. With a shift of focus towards constructionism, authors of many other chapters analyse how speakers use language to construct social difference, for example constructing their own personal and social identities, or constructing particular qualities of social relationships. Either way, the main emphasis has been on 'what people do sociolinguistically' and on its social consequences or achievements. The main research method has been observation – recording and analysing language in use. Observing and analysing language in use is the methodological mainstay of Sociolinguistics, even though we have seen some radically different approaches to this process, some more qualitative and some more quantitative.

In addition, however, Sociolinguistics has always recognized the importance of collecting data on people's *judgements* and *opinions* about language use. We all know that different ways of speaking are regularly subject to assessment, sometimes prejudicially, and we are probably most aware of this in relation to local vernacular accents and dialects, which are often stigmatized and considered to be 'ugly', 'common' or 'incorrect'. Even though sociolinguists believe strongly in the *linguistic equivalence* of all speech varieties – that is, that, on purely linguistic grounds, there is no reason to say that one variety is inherently superior to another – they are acutely aware of how linguistic varieties are socially *non*-equivalent. Social attitudes to linguistic diversity have an important bearing not only on how speakers use language, but also on how linguistic varieties acquire, maintain or lose status over time. These

341

considerations are centrally important in research into minority languages, multilingualism, language rights, language death and global shifts in language use (see Part V). But social evaluation is relevant in *all* contexts of language use, and in this part of the Reader we see how Sociolinguistics has developed different perspectives on it.

The study of *language attitudes* has been a very productive theme in the Social Psychology of Language. In and after the 1970s there was a steady stream of studies designed to survey people's responses to different linguistic varieties, especially 'standard' versus 'non-standard' accents and dialects, and minority versus majority languages. Many of these studies used quite direct methods, presenting short snippets of audio-recorded speech to large groups of listeners, who would then note down their reactions in terms of numerical scales, indicating to what extent they found a speech style or its speaker 'attractive', 'prestigious', 'dynamic', and so on. Quite early on it was established that speakers of 'standard' varieties tended to be judged relatively positively, especially on social dimensions related to intelligence and superiority, even though they might do less well than others on social dimensions related to social attractiveness. Studies of this sort have been very revealing, although there are known problems involved in selecting valid samples of spoken data and in choosing groups of people as 'judges' (since judgments may well vary as much as ways of speaking do). Again, it is difficult for language attitudes studies to reflect the influence of local social contexts upon social judgments. If we acknowledge that social evaluations made of speakers and varieties are very sensitive to the precise circumstances of speaking and listening, then we would be concerned that we were getting only quite generalized patterns of social evaluation in controlled, experimental studies.

Even so, these general patterns can themselves be informative. In Chapter 24 we reproduce John Edwards' early study of the perception of gender and social class in young children's speech. This is a very good example of the experimental tradition in which language attitudes in general tended to be investigated by social psychologists. The starting point for the study is that young children's prepubescent voices lack the pitch differences that distinguish boys form girls after boys' voices have 'broken' – a process whereby boy's larynxes become bigger and their vocal folds longer, producing lower-frequency sounds. Edwards is interested in the accuracy with which people can distinguish prepubescent boys and girls from their voices alone, but mainly in the social norms that are revealed when they make their assessments of sex and social class from voice. It turns out that the adult 'judges' in Edwards's study were quite good at identifying the children's sex, but there were interesting patterns among the *incorrect* assessments. There was a tendency for working-class voices (which included girls' as well as boys' voices) to be heard as boys' voices, and for middle-class voices to be heard as girls' voices.

Edwards' study therefore gives us information about the cultural norms and assumptions that come into play interpretively when we listen to voices – particularly the voices of people we don't know. As he says, there appears to be a tacit understanding that working-class speech is 'rougher' and 'more masculine' than middle-class speech. This is an *ideological* understanding about language – a *language ideology* with political implications, linked to themes of Part II of the *Reader*. Assuming Edwards' informants are not exceptional (and there is no reason to think that they are), this language ideology is available to members of the culture and structures their/our engagement with linguistic diversity. The concept of language ideology is in fact the main focus of this part of the Reader and it has become a key concept in modern Sociolinguistics, following important theoretical and empirical initiatives by linguistic anthropologists. Before considering it in more detail we should note Nancy Niedzielski and Dennis Preston's argument in Chapter 25 that, in fact, studying ideological values for language has a long and distinguished track-record, from Henry Hoenigswald onwards, albeit with slightly different emphasis and under a different heading – *folk linguistics*.

For Niedzielski and Preston, folk linguistics is the study of *overt* public commentary on language, although the analytic interest has always been on how non-specialists 'make sense of language'. The authors start with a very useful diagram that identifies different ways in which cognitive and subjective processes impinge on language use. Folk linguistics is concerned with ordinary people's conscious *metalinguistic* comments – how they characterize language in their own linguistic terms – and it presumes that sociolinguists need to be aware of 'the folk's' linguistic awareness and judgments. Niedzielski and Preston argue, for example, that real-world decisions about language use and language learning are influenced by everyday beliefs, perceptions and evaluations of language use. To that extent, 'folk' orientations may have more explanatory value than specialist linguists' orientations.

The authors then give examples of different research methods that can be used to *elicit* (as opposed to simply observing) people's beliefs about language, including map-drawing and map-labeling techniques of the sort they have used in connection with USA dialects of English. Niedzielski and Preston get large groups of informants to draw boundary lines on blank maps to represent dialect differences, and then to label and characterize the different dialect zones that they have marked. It is striking how, in their data, speech differences that sociolinguists describe in neutral, geographical and social terms (such as 'Southern USA English') are described by young informants in much more evaluative terms, such as 'casual', 'friendly' and 'drawling'. Informants have a strong sense of whose speech is more and less 'correct', and of where these differences are to be found. The everyday social worlds of language evaluation, as the early language attitudes studies revealed, are clearly far more vivid and judgmental than the descriptive repertoires of academic sociolinguists.

In their short chapter (26) Judith Irvine and Susan Gal make the point, however, that linguists' own ideologies need to be taken into account as well as those of ordinary people – the people that linguists typically observe participating in social encounters. As they say, 'there is no "view from nowhere"' (p. 374), and linguists' perspectives must therefore be ideological too. *Language-ideological research* exists in order to explore how particular sets of beliefs and assumptions about language influence language change, and how they impact on other sorts of actions and policies to do with language in social life. But this approach is also able to comment critically on how we study language. Irvine and Gal set out three semiotic processes that they say are the means by which people construct ideological representations of linguistic differences: *iconization, fractal recursivity* and *erasure*. These abstract categories refer to quite familiar 'ways of seeing' or 'ways of talking about' language. *Iconization* means treating a linguistic variety as if it defines the essence of a social group (see our discussion of essentialism in the general Introduction). An example is when, in Niedzielski and Preston's data, Southern USA speech is said to *be* 'casual speech', or when Birmingham-accented speech in the UK is said to *be* 'ugly'. *Fractal recursivity* is when some sort of distinction is reapplied 'recursively' in other situations, for example when a value-distinction such as 'friendly versus unfriendly', which seems to apply to a particular and fleeting relationship between individuals, is transferred onto whole communities. So we might end up with the ideological assumption that 'local people are friendly', or that 'Scots are unfriendly'. *Erasure* is the ideological cancelling or ignoring of a social or sociolinguistic distinction, for example when a complex social profile of a group of people, known from experience, is reduced down to a gross stereotype. We may well have experienced the fact that Scottish people are in fact highly diverse, and not uniformly either 'friendly' or 'unfriendly'. But that evidence gets erased in the ideological representation of the social group, for some local purpose.

In her chapter (27) Sally Johnson analyses how language-ideological processes were implicated in the reforming of German orthography in Germany, in and after 1996. Spelling is a notorious arena for entrenched language ideologies. It is not at all uncommon for people to feel that 'good spelling' is not only an index of 'correct' linguistic practice but even a matter of moral worth! In contrast, linguists have always emphasized how spelling is an 'overlaid', secondary mode of using a language, and how there are many random aspects to spelling systems, as well as some regularities that tend to go unnoticed. For most linguists spelling is primarily a recoding of spoken language that allows us to communicate via written text, where the system characteristics of writing are less important than what the system functionally achieves. On the other hand, public debates about spelling, and about spelling reform in particular, are liable to be conducted in terms of 'logic', 'elegance', 'tradition', 'modernity', 'correctness', 'authority', and so on. These are the sorts of ideological formations that Johnson analyses in the German case.

Johnson shows how evaluative discourses about German spelling served different interest-groups in the debates about reform that she analysed, and how different groups in competition with each other *rationalised* the question of orthography quite differently. People in favour of reforming German spelling argued that there needed to be a 'more coherent' and 'valid' spelling system, while people opposing reform argued that re-standardization was itself a threat to 'coherence'. Values that were related to historical, visual and aesthetic continuity were propounded by people opposing reform, while linguists in the pro-reform group took a more 'scientific' line. In general a conservative ideology of standardization was deployed as a way of resisting reform, while reformers took much more pragmatic and efficiency-oriented stances, even though both camps – in some ways and on their own terms – agreed there was a need for standardization.

So far in this part of the book we have been examining approaches to language attitudes and ideologies that maintain some distance between subjective orientations towards language use and the details of language use itself. But attitudes and ideologies are of course also *part of* the process of *using* language. To put this another way, using language has an inherent metalinguistic and *metapragmatic* components. Speakers and listeners conduct interaction against the backdrop of an evolving set of beliefs, evaluations and assumptions, as they communicate. Strategizing *about* communication (strategies, outcomes, identities, relationships and so on) is all part of what communication *is*. This is a point that Alexandra Jaffe makes in the short review of perspectives on language ideology with which she begins her chapter (28) and it is the theoretical basis of her detailed analysis of the use of French and Corsican languages in a bilingual school in Corsica.

Corsican language planning initiatives have led to a situation where explicit ideological support is, institutionally speaking, being given for an increased use of Corsican, including in the school setting that Jaffe is investigating. In that school Corsican is foregrounded as 'the language of school identity', and there is a rule that children should live their school lives in the context of 50:50 use of Corsican and French. But at the level of practice – kids and teachers using language in school activities – Jaffe identifies patterns that hark back to the dominant *diglossic* relationship between French and Corsican (on diglossia see Charles Ferguson's Chapter 31, in Part V), where French has been established as the high-status language used for public communication, with Corsican functioning more as a low-status language of social solidarity. Abstract hierarchies between language codes, like those imposed in language planning regimes, may or may not be the relationships actually experienced and 'lived out' interactionally by language users. The significant properties of language codes, Jaffe argues, are the ones that people experience and perform in ideological dimensions of discourse practice.

We end Part IV with Elinor Ochs's theoretically rich discussion of *indexicality, stance, identity* and *interaction* (Chapter 29), which expands Jaffe's main line of argument about the link between ideology and interactional practice. The context for Ochs's discussion is *language socialization*, the process by which 'novices' (obviously including young children) are socialized into the ways of speaking and ways of meaning of particular cultures. She uses data from American but also Western Samoan cultural settings to illustrate how novices have to learn potentially culture-specific indexical relationships between communicative acts, stances and identities. For example, in learning and using Samoan versions of the verbal imperatives meaning 'come', 'go' and 'give', Samoan children learn that the imperatives 'come' and 'go' can only be used by superiors to inferiors, while the imperative 'give' can be used to people of any rank. This is because 'give' is used in the social and interactional context of begging: 'give (to me)', which involves the speaker making an overture to people generally above her or his own status. Social practices and role-relationships therefore underpin the acquisition of lexical forms in Samoan. Ochs also points out that cultural learning is not a simple matter of having cultural norms handed down to one. Rather, socialization is a constitutive process (social constructionism again): 'every social interaction in this sense has the potential for both cultural persistence and change, and past and future are manifest in the interactional present' (Ochs, p. 412).

Ochs's theoretical ideas are ones we can use in referring back to earlier chapters, particularly those dealing with the social and stylistic construction of identities (for example, in Part III), also in looking forward to later chapters, particularly those dealing with culture and interaction (particularly in Part VI). Ochs's chapter would be fully at home in Part VI, but it can also inform the sociolinguistic analysis of bilingualism and multilingualism in the section that follows this one. These overlaps and resemblances are the ones we had in mind when, in our general Introduction, we suggested that modern Sociolinguistics is coalescing around a relatively finite set of conceptual resources and perspectives whose value is recognized in most branches of sociolinguistic inquiry.

One concept that merits emphasizing in Ochs's chapter is *stance* and its relationship to *social identity*. In Ochs's conception, stances that speakers adopt in interaction are related to social identities that might more durably define those speakers, but only indirectly so. She gives the example of Rundi culture where the affective (emotional) stance of 'impassivity' – being silent and unruffled in all social contexts – is associated with the social identity of being 'upper caste'. As Ochs points out, in mainstream USA culture, the social identity and role of 'being a medical doctor' might for many people be associated with the stance of 'being caring', although in this case the stance-identity link might be an ideological assumption made only by people who are *not* doctors – doctors themselves might see the relationship quite differently! The important point is, therefore, that interactional and relational stances are linked to social identities only in ideological processes of *ascription* – when people ascribe the stance of 'being caring' to 'doctors', and perhaps the stance of 'being accommodative' to 'women' and the stance of 'being aggressive' to 'men'. We should be wary of assuming that social groups can essentially be defined by the stances that they sometimes take in interaction, which is a generalization we discussed critically in relation to language and gender in Part II.

CHAPTER 24

Social Class Differences and the Identification of Sex in Children's Speech

JOHN R. EDWARDS

Introduction

It is a truism that, in learning and using language, people are susceptible to social influences in their environment. At a gross level this is shown by the fact that, for example, Chinese children learn Chinese and American children learn English. Within such broad linguistic categories, however, there may exist many regional and social accent and dialect varieties. In addition, varying degrees of prestige and value attach to different language varieties (see, for example, Giles and Powesland 1975 and see Chapter 25 in this volume). Thus within a given society the social conventions relating to language may be many and varied.

One important dimension along which linguistic perceptions may vary is that of social class. In both America and Britain, for example, an association between working-class speech and masculinity and 'toughness' has been noted. Labov (1966) pointed to the positive masculine values associated with working-class speech patterns in New York City. Perception of these values is apparently not restricted to members of the working class, but is shared to some degree by middle-class speakers as well. Whether speakers are aware of these values or whether, because of middle-class pressures, they do not readily admit to them, such values do appear to have general appeal. Thus Labov noted that 'masculinity is unconsciously attributed to the unmodified

Source: 'Social Class Differences and the Identification of Sex in Children's Speech', by Edwards, J. R. in *Journal of Child Language*, **6** (1979) (Cambridge: Cambridge University Press) pp. 121–7, table 22.1, figure 22.2.

native speech pattern of the city' (1966: 501). The attribution of masculinity to working-class speech has been termed 'covert prestige', which seems apt, both in view of what has just been mentioned and, as well, in the light of information deriving from a study of English in Norwich (Trudgill 1972). Here, among both working-class and middle-class males, covert prestige was demonstrated by the fact that as many as 54% *claimed* to use non-standard speech forms (e.g. for the word *tune,* use of [tu:n]) rather than [tju:n]), even when they did not actually do so.

The covert prestige of working-class speech obviously attracts men rather than women. Indeed, Labov (1966) noted that the positive masculine associations of working-class speech for men do not appear to be balanced by any similar positive values ascribed by women to non-standard speech. Female speech, in general, has been found to be more disposed towards standard, middle-class styles (Fischer 1958; Thorne and Henley 1975; Trudgill 1972, 1974). Allowing for social class and age, women tend to produce 'politer' and more 'correct' speech than their male counterparts. Thus it appears that, as Trudgill (1974) has suggested, covert prestige is more powerful for men and standard prestige is more powerful for women.

Further to this, Mattingly (cited in Sachs 1975) has suggested that linguistic conventions relating to men's and women's speech may cause, in adults, exaggeration of voice differences beyond those accounted for physiologically. Similar conventions may operate for children's speech as well (Meditch 1975). In general, children's early learning of social conventions can hardly be doubted. In the learning of sex-trait stereotypes, for example, Williams, Giles and Edwards (1977) have shown that children as young as five years of age may be quite aware of socially determined stereotypes concerning characteristics of men and women.

Among prepubertal children, certain physiological sex differences relating to speech production are not very marked; the lower fundamental frequency (pitch) typical of male speech, for instance, is produced with the onset of puberty. Similarly, formant (overtone) frequencies are, physiologically, unlikely to be very different among prepubertal boys and girls (Sachs, Lieberman and Erickson 1973). Nevertheless, the sex of prepubertal children can be identified with a high degree of accuracy by judges listening to tape-recorded speech samples. Thus, Weinburg and Bennett (1971) reported 74% accuracy with five- and six-year-olds; Meditch (1975) found 79% correct guesses made of the sex of three- to five-year-old children; Sachs et al. (1973) recorded 81% accuracy in judges' identifications of the sex of children whose ages ranged from four to fourteen years. It seems likely that, as Sachs (1975) has suggested, the cues in the speech of prepubertal children which allow accurate identification of sex are at least partly related to children's early conformity to appropriate social norms.

If young children reflect social norms in their speech, and if these norms themselves vary along sex and social class dimensions, then one might expect judgements of prepubertal children's sex to illuminate these phenomena. The purpose of the present study, therefore, was to consider whether differences in the accuracy of sex identification may be related to the social class of the speaker. In addition, the nature of the investigation suggested that the sex of those making the identifications might also prove relevant. Meditch (1975), for example, found that female judges were more accurate in sex identification than were males. Therefore, both male and female judges participated in this study. In order to be better able to interpret any findings showing differences related to social class, attention was also given to the perceptions of middle-class and working-class speech along the masculinity–feminity dimension.

Overall, this study sought to give some practical insights concerning the identification/misidentification of children's sex which may be useful to workers in the general area of child language. Condry and Condry (1976) have provided a general example of the influence of sex stereotypes; ratings of the emotions suggested by the videotaped behaviour of a nine-month-old were quite different, according to whether judges thought they were observing a boy or a girl. More specifically, a recent review by Thorne and Henley (1975) has shown that sex stereotypes operate in connection with speech. In general, the sex (actual or guessed) of a child whose language is under study may be a potent factor in any interpretations of speech behaviour, and one worthy of investigation.

Method

The subjects comprised 20 lower-working-class children and 20 middle-class children, whose average age was 10 years (SD approximately 6 months).[1] Within each group were 10 boys and 10 girls. Each child read a prose passage – a 99-word description of school life – which was selected with the assistance of teachers. All the children were given a practice trial following which their second reading was tape-recorded. The reading took place at school, where the investigator was a familiar figure, and the children appeared at ease; the reticence sometimes shown by working-class children in such situations was not evident here (see also Edwards 1976). The judges in this study were 14 teachers-in-training at a Dublin college. There were seven females and seven males. All judges heard all the children's taped voices, in a randomized order, and were asked to identify the sex of each child. Five other adults (2 males and 3 females) were asked to listen to all the voices and to rate each one, using 7-point scales, on four traits: rugged–delicate, low–high, masculine–feminine, rough–smooth. These scales were taken from Sachs (1975) and were included here to see whether, over both boys and girls, working-class speech was in fact perceived as more masculine in character than middle-class speech. The scales were scored by averaging the ratings (from 1 to 7) given by the judges for each child.

Results

Overall, the judges showed 83.6% accuracy in identifying the children's sex, which is of the same order as that obtained in previous studies (see above). The major interest here, however, arises from the distribution of the incorrect identifications; there were 92 errors made in all, 16.4% of the total number of guesses (14 × 40 = 560). An analysis of variance was performed on the errors (3-way: social class × child sex × judges' sex) in which the last factor was a replicated one. The cell totals for this analysis are shown in Table 24.1. The main effect due to the judges' sex was found to be significant ($F = 15.83$, d.f. = 1, 36, $p < 0.01$) – the female judges being more accurate overall than were their male colleagues. There was also a significant interaction found between social class and child sex ($F = 10.80$, d.f. = 1, 36, $p < 0.01$). This interaction is depicted in Figure 24.1. It is apparent that relatively few errors were made in identifying the sex of working-class boys; more were made with girls. For the middle-class children, the pattern is reversed with more errors being made with boys than with girls.

On each of the four rating scales, the means for the middle-class and working-class groups were compared using one-tailed t-tests. On the scale rugged–delicate, although there was a tendency for working-class children's voices to be perceived as more rugged, no significant different was detected ($t = 1.57$, d.f. = 38, $p > 0.05$). However, looking at the other three dimensions, the working-class children were seen as having lower voices ($t = 1.72$, $p < 0.05$), rougher voices ($t = 4.35$, $p < 0.01$) and more masculine voices ($t = 1.86$, $p < 0.05$) than their middle-class counterparts.

Table 24.1 Errors made in the identification of children's sex

		Male judges	Female judges
Working class	Boys	3	1
	Girls	21	9
Middle class	Boys	26	17
	Girls	10	5

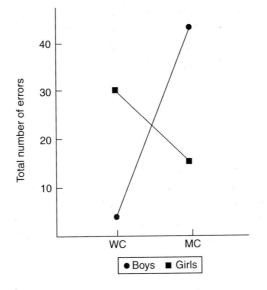

Figure 24.1   Interaction between social class (WC = working class; MC = middle class) and child sex in terms of errors of sex identification

Discussion

The finding that female judges were more accurate than the males in identifying the children's sex is in accord with similar results reported by Meditch (1975). Although there is little in the literature on this specific point, Mazance and McCall (1976) found that females were more sensitive than males in interpersonal relationships, especially with regard to verbal styles. If this is the case, then the present results are at least partly explicable (see also Kramer 1977).

Of greater interest here, however, is the interaction, shown in Figure 24.1, between social class and child sex. Among the working-class children, few boys were mistaken as girls; this is consistent with a view of working-class speech as rougher and more masculine than that of the middle class. This view received additional support in the present study from the results of the subjective ratings of the speech samples: the working-class voices were perceived as being lower, rougher and more masculine than the middle-class voices. The fact that more working-class girls were mistaken as boys is interesting, since there is evidence from several sources (see above) that female speech is politer and more correct (i.e. more approaches a middle-class standard) than that of males. In this connection, Labov (1966) has noted that, in showing a tendency towards more standard speech, females exhibit much greater linguistic insecurity than males. It is possible, of course, that status-consciousness of this sort is not highly developed among young girls, although early learning of social norms seems fairly general. In addition, Fischer's (1958) results would seem to belie such a view. He found, among children aged between three and ten years, that girls were much more likely than boys to use the more standard -*ing* rather than -*in* for the ending of the present participle. It may, in fact, be the case that working-class girls are misidentified as boys because the general masculinity of working-class speech is strong enough to cover any stratus strivings on the girls' part. And, in his work on covert prestige, Trudgill (1972) has noted that, although covert prestige itself is primarily a male phenomenon, it is also evident among younger females. It remains to be seen, according to Trudgill, whether the attraction of covert prestige for females is repeated by the youth of each generation or whether it is a new, and perhaps stable, change.

Among the middle-class children, more errors were made with the boys than with the girls. Even though, physiologically, prepubertal boys and girls are more or less equivalent in terms of speech production, the observation that 'boys sound like girls' is more common, perhaps, than 'girls sound like boys'. This is presumably because it is the boys' speech which is going to change markedly at puberty, developing into stereotypical male adult speech, while the differences between girls' and women's speech are less marked. In general terms, of course there is also the fact that, if working-class speech is seen as relatively more masculine than middle-class speech, then the other side of the coin is that middle-class speech is relatively more feminine. Trudgill (1974) pointed out that some males may associate standard speech with feminity, and has also suggested (1972) that middle-class speech may carry feminine connotations because schools, which generally support middle-class speech, are staffed largely by women. In general, the findings reported here support the view that working-class speech is characterized as more masculine than middle-class speech, and this is reflected in the way errors in sex identification are made.[2]

The results of the present study have some implications for those who work with children's speech. Condry and Condry (1976), in their discussion of the influence of sex stereotypes upon the observation of a child's behaviour (see Introduction), suggested caution in interpreting studies of children in which the sex is known, and in which the behaviour has some relation to commonly held sex stereotypes. Such stereotypes are clearly important in the area of speech (Sachs 1975; Thorne and Henley 1975). Where the sex of the child is known, one may at least attempt to interpret results in the light of sex stereotypes which can themselves be investiged. Where the sex is unknown, however, interpretation may be more difficult since, although stereotypes still operate, one cannot be sure if judges have accurately identified the child's sex. The present study indicates that, although there may be a high overall degree of accuracy in guessing the sex of prepubertal children from speech samples, errors made may not be randomly distributed. Consequently, unless they have specific reasons for not doing so, researchers may wish to ensure that the sex of children is known to those who are to assess or interpret some aspects of the children's language.

NOTES

1. The author is aware that terms like 'working class' and 'middle class' are very general. Considerable background data, available upon request, show that for the children in the present study the terms are reasonably applied and reflect such indices as the overall socioeconomic status of the home, characteristics of the home area, parental occupation, etc.
2. An interesting extension of this work would be to employ working-class judges.

REFERENCES

Condry, J. and S. Condry. 1976. Sex differences: A study of the eye of the beholder. *Child Development* 47: 812–819.

Edwards, A. D. 1976. Social class and linguistic choice. *Sociology* 10: 101–110.

Fischer, J. L. 1958. Social influences on the choice of a linguistic variant. *Word* 14: 47–56.

Giles, H. and P. F. Powesland. 1975. *Speech Style and Social Evaluation*. London: Academic Press.

Kramer, C. 1977. Perceptions of female and male speech. *Language and Speech* 20: 151–161.

Labov, W. 1966. *The Social Stratification of English in New York City*. Washington, D.C.: Center for Applied Linguistics.

Mazanec, N. and G. J. McCall. 1976. Sex forms and allocation of attention in observing persons. *Journal of Psychology* 93: 175–180.

Meditch, A. 1975. The development of sex-specific speech patterns in young children. *Anthropological Linguistics* 17: 421–433.

Sachs, J. 1975. Cues to the identification of sex in children's speech. In B. Thorne and N. N. Henley. (eds.) *Language and Sex: Difference and Dominance*. Rowley, Massachusetts: Newbury.

Sachs, J., P. Lieberman and D. Erickson. 1973. Anatomical and cultural determinants of male and female speech. In R. W. Shuy and R. W. Fasold (eds.) *Language Attitudes: Current Trends and Prospects*. Washington, D.C.: Georgetown University Press.

Thorne, B. and N. Henley. (eds.) 1975. *Language and Sex: Difference and Dominance*. Rowley, Massachusetts: Newbury.

Trudgill, P. 1972. Sex, covert prestige and linguistic change in the urban British English of Norwich. *Language and Society* 1: 179–195.

Trudgill, P. 1974. *Sociolinguistics: An Introduction*. Harmondsworth: Penguin.

Weinburg, B. and S. Bennett. 1971. Speaker sex recognition of 5- and 6-year-old children's voices. *Journal of the Acoustical Society of America* 50: 1210–1213.

Williams, J. E., H. Giles and J. R. Edwards. 1977. Comparative analyses of sex-trait stereotypes in the United States, England and Ireland. In Y. H. Poortinga (ed.) *Basic Problems in Cross-cultural Psychology*. Amsterdam: Swets and Zeitlinger.

CHAPTER 25

Folk Linguistics

NANCY NIEDZIELSKI AND DENNIS R. PRESTON

It's like D's family, they all talk funny I think.

Now it is true you can be a math person and have difficulty with the English language. For every rule there are twenty exceptions.

I think to teach Black English in a school isn't right because... it's not the English language anymore.

I thought German was supposed to be one of the harder languages to learn. I don't know if it's because they gurgle when they talk or... you know. ... It's like you're trying to clear your throat while you're speaking. I mean that would really be hard for me.

Folk Linguistics (FL) aims to discover and analyze beliefs about and attitudes towards language by collecting and examining overt comment about it by nonlinguists. This pursuit also includes a search for the organizing principles behind such beliefs and goals as presented in Niedzielski and Preston (2000).

The re-emergence of interest in FL in the United States dates from a 1960 conference in California; Henry Hoenigswald said that

> we should be interested not only in (*a*) what goes on (language), but also in (*b*) how people react to what goes on (they are persuaded, they are put off, etc.) and in (*c*) what people say goes on (talk concerning language). It will not do to dismiss these secondary and tertiary modes of conduct merely as sources of error. (1966: 20)

Researchers in FL have employed a number of techniques in their attempts to elicit these 'secondary and tertiary modes of conduct', several illustrated and commented on below. In general, respondents are presented with and/or encouraged to discuss or respond to areas of language concern that expose not merely their traditional, prepackaged notions but also the processes that govern their thinking. Folk belief about language is considered to be a dynamic process that allows nonspecialists to make sense of their linguistic environments.

The relation of FL to other approaches to the study of language is illustrated in Figure 25.1.

The top of this triangle (a) characterizes Hoenigswald's 'what goes on', and the a' above it is the explanatory area that represents the bulk of what most subfields of linguistics are concerned with: linguistic *competence*. The bottom line of the triangle (b1 – bn) represents a continuum of consciousness. The rightmost side (bn) is the traditional domain of the Social Psychology of Language or language attitude studies and focuses on automatic processes, those largely outside conscious awareness. The leftmost side (b1) is the primary area of concern in FL and is made up of conscious, deliberative acts. Although the boundary between the two is fuzzy, and recent work in more cognitively oriented Social Psychology, particularly in the study of attitudes, questions positing different background beliefs for the two (for example, Bassili and Brown 2005), the distinction is still worth maintaining, particularly since work on language, as in other areas, often finds a mismatch between implicit and explicit attitudes (for example, Kristiansen 2006). Finally, just as there is an a', there is a b' – the underlying beliefs and belief systems which lie behind folk expression about language.

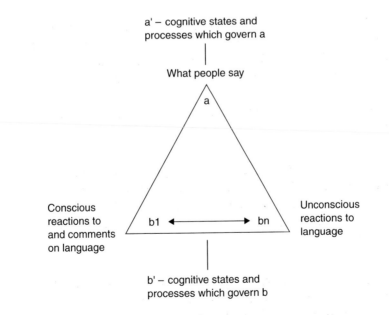

Figure 25.1   The position of folk linguistics and language attitudes in the general study of language

In FL, however, the dichotomy between the conscious and unconscious does not do justice to the levels and types of awareness of the linguistic units that may stimulate responses. The availability of different structural units of language has been extensively commented on (for example, Silverstein 1981), and, recently, Preston (1996a) has listed both levels and modes of such awareness: topics can be *unavailable* (those the folk will not comment on); *available* (discussed only if they are carefully described); *suggestible* (although seldom initiated by the folk, nevertheless commented on without elaborate description), and *common* (frequent public topics of folk linguistic discussion). It is also the case that the folk may or may not be *accurate* in their discussion of linguistic phenomena (although, as in all ethnographic studies, this has no bearing on the value of the data). In addition, the *detail* of folk awareness of an object may be either *global* or *specific*. For example, an accent may be described globally (*... they all talk funny...*), while some linguistic phenomena are characterized with great specificity (*... It's like you're trying to clear your throat while you're speaking*). Finally, the degree of *control* that a respondent possesses in the performance of a linguistic unit under discussion is variable and might not be correlated with any of the other types of awareness. A respondent who says someone 'talks funny' might not be able to mention any specific feature that contributes to that characterization, but might be able to give a convincing imitation. In short, FL awareness is not only a matter of degree of consciousness, but one of mode or type as well. Even an inaccurate characterization of a linguistic fact or a poor mimicry of a variety demonstrates some kind of awareness, and for every act of language perception, the mode and degree of awareness is an open and interesting question.

Furthermore, awareness of linguistic phenomena is also governed by salience factors, regardless of the level of availability of a structural type or the kind of response elicited. Sibata (1971), for example, suggests that attention is drawn to language primarily when it differs from one's own, although we suspect that notice is also triggered by a speaker's using a form different from that which a hearer expects him or her to use. Whatever the triggering event, it must somehow move the respondent away from the normal practice of language, which is communicative.

Although FL typically studies more deliberative responses, it owes much to early work in the Social Psychology of Language – the focus on bn. Matched guise studies (for example, Lambert et al. 1960) examined attitudinal responses to language varieties by collecting ratings of performances of such varieties by the same speaker along evaluative dimensions represented by a number of opposed adjective pairs. This technique was borrowed from the *semantic differential* work of Osgood et al. (1957) and led to such findings as the one that suggests that local varieties are valued along measures of *solidarity* – involving such concepts as 'warm', 'honest' and 'down-to-earth', while standard varieties are valued for *status* – scoring higher on such values as 'well-educated', 'industrious' and 'diligent' (for example, Ryan et al. 1982: 8). This research laid the groundwork for further explorations into attitudes towards language phenomena at both global and the specific levels, and FL supplements those findings by providing a more explanatory basis for attitudinal rankings based on underlying folk theories.

FL owes perhaps its greatest debt to ethnographers of speaking, whose work in a variety of contexts has led to an enriched understanding of linguistic behavior. On the other hand, FL also benefits the ethnography of speaking by providing richer detail about the folk belief surrounding language itself, an ethnography perhaps too often earlier derived from the observation of performance than from the elicitation of opinion. It is clear, however, that FL subject matter has been valued in the ethnographic tradition.

> If the community's own theory of linguistic repertoire and speech is considered (as it must be in any serious ethnographic account), matters become all the more complex and interesting. (Hymes 1972: 39)

FL research has also contributed to a and a' – the General Linguistics peak of the triangle. Plichta (2004), for example, noted that folk comment on the 'nasal' character of Northern, urban US pronunciation was ignored by linguists on the basis of its unscientific character (for example, Labov's discussion in Hoenigswald 1966: 23–24). After a careful acoustic investigation of two vowels involved in the Northern Cities Chain Shift, however, Plichta discovered that a nasal formant was, in fact, a feature that accompanied the repositioning of these vowels, a strong confirmation of the utility of folk comment even in matters of general and descriptive linguistics.

Although it is not directly represented in the triangle of Figure 25.1, work in language variation and change also benefits from FL research. Since FL is an integral part of the ethnography of a speech community, any research that depends on an understanding of a community will need FL information as much as it needs any other demographic and/or linguistic characterization. It is difficult to imagine not wanting to know what members of a speech community believe about the linguistic phenomena that are under investigation in the study of variation and change. For example, FL evidence provided by imitation of language varieties reveals that even if the folk are not aware of (or do not have labels for) some variety differences, they are capable of manipulating some such differences in a systematic way, suggesting that there is at least some level of awareness of items involved in language variation. In addition, an analysis of which groups demonstrate control over which specific features may contribute to an understanding of how particular features spread across individuals and communities.

Finally, FL clearly contributes to applied linguistics. An obvious application is to language learning issues, given that the folk express numerous concerns in their discussions of second language learning. It seems logical to suggest that what people believe about how they learn language, how difficult the target language is, and what particular talents they believe they have or lack in learning a second language, as well as what the social outcomes of learning are will aid those designing curricula, training teachers and writing textbooks in order to adapt to or at least reflect an understanding of the learner's conception of the language learning process (for example, Pasquale and Preston 2006).

We turn now to examples of a variety of different methodologies and approaches that have been employed in FL. In a sub-branch of the field known as *perceptual dialectology*, Preston (1996b) asked respondents to carry out several tasks related to the distribution of regional speech in the United States. The *hand-drawn map* task required respondents to draw outlines of areas where people 'spoke differently' and to give labels to these areas. Figure 25.2 shows the results of such a task for a respondent from Illinois (Chicago) and Figure 25.3 for one from South Carolina.

The first thing to notice about these maps is the ethnographic richness. The Chicagoan calls his own region 'normal' while the South Carolinian refers to all Southerners as 'God's people'. Perhaps just these two maps already provide a clue to the social psychological divide between a preference for status-based as opposed to solidarity-based associations suggested above, and we will return to that theme. We do not have the space here to comment on the detailed ethnographic content of these maps, but the reader may consult Preston (1989, 1999), Niedzielski and Preston (2000) and the references in those works as well as the content of Long and Preston (2002) for many examples. Canobbio and Iannàccaro (2000) supplements Preston (1999) for a bibliography in this general research area.

When a large number of these maps are combined for members of the same speech community, we may be able to assert that we have determined a folk 'mental dialect map' of that group. Preston and Howe (1987) devised a computer-based technique for such combination, and Figure 25.4 shows the composite map for a large number of hand-drawn maps from southeastern Michigan.

This quantitative approach raises questions about why some areas were so often outlined and others were not. The southeastern Michigan respondents clearly found the US South to be the most salient area in their task; more than 90 percent of the respondents outlined such an area (#1 in Figure 25.4). The next two most frequently outlined areas were the local one (#2, 61 percent) and an area around New York City (#3, 54 percent). The ethnographic details of many of the hand-drawn maps gave a direct clue for this general pattern of responses.

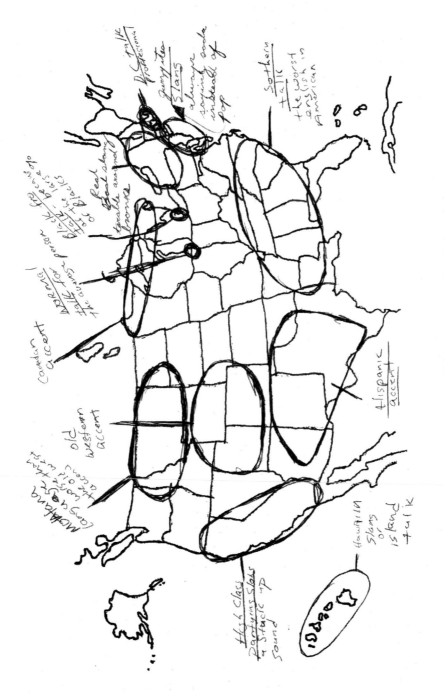

Figure 25.2 A young, male Chicago respondent's hand-drawn map

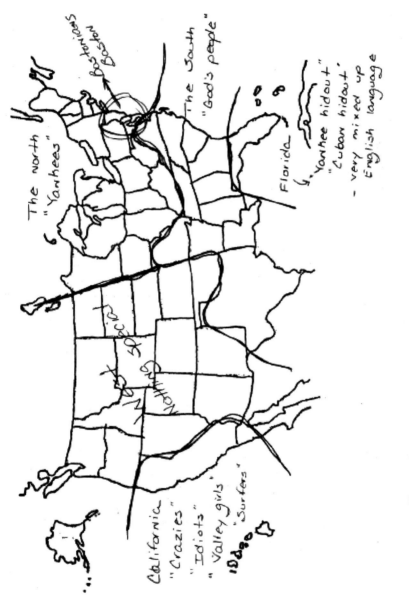

Figure 25.3 A middle-aged, male South Carolina respondent's hand-drawn map

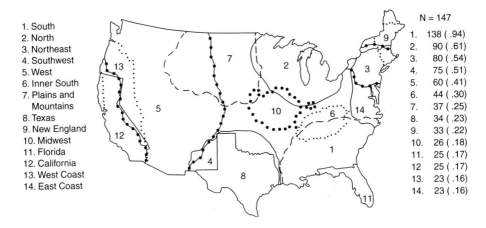

1. South
2. North
3. Northeast
4. Southwest
5. West
6. Inner South
7. Plains and Mountains
8. Texas
9. New England
10. Midwest
11. Florida
12. California
13. West Coast
14. East Coast

N = 147

1.	138 (.94)
2.	90 (.61)
3.	80 (.54)
4.	75 (.51)
5.	60 (.41)
6.	44 (.30)
7.	37 (.25)
8.	34 (.23)
9.	33 (.22)
10.	26 (.18)
11.	25 (.17)
12.	25 (.17)
13.	23 (.16)
14.	23 (.16)

Figure 25.4   Computer-assisted composite of hand-drawn maps of US dialect areas by southeastern Michigan respondents

Respondents were not directly answering our request to outline areas where people speak differently (a wording purposely used to avoid the stigmatized label *dialect*); they were identifying distinct areas on the basis of where people spoke more and less correct English, as the labels in Figure 25.1 in particular make clear. In many of the hand-drawn maps from which the generalization in Figure 25.4 was derived, the southeastern Michigan respondents identified the South as an area of nonstandard speech, but they identified their own area as one supporting 'standard English', 'correct English' or simply 'normal'. They also rated New York City and the surrounding area as another area where 'Bad English' was common.

When FL discovers that an underlying principle (here 'correctness') is at work, an obvious strategy is to engage respondents in that concept directly. Another perceptual dialectology task, therefore, required respondents to rank the 50 states (and New York City and Washington, D.C.) on a correctness scale. Figure 25.5 shows how raters similar to those who drew the maps from which Figure 25.4 was derived performed on this task. Just as the hand-drawn maps suggest, the local area is best rated, and the South and New York City are worst rated, but this task more directly makes use of the respondents' own concept of regional differentiation, one apparently based on prescriptive notions.

Since many of the hand-drawn maps (for example, Figure 25.2 above) suggested that a dimension other than language correctness was at work (and since previous work in the Social Psychology of Language also suggested such a dimension, for example, Ryan et al. 1982), the same respondents who

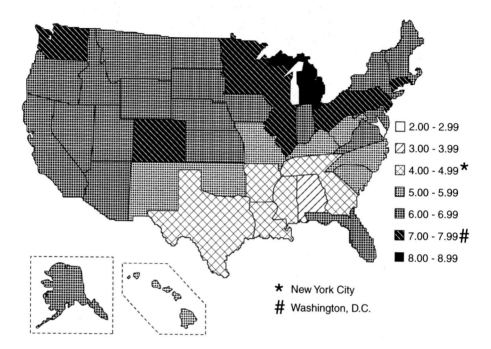

Figure 25.5   Southeastern Michigan ratings of the fifty states, New York City, and Washington, D.C. on a scale of I (least correct) to 10 (most correct) for language correctness

provided the data in Figure 25.5 were also asked to rate areas for *pleasantness*. Figure 25.6 shows those results.

Although these Michigan raters still find their region most pleasant, they do not find it uniquely so, and the degree of pleasantness is in the 7.00 range (not 8.00, as it was for correctness). They also find the worst rated state of the South (Alabama) less unpleasant (4.00) than it was incorrect (3.00). This finding led us to believe that linguistically secure Michigan raters perhaps had more invested in the notion of correctness than that of pleasantness. To see whether that relationship would hold for Alabama, the apparently most prejudiced-against state, at least by Michigan raters, we asked raters from Alabama to carry out the same two tasks.

As Figure 25.7 shows, Alabamians care very little for language correctness. Where Michigan raters found enormous local preference and great disparity between the two states, Alabamians regarded both states (and all in between) as mediocre for language correctness (5.00). But when asked about pleasantness, Alabamians responded with the same local security that Michiganders had for correctness: Alabama (and only Alabama) scored in the 8.00 range (Figure 25.8).

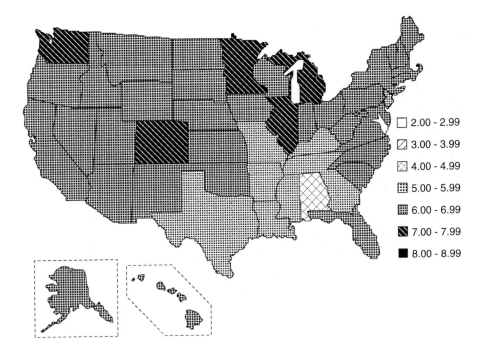

Figure 25.6 Southeastern Michigan ratings of the fifty states, New York City, and Washington, D.C. on a scale of 1 (least pleasant) to 10 (most pleasant) for language pleasantness

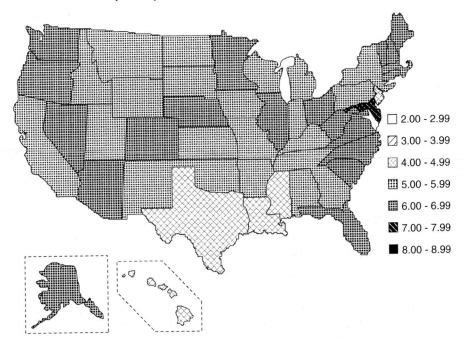

Figure 25.7 Alabama ratings of the fifty states, New York City, and Washington, D.C. on a scale of 1 (least correct) to 10 (most correct) for language correctness

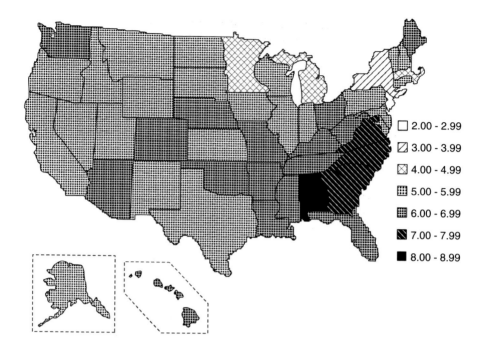

Figure 25.8 Alabama ratings of the fifty states, New York City, and Washington, D.C. on a scale of 1 (least pleasant) to 10 (most pleasant) for language pleasantness

FL study supports, therefore, the social psychological notion that there are differences in speech communities with regard to status versus solidarity in linguistic matters. Areas of great linguistic security (for example, Michigan) find the status dimension strongest; prejudiced-against areas (for example, Alabama) take comfort in solidarity.

It is not clear however, whether the single terms 'correctness' and 'pleasantness' revealed the complexity of this distribution. Ryan et al. (1982) suggest that contrasts might exist (see Table 25.1).

The early FL findings in perceptual dialectology reported above make it seem that the United States is a 'Type B', although the ratings add a more sophisticated degree: Michiganders strongly prefer their LV1 variety for 'Status' and weakly prefer it for 'Solidarity', and Alabamians weakly prefer some LV1 varieties for 'Status' but strongly prefer their own LV2 for 'Solidarity'.

We worried, however, that 'correctness' and 'pleasantness', the terms we selected in this research for the 'status' and 'solidarity' dimensions, might not elicit the same responses that those drawn from folk terminology would. We therefore provided Michigan respondents with a map based on Figure 25.3

Table 25.1 Types of preferences for varieties by prestige variety (LVI) and nonprestige variety (LV2) speakers

Type of preference	Judges			
	LVI speakers		LV2 speakers	
	Status	Solidarity	Status	Solidarity
A. Majority group	LVI	LVI	LVI	LVI
B. Majority group for Status/ in-group for solidarity	LVI	LVI	LVI	LV2
C. In-group	LVI	LVI	LV2	LV2
D. Majority group for status/ minority group for solidarity	LVI	LV2	LVI	LV2

Source: Ryan, Giles, and Sebastian 1982: 9.

and asked them to provide words and phrases to characterize the way people spoke in these different areas. Since this elicitation of labels was based on a mental map drawn from similar respondents, we had some confidence that subsequent use of these labels in ranking experiments would be better rooted in folk reality, and the procedure is well established in classic language attitude research (for example, Shuy and Fasold 1973).

Another group of Michiganders were again shown a map based on Figure 25.3 and asked to rate each region on a six-point scale for the following twelve opposites, essentially the terms and notions acquired from the folk respondents:

slow – fast	formal – casual	educated – uneducated
smart – dumb	polite – rude	snobbish – down-to-earth
nasal – not nasal	normal – abnormal	friendly – unfriendly
drawl – no drawl	twang – no twang	bad English – good English

Although all the regions outlined in Figure 25.3 were rated, we are concerned here only with the ratings for region 1 (the South) and region 2 (the local area). The results are shown in Table 25.2.

Michigander ratings of the 'North', the local area, are shown on the right hand side of Table 25.2, and the highest rated concepts, shown on the lower right, are no surprise. These Michiganders gave excellent to fair ratings on all the items that a factor analysis placed in group #1, one clearly associated with status. In contrast, the same concepts get the very lowest ratings for southern speech (lower left). In fact, a rank ordering comparison will show a nearly perfect negative correlation: the highest ranked notion for the 'North' was 'Drawl' (indicating 'no drawl') while the same feature was lowest ranked for the 'South'.

The more interesting details, however, are found in the upper half of Table 25.2. The scores for factor group #2 (clearly notions of solidarity) are, in general, higher for the 'South' than they are for the 'North', even though the raters are exclusively residents of the latter area. Southerners are 'More Casual', and they are rated higher for 'Friendly', 'Down-to-earth', 'Polite' and 'Not nasal' (see the work by Plichta 2004 cited above).

This finding prompts us to suggest that the United States is perhaps a 'Type D' place (see Table 25.1) and that, although our findings in other modes of perceptual dialectology were not in error, they did not tease out the full spectrum of associations that this last one did with its dependence on folk labels and, presumably, beliefs. This finding is, in fact, in line with a great deal of work being conducted on emerging norms worldwide. Speakers of all ages of local majority standard varieties appear to be borrowing from nonstandards, whether such varieties are those of long-standing local groups or of newer immigrant populations (for example, Rampton 1995, although this phenomenon is hardly restricted to London or even Europe and North America).

FL has also formed an affinity with sociophonetic research. The earliest work on perceptual dialectology was seen as corrective to much language attitude research that did not determine the folk concepts and mental maps of persons asked to respond to voice samples from various regions and/or groups. Preston (1989), for example, argued that it was important to know where people 'thought' sample voices could be from (their mental linguistic maps) and

Table 25.2 Mean scores, ranks, and factor group membership for the local area ('North') and the 'South' on a trait ranking test (on a six-point scale) by southeastern Michigander respondents

	Mean scores (ordered) Southern				Mean scores (ordered) North		
Factor	Mean	Attribute	Rank	Rank	Factor	Mean	Attribute
−1&2	4.66	Casual	1	12	−1&2	3.53	Casual
2	4.58	Friendly	2	9.5	2	4.00	Friendly
2&−1	4.54	Down-to-earth	3	6	2&−1	4.19	Down-to-earth
2	4.20	Polite	4	9.5	2	4.00	Polite
∅	4.09	Not nasal	5	11	∅	3.94	Not nasal
1&2	3.22	Normal	6	3	1&2	4.94	Normal
1	3.04	Smart	7	4	1	4.53	Smart
1	2.96	Twang	8	2	1	5.07	Twang
1	2.86	Good English	9	5	1	4.41	Good English
1	2.72	Educated	10	8	1	4.09	Educated
1	2.42	Fast	11	7	1	4.12	Fast
1	2.22	Drawl	12	1	1	5.11	Drawl

where they actually 'believed' them to be from (their folk identification abilities). Early sociolinguistic work pointed the way to studies that focused on specific elements in a variety repertoire that could elicit identification (for example, Graff et al. 1983). Recent work, therefore, has focused on elements of pronunciation that are likely to trigger folk identifications and responses, whether at conscious or unconscious levels. In one such study, for example, Niedzielski (1999) focuses on perception of the low-front vowel in the same area of southeastern Michigan in which most of the perceptual dialectological work reported on above was carried out. She asked local respondents to identify which of three versions of the low-front vowel [æ] (the TRAP vowel) matched a sample they had just heard when it was suggested to them that the speaker was a local Michigander. The sample was a raised and fronted version of that vowel, a part of the 'Northern Cities Chain Shift', a vowel rotation considerably advanced in the area. The respondents then heard exactly the same raised and fronted version (called 'Actual'), a second version at the more common English position for this vowel (called 'Canonical'), and an exaggeratedly lower and backer one, one actually approaching the usual position of American English 'hot' ([ɑ], called 'Hyper-standard', reflecting a fairly common US belief that lower and backer versions of this vowel are somehow 'posher', probably an association with British English). Table 25.3 shows the results.

As Table 25.3 shows, no respondent (out of 42) got the test right. Of the respondents, 90 percent believed that the speaker had actually uttered the canonical vowel and 10 percent even suggested that the hyper-correct version matched the original. This dramatic failure to hear a clearly different acoustic signal can be explained only by an appeal to the folk belief of the respondents. As the earlier work on US perceptual dialectology has shown, Michiganders are convinced that their local variety is a standard one. They 'hear', therefore, local speakers uttering a canonical form even when the acoustic evidence is to the contrary, and we suspect that a great deal of perceptual mishearing has its roots in the ideologies and beliefs exposed by FL research.

We also believe that work with items at other linguistic levels (morphosyntactic, lexical, pragmatic) might also show such interesting correlations,

Table 25.3   Respondent matching results for the vowel in *last*

1 *hyper-* *standard*	*2* *canonical* */æ/*	*3* *actual* *token*	*Total*
10% n= 4	90% 38	0% 0	42

and we hope that researchers in the field will continue to seek the triggering of FL reactions by specific linguistic units.

At the other end of the spectrum, discourses comprise a great deal of the data used in FL investigation. In most such studies, a network model of the participant-observation technique was employed in which fieldworkers chose a network that they are already a member of and recorded conversational data which touched on linguistic topics. During such conversations, the fieldworker can choose to either directly ask questions regarding linguistic phenomena or to suggest topics through more indirect means.

The difficulty in working with discoursal data is not in acquiring it; respondents are eager to talk about many aspects of language structure, use, and even psycholinguistic embedding. For linguists interested in FL, however, the difficulty is in interpretation. We are not essentially interested in discourse structure, but we want to determine the elements in a discourse that relate to the superficial and/or underlying folk beliefs of the speaker. We do not believe that the use of a passive, for example, necessarily points to a desire on the part of a speaker to 'hide something', and, although that is an interesting folk belief (for example, Niedzielski and Preston 2000), it is hardly a sophisticated linguistic one.

There are, however, analytic procedures that take structural elements into consideration that also seem to shed light on folk belief. In a discussion of African American English (called 'Black English' at the time of the interview), an African American respondent does not agree with what the interviewer appears to believe is a shared presupposition: that Black English is a 'dialect'. We find support for our interpretation in the marshalling of information strategies after this initial disagreement surfaces. If 'Black English' had been agreed on by the conversational participants, it would have been topicalized and would have been realized in the following stretch of the conversation as a 'topic' with the typical linguistic strategies associated with old information (for example, pronominalization, deletion or ellipsis, co-occurrence with the article 'the' or demonstrative 'this' or 'that'). In fact, a study of the subsequent references to the variety during this period of disagreement show that such topicalization strategies were not used for the next several references (Preston 1993), proof from the information structure of the discourse about the status of the respondent's beliefs regarding the variety in question.

There is no room here to explore other analytic approaches to discourse that can help uncover FL belief and how it is instantiated in discourse. A summary of several techniques is outlined and exemplified in Preston (1993), but we believe an advantage in working with discoursal data is that it highlights the process of the application of linguistic folk belief to a specific setting, making it clear that a wide range of beliefs, even apparently contradictory ones, is available for application to linguistic objects in an individual. Discoursal data often more dramatically reveal the process of selecting from that range for a specific application.

We have, however, also simply taken the mention of folk belief at face value from discoursal and quantitative surveys and tried to catalog them for their topics and what they reveal about the kinds of beliefs the folk hold about language in general. One of our aims in doing this has been to suggest that a general folk theory of language is often the accompaniment to any expression of folk belief. Although we do not claim to have the final word on such a theory, we believe a great deal of our quantitative and discoursal data from the United States suggests that an underlying folk theory of language stands in stark contrast to the one held by most professional linguists. Figure 25.9 shows this relationship.

Linguists believe that language is a concrete instantiation in the mind/brain space of individuals; it most certainly has social effects, but its 'home' is within the individual. Linguists abstract from this concreteness to such notions as 'dialect' and 'language', but anyone who has ever struggled with

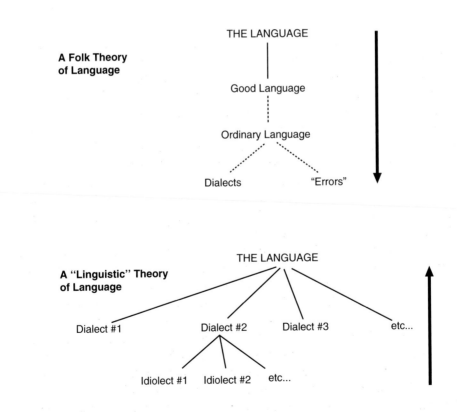

Figure 25.9 Folk and linguistic theories of language

the distinction between the two will agree that the question of which closely related varieties are dialects and which are languages is resolved by political, geographical and even religious norms, not by structural ones.

Not so the folk, at least not the US folk we have investigated. For them, the language has a cognitively exterior reality: although they know that individuals possess something language-like, that possession may either (responsibly) reflect the abstraction that is the real language or it may (irresponsibly) diverge farther and farther from it until it reaches the ultimate linguistic irresponsibility of 'dialect' or simply 'error'. We believe the search for such underlying theories helps us understand a great deal of folk involvement in public questions about language (teaching, learning, evaluating others' behavior, even judging their intellect), and that, even if FL did not shed light on questions that more often engage professionals, the important revelations it may make about language and public life would make its pursuit worthwhile.

REFERENCES

Bassili, John N. and Rick D. Brown. 2005. Implicit and explicit attitudes: Research, challenges, theory. In Dolores Albarracín, Blair T. Johnson and Mark P. Zanna (eds.) *The Handbook of Attitudes*. Mahwah, New Jersey: Lawrence Erlbaum. 543–574.

Canobbio, Sabina and Gabriele Iannàccaro (eds.). 2000. *Contributo per una bibliografia sulla dialettologia percettiva (Atlante Linguistico ed Etnografico del Piemonte Occidentale 5)*. Turin: Università degli Studi di Torino, Departimento di Scienze del Linguaggio, Consiglio Nazionale delle Recerche, Edizioni dell'Orso.

Graff, David, William Labov and Wendell A. Harris. 1983. Testing listeners' reactions to phonological markers of ethnic identity: A new method for sociolinguistic research. In David Sankoff (ed.) *Diversity and Diachrony*. Amsterdam/Philadelphia: John Benjamins. 45–58.

Hoenigswald, Henry. 1966. A proposal for the study of folk-linguistics. In William Bright (ed.) *Sociolinguistics*. The Hague: Mouton. 16–26.

Hymes, Dell. 1972. Models of the interaction of language and social life. In John J. Gumperz and Dell Hymes (eds.) *Directions in Sociolinguistics: The Ethnography of Communication*. New York: Holt, Rinehart, and Winston. 35–71.

Kristiansen, Tore. 2006. Social meanings and subjective processes: A presentation of theories and methods from the Næstved studies. Paper presented to Approaches to the Study of Folk Linguistics, Sociolinguistic Awareness and Language Attitudes. The Third Symposium within the Series of Faculty Seminars Arranged by The Centre for Research on Bilingualism, Stockholm University.

Lambert, Wallace E., R. C. Hodgsen, Robert C. Gardner and Samuel Fillenbaum. 1960. Evaluation reactions to spoken language. *Journal of Abnormal and Social Psychology* 60: 44–51.

Long, Daniel and Dennis R. Preston (eds.). 2002. *Handbook of Perceptual Dialectology. Volume 2*. Amsterdam/Philadelphia: John Benjamins.

Niedzielski, Nancy. 1999. The effects of social information on the perception of sociolinguistic variables. *Journal of Language and Social Psychology.* 18: 62–85.

Niedzielski, Nancy and Dennis R. Preston. 2000. *Folk Linguistics.* Berlin: Mouton de Gruyter.

Osgood, C. E., G. J. Suci and P. H. Tannenbaum. 1957. *The Measurement of Meaning.* Urbana, Illinois: The University of Illinois Press.

Pasquale, Michael and Dennis R. Preston. 2006. The folk linguistics of language teaching and learning. Paper presented to the 2006 SLRF (Second Language Research Forum). Seattle, Washington: University of Washington.

Plichta, Bartłomiej. 2004. Interdisciplinary perspectives on the Northern Cities Chain Shift. Unpublished PhD dissertation. East Lansing, Michigan: Michigan State University.

Preston, Dennis R. 1989. *Perceptual Dialectology: Nonlinguists' Views of Areal Linguistics.* Dordrecht: Foris Publications.

Preston, Dennis R. 1993. The uses of folk linguistics. *International Journal of Applied Linguistics* 3: 181–259.

Preston, Dennis R. 1996a. Whaddayaknow?: The modes of folk linguistic awareness. *Language Awareness* 5: 40–74.

Preston, Dennis R. 1996b. Where the worst English is spoken. In Edgar Schneider (ed.) *Focus on the USA.* Amsterdam/Philadelphia: John Benjamins. 297–360.

Preston, Dennis R. (ed.). 1999. *Handbook of Perceptual Dialectology. Volume 1.* Amsterdam/Philadelphia: John Benjamins.

Preston, Dennis R. and George M. Howe. 1987. Computerized studies of mental dialect maps. In Keith Denning, Sharon Inkelas, Faye C. McNair-Knox and John Rickford (eds.) *Variation in Language: NWAV-XV at Stanford.* Stanford, California: Department of Linguistics, Stanford University. 361–378.

Rampton, Ben. 1995. *Crossing: Language and Ethnicity among Adolescents.* London: Longman.

Ryan, Ellen Bouchard, Howard Giles and Richard J. Sebastian. 1982. An integrated perspective for the study of attitudes toward language variation. In Ellen Bouchard Ryan and Howard Giles (eds.) *Attitudes Towards Language Variation.* London: Edward Arnold. 1–19.

Shuy, Roger W. and Ralph W. Fasold. 1973. *Language Attitudes: Current Trends and Prospects.* Washington, D.C.: Georgetown University Press.

Sibata, Takesi. 1971. Kotoba no kihan ishiki. *Gengo Seikatsu* 236 (May): 14–21. [English quotations and page references are taken from this article translated as Consciousness of language norms, Chapter 22 in Tetsuya Kunihiro, Fumio Inoue, and Danny Long (eds.). 1999. *Takesi Sibata: Sociolinguistics in Japanese contexts.* Berlin: Mouton de Gruyter. 371–377.]

Silverstein, Michael. 1981. The limits of awareness. *Sociolinguistic Working Paper No. 84.* Austin, Texas: Southwest Educational Development Laboratory.

CHAPTER 26

Language-Ideological Processes

JUDITH T. IRVINE AND SUSAN GAL

A language is simply a dialect that has an army and a navy – so goes a well-known saying in linguistics. Although only semiserious, this dictum recognizes an important truth: The significance of linguistic differentiation is embedded in the politics of a region and its observers. Just as having an army presupposes some outside force, some real or putative opposition to be faced, so does identifying a language presuppose a boundary or opposition to other languages with which it contrasts in some larger sociolinguistic field. In this chapter we focus on the ideological aspects of that linguistic differentiation – the ideas with which participants and observers frame their understanding of linguistic varieties and map those understandings onto people, events, and activities that are significant to them. We call these conceptual schemes *ideologies* because they are suffused with the political and moral issues pervading the particular sociolinguistic field and are subject to the interests of their bearers' social position.

Linguistic ideologies are held not only by the immediate participants in a local sociolinguistic system. They are also held by other observers, such as the linguists and ethnographers who have mapped the boundaries of languages and peoples and provided descriptive accounts of them. Our attention here is therefore just as appropriately directed to those mappings and accounts as to their subject matter. There is no 'view from nowhere', no gaze that is not positioned. Of course, it is always easier to detect positioning in the views of others, such as the linguists and ethnographers of an earlier era, than in one's own. Examining the activities of linguists a century or more ago reveals, via the wisdom of hindsight or at least via historical distance, the ideological dimensions of their work in drawing and interpreting linguistic boundaries.

Source: 'Language Ideology and Linguistic Differentiation', by Irvine, J. T. and Gal, S. in Kroskrity, P. V. (ed.) *Regimes of Language: Ideologies, Polities, and Identities* (2000) (Santa Fe, New Mexico: School for American Research Press) pp. 35–79.

This historical inquiry also has a contemporary relevance, to the extent that early representations of sociolinguistic phenomena influenced later representations and even contributed to shaping the sociolinguistic scene itself.

Our discussion is less concerned with history per se, however, than with the dynamics of a sociolinguistic process. In exploring ideologies of linguistic differentiation, we are concerned not only with the ideologies' structure but also, and especially, with their consequences. First, we explore how participants' ideologies concerning boundaries and differences may contribute to language change. Second, we ask how the describer's ideology has consequences for scholarship, how it shapes his or her description of language(s). Third, we consider the consequences for politics, how linguistic ideologies are taken to authorize actions on the basis of linguistic relationship or difference.

To address these questions we have examined ethnographic and linguistic cases from several parts of the world, involving different kinds of linguistic differentiation. Since Africa and Europe are the sites of our own research, we have looked most particularly to these regions for examples of relevant ethnography, linguistics, and historical investigation. But whether in these parts of the world or elsewhere, in all the cases we have examined we find some similarities in the ways ideologies 'recognize' (or misrecognize) linguistic differences: how they locate, interpret, and rationalize sociolinguistic complexity, identifying linguistic varieties with 'typical' persons and activities and accounting for the differentiations among them. We have identified three important semiotic processes by which this works: iconization, fractal recursivity, and erasure.

Before we offer more specific discussions of what these three processes are, let us note that all of them concern the way people conceive of links between linguistic forms and social phenomena. Those conceptions can best be explicated by a semiotic approach that distinguishes several kinds of sign relationships, including (as Peirce long ago suggested) the iconic, the indexical, and the symbolic. It has become a commonplace in Sociolinguistics that linguistic forms, including whole languages, can index social groups. As part of everyday behavior, the use of a linguistic form can become a pointer to (index of) the social identities and the typical activities of speakers. But speakers (and hearers) often notice, rationalize, and justify such linguistic indices, thereby creating linguistic ideologies that purport to explain the source and meaning of the linguistic differences. To put this another way, linguistic features are seen as reflecting and expressing broader cultural images of people and activities. Participants' ideologies about language locate linguistic phenomena as part of, and evidence for, what they believe to be systematic behavioral, aesthetic, affective, and moral contrasts among the social groups indexed. That is, people have, and act in relation to, ideologically constructed representations of linguistic differences. In these ideological constructions, indexical relationships become the ground on which other sign relationships are built.

The three semiotic processes we have identified are thus the means by which people construct ideological representations of linguistic differences.

Iconization involves a transformation of the sign relationship between linguistic features (or varieties) and the social images with which they are linked. Linguistic features that index social groups or activities appear to be iconic representations of them, as if a linguistic feature somehow depicted or displayed a social group's inherent nature or essence. This process entails the attribution of cause and immediate necessity to a connection (between linguistic features and social groups) that may be only historical, contingent, or conventional. The iconicity of the ideological representation reinforces the implication of necessity. By picking out qualities supposedly shared by the social image and the linguistic image, the ideological representation – itself a sign – binds them together in a linkage that appears to be inherent.

Fractal recursivity involves the projection of an opposition, salient at some level of relationship, onto some other level. For example, intra-group oppositions might be projected outward onto intergroup relations, or vice versa. Thus the dichotomizing and partitioning process that was involved in some understood opposition (between groups or linguistic varieties, for example) recurs at other levels, creating either subcategories on each side of a contrast or supercategories that include both sides but oppose them to something else. Reminiscent of fractals in geometry and the structure of segmentary kinship systems – as well as other phenomena anthropologists have seen as involving segmentation or schismogenesis, such as nationalist ideologies and gender ritual – the myriad oppositions that can create identity may be reproduced repeatedly, either within each side of a dichotomy or outside it. When such oppositions are reproduced within a single person, they do not concern contrasting *identities* so much as oppositions between *activities* or *roles* associated with prototypical social persons. In any case, the oppositions do not define fixed or stable social groups, and the mimesis they suggest cannot be more than partial. Rather, they provide actors with the discursive or cultural resources to claim and thus attempt to create shifting 'communities', identities, selves, and roles, at different levels of contrast, within a cultural field.

Erasure is the process in which ideology, in simplifying the sociolinguistic field, renders some persons or activities (or sociolinguistic phenomena) invisible. Facts that are inconsistent with the ideological scheme either go unnoticed or get explained away. So, for example, a social group or a language may be imagined as homogeneous, its internal variation disregarded. Because a linguistic ideology is a totalizing vision, elements that do not fit its interpretive structure – that cannot be seen to fit – must be either ignored or transformed. Erasure in ideological representation does not, however, necessarily mean actual eradication of the awkward element, whose very existence may be unobserved or unattended to. It is probably only when the 'problematic' element is seen as fitting some alternative, threatening picture that the semiotic process involved in erasure might translate into some kind of practical action to remove the threat, if circumstances permit.

By focusing on linguistic differences, we intend to draw attention to some semiotic properties of those processes of identity formation that depend on defining the self as against some imagined 'Other'. This is a familiar kind of process, one by now well known in the literature. Anthropologists, at least, are now well acquainted with the ways in which the Other, or simply the other side of a contrast, is often essentialized and imagined as homogeneous. The imagery involved in this essentializing process includes, we suggest, linguistic images – images in which the linguistic behaviors of others are simplified and seen as if deriving from those persons' essences rather than from historical accident. Such representations may serve to interpret linguistic differences that have arisen through drift or long-term separation. But they may also serve to influence or even generate linguistic differences in those cases where some sociological contrast (in presumed essential attributes of persons or activities) seems to require display.

CHAPTER 27

Language Ideology and Spelling Reform: Discourses of Orthography in the Debate over German

SALLY JOHNSON

In 1995, the German Standing Conference of Ministers for Education and Cultural Affairs – the *Kultusministerkonferenz* or *KMK* – announced that a reform of German orthography had been approved. The proposed changes were an attempt to harmonise what was perceived to be a complex and inconsistent set of orthographic rules that were causing unnecessary problems for language users of all ages, particularly for young school children.[1] The reform was to be introduced from 1 August 1998 to coincide with the start of the new school year, and this would be followed by a seven-year transitional period until 31 July 2005, during which time the old orthography would be considered 'outdated' (*überholt*) but not 'wrong' (*falsch*).

The decision to reform German orthography had not been taken lightly. Given that the first and hitherto only set of official guidelines for all the German-speaking countries had been agreed in 1901/1902, the final proposal for their revision in 1996 was the result of almost a century of often heated debate among linguists, politicians, educationalists, lexicographers, writers, journalists and other interested parties. Nor was the 1996 reform an exclusively German affair. From the mid-1970s in particular there had been close liaison between what were then the four main German-speaking states – the

Source: The text is adapted from Chapters 1 and 6 of *Spelling Trouble? Language, Ideology and the Reform of German Orthography* by Johnson, S. (2005a) (Clevedon: Multilingual Matters). The author and editors are grateful to Multilingual Matters for kindly allowing us to re-print this material.

Federal Republic of Germany, the German Democratic Republic, Austria and Switzerland – a process that was subsequently facilitated by the unification of Germany in 1990. At various points there had also been input from representatives from Liechtenstein, Belgium, Luxembourg, Denmark, Italy, Romania, and Hungary. On 1 July 1996, delegates met in Vienna to sign the so-called Vienna Declaration of Intent (*Wiener Absichtserklärung*), thereby agreeing to implement the new guidelines.

Although the disputes surrounding state involvement in the standardisation of German orthography had never entirely abated since they first began in the mid-nineteenth century, by the time the Vienna Declaration was signed in 1996, a new round of protest had already gathered momentum. In May of that year, Rolf Gröschner, professor of law at the University of Jena and his 14-year-old daughter took their case to the Federal Constitutional Court (*Bundesverfassungsgericht* – BVerfG) in Karlsruhe. Even though the Court rejected their claim that the reform was at odds with the German Basic Law (*Grundgesetz*), their highly publicised campaign helped to fan the flames of what might reasonably be characterised as a traditional public antipathy to the idea of orthographic reform. In October of the same year, a group of eminent writers and intellectuals, including the subsequent Nobel laureate Günter Grass, put their signatures to a petition circulated at the annual Frankfurt Book Fair, a protest that attracted considerable media interest, culminating in a front-cover story by the German news magazine, *Der Spiegel* (see Johnson 2007).

In the meantime many parents had begun to challenge the reform in the regional courts. By spring 1998, some 30 cases had been heard and in May of that year the issue was referred back to the Federal Constitutional Court for a final hearing. But even when this court ruled definitively in favour of the reform in July 1998, and all schools and official authorities were instructed to proceed with its implementation, the popular protest continued. In September, the electorate of the most northerly German state, Schleswig-Holstein, voted in a referendum to opt out of the reform. However, it was a situation which would not – and probably could not – be tolerated for long, and following the intervention of the regional parliament, the referendum result was overturned one year later, and schools in Schleswig-Holstein were once again instructed to teach the new spellings.

By this point, it began to look as though the legal dispute over German orthography had finally run its course. However, popular dispute persisted, and many anti-reform groups, such as the 'Organisation for German Spelling and Language Cultivation' (*Verein für deutsche Rechtschreibung und Sprachpflege*), continued to call for a reversion to the old orthography. Moreover, the exact status of the new rules following the end of the interim period in 2005 remains uncertain – if not for schools and official authorities, then at least for many individual members of the wider speech community (see Johnson 2005b).

In a historical survey of written German, Wolfgang Werner Sauer and Helmut Glück (1995: 69) declared: 'Orthography is boring. It is a subject for elderly folk who love order, vote Conservative, and always keep their dog on a lead.' Their heavily ironic comment, as they then proceeded to demonstrate, could not be further from the truth. Indeed the dispute over the 1996 reform of German orthography provides ample evidence that the group of those who do not find such issues boring extends way beyond order-loving Conservatives who take their dogs for walks on leads. The key question, however, is *why*?

Orthography as Language Ideological Debate

The disputes surrounding German orthography constitute a prime example of what Jan Blommaert (1999) has referred to as a *language ideological debate*. Blommaert describes such debates as occurring in specific times and places where real social actors or *ideological brokers* have collectively disputed the nature and function of language. These ideological brokers can then be said to have engaged in the production and reproduction of competing *language ideologies*, that is, 'sets of beliefs about language articulated by users as a rationalisation or justification of perceived language structure and use' (Silverstein 1979: 193). At the same time, such ideological brokerage can be theorised in terms of 'bids' for *authoritative entextualisation* (Silverstein and Urban 1996: 11), in other words, as concrete attempts to secure closure in a given debate, according to which a particular view of language would eventually achieve a naturalised, common sense status. Here we see how language ideologies represent not only *perceptions* of language and discourse, but perceptions that are themselves 'constructed in the interest of a specific social or cultural group' (Kroskrity 2000: 8). It is in this sense that the concerns of language ideology theorists meld with those of critical discourse analysts, who are similarly concerned with hegemonic 'struggles to legitimise claims for the universality of perspectives, interests, projects, etc. which are particular in their origins' (Fairclough 2003: 79).

Writing at the beginning of the 1990s, Kathryn Woolard noted how 'the topic of language ideology may be one much-needed bridge between work on language structure and language politics, as well as between linguistic and social theory' (1992: 236). However, Blommaert's point of departure for the analysis of language ideological *debates* is his contention that, while there is now a substantial literature on language ideology generally and historians of language have also touched upon related issues: 'the *historiography of language ideologies* is something that remains to be constructed' (1999: 1; original emphasis). For, in any attempt to understand how and why some views of language gradually emerge as dominant, while others are suppressed and marginalised, we need to attend to the historical processes that inform the dynamics of social power as these obtain in particular times and places. This is because

> ideologies do not win the day just like that, they are not simply picked up by popular wisdom and public opinion. They are being reproduced by means of a variety of institutional, semi-institutional and everyday practices: campaigns, regimentation in social reproduction systems such as schools, administration, army, advertisement, publications (the media, literature, art, music) and so on …. These reproduction practices may result – willingly or not – in *normalization*, i.e. a hegemonic pattern in which the ideological claims are perceived as 'normal' ways of thinking and acting. (Blommaert 1999: 10–11; original emphasis)

A focus on *orthography* – literally the assumption that there is only one correct way of writing – lends itself particularly well to the kind of historiographical approach to language ideologies advocated by Blommaert. It is, moreover, in tune with an emerging literature within Sociolinguistics and linguistic anthropology that emphasises the contingent nature of orthographic practices generally (Sebba 2007). Mark Sebba (1998: 35–40), for example, describes how the dominant view of orthography has traditionally been that of a neutral, technical accomplishment whose primary function is little more than the 'reduction of speech to writing'. Yet, drawing on Brian Street's (1984) now classic distinction between 'autonomous' and 'ideological' views of *literacy*, Sebba argues how an autonomous approach to orthography similarly masks the ideological nature of the choices made by real social actors in the creation and revision of writing systems. In his study of British Creole, Sebba (1998) then explores the ways in which a number of writers of Caribbean origin have tried to capture in written form a variety of speech for which there is no standard orthography. Especially interesting are the choices made by such writers in those cases where there is no *phonemic* motivation for adopting a spelling which diverges from that of the lexifier language, English, for example, <tuff> (tough) or <dhu/duh> (do) (Sebba 1998: 27). This suggests that Caribbean writers are opting for spellings that implicitly *construct* a difference between British Creole and standard English as a way of highlighting their own distinctiveness from mainstream cultural practices.

Similar uses of orthography as a means of styling both Self and Other in the representation and construction of ethnic, regional, national, gender and/or age-related identities have been explored in the context of many languages (for references and further discussion see Johnson 2005a). It is interesting to note, however, the way in which this somewhat disparate body of recent work in what Sebba (2000: 926) refers to as 'the sociolinguistics of orthography' has focussed on orthographic practices and values primarily in the context of *emergent, nonstandard* or *endangered* varieties of written language. This is perhaps inevitable when one considers that such varieties present particularly rich opportunities for observing the production of ideologies, and the construction of social identities, against the backdrop of a typically tense relationship with mainstream standards. Yet such opportunities are arguably less in evidence in the context of those varieties of written language that are already both highly standardised and widely used. This is because it is here that what James and Lesley Milroy (1999) have referred to as 'standard language ideology' – the promotion of an idealised standard perpetuating the interests of dominant social groups – is probably at its most naturalised. And even though processes of standardisation can have never been entirely finished, once a standard variety has been widely accepted, diffused, prescribed and codified, notions of orthographic (in)correctness can appear so utterly self-evident that their status as common sense is often considered – quite literally – *beyond debate*. It is therefore perhaps only when such conventions are subject to a form of revision or re-standardisation, as in the 1996 reform of German, that popular awareness of the contingency of orthographic norms resurfaces and the relevant language ideological debates are triggered once again.

Competing Discourses of Orthography

One way of approaching the disputes surrounding the reform of German is to see the various groups of ideological brokers as drawing on and/or re-producing competing *discourses* of orthography. This is an approach adopted by Christina Eira (1998) in her analysis of the selection of an orthographic system for Hmong, a language spoken by descendants of Chinese migrants, in Coolaroo, near Melbourne, Australia. Eira proposes how, when trying to unravel the complex disputes that typically ensue in debates over the creation or revision of orthographic systems, it can be useful to explore the manner in which social actors draw upon disparate discourses as competing *sites of authority*. Working with a concept of discourse as 'an underlying set of cultural belief frameworks', she then argues how 'the basis for orthography selection is fundamentally a question of the location of authority, which is in turn a function of the prevailing discourse' (Eira 1998: 172). Accordingly, disputes over orthography can to a considerable extent be explained in terms of 'disagreement on discourse allegiance', whereby she sketches a number of potential discourses as follows.

1. The **Scientific Discourse** is the one that is traditionally drawn upon by professional linguists working on orthography selection and revision, and is characterised by an overriding concern with the representation of sound

and/or meaning. Within this discourse, the optimal writing system is typically posited as one characterised by phoneme-grapheme correspondence and/or the systematic representation of morphemes (see also Stebbins 2001: 186–187). As Eira (1998: 176) notes: 'Whether or not one can propose principles for a linguistically optimal writing system, it does not at all follow that linguistic efficacy is the only or the most significant factor in the creation of orthography, defined as the accepted standard for writer/ readers of the language'. That said, the Scientific Discourse has traditionally enjoyed a privileged and dominant status in Western academic debates over orthography, a status that, as Eira suggests has typically masked its nature *as discourse*, thereby allowing (or even encouraging) its exponents 'to pass off any motivation other than the scientific as "superstitious" or "unenlightened"' (Eira 1998: 177).

2. The **Political Discourse** is rooted in the principle whereby the social inclusion and exclusion of individuals and groups are indexed by orthographic practices and values in such a way that national/cultural boundaries are constructed or maintained (see also Stebbins 2001: 187–189). Here Eira (1998: 177) points out how orthographies come to 'symbolise the validity or supremacy of the relevant cultural group [whose] usage must therefore reflect the nationalist/culturalist position at hand'. For example, while the Chinese character script serves the crucial purpose of unifying a number of otherwise diverse language communities, both British and American users of English can often be seen fiercely defending the small number of differences between their respective orthographies as indices of their own, arguably superior, cultural identities. As Eira concludes: 'Unification and differentiation, assimilation and repression, language/culture maintenance, and official recognition are all functions of the Political Discourse, and therefore have ramifications for ensuring lasting relevance of an orthography for a given language/culture group' (Eira 1998: 178).

3. The **Historical Discourse**, according to Eira (1998: 175), typically manifests itself as a conservative, perhaps even nativist, movement dedicated to the resistance of change, and is therefore likely to be of greater relevance in debates over the revision (as opposed to selection) of orthographic systems. Within this discourse, considerable emphasis is placed on the cultural continuity of the language with a concomitant concern for historical, visual and aesthetic factors as embodied, not least, in the literary heritage. In this regard, there may be an overlap with the **Religious Discourse**, whereby orthographies or scripts have, over time, been 'endowed with sacred status', not least in view of the traditional links between the use of a given orthography or script (for example, the Roman alphabet) and canonical renderings

of a sacred text (for example, the Bible) (1998: 178). However, in the case of highly standardised languages, the perception of a 'spiritual' relationship between not only the original content but also the *form* of sacred works may be so thoroughly naturalised that a deity is no longer called upon as the source of legitimation. In this context, Eira notes how 'the *status quo* of the orthography may be regarded as sacred, i.e. as something in which change is perceivable only as degradation' (1998: 180; my emphasis).

4. The **Pedagogical Discourse** revolves primarily around a concern for the ease with which a given orthography can be acquired by learners, and as such may be linked to debates over literacy more generally. According to Stebbins (2001: 184–185), exponents of this discourse (typically teachers) tend to view the consistency and uniformity of orthographies as a pre-condition for ease of acquisition. In this sense there are overlapping concerns with the Scientific and Historical Discourses, although there may be less emphasis on phoneme-grapheme equivalence as the key to systematicity. Moreover, there is often a general hostility towards variant spellings, which are widely considered a burden to learners.

This taxonomy of the potential discourses that may be invoked by participants in debates over orthography is by no means exhaustive. Eira (1998: 175) herself refers further to a **Technological Discourse**, according to which the efficacy of an orthography in the context of global electronic communication may be foregrounded in conjunction with the more general pursuit of linguistic or political modernity. Meanwhile, Stebbins (2001: 189–190) identifies a so-called **Community Discourse** where the cultural values of a community (as opposed to a region or nation) may be inscribed in orthographic practices and values. Moreover, as Eira (1998: 175) notes: 'In real-world circumstances, these fields are never neatly separate, but occur in layers and hierarchies which reflect the belief system structure of the culture(s) concerned.' In this regard, it is not simply the case that different groups of social actors draw exclusively on disparate discourses: what is of interest is the way in which such discourses are variously assembled by those groups when presenting a case for, or against, a particular orthography.

Competing Discourses in the Debate over German

Eira's notion of competing discourses as sites of *authority* in disputes over orthography melds well with Blommaert's (1999) concept of a language ideological debate. While it is clear that social actors are differently positioned in terms of the power they have to secure the normalisation of their particular viewpoints, the notion of competing discourses also allows us to explore the possibility that disparate groups of ideological brokers may in fact be *differently rationalising* the question of orthography. Put simply: we might see the linguists behind the 1996 reform of German as drawing on (and re-producing) a Scientific Discourse of orthography. The opponents' arguments, by contrast, were mostly couched in terms of a Historical Discourse with its focus on orthography as a symbol of cultural continuity, combined with secular dimensions of the Religious Discourse, according to which written German was viewed as sacred and immutable. But as Eira (1998: 174) emphasises, it is not only an allegiance to conflicting discourses that can account for disputes. A key source of disagreement can be the manner in which social actors draw upon the same basic discourse, albeit in different ways. And it is in relation to the Political Discourse, with its focus on the unificatory and disciplinary functions of orthography, that we encounter some of the more complex dimensions of the language ideological debate surrounding German orthographic reform.

At this juncture it is useful to return to the stated aim of the reform as laid down in the 1996 guidelines:

> to regulate spelling within those institutions (schools, official authorities) for which the state has jurisdiction with regard to orthography. In addition, the guidelines will function as a model, thereby securing a unified orthography, for all those who wish to orientate themselves toward an orthography with general validity (i.e. businesses, especially printers, publishers, editorial boards – but also private individuals). The new rules replace those of 1902 and all subsequent modifications.

The new guidelines are based on the following principles:

> An attempt to achieve a modest simplification of orthographic content with the aim of removing a series of exceptions, thereby extending the validity of the basic rules.
> A commitment to a re-formulation of the rules according to a unified concept [of orthography].(Deutsche Rechtschreibung 1996: 10; my translation)

Here we encounter a clear commitment on the part of the reformers to the *unificatory* function of the Political Discourse. From their perspective, this unity was then best achieved via the kind of *linguistic* systematicity associated with the Scientific Discourse. Of course, the aim of maintaining orthographic coherence was shared by the reform's opponents. However, their protest was fuelled largely by a concern that it was the re-standardisation process *itself* that posed a threat to such coherence. A further difference was that whereas the opponents' concept of unity was allied to a Historical Discourse that explicitly foregrounded the historical, visual and aesthetic dimensions of German orthography, these were the very factors formally excluded by the Scientific Discourse that underpinned the theoretical models drawn upon by the linguists. In other words, the linguists declared historical, visual and aesthetic issues to be largely irrelevant to the formal language planning process.

These competing rationalisations of the unificatory function of the Political Discourse have, in turn, repercussions for its *disciplinary* dimension. Here orthographic practices and values function as a symbolic means of constructing and maintaining not only in-/out-group boundaries vis-à-vis *horizontal* social relations. They also help to consolidate such boundaries in relation to *vertical* (that is, social class) relations, a function that then overlaps with the Pedagogical Discourse. In other words, the reformers saw the re-standardisation process to some extent as a means of challenging the ways in which incorrect spelling was typically used to index vertical social relations. This was to be achieved by making German orthography more linguistically systematic – and hence easier to learn – for those groups who had traditionally struggled to acquire the correct forms, such as young people or those with lower levels of exposure to the written language. This compared markedly to the views of the opponents, who were more concerned to *maintain* the symbolic function of orthography in relation to educational achievement and/or social class. At the same time, the linguists viewed the reform as an opportunity to enhance the pedagogic efficacy of what they knew to be an *arbitrary* standard, again by attempting to make that standard easier to acquire.

This compared to the opponents, who were not only concerned that the reform failed to achieve its basic aim of improving the teachability and learnability of German orthography. For them, the standard was not an arbitrary phenomenon: it was a *minimum* standard to which *all* users should aspire in view of its status as a 'historical-cultural product' (*Kulturgut*) that had evolved over many centuries as embodied in what is considered to be the great literary works of, say, Goethe and Schiller. In this sense any alteration to German spelling not only constituted a lowering of that standard – it implicitly threatened to relativise notions of correctness, thereby diminishing both the disciplinary and unificatory value of orthography for future generations of language users. This was insofar as the symbolic investment made by those who had already learned to use the old standard correctly which was now clearly under threat. Put simply: if what counts as correct can be seen to change over time, how is it possible to claim that there is only one form of correct spelling and punctuation, the very essence of the notion of *ortho*-graphy?

We have seen thus far how the reformers and their opponents differently interpreted the functions of the Political Discourse in relation to German orthography. However, it is not only the differences in their respective standpoints that are of interest, but also the similarities. What united the two groups throughout this dispute was their marginalisation of the political dimensions of the reform with recourse to the other Discourses on which they drew as potential sites of authority. In other words, both parties were concerned to demonstrate how orthography was *not* in fact a political issue. For the linguists, this was shored up by arguments rooted in the *Scientific* Discourse, with its autonomous view of orthography as a structurally self-referential, bounded system, whereby systematicity and correctness were merely technical, 'linguistic' issues (though this, of course, clashed with the reformers' own attempts to make the learning of orthography easier for certain marginalised social groups – clearly a political aim). Meanwhile, for the opponents, it was the invocation of the *Historical* Discourse, with its emphasis on orthography as symbolising an organic culture and aesthetic, that was similarly invoked as a means of de-politicising their own objections to the reform. In other words, German orthography was presented as standing outside of politics, bearing no relation to issues of power and privilege, having merely evolved over time without recourse to explicit political intervention (a view that was again misguided when one considers the involvement of powerful individuals and groups throughout the long and complex history of the standardisation of German). In sum, while both groups subscribed to the functions of the Political Discourse, each attempted to legitimise its own particular standpoint via a process of *de*-politicisation. This process was underpinned, however, by a differing discourse allegiance – the Scientific Discourse in the case of the reformers, the Historical Discourse in the case of the opponents.

In spite of their invocation of competing discourses of orthography, on the one hand, or disparate interpretations of the same basic discourse, on the other, it is crucial to note how neither of the two main groups of ideological brokers was at any point explicitly contesting the need for a standard orthography per se. As such, we see how no group called into question the political instrumentalisation of orthography that was implicit in the (re-)standardisation project as a whole. This was insofar as no group challenged the underlying unificatory purpose of a standard orthography in relation to a much longer-term attempt on the part of the German state to modernise the language as an index of the purported homogeneity of its community of users. Nor was the basic disciplinary function of a standard orthography questioned in any tangible way, such that even the post-1996 guidelines will continue to act as a means of benchmarking the educational achievement and intellectual standing of language users, not least that of school-pupils. Accordingly, we see how both of the two main groups of ideological brokers operated throughout this dispute within an overarching 'ideology of standardisation'. And it was in this way that the very idea of a standard German orthography (whether the old or new variant) was able to retain its status as a seemingly normal, natural and inevitable fact of language. This was a view that was *re*-produced, moreover, in the course of the legal dispute, bolstered not least by the third group of ideological brokers in this debate, the judges of the Constitutional Court, who proceeded to give the reform their full legal backing.

Conclusion

While the authority of the state in relation to German orthography was left firmly intact in the course of the dispute described in this chapter, we might see the language ideological debate that ensued as a relatively predictable challenge to the legitimacy of that authority. It was in many ways 'predictable' because, as Blommaert (1999: 8) reminds us, in any situation where language is seized upon as a symbolic resource: 'What counts for power also counts for its results: conflict, inequality, injustice, oppression, or delicate and fragile status-quo.' In conclusion, therefore, we might interpret the dispute over German orthography as a public re-articulation of the self-same social conflicts that are metaphorically inscribed in the practices and values of a standard orthography per se. And in this sense, we could argue that the dispute was merely a case of the state reaping the inevitable consequences of such conflicts, the seeds of which were sown when it first embarked on the formal codification of German orthography almost one hundred years earlier.

NOTE

1. The changes can be categorised into six main groups as follows: (i) sound-letter classifications (for example, *Känguruh → Känguru* 'kangaroo'); (ii) separate and compound spelling (for example, *radfahren→ Rad fahren* 'to cycle'); (iii) hyphenation (for example, *Hair-Stylist → Hairstylist/Hair-Stylist*); (iv) capitalisation (for example, *in bezug auf →* *in Bezug auf* 'with respect to'); (v) punctuation (that is, a reduction in the number of formal punctuation rules); and (vi) the separation of words at the ends of lines (for example, *Zuk-ker→ Zu-cker* 'sugar') (for further details and discussion, see Johnson 2005a: 45–86).

REFERENCES

Blommaert, Jan (ed.). 1999. *Language Ideological Debates*. Berlin: Mouton de Gruyter.

Deutsche Rechtschreibung. 1996. *Regeln und Wörterverzeichnis. Text der amtlichen Regelung*. Tübingen: Gunter Narr Verlag.

Eira, Christina. 1998. Authority and discourse: Towards a model for orthography selection. *Written Language and Literacy* 1: 171–224.

Fairclough, Norman. 2003. *Analysing Discourse: Textual Analysis for Social Research*. London: Routledge.

Johnson, Sally. 2007. The iconography of orthography: representing German spelling reform in the news magazine *Der Spiegel*. In Sally Johnson and Astrid Ensslin (eds.) *Language in the Media: Representations, Identities, Ideologies*. London/New York: Continuum. 91–110.

Johnson, Sally. 2005a. *Spelling Trouble? Language, Ideology and the Reform of German Orthography*. Clevedon: Multilingual Matters.

Johnson, Sally. 2005b. 'Sonst kann jeder schreiben, wie er will...'? Orthography, legitimation, and the construction of publics. In Sally Johnson and Oliver Stenschke (eds.) Special issue on the German spelling reform. *German Life and Letters* 58: 453–470.

Kroskrity, Paul (ed.). 2000. *Regimes of Language: Ideologies, Polities and Identities*. Santa Fe, New Mexico: School of American Research Press.

Milroy, James and Lesley Milroy. 1999. *Authority in Language: Investigating Standard English*. 3rd edition. London: Routledge.

Sauer, Wolfgang Werner and Helmut Glück. 1995. Norms and reforms: Fixing the form of the language. In Patrick Stevenson (ed.) *The German Language and the Real World*. Oxford: Clarendon Press. 66–93.

Sebba, Mark. 1998. Phonology meets ideology: The meaning of orthographic practices in British Creole. *Language Problems and Language Planning* 22: 19–47.

Sebba, Mark. 2000. Orthography and ideology: Issues in Sranan spelling. *Linguistics* 38: 925–948.

Sebba, Mark. 2007. *Orthography and Society: The Cultural Politics of Spelling around the World*. Cambridge: Cambridge University Press.

Silverstein, Michael. 1979. Language structure and linguistic ideology. In P. Clyne et al (eds.) *The Elements: A Parasession on Linguistic Units and Levels*. Chicago: Chicago Linguistic Society. 193–247.

Silverstein, Michael and Greg Urban (eds.). 1996. *Natural Histories of Discourse*. Chicago: University of Chicago Press.

Stebbins, Tonya. 2001. Emergent spelling patterns in Sm'algyax (Tsimshian, British Columbia). *Written Language and Literacy* 4: 163–193.

Street, Brian. 1984. *Literacy in Theory and Practice*. Cambridge: Cambridge University Press.

Woolard, Kathryn. 1992. Language ideology: Issues and approaches. *Pragmatics* 2: 235–250.

CHAPTER 28

The Production and Reproduction of Language Ideologies in Practice

ALEXANDRA JAFFE

Introduction

Over the past fifteen years, language ideologies have become a significant focus of analysis in Linguistic Anthropology and Sociolinguistics. This now significant body of research has extended our understandings of the systematic nature of linguistic behavior to people's *ideas* about language. It has also provided analytical models for tracing the connections between talk as social action and broader social and political structures and processes (Irvine and Gal 2000) by showing the role that language ideologies play in 'constituting ... linguistic and discursive forms as indexically tied to features of their sociocultural experience' (Kroskrity 2004: 507). In this chapter, I briefly review some of the main themes in language ideological research and then go on to explore the structure of a specific web of ideological relations surrounding the experience and conceptualization of diglossia on Corsica. I then explore how this ideological system structures both teacher practices and children's metalinguistic behavior in a bilingual Corsican school. The emphasis is on how this data reveals processes of indexicalization in action, and on the way that specific, local language ideologies index foundational ideologies about the nature of language and its relation to identity.

Language Ideological Research

Language ideologies relate to a wide range of phenomena that include (1) ideas about the nature of language itself; (2) the values and meanings attached to particular codes, genres, media and discourses; (3) hierarchies of linguistic value (from how particular codes are ranked to more general esthetic criteria used to evaluate spoken and written language); and (4) how specific linguistic codes or forms are connected to identities (both individual and collective and at all levels) as well as sociocultural roles and stances.

Ideologies are present both in the specific content of these four areas and in the nature of the connections posited in (4). From an analytical perspective, these connections are indexical, situated and contingent. However, through repeated practice these connections are subject to 'iconization' (Irvine and Gal 2000, Chapter 26). That is, as Wortham points out in his discussion of the role of language ideologies in the mediation of social identity, 'people rely on their construals of what particular linguistic patterns mean in order to identify speakers as occupying recognizable social positions ... [C]onsistent positioning over time can establish more enduring identities for individuals and groups' (2001: 256). It is thus crucial to incorporate the dimension of time in ideological analysis and to look at how, in specific historical contexts, multiple ideologies jockey for position in social life, and how particular language ideologies become hegemonic or 'naturalized' – or, alternatively, get challenged, contested or modified (see Blommaert 1999a; this volume, Chapter 38; and Kroskrity 2004 on the importance of a historical time frame; Blommaert's 1999b edited volume *Language Ideological Debates*; Irvine and Gal 2000; Irvine 2001; Kroskrity 1998; Jaffe 1999; Swigart 2000 and Woolard 1998 for some examples of analyses of the historical production and reproduction of dominant and alternative ideologies).

Language ideologies are also productive with respect to the social world because they are systems of classification, and as such, they can be mobilized to make social or cultural sense at multiple levels and in multiple contexts. Gal and Irvine refer to this property as 'recursivity', defined as the 'projection of an opposition, salient at one level of relationship, onto some other level. It is the process by which meaningful distinctions (between groups, or between linguistic varieties, etc.) are reproduced within each side of a dichotomy or partition, creating subcategories and subvarieties; or, conversely, by which intragroup oppositions may be projected outward onto inter-group relations ... This is the process that links subtle forms of distinctiveness with broader contrasts and oppositions' (Irvine 2001: 33).

Finally, we find the empirical traces of language ideologies in multiple types and levels of data. Language ideologies are reflected in explicit statements about language (in metalinguistic discourse); they are refracted in practices that orient towards or draw upon ideologies as resources, and are also embedded as presuppositions of discourses.

From the General to a Specific Case: Corsican Diglossia

Figure 28.1 is a sketch of the way that foundational ideologies of language frame general ideologies of linguistic-social differentiation, and give sociolinguistic variation its meaning potential. That is, only bounded, homogenous codes can be equated to or differentiated from other relevant codes within systems of value ('Ideology 2'). Only opposable, rankable codes can be mobilized to do the work of social identification/differentiation through a process

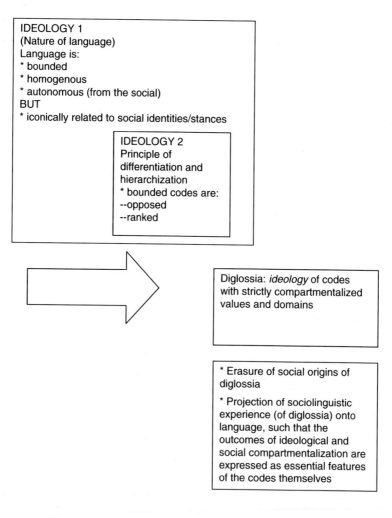

Figure 28.1　Ideological frameworks: Diglossia

of iconization. And the only way to fully accomplish the process of iconization (to completely naturalize the connections between the linguistic and the social) is to maintain an ideology of the autonomy of linguistic systems.

The arrow in the diagram indicates the way that these foundational ideological frames structure the experience and representation of diglossia (see Ferguson, Chapter 31, this volume) that I have documented on Corsica. Notice that I am treating diglossia as an ideology of strict compartmentalization of domains of use and value associated with two codes, not just as a label describing an objective sociolinguistic situation. It is worth tracing the process of iconization as it takes place through the filter of these foundational ideologies. As Kroskrity writes, 'ideas about language emerge from social experience and profoundly influence the perception of linguistic and discursive forms' (2004: 508). The social experiences that are key to my analysis of language ideologies on Corsica involve the compartmentalization of linguistic experiences. On Corsica, as in many other minority language contexts, the dominant language (French) was the only legitimate language of the public, official sphere and powerful institutions like the school. In the early part of the twentieth century, these were the only domains in which Corsicans used and experienced French; Corsican was the exclusive language of the 'inner sphere' of the home and family. In other words, we see lived experience setting up the conditions described in the box labeled 'Ideology 2'. The Corsican diglossic experience was also profoundly influenced by dominant French ideologies of the iconic relationship between language and citizenship, so that any opposition between French and Corsican was simultaneously an opposition between Frenchness and Corsicanness (the principle of recursivity). All of this social experience takes place against the backdrop of an autonomous view of language which does not view people's experiences of language as social but as linguistic in origin.

It is this combination of experiential and ideological conditions that makes it possible for Corsicans to project their socially mediated experiences of compartmentalized use and value onto French and Corsican as essential, 'natural' features of the codes themselves. Note that this does not mean that we can treat experience (or sociolinguistic practices or context) as having some essential nature. On the contrary, I want to emphasize the ways in which experience itself is ideologized and selectively filtered. For example, while it is true that French was represented as the only legitimate language of the school, and many teachers insisted that students speak French and punished them for speaking Corsican, there were also teachers who tolerated the use of Corsican among the children and/or used it themselves in school contexts. In Scott's terms (1992), the ideologized account of experience that is mobilized in iconization of the relationship between language, domain, function and value concerns only the 'official transcript'; in Gal and Irvine's terms, the 'unofficial transcript' is 'erased'.

This account illustrates the process through which foundational ideologies about what language is, and key principles of differentiation and hierarchization create the conditions in which ideologies associated with specific codes come into being. This brings us to the question of how these ideologies behave over time; including the extent to which they structure linguistic behavior under different conditions from those in which they developed as well as the way that changing conditions may reconfigure language ideological space. Here, we can return to the subject of diglossia on Corsica and how it has played out in recent Corsican sociolinguistic history, which is characterized by continuing language shift towards French and, in response, a rise in language planning efforts designed to increase the use and status of Corsican. Below, I explore data collected in a Corsican bilingual school in 2000. The micro-level analysis of language choice, teacher and student stances offers some insights on the process of indexicalization, as well as on the ways that language ideologies are inscribed and naturalized in practice. This approach treats these ideologies as 'habitus': as a system of 'durable, transposable dispositions' that serve a structuring role in generating and organizing both practices and representations (Bourdieu 1991: 53).

Corsican Bilingual Education: The Production and Uptake of Language Ideologies

Since its inception in 1996, Corsican bilingual education has had a relatively explicit ideological component related to its intended role in the revitalization of the Corsican language. The generation of language activists involved in setting up bilingual programs and policy was influenced by Corsican sociolinguists such as Jacques Thiers (1984, 1989), Fernand Ettori and Jacques Fusina (1980) and Jean-Baptiste Marcellesi (1989). These sociolinguists popularized the notion of diglossia and identified it as a catalyst for language attitudes that contributed to language shift. They emphasized that both Corsicans' linguistic insecurity in French and their sense of linguistic inferiority relative to Corsican were outcomes of the collective psychosocial effects of French language domination and the experience of diglossia. With respect to the model that I sketched above, they worked hard to put the social and the historical back into the equation, and thus to decouple the essential or iconic relationships between the two languages and the domains of use and value with which they had become associated. Corsican language education has thus always had a strong status planning dimension, aimed at reallocating languages in Corsican sociolinguistic space and dislodging the hold of French on high-status, public, institutional domains of use. Within bilingual schools, this has translated into an effort to maintain functional parity between Corsican and French. In the school that I studied, teachers used both languages for all pedagogical and social functions, and both languages were used in the teaching of all the subjects in the curriculum. This was explained quite explicitly by the teachers as a form of resistance to diglossia, which they saw refracted in some of their colleagues' insecurities and reticence related to the teaching of math and science in Corsican. At the same time, Corsican had a special status in this school as a language of cultural heritage, whose affective and social value was defined at least in part by differentiation from French. As I discuss below, this translated into some contrasts in classroom practice between the participant structures, forms of evaluation of language competence and representational roles of Corsican vs. French. To the extent that these contrasts represented Corsican as the language of greater intimacy and solidarity, they also reproduced elements of the diglossic system.

As a site of language ideological production, then, the bilingual school where I studied was multiple and complex. This raises a question about ideological reproduction: how students experience and interpret the language ideological content of their education. In the following analysis, I examine the way that students' sociolinguistic practices reveal their understandings of the relative statuses and roles of Corsican and French. I go on to explore the link between the specific local ideologies established in the classroom and some of the foundational ideologies about the nature of language itself that I have outlined above. I will be drawing on three kinds of data: ethnographic observations and recordings, questionnaires/interviews and experimental data.

Corsican as Preferred: Multiple Lines of Evidence

The village school I studied had two multi-age classrooms, one for the 3–6-year-olds and the other for the 7–11-year-olds. The following transcript is an extract of approximately four minutes of an audio recording made in the younger children's classroom at the four-year-old's table before the official start of the school day. Five four-year-olds were talking and playing with no teacher supervision. Petru, five, joined the table bringing a box of Corsican flash cards he had gotten from a shelf. He took them out one by one and attempted to gain the children's attention and to engage them in providing names for each of the pictures. While the children's attention to Petru fluctuated, he maintained enough of an audience to keep up the activity for ten minutes.

Extract 1: (5/2000) In this and following extracts, Corsican is represented in boldface. Items that are boldface and italic represent nonsense or invented words. AMJ = author.

1	Petru	Charles, qu'est-ce que c'est? qu'est-ce	Charles, what's this ? what's this ?
2		que c'est? *(showing a card)*	
3	Charles	**Portamuneta**	**Purse**
4	Petru	Bien, **portamuneta**, aheh !	Good, **purse**, aheh!
5	Child	*hard to hear : seems to be challenging Charles's answer*	
6	Petru	C'était **portamuneta** il a dit. Il l'a dit en	It was **purse** he said. He said it in
7		corse. **Portamuneta.**	Corsican. **Purse.**
8	Children	*children's talk continues at table 10 seconds*	
9	Petru	**Chì ghjè ?**	**What's this?**
10	Children	*talk continues, overlapping with following two answers*	
11	Child 1	**Una casa**	**a house**
12	Child 2	**Una casa**	**a house**
13	Petru	Non, eh ... oui. **Ghjè una casa**	No, oh..yes, **It's a house**
14	AMJ	**Ghjè una scola**	**It's a school.**
15	Petru	Non, **una casa**	No, **a house**
16	AMJ	non, **scola**	No, **school**
17	Petru	ah, oui, **scola.**	ah, yes, **school**
		children continue to chat. Petru takes out another card	
18	Petru	**E que?**	**And this?**
19	J-Pierre	Ça, c'est qui?	Who's that?
20	Petru	ça, c'est pour les petits.	That's for the little kids.
21	Girl	Alexandre et moi, on parte	Alexander and I, we're going
22	Child	(unintelligible) haricots	(?) beans
23	Petru	En corse, en corse !	In Corsican ! In Corsican !
		Petru displays another card	
24		**Chì ghjè què ?** ...	**What's this ?**
25	Children	**una moto**	**a motorcycle**
26		**una moto**	**a motorcycle**
27		*una mobiletta*	*a mobyletta*
28		*una moballa*	*a moballa*
29		*una motota*	*a motota*
30	Petru	*una moto:ta, una tota*	*a moto:ta, a tota*
31	Girl	une moto ! une moto ! une moto !	a motorcycle! a motorcycle ! a motorcycle !
32	Petru	En corse s'il te plait ma cocotte	In Corsican please my dear

Even without knowing anything about Petru or this classroom, we can tell from this transcript that he is playing teacher. We see him both taking up a teacher's authoritative stance and an adult's affective stance (the use of *ma cocotte* in line 32 would normally be reserved for use by adults towards children). This shows that he has made the (indexical) connection between particular kinds of speech acts (being the initiator and evaluator in the Initiation-Response-Evaluation sequence and using specific terms of endearment) and specific social roles and prerogatives.

With respect to Petru's language choices as he inhabits this role, he uses both Corsican and French to ask questions (line 1 in French; lines 9, 18 and 24 in Corsican). In evaluative moves, all his one-word tokens ('yes', 'no', 'good') are exclusively in French, but he ratifies correct answers through repetition in Corsican in lines 4, 6, 7 and 13. Even when he uses French, the content of his evaluations explicitly identifies Corsican as the only legitimate code for answers. On line 6, he defends Charles's answer as right by insisting that he 'said it in Corsican'; on lines 23 and 32 he admonishes the other children to speak Corsican. These kinds of explicit directives about and judgements of language choice were repeated on two other occasions in the course of this ten-minute activity. On one occasion he commented, to no-one in particular, that *il faut, il faut qu'ils le disent en corse*, 'They have, they have to say it in Corsican'; in another instance a child used the French word *ballon* and he replied *En corse et pas en français*, 'In Corsican and not in French'. Petru's *simultaneous* enactment of the teacher's role and his choice of Corsican as the gold language standard thus show that he considers Corsican to be the preferred language of school.

This leads us to consider where Petru acquired this local ideology about the relative status of French versus Corsican. To answer this question, we can turn to biographical, sociolinguistic and interactional data. Petru entered this school at age three as an almost monolingual Corsican speaker. This is very unusual; most Corsican children enter school either French-monolingual or French-dominant. However, Petru's parents were committed Corsican nationalists, and had made an explicit choice to bring their children up in Corsican. While official guidelines prescribed a 50–50% use of Corsican and French in bilingual schools, the curriculum for children of age 3–6 in this particular school was Corsican-heavy. After about a year of school (and constant play with other children through the medium of French) Petru had acquired completely age-appropriate oral skills in French. This meant that at the time of the recorded interaction, he had spent over a year being one of the very small number of children in the class who were able to participate with an equal level of competence in the Corsican and French parts of the curriculum. In my observations, the teacher never rewarded Petru just for speaking Corsican if his answer (or some other aspect of his behavior – like calling out) was not appropriate, and being an easily distracted child who liked to call out loudly, he was frequently chastised. Nevertheless, whenever the teacher asked questions, or provided opportunities to speak in Corsican where she had not previously established relevant vocabulary and structures for the whole class, Petru was at an advantage, and his voice was heard. In short, in his personal experience as a Corsican speaker in a bilingual classroom, he learned that Corsican language competence was a scarce and valued resource that had currency in the school reward structure, defined in terms of access to the floor and teacher ratification.

We can also understand Petru's interpretation of Corsican as the preferred language in the context of the relationship between the school and the wider sociolinguistic context. That is, the high frequency of Corsican language use in the school contrasted sharply with practices outside the school, where most adults used French most of the time with most children. In a society in which speaking French with children has become an unmarked practice, speaking Corsican with children is very clearly a deliberate and voluntary choice. That is, even if Corsican bilingual teachers were to have used Corsican and French for exactly the same amount of time and for identical functions in school, their choice to speak Corsican 50 percent of the time could be interpreted as a strong preference.

It was also the case that the teachers did *not* use Corsican and French in exactly the same way; nor did they evaluate children's competencies and performance in the two languages using exactly the same criteria. While children were held more accountable for specific linguistic knowledge in French than in Corsican, Corsican had a privileged status as the language of collective representation. Corsican was used for most documents sent outside the school; it was the language of school plays, poster displays, poetry and songs. It was also the language of media representations; as I have explored elsewhere (Jaffe 2007), during the filming of a television documentary on the school, children increased their use of Corsican in comparison to their everyday practices. In fact, Petru was not alone in his explicit assessment of language preference. All of the children in this school identified Corsican as the language that their teachers preferred and spoke the best in an oral survey that I conducted with them. (They were shown photographs of themselves, their teachers and all of their classmates and asked to identify which language(s) each person spoke, spoke best, understood and preferred.)

Subtle Forms of Resistance and the Indexing of Language Ideologies

There is another element of Extract 1 that merits our attention as an index of children's uptake of language ideological frameworks: the word and sound play on lines 27–30 by the children who are cast in student roles by Petru's teacher performance. In these lines, '*mobiletta*' is a plausible corsicanization of the word 'mobylette', which is a specific kind of motorized bicycle and thus a possible label for the picture Petru displayed. However, '*moballa*' and '*motota*' are nonsense words. They were also delivered with great gusto and volume. Their expressive value prompted Petru to briefly change his footing and align himself with his peers on line 30 by repeating '*motota*' with two variations: a lengthened vowel and then clipping (to '*tota*') before returning to his teacher role. As I have mentioned, this whole sequence took place outside the margins of 'official' school time, and outside of any teacher supervision (I was the only adult to intervene in any way). The scene at the table was relatively noisy and chaotic, with only one or two children at any one time attending in any way to Petru's agenda. Language play could, therefore, have had a purely ludic origin and function. However, other data from the same children's interactions with the teacher suggest that playing with the form and sound of the 'right' answer was a form of mild resistance to the imposition of 'teacher' norms and rules and/or to the school agenda in general (see Rampton 1999).

The following extracts are taken from both field notes and recordings made in October and November of 2000. Anne, Letizia, Saveriu and Charles were five years old and Petru was now six. The speech act in question in Extracts 3, 4 and 5 was in fact a frequent and ritualized one: the teacher in this classroom required children to ask permission to blow their noses (and to go to the toilet) and required them to ask in Corsican. This particular question (as well as the non-ritualized question in Extract 2) demanded the use of a reflexive verb, and because the placement of the reflexive pronoun differs in French vs. Corsican interrogatives, led to repeated corrections by the teacher of the sort represented in line 2 of Extract 3. In fact, we can see allusions to the fact that these kinds of interactions have taken place before in the teacher's comment in Extract 3 (directed at a student intern who was observing the class that day) that 'we manage to communicate' as well as in her reaction to Saveriu in line 2 of Extract 5: by calling him a clown, she defines his incorrect pronoun placement as a deliberate repetition of past behavior rather than as an unintentional error.

Extract 2: 10/27/00

1	Anne	Possu andà à mi vestà?	Can I go to myself dress? [put coat on]
2	Teacher	à vesteti	to dress yourself
3	Petru	à mi vestà	to dress myself
4	Charles	Possu andà à *piscià, puscià, pascià*?	Can I go pee, pie, pay?

Extract 3: 11/23/00

1	Letizia	Possu mi scuscià ?	Can I my nose blow?
2	Teacher	'Possu sciusciami' o 'mi possu	'Can I blow my nose?', or 'my nose, can I
3		sciuscià?	blow it?'
4	Letizia	Je peux me *schiusher?*	Can I *shoosh my nose?*
5	Teacher	On arrive à se comprendre!	We manage to communicate!

Extract 4: 11/27/00

1	Petru and Charles, (to Letizia)	Tu as dit, 'je peux me *schiusher?'*	You said, 'can I *shoosh* my nose?'
2	Saveriu	Mi possu sciusciammi ?	Can I myself blow my nose?

Extract 5: 11/29/00

1	Saveriu	Possu mi sciuscià ?	Can I my nose blow?
2	Teacher	O falzò !	You clown!
3	Saveriu	Mi possu sciuscia ?	My nose, can I blow it?
4	Letizia	Il le dit comme moi !	He says it like me!

The word play in these extracts involves both sound and structure. In Extract 2, the teacher corrects Anne, but does so in her own voice (using the second person pronoun for Anne). Petru then repeats Anne's question in Anne's (or any student's) voice, using the correct reflexive pronoun placement. Charles follows by asking another question (with no reflexive pronoun) but clowns around with vowel substitutions, producing two nonsense words. This introduces a humorous key (Rampton 1999: 487) that doesn't challenge the teacher's authority directly but takes away her prerogative to define the tone of the interaction and to maintain a serious frame. In Extract 3, Letizia responds to the correction of her Corsican by switching into French (where she maintains French reflexive pronoun placement) and using an invented gallicization 'schiusher' of the Corsican verb 'sciuscià'. This both undermines the teacher's prerogative to choose the language of the interaction and violates code boundaries. It was also, I should point out, quite self-conscious (done with a mischievous smile) and playful, and was taken as such by the teacher. At this point, the word '*schiusher*' entered the classroom vocabulary, and, as we see by the dates on the extracts, was recycled several days later by Petru and Charles. It was also at this point that the interactions around the issue of reflexive pronoun placement for this verb became a focus of explicit meta-sociolinguistic commentary, which we see in Extracts 4 and 5. It is of course not possible to assess Saveriu's linguistic knowledge/conscience in these two extracts with absolute certainty; he may have been uncertain about which form to use. However, as discussed above, we can see that he is *treated as* making a stylistic choice rather than making an error.

These practices index both specific/local and general ideologies of language. First of all, any behavior understood as resistant (mild or otherwise) indexes what it resists. All of the instances of language play in Extracts 1 through 5 are responses to overt acts of negative evaluation by a teacher (or a child playing a teacher) that impose a Corsican-only norm (Petru) or a Corsican language standard (the teacher). Acts of resistance, therefore, are indirect indices of the authority and preferential status attributed to Corsican within the bilingual classroom.

Implications for Ideological Reproduction

If we take all of this data together, we can see that the introduction of Corsican into bilingual schooling has in fact resulted in a change in a specific language ideology related to the relative status of the two languages in the school. At one level, the identification of Corsican as the language of preference upsets the diglossic model by reversing the status of Corsican and French in the school in some important ways. This change, however, is neither straightforward nor complete. At the local level, I have noted that while Corsican is used for all of the same high-status pedagogical functions as French, it is still differentiated from French along lines that relate to its status within the diglossic system as the language of solidarity, intimacy and cultural identity. This is reflected in differences in standards of performance and evaluation in Corsican vs. French. In French, children are held individually accountable for testable knowledge of Standard French spelling and grammar; in Corsican they are held collectively accountable for good-faith participation in a shared social and pedagogical agenda that includes Corsican but does not demand the same level of formal language competence from everyone. Corsican is also differentiated from French as *the* language of school identity; it is the code that is put on display in school documents, creative activities and performances.

Beyond these specific elements of a diglossic ideological model, school practice also reproduces several other important elements of what I have labeled Ideology 1 and Ideology 2 in Figure 28.1. Ideology 2 is reflected in the behaviors of Andria and the teacher, who both police the boundaries between Corsican and French in their imposition of Corsican as the preferred language choice and in the teacher's efforts to stop French pronominal usage from influencing the children's Corsican language structure. I have to emphasize that this was not always the case in this school, and teachers were in many instances very tolerant with respect to language choice and language mixing. However, these particular interactions show that Corsican and French were always *potentially* opposable. Furthermore, we see that those oppositions were always available to be mapped on to other socially relevant identities and stances, such as complying with the school agenda, being a good citizen and so on (the principle of recursivity).

The principle of hierarchization in Ideology 2 is also in evidence in these interactions, where there is a single right answer and a single right language. Again, I have to add that the ritualized requirement to ask to get a Kleenex in Corsican was not representative of this particular teacher's overall approach, in which she emphasized student inquiry and engaged in many activities in which students were invited to propose and discuss multiple possible rationales, answers and positions. However, she also made a choice to impose the use of Corsican for routine requests to blow one's nose or go to the toilet as a counterbalance to her general tolerance for children's use of French in the classroom.

It is also the case that hierarchization is built into the experience of schools themselves, in their social function of selection and ranking. In other research with the children in the older class, I found that while teacher's practice embodied a high tolerance/value on the expression of Corsican dialectal variation in orthography, students tended to view orthographic standards as much more rigid (Jaffe 2003). In this sense, we can see how students' experiences of school as an institution act as an ideological filter for their understandings of the nature and status of languages in the bilingual program. That is, when Corsican becomes a school subject, it is assimilated into children's experiences of testing and evaluation of school subjects in general, and is assumed to be governed by single, institutional standards.

What we see here is a principle of recursivity built into ideological systems. Put another way, the relationships between elements of an ideological web have a *metonymic* property: each time one part of the system is enacted in practice, it indexes the whole. It is this process of ideological entailment that makes dominant language ideologies resistant to change. The metonymic principle is also what makes processes of indexicalization so powerful. That is, people *experience* and perform properties of codes, identities and relationships simultaneously in practice. This experiential simultaneity may be at the heart of the process of iconization. This is why, as I have argued elsewhere, forms of resistance to dominant language ideologies that do not challenge foundational language ideologies (1 and 2 in Figure 28.1) and processes of differentiation tend to reproduce forms of social and linguistic hierarchy (Jaffe 1999). At the same time, the interconnection between experiences and ideology allows us to locate the potential for ideological change in systems of practice. In the school that I studied, everyday practices which decentered issues of language boundaries and choice provided that potential, a potential that is discernible in the children's language play described above, but whose long-term effects on the habitus of bilingual schools remains to be determined.

REFERENCES

Blommaert, Jan. 1999a. The debate is open. In Jan Blommaert (ed.) *Language Ideological Debates*. Berlin: Mouton de Gruyter. 1–38.

Blommaert, Jan (ed.). 1999b. *Language Ideological Debates*. Berlin: Mouton de Gruyter.

Bourdieu, Pierre. 1991. *Language and Symbolic Power*. Cambridge, Massachusetts: Harvard University Press.

Ettori, Fernand and Jacques Fusina. 1980. *Langue corse: incertitudes et paris*. Ajaccio: A Stampa.

Irvine, Judith. 2001. Style as distinctiveness: The culture and ideology of linguistic differentiation. In Penelope Eckert and John Rickford (eds.) *Style and Sociolinguistic Variation*. Cambridge: Cambridge University Press. 21–43.

Irvine, Judith and Susan Gal. 2000. Language ideology and linguistic differentiation. In Paul V. Kroskrity (ed.) *Regimes of Language*. Santa Fe, New Mexico: School of American Research. 35–83.

Jaffe, Alexandra. 1999. *Ideologies in Action: Language Politics on Corsica*. Berlin: Mouton de Gruyter.

Jaffe, Alexandra. 2003. Misrecognition unmasked? 'Polynomic' language, expert statuses and orthographic practices in Corsican schools. *Pragmatics* 13: 515–538.

Jaffe, Alexandra. 2007. Corsican on the airwaves: Media discourse, practice and audience in a context of minority language shift and revitalization. In Sally Johnson and Astrid Enslin (eds.) *Language in the Media*. London: Continuum Press. 149–172.

Kroskrity, Paul V. 1998. Arizona Tewa speech as a manifestation of a dominant language ideology. In Bambi B. Schieffelin, Kathryn Woolard and Paul V. Kroskrity (eds.) *Language Ideologies: Practice and Theory*. New York: Oxford University Press. 102–122.

Kroskrity, Paul V. 2004. Language ideologies. In Alessandro Duranti (ed.) *A Companion to Linguistic Anthropology*. Malden, Massachusetts: Blackwell Publishing. 496–517.

Marcellesi, Jean-Baptiste. 1989. Corse et théorie sociolinguistique: reflets croisés. In G. Ravis-Giordani (ed.) *L'île miroir*. Ajaccio: La Marge. 165–174.

Rampton, Ben. 1999. Deutsch in Inner London and the animation of an instructed foreign language. *Journal of Sociolinguistics* 3: 480–504.

Scott, James. 1992. *Domination and the Arts of Resistance*. New Haven, Connecticut: Yale University Press.

Swigart, Leigh. 2000. The limits of legitimacy: Language ideology and shift in contemporary Senegal. *Journal of Linguistic Anthropology* 10: 90–130.

Thiers, Jacques. 1984. Diglossie corse et dysfonctionnement du langage. In Sébastien Giudicelli (ed.) *La Corse et la Folie*. Marseilles: Editions du Quai. 37–40.

Thiers, Jacques. 1989. *Papiers d'Identité(s)*. Levie: Albiana.

Woolard, Kathryn. 1998. Simultaneity and bivalency as strategies in bilingualism. *Journal of Linguistic Anthropology* 8: 3–29.

Wortham, Stanton. 2001. Language ideology and educational research. *Linguistics and Education* 12: 253–259.

CHAPTER 29

Linguistic Resources for Socializing Humanity*

ELINOR OCHS

The Indexicality Principle

The fields of pragmatics, linguistic anthropology, Sociolinguistics, conversation analysis, and ethnomethodology all articulate ways in which the meaning of cultural forms, including language, is a function of how members engage these forms in the course of their social conduct. By now it is generally appreciated that members use cultural forms, including linguistic forms within their code repertoires, variably according to their conceptualization of the social situation at hand. In the social sciences 'situation' is usually broadly conceived and includes socio-cultural dimensions a member activates to be part of the situation at hand such as the *temporal and spatial locus* of the communicative situation, the *social identities* of participants, the *social acts* and *activities* taking place, and participants' *affective and epistemic stance*. For purposes of this discussion, situational dimensions other than space and time are preliminarily defined as follows:

> *social identity* encompasses all dimensions of social personae, including roles (e.g. speaker, overhearer, master of ceremonies, doctor, teacher, coach), relationships (e.g. kinship, occupational, friendship, recreational relations), group identity (e.g. gender, generation, class, ethnic, religious, educational group membership), and rank (e.g. titled and untitled persons, employer and employee), among other properties;

> *social act* refers to a socially recognized goal-directed behavior, e.g. a request, an offer, a compliment;

Source: 'Linguistic resources for socializing humanity', by Ochs, E. in Gumperz, J. J. and Levinson, S. C. *Rethinking Linguistic Relativity* (1996) (Cambridge: Cambridge University Press) pp. 407–37.

activity refers to a sequence of at least two social acts, e.g. disputing, storytelling, interviewing, giving advice;

affective stance refers to a mood, attitude, feeling, and disposition, as well as degrees of emotional intensity vis-à-vis some focus of concern (Labov 1984; Levy 1984; Ochs and Schieffelin 1984);

epistemic stance refers to knowledge or belief vis-à-vis some focus of concern, including degrees of certainty of knowledge, degrees of commitment to truth of propositions, and sources of knowledge, among other epistemic qualities (Chafe and Nichols 1986).

Every novice enters a fluid, sometimes volatile, social world that varies in certain conventional, non-random ways. Membership is accrued as novices begin to move easily in and out of linguistically configured situations. As they do so, novices build up associations between particular forms and particular identities, relationships, actions, stances, and the like. A basic tenet of language socialization research is that *socialization is in part a process of assigning situational, i.e., indexical, meanings* (e.g. temporal, spatial, social identity, social act, social activity, affective or epistemic meanings) to particular forms (e.g. interrogative forms, diminutive affixes, raised pitch and the like). I will refer to this tenet as the Indexicality Principle. To index is to point to the presence of some entity in the immediate situation at hand. In language, an index is considered to be a linguistic form that performs this function (Lyons 1977; Peirce 1955). Peirce, for example, defines index as follows:

> [An index is] a sign, or representation, which refers to its object not so much because of any similarity or analogy with it, nor because it is associated with general characters which that object happens to possess, as because it is in dynamical (including spatial) connection both with the individual object, on the one hand, and with sense or memory of the person for whom it serves as a sign, on the other hand. (Peirce 1955: 107)

A linguistic index is usually a structure (e.g. sentential voice, emphatic stress, diminutive affix) that is used variably from one situation to another and becomes conventionally associated with particular situational dimensions such that when that structure is used, the form invokes those situational dimensions.[1]

An example of linguistic indexing of *affective stance* is provided in (1) below. Affect is richly indexed in all languages of the world (see Ochs and Schieffelin 1984). In addition to indexing particular kinds of affect (e.g. positive affect, negative affect), languages also index degrees of affective intensity. 'Intensity operates on a scale centered about the zero, or unmarked expression, with both positive (aggravated or intensified) and negative (mitigated or minimized) poles' (Labov 1984: 44). In (1), a stance of heightened affect is indexed in the immediate situation through the use of the following structures in English: quantifiers ('all over', 'a lot') as well as emphatic stress (e.g. 'a lot', 'that long'), phonological lengthening (e.g. 's::-so', 'jus::t'), interjections ('Go:d'), laughter, and repetition (e.g. 'I didn't eat one bit I didn't take one bite').[2]

(1) *Mother approaches her two children (Jimmy and Janet), who are eating dinner. Jimmy has just commented that Janet has drowned her meat in A1 sauce and compares this with how he used to drown his pancakes in syrup*:

→ Jimmy   when I had pancakes one- pancakes (that) one time?
→   I like syrup? I put syrup? – <u>all over</u> my pancakes
→   and a <u>lot</u> – an – I didn't eat one bit I didn't take one
→   bite – I took some bites but =
      Mother: = when was that?
      Jimmy: a long time ago? – bout ((tosses head)) ten? – ten years old?
               - a:nd – the: [(Ja)
→ Mother: [(that wasn't <u>that</u> long
→ Jimmy: (well who knows) – but um th- the <u>pancake</u>- it was
→   s::-so soft (you) could – like (break) it with your -
→   – ju::st (pull it off) – <u>Go:d</u> hh
               ((pause))
      Jimmy: (I) tried to scrape some of it <u>off</u> but hchehe
               ((pause)) ((TV going))
      Mother: just sinks in

A second example of indexicality focuses on the indexing of *social identity*. This example is taken from interaction between two siblings in a Western Samoan household. Western Samoan society is elaborately hierarchical, with ranking on the basis of title, generation, and age among the variables. Traditional expectations assume that higher-ranking parties to an interaction will be less physically active than lower-ranking parties. Hence directives using the deictic verbs *sau*, 'come', and *alu*, 'go', are appropriately addressed to those of lower rank (Platt 1986). Within the analytic framework of the present chapter, we consider these verbs to index not only spatial dimensions but social relational dimensions of the social situation as well. In particular, the verbs *sau* and *alu* index that the speaker is of a higher rank than the addressee. In example (2), Mauga addresses her younger sibling Matu'u (2 years 2 months), with each instance of the deictic verbs indicating the asymmetrical nature of their relationship:

(2) *Matu'u's older sister, Mauga, is sitting at the front edge of the house. Matu'u is at the back of the house*:

→ Mauga: *Matu'u sau*
            Matu'u, come here.

→   *Matu'u sau*
           Matu'u, come here.
           ((Matu'u goes to Mauga))

→   *alu mai sau 'ie*
           'Go get a piece of clothes (for you).'

→   *Alu amai le mea solo ai lou isu*
           'Go get it to wipe your nose.'

→   *kamo' e, alu e amai le solosolo 'ua e loa 'ua e loa*
           'Hurry, go get the handkerchief, you know, you know.'

When we examine the situational meanings linguistic structures index, certain situational dimensions appear to be grammaticized more than other dimensions across language communities. Pragmatic studies attest to rich indexical systems referring to *time* and *space* (Fillmore 1982; Hanks 1990; Lyons 1982; Talmy 1983). Less recognized is the fact that, in many languages, *affective* and *epistemic stance* is encoded at many levels of linguistic structure. For example, degrees of certainty are indexed through sentential adverbs, hedges, presuppositional structures (e.g. cleft constructions, determiners), and sentential mood (e.g. interrogative mood indexing uncertainty/unknowing state), among other structures. As example (1) attests, affective stance is also elaborately indexed through grammatical structures such as diminutives, augmentatives, quantifiers, verb voice, sentential adverbs, and intonation (see Labov 1984; Ochs and Schieffelin 1984). While *social identity* is indexed across the world's language communities through pronominal systems and honorific morphology among the structures, social identity does not appear to be grammaticized through a wide diversity of grammatical structures, in comparison to grammatical resources for indexing time, space, and affective/epistemic stance.

Furthermore, other situational dimensions such as *social acts* and *social activities* are even less widely grammaticized. Thus while *act* meanings may be indexed through sentential mode, e.g. interrogatives (which might, in certain circumstances, for example, index that one is performing the act of asking a question), imperatives (which might, in certain circumstances, for example, index that one is performing the acts of commanding or reprimanding), and declaratives (which might, in certain circumstances, index that one is performing the act of asserting), relatively few grammatical structures directly index act meanings. Indeed a case could be made that interrogative, imperative, and declarative modes are not indexing act meanings but instead epistemic stance meanings, e.g. interrogative foregrounding relative uncertainty. (The relation between stance and social act meanings will be discussed below.)

Similarly, while the use of specialized lexicons, e.g. legalese, may index particular social activities, e.g. a trial, it is difficult to locate grammatical structures that directly index activity meanings. Are there grammatical structures that directly index that one is having an argument, making a decision, giving directions, coaching, or attempting to solve a problem at hand? As will be discussed below, the indexing of social activities may be accomplished through the indexing of other situational dimensions, e.g. the indexing of narrative activity may be accomplished through the indexing of historical present time.

It is important to stress at this point that the assignment of situational meanings is a complex, interactionally accomplished process. Interlocutors have available to them a reserve of linguistic structures – some grammatical, others discursive – that are conventionally associated with particular situational dimensions. Interlocutors may use these structures to index a particular identity, affect, or other situational meaning; however, others co-present may not necessarily assign the same meaning. This circumstance is captured by Searle's distinction between illocutionary act (act meaning intended by performer) and perlocutionary act (act meaning interpreted by others) where illocutionary and perlocutionary act meanings are not the same (Searle 1970). Cases of indexical breakdown have also been central to Gumperz's study of 'crosstalk' wherein interlocutors project different contexts of situation from linguistic 'contextualization cues' (Gumperz 1982, Chapter 40). In some cases of crosstalk, the discrepancy in interpretation goes by unnoticed as interlocutors strive to interact as if they do understand one another. In other cases, mutual understanding may be sought and sometimes jointly achieved through conversational devices such as repair structures (Schegloff, Jefferson and Sacks 1977) or other types of negotiation.

It is also important to note before going on that assignment of indexical meaning involves more than perception of a single linguistic form alone. Rather, the situational interpretation of any one linguistic form is an outcome of its relation to co-occurring linguistic forms in the prior and present discourse structure, to subjective understandings of the propositional content of the utterances thus far and of the activity those utterances are constituting as well as subjective understandings of gestures and other dimensions of the non-vocal setting (see Brown and Levinson 1979; Ochs 1988, 1990, 1992; Silverstein 1987).

Indexical knowledge is at the core of linguistic and cultural competence and is the locus where language acquisition and socialization interface (Ochs 1990). A novice's understanding of linguistic forms entails an understanding of their indexical potential (i.e. the situational constellations of by whom, for what, when, where and to what ends forms are conventionally employed) in co-ordination with co-occurring linguistic forms and other symbolic dimensions of the situation at hand. A novice's understanding of social order similarly crucially relies on an understanding of how that order is linguistically realized moment-by-moment over interactional time.

As early as the first year of life, infants begin to be attuned to the indexical meanings of particular structures. For example, infants confronting novel objects will monitor the voice quality and intonation of significant others (along with facial gestures) as indexes of their stances towards that object, an activity developmentalists call 'social referencing' (Campos and Stenberg 1981; Klinnert, Campos, Sorce, Emde and Svejda 1983). This observation is supported by developmental phonologists, who note that children at the single-word stage can discern and respond appropriately to culturally relevant emotional stances indexed by diverse intonational contours (Cruttenden 1986; Halliday 1973; Peters 1977). Young children also grasp indexical meanings of morphological structures. For example, Platt's observations of children at the single-word and two-word stage in Western Samoa suggest that they have considerable understanding of the social rank indexed by specific verbs (Platt 1986). In particular, Samoan children grasp that the deictic verbs *sau*, 'come', and *alu*, 'go', can be used in directives only to inferiors, but that *aumai*, 'give', in the imperative (begging) can be directed to kin regardless of status. As a consequence, Samoan children produce the semantically more complex form 'give' earlier and more often than the less complex forms 'come' and 'go'. Children at this stage of life appropriately address 'come' to animals, the only appropriate lower-status creatures. At this same period of development, Samoan children are able to appropriately switch between two different phonological registers and use competently the affect-marked (sympathy stance) pronoun *ta 'ita*, 'poor me', to index stance (Ochs 1988). Similarly, Kaluli children in Papua New Guinea master the affect-marked (appeal stance) pronoun *nel*, 'to me (appeal)', by two years of age (Schieffelin 1990).

Researchers have also observed that two- to four-year-old English-speaking children understand so-called indirect act meanings (e.g. indirect requests) indexed by co-occurring grammatical structures (e.g. indirect word order, pronouns) (Shatz 1983), and children as young as four vary linguistic structures according to social status of addressee (Shatz and Gelman 1973). By the age of five, English-speaking children understand and use productively linguistic forms that index social relationships such as doctor–patient, teacher–student, parent–child, and native–foreigner (Andersen 1977).

Indexical Property of Constitutiveness

The Sapir–Whorf hypothesis promotes the notion that language does not merely mirror 'reality', it also shapes it. While deterministic interpretations of this generalization have been refuted, there lingers among anthropologists and sociologists of language the notion that nonetheless language does structure the phenomenological world. This notion is foregrounded in Austin's notion of performatives as verbal predicates that bring about social actions through their utterance (Austin 1962), in conversation analyses of how turn organization structures future interactional moves (Goodwin and Goodwin 1987; Sacks, Schegloff and Jefferson 1974; Schegloff 1987), and in studies of how situationally bound linguistic forms bring into being particular social situations (Brown and Levinson 1979; Goodwin and Duranti 1992; Hanks 1990; Ochs 1988, 1990, 1992; Silverstein 1993). In some cases the linguistic forms may bring about the same situational definition for all participants but, in other cases, participants may use the linguistic forms to construct divergent situations (Gumperz 1982).

This property of language means that, when interlocutors use indexical forms, they may *constitute* some social structure in the immediate situation at hand. For example, in (2), Mauga uses the deictic verbs not only to indicate that she is of higher rank than her younger sibling, Matu'u, but also to bring that ranking into the situation at the moment. In using the deictic verbs, Mauga is both attempting to define her relationship with Matu'u and socializing Matu'u into the social indexical scope of these grammatical forms. When Matu'u complies with Mauga's directives to 'come' and 'go', she ratifies Matu'u's definition of the relationship for that moment. This is not to say that all socialization is characterized by compliance and ratification on the part of the children and other novices. In some cases, novices (including children) struggle to redefine, i.e., to reconstitute, their relationship to more knowing members of the community. The important point is that interlocutors, including experts and novices, build up definitions of situations turn-by-turn, moment-by-moment, in the course of their interaction.

In this perspective, members of societies are agents of culture rather than merely bearers of a culture that has been handed down to them and encoded in grammatical form. The constitutive perspective on indexicality incorporates the post-structural view that the relation between person and society is dynamic and mediated by language. In an intellectual era that has brought paradigms such as practice theory and cultural psychology into academic parlance, we have come to entertain the notion that, while person and society are distinguishable, they are integral. Person and society enter into a dialectical relation in that they act on each other, draw upon each other, and transform each other. In such paradigms, while society helps define a person, a person also helps to (re)define society.

Socialization in this constitutive view is not a uni-directional transaction from member to novice but rather a *synthetic, interactional achievement* where novice is an active contributor. In this view as well, while language is a socio-historical product, language is also an instrument for forming and transforming social order. Interlocutors actively use language as a semiotic tool (Vygotsky 1978) to either reproduce social forms and meanings or produce novel ones. In reproducing historically accomplished structures, interlocutors may use conventional forms in conventional ways to constitute the local social situation. For example, they may use a conventional form in a conventional way to call into play a particular gender identity. In other cases, interlocutors may bring novel forms to this end or use existing forms in innovative ways. In both cases, interlocutors wield language to (re)constitute their interlocutory environment. Every social interaction in this sense has the potential for both cultural persistence and change, and past and future are manifest in the interactional present.

Indexical Valences

Many pragmatic and anthropological linguistic studies of indexicality tend to focus on only *one* situational dimension associated with *one* set of linguistic forms. For example, several decades ago, Whorfian-inspired research tended to analyse a single ethno-semantic situational domain, such as time (Whorf 1956). Pragmatic studies within linguistics and philosophy also analyse lexical and grammatical systems that appear to index a single situational dimension, e.g. pragmatic studies of honorific systems that index social identity (Comrie 1976; Kuno 1973), evidential systems that index epistemic stance (Chafe and Nichols 1986), or performative predicates that index social acts (e.g. Austin 1962; Searle 1970). The situational dimension chosen for analysis is usually grammaticized or lexically expressed in complex and interesting ways. Further, that situational dimension seems to be the foreground semantic field – i.e., the conventional, recognized meaning – that is associated with those particular linguistic forms.

In all societies, however, members have knowledge of norms, preferences and expectations that relate particular indexical dimensions to one another. That is, in all societies, members have tacit understandings of norms, preferences, and expectations concerning how situational dimensions such as time, space, affective stance, epistemic stance, social identity, social acts, and social activities cluster together. For example, the Rundi as described by Albert (1972: 82) expect high-ranking men in public settings to exhibit a detached stance:

> Caste stereotypes represent those in the upper strata of society as never raising their voices or allowing anger or other emotions to show ... That total, glacial silence of a perfectly immobile Mututsi who has chosen not to speak has to be experienced to be appreciated. To all appearances, the silence can be maintained indefinitely and in the face of every known technique of provocation, domestic or imported.

To consider another example, in middle-class American families, the role of mother is associated with the acts of eliciting and initiating family stories during family dinnertime (Ochs and Taylor 1992). Performing these acts is part of what is expected of a middle-class mother. Other acts associated with mothers of this social group include praising children and verbally guessing at their unintelligible utterances (Ochs 1988). One way of considering such cultural associations is to think of particular situational dimensions as linked to other situational dimensions through socially and culturally constructed *valences*. Somewhat like elements in a chemical compound, these valences show how a particular situational dimension is linked to other situational dimensions (e.g. among the Rundi, the situational display of detachment has valences that link it to high status). Fundamental to membership in a community is knowledge of the valences that link one situational circumstance to another.[3]

Because particular situational dimensions (e.g. particular stances, acts, statuses etc.) are linked through socio-cultural valences, the realization of any one situational dimension (e.g. the linguistic indexing of a particular stance) may invoke or *entail* (for members of particular communities) other culturally relevant situational dimensions (Ochs 1990, 1992; Silverstein 1993). While a number of studies of language use dwell on the relation of linguistic forms to only one situational dimension and ignore situational dimensions socio-culturally linked to that dimension, other studies – predominantly linguistic anthropological studies – consider a range of situational dimensions socio-culturally entailed by a set of linguistic forms (see Brown and Levinson 1979, 1987; Duranti 1984, 1990; Gumperz 1982; Hanks 1990; Haviland 1989; Ochs 1988, 1992; Sehieffelin 1981, 1990; Silverstein 1993). From a current linguistic anthropological perspective, indexicality does not stop at one situational domain. For example, for members of Rundi society, the linguistic forms that index an affective stance of detachment also index (because of socio-cultural valences that link situational dimensions) a particular social status. In other communities, reported speech forms (e.g. 'they say') index more than an epistemic stance (indirect knowledge). Depending on community and circumstance within the community, reported speech forms may also index a range of situational dimensions including the act of reporting and/ or some degree of authoritative status of the speaker vis-à-vis the expressed proposition. Relations of entailment among situational dimensions may vary across social groups even within the same language community. For example, for certain patients in the United States, knowledge that some party is a medical doctor may entail the stances of being knowledgeable, objective, and caring, and a set of actions and activities (medical procedures). On the other hand, for the community of medical personnel, such entailments do not necessarily hold. Indeed medical personnel assume medical doctors will display a range of knowledgeability, acts, and activities, and, in certain contexts (e.g. in grand rounds), will scrutinize one another's stance and practices (Cicourel 1989).

It is important to distinguish the range of situational dimensions that a form (set of forms) *potentially* indexes from the range of situational dimensions that a form (set of forms) *actually* indexes in a particular instance of use (in the mind of any participating interlocutor – speaker, addressee, overhearer, etc). The indexical potential of a form derives from a history of usage and cultural expectations surrounding that form. When a form is put to use in dialog, the range of situational dimensions that particular form indirectly helps to constitute and index is configured in a particular way. Not all situational meanings are necessarily entailed.

Indexical valences and entailed indexicality are useful constructs in understanding linguistic relativity, for they are powerful linguistic vehicles for socializing novices into the cultural structuring of everyday life. Knowledge of entailed situated meanings of particular indexical forms offers a wedge into how members construe their local worlds. Language acquisition and language socialization can be seen as unfolding understanding of the indexical potential of particular linguistic forms and the skill to apply that understanding to construct situations with other interlocutors.

The Centrality of Stance

The previous section stresses the point that situational dimensions are linked by socio-cultural valences (i.e. expectations, preferences, norms) such that the calling into consciousness of one particular dimension may culturally entail other relevant dimensions. A way of recouching relations of entailment that obtain among situational dimensions (for members of a social group) is to view situational dimensions entailed by some other situational dimension as components that help to constitute the meaning of that situational dimension. Thus, in the case of the Rundi, a component of the meaning of upper caste (social identity) is impassivity (affective stance) in public. Or the converse: a component of the meaning of impassivity (affective stance) is the social identity of upper caste (as well as any other social identity to which those stances are linked). Similarly, as noted earlier, in the minds of many patients in the United States part of the meaning of medical doctor (social identity) is the set of stances of being knowledgeable, objective, and caring, as well as the activity of diagnosis (Cicourel 1989). Or the converse: part of the meaning of the cluster of stances 'knowledgeable, objective, and caring' is the social identity of medical doctor (as well as any other social identity to which those stances are linked). Likewise, particular temporal dimensions are socio-culturally linked to affective stances (Hanks 1990) and as such can help to constitute the meaning of particular affective stances. For example, for many speakers of English, the temporal dimension of the present moment, 'now', may help to constitute a stance of affective intensity (as in the utterance

'Now look at what you have done'). And as well, for many speakers of English, the stance of affectivity/intensity is part of the meaning of 'now'.

Any situational dimension (any temporal/spatial dimension, affective/epistemic stance, social act, social activity, social identity) can in theory help to constitute the meaning of any other situational meaning. In this section, I focus on affective and epistemic stance and propose that these stances are central meaning components of social acts and social identities and that linguistic structures that index epistemic and affective stances are the basic linguistic resources for constructing/realizing social acts and social identities. Epistemic and affective stance has, then, an especially privileged role in the constitution of social life. This role may account in part for why stance is elaborately encoded in the grammars of many languages.

Stance as a Component of Social Acts

Affective stance

In all communities, affective stances are socio-culturally linked to social acts, in the minds of speakers (illocutionary acts), of hearers (perlocutionary acts), or of both speakers and hearers. For example, sadness may be conventionally linked to condolences, negative affect to complaints, positive affect to praises, and so on. We can think of these relations constitutively in the sense that particular affects help to constitute the meaning of particular acts. Where these affects are indexed by a linguistic form, that form may also constitutively index associated social acts. Example (3) illustrates an interaction between a Samoan mother and child in which the selection of a particular variant of the Samoan first person pronoun *ta 'ita* conventionally indexes the affective stance of sympathy or love for the referent ('poor me'). This affective stance, however, helps to constitute the meaning of the act performed in (3), namely begging. In (3), the use of *ta 'ita* then not only indexes sympathy/love, it also constitutes and indexes the social act of begging:[4]

(3)   K (1 year 7 months) with mother, who holds food

K	Mother
((crying)) *//mai /*	*//(leai) leai/*
'give (it)'	'(no) no'
((calls name of mother))	
	'o le a
	'what is it?'

→   *(i)ta/*
    '(for) dear me'

In Samoan, there are two alternate forms (*a'u*, 'I' and *ta 'ita* 'dear me') for referring to the first person. Only *ta 'ita* indexes a sympathetic affective stance. *Ta 'ita* is conventionally used by Samoan speakers to both give and elicit sympathy. It is used to console and to appeal. In this segment of interaction, K first uses the verb *mai*, 'give', with a crying tone of voice. These structures help to constitutively index a demand, which the mother rejects. K then elicits his mother's attention again and utters the sympathy-marked pronoun *ita* (a form of *ta 'ita*). While foregrounding the affect of sympathy for self, this form in this context (i.e. following the expression of *mai*, 'give') transforms the demand into begging. If the child had used the more affect-neutral pronoun *a' u*, 'I', the act might not be necessarily interpreted as begging despite the child's use of crying. *Ita* alters the meaning of the utterance sequence to cumulatively mean something like 'Have pity and give it to this wretched soul.' A similar pronoun in Kaluli (Papua New Guinea), *nel* 'to me (appeal)', not only indexes sympathetic affect but is central to defining acts of appeal, and is frequently used by two-year-olds in appealing for the breast (Schieffelin 1990).

In much the same way as the affect markers *ta 'ita* in Samoan and *nel* in Kaluli are central to constituting the acts of begging/appeal, so the use of respect vocabulary in Samoan and many other languages may be a central affective component of requests. The potential range of act meanings entailed by respect vocabulary, as with other affective forms, is large. Depending upon other co-occurring structures and circumstances, interlocutors hearing a switch from everyday to respect vocabulary try to interpret the nature of the social act being constituted through this display of deferential affect. In the course of fieldwork, our research group was often visited by members of the Samoan community who knew us well and spoke to us informally. Occasionally these same folks approached using respect vocabulary. During these occasions, we came to understand that these expressions of deference (e.g. *maalie lou finangalo*, 'please your wish') were helping to constitute a request for an item of some magnitude such as a loan or a ride into town.

Linguistic structures that index affective *intensity* also help to define acts. In the examples below taken from American family interactions, intensity markers such as emphatic stress, loudness, syllable lengthening, intensifying adverbs ('freezing cold'), interjections ('BU::::RR'), as well as repetition, index not only affect but also the act of *complaining*:

(4) *Mother, Father, and Grandfather, and three children [Heddi, Sharon, and Kit] are eating dinner:*

→	Heddi:	the PEAS are <u>CO:::LD</u>!
	Mother:	what ((*to Heddi*))
	Sharon:	((*while tapping plate with fork*)) [( )
	Kit	[mu mu mu mu mum

$\rightarrow$ Heddi: [these peas are cold!
    Mother: (it won't hurt/okay) –
             ((*to Father*)) were- were <u>your</u> peas [cold when you ate 'em?
    Kit: ((*Kit continues to struggle and whimper*))
    Father: I didn't eat 'em – I (haven't had/didn't have) any yet
             ((*pause*))
    Mother   ((*to Kit*)) just a <u>minu</u>te I'll get you some mo:re
$\rightarrow$ Sharon: <u>BU:::[:RR!</u>
    ?:   (what's a matter Sharon)
$\rightarrow$ Sharon   bur[r these peas are cold!
    Heddi: [they're f- ((*as she looks into pan for more food*))
    Mother: oh=
$\rightarrow$ Heddi: = they're <u>freezing</u> co::ld!

Other examples, from this same family dinner, of affect intensifiers (e.g. emphatic stress) that help constitute complaints include:

(5) *Heddi's complaint about the spare rib she is eating*:

    Heddi: this huge thing, I <u>can't</u> even <u>chew</u> it ((*throws down bone on plate*))

(6) *Father's complaint about the way in which Heddi is choosing a slice of cantaloupe from the serving bowl*:

    Heddi: ((*Heddi is searching bowl for a slice and looks several times to compare sizes with Sharon's slice*))
$\rightarrow$ Father: ((*annoyed*)) <u>Pick</u> one Heddi and <u>stop</u> (this) diggin' around.

Epistemic stance

As noted earlier, epistemic stance includes qualities of one's knowledge, such as degrees of certainty as to the truth of a proposition and sources of knowledge, including perceptual knowledge, hearsay knowledge, common-sense knowledge, and scientific knowledge, among other phenomena. These stances in turn may be constitutive of social acts. For example, in example (7) below, the use of the epistemic indexical term 'maybe' as a postscript to the earlier utterance 'finish chewing and then you may talk' constitutively indexes not only relative uncertainty but also an act meaning something on the order of an implied threat or perhaps a warning:

(7) *Mother, Father, and two children (Susan and Artie) are eating dinner. Susan talks with food in her mouth*:

    Mother: ((*deliberately, to Susan*)) finish chewing, and then you may talk
    Artie: ((*takes a noisy gasp for air*))
$\rightarrow$ Mother: ((*continuing in same tone of voice to Susan*)) <u>may</u>be

Samoan has a sentence-final particle e which functions in a similar way to this post-completion use of 'maybe' in English, as illustrated in (8):[5]

(8) *In a Samoan house, a mother is talking with one of her three children who is acting selfishly towards his siblings.*

	Mother:	e	le	koe	fa'akau aa	mai
		TA	NEG	again	buy	EMPH DEICT.PRT
		aa	sau	fagu	e:!	
→		EMPH ANY.YOUR GUN EMPH			

'she won't buy again any water pistol for you (unless you shape up)!'

Here the Samoan particle *e* marks a future world that might come true if certain behaviors continue that the speaker does not condone. As with the use of 'maybe' in example (7), the particle helps to constitute the utterance as a conditional threat or a warning. In both examples (7) and (8), the speaker is threatening to possibly withdraw something the addressee desires: in (7), to talk, in (8), to have a water pistol.

The monograph by M. H. Goodwin (Goodwin 1990) about the discourse of pre-adolescent Black children vividly displays how these speakers lace their utterances with epistemic forms that lend definition to the act meanings in play. In (9) below, Ruby uses the epistemic verb 'know' both to constitutively index her certain knowledge about the proposition 'it's a free world' and to construct a *challenge* to Stacey's possible assumption that 'it's a free world' is news to Ruby:

	(9) Stacey:	Fight yourself.
	Ruby:	Well you <u>make</u> me fight myself.
	Stacey:	I can't <u>make</u> you. Cuz it's a free world.
→	Ruby:	I <u>know</u> it's a free world. (Goodwin 1990: 154)

Similarly, the children used modal verbs such as 'can' and 'could' to constitutively index not only the epistemic stance of possible or uncertain worlds but also the act of *suggesting*, as displayed in the following utterances:

	(10)a.	
→	Bea:	We could go around looking for more bottles.
	(10)b.	
		((*Discussing where to break bottle rims*))
→	Martha:	We <u>could</u> use a sewer.
		((*Discussing keeping the activity secret from boys*))
→	Kerry:	We can <u>l</u>imp back so nobody know where we gettin' them from. (Goodwin 1990: 111)

Stance as a component of social identity

As noted earlier, 'social identity' encompasses participant roles, positions, relationships, reputations, and other dimensions of social personae. In all societies, these identities are conventionally linked to affective and epistemic stances. One way of considering affective and epistemic stances is to see them as perspectives independent of social identities, which members expect of those who hold those identities. For example, we might consider the stances of being knowledgeable, objective, and caring as perspectives independent of the social identity of medical doctor in the United States. Similarly, we might consider the stances of hesitancy and delicacy as independent of female gender identity in Japanese society (Cook 1988). On the other hand, another way of considering stances is to view them as not outside the category of social identity. They do not merely point to a social identity but rather *help to constitute* that identity. In the case of medical doctor, one may display the stances of knowledgeability, objectivity, and care to build a certain kind of medical professional identity. In radically different circumstances, a Japanese woman may display hesitancy and delicacy to create a female gender identity for the situation at hand.

In all societies, members may vary which stances they display and in so doing build different sorts of social identities. In Japanese society, females do not necessarily display hesitancy and delicacy in every situation but rather select when to display these stances. Women the world over may play up or play down their female gender identity. They build their social personae using stance displays variably within and across social interactions (Cook 1988). In West and Zimmerman's language (1987), a woman may choose to 'do gender' or 'do being female' to varying degrees and in different ways. In like manner, one may opt for 'doing being mother', 'doing being son-in-law', 'doing being grandparent', or even 'doing being baby' (as when two-year-old 'reverts' to a baby identity when an infant sibling arrives home from the hospital).

Fluidity in stance and social identity is characteristic of institutional interactions as well. For example, a medical doctor may vary his or her stances within the same interaction with a patient or with a medical peer to create different professional identities at the moment, e.g. shifting between stances of greater or lesser certainty to create more or less authoritarian professional identities (Cicourel 1989; Fisher 1991). Similarly, Jacoby and Gonzales (1991) document how the director of a physics laboratory in the United States and the graduate students within the laboratory fluctuate between the role of expert and that of novice by modulating their displays of epistemic stance from certainty to uncertainty even while on the same topic in the same laboratory meeting. Even in highly prescribed, formal interactions, participants have some fluidity in the social identities they enact. In highly formal decision-making councils (*fono*) in Western Samoa, for example, all the participants have the title of orator or high chief and each of these titles is ranked with respect to another tradition. Yet in any one meeting or even at any one point in the meeting, the participants may constitutively index themselves in a different, usually lower, status through the stances they linguistically and non-linguistically display (Duranti 1981).

NOTES

* I am grateful to the following institutions for their support of this study: The National Institute of Child Health and Development (1986–1990), The National Science Foundation (1986–1990), and The Spencer Foundation (1990–1993). This essay has also benefited from the careful reading of earlier drafts by Alessandro Duranti, Patrick Gonzales, Sally Jacoby, Carolyn Taylor, and the editors of the source volume.

1. A number of social scientists have examined different dimensions of indexicality and have created distinct terms in their analyses. The reader is referred to the essays of Bühler on 'shifters' and 'pointing words' (1934), Goffman on 'keys', 'frames' (1974), and 'footing' (1981), Gumperz on 'contextualization cues' (1981, 1982, this volume), Hanks on 'deictic fields' and 'deictic zones' (1990), Rommetveit on 'co-ordinates' of the act of speech (1974), and Silverstein on presuppositional and creative indexicality (1987, 1993).

2. The transcription notation uses the following symbols.
    Square brackets denote the onset of simultaneous and/or overlapping utterances, for example:

Jimmy:	a long time ago? – bout ((*tosses head*)) ten? – ten
	years old? – a:nd – the: [(Ja)
Mother:	[(that) wasn't <u>that</u> long

    Equals signs indicate contiguous utterances, in which the second is latched onto the first; or an utterance that continues beyond an overlapping utterance:

| | Mother: | oh= |
| → | Heddi: | = they're freezing co::ld! |

    One or more colons represent an extension of the sound syllable it follows ('co::ld'); underlining indicates emphasis ('<u>freezing</u>'); capital letters indicate loudness ('BU::::RR'); audible aspirations (hhh) and inhalations (.hhh) are inserted where they occur ('Go:d hh'); pauses and details of the conversational scene or various characterizations of the talk are inserted in double parentheses (((*pause*)) ((*TV going*))); items enclosed within single parentheses indicate transcriptionist doubt ('jus::t (pull it off)').

3. In cognitive science paradigms, these valences might be seen as structuring situational schemata (cf. Johnson 1987).

4. In Samoan child language transcripts using parallel columns to represent speakers' turns, the notation '/' marks the end of an utterance and '//' marks a point of overlap across turns.

5. TA marks tense/aspect; DEICT.PRT marks deixis: EMPH. marks emphasis: NEG marks negation.

REFERENCES

Albert, E. 1972. Cultural patterning of speech behaviour in Burundi. In J. J. Gumperz and D. Hymes (eds.) *Directions in Sociolinguistics: The Ethnography of Communication.* New York: Holt, Rinehart and Winston. 72–105.

Anderson, E. S. 1977. Learning to speak with style: A study of the sociolinguistic skills of children. PhD dissertation. Palo Alto, California: Stanford University.

Austin, J. L. 1962. *How to Do Things with Words.* Oxford: Oxford University Press.

Brown, P. and S. C. Levinson. 1979. Social structure, groups, and interaction. In H. Giles and K. Scherer (eds.) *Social Markers in Speech.* Cambridge: Cambridge University Press. 291–341.

Brown, P. and S. C. Levinson. 1987. Politeness: Some universals in language usage. *Studies in Interactional Sociolinguistics* 4. Cambridge: Cambridge University Press.

Bühler, K. 1934. *Sprachtheorie: die Darstellungsfunktion der Sprache.* Jena: Gustav Fischer.

Campos, J. and C. Stenberg. 1981. Perception, appraisal, and emotion: The onset of social referencing. In M. E. Lamb and L. R. Sherrod (eds.) *Infant Social Cognition.* Hillsdale, New Jersey: Lawrence Erlbaum.

Chafe, W. and Nichols J. (eds.) 1986. *Evidentiality: The Linguistic Coding of Epistemology.* Advances in Discourse Processes. Norwood, New Jersey: Ablex.

Cicourel, A. 1989. Medical speech events as resources for getting at differences in expert–novice diagnostic reasoning. Paper prepared for the American Anthropological Association Meetings. Washington, D. C., November 1989.

Comrie, B. 1976. Linguistic politeness axes: Speaker–addressee, speaker–reference, speaker–bystander. *Pragmatics Microfiche* 1: A3–B1.

Cook, K. W. 1988. A cognitive analysis of grammatical relations, case and transitivity in Samoan. PhD. Dissertation. San Diego, California: University California.

Cruttenden, A. 1986. *Intonation.* Cambridge: Cambridge University Press.

Duranti, A. 1981. *The Samoan Fono: A Sociolinguistic Study.* Pacific Linguistics Monographs, series B, 80. Canberra: Australian National University, Department of Linguistics.

Duranti, A. 1984. The social meaning of subject pronouns in Italian conversation. *Text* 4: 277–311.

Duranti, A. 1990. Politics and grammar: Agency in Samoan political discourse. *American Ethnologist* 17: 646–666.

Fillmore, C. 1982. Towards a descriptive framework for spatial deixis. In R. Jarvella and W. Klein (eds.) *Speech, Place and Action: Studies in Dexis and other Related Topics.* New York: John Wiley and Sons. 31–59.

Fisher, S. 1991. A discourse of the social: Medical talk/power talk/oppositional talk. *Discourse and Society* 2: 157–182.

Goffman, E. 1974. *Frame Analysis. An Essay on the Organization of Experience.* New York: Harper and Row.

Goodwin, C. and A. Duranti. 1992. Rethinking context: An introduction. In A. Duranti and C. Goodwin (eds.) *Rethinking Context: Language as an Interactive Phenomenon.* Cambridge: Cambridge University Press. 1–42.

Goodwin, M. H. 1990. *He-Said-She-Said: Talk as Social Organization among Black Children.* Bloomington, Indiana: Indiana University Press.

Goodwin, M. H. and C. Goodwin. 1987. Children's arguing. In S. Philips, S. Steele and C. Tanz (eds.) *Language, Gender, and Sex in Comparative Perspective*. Cambridge: Cambridge University Press. 200–248.

Gumperz, J. J. 1981. *Language and Social Identity*. Cambridge: Cambridge University Press.

Gumperz, J. J. 1982. *Discourse Strategies*. Cambridge: Cambridge University Press.

Halliday, M. 1973. *Explorations in the Functions of Language*. London: Arnold.

Hanks, W. 1990. *Referential Practice: Language and Lived Space among the Maya*. Chicago: University of Chicago Press.

Haviland, J. B. 1989. 'Sure sure': Evidence and affect. *Text* 9: 27–68.

Jacoby, S. and P. Gonzales. 1991. The constitution of expert-novice in scientific discourse. *Issues in Applied Linguistics* 2: 149–182.

Klinnert, M., J. J. Campos, J. F. Sorce, R. N. Emde and M. Svejda. 1983. Emotions as behavior regulators: Social referencing in infancy. In R. Plutchik and M. Kellerman (eds.) *Emotion: Theory, Research, and Experience*. New York: Academic Press. 257–285.

Kuno, S. 1973. *The Structure of the Japanese Language*. Cambridge, Massachusetts: Harvard University Press.

Labov, W. 1984. Intensity. In D. Schiffrin (ed.) *Meaning, Form, and Use in Context: Linguistic Applications, GURT '84*. Washington, D. C.: Georgetown University Press. 43–70.

Levy, R. 1984. Emotion, knowing and culture. In R. Shweder and R. Levine (eds.) *Culture Theory: Essays on Mind, Self, and Emotion*. Cambridge: Cambridge University Press. 214–237.

Lyons, J. 1977. *Semantics*. 2 vols. Cambridge: Cambridge University Press.

Lyons, J. 1982. Deixis and subjectivity: Loquor, ergo sum? In R. Jarvella and W. Klein (eds.) *Speech, Place, and Action: Studies in Deixis and other Related Topics*. New York: John Wiley and Sons. 101–125.

Ochs, E. 1988. *Culture and Language Development: Language Acquisition and Language Socialization in a Samoan Village*. Cambridge: Cambridge University Press.

Ochs, E. 1989. Language has a heart. *Text* 9: 7–25.

Ochs, E. 1990. Indexicality and socialization. In J. W. Stigler, R. Shweder and G. Herdt (eds.) *Cultural Psychology: Essays on Comparative Human Development*. Cambridge: Cambridge University Press. 287–308.

Ochs, E. 1992. Indexing gender. In A. Duranti and C. Goodwin (eds.) *Rethinking Context: Language as an Interactive Phenomenon*. Cambridge: Cambridge University Press. 335–358.

Ochs, E. and B. Schieffelin. 1984. Language acquisition and socialization: Three developmental stories and their implications. In R. Shweder and R. Levine (eds.) *Culture Theory: Essays on Mind, Self, and Emotion*. Cambridge: Cambridge University Press. 276–320.

Ochs, E. and C. Taylor. 1992. Family narrative as political activity. *Discourse and Society* 3: 301–344.

Peirce, C. 1955. *Philosophical Writings of Peirce*. New York: Dover Publishers.

Peters, A. 1977. Language learning strategies. *Language* 53: 560–573.

Platt, M. 1986. Social norms and lexical acquisition: A study of deictic verbs in Samoan child language. In Schieffelin and Ochs (eds.) *Language Socialization Across Cultures*. Cambridge: Cambridge University Press. 127–151.

Rommetveit, R. 1974. *On Message Structure: A Framework for the Study of Language and Communication*. New York: John Wiley and Sons.

Sacks, H., E. A. Schegloff and G. Jefferson. 1974. A simplest systematics for the organization of turn-taking for conversation. *Language* 50: 696–735.

Schegloff, E. A. 1987. The routine as achievement. *Human Studies* 9: 111–151.

Schegloff, E. A., G. Jefferson and H. Sacks. 1977. The preference for self–correction in the organization of repair in conversation. *Language* 53: 361–382.

Schieffelin, B. 1981. Talking like birds: Sound play in a cultural perspective. In J. Ley (ed.) *The Paradoxes of Play*. New York: Leisure Press. 177–184.

Schieffelin, B. 1990. *The Give and Take of Everyday Life: Language Socialization of Kaluli Children*. Cambridge: Cambridge University Press.

Searle, J. 1969. *Speech Acts, an Essay in the Philosophy of Language*. Cambridge: Cambridge University Press.

Shatz, M. 1983. Communication. In *Handbook of child psychology (fourth edition)*, vol. III: *Cognitive Development*. New York: John Wiley and Sons. 841–890.

Shatz, M. and R. Gelman. 1973. *The Development of Communication Skills: Modifications in the Speech of Young Children as a Function of Listener*. Monographs of the Society for Research in Child Development, 38, no. 152.

Silverstein, M. 1987. The three faces of 'function': Preliminaries to a psychology of language. In M. Hickmann (ed.) *Social and Functional Approaches to Language and Thought*. New York: Academic Press. 17–38.

Silverstein, M. 1993. Metapragmatic discourse and metapragmatic function. In J. Lucy (ed.) *Reflexive Language*. New York: Cambridge University Press. 3–58.

Talmy, L. 1983. How language structures space. In H. Pick and L Acredolo (eds.) *Spatial Orientation: Theory, Research and Application*. New York: Plenum Press. 225–282.

Vygotsky, L. S. 1978. *Mind in Society: The Development of Higher Psychological Processes*, ed. and trs. M. Cole, V. John-Steiner, S. Scribner, and E. Souberman. Cambridge, Massachusetts: Harvard University Press.

West, C. and D. H. Zimmerman. 1987. Doing gender. *Gender and Society* 1: 125–151.

Whorf, B. L. 1956. *Language, Thought and Reality: Selected Writings of Benjamin Lee Whorf*, ed. J. B. Carroll. Cambridge, Massachusetts: MIT Press.

PART V
MULTILINGUALISM, CODE-SWITCHING AND DIGLOSSIA

Editors' Introduction to Part V

The Reader has already presented several chapters that deal with (a) social environments where more than one language code is culturally embedded, and (b) particular speakers who use the resources of more than one language code (see Chapters 20, 23, 28, 29). Taken together, (a) and (b) are the twin concerns in the Sociolinguistics of *bi- and multilingualism*, implying that we have to define these terms simultaneously at social (a-type) and individual (b-type) levels. Multilingualism was one of the earliest themes in Sociolinguistics, simply because it is one of the most obvious types of linguistic diversity and change, and one where issues of identity are rarely far form the surface.

Early sociolinguistic research on multilingualism was done under the sub-heading of the Sociology of Language, and we start Part V with a chapter (30) by Joshua Fishman, its earliest leading exponent. Fishman debates some of the political and moral questions surrounding *language and ethnicity* (a short-form for ethnic identity). His celebratory view of linguistic and ethnic diversity has been very influential in Sociolinguistics, and it has also become controversial in some regards. But he has without doubt helped to establish the importance of sociolinguistic ideas in key areas of social and political life. The most important of these is *language planning*, a term that refers to any systematic attempt to intervene directly in the future 'health' or *vitality* of a language. Fishman's lifelong commitment has been to the protection and revitalizing of threatened minority languages, and to *reversing language shift* (reversing the decline of minority languages). His chapter is a frank and personal, but also wide-ranging and philosophical, essay. Fishman exposes his own ideological stances, for example on the 'creative and healing' potential of ethnicity. But he also points to the 'irrational', damaging and dangerous side of ethnicity, in its propensity to surface as xenophobia and racism. The study of multilingual nations and states has revealed the dangerous myth of 'one nation, one state, one language' which became well-established in the nineteenth-century Europe and has persisted in the political and popular conception of nationhood until late-modern times. Today, such an ideology can too easily be a tool of reactionary propaganda, in the rhetoric of such right-wing groups as 'English Now' in the USA, whose aim is to 'cleanse' America linguistically by imposing English as its official language. Such legislation could lead to a ban on bilingual education and might also spark off some version of ethnic cleansing on the grounds of the alleged superiority of English over other languages spoken in America. In Fishman's terms, this form of linguistic discrimination is indeed a form of *racism*.

We suggested in the general Introduction that it is probably no longer necessary to hold on to the various original sub-divisions of Sociolinguistics, because the discipline has moved ahead and developed much more integrated approaches to, for example, monolingual variation and multilingual variation. We find very much the same social, political and interactional issues arising when we look at each 'level' of diversity, and we need very much the same explanatory theories and concepts to understand each of them. Also, we have commented critically on the assumption that 'a language' is a neatly bounded linguistic or social unit, even though there are ideological forces that sometimes conspire to keeping languages neatly separated form each other (see Jaffe's Chapter 28). To this extent it might be true that we no longer need to treat the Sociology of Language as a separate field, and we might have reservations about the most basic terms that it uses: is the sociolinguistic experience of 'multilingualism' really so different from that of 'monolingualism'?

Even so, the political sensitivities that we saw around language ideologies (in Part IV) are very much a legacy of the fusion of critical analysis and activism that Joshua Fishman has always embodied. It is common nowadays to critique the notion of *essentialism*, and in the early work in the Sociology of Language we do find assumptions being made about the inherent value of (minority) language codes in defining the essence of cultural experience. But of course, there are many circumstances and many people for whom linguistic diversity *does* define an essential sense of socio-cultural identity. Sociolinguistic research has become wary of making this assumption as a given, and it has become more aware of the local contingencies and complexities of social identification that are often involved. The constructionist perspective that we have seen coming through sociolinguistic analysis so pervasively redirects our attention onto the constitutive practices around language use. It has become less tenable to claim that single languages enshrine singular identities, and particularly so under conditions of accelerating global interdependencies (see Blommaert's and Jaworski's chapters in Parts V and VI, respectively). But Fishman reminds us that a sense of entitlement to 'one's own language', for some people remains a powerful motivating force.

Charles Ferguson's analysis of *diglossia* (Chapter 31) is a landmark contribution to the description of how language may relate to each other systemically in bilingual settings. Based mainly on his own experience in these settings, Ferguson considers four pairs of languages – paired in the sense of being linked as varieties: Classical and Egyptian Arabic, Standard and Swiss German, Standard and Haitian Creole French, and High and Low Greek. He is able to show that, despite the cultural unrelatedness of the four cases, each pair of languages is sociolinguistically organized in a very similar way. Each pair comprises what Ferguson calls H (high) and L (low) varieties. H varieties are used in social domains linked to a particular range of public communicative functions, while L varieties are used for a set of non-overlapping, more private or informal, domains and functions. Ferguson argues that diglossic situations of this sort are *stable* sociolinguistic environments, in the sense that the systemic relationships between varieties are known and adhered to and not easy to challenge (although see Dorian's Chapter 37 for a critique). Fishman later went on to point out that community-level diglossia might be based on either high levels of bilingual competence (when most speakers have command of both H and L varieties) or alternatively on how levels of bilingual competence (when most speakers speak either H or L, but not both). The implications are of course significant, in that 'diglossia without bilingualism' points to a society that is strongly divided in terms of social status.

Multilingual societies are sometimes quite volatile rather than stable, and people's language preferences are often made in relation to changing social circumstances. One of the most influential studies of dynamic shifts in language choice was Susan Gal's analysis of Oberwart in Eastern Austria (Chapter 32). Gal studied the Hungarian-speaking population of Oberwart, mainly low-status agricultural or industrial workers, at a time when Hungarian-German bilingualism had become common and when German-speaking in-migrants were rapidly swelling the size of the town. She found that using Hungarian was associated with the socio-cultural meaning of 'peasant', even though younger speakers who also spoke Hungarian thought of themselves as 'workers' (and *not* as 'peasants'). Gal's main empirical work is then devoted to analysing bilingual speakers' reported patterns of language selection – between Hungarian and German or both languages – across a range of social situations, corroborated by her own observations.

Gal's findings reveal what can be called an *implicational scale,* a pattern where a choice at one point on a scale implies a similar choice on other scales – see Gal's first Table. There are interesting parallels to be drawn between the social situations that Gal presents to her informants and those discussed by Ferguson in connection with diglossia. Bilingual women in Oberwart reported that talking 'to doctors' was most heavily associated with use of German, while talking 'to God' was most heavily associated with use of Hungarian (and this gives us a further perspective on the processes of audience design and interpersonal accommodation that we discussed in Part III of the Reader). There was also a clear pattern according to informants' age, whereby younger women were regularly more likely than older women to say they would use German across a wide range of social situations. In fact, young women were clearly motivated to refute their associations with peasant culture, and with Hungarian as a sociolinguistic index of 'peasantness'. In other parts of the study Gal goes on to consider men's responses and other factors, including informants' social networks that appear to influence their responses.

In this relatively early study we are once again back in a sociolinguistic world of fixed categories and quantitative methods, but, as in variationist research, it would not have been possible to establish generalizations about language preferences without these design characteristics. Gal's study implies that bilingual speakers have a facility to switch between the various language codes in their repertoire, and to do so in socially meaningful and socially motivated ways, under the influence of ideological values and pressures. The study of code-switching quickly became an important theme in the Sociolinguistics of multilingualism and it emphasized the point that speakers rarely keep their linguistic varieties clearly compartmentalized in actual usage. As we noted above, there is a widespread ideological assumption – part of *standard language ideology* as it is entertained by conservative purists – that it is 'best' or 'most logical' to 'keep different languages separate', but this proves *not* to be a principle that multilingual speakers adhere to.

In her chapter (33), Carol Myers-Scotton overviews some of the current debates about how to approach the sociolinguistic analysis of code-switching. This phenomenon is a regular and probably inevitable function of any speaker who is a competent user of more than one language, though the degree of competence in their command of each of the codes may vary quite significantly. And *bi-* or *multilingualism* (ability to speak two or more languages, respectively), is far more prevalent in the world than monolingualism (ability to speak only one language), assuming we tolerate these descriptions. It is worth emphasizing, then, that the phenomenon of code-switching (CS) is a 'natural' outcome of a highly commonplace sociolinguistic environment; it is not an aberration or a linguistic deficiency, as some purists may still argue. Myers-Scotton mentions some of the most eminent linguists' misconceptions of CS, and we see a continuing monolingual bias in some of the current linguistic work concerned primarily with the study of idealized, decontextualized language data. 'Switching' does not only happen between distinct language codes, however defined (see our discussion in the general Introduction of the theoretical, cultural, and political problems in defining and distinguishing 'languages' from 'dialects', for example). Monolingual conversations and speech events are frequently sites of switching (or shifting) between different varieties of the same language (dialects or registers), with significant consequences in creating social meaning (see, for example, Barrett's chapter in Part II and his discussion of African American drag queens' style-shifting performances).

Sociolinguists embraced CS as a systematic area of investigation in the early 1970s, particularly in response to Jan-Petter Blom and John Gumperz's study of code-switching in a small fishing village of Hemnesberget (see also Rampton's chapter in Part III). Since then, CS has attracted much attention from all corners of Sociolinguistics, with researchers applying their preferred frameworks and approaches to its study, focusing either on the more linguistic/structural aspects of code-switched language, or its social consequences (as far as these can be separated). Some examples of diverse methodologies in CS studies represented in the Reader are Discourse Analysis and Conversation Analysis (see Auer's Chapter 34, in this part), ethnography (see Rampton's Chapter 20, in Part III), and accommodation theory (see Cheshire's Chapter 9, in Part I, in which she uses this approach to analyse her style-shifting data). Myers-Scotton's own approach to CS is known as the *markedness model*, which deals with the socio-psychological motivations for CS and generalizations about how these motivations are interpreted. The model is based on the idea that one of the language codes in the community of speakers is interpreted as 'unmarked' (implying predictable, expected usage), while the other or others are 'marked' (implying unexpected usage). Thus, in any given interaction, a switch to an unmarked variety tends to index an expected relationship between the speaker and other participants, while a switch to a marked variety is a bid for another relationship.

Myers-Scotton compares her model mainly to the Conversation Analytic and Discourse Analysis approaches. The first of these is concerned mainly with the interpretation of CS in terms of its sequential organization within a conversation , while the second is concerned with more perfomative aspects of CS and their social meanings. Finally, Myers-Scotton discusses different approaches to the grammatical structure of CS.

Peter Auer's approach to the study of bilingualism and CS (in Chapter 34) is in the Conversation Analysis tradition. In his analysis of German/Italian CS among children and adolescents in a family of Italian origin living in Germany, Auer resists the idea of ascribing predetermined meanings to the use of either language at any particular point in conversation, on the grounds that too many possible interpretations are possible. Rather, he examines the *position* of a switch in the sequential order of conversation, and this allows him to establish the emerging context of talk. Based on the details of the *sequential embeddedness* of language choice and language alternation, he then formulates a *procedural model* of CS.

Auer proposes the following two pairs of analytic procedures for the interpretations of CS: *discourse-* versus *participant-related* CS, and *insertional* versus *alternational* CS. In the former pair, the first type of code-switching *contextualizes* ongoing interaction (see Gumperz, Chapter 40, in Part VI), or provides cues about its overall cohesion, organization, the specific type of relationship (or *footing*) that is being enacted between the social actors, or the type of activity that the participants are being engaged in. The second element signals specific attributes of the speaker, for example, his/ her competence, norms and preferences for the choice of one language over another in a particular situation. In the other contrast, *insertional* CS refers to relatively brief uses of another language in a stretch of talk, while *alternational* code-switching signals a re-negotiation of the language of interaction. This matrix for the interpretation of code-switching allows Auer to account for a diverse range of data relying on the locally (sequentially) defined context and attending to the participants' shared procedural knowledge deployed in the course of interaction.

The chapters we have reviewed so far in this part of the Reader point to one basic social aspect of bi-, multilingualism and code-switching – *language contact*, which has been recognized as one of the major forces driving language change. Of course, language contact really means contact between *speakers* of different languages or speakers who have varied linguistic repertoires. One of the most tangible and well-documented effects of language contact situations is the emergence of *pidgin and creole languages*. Jeff Siegel's Chapter (35) gives a rich account of one such language, Tok Pisin (or New Guinea Pidgin). Having originated like most other pidgins around the world as a *trade language* used between groups of people who did not share a common language, Tok Pisin started as a simplified version of English used for some limited business purposes between Europeans and Melanesians – pidgins usually take the language of the politically and economically dominant group as their source or *lexifier* (vocabulary-donating) *language*. Later, as Siegel describes, the lexicon, grammar, functions and speaker groups of the pidgin became more complex and broadened to the point that the pidgin acquired native speakers (children of parents whose only common language was the pidgin), and Tok Pisin therefore became technically a *creole* language, although the status of Tok Pisin in this regard is still under dispute. At this point it no longer is a 'simplified' version of any other language but, in structural and functional terms, a fully developed linguistic system and code.

Siegel describes in some detail the linguistic structure of Tok Pisin at every linguistic level: phonology (sounds), lexicon (vocabulary), morphology and syntax (grammar). He discusses the functional spread of Tok Pisin in the media, politics, religion and education, and captures some of the *language ideological debates* about its status (see also chapters in Part IV). This is an excellent example of how frequently negative claims made by various individuals and institutions about the status, 'correctness', or 'suitability' of some linguistic varieties for 'proper' communication in 'serious' contexts are really powerful political moves drawing boundaries between self and other. They are efforts to deny specific groups cultural status and *capital*, by implying or proclaiming that the way they speak is 'worthless'. However, as Siegel's chapter makes clear, although Tok Pisin is a site of an ongoing ideological struggle, its speakers are not just helpless victims of linguistic and political discrimination. They actively contest hegemonic ideologies privileging English as a 'superior' and 'standard' language.

The ideological struggle over Tok Pisin can be described in terms of Stephen May's Chapter (36) as an issue of *language rights*. The main impetus for work in the area of language rights comes from sociolinguists' concern with the growing disappearance of many languages of the world, or *language death* (see Dorian's Chapter 37). As Ferguson's chapter on Diglossia and Siegel's chapter on Tok Pisin have demonstrated, in multilingual societies the social status of different languages is unequal to the point that, in some communities, the dominant, often majority language may gradually replace and eradicate the dominated minority language from all of its contexts of use. As a result, language death or language shift may follow (see Gal, Chapter 32). May balances a number of arguments put forward in favor of active political and legal protection of minority languages, frequently compared to the endangered plant and animal species via a *language ecology* metaphor. He notes how relatively recent processes (dating back to the nineteenth century) of creating national ideologies and identities in Europe went hand-in-hand with the privileging of some languages as having 'national' status, while 'minoritising' others. Hence, while some languages may enjoy the status of national languages in one part of the world (for example, Spanish in Spain), they may be treated as minority languages elsewhere (for example, Spanish in the USA). Some languages, for example Kashubian in Poland, have only a 'minority' status. Another factor in the loss of status and replacement of local languages (also in a majority context) is the spread of English as a global language. For example, a very large proportion of academic publication in many countries is in English, even though English is not recognized as one of their official languages.

However, as May points out, the biological/ecological analogy in the study of language rights has also been criticized for essentializing the role of (minority) languages, treating them as static and reified, deterministically linked to (ethnic) minorities, which are treated as homogeneous and their identities as immutable. In response to this criticism, some scholars involved in language rights research adopted a more critical stance, considering language to be only one possible resource available to minorities for self-identification, and taking into account a broader social and historical context in analysing the spread of dominant national and language ideologies.

Nancy Dorian's Chapter (37), reprinted here from her classic study of language death concerning *East Sutherland Gaelic* (ESG, a Scottish Gaelic dialect), documents some of the sociolinguistic processes involved in the extinction of a language in a small fishing community in Scotland. This process can be seen as a reversal of the process described by Siegel in his discussion of the *birth* of a pidgin and its subsequent development and success in becoming a national language. What both types of situation have in common is, once again, language contact, East Sutherland witnessing a shift from near universal monolingualism in Gaelic to near universal monolingualism in English. At the time of Dorian's fieldwork, the few remaining bilingual speakers used mostly an archaic and conservative variety of Gaelic of a religious or folkloristic nature. Code-switching was prevalent, with the societal norms changing in favor of switching to English at an increasingly wide range of points in interaction (cf. Auer's participant-related switching, in Chapter 34). Gaelic was also marked by frequent use of English loanwords or 'interference'. However, as Dorian also points out, the disappearance of ESG was inevitably ideologically highly charged, with the remaining (older) speakers of ESG displaying 'pride' in speaking it and showing scorn for the Gaelic speakers who chose not to use it, interpreting their choice of English as betrayal of community solidarity and values. On the other hand, many Gaelic-speaking parents of young children would only address their children in English, assuming that English monolingualism was the best way forward in ensuring the children's upward mobility.

We end this part of the Reader with Jan Blommaert's plea for a sociolinguistic theory of *globalization* (Chapter 38). Although Blommaert's piece is not strictly focused on aspects of global multilingualism, we have included his chapter in this section because he is concerned here with Dell Hymes's notion of *ways of speaking* (see Chapter 39), which may involve different styles, genres as well as language codes, and their place and value in the sociolinguistic system, that is, how language *functions* in its social context. The social context of globalization requires sociolinguists to examine linguistic *flows* across global contexts, and for this purpose Blommaert invokes the work of Immanuel Wallerstein on *World System Analysis*. The *system* locates nations and regions in terms of three main categories: 'core', 'semi-periphery' and 'periphery'. This division is based on nations' or regions' political and economic organization, their relative position in the economic hierarchy of the world, and the asymmetrical relations of the division of labor across the spectrum. Due to the exploitative relation between the core and peripheral regions, with the former maximizing their profits at the expense of the latter, the system is founded on *neo-colonial* forms of discrimination and control. As Blommaert argues, the differences in wealth and status between these strata are responsible for the fact that '*inequality, not uniformity, organizes the flows* across the "globe"' (p. 564, his emphasis). Blommaert's text reminds us that the long-standing concern that sociolinguists have had with social inequalities around language will have to be up-dated to take into account new forms of discrimination in a 'shrinking' and ever more inter-dependent world.

CHAPTER 30

Language, Ethnicity and Racism

JOSHUA A. FISHMAN

Language and Ethnicity: Overlooked Variables in Social Theory and Social History

Many discussions of ethnicity begin with the struggle to define 'it'. While I am certainly interested in defining (or delimiting) ethnicity, I am even more interested in what the definitional struggle in this day and age reveals, namely, that the social sciences as a whole still lack an intellectual tradition in connection with this topic. Social scientists and social theorists have neither reconstructed nor developed with respect to ethnicity (nor, indeed, with respect to language and ethnicity) either a sociology of the phenomenon *per se* or a sociology of knowledge concerning it, much less a synchronic view of the link between the two, in any major part of the world of social life and social thought. Thus, here we are, in the late twentieth century, with God only knows how few or how many seconds remaining to the entire human tragicomedy on this planet, still fumbling along in the domain of ethnicity, as if it had just recently appeared and as if three millenia of pan-Mediterranean and European thought and experience in connection with it (to take only that corner of mankind with which most of us are most familiar) could be overlooked. Obviously that is not our attitude toward other societal forms and processes such as the family, urbanization, religion, technology, etc. For all of these we manifestly delight in the intellectual traditions surrounding them. I must conclude that our intellectual discomfort and superficiality with respect to ethnicity and our selective ignorance in this connection are themselves ethnicity-related phenomena, at least in part, phenomena which merit

Source: 'Language, Ethnicity and Racism', by Fishman, J. A. in Saville-Troike, M. (ed.) *Georgetown University Round Table on Languages and Linguistics (GURT) 1977: Linguistics and Anthropology* (Georgetown University Press) pp. 297–309.

consideration if we are ultimately to understand several of the dimensions of this topic that are still waiting to be revealed.

This is not the place to undertake so grand an expedition, nor have I the ability to take you everywhere that this topic (the sociology of language and ethnicity and the sociology of knowledge with respect to it) must lead us. Suffice it to say that we must try to carry both the reconstruction and the analysis of social history and social theory from classical Hebrew and Greek times through to the twentieth century, up to and including the 'rebirth of ethnicity' in many Western locales during the past decade. In the process we must attend to the Roman Empire, both in the West and in the East; to the early Church and the Church Fathers; to Islam as a Euro-Mediterranean presence, to medieval and renaissance life and thought throughout Europe; to the reformation and counter-reformation; to the commercial and industrial revolutions viewed both as social change/continuity and as stimulants to social thought and social theory; and finally, to the rise of modern intellectual schools and social movements. In this last we must particularly examine the capitalist–Marxist clash, and the Marxist–Herderian–Weberian differences in sociological and anthropological thought and in political and economic action, both in the ominous nineteenth and in the cataclysmic twentieth centuries. At this time I can only try to select a few themes here and there that may provide some clues to language and ethnicity viewed in such a perspective.

What is Ethnicity?

Since one of my objectives (in what might very well be a life-time task in and of itself) is to disclose what social theorists have said about ethnicity, including how they have defined it, my initial definitional passions can be satisfied at a general orientional level which gives me as much latitude as possible to attend to all forms and definitions of ethnicity (see Isajiw 1974, for detailed attention to the definitional issue). What I am interested in is both the sense and the expression of 'collective, intergenerational cultural continuity', i.e. the sensing and expressing of links to 'one's own kind (one's own people)', to collectivities that not only purportedly have historical depth but, more crucially, share putative ancestral origins and, therefore, the gifts and responsibilities, rights and obligations deriving therefrom. Thus, what I am interested in may or may not be identical with all of society and culture, depending on the extent to which ethnicity does pervade and dictate all social sensings, doings and knowings, or alternatively (and as is increasingly the case as society modernizes) only some of these,[1] particularly those that relate to the questions: Who are we? From where do we come? What is special about us? I assume (together with Le Page and Tabouret-Keller 1982) that these questions can be answered differently at different times by the same respondents (and, all the more so, by different respondents). It is in this context that I also want to monitor whatever link there may be to language as an aspect of presumed ethnic authenticity.

The Theme of Fundamental 'Essence'

Both ancient Israel and ancient Greece conceived of the world as made up of a finite number of ethnicities with characteristic and fundamental biological 'essences' and, therefore, histories or missions of their own. This theme, with its undercurrent of bodily continuity and triumph over death, has its counterpart in modern Herderian and nationalist thought and has been continually present in the pan-Mediterranean and European world, as well as in much of the African, Asian, and Native American worlds. This essence is transcendental and ultimately of superhuman origin, and language is naturally a co-occurring part of the essential blood, bones, or tears. Thus, the view that the deity (or deities) necessarily speak(s) to each ethnicity in its own language and could not conceivably do otherwise, is also a recurring view (albeit one that is not always accepted and, therefore, one that is also contradicted). It is a view related to a cosmology in which language-and-ethnicity collectivities are seen as the basic building blocks of all human society. In more modern thought, the superhuman origin of this co-occurrence and its dependence on biological essences are questioned. However, many theoreticians and philosophers still hold that ethnicity and ethnogenesis (i.e. the coming into being of ethnicities and of language-and-ethnicity linkages) is a natural and necessary fact of human social life (for a Soviet view along these very lines, see Bromley 1974). Eastern European and Eastern Mediterranean thought is particularly noteworthy along these latter lines (Jakobson 1945) and it is here in the Euro-Mediterranean complex that we find today most generally and insistently the view that language authenticity is a natural and necessary part of a mystically inescapable physical/cultural collective continuity.

The Theme of Metamorphosis

Seemingly at odds with the above view, but at times syncretistically subscribed to in addition to it, is the view that ethnicities can be transcended and that new or 'higher' levels of ethnic integration can be arrived at, including the level of terminal de-ethnicization, i.e. of no ethnicity at all. The argument between those who view ethnicity as fixed and god-given and those who view it as endlessly mutable begins with Plato and Aristotle, the former proposing that a group of de-ethnicized Guardians of the City be created so that uncorrupted and uncorruptable, altruistic and evenhanded management of the polity could be attained. There would be no husband– wife relationships among them since all women would belong to all men and vice versa. Similarly their offspring would have no fathers and no mothers since all male adults would be fathers to all children, all female adults would be their mothers, all children would belong equally to all adults and vice versa. Only a group such as this – a group whose members had no differentiating intergenerational biological continuities – could devote itself to the public weal, since, having neither property nor family, it could view the general need without bias, without favoritism, without greed, without conflict of interest, all of which Plato considered necessary accompaniments of ethnicity. Aristotle hotly contested this view and stressed that, whatever the dangers of ethnicity might be, those who do not initially love and feel uniquely bound to specific 'others' could not then love mankind nor have the benefit of generalized 'others' firmly in mind. A child who belongs equally to one and all belongs to no one. The challenge of ethnicity, as Aristotle saw it, was one of augmenting familial love, expanding the natural links to one's own 'kind', so that these links also include others who are more distantly related, rather than doing away with the initial links and bonds as such.

This theme too is developed consistently – the expansion and transmutation of language and ethnicity to a higher, more inclusive level of both being repeatedly expressed by early Christian thought, e.g. St. Augustine, Roman thought, medieval thought (including much of moral philosophy) and by capitalist statism. Going even further, de-ethnicization and linguistic fusion are expressed as ultimate, millenial goals by some modern Christian social theorists, by classical Marxists as well as classical capitalists, and as inevitable if regrettable outcomes of modern industrial society by Weber and the entire 'grand tradition' of modern social theory from Saint-Simon to Parsons.

Ethnicity as Disruptive, Irrational, and Peripheral

The darker side of ethnicity is commented on by almost all ancient and medieval thinkers, but usually as only one side of the coin, i.e. as only half of the entire phenomenon which has both positive and negative features. However, the more completely negative view begins with Plato, as already mentioned, in relation to matters of state. In this connection it receives its quintessential formulation by Lord Acton, John Stuart Mill, and other establishment-oriented defenders of Western capitalist democracy. For them, state-forming ethnicity was nothing but the democracy. For them, state-forming ethnicity was nothing but the disrupter of civility, a base passion, a nightmare, a wild evil that still lurked in the backward parts of Europe but that had, thank God, already been tamed and superseded in Great Britain, France, Spain, Holland, and in the other early and enlightened beneficiaries of political consolidation and econo-technical growth.

This view coincided with a developmental theory defining 'legitimate' language-and-ethnicity, namely, that the link between them and the currency that they both enjoyed *in the West* were by-products of political and economic stability. That is, they were the legitimate creations of centuries of continuous governmental, commercial, military, and religious stability. This view, that the benign, wise and stable state creates its corresponding and legitimate nationality, was long the dominant view in the West. The thought that the nationality might undertake to create a state for itself was anathema, viewed as unnatural, unjust, unwise, and simply a wild and wanton disruption of peace and civility. The thought of a Breton or Romanian ethnicity was as roundly abhorred by 'proper' society *then* as the thought of a Quebecois ethnicity is in some circles *today*. Indeed, the evil, instinctual penchant of 'illegitimate' language-and-ethnicity movements to undertake disruptive state-formation was thought to be the basic negative dynamic of minority ethnicity, and so it is for some to this very day. Thus, the confusion of ethnicity with politically troublesome collectivities, with rambunctious minorities, with 'difficult' peripheral and vestigial populations, began long ago.

However, classical Marxism was not very different from capitalist establishment statism in this respect. Mill had held that the language and ethnicity movements, particularly in their nationality-into-state phase, were despicable 'irrationalities' that had to be contained at all costs, evils to be compromised with only grudgingly if the established political order was to be maintained (note, for example, the compromise escape clause of 'once defeated but historical nations' as an interstitial category between Mill's and Acton's two major categories: 'goodies': 'peoples with histories', and 'baddies': 'peoples without histories'). Initially, Marx and Engels were equally vituperative with respect to nation-into-state language and ethnicity movements (and, ultimately, made equally grudging and opportunistic exceptions in connection with them), due to their obviously disruptive impact on the class struggle and on proletarian unity. However, if language-and-ethnicity movements for Mill were merely vile passions, they were for Marx and many of his followers also vile figments, lies, and chimeras, objectively no more than mere by-products of more basic economic causes, phantoms manipulated by leading capitalist circles in order to fragment and weaken the international proletariat.

Needless to say, both Mill and Marx have their followers today, who ascribe to language and ethnicity linkages all manner of evil and evil alone, including genocide. Furthermore, this purportedly objectivist view is still very much alive among these social scientists who deny any subjective validity or functional need for ethnicity, and who see it only as an essentially manipulated (and therefore, basically inauthentic), manufactured byproduct of élitist efforts to gain mass support for political and economic goals (Gellner 1964). They basically sympathize with Engels's lament of more than a century ago (1866):

> There is no country in Europe where there are not different nationalities under the same government. The Highland Gaels and the Welsh are undoubtedly of different nationalities to what the English are, although nobody will give to these remnants of people long gone by the title of nations, any more than to the Celtic inhabitants of Brittany in France... The European importance, the vitality of a people, is as nothing in the eyes of the principle of nationalities; before it the Roumans [sic] of Wallachia, who never had a history, nor the energy required to have one, are of equal importance to the Italians who have a history of 2,000 years, and an unimpaired national vitality: the Welsh and Manxmen, if they desired it, would have an equal right to independent political existence, absurd though it be, with the English! The whole thing is absurdity. The principle of nationalities, indeed, could be invented in Eastern Europe alone, where the tide of Asiatic invasion, for a thousand years, recurred again and again, and left on the shore those heaps of intermingled ruins of nations which even now the ethnologist can scarcely disentangle, and where the Turk, the Finnic Magyar, the Rouman, the Jew and about a dozen slavonic tribes live intermixed in interminable confusion.

To this very day ethnicity strikes many Westerners as being peculiarly related to 'all those crazy little people and languages out there', to the unwashed (and unwanted) of the world, to phenomena that are really not fully civilized and that are more trouble than they are worth.

Ethnicity as Creative and Healing

Autochthonous ethnicity theories commonly refer to the responsibilities incumbent upon the carriers of the intergenerational essence, i.e. to the duties that those of 'one's own kind' have, duties to be and to do in particular authentic ways; and of course, these theories also refer to the individual and collective rewards of such faithfulness. However, various more generalized ethnicity theories have taken this kind of thinking a step higher. Classical Hebrew thought contains a recurring emphasis on the perfectability of ethnicity, i.e. an emphasis on its highest realization via sanctification. It was not only Jewish ethnicity which could be so elevated and attuned with the Creator's designs and expectations (Fishman, Mayerfeld and Fishman 1985), although Hebrew thought is, understandably, repeatedly more concerned with the theoretical perfectability of Hebrew ethnicity (just as it is with the actual shortcomings of Hebrew ethnicity). Hebrew thought is an early source for the recurring message that sanctified ethnicity is ennobling, strengthening, healing, satisfying. Its thought proclaims the message of the joy, the wholeness, the holiness of embodying and expressing language-and-ethnicity in accord with the commandments of the Master of the Universe: 'for they are our life and the length of our days'. Whosoever lives in the midst of his own kind, speaking his own language and enacting his own most divinely regulated traditions in accord with these imperatives, has all that one could hope for out of life (also see Fishman 1978).

The joys of one's own language and ethnicity are subsequently expressed over and over again, from every corner of Europe and in every period. In modern times this feeling has been raised to a general principle, a general esthetic, a celebration of ethnic and linguistic diversity *per se,* as part of the very multisplendored glory of God, a value, beauty, and source of creative inspiration and inspiring creativity – indeed, as the basic human good. It is claimed that it is ethnic and linguistic diversity that makes life worth living. It is creativity and beauty based upon ethnic and linguistic diversity that make man human. Absence of this diversity would lead to the dehumanization, mechanization, and utter impoverishment of man. The weakening of this diversity is a cause for alarm, a tendency to be resisted and combated. In Herder and in Mazzini, in the Slavophiles and in Kallen – indeed, in much of modern Anthropology – the theme of ethnic diversity and the sheer beauty of cultural pluralism provide an unending rhapsody. This view both tantalizingly merges with and also separates from general democratic principles, with the rights of man, and the inalienable privilege to be one's self, *not only to be free but to be free to be bound together with 'one's own kind'* (Talmon 1965). On the one hand, democracy also subsumes an alternative right, namely, to be free from ethnicity, i.e. the right and opportunity to be a citizen of the world rather than a member of one or another traditioned ethnic collectively. On the other hand, democracy guarantees the right to retain one's own ethnicity, to safeguard collective ethnic continuity, to enable one's children to join the ranks of 'one's own kind', to develop creatively, and to reach their full potential without becoming ethnically inauthentic, colorless, lifeless, worse than lifeless: nothingness.

Dimensions of Language-and-Ethnicity

The foregoing themes provide us with many insights into language and ethnicity, and into how language and ethnicity have been viewed in a particularly influential part of the world as well. The themes themselves are not independent of each other. Many of them relate to a putative ethnic essence that is intergenerationally continuous among 'one's own kind' and is absorbed via the mother's milk. Thus, there is commonly a 'being' component to ethnicity, a bodily mystery, a triumph over death in the past as well as a promise of immortality in the future, as the putative essence is handed on generation after generation. There are a few escape hatches in, and a few escape hatches out, and a terrifying state of liminality in between, but the physical continuity of a *corpus mysticum* continues. And language is part of that corpus. It issues authentically from the body, it is produced by the body, it has body itself (and, therefore, does not permit much basic modification).

Just as commonly, language is part of the authentic 'doing' constellation and the authentic 'knowing' constellation that are recurringly assumed to be dimensions of ethnicity. Ethic doing and knowing are more mutable and, therefore, in danger of inauthenticity. Ethnic doing is a responsibility that can be shirked. Ethnic knowing is a gift that can be withheld. The basic desideratum, ethnic being, is necessary but not sufficient. There is everything to be gained and everything to be lost, and language is recurringly part and parcel of this web (Fishman 1977). In premobilization ethnicity it is naturally, unconsciously so (Fishman 1965), whereas in mobilized ethnicity it is a rallying call, both metaphorically and explicitly (Fishman 1972).

Autochthonous theories gravitate toward the metaphorical and metaphysical views of the language and ethnicity link. External objectivists reduce the mystery to the needs of the military and the economy, with the school system merely exploiting language and ethnicity in preparing recruits for both. Autochthonists see language and ethnicity as initial essences, or causes. External objectivists see them as manipulable by-products. However, both agree that they are generally there together. Hovering over them both is the problem of how to interpret the 'we–they' differences that are, unconsciously or consciously, part of the experience of ethnicity, which brings me to racism.

Ethnicity and Racism

Racism is one of many words that have been so broadened in modern, popular usage as to have lost their utility. Democracy and socialism are two other such terms, but whereas the latter have become all-purpose terms of approbation (viz., people's democracy, guided democracy, National Socialism, etc.), the former has become an all-purpose put-down. I would like to rescue *racism* from that dubious distinction, to limit its semantic range, in order more clearly to distinguish between ethnicity and racism as social phenomena and as social theories, and thereby, to focus pejorative usage more tellingly.

Relative to ethnicity, racism is not only more focused on the 'being' component (therefore having even fewer escape hatches from it than does ethnicity), but it also involves an evaluative ranking with respect to the discontinuity between ethnic collectivities. Ethnicity is an enactment (often unconscious) and a celebration of authenticity. Racism inevitably involves more heightened consciousness than does ethnicity, not only because it is an 'ism', but because its focus is not merely on authenticity and the celebration of difference or collective individuality, but on the evaluation of difference in terms of inherent better or worse, higher or lower, entirely acceptable and utterly objectionable. Ethnicity is less grandiose than racism. It has no built-in power dimension while racism, being essentially hierarchical, must have the concept of dominance in its cosmology and requires the constructs of superior races, dominant stocks, master peoples. By their words and deeds, ethnicity and racism are importantly different.

Herder, though anti-French to the hilt (like many German intellectuals struggling against French cultural hegemony within the disunited German princedoms at the beginning of the nineteenth century), is rarely, if ever, racist. He proclaims:

> No individual, no country, no people, no history of a people, no state is like any other. Therefore, the true, the beautiful and the good are not the same for them. Everything is suffocated if one's own way is not sought and if another nation is blindly taken as a model. (Herder, *Sammtliche Werke*, v. 4: 472).

Is not this still a dominant ethic and motivating dynamic in cultural anthropology to this very day? Herderian views must be understood as a plea and a rhapsody for an ethnically pluralistic world in which each ethnicity can tend its own vineyard as a right, a trust, and a point of departure for new beauty and creativity yet undreamed of. Such pluralism is, however, strange to racism, since the dynamics of racism represents a call and rationale for domination rather than for coexistence. While ethnicity can proclaim live and let live, racism can proclaim only bondage or death to the inferior.

Of course, every ethnicity runs the risk of developing an ethnocentrism, i.e. the view that one's own way of life is superior to all others. It may even be true that some degree of ethnocentrism is to be found in all societies and cultures, including the culture of secular science itself, to the degree that they are all-encompassing in defining experience and perspective. The antidote to ethnocentrism (including acquired anti-ethnic ethnocentrism, which may be just as supercilious and uncritically biased as is ethnic conditioning) is thus comparative cross-ethnic knowledge and experience, transcending the limits of one's own usual exposure to life and values (a theme which has long appeared in the literature on ethnicity). Characteristic of postmodern ethnicity is the stance of simultaneously transcending ethnicity as a complete, self-contained system, but of retaining it as a selectively preferred, evolving, participatory system. This leads to a kind of self-correction from within and from without, which extreme nationalism and racism do not permit.

The modern heroes of racism are Gobineau in France (see, for example, Biddess 1966, 1970a, b), Houston Stewart Chamberlain (1899) in England, and a chorus of German philosophers, scientists, and politicians (see, for example, Barzun 1937; Gasman 1971; Mosse 1966; Weinreich 1946). From their works it becomes clear that the language link to racism is an invidious as racism *per se*. Hermann Gauch, a Nazi 'scientist', was able to claim:

> The Nordic race alone can emit sounds of untroubled clearness, whereas among non-Nordics the pronunciation is...like noises made by animals, such as barking, sniffing, snoring, squeaking...That birds can learn to talk better than other animals is explained by the fact that their mouths are Nordic in structure. (quoted in Mosse 1966: 225)

Here we have the ultimate route of racist thought: the demotion of the 'others' to a subhuman level. They are animals, vermin, and are to be subjected to whatever final solution is most effect and efficient.

Concluding Sentiments

These remarks must not be taken simply as a defense of ethnicity. Ethnicity has been recognized since ancient times as capable of excess, corruption, and irrationality, this capacity being one of the basic themes accompanying its preregrination across the centuries. The very term *ethnicity,* derived from the Greek *ethnos* (used consistently in the Septuagint to render the Hebrew *goy,* the more negative term for nationality, as distinct from *am,* the more positive term), has a decided negative connotation in earliest English usage (see OED: *ethnic* 1470, *ethnist* 1550 and 1563, *ethnicize* 1663, *ethnicity* 1772, *ethnize* 1847). These connotations – heathenness, superstition, bizarreness – have not fully vanished even from modern popular usage, e.g. ethnic dress, ethnic hair-dos, ethnic soul. Thus, we need not fear that the excesses of ethnicity will be overlooked.

Racism itself is one of the excesses into which ethnicity can develop, although racism has often developed on pan-ethnic and perhaps even on nonethnic foundations as well.[2] However, the distinction between ethnicity and racism is well worth maintaining, particularly for those in the language-related disciplines and professions. It clarifies our goals, our problems, and our challenges as we engage in bilingual education, in language planning, in language maintenance efforts, and in a host of sociolinguistic and anthropological enterprises. The distinctions between religion and bigotry, sexuality and sexism, socialism and communism, democracy and anarchy, are all worth maintaining. No less worthwhile is the distinction between ethnicity and racism. Unfortunately, we know more about racism that about ethnicity, and more about the conflictual aspects of ethnicity than about its integrative functions. This is a pity, particularly for American intellectuals, since we too (regardless of our pretense to the contrary) live in a world in which the ethnic factor in art, music, literature, fashions, diets, childrearing, education and politics is still strong, and needs to be understood and even appreciated. Not to know more about ethnicity, about the ethnic repertoires of modern life, the endless mutability of ethnicity since the days of ancient Israel, the variety of prior thought concerning ethnicity (e.g. the various and changing views as to its power or centrality as a factor in societal functioning and social behavior) is also to limit our understanding of society and of the role of language in society. Language and ethnicity have been viewed as naturally linked in almost every age of premodern pan-Mediterranean and European thought. When ethnicity disappeared from modern social theory in the nineteenth century, language, too, disappeared therefrom. We may now be at the point of reappearance of both in modern social theory and we must prepare ourselves, accordingly, to benefit from and to contribute to the sensitivities and perspectives that a knowledge of language and ethnicity can provide, without overdoing them. Only in this way can the 'ethnic revival' in the United States be fully understood.

NOTES

1. For an account of racism's more complete domination of modern culture, see Banton's paper in Zubaida (1970). For a preliminary differentiation between ethnicity and racism, see the penultimate section of this chapter.
2. The terminology of ethnicity often included the word *race* (e.g. *raza*) in the sense of ethnicity as employed in this chapter. This is but one of the semantic alternatives that a sociology and a sociology of knowledge pertaining to ethnicity must be aware of and must hurry to illuminate.

REFERENCES

Barzun, J. 1937. *Race: A Study in Superstition*. New York: Harper.
Biddess, M. D. 1966. Gobineau and the origin of European racism. *Race: Journal of the Institute of Race Relations* 7: 225–270.
Biddess, M. D. (ed.). 1970a. *Gobineau: Selected Political Writings*. London: Cape.
Biddess, M. D. 1970b. *Father of Racist Ideology: The Social and Political Thought of Count Gobineau*. London: Weidenfeld and Nicolson.
Bromley, Yu V. 1974. Soviet Ethnology and Anthropology. *Studies in Anthropology I*. The Hague: Mouton.

Chamberlain, H. S. 1899. *The Foundations of the Nineteenth Century*. New York: Fertig.

Engels, F. 1866. What have the working class to do with Poland? *Commonwealth* 24, 31 March and 5 May.

Fishman, D. E., R. Mayerfield and J. A. Fishman. 1985. *Am* and *Goy* as designations for ethnicity in selected books of the Old Testament. In J. A. Fishman, et al. *The Rise and Fall of the Ethnic Revival*. Berlin: Mouton de Gruyter. 15–38.

Fishman, J. A. 1965. Varieties of ethnicity and varieties of language consciousness. *Georgetown University Roundtable on Languages and Linguistics, 1965*, Kreidler, C. W. (ed.) 69–79.

Fishman, J. A. 1972. *Language and Nationalism*. Rowley: Newbury House.

Fishman, J. A. 1977. Language and Ethnicity. In H. Giles (ed.) *Language and Ethnicity in Intergroup Relations*. New York: Academic Press. 15–57.

Fishman, J. A. 1978. Positive bilingualism: Some overlooked rationales and forefathers. *Georgetown University Roundtable on Languages and Linguistics, 1978*, Atlantis, J. E. (ed.) 42–52.

Gasman, D. 1971. The scientific origins of national socialism. *Social Darwinism in Ernest Haeckel and the German Monist League*. London: Macdonald.

Gellner, E. 1964. *Thought and Change*. Chicago, Illinois: University of Chicago Press.

Herder, J. G. *Sammtliche Werke*. 33 vols. Suphan, B., Redlich, E. et al. (eds.) Berlin. 1877–1913.

Isajiw, W. W. 1974. Definitions of ethnicity. *Ethnicity* 1: 111–124.

Jakobson, R. 1945. The beginnings of national self-determination in Europe. *Review of Politics* (1968) 2: 29–42. Reprinted in Fishman, J. A. (ed.) *Readings in the Sociology of Language*. The Hague: Mouton.

Le Page, R. B. and A. Tabouret-Keller. 1982. Models and stereotypes of ethnicity and language. *Journal of Multilingual and Multicultural Development* 3: 161–192.

Mosse, G. L. 1966. *Nazi Culture: Intellectual, Cultural and Social Life in the Third Reich*. London: W. H. Allen.

Talmon, J. L. 1965. *The Unique and the Universal*. London: Secker and Warburg.

Weinreich, M. 1946. *Hitler's Professors: The Part of Scholarship in Germany's Crimes against the Jewish People*. New York: Yiddish Scientific Institute-YIVO.

Zubaida, S. (ed.) 1970. *Race and Racism*. London: Tavistock.

CHAPTER 31

Diglossia

CHARLES A. FERGUSON

In many speech communities two or more varieties of the same language
are used by some speakers under different conditions. Perhaps the most
familiar example is the standard language and regional dialect as used, say,
in Italian or Persian, where many speakers speak their local dialect at home
or among family or friends of the same dialect area but use the standard
language in communicating with speakers of other dialects or on public
occasions. There are, however, other, quite different examples of the use
of two varieties of a language in the same speech community. In Baghdad
the Christian Arabs speak a 'Christian Arabic' dialect when talking among
themselves but speak the general Baghdad dialect, 'Muslim Arabic', when
talking in a mixed group. In recent years there has been a renewed interest in studying the development and characteristics of standardized languages, and it is in following this line of interest that the present study
seeks to examine carefully one particular kind of standardization where
two varieties of a language exist side by side throughout the community,
with each having a definite role to play. The term 'diglossia' is introduced
here, modeled on the French *diglossie*, which has been applied to this situation, since there seems to be no word in regular use for this in English;
other languages of Europe generally use the word for 'bilingualism' in this
special sense as well.

It is likely that this particular situation in speech communities is very widespread, although it is rarely mentioned, let alone satisfactorily described. A full
explanation of it can be of considerable help in dealing with problems in linguistic description, in historical linguistics, and in language typology. The present
study should be regarded as preliminary in that much more assembling of
descriptive and historical data is required; its purpose is to characterize diglossia
by picking out four speech communities and their languages (hereafter called
the defining languages) which clearly belong in this category, and describing

Source: 'Diglossia', by Ferguson, C. A, in Diver, W., Martinet, A. and Weinreich, U
(eds.) *Word: Journal of the Linguistic Circle of New York* (15) (1959) (New York: The
Linguistic Circle of New York).

features shared by them which seem relevant to the classification. The defining languages selected are Arabic, Modern Greek, Swiss German, Haitian Creole.

Before proceeding to the description it must be pointed out that diglossia is not assumed to be a stage which occurs always and only at a certain point in some kind of evolution, e.g. in the standardization process. Diglossia may develop from various origins and eventuate in different language situations. Of the four defining languages, Arabic diglossia seems to reach as far back as our knowledge of Arabic goes, and the superposed 'Classical' language has remained relatively stable, while Greek diglossia has roots going back many centuries, but it became fully developed only at the beginning of the nineteenth century with the renaissance of Greek literature and the creation of a literary language based in large part on previous forms of literary Greek. Swiss German diglossia developed as a result of long religious and political isolation from the centers of German linguistic standardization, while Haitian Creole arose from a creolization of a pidgin French, with standard French later coming to play the role of the superposed variety. Some speculation on the possibilities of development will, however, be given at the end of the paper.

For convenience of reference the superposed variety in diglossia will be called the H ('high') variety or simply H, and the regional dialects will be called L ('low') varieties or, collectively, simply L. All the defining languages have names for H and L, and these are listed in the accompanying table.

		H is called	L is called
Arabic	Classical (= H)	*'al-fuṣḥā*	*'al-ᶜāmmiyyah, 'ad-dārij*
	Egyptian (= L)	*ᶜil-faṣiḥ, 'in-naḥawi*	*'il-ᶜammiyya*
Swiss German	Standard German (= H) Swiss (= L)	*Schriftsprache [Schweizer] Dialekt, Schweizerdeutsch*	*Hoochtüütsch Schwyzertüütsch*
Haitian Creole	French (=H)	*français*	*créole haitien*
Greek	H and L	*katharévusa*	*dhimotiki*

1. Function One of the most important features of diglossia is the specialization of function for H and L. In one set of situations only H is appropriate and in another only L, with the two sets overlapping only very slightly. As an illustration, a sample listing of possible situations is given, with indication of the variety normally used:

	H	L
Sermon in church or mosque	x	
Instructions to servants, waiters, workmen, clerks		x

Personal letter	x	
Speech in parliament, political speech	x	
University lecture	x	
Conversation with family, friends, colleagues		x
News broadcast	x	
Radio 'soap opera'		x
Newspaper editorial, news story, caption on picture	x	
Caption on political cartoon		x
Poetry	x	
Folk literature		x

The importance of using the right variety in the right situation can hardly be overestimated. An outsider who learns to speak fluent, accurate L and then uses it in a formal speech is an object of ridicule. A member of the speech community who uses H in a purely conversational situation or in an informal activity like shopping is equally an object of ridicule. In all the defining languages it is typical behavior to have someone read aloud from a newspaper written in H and then proceed to discuss the contents in L. In all the defining languages it is typical behavior to listen to a formal speech in H and then discuss it, often with the speaker himself, in L.[1]

The last two situations on the list call for comment. In all the defining languages some poetry is composed in L, and a small handful of poets compose in both, but the status of the two kinds of poetry is very different, and for the speech community as a whole it is only the poetry in H that is felt to be 'real' poetry.[2] On the other hand, in every one of the defining languages certain proverbs, politeness formulas, and the like are in H even when cited in ordinary conversation by illiterates. It has been estimated that as much as one-fifth of the proverbs in the active repertory of Arab villagers are in H.

2. Prestige In all the defining languages the speakers regard H as superior to L in a number of respects. Sometimes the feeling is so strong that H alone is regarded as real and L is reported 'not to exist'. Speakers of Arabic, for example, may say (in L) that so-and-so doesn't know Arabic. This normally means he doesn't know H, although he may be a fluent, effective speaker of L. If a non-speaker of Arabic asks an educated Arab for help in learning to speak Arabic the Arab will normally try to teach him H forms, insisting that these are the only ones to use. Very often, educated Arabs will maintain that they never use L at all, in spite of the fact that direct observation shows that they use it constantly in all ordinary conversation. Similarly, educated speakers of Haitian Creole frequently deny its existence, insisting that they always speak French. This attitude cannot be called a deliberate attempt to deceive the questioner, but seems almost a self-deception. When the speaker in question is replying in good faith, it is often possible to break through these attitudes by asking such questions as what kind of language he uses in speaking to his children, to servants, or to his mother. The very revealing reply is usually something like: 'Oh, but they wouldn't understand [the H form, whatever it is called].'

Even where the feeling of the reality and superiority of H is not so strong, there is usually a belief that H is somehow more beautiful, more logical, better able to express important thoughts, and the like. And this belief is held also by speakers whose command of H is quite limited. To those Americans who would like to evaluate speech in terms of effectiveness of communication it comes as a shock to discover that many speakers of a language involved in diglossia characteristically prefer to hear a political speech or an expository lecture or a recitation of poetry in H even though it may be less intelligible to them than it would be in L.

In some cases the superiority of H is connected with religion. In Greek the language of the New Testament is felt to be essentially the same as the *katharévusa,* and the appearance of a translation of the New Testament in *dhimotiki* was the occasion for serious rioting in Greece in 1903. Speakers of Haitian Creole are generally accustomed to a French version of the Bible, and even when the Church uses Creole for catechisms, and the like, it resorts to a highly Gallicized spelling. For Arabic, H is the language of the Qur'an and as such is widely believed to constitute the actual words of God and even to be outside the limits of space and time, i.e. to have existed 'before' time began with the creation of the world.

3. Literary heritage In every one of the defining languages there is a sizable body of written literature in H which is held in high esteem by the speech community, and contemporary literary production in H by members of the community is felt to be part of this otherwise existing literature.

The body of literature may either have been produced long ago in the past history of the community or be in continuous production in another speech community in which H serves as the standard variety of the language. When the body of literature represents a long time span (as in Arabic or Greek) contemporary writers – and readers – tend to regard it as a legitimate practice to utilize words, phrases, or constructions which may have been current only at one period of the literary history and are not in widespread use at the present time. Thus it may be good journalistic usage in writing editorials, or good literary taste in composing poetry, to employ a complicated Classical Greek participial construction or a rare twelfth-century Arabic expression which it can be assumed the average educated reader will not understand without research on his part. One effect of such usage is appreciation on the part of some readers: 'So-and-so really knows his Greek [or Arabic]', or 'So-and-so's editorial today, or latest poem, is very good Greek [or Arabic]'.

4. Acquisition Among speakers of the four defining languages adults invariably use L in speaking to children and children use L in speaking to one another. As a result, L is invariably learned by children in what may be regarded as the 'normal' way of learning one's mother tongue. H may be heard by children from time to time, but the actual learning of H is chiefly accomplished by the means of formal education, whether this be traditional Qur'anic schools, modern government schools, or private tutors.

This difference in method of acquisition is very important. The speaker is at home in L to a degree he almost never achieves in H. The grammatical structure of L is learned without explicit discussion of grammatical concepts; the grammar of H is learned in terms of 'rules' and norms to be imitated.

It seems unlikely that any change toward full utilization of H could take place without a radical change in this pattern of acquisition. For example, those Arabs who ardently desire to have L replaced by H for all functions can hardly expect this to happen if they are unwilling to speak H to their children

5. Standardization In all the defining languages there is a strong tradition of grammatical study of the H form of the language. There are grammars, dictionaries, treatises on pronunciation, style, and so on. There is an established norm for pronunciation, grammar, and vocabulary which allows variation only within certain limits. The orthography is well established and has little variation. By contrast, descriptive and normative studies of the L form are either non-existent or relatively recent and slight in quantity. Often they have been carried out first or chiefly by scholars *outside* the speech community and are written in other languages. There is no settled orthography and there is wide variation in pronunciation, grammar, and vocabulary.

In the case of relatively small speech communities with a single important center of communication (e.g. Greece, Haiti) a kind of standard L may arise which speakers of other dialects imitate and which tends to spread like any standard variety except that it remains limited to the functions for which L is appropriate.

In speech communities which have no single most important center of communication a number of regional L's may arise. In the Arabic speech community, for example, there is no standard L corresponding to educated Athenian *dhimotiki*, but regional standards exist in various areas. The Arabic of Cairo, for example, serves as a standard L for Egypt, and educated individuals from Upper Egypt must learn not only H but also, for conversational purposes, an approximation to Cairo L. In the Swiss German speech community there is no single standard, and even the term 'regional standard' seems inappropriate, but in several cases the L of a city or town has a strong effect on the surrounding rural L.

6. *Stability* It might be supposed that diglossia is highly unstable, tending to change into a more stable language situation. This is not so. Diglossia typically persists at least several centuries, and evidence in some cases seems to show that it can last well over a thousand years. The communicative tensions which arise in the diglossia situation may be resolved by the use of relatively uncodified, unstable, intermediate forms of the language (Greek *mikti*, Arabic *al-luǧah al-wusṭā*, Haitian *créole de salon*) and repeated borrowing of vocabulary items from H to L.

In Arabic, for example, a kind of spoken Arabic much used in certain semi-formal or cross-dialectal situations has a highly classical vocabulary with few or no inflectional endings, with certain features of classical syntax, but with a fundamentally colloquial base in morphology and syntax, and a generous admixture of colloquial vocabulary. In Greek a kind of mixed language has become appropriate for a large part of the press.

The borrowing of lexical items from H to L is clearly analogous (or for the periods when actual diglossia was in effect in these languages, identical) with the learned borrowings from Latin to Romance languages or the Sanskrit *tatsamas* in Middle and New Indo-Aryan.

7. *Grammar* One of the most striking differences between H and L in the defining languages is in the grammatical structure: H has grammatical categories not present in L and has an inflectional system of nouns and verbs which is much reduced or totally absent in L. For example, Classical Arabic has three cases in the noun, marked by endings; colloquial dialects have none. Standard German has four cases in the noun and two non-periphrastic indicative tenses in the verb; Swiss German has three cases in the noun and only one simple indicative tense. *Katharévusa* has four cases, *dhimotiki* three. French has gender and number in the noun, Creole has neither. Also, in every one of the defining languages there seem to be several striking differences of word order as well as a thorough-going set of differences in the use of introductory and connective particles. It is certainly safe to say that in diglossia *there are always extensive differences between the grammatical structures of H and L*. This is true not only for the four defining languages, but also for every other case of diglossia examined by the author.

8. *Lexicon* Generally speaking, the bulk of the vocabulary of H and L is shared, of course with variations in form and with differences of use and meaning. It is hardly surprising, however, that H should include in its total lexicon technical terms and learned expressions which have no regular L equivalents, since the subjects involved are rarely if ever discussed in pure L. Also, it is not surprising that the L varieties should include in their total lexicons popular expressions and the names of very homely objects or objects

of very localized distribution which have no regular H equivalents, since the subjects involved are rarely if ever discussed in pure H. But *a striking feature of diglossia is the existence of many paired items, one H one L, referring to fairly common concepts frequently used in both H and L, where the range of meaning of the two items is roughly the same, and the use of one or the other immediately stamps the utterance or written sequence as H or L.* For example, in Arabic the H word for 'see' is *ra'ā*, the L word is *šāf.* The word *ra'ā* never occurs in ordinary conversation and *šāf* is not used in normal written Arabic. If for some reason a remark in which *šāf* was used is quoted in the press, it is replaced by *ra'ā* in the written quotation. In Greek the H word for 'wine' is *ínos*, the L word is *krasí.* The menu will have *ínos* written on it, but the diner will ask the waiter for *krasí.* The nearest American English parallels are such cases as *illumination ~ light, purchase ~ buy*, or *children ~ kids*, but in these cases both words may be written and both may be used in ordinary conversation: the gap is not so great as for the corresponding doublets in diglossia. Also, the formal–informal dimension in languages like English is a continuum in which the boundary between the two items in different pairs may not come at the same point, e.g. *illumination, purchase,* and *children* are not fully parallel in their formal–informal range of usage.

9. Phonology It may seem difficult to offer any generalization on the relationships between the phonology of H and L in diglossia in view of the diversity of data. H and L phonologies may be quite close, as in Greek; moderately different, as in Arabic or Haitian Creole; or strikingly divergent, as in Swiss German. Closer examination, however, shows two statements to be justified. (Perhaps these will turn out to be unnecessary when the preceding features are stated so precisely that the statements about phonology can be deduced directly from them.)

(a) The sound systems of H and L constitute a single phonological structure of which the L phonology is the basic system and the divergent features of H phonology are either a subsystem or a parasystem. Given the mixed forms mentioned above and the corresponding difficulty of identifying a given word in a given utterance as being definitely H or definitely L, it seems necessary to assume that the speaker has a single inventory of distinctive oppositions for the whole H–L complex and that there is extensive interference in both directions in terms of the distribution of phonemes in specific lexical items.

(b) If 'pure' H items have phonemes not found in 'pure' L items, L phonemes frequently substitute for these in oral use of H and regularly replace them in tatsamas. For example, French has a high front rounded vowel phoneme /ü/; 'pure' Haitian Creole has no such phoneme. Educated speakers of Creole use this vowel in *tatsamas* such as *Luk* (/lük/ for the Gospel of St. Luke), while they, like uneducated speakers, may sometimes use /i/ for it when speaking French. On the other hand, /i/ is the regular vowel in such *tatsamas* in Creole as *linèt* 'glasses'.

In cases where H represents in large part an earlier stage of L, it is possible that a three-way correspondence will appear. For example, Syrian and Egyptian Arabic frequently use /s/ for /θ/ in oral use of Classical Arabic, and have /s/ in tatsamas, but have /t/ in words regularly descended from earlier Arabic not borrowed from the Classical.

Now that the characteristic features of diglossia have been outlined it is feasible to attempt a fuller definition. (DIGLOSSIA *is a relatively stable language situation in which, in addition to the primary dialects of the language (which may include a standard or regional standards), there is a very divergent, highly codified (often grammatically more complex) superposed variety, the vehicle of a large and respected body of written literature, either of an earlier period or in another speech community, which is learned largely by formal education and is used for most written and formal spoken purposes but is not used by any sector of the community for ordinary conversation.*)

With the characterization of diglossia completed we may turn to a brief consideration of three additional questions: How does diglossia differ from the familiar situation of a standard language with regional dialects? How widespread is the phenomenon of diglossia in space, time, and linguistic families? Under what circumstances does diglossia come into being and into what language situations is it likely to develop?

The precise role of the standard variety (or varieties) of a language vis-à-vis regional or social dialects differs from one speech community to another, and some instances of this relation may be close to diglossia or perhaps even better considered as diglossia. As characterized here, diglossia differs from the more widespread standard-with-dialects in that no segment of the speech community in diglossia regularly uses H as a medium of ordinary conversation, and any attempt to do so is felt to be either pedantic and artificial (Arabic, Greek) or else in some sense disloyal to the community (Swiss German, Creole). In the more usual standard-with-dialects situation the standard is often similar to the variety of a certain region or social group (e.g. Tehran Persian, Calcutta Bengali) which is used in ordinary conversation more or less naturally by members of the group and as a superposed variety by others.

Diglossia is apparently not limited to any geographical region or language family. Three examples of diglossia from other times and places may be cited as illustrations of the utility of the concept. First, consider Tamil. As used by the millions of members of the Tamil speech community in India today, it fits the definition exactly. There is a literary Tamil as H used for writing and certain kinds of formal speaking, and a standard colloquial as L (as well as local L dialects) used in ordinary conversation. There is a body of literature in H going back many centuries which is highly regarded by Tamil speakers today. H has prestige, L does not. H is always superposed, L is learned naturally, whether as primary or as a superposed standard colloquial. There are striking grammatical differences and some phonological differences between the two varieties. The situation is only slightly complicated by the presence of Sanskrit and English for certain functions of H; the same kind of complication exists in parts of the Arab world where French, English, or a liturgical language such as Syriac or Coptic has certain H-like functions.

Second, we may mention Latin and the emergent Romance languages during a period of some centuries in various parts of Europe. The vernacular was used in ordinary conversation but Latin for writing or certain kinds of formal speech. Latin was the language of the Church and its literature, Latin had the prestige, there were striking grammatical differences between the two varieties in each area, etc.

Third, Chinese should be cited because it probably represents diglossia on the largest scale of any attested instance. The *weu-li* corresponds to H, while Mandarin colloquial is a standard L; there are also regional L varieties so different as to deserve the label 'separate languages' even more than the Arabic dialects, and at least as much as the emergent Romance languages in the Latin example. Chinese, however, like modern Greek, seems to be developing away from diglossia toward a standard-with-dialects in that the standard L or a mixed variety is coming to be used in writing for more and more purposes, i.e. it is becoming a true standard.

Diglossia is likely to come into being when the following three conditions hold in a given speech community: (1) There is a sizable body of literature in a language closely related to (or even identical with) the natural language of the community, and this literature embodies, whether as source (e.g. divine revelation) or reinforcement, some of the fundamental values of the community. (2) Literacy in the community is limited to a small elite. (3) A suitable period of time, on the order of several centuries, passes from the establishment of (1) and (2). It can probably be shown that this combination of circumstances has occurred hundreds of times in the past and has generally resulted in diglossia. Dozens of examples exist today, and it is likely that examples will occur in the future.

NOTES

1. The situation in formal education is often more complicated than is indicated here. In the Arab world, for example, formal university lectures are given in H, but drills, explanation, and section meetings may be in large part conducted in L, especially in

the natural sciences as opposed to the humanities. Although the teachers' use of L in secondary schools is forbidden by law in some Arab countries, often a considerable part of the teacher's time is taken up with explaining in L the meaning of material in H which has been presented in books or lectures.

2. Modern Greek does not quite fit this description. Poetry in L is the major production and H verse is generally felt to be artificial.

CHAPTER 32

Language Change and Sex Roles in a Bilingual Community

SUSAN GAL

Introduction

Linguistic differences between men and women can appear at various levels of grammar: in phonology, in syntax and pragmatics, in choice of lexical items, in choice of language by bilinguals, as well as in patterns of conversational interaction.

However, the effects of such sex differences on linguistic *change* have so far been noted only with respect to phonology, where it has been demonstrated that, along with other social correlates of synchronic linguistic diversity such as class and ethnicity, 'the sexual differentiation of speech often plays a major role in the mechanism of linguistic evolution' (Labov 1972: 303). The substantive aim of this chapter is to describe the way in which the women of a Hungarian–German bilingual town in Austria have contributed to a change in patterns of language choice. The entire community is gradually and systematically changing from stable bilingualism to the use of only one language in all interactions. Sex-linked differences in language choice have influenced the overall community-wide process of change.

In the language usage patterns to be described here, young women are more advanced or further along in the direction of the linguistic change than older people and young men. This is one of the patterns which has been noted

Source: 'Peasant Men Can't Get Wives: Language Change and Roles in a Bilingual Community', by Gal, S. in *Language in Society*, 7 (1) (1978) (Cambridge: Cambridge University Press) pp. 1–16, tables 29.1–29.4.

in correlational studies of phonological change in urban areas. Most such studies report that women use the newer, advanced forms more frequently than men. Newly introduced forms used mostly by women are sometimes prestigious (Trudgill 1972) and sometimes not (Fasold 1968). In many cases women, as compared to men of the same social class, use more of the new non-prestigious forms in casual speech, while moving further towards prestige models in formal speech. In other cases women do not lead in the course of linguistic change (reported in Labov 1972).

Although such findings are well documented, adequate explanations of them have not been offered. General statements about the linguistic innovativeness or conservatism of women will not account for the data. Neither Trudgill's (1972) suggestion that women are 'linguistically insecure', nor Labov's (1972) allusion to norms of linguistic appropriateness which allow women a wider expressive range than men, can convincingly explain why women are linguistically innovative in some communities and not in others (Nichols 1976). Women's role in language change has rarely been linked to the social position of women in the communities studied and to the related questions of what women want to express about themselves in speech. In the present study, men's and women's ways of speaking are viewed as the results of strategic and socially meaningful linguistic choices which systematically link language change to social change: linguistic innovation is a function of speakers' differential involvement in, and evaluation of, social change.

Specifically, in the linguistic repertoire of the bilingual community to be described here, one of the languages has come to symbolize a newly available social status. Young women's language choices can be understood as part of their expression of preference for this newer social identity. The young women of the community are more willing to participate in social change and in the linguistic change which symbolizes it because they are less committed than the men to the traditionally male-dominated system of subsistence agriculture, and because they have more to gain than men in embracing the newly available statuses of worker and worker's wife. In order to make this argument in detail several words of background are necessary, first about the community and second about its linguistic repertoire.

The Community

Oberwart (Felsöör) is a town located in the province of Burgenland in eastern Austria. It has belonged to Austria only since 1921 when as part of the post-World War I peace agreements the province was detached from Hungary. The town itself has been a speech island since the 1500s when most of the original Hungarian-speaking population of the region was decimated by the Turkish wars and was replaced by German-speaking (and in some areas Croatian-speaking) settlers. In Oberwart, which was the largest of the five remaining Hungarian-speaking communities, bilingualism in German and Hungarian became common.

During the last thirty years [i.e. thirty years before 1978 - eds.] Oberwart has grown from a village of 600 to a town of over 5000 people because, as the county seat and new commercial centre, it has attracted migrants. These new settlers have all been monolingual German speakers, mainly people from neighboring villages, who have been trained in commerce or administration. The bilingual community today constitutes about a fourth of the town's population.

The indigenous bilinguals who will be the focus of this discussion have until recently engaged in subsistence peasant agriculture. Since World War II, however, most of the agriculturalists have become industrial workers or worker-peasants. By 1972 only about one-third of the bilingual population was employed exclusively in peasant agriculture.

In short, Oberwart is an example of the familiar post-war process of urbanization and industrialization of the countryside often reported in the literature on the transformation of peasant Europe (e.g. Franklin 1969).

The Linguistic Repertoire

Bilingual communities provide a particularly salient case of the linguistic heterogeneity which characterizes all communities. In Oberwart the linguistic alternatives available to speakers include not only two easily distinguishable languages but also dialectal differences within each language. These 'dialects' are not homogeneous, invariant structures, but rather are best characterized as sets of covarying linguistic variables which have their own appropriate social uses and connotations (cf. Gumperz 1964; Ervin-Tripp 1972). It is possible for bilingual Oberwarters to move along a continuum from more standard to more local speech in either of their languages (cf. Gal 1976).

Of the many functions that code choice has been shown to serve in interaction (Hymes 1967) this paper focuses on just one and on how it is involved in change. As Blom and Gumperz (1972) have argued, alternate codes within a linguistic repertoire are usually each associated with subgroups in the community and with certain activities. It has been pointed out that a speaker's choice of code in a particular situation is part of that speaker's linguistic presentation of self. The speaker makes the choice as part of a verbal strategy to identify herself or himself with the social categories and activities the code symbolise. The choice, then, allows the speaker to express solidarity with that category or group of people.

The Meaning of Codes

Although bilingual Oberwarters use both standard and local varieties of German as well as of Hungarian, and although the choice between local and standard features in either language carries meaning in conversation, here we will be concerned only with the symbolically more important alternation between German of any sort (G) and Hungarian of any sort (H).

Today in Oberwart H symbolizes peasant status and is deprecated because peasant status itself is no longer respected. 'Peasant' is used here for a native cultural category that includes all local agriculturalists and carries a negative connotation, at least for young people. Young bilingual workers often say, in Hungarian, that only the old peasants speak Hungarian. There is no contradiction here. The young workers know that they themselves sometimes speak Hungarian and they can report on their language choices accurately. The saying refers not to actual practice but to the association of the Hungarian language with peasant status. All old peasants do speak Hungarian and speak it in more situations than anyone else.

The preferred status for young people is worker, not peasant. The world of work is a totally German-speaking world, and the language itself has come to represent the worker. The peasant parents of young workers often say about their children 'Ü má egisz nímët' ('He/she is totally German already').[1] This is not a reference to citizenship, nor to linguistic abilities. Oberwarters consider themselves Austrians, not Germans, and even young people are considered bilingual, often using Hungarian in interactions with elders. The phase indicates the strong symbolic relationship between the young people's status as workers and the language which they use at work.

German also represents the money and prestige available to those who are employed, but not available to peasants. German therefore carries more prestige than Hungarian. The children of a monolingual German speaker and a bilingual speaker never learn Hungarian, regardless of which parent is bilingual. In addition, while in previous generations the ability simply to speak both German and Hungarian was the goal of Oberwarters, today there is a premium not just on speaking German, but on speaking it without any interference from Hungarian. Parents often boast that in their children's German speech 'Nëm vág bele e madzsar' ('The Hungarian doesn't cut into it'). That is, passing as a monolingual German speaker is now the aim of young bilingual Oberwarters.

Such general statements about symbolic associations between languages, social statuses and the evaluations of those statuses do not in themselves predict language choice in particular situations. For instance, although H is negatively evaluated by young people it is nevertheless used by them in a number of interactions where, for various reasons, they choose to present themselves as peasants. Besides the values associated with languages, the three factors which must be known in order to predict choices and to describe the changes in these choices are the speaker's age and sex and the nature of the social network in which that speaker habitually interacts.

How do Language Choice Patterns Change?

In any interaction between bilingual Oberwarters a choice must be made between G and H. While in most situations one or the other language is chosen, there are some interactions it is impossible to predict which language will be used by which speaker and both are often used within one short exchange. Gumperz (1976) has called this conversational code-switching. When both languages may appropriately be used Oberwarters say they are speaking 'ehodzsan dzsün' ('as it comes'). A description of language choice in such situations must include such variation and in this sense is comparable to the rule conflicts described for syntactic change by Bickerton (1973).

In predicting an individual's choice between the three possibilities – G, H or both – the habitual role-relationship between participants in the interaction proved to be the most important factor. Other aspects of the situation such as locale, purpose or occasion were largely irrelevant. Therefore, specification of the identity of the interlocutor was sufficient to define the social situation for the purposes of the present analysis.

We can think of informants as being ranked along a vertical axis and social situations being arranged along a horizontal axis, as in Tables 32.1 and 32.2. Note that all speakers listed in these tables are bilingual. The information is drawn from a language usage questionnaire which was constructed on the basis of native categories of interlocutors and linguistic resources. Similar scales based on systematic observation of language choice were also constructed. There was a high degree of agreement between observed usage and the questionnaire results (average agreement for men 86%, for women 90%). That is, the questionnaire results were corroborated by direct observation of language choice.

The language choices of a particular informant in all situations are indicated in the rows of Tables 32.1 and 32.2 and the choices of all informants in a particular situation are indicated in the columns. The choices of Oberwarters, arranged in this way, form a nearly perfect implicational scale. Note that for all speakers there is at least one situation in which they use only H. For almost all speakers there are some situations in which they use both G and H and some in which they use only G. Further, for any speaker there are no bilingual interlocutors with whom she or he speaks both G and H unless

Table 32.1   Language choice pattern of women

Informant	Age	1	2	3	4	5	6	7	8	9	10	11
				Social situations (identity of participant)								
A	14	H	GH		G	G	G			G		G
B	15	H	GH		G	G	G			G		G
C	25	H	GH	GH	GH	G	G	G	G	G		G
D	27	H	H		GH	G	G			G		G
E	17	H	H		H	GH	G			G		G
F	39	H	H		H	GH	GH			G		G
G	23	H	H		H	GH	H		GH	G		G
H	40	H	H		H	GH		GH	G	G		G
I	52	H	H	H	GH	H		GH	G	G	G	G
J	40	H	H	H	H	H	H	GH	GH	GH		G
K	35	H	H	H	H	H	H	H	GH	H		G
L	61	H	H		H	H	H	H	GH	H		G
M	50	H	H	H	H	H	H	H	H	H		G
N	60	H	H	H	H	H	H	H	H	H	GH	G
O	54	H	H		H	H	H	H	H	H	GH	H
P	63	H	H	H	H	H	H	H	H	H	GH	H
Q	64	H	H	H	H	H	H	H	H	H	H	H
R	59	H	H	H	H	H	H	H	H	H	H	H

Note:

No. of informants = 18

Scalability = 95.4%

1 = to god
2 = grandparents and their generation
3 = bilingual clients in black market
4 = parents and their generation
5 = friends and age-mate neighbors
6 = brothers and sisters
7 = spouse
8 = children and their generation
9 = bilingual government officials
10 = grandchildren and their generation
11 = doctors

G – German, H – Hungarian, GH – both German and Hungarian.

there are some, listed to the left of that interlocutor, with whom the speaker uses H. With few exceptions, if G is used with an interlocutor then only G is used to interlocutors listed to the right of that, and GH or H are used with those listed to the left. The occurrence of any of the three linguistic categories in a cell implies the occurrence of particular others in the cells to the left and right.

Table 32.2 Language choice pattern of men

		Social situations (identity of participant)										
Informant	Age	1	2	3	4	5	6	7	8	9	10	11
A	17	H	GH		G	G	G			G		G
B	25	H	H		GH	G	G			G		G
C	42		H		GH	G	G	G	G	G		G
D	20	H	H	H	H	GH	G	G	G	G		G
E	22	H	H		H	GH	GH			G		G
F	62	H	H	H	H	H	H	GH	GH	GH	G	G
G	63	H	H		H	H	H	H		GH		G
H	64	H	H	H	H	H	H	H	GH	GH		G
I	43	H	H		H	H	H	H	G	H		G
J	41	H	H	H	H	H	H	H	GH	H		H
K	54	H	H		H	H	H	H	H	H		G
L	61	H	H		H	H	H	H	H	G	GH	G
M	74	H	H		H	H	H	H	H	H	GH	H
N	58	G	H		H	H	H	H	H	H	H	H

Note:
No. of informants = 14
Scalability = 95.2%
Situations 1–11 are defined as in Table 32.1

In addition, looking at the columns instead of the rows in Tables 32.1 and 32.2, and considering not one speaker at a time but the group of speakers as a whole, we see that if a speaker high on the list uses both G and H in a particular situation, then speakers lower down can be expected to use H or both in that situation. But if the speaker at the top of the list uses H, then all others use H in that situation as well. The presence of any one of the three linguistic categories in a cell restricts which of the three may occur in the cells above and below that one. When one speaker's choice of language in a particular situation is known it also gives information about the possibilities open to those lower on the list and those higher on the list. The closer an informant is to the top of the list the more situations there are in which he or she uses G. The closer to the bottom, the more H he or she uses. Tables 32.1 and 32.2 have scalabilities of 95.4% and 95.2% respectively, showing that there are only a few exceptions to these generalizations.[2]

Given this, it is worth considering the factors that determine the place of a speaker on the scale. Two factors determine the degree to which a person uses H as opposed to G: the person's age and her or his social network. Because historical evidence (cf. Imre 1973; Kovács 1942: 73–76) shows that present-day age differences are not due to age-grading of language choice, we can take age (apparent time) as a surrogate for repeated sampling over real time (cf. Labov 1972 for details of this strategy).

Social network is defined here as all the people (contacts) an individual spoke to in the course of a unit of time. The average amount of time for all informants was seven days. Each of these network contacts was assigned to one of two categories: (a) those who lived in households which owned either pigs or cows, (b) those who lived in households which owned neither pigs nor cows. Oberwarters themselves define those who own cows and pigs as peasants. The peasantness of a person's network, expressed as the percentage of contacts who fit into category (a) is, in effect, a measure of that person's social involvement with the category of persons with which the use of H is associated.

The more peasants the individual has in her or his social network the greater the number of social situations in which that individual uses H. In fact, in most cases a *person's own status*, whether peasant, worker or some gradation in between, *was not as accurate a predictor of his or her choices as the status of the person's social contacts*. These results lend support to the notion that social networks are instrumental in constraining speakers' linguistic presentation of self.

The three-way relationship between language choices, age, and peasantness of social network can be demonstrated by ranking informants on each of the measures and then correlating the rankings with each other. Table 32.3 shows the correlations for this sample of informants. All are significant at the 0.01 level. Note that this group of informants was not formally selected as a representative sample of the bilingual community, but rather was chosen to represent the entire range of the two variables – age and social network – so that conclusions could be drawn about the effect of each variable on changing language choices. In order to distinguish the effects on language choice of time on the one hand and the effects of changing social

Table 32.3　Correlations between language choice and age, language choice and peasantness of network[*]

	All informants	Women	Men
Language choice and age	0.82	0.93	0.69
Language choice and peasantness of network	0.78	0.74	0.78
	N = 32	N = 18	N = 14

Note:
[*]Spearman rank correlation coefficients all significant at the 0.01 level.

networks on the other, both old people who had never been totally involved in peasant agriculture and young people who were very much involved were included in the sample.

On the basis of the rank correlations the following brief outline of the synchronic pattern of language choice can be drawn. For the sample as a whole, the more peasants in one's social network the more likely it is that one will use H in a large number of situations. The older one is the more likely it is that one will use H in a large number of situations. Young people who interact only with workers use the least H, older people who interact mostly with peasants use the most H. Older people who associate mostly with workers are closest in their language choices to people much younger than themselves, while very young people who associated mostly with peasants use more H than others their own age.

Because historical evidence rules out the possibility of age-grading and because the sample allows one to disentangle the effects of time and that of networks, it is possible to hypothesize the following process of change. Changes in language choices occur situation by situation. The rule for one situation is always first categorical for the old form (H), then variable (GH), before it is categorical for the new form (G). As speaker's networks become less and less peasant they use H in fewer and fewer situations. And, in a parallel but separate process, as time passes new generations use H in fewer and fewer situations regardless of the content of their social networks.

Differences between Men and Women

The implicational scales describing choices seem to indicate no differences between men and women. Both men and women show the same kinds of implicational relationships in the same ordered list of situations. However, the rank correlations of language choice, age and peasantness of network, summarized in Table 32.3, present a more complicated picture. Here the issue is whether age and social networks are equally well correlated with language choice for men and women. In fact they are not: for men the correlation between social network and language choice is about the same as the correlation between age and language choice (0.78 and 0.69 respectively). For women age alone is more closely correlated with language choice (0.93) than is the social network measure (0.74). This difference between men and women is significant at the 0.05 level.

In short, there is a difference between men and women in the way each is going through the process of change in language choice. If we distinguish three twenty-year generations, separate the men from the women and those with very peasant networks from those with non-peasant networks, it is possible to illustrate the process at work. Informants' networks ranged from 13 per cent peasant contacts to 94% peasant contacts. This continuum was divided into two parts. All those scoring at or above the median were put in the peasant network category in Figure 32.1, all those scoring below the median were in the non-peasant network category.

Figure 32.1 illustrates the fact that for men there is a very regular pattern in the correlations. From the oldest to the youngest generation use of G increases, but for each generation this increase is greatest for those whose

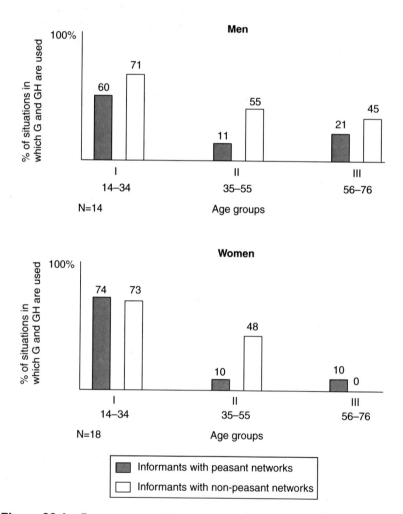

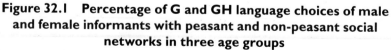

Figure 32.1   Percentage of G and GH language choices of male and female informants with peasant and non-peasant social networks in three age groups

social networks include a majority of non-peasants. Among the men the youngest group as a whole uses less H than any of the others. But those young men with heavily peasant networks do use more H. Regardless of the negative evaluations, for these young men expression of peasant identity is still preferred for many situations.

For women the process is different. First we find that in the oldest generation this sample includes not one person with a non-peasant network.

This is not a sampling error but reflects the limited range of activities, and therefore of social contacts, open to women before World War II. In the middle generation the women's pattern matches that of men exactly. Many women of the generation reaching maturity during and after World War II left the peasant home, if only temporarily, to work in inns, factories and shops. Often they remained in contact with those they befriended. As with the men, those who have heavily peasant networks use more H than those who do not.

The youngest generation of women differs both from the older women and from the men. First, these youngest women use more G and less H than anyone else in the community, including the youngest men. In addition, for these women, *peasantness of social network makes no difference in language choice.* Young women with peasant networks use Hungarian as rarely as young women with non-peasant networks. Recall that for all the men, including the youngest, peasantness of network did make a difference since it was associated with more use of H.

To understand these differences it is necessary to go back to the activities from which the languages derive their meanings and evaluations. For the most recent generation of women, peasant life is a much less attractive choice than it is for men. Now that other opportunities are open to these young women, they reject peasant life as a viable alternative. It will be argued here that their language choices are part of this rejection.

There are some young men who, despite a general preference for industrial and commercial employment, want to take over family farms. Some of these young men have the newly developing attitude that farming can be an occupation, a 'Beruf', like any other. These are men whose families own enough land to make agriculture if not as lucrative as wage work at least a satisfactory livelihood. In contrast, young women, since World War II, have not been willing to take over the family farm when this opportunity is offered to them. More importantly, they specifically state that they do not want to marry peasant men. The life of a peasant wife is seen by Oberwart young women as particularly demeaning and difficult when compared to the other choices which have recently become available to them.

Let us compare the choices open to Oberwart young men and women as they see them. For men the life possibilities are (a) to be an industrial or construction worker (usually a commuter coming home only on weekends),

(b) to be a peasant-worker, holding two full-time jobs, and (c) to be a full-time agriculturalist. This last is felt by Oberwart men to have the advantage of independence – no orders from strangers – and the disadvantage of lack of cash and prestige. But it is generally agreed that while agricultural work was once more grueling and difficult than factory and construction work, this is no longer the case. Although peasant men still work longer hours than those in industry, machines such as the tractor and the combine make men's farm work highly mechanized and considerably less difficult than it once was.

For women the life possibilities depend mainly on whom they marry. The peasant wife typically spends the day doing farm work: milking, feeding pigs, hoeing, planting and harvesting potatoes and a few other rootcrops. Her evenings are spent doing housework. Industriousness is traditionally considered a young peasant wife's most valuable quality.

There are machines now available which lighten the work of the peasant wife considerably, including the washing machine, the electric stove and the silo (which eliminates the need for rootcrops as cattle feed). But in peasant households the male labor-saving machines are always acquired before any of the ones which lighten women's work. For instance the silo, which is perhaps the most substantial work-saver for the peasant wife, is never built before a combine is purchased, and the combine itself is among the last and most expensive of the machines acquired. In this Oberwart exemplifies the pattern all over Europe, where, for instance, the German small peasant's wife in 1964 averaged over the year 17 more work hours per week than her husband (Franklin 1969: 37–44). In addition, although peasant life in Oberwart is less male-dominated than, for instance, in the Balkans (compare Denich 1974 with Fél and Hofer 1969: 113–144), nevertheless for the peasant wife the independence which is said to compensate the peasant man for his work is not freely available. In fact, being a young peasant wife often means living under the authority of a mother-in-law who supervises the kitchen and women's farm work generally.

In marked contrast, marriage to a worker involves only household tasks and upkeep of a kitchen garden. Wives of workers are sometimes employed as maids or salespersons, but mostly they hold part-time jobs or are not employed at all. Because of the increased access to money, because agricultural equipment is not needed and because some of the women themselves contribute part of the money, electric stoves and washing machines are among the first appliances bought by working married couples, thereby further lightening the wife's work load. Peasant wives work far more than peasant men. Peasant men work more hours than worker men. Worker's wives, especially if not employed, often work fewer hours than their husbands.

This contrast is not lost on young Oberwart women. When discussing life choices they especially dwell on the dirtiness and heaviness of peasant work.

Rejection of the use of local Hungarian, the symbol of peasant status, can be seen as part of the rejection, by young women, of peasant status and life generally. They do not want to be peasants; they do not present themselves as peasants in speech.

Mothers of marriageable daughters specifically advise them against marriage to peasants. Oberwarters agree that 'Paraszt legin nëm kap nüöt' ('Peasant lads can't get women'). For instance, in reference to a particular young couple an old man remarked: 'Az e Trüumfba jár, az fog neki tehen szart lapáni? Abbu má paraszt nëm lesz, az má zicher!' ('She works at the [local bra factory], *she*'s going to shovel cow manure for him? She'll never be a peasant, that's for sure'.) Although the young men themselves are usually also reluctant to become peasants, for those who nevertheless choose family agriculture as their livelihood, the anti-peasant attitudes of the community's young women present a problem.

If in recent years Oberwart young women have not wanted to marry peasant men, and if they have acted on this preference, then Oberwart peasant men must have found wives elsewhere. The town's marriage records should provide evidence for the difference in attitudes between young men and young women.

The general trend in Oberwart in the post-war years has been away from the traditional village endogamy and towards exogamy. For instance, Table 32.4 shows that between 1911 and 1940 72% and 1940 72% of the marriages of bilinguals in Oberwart were endogamous. Between 1961 and 1972 only 32% were. But for the bilingual peasant men of Oberwart the figures are different. As Table 32.4 indicates, between 1911 and 1940 a larger percentage of peasant men married endogamously than all bilingual Oberwarters (87%). Between 1941 and 1960, however, this was reversed. Finally, by 1961–1972, when 32% of all bilingual Oberwarters married endogamously, not one peasant man married endogamously. Those peasant men who did marry during those years found wives in the neighboring small German monolingual villages where being a peasant wife has not been negatively valued. In short, the marriage records provide evidence that young Oberwart women's stated

Table 32.4 Endogamous marriages of all bilingual Oberwarters and bilingual male peasant Oberwarters

	% Endogamous marriages of all marriages	*% Endogamous marriages of male peasants*
1911–1940	71%	87%
1941–1960	65	54
1961–1972	32	0

Source: Marriage Register, City of Oberwart.

attitudes towards peasant men have been translated into action. The effect of this is discussed below.

Conclusion

There are two ways, one direct and one indirect, in which the attitudes and choices of young bilingual women are changing the language usage pattern in this community. Directly, the young women, even those with heavily peasant networks, refuse, in most situations, to present themselves as peasants by using H. This contrasts with the language choices of older women and has the general effect that more German is used in more interactions in the community. It also contrasts with the choices of young men, who use Hungarian in more interactions than the young women and who are constrained by the peasantness of their social networks so that those with heavily peasant networks choose local Hungarian in more interactions than those with non-peasant networks.

Indirectly, young women's marriage preferences are also having a linguistic effect. They refuse to marry local peasant men, preferring workers instead. As a result, exactly that small group of young men most likely to be using Hungarian in many situations, that is the ones engaged in peasant agriculture, are the ones who have married German monolingual women with the greatest frequency in the last decade or so. Because the children of marriages between monolingual German speakers and bilingual Hungarian–German speakers in Oberwart rarely if every learn Hungarian, in an indirect way the present generation of young women is limiting the language possibilities of the next generation.

In exploring the reasons for the difference between young men's and young women's language choices, evidence was presented showing that in their stated attitudes and their marriage choices the women evaluate peasant life more negatively than the men and reject the social identity of peasant wife. The women of Oberwart feel they have more to gain then men by embracing the new opportunities of industrial employment. Also, considering the male-dominated nature of East European peasant communities generally and the lives of Oberwart women in particular, women have less to lose in rejecting the traditional peasant roles and values.

This paper has argued that women's language choices and their linguistic innovativeness in this community are the linguistic expressions of women's greater participation in social change. The linguistic pattern is best understood by considering the social meanings of the available languages and the strategic choices and evaluations which men and women make concerning the ways of life symbolized by those languages.

Acknowledgement

The data reported here were gathered during 1974 as part of dissertation fieldwork supported by a NIMH Anthropology Traineeship at the University of California, Berkeley. My thanks to Paul Kay, John Gumperz and E. A. Hammel for their many suggestions. An earlier version of this paper was presented at the symposium on 'Language and Sex Roles' at the 74th Annual Meeting of the AAA, December 1975.

NOTES

1. The orthography is a modified version of Imre (1971) and of the Hungarian dialect atlas.
2. 'Scalability' is the proportion of cells that fit the scale model. Inapplicable cells (those left empty in Tables 32.1 and 32.2) were omitted from the denominator.

REFERENCES

Bickerton, D. 1973. The nature of a Creole continuum. *Language* 44: 640–669.

Blom, J. P. and J. J. Gumperz. 1972. Social meaning in linguistic structures: Code switching in Norway. In J. J. Gumperz and D. Hymes (eds.) *Directions in Sociolinguistics*. New York: Holt, Rinehart and Winston.

Denich, B. 1974. Sex and power in the Balkans. In M. S. Rosaldo and L. Lamphere (eds.) *Woman, Culture and Society*. Stanford, California: Stanford University Press.

Ervin-Tripp, S. 1972. On sociolinguistic rules: Alternation and co-occurrence. In J. J. Gumperz and D. Hymes (eds.) *Directions in Sociolingusitics*. New York: Holt, Rinehart and Winston.

Fasold, R. 1968. 'A sociolinguistic study of the pronunciation of three vowels in Detroit Speech'. Washington, D. C.: Center for Applied Linguistics. Mimeo.

Fél, E. and T. Hofer. 1969. *Proper Peasants*. Chicago, Illinois: Aldine.

Franklin, S. H. 1969. *The European Peasantry*. London: Methuen.

Gal, S. 1976. *Language Change and its Social Determinants in a Bilingual Community* Ann Arbor, Michigan: University Microfilms.

Gumperz, J. J. 1964. Linguistic and social interaction in two communities. *American Anthropologist* 66 Part II: 137–154.

Gumperz, J. J. 1976. The sociolinguistic significance of conversational code-switching. Ms.

Hymes, D. 1967. Models of the interaction of language and social setting. *Journal of Social Issues* 23: 8–28.

Imre, S. 1971. A Felsoori Nyelvjárás (The Oberwart Dialect). *Nyelvtudományi Értekezések* 72 (Budapest).

Imre, S. 1973. Az Ausztriai (Burgenlandi) Magyar Azorványok (The Hungarian Minority Group in Austria). In *Népi Kultura – Népi Társadalom* (Folk Culture – Folk Society). Budapest: Akadémiai Kiadó.

Kovács, M. 1942. *A Felsoori Magyar Népsziget* (*The Hungarian Folk-Island of Oberwart*). Budapest: Sylvester-Nyomda.

Labov, W. 1972. *Sociolinguistic Patterns*. Philadelphia, Pennsylvania: University of Pennsylvania Press.

Nichols, P. 1976. Black women in the rural South: Conservative and innovative. Paper presented to the Conference on the Sociology of the Languages of American Women. New Mexico: Las Cruces.

Trudgill, P. 1972. Sex, covert prestige and linguistic change in the urban British English of Norwich. *Language in Society* 1: 179–195.

CHAPTER 33

Code-switching

CAROL MYERS-SCOTTON

Introduction

Code-switching (CS) is most generally defined as the use of two language varieties in the same conversation, not counting established borrowed words or phrases from one variety into the other. Some researchers use other terms while still referring to utterances with surface-level elements from two varieties; for example, 'code mixing' is often used, or even 'transference' when emphasis is on structural or semantic changes in one variety under the influence of another (see also Auer this volume, Chapter 34).

Under any of these rubrics, the varieties can occur in a number of structural configurations, but there are two general types, *inter-sentential CS*, which is most often studied for its social features, and *intra-sentential CS*, which is more studied for its grammatical structure. Both types may occur in the same discourse. Inter-sentential CS includes switching between monolingual sentences from the participating varieties, as in Extract 1. The extent of an inter-sentential switch can be one sentence or many more in an extended discourse.

> **Extract 1**: Policeman to heckler in crowd in Nairobi, switching from Swahili to English for one sentence; Swahili is in bold. (Source: Myers-Scotton 1993: 77).
>
> How else can we restrain people from stealing except by punishment? **Wewe si mtu kutuambia vile tutafanya kazi – tuna sheria yetu.**
>
> Translation of Swahili sentence: 'You aren't [the] person to tell us how to do our work – we have our laws.'

Intra-sentential CS includes bilingual constituents within a single sentence. Extract 2a is a bilingual sentence consisting of two monolingual clauses.

Extract 2b is a sentence that is a single bilingual clause. Arguably, the clause (or, projection of complementizer, CP), not the sentence, is the best unit for analysis of constraints on constituent structure, because sentences do not necessarily consist of equal structures. Further, it is within the clause that participating languages are really in contact.

Extract 2a: Palestinian Arabic-English.

I am not going,	**liʔanni**	**taʕbani**
	because/1s	GERUND/F/S/tired

'I am not going, because I am tired.'

Extract 2b: American Finnish-English (Source: Halmari 1997: 80).

Onks	sulla	vähän	**napkin**-eitä?
Have.INTEROG	you/ADDESSIVE	some napkin-PL/PARTITIVE	

'Do you have some napkins?'

Main Approaches to Code-switching

Researchers of CS fall into two groups, those interested in the social motivations for and/or the discourse functions of CS, and those interested in characterizing or explaining the grammatical structure of CS (e.g. the constraints on two varieties in the same clause). This overview emphasizes research on the more social side of CS (see also Auer this volume, Chapter 34), but will briefly survey attempts to characterize grammatical constraints on CS structure. CS sometimes involves more than two varieties; but for brevity, this overview refers to CS with two varieties. Also, it deals only with CS between varieties that are recognized as not mutually intelligible (i.e. the speakers are considered bilingual or multilingual), but participating varieties are not necessarily the standard dialect of a given language. It is worth emphasizing that the topic of CS is relevant to all communities, because the phenomenon of using two varieties in the same conversation or written work occurs between dialects and styles or registers of the same language; this sometimes is called style-shifting or style switching. Such switches occur much more often in written work, fictional or non-fictional, than is generally recognized, contributing to the pragmatics of any linguistic string.

Code-switching Arrives on Linguists' Radar Screens

As background, I offer a very brief sketch of CS today and attitudes towards CS. CS has been the norm in many communities, yet was often unnoticed by outsiders. Recently, it has attracted attention because it has surfaced in new places, due to social changes, most notably increased immigration and globalization. Winford (2003) lists three types of situations that promote CS today: (1) long-term stable bilingual communities (he mentions European examples, but there are many others, especially in Africa and Asia); (2) colonization in the developing world that introduced European languages that today are often official languages of administration and education; and (3) immigration into industrialized nations, because of either political unrest at home or better economic incentives elsewhere.

Yet, up until the last quarter of the twentieth century, few linguists even recognized CS as a subject to study, and when they commented on it at all, it was in negative terms. For example, in his classic study of language contact, Weinreich (1953, 1967) is often quoted as having written this dismissal of CS: 'The ideal bilingual switches from one language to the other according to appropriate changes in the speech situation (interlocutors, topics, etc.), but not in an unchanged speech situation and certainly not in the same sentence' (73).

If linguists even recognized CS's existence, it was lumped under terms such as 'interference'. Such views, of course, reflect the still prevailing public view in some bilingual communities that CS is nothing but a 'broken language', leading many parents and educators to conclude they should shield children from it. Against this backdrop, some linguists at least became interested in bilingual communities, if not CS, in the late 1960s and 1970s, as journal articles about the allocation of language varieties in such communities began to appear frequently.

But few researchers even recognized in print that CS existed in these bilingual communities. Real consideration of CS as a worthy research topic had to wait for Blom and Gumperz (1972), which dealt with CS between dialects in a Norwegian fishing village. What began to attract linguists interested in the social side of language use to studying CS was that Blom and Gumperz presented CS as a type of skilled performance with social messages as much as semantic ones.

The result is that from the late 1970s onwards, many studies attempting to characterize the social functions of CS appeared. Some of the first looked at CS between Spanish and English in the American southwest. At the same time, analyses of CS in indigenous European communities began appearing. Other researchers 'discovered' CS in multilingual areas all over the globe, such as in African cities. By the 1980s, a number of publications on immigrant to Western nations began to appear.

Socially Oriented Approaches to Code-switching

Up until today, the motivations for CS remain a major research topic for linguists and linguistic anthropologists interested in linguistic choices as a social phenomenon. Sociolinguistics textbooks contain lengthy sections on CS. Also, the journals that publish on bilingual topics continue to contain many articles on CS (e.g. *International Journal of Bilingualism* and *Bilingualism: Language and Cognition*) and other more mainstream journals also contain such articles (e.g. *Journal of Sociolinguistics, Language in Society,* and *Linguistics*). Most recently, papers on CS in electronic forms on the web are appearing.

Many of these studies remain at the descriptive level, but there are at least two models that offer explanations for CS when it occurs within a discourse: a conversation analysis approach (CA), most closely identified with Auer (e.g. 1984, 2005, this volume) and more recently Li (2002), and the markedness model (MM) of Myers-Scotton (e.g. 2002a). A third grouping of analysts more or less aligned with CA emphasize the speaker's creative agency behind why and where CS occurs. They include Stroud (2004) and Gafaranga (2005), as well as Rampton (1995). In addition, Speech Accommodation Theory (e.g. Giles and Coupland 1991) has the potential to provide analyses of CS corpora, although not many researchers have taken the theory in that direction (but see Bourhis et al. 1979 on switching under experimental conditions). Linguists following this approach, now called Communication Accommodation Theory, study switching between styles within a language (cf. Bell 1984, 2001, this volume on 'audience design', and the 'style as self-identity' approach of Coupland 2001, this volume).

Most space in this section is devoted to the CA and MM approaches. But for most discussions of CS, a starting point is Gumperz's notion that CS is one of the possible 'contextualization cues' that speakers/writers employ to signal socially relevant meanings (1982, this volume). Also, whatever their theoretical orientation, analysts often refer to Goffman (1981) and his concept of *footing*, changes in an actor's stance that may consist of CS in a given interaction. Another writer that many current researchers link to their own approaches is Bakhtin (1986). What attracts researchers is his notion that speakers have access to a number of *voices* that they make their own; these voices are echoes of earlier utterances, but especially the utterances of others.

In producing Gumperz's contextualization cues, Goffman's changes of footing, or Bakhtin's recycled voices, speakers can and do produce meaningful switches without necessarily doing any conscious planning. Certainly, most CS researchers assume that when CS occurs, it is largely unconscious. Also, most researchers agree that speakers seldom intend a single meaning when they shift codes; instead, both speaker and addressee seem almost to expect that switching will create potentially ambiguous or multiple meanings because it taps into another language's semantic and pragmatic components.

The Markedness Model

The MM attempts to explain the socio-psychological motivations for CS. But its goal is not to detail the macro-level social factors that serve as motivations, whether in an entire community or in specific interactions. Rather, what the MM offers is a generalization about how motivations are interpreted. This generalization is that, in any interaction, speakers and listeners employ a cognitively based continuum of unmarked to marked choices as the main mechanism that aids them in interpreting any linguistic choice. Within a community, a switch is interpreted as 'unmarked' (implying predictable, expected usage) or 'marked' (implying unexpected usage). That is a choice is more unmarked or marked in terms of the extent to which it indexes the Rights and Obligations Set (ROS) that is expected in that community from conversational participants in a given interaction. Thus, readings of markedness are not only community-specific, but also reflect specific relationships and interactions.

Switches to an unmarked variety index an expected relationship between the speaker and other participants; switches to a marked variety are bids for another relationship. A largely unspoken consensus indicates what is 'expected', but that consensus often follows the views of persons in power in the relevant community. Markedness is a gradient feature; that is, potential choices fall along a continuum from unmarked to marked. The details of this continuum are 'known' to participants, based on their cognitive abilities to evaluate and organize past experiences. Further, no choices are always marked or unmarked; rather, choices receive readings of markedness that are specific to different types of interactions.

Switching as a Pragmatic Message

The MM is cognitively based in the sense that it depends on pragmatic competence, the part of any person's general cognitive structure paralleling grammatical competence. Speakers rely on their pragmatic competence to arrive at interpretations of intended meanings in any utterance. Thus, this competence enables participants to interpret the indexicality of any linguistic choice in relation to the expected ROS between participants in a given interaction. Indexicality develops between a given ROS and a linguistic variety because the two become associated through use. When speakers make 'unmarked' choices, they are using this linkage to guide them to the expected choice in a given interaction, a choice they often make because it is the 'safest' in a given interaction.

The heart of the MM is that speakers are actors and are thus free to make marked choices. If they do this, the effect is to call up linkages that would be in effect in another interaction type than the current one. The notion that marked choices and negotiations exist is akin to Denison's comment in the 1970s that 'It is because there are sociolinguistic norms of expectation that participants are able to some extent to *create* social situations by skilful switching of diatypes' (1971: 178).

Recent presentations of the MM emphasize features that are akin to Rational Choice Models in the social sciences. Specifically, they emphasize that switching is a subjective strategy, one that speakers select as individuals depending on how they weigh alternatives and make choices that they judge will bring them the most rewards in the current interaction. Thus, Myers-Scotton and Bolonyai argue that speakers' creativity resides in making the most of their choices: 'Speakers operate with the expectation that what they say will be available evidence for others ... [they] collect, pay attention to, and take account of all these sources of available evidence in calculating the possible outcomes of their decisions regarding *how* to speak' (2001: 22).

An Analysis Following the MM Approach

Home conversations between an African graduate student studying in the United States, his wife, and their children illustrate how speakers use their knowledge of markedness strategically (Myers-Scotton 2002b). Chichewa is an L1 for all family members, and a quantitative analysis shows that it is the unmarked choice of the mother and father for family interactions, even though they both speak very fluent English and use it constantly outside the home. Chichewa is an official language in the south-central African nation of Malawi where it is widely spoken as an L1 or L2. For the mother, 67 percent of her clauses (288/429) are all in Chichewa, 7 percent are English only, and 26 percent show CS. In contrast, for the two boys, aged 10 (Peter) and 7 (Thengo), English is their unmarked family choice; clearly, they align themselves much more with the society in which they are living than do their parents. For example, 73 percent of Peter's clauses are all in English (141/194); 16 percent are Chichewa only, and 11 percent show CS.

But when Peter wants to tell his father about Thengo's behavior, it is no surprise that he begins in Chichewa, even though this is a marked choice for him. One interpretation is that he steps out of his own unmarked role (i.e. using mostly English) in order to get his father's attention, to please him (as a dutiful son), and to get his father on his side in his quarrel that ensues with Thengo.

Extract 3: (Source: Myers-Scotton 2002b: 215–216)

Peter: Atata, mufuna mudziwe...Thengo, **All he thinks about in class**...kumangoumbuzana ndi anthu.

'Daddy [honorific], do you want to know....Thengo, all he thinks about in class is fighting with people.'

After his father responds in Chicheŵa, Peter's next turn is also largely in Chicheŵa:

Peter: Amangochita **think about** kumaaumbiza anthu.

            'He just thinks about beating up people.'

Thengo: **No, I don't.**

Peter: kumapanga 'phaa'!

            'He does [makes a gesture].'

In another conversation in the same family, the mother is getting ready to leave home for her job as a secretary. She is instructing Peter about kitchen matters. But then she switches to a final clause that is all in English. This switch – as she is physically leaving home – is a marked choice for her, but it is as if she is saying 'I'm a different person when I go out this door and I can use this common casual expression in English to show it.'

Extract 4: (Source: Myers-Scotton 2002b: 217)

Mother: Ok, ukangoyang'ana ma-**drink** amene ali mu-**fridge**-mo...

       'Ok, just go and look at [the] drinks that are in [the] fridge ...'

       ...ukachape uyu. [now on her way out the door] **And then I'm out of here.**

       'Go and wash this one, and then I'm out of here.'

Conversation Analysis and Code-switching

In contrast to the MM, CA approaches to CS mainly look to the sequential organization of the interaction itself as the basis for interpretations. They rely much less on cognitively based inferences or societally based associations. Further, CA analysis is much more inductive; it is very much a bottom-up, empirical approach. Analysts find evidence of intended social messages in every nuance of the interaction, such as how a switch is positioned in relation to pauses and their length, as well as to other speakers' contributions. They argue that any interpretation of a switch must be situated in the interaction. Applying CA approaches to CS originally was most associated with Auer (1984, this volume).

This emphasis on detail is related to a major goal that CA analysts have – to demonstrate how 'orderly' ordinary conversation is. Gafaranga, who favors a CA approach, writes, 'The task...is to account for the orderliness of conversation as an activity in its own right' (2005: 291). Like many other CA analysts, he also is very clear in arguing for the primacy and autonomy of conversational structure in analyses of CS. In this sense, CA analysis resembles a 'discovery procedure' based on the premise that not only is there order in conversation, but that within that order, the speaker's own interpretation behind his or her turn is revealed.

The Discourse-Specific Basis of Meaning

Emphasis on the fluid nature of meanings also characterizes recent work that is not specifically identified with CA approaches, but which often seems to be very much within the CA fold. For example, Stroud stresses that 'meaning itself is performatively constructed' (2004: 150). He also speaks out against accounts of CS 'that construe language as mimetic of social structure' or meaning that is 'permanently, authoritatively and systematically determined prior to the speech moment' (ibid.). However, Stroud also speaks of 'appropriating utterances and infusing them with new meanings ...' (ibid.: 150). This implies that some choices do have expected meanings.

Stroud is among analysts who view an analysis of conversational structure only complete if that analysis includes considerations of the prevailing societal and ideological structures in a community. In their writings, one sees a blending of how CS is interpreted: it becomes not just the CA analysts' presentation of a speaker's CS as an expression of a personal identity, but also of a personal political ideology. Thus, in writing about the conversation of market women in Mozambique he concludes that 'framed in the expression of disillusionment of the powers that be in Mozambique, Portuguese is reconstituted in the mouths of these women to carry meanings and contrast identities in direct opposition to those conventionally associated with the language of the elites' (ibid.: 154).

Summarizing the Differences

Five overlapping generalizations capture differences in the various approaches. I refer specifically to the MM model and CA analyses, but the same questions can be asked of any approach to CS. First, what is the mechanism that provides evidence for social messages? The MM views the unmarked–marked continuum as an important mechanism through which speakers can provide evidence of their intended inferences. The model's basic premise is that speakers fashion their utterances as they do (in terms of markedness) because they are aware that listeners will make inferences about their intended meanings. These inferences will be based not just on the semantic and syntactic nuts and bolts of the speaker's utterances, but also on the listeners' conceptual resources. These resources include memories about previous like interactions, but also about the speaker's identity and therefore his/her likely goals in regard to self-presentation and relationship with others present. In contrast, CA has a different focus regarding how social messages receive interpretations. Rather than depend on cognitively based pragmatic abilities for interpretations, CA looks for meanings in the dissected empirical evidence. Social messages are derived primarily from the utterances that speakers actually produce in a given conversational exchange and the nature of responses that other speakers produce. Thus, for CA, the basic premise is that because conversations are orderly, social messages will reveal themselves in the way that a discourse is organized. Still other researchers continue in the more traditional descriptive approach of early studies. They rely more exclusively on pointing out correlations between macro-features (i.e. the situation) or sociolinguistic profiles (i.e. a speaker's education, age, gender, etc.) and instances of CS.

A second, related point that divides not just CA and the MM, but much recent, unaligned work, is the use of word 'strategy'. What counts as a strategy? For many, including the MM, if CS is a *strategy*, it comes with the implication that CS carries messages of intentionality. In contrast, CA models downplay even unconscious planning in discourse and intentionality. Li (2002) stresses the 'emergence' of meaning in a conversation, not the speaker's *a priori* expectations about the meaning of a switch. He writes, 'Meaning emerges as a consequence of bilingual participants' contextualization work and thus is "brought about" by speakers through the very act of code-switching' (Li 2002: 167). That is, CA highlights the order it finds in how conversations are organized, not the cognitive activity behind conversational contributions. (For an overview of the sense in which CS is seen as strategic, see Woolard 2005.)

A third difference concerns the role of the speaker's creativity. For CA analysts, where a speaker places a switch is an act of creativity because the switch's meaning depends on how it is sequentially located in the discourse. For MM analysts, creativity is making cognitive calculations and deciding (unconsciously) whether making the unmarked (expected) choice or a marked choices will give speakers the best 'return' in a specific interaction type.

A fourth difference among models is their answer to this question: What role does a variety's social meaning in the wider societal context have in motivating a speaker to make a specific switch? As just noted, all approaches agree that speakers can be creative in some sense, but not all agree with the MM that speakers are operating with awareness of the social consequences of choices. Thus, the MM links a speaker's choices to what the speaker 'knows' about macro-level associations of the varieties *outside the interaction at hand but in the relevant community*. In contrast, CA approaches argue the motivation for choices *lies within the interaction in which the choice occurs*. Showing skepticism about the MM's notion that CS is an index of the speaker's motivations that take account of macro-factors in the community, Auer poses these questions: 'what kind of identity predicates (membership categories) can the alternating use of two languages be an index *of* in conversation? And second, how, exactly can such an index be shown to be interpretively relevant?' (2005: 404).

A fifth difference is how the models arrive at their analyses. A shortcoming of all approaches is that the analyst makes interpretations about the social meaning of speakers' CS choices that are more or less subjective. CA analysts would say 'no' to this statement; they claim that they are only offering the speaker's own interpretation, which is revealed through the switch and its placement in the conversation. Adherents of the MM would say 'yes, admittedly, cognitive calculations are not available for inspection, but claims about our analyses are based on the empirically verifiable associations that the speaker's community makes between speaking one variety rather than another in a given context.'

Evaluation of the MM and CA

In an overview of approaches to socially oriented models of CS, Woolard (2005) sees the MM as circular in regard to its use of the notion of 'unmarked choices'. She compares the MM model's notion of markedness to that in Greenberg (1966) where the 'cause' of a linguistic element's frequency is an 'effect' of its linguistic form (i.e. unmarked forms turn out to be more frequent). The difference is that what defines an unmarked choice as unmarked under the MM is not its linguistic form, but its frequency. Woolard correctly sees that this 'leaves markedness itself no autonomous status' (ibid.: 80). But this does not make the model circular. When speakers frequently choose a variety, they are, in effect, recognizing it already has a status as frequently chosen. Also, when individuals select the unmarked choice, this is a separate phenomenon from the group statistic that caused it to be labeled the unmarked choice.

The MM also receives criticism from Coulmas (2005: 122). He sees the MM as making a static link between linguistic varieties in a community's repertoires and specific associations – although the MM wasn't intended to make the 'neat correlation of varieties and types of relationships' that he attributes to it. What the model's markedness framework does is offer an evaluation procedure. Speakers and listeners base their evaluations of potential and actual choices on various types of information, including correlations that they see existing. But the model itself only offers the means to make correlations. Coulmas does recognize the intended significance of the MM's notion of marked choices as 'the speaker's strategic use of a new code'. Still, he argues for a more locally based analysis, similar to that in CA-oriented approaches, that somehow might supply 'a universally applicable answer to the question of why a speaker may choose not to conform to societal norms' (ibid.).

While also recognizing the value of a locally based approach in which the discourse contextualizes, Coupland and Jaworski argue that 'social interaction *is*, as well as contextualizing, *contextualized* [italics added] by prior expectations and assumptions, which must be carried cognitively, as Gumperz, Hanks, Silverstein and others have argued by their appeals to concepts like conversational "framing", "inferencing" and indeed "social meaning" itself' (2004: 26).

In his recent study of discourse analysis, Blommaert (2005) finds two problems with CA approaches. First, Blommaert discusses CA analysts' often-stated claim that CA analysis is free of the biases of the analyst, relying only on the text itself. He writes, 'This core methodological argument – the "naturalness" of data – is circular because the notional erasure of the analyst's voice depends on the analyst's observations of speakers' regularities in behavior. These regularities have been established by CA by means of analytically focused and empirically grounded claims, i.e. by using the analyst's voice' (Blommaert 2005: 54).

Second, Blommaert faults CA for its strong emphasis on the current interaction as the main relevant context. He comments that '... analysis should not start, so to speak, as soon as people open their mouths. It should have started long before that' (2005: 67). He also notes the need to link linguistic choices with the macro-social messages that they are embedded in. He writes that analysis 'must also be concerned with invisible, hegemonic, structural, and normalised power sedimented *in* language itself as an *object* of inequality and hegemony' (Blommaert 2005).

The Grammatical Structure of Code-switching

Most current efforts that consider the grammar of CS look at such structures exclusively, if they mention the social context at all. These studies attempt to answer the question, 'What are the constraints on switching languages within a sentence/clause?' They began in earnest in the 1980s although there were scattered efforts in the 70s. Current efforts can be divided into four groups: (1) studies emphasizing surface-level differences; (2) those that extend the dominant generative syntactic theory to code-switching; (3) those that link CS to a morphological theory and/or psycholinguistic models of language production. These are discussed in more detail below.

In addition, another group of researchers are beginning to emphasize CS as a force in contact-induced language change (e.g. Backus 2004; Winford 2003).

Most approaches today offer some quantitative evidence to back up individual examples and claims; to date, purely judgment-based approaches are an exemption, typically offering only single grammaticality judgments along with examples. For the sake of brevity, I call the language supplying the grammatical frame of the bilingual clause the Matrix Language (ML) and the other participating language the Embedded Language (EL). The three main approaches to CS mentioned above deal with what I call classic CS. Classic CS is defined as a bilingual clause with only one of the participating varieties as the source of the abstract structure of the morpho-syntactic frame.

Composite CS contrasts with classic CS in that both participating varieties supply some of the abstract structure of the frame. Even so, one language dominates in supplying structure and surface-level realizations. Studying composite CS represents a new frontier for researchers; Muysken (2000) and Clyne (2003) are the only main figures in the field who go beyond classic CS, although composite CS is attracting more interest.

Representative Grammatical Models of Code-switching

The central differences between the main grammatical models of CS are as follows:

(1) Poplack (1980) maintains that switching only occurs at points where the ML and the EL share equivalent syntactic structures; also, intra-word combinations of languages are prohibited. In line with this constraint, Poplack claims that most singly occurring elements from the EL, including those inflected with ML affixes or other system morphemes, are 'nonce borrowings'. I dispute this interpretation of the data, arguing that these singly occurring EL forms have the same distribution as EL phrases (e.g. *house* and *new houses*, cf. Myers-Scotton 2006: 257–260).

(2) The Matrix Language Frame (MLF) model claims that CS can best be explained by starting at an abstract level, differentiating the roles of participating languages and morpheme types (Myers-Scotton 1997, 2002a). It emphasizes asymmetry in both cases, claiming most crucially that only one of the participating languages supplies morpho-syntactic structure to the bilingual clause. That is, the EL does not frame any phrases containing ML morphemes; its role is limited to providing content morphemes in mixed constituents and EL islands. A newer, related model, the 4-M model of

morpheme classification, is not a model of CS, but it is relevant to constraints on CS because it ties in morpheme distribution in bilingual speech to a language production model, arguing that different types of morpheme are salient at different levels in production (Myers-Scotton 2005).

(3) MacSwan (e.g. 2005) and others who apply Chomsky's approaches to monolingual syntax to CS claim that there is no need to posit any grammatical operations beyond those that apply in syntactic models for analyzing monolingual data. Following Chomsky's Minimalist Program (1995), MacSwan argues that CS is possible and can be explained if certain features of all participating languages are checked for convergence (as defined by the MP) in the same way that monolingual features are checked. The implication is that this checking will indicate which language will always supply the grammatical frame in bilingual constituents. In contrast, Jake et al. (2002, 2005) argue that MacSwan's approach under-predicts what actually occurs in CS data. They argue selection of the ML is not based on its inherent features; *a priori*, either language could supply the grammatical frame in bilingual speech. In fact, it is in the selection of the ML that the social context assumes importance.

Recognizing Social Messages in Grammatical Structures

In many ways, it is problematic to consider these approaches under the rubric, Sociolinguistics. These researchers all recognize that CS takes place in a social context, but to varying degrees; they would argue that this context has little to do with the grammatical structure of CS. There are exceptions, such as Bentahila and Davies (1992), who look at CS patterns across generations, or Gardner-Chloros (Gardner-Chloros and Edwards 2004), who argue more explicitly that the social context or discourse structure and grammatical outcomes are linked.

Also, the MLF model of grammatical constraints often coincides with the MM model in an important way: The ML, a grammatical construct for the variety that supplies the morpho-syntactic frame of the bilingual clause, is often the variety that would be the expected unmarked choice for the interaction in which CS takes place. This may be the socially dominant language in the relevant community, but it is generally whatever receives a consensus as an appropriate choice for the given interaction. This may well be the speakers' L1, but it is not always.

The MLF model suggests that when the ML is designated at the conceptual (pre-linguistic) level, speakers who engage in CS take account of the societal roles of the languages. They also consider other participants' proficiencies in the available languages. This view implies that the speaker's intentions and assessments of social factors are important in determining the ML, not any cross-linguistic grammatical differences.

Interpreting Alternation between Languages in Code-switching

In Extract 5 from Xhosa-English CS, the speaker alternates between monolingual clauses in Xhosa and English, although throughout the entire discourse (not shown here), most of the clauses have a morpho-syntactic frame from Xhosa with some English elements. The speaker is an L1-speaker of Xhosa who also is very proficient in English. She is in her late thirties and has some post-secondary education. She works in a government office and lives in Soweto near Johannesburg (Myers-Scotton 2005). This example contains the first part of her response to the question (in Xhosa and from a Xhosa L1-speaker who was the interviewer), *E-bebula-wa yintoni utata?* 'What caused the death of your father?' The interviewee's first clause is in English, followed by two bilingual clause framed by Xhosa. Then she says '*there was no help*' entirely in English and finishes with a monolingual clause in Xhosa.

> **Extract 5**: (Source: Myers-Scotton 2005)
> i-**cancer, he had cancer of the lungs ...** i-**cancer** yamgulisa
> 'Cancer, he had cancer of the lungs ... cancer made him sick
> yamphatha kakubi se-yi-**spread**-ile emzimbeni
> it was really bad on him after spreading throughout his body ...'
> **There was no help.** Beyekho enyindlela bebengamphilisa ngayo.
> 'There was no help. There was no other way to keep him alive.'

An analysis under the MLF model concentrates on the divisions between Xhosa and English in supplying grammatical elements in the bilingual clauses. Clearly, Xhosa is the ML of these clauses because all grammatical elements come from Xhosa, not just those specified in the MLF model. For example, note how the English verb *spread* is inflected with a Xhosa aspectual prefix *se-* and a subject-verb AGR prefix *yi-* that agrees with *i-cancer*. It also has the perfective suffix *-ile*.

A socially oriented analysis of these clauses might note how English clauses carry the bad news while Xhosa is used to explain the details of the disease. Do the clauses in English, the non-L1 language and the language of socio-economic mobility and political power in South Africa, add a sense of finality and even credibility to the referential content? One can see how such an argument can explain alternations across the continuous discourse of even one person.

Conclusion

Code-switching (CS) is arguably the most widely researched topic in the field of language contact today. Ironically, it wasn't so long ago that CS was not even considered worthy of study. Since then, many researchers have suggested reasons why speakers engage in CS. This overview has devoted the most space to contrasting approaches to this study.

Some see importance in the sequential positioning of CS in a discourse as important in interpreting the motivations as well as the effects of CS. Others suggest that speakers perceive CS as a resource with pragmatic consequences; they engage in CS when they calculate that it offers a desirable outcome, given the context and the available choices. Other researchers who also study CS are more concerned with explaining the division of labor between the participating varieties regarding the grammatical structure of bilingual clauses. Again, approaches differ considerably. Whether CS is studied as a signal of socially relevant meanings or for its insights into the grammatical structure of bilingual speech, the vigor with which different researchers promote their views is evidence that CS will continue as a well-studied phenomenon.

REFERENCES

Auer, Peter. 1984. *Bilingual Conversation*. Amsterdam/Philadelphia: John Benjamins.

Auer, Peter. 2005. A postscript: Code-switching and social identity. *Journal of Pragmatics* 37: 403–410.

Backus, Ad. 2004. Converegence as a mechanism of language change. *Bilingualism, Language and Cognition* 7: 179–181.

Bakhtin, Mikhail M. 1986. *Speech Genres and Other Late Essays*. Edited by Caryl Emerson and Michael Holquist, translated by Vern W. McGee. Austin: University of Texas Press.

Bell, Allan. 1984. Style as audience design. *Language in Society* 13: 145–204.

Bell, Allan. 2001. Back in style: Reworking audience design. In Penelope Eckert and John Rickford (eds.) *Style and Sociolinguistic Variation*. Cambridge: Cambridge University Press. 139–169.

Bentahila, Abdelali and Eirlys Davies. 1992. Code-switching and language dominance. In Richard J. Harris (ed.) *Cognitive Processing in Bilinguals*. Amsterdam: Elsevier. 443–447.

Blom, Jan-Petter, and Gumperz, John. 1972. Social meaning in linguistic structures: Code-switching in Norway. In John Gumperz and Dell Hymes (eds.) *Directions in Sociolinguistics*. New York: Holt, Rinehart & Winston. 407–434.

Blommaert, Jan. 2005. *Discourse: A Critical Introduction*. Cambridge: Cambridge University Press.

Bourhis, Richard Y., Howard Giles, Jacques Leyens and Henri Tajfel. 1979. Psycholinguistic distinctiveness: Language divergence in Belgium. In Howard Giles and Robert St. Clair (eds.) *Language and Psychology*. Oxford: Blackwell. 158–185.

Chomsky, Noam. 1995. *The Minimalist Program*. Cambridge, Massachusetts: MIT Press.

Clyne, Michael. 2003. *Dynamics of Language Contact*. Cambridge: Cambridge University Press.

Coulmas, Florian. 2005. *Sociolinguistics: The Study of Speakers' Choices*. Cambridge: Cambridge University Press.

Coupland, Nikolas. 2001. Language, situation, and the relational self: Theorizing dialect-style in sociolinguistics. In Penelope Eckert and John Rickford (eds.) *Style and Sociolinguistic Variation*. Cambridge: Cambridge University Press. 185–210.

Coupland, Nikolas and Adam Jaworski. 2004. Sociolinguistic perspectives on metalanguage: Reflexivity, evaluation and ideology. In Adam Jaworski, Nikolas Coupland and Dariusz Galasiński (eds) *Metalanguage: Social and Ideological Perspectives*. Berlin: Mouton de Gruyter. 15–51.

Denison, Norman. 1971. Some observations on language variety and plurilingualism. In Edwin Ardener (ed.) *Social Anthropology and Language*. London: Tavistock. 157–185

Gafaranga, Joseph. 2005. Demythologising language alternational studies: Conversational structure vs. social structure in bilingual interaction. *Journal of Pragmatics* 37: 281–300.

Gardner-Chloros, Penelope and Malcolm Edwards. 2004. When the blueprint is a red herring: assumptions behind grammatical approaches to code-switching. *Transactions of the Philological Society*. 102: 103–129.

Goffman, Erving. 1981. Footing. In *Forms of Talk*. Philadelphia, Pennsylvania: University of Pennsylvania Press. 124–159.

Greenberg, Joseph H. 1966. Some universals of grammar with particular reference to the order of meaningful elements. In J. H. Greenberg (ed.) *Universals of Language*. Cambridge, MA. and London: MIT Press. 73–113.

Gumperz, John J. 1982. *Discourse Strategies*. Cambridge: Cambridge University Press.

Halmari, Helena. 1997. *Government and Codeswitching: Explaining American Finnish*. Amsterdam/Philadelphia: John Benjamins.

Jake, Janice, Carol Myers-Scotton and Steven Gross. 2002. Making a minimalist approach to codeswitching work: Adding the Matrix Language. *Bilingualism, Language and Cognition* 5: 69–91.

Jake, Janice, Carol Myers-Scotton and Steven Gross. 2005. A response to MacSwan (2005): Keeping the Matrix Language. *Bilingualism, Language and Cognition* 8: 1–6.

Li, Wei. 2002. 'What do you want me to say?' On the conversational analysis approach to bilingual interaction. *Language in Society* 31: 159–180.

MacSwan, Jeff. 2005. Codeswitching and generative grammar: A critique of the MLF model and some remarks on 'modified minimalism'. *Bilingualism, Language and Cognition* 8: 1–22.

Muysken, Pieter. 2000. *Bilingual Speech: A Typology of Code Mixing*. Cambridge: Cambridge University Press.

Myers-Scotton, Carol. 1997. *Duelling Languages, Grammatical Structure in Codeswitching*. 2nd edition. Oxford: Oxford University Press.

Myers-Scotton, Carol. 2002a. *Contact Linguistics: Bilingual Encounters and Grammatical Outcomes*. Oxford: Oxford University Press.

Myers-Scotton, Carol. 2002b. Frequency and intention in (un)marked choices in code-switching. *International Journal of Bilingualism* 6: 205–219.

Myers-Scotton, Carol. 2005. Xhosa-English codeswitching corpus. Unpublished.

Myers-Scotton, Carol. 2006. *Multiple Voices: An Introduction to Bilingualism*. Oxford: Blackwell Publishing.

Myers-Scotton, Carol and Agnes Bolonyai. 2001. Calculating speakers: Codeswitching in a Rational Choice Model. *Language in Society* 30: 1–28.

Poplack, Shana. 1980. 'Sometimes I'll start a sentence in Spanish y termino en español: Toward a typology of code-switching. *Linguistics* 18: 581–618.

Rampton, Ben. 1995. *Crossing: Language and Ethnicity among Adolescents*. London: Longman.

Stroud, Christopher. 2004. The performativity of codeswitching. *International Journal of Bilingualism* 8: 145–166.

Weinreich, Uriel. 1967. *Languages in Contact*. The Hague: Mouton. [Originally published in 1953, *Publications of the Linguistic Circle of New York*, 1.]

Winford, Donald. 2003. *An Introduction to Contact Linguistics*. Cambridge: Cambridge University Press.

Woolard, Kathryn. 2005. Codeswitching. In Alessandro Duranti (ed.) *A Companion to Linguistic Anthropology*. Blackwell Publishing: 73–94.

CHAPTER 34

Bilingual Conversation

Peter Auer

Bilingualism and Conversation Analysis

For a long time, the analysis of conversational code-switching has been restricted to enumerating the types of functions the juxtaposition of two languages can achieve in discourse. This seems inadequate for a number of reasons. To begin with, it is a futile endeavour to give a closed classificational scheme for code-switching, since an indeterminate number of interpretations can be arrived at. What exactly a bilingual participant is doing when he or she switches languages is closely tied to the specific, never-identical circumstances in which this switching occurs. To be sure, there are interpretations that recur, and it can be instructive to know about these most frequent functions of language switching in discourse. Even so, participants do not just choose one type from some fixed set of alternatives. This brings us to the second point against a classificational approach to code-switching. If the number of types of language alternation is not finite, then *how* do participants agree on one interpretation or the other *in loco*? It is this question which seems to be of primary importance, and it is one left unanswered by all classificational systems.

I suggest that the classification of code-switching types must be subordinated to the analysis of the *procedures* used by participants to arrive at it. The procedural interest is one in *members'* methods. Its starting point is the embeddedness of code-switching in the sequential organization of interaction. The seemingly trivial fact that language choice (whatever the linguistic activity on which it occurs) is preceded and followed by the choice of the same or other language will turn out to be one of the cornerstones of the explanation of the meaning of conversational code-switching. We will see that under close scrutiny, the details of the sequential embeddedness of language choice and language alternation permit us to formulate the coherent procedural model we are looking for.

490

It is necessary to turn to some definitional issues at this point. First, there is the question of *defining bilingualism*. Linguists have generated an extensive literature in their inconclusive discussion of exactly how competent someone has to be to be 'bilingual'. Dozens of attempts have been made to come to a definition, ranging from minimal ('use of two languages') to maximal ones ('native-like control of two languages'). The impasse can only be overcome if bilingualism is no longer regarded as 'something inside speakers' heads, that is, a mental ability, but as a displayed feature of participants' everyday linguistic behaviour. Bilingualism must be looked upon primarily as a set of complex linguistic activities, and only in a 'derived' sense as a cognitive ability. Consequently there is no one definition of bilingualism: bilingualism becomes an interactionally constructed predicate.

A second issue concerns the definition of the term *code-switching*. I will use the term for all instances of *locally functional use of two languages in an interactional episode*. Code-switching may occur between two turns, or turn-internally; it may be restricted to a well-defined unit or change the whole language of interaction; it may occur within a clause (although this is the rare case), or between clauses. The distinction between functional and (locally) non-functional language alternation is important for setting off code-switching against 'code-mixing'. In the latter case, the frequent variation between the two 'codes' has become a 'mode of interaction' in its own right, that is, a new code with 'rules' and regularities of its own (see also Myers-Scotton this volume, Chapter 33).

Two Basic Procedures for the Production and Interpretation of Code-Switching

Two basic pairs of procedures will be introduced here; they provide the 'underlying' procedural apparatus for arriving at local interpretations of code-switching in their context. These are the pairs *insertional* versus *alternational code-switching* and *participant* versus *discourse-related* code-switching. From a hearer's point of view, we can reformulate them in the form of the following problems for which the speaker must provide hints to solutions:

1. Is the switch in question tied to a particular linguistic structure (for instance, a word, a sentence, or a larger unit: insertional switching), or is it tied to a particular point in conversation (alternational code-switching)?
2. Is the code-switching in question providing cues for the organization of the ongoing interaction (that is, is it discourse-related), or about attributes of the speaker (participant-related)?

In what follows, these procedures will be discussed in more detail on the basis of some data extracts taken from an investigation of bilingual conversations among bilingual children and adolescents of an Italian family background, living in a small town in Southern Germany.

Discourse- versus Participant-Related Code-Switching

The first extract is taken from a conversation over lunch between Daniela, a 14-year-old girl, her younger sister Fiorella (who does not take part in the following exchange) and two young bilingual women, one of Italian and the other of German background (Angela and Beate). The data (as all the subsequent ones) were recorded in the early eighties of the last century in a small southwest German town with a large proportion of immigrants from Italy. Daniela and Fiorella have an Italian family background and were born and/or brought up in Germany (German in capital letters, Italian or Italian dialect otherwise).

Extract 1: Daniela (D) is talking about the drinking habits of her sister Fiorella.

01	D:	perché lei è- riempë il bicchiere no, =
		because she is- fills her glass you know
02		quando mangia: (–)
		when she eats
03	B:	°°mhm,°°=
04	D:	=e poi lo lascia sta:re;
		and the she leaves it
05	A:	mm,
06		(0.5)
07	D:	[poi devo: be- (–) eh=bevo io e mi madre
		then I have to dr- (–) I drink it and my mother
08	?:	[°° (..............)°°
09	D:	io non (ne) voglio; (–) °quindi si butta°,
		I don't want it so it's thrown away
10	A:	Mm
11		(2.0)
→ 12	D:	DIE NUDELN SCHMECKEN BESSER,
		the noodles taste better
13		(1.0)
14		ALS ALLES
		than anything

(Conversation continues in German about the meal.)

Extract 2: Beginning of an interactive episode; adult Manuele (M) approaches Francesca (F) and her younger cousin Luca (L).

	01	M:	che bella giornata oggi=eh?
			what a nice day it is isn't it?
	02	F:	°mm:,°
	03	M:	cosa facciamo oggi? (–) restiamo dentro;
			what shall we do today shall we stay inside
	04		facciamo qualche [gioco (dien)? (–) n [o;
			shall we play a game (inside) *no*
	05	L:	[NÖ=Ä [Ä::
			no uhm uhm
	06	M:	eh?
	07	L:	°uno° (– –)
			one
	08	M:	cosa vuoi fare LUKAS;
			what do you want to do Lukas
→	09	F:	°AUSGEHE°
			go out
	10	L:	IN DE WALD,
			into the forest
	11	M:	JA?
			Really
	12	L:	ÄÄH (–) IN DER WALD,
			uhm into the forest
	13	F:	°LANGWEILIG°
			boring
	14	L:	(WO DE:NN)
			Where
	15		(1.5)
	16		e::m:
	17		(0.5)
	18		IN.N PA:RK
			to the park
	19		(1.0)
	20	F:	<<più f>AM LIEBSCHTE SCHWIMME;> (–)
			(I love best) to go swimming
	21	L & F:	((laughter))
→	22	M→F:	vuoi andare a nuotare
			you want to go swimming

	23		(1.0)

→ 24   L→F: DANN GEH DOCH IN DE BODESEE

        then why don't you go into Lake Constance

25   M: h e h e h e h e h i h i

26   F →   WENN MORGE NO SCHÖNS WETTER ISCH=(DARF I MAMA)

     M: *if we still have fine weather tomorrow (I can sometimes*

         SCHIM.M IM JAKOB)

        go swimming in the Jacob (pool))

27   (0.5)

28   L: AH SCHÖN WÄR DES GU:T

        great that would be fine

→ 29   M: <<f>sapete nuotare voi due> (– –)

        do you two know how to swim?

▶ 30   F: <<lento> [↑lu:i ↓no ↑lu:i ↓no:> <<acc> ↑lui ↓no >

        he doesn't he doesn't he doesn't

→ 31   L: [DOCH (–) ICH (HABS NICHT)

                    yes   I   (haven't)

→ 32   M: tu [no?

        you don't?

33   F: [no! non vuol fa:r mala figu:ra

        no he   doesn't want to give a bad impression

34   pirciò dice se:mbre si:=

        therefore he always says yes

35   M: = ↑ah:::[:

▶ 36   L: [perché: (io va::i: in) ië no(n); (–)

        because (I go to)   I don't

37   (kon) volevo emparra:re voglio

        want(ed) to learn it

38   M: bravo Lukas (–) perché non vuoi imparare

        good Lukas why   don't you want to learn it

39   L: perché voglio: (– –) porché non voggio.

        because I want   because I don't want to

40   M: he he he he he 'h 'h

41   F: io si

        I do

The extract begins in the middle of topic 'having lunch at Daniela's home'. In lines 01–02, Daniela explains to Angela and Beate why her mother does not like her younger sister Fiorella to have wine with the meals: it always gets thrown away, for Fiorella does not empty her glass. The point in the sequential development of that interaction which we will focus on is reached in line 12. Here, Daniela proposes to change the *footing* of the conversation (Goffman 1979) at that moment: a 'change of gears' (2) and a 'change in our frame for events' (5) which, as Goffman points out, is often accompanied and achieved by a change of code. More precisely, in our case, the speaker proposes a new conversational topic, in talking no longer about Fiorella and her drinking habits, but about the lunch she and Angela and Beate are having together. She returns from displaced speech into deictic speech, embedded into the situation at hand. At the same time, she switches from Italian into German.

What is the relationship between code-switching from Italian into German, and the new footing? One way of conceptualizing this relationship would be to see code-switching as a *consequence* of the change of topic. According to such a view, switching is *caused* by a change of topic. If we were to conceptualize code-switching in such a way, we would deny its functionality; being caused by the new footing, it could hardly be said to have any meaning for the development of the conversation. However, in most speech communities, there is no one-to-one relationship between language choice and utterance type. In order to come to a more satisfactory conceptualization of the relationship between code-switching and the new footing in a case such as the one documented in the data extract, it is useful to invoke Gumperz' notion of *contextualization* (cf. Gumperz 1982, this volume, Chapter 40). Gumperz' basic idea is that conversationalists need to provide their hearers not only with propositional content in order to communicate what they want to say, they also have to provide a context in which these propositions can be embedded and in which they become interpretable. Contextualization refers to participants' joint efforts to establish and make relevant such contexts. Thus, the notion of contextualization goes a considerable step beyond the commonplace linguistic formula that interpretations of utterances 'depend' on their context. It brings into focus the fact that such a context is not something given and available in itself, but has to be created and maintained by participants in addition to what they say (in the restricted, referential sense).

Apart from code selection and switching, contextualization strategies rely on prosodic cues (intonation, rhythm, accent, etc.), gestural and kinesic cues, eye contact, etc. Code-switching is one way of contextualizing verbal activities, that is, of informing co-participants about the ever-relevant question 'what are we doing now?' – even though its contribution to answering it may be restricted to the information 'something different than before'. Whenever a feature of the discourse is changed in such a way, I will speak of discourse-related code-switching.

Consider in this context Extract 3, taken from the same conversation as Extract 1:

Extract 3

01	D:	e tere:sa (–) è scesa: giù. (–) allo:ra si ë- (–)
		and Teresa came down so if
02		fin=alle: (–) il=una meno un quarto: abbiamo
		until quarter to one we
03		parla:to cossì=no (–) fa (mori: d- dë-) uh
		talked like that make (... ... ...) uhm
04	A:	mm
05		(dello di) barzelle:tt, (–)
		(of the) jokes
→ 06		<<f> KENNSCH DU WITZLE?>
		do you know jokes?
07	B:	<<mp> poche>
		few

Participants are the same as above. Again, Daniela proposes a new activity, that is, the telling of jokes (line 06). Again, this proposal is accompanied and signalled by code-switching into German. As in Extract 1, Daniela not only invites Beate to engage in a different activity/topic, she also invites her to switch into German for the following stretch of conversation. However, whereas in Extract 1 both the new topic and the new language were accepted, Beate declines Daniela's invitation to change the language of interaction in Extract 3. In addition, the new topic/activity is only responded to in a very 'unenthusiastic' fashion (cf. the low amplitude of Beate's response in contrast to Daniela's *forte* proposal, and the scaling down on the lexical level – 'few' as opposed to 'oh yes a lot' or something similar). Beate's non-cooperation at the level of language choice parallels her non-enthusiastic cooperation at the topical/activity type level: again, the former is used to signal the latter. Again, this provides evidence for our claim that code-switching is employed as a contextualization strategy to initiate new footings, while a causal interpretation of code-switching as a consequence of topic change fails to explain its meaning.

Turning to Extract 2 now, a different member's procedure for making the juxtaposition of two languages can be observed. Manuele, an adult bilingual

Italian, has met Luca aged nine, and his cousin Francesca aged 12 in the *Centro Italiano* of the town. The three start to plan the afternoon. Francesca wants to go swimming, so Manuele inquires if the two children know how to swim at all. The girl does, but Luca does not and has to defend himself against his cousin's teasing.

In this extract, code-switching is quite frequent (cf. the arrowed lines); however, it does not appear to coincide with frequent changes of footing. The contributions 'marked' by new language are conversationally 'unmarked'. Another difference is that code-switching is not done by one speaker in his or her contribution, but between turns, and that this inter-turn switching is due to participants' consistent use of one language (Italian for Manuele, German for Francesca and Luca). Thus, on a turn-by-turn basis, we can speak of code-switching, but from the perspective of the individual speaker, there is no switching at all. Such a sequence I call a *language negotiation sequence*. It begins with a disagreement between two or more parties about which language to use for interaction, and ends as soon as one of them 'gives in' to the other's preferred language (if that happens at all).

At a closer look, the extract turns out to be composed of two of such language negotiation sequences. Manuele's initial question (01, *che bella giornata oggi=eh?* 'what a nice day it is isn't it?') and his following questions about what should be done that afternoon (03–04) only receive minimal responses which mostly cannot be attributed to either language. The first fully-fledged utterance of one of the children is produced in line 08, when Manuele addresses Luca directly (using the German form of his name, *Lukas*). In his place, his cousin makes a proposal in German to 'go out' (*ausgehe*), which is collaboratively completed/supplemented by Luca's *in de Wald* ('into the forest'). Manuele's German surprise marker *ja?* terminates this first language negotiation sequence in favour of the children's preference. After some German turns by Luca and Francesca, Manuele returns into Italian in line 22 by reformulating Francesca's proposal to 'go swimming' (*am liebschte schwimme*). This reformulation starts a second language negotiation sequence. However, Francesca does not respond; instead, she turns to her cousin (line 24), and only in line 30 back to Manuele, in both cases using German. M insists on Italian in his next question (line 29, *sapete nuotare voi due* 'do you two know how to swim?'). At this point, the two children, who have both displayed a preference for German, split. Francesca switches into Italian and terminates the language negotiation between herself and Manuele in favour of Italian; whereas Luca remains with German until line 39 when he, too, 'surrenders' to the other two participants' language choice.

Switching in the arrowed lines of this transcript does not contextualize new activities, topics, etc. Also, it does not contrast something that has been done before with something that will be done now; on the contrary, different language choice by the participants establishes some sort of coherence – not between adjacent turns, but between same-speaker turns (or, to be more precise, between Manuele's turns on the one hand, and Francesca's and Luca's turns on the other). In Sacks' terms, code-switching 'skip-connects' utterances and thereby provides a particular type of 'tying' (Sacks, 1992). As to the interactional function or meaning of such a case of code-switching, the object of signalling processes is a different one than in Extract 1. Whereas in the case of discourse-related switching a new footing is marked by language choice, switching of the second type signals a speaker's preference for one language over the other. In the first place, it tells co-participants something about the code-switching party and his or her linguistic preferences. Here, the term *participant*-related language alternation will be used.

Preference for one language over the other as displayed by a co-participant in such a way may be of the relatively stable, individualistic kind. However, it may also be bounded to and hint at characteristics of the episode, that is, a speaker may demonstrate that he or she finds it appropriate to use a given language in the present context (for instance, in the present constellation of participants, for interaction in the presently relevant institutional context for the kind of interaction to be carried out, etc.). Such a more restricted interpretation of participant-related code-switching invokes or alludes to larger scale 'norms' for the uses of the two languages of the bilingual community. Different speech communities diverge in their developing of such 'norms', in their generality and in the strictness in which they require them to be followed.

Line 30 (Francesca's *lui no lui no* 'he doesn't he doesn't') needs some further commenting. Here, intuitively, the interaction seems to have reached a turning point. As noted above, Francesca for the first time uses Italian and gives up her language preference in favour of Manuele's preference for Italian. There is something more substantial and less formal at stake though. We have to see Francesca's factual answer to Manuele's question *sapete nuotare voi due* 'do you two know how to swim?' as a selection out of a set of at least two possibilities. Let us suppose that the 'facts' require a different answer for Francesca and for Luca. Then the girl can at least choose between answer *io si* 'I do', with an implicature 'but he doesn't', and *lui no* 'he doesn't' with an implicature 'but I do'. In terms of truth values, both answers are equivalent. In terms of how language works in and for communication, they are not. To see why this is so, one must take into account that competences of almost all kinds are evaluated positively in the cultures in question; this is demonstrated, among other things, by the preferred character of (other-)ascriptions of competence over (other-)ascriptions of incompetence. Accordingly, the set of alternatives available to Francesca in formulating her answer contains a preferred, 'politer' version avoiding an explicit other-ascription of incompetence (*io sì*) and a dispreferred, 'ruder' one exposing the other's incompetence (*lui no*). In addition to choosing the 'ruder' alternative, the girl employs prosodic means to mark *lui no* and its repetition as a *teasing*, such as slow delivery and syllable-by-syllable switching between a high and a low pitch level. That Francesca's turn is hearable as a teasing is also confirmed by Luca's responses: he first attempts to contradict her (line 31), but when Francesca reveals this move as a strategic lie (lines 33–34), he tries to justify himself and find a reason why he cannot swim (*perché non voglio* 'because I don't want to').

If it is correct that there is an antagonism developing in these lines between Luca and Francesca, this throws a new light and the girl's switching into Manuele's preferred language: by 'surrendering' in the language negotiation sequence with the adult, Francesca changes her allegiance. Instead of insisting together with Luca on German, she symbolically takes Manuele's side and 'isolates' the boy. As this is done together with exposing his incompetence, Luca is 'under attack' both on the level of the activity and on the level of language choice. So language choice is discourse-related, or 'strategic', in this extract. However, it is not code-switching (on the turn-by-turn basis) which is functional – for this phenomenon, as we have seen, is to be interpreted as signalling participants' preferences – but the *termination of a language negotiation sequence* by one of the opponents' having given in to the other. Francesca uses it to symbolically 'switch sides'.

One further step has to be made in this reconstructive analysis of participant-related code-switching as a basic way of using language alternation. In order to understand a sequence as a 'language negotiation', or in terms of 'diverging language preferences', we (and participants) start from the assumption that there is a *preference for same language talk*. Only on the basis of such an expectation does it make sense to speak of a tension between participants using different languages, one which is resolved by one participant giving up his or her preference. As analysts, our evidence for participants' orientation to such a preference (as opposed to, say, everyone-use-whatever-s/he-wants preference) is, in addition to the regular occurrence of sequences of the type

$$A_i, B_g, A_i, B_g, \ldots // A_i, B_i, A_i, B_i, \ldots \text{ or}$$
$$// A_g, B_g, A_g, B_g, \ldots$$

(where A and B are participants, and *i* and *g* languages), the way in which the transition between the dispreferred and the preferred pattern of language use ('//' in the above formula) can become functional for answering the question 'what is going on?'. B's non-acceptance of Daniela's new language choice *and* of her proposal for further conversational activities in Extract 2 is also telling here. For according to the preference for same language talk, the other parties' accepting of the code-switching party's language choice is 'unmarked'. Doing what is 'marked', and employing it for some purpose, underlines the oriented-to status of the postulated preference for same language talk. Obviously, the preference for same language talk is nothing like a universal.

Discourse- and participant-related code-switching can be seen as methods to come to grips with two general types of conversational tasks. One of them concerns the organization of conversation, that is, turn-taking, topical cohesion, tying, sequencing of activities, repair, overall organization, etc. In addition to whatever means there are available to monolingual conversationalists to carry out these tasks, bilinguals can make use of the two or more languages in their linguistic repertoire by employing language alternation as a contextualization strategy. This is what has been called discourse-related code-switching here. A second type of task concerns finding/negotiating the proper language for the interaction, that is (in the ideal case), one that is situationally adequate, that accommodates all parties' competence and preferences, etc. It also includes finding out whether the other has more than one variety at his or her disposal at all. All instances of language switching serving this second type of task have been called participant-related.

Insertion versus Alternation

The second basic procedural distinction, that is, that between alternation and insertion, crosscuts the one already introduced. Up to now, only examples of alternational code-switching have been considered. In order to illustrate insertion, compare Extract 1 with the following two instances taken from a conversation between Manuele and four adolescent boys (Clemente, Alfredo, Camillo and Alberto), all with an immigrant background and living in Germany:

Extract 4: Clemente (CL) and Alfredo (AL) are complaining about two older people living in the same house.

```
01   M:   perché non lavorano però eh stanno tutto [il giorno a casa
          because they don't work so they stay at home all through the day
02   AL:                                           [che è vecchië e già
          penzionann nun hannë figlië; =
          he is old and retired already they don't have children
05   M:   =he [ ::
```

```
06   CL:      [NA ABER NICHT DER MANN; (–) [DER MANN SCHAFFT NO;
              no but not the husband      the husband still goes to work
07   AL:                                  [u mo u mo
                                          the husband the husband
08           u MANN  è:: chiste:  chiù SCH (–) chiù SCHLIMM angora;
             the husband is this one (is) more w  even worse
09           (1.0)
10           na vo:t (.) ((follows story))
             once
11   M:      °°mhm°°
```

Extract 5: Narrative about a television film about a dog.

```
01   M:      ma ma era era in guerra era
             but but this was this was during the war it was
02   CM:     no, allorë (–) lui era (–) ahm (–) DRESSIERT, (–)
             no well      he was            trained
03           °come si dice°
             how do you say
04   M:      hm, (–) si si si si.
                  yes yes yes yes
```

Looking at the German items *dressiert* 'trained' and *Mann* 'husband' or 'man' in these extracts, the following differences are readily observed: (a) in Extract 1, a whole sentence is produced in German by the code-switching speaker, but only single lexemes are in Extracts 4 and 5; (b) after the present speaker's language alternation, talk in the switched-to language follows in Extract 1, whereas the speaker resumes talk in Italian in Extracts 4 and 5; (c) there are functional differences: in particular, the insertion of *dressiert* seems to correspond to a speaker's difficulties to 'find the right word' in Italian, and *Mann* ties back anaphorically to the first mention of the word in line 06 by another participant, that is, it establishes topical cohesion between two adjacent turns. More generally, I call code-switching at a certain point in the conversation without a structurally determined (and therefore predictable) return into the first language *alternational* code-switching; any code-switching on a certain structural unit with a structurally provided point of return into the first language coinciding with that unit's completion I call an *insertion*.

Polyvalent Local Meanings

The local application of the two dichotomously organized procedural distinctions leads to those local meanings of language alternation that are maximally 'distant' from each other and therefore represent 'clearest' and 'most obvious' cases. However, only a part of the data of our (and presumably of any other) corpus on language alternation can be accounted for by using these prototypes. At least some instances will be polyvalent in the sense of showing characteristics of more than one prototype, or in the sense of showing only some features of the 'nearest' prototype.

It must not be seen as a weakness of our procedural model, but as its natural outcome that the four prototypes do not exhaustively classify the data. Bilingual participants are equipped with the distinctions alternational versus insertional and participant versus discourse-related code-switching. They are means to arrive at local interpretations of code-switching; however, they do not determine them.

Between Participant- and Discourse-Related Switching

I will start out with analyses of a case of polyvalence in which features both of discourse and of participant-related code-switching are present. In the first case, it is the renewed insisting of a party on his or her individualistic language preference in a certain environment which gives code-switching a discourse-related meaning.

In the following extracts, Daniela switches to German for a very short passage (a *jaja* in Extract 6, an *ah so* in Extract 7), which, however, clearly deviates from the established language of interaction (Italian). According to the types of code-switching that have been discussed so far, they are difficult to analyse. On the one hand, they do not seem to build up a contrast between something that has been said before and something that is going to be said now; on the other hand, they are quite ineffective at the level of renegotiating the language of interaction, and the *loci* in which the switching occurs is surely 'critical' for the interaction.

Extract 6: Daniela is telling a joke about Tarzan and Jane to Angela and Beate.

01	D:	allora: c=era questo: m- staváne passeggiando:
		well there was this m they were having a walk
02		no (–) era u[n (– –)
		you know it was a
03	A:	[un tarz[an
		a Tarz an

04	D:	[un giorno caldo (–)

a warm day

05		(1.5)
06		e dice Jane a Tarzan (–) Tarzan (– – –)

and Jane says to Tarzan Tarzan

| 07 | | no Jane (–) Jane dice a Tarzan si (–) dice Tarzan |

no Jane Jane says to Tarzan yes she says (to) Tarzan

| 08 | | a me mi fa: (–) fa caldo (–) me dë (–) be:- (–) e |

I am I'm warm I (ha) (ok) so

| 09 | | spogliati no (– –) |

take off something

| 10 | A: | hi hi hi hi nella foresta |

in the forest

| 11 | D: | e: (–) e soltano: quello di sopra lei no (–) |

(yes) (she has) only this thing on top you know

| 12 | | e a detto ma che fa (–) quelli che co:sa (...............) (–) |

and he said but what do you do what are these (.......)

| 13 | | sono le (–) mie: due lu:ci no, (–) |

they are the my two lanterns you know,

14	A:	ah.
15	D:	e[:
16	A:	[le mammelle

the breasts

→	17	D:	eh hi hi ['h JAJA 'h 'h 'h 'h ['h°

yesyes

18	B:	[°↑ hnhn hn hn hi [hi hi°
19	A:	[ehn
20	D:	allo:ra ((Daniela continues to tell the joke))

so

Extract 7: Daniela and Angela discuss the idea of having a boyfriend.

01	D:	[tu non ce l=hai il fidanza:to;

you haven't got a boyfriend

02	A:	[((singing, pp))
03		<<very short and dry, pp> no>

No

04	D:	peccatë hn?

that's a pity isn't it?

05		(1.0)

06	A:	°(perché (–) è un peccato?)°
		(why is it a pity)
07		(1.0)
08	D:	<<mf>non lo non lo ne vuoi>
		you you don't want one?
09	A:	ʹmʹm ((negation))
10		(2.0)
11	D:	<<presto> perché>
		why
12	A:	perché gli uomini mi hanno rotto le scatole,
		because men get on my nerves
13		(0.5)
→	14	D:	AH SO:: ʹhe he
		I see
15	A:	<<p>tutti uguali,> (– –) <<mp>tu lo vuoi?>
		all the same you want one?
16	D:	no; ʹh
		no
01	A:	perché
		why
02	D:	he he h ha ha ʹh ((ʹembarrassedʹ))

What is going on here? In Extract 6, Daniela is just about to tell a joke to the two young women Angela and Beate with whom she is interacting. Soon, it turns into a 'dirty' joke. How its 'dirty' character is being established by co-participants is highly relevant to the analysis of Daniela's switching into German in line 17. The use of obscene words is obviously not responsible; for as in many jokes of this type, there are no 'obscene' words to be found in it. There must be other reasons then for which we can see the joke turning into a dirty one.

After the general setting has been given (Tarzan and Jane are on a walk through the jungle), the central part of the joke starts with the reconstruction of an interaction between the two story characters. Extract 6 documents the first step in a three-step sequence in which Jane introduces 'innocent' code names for sexual organs. Jane takes off her blouse and explains to Tarzan (the strong but naïve lover) what her breasts are: *le mie due luci* 'my two lanterns'. Further steps in the coding sequence will introduce 'jungle' for vagina and 'serpent' for penis. The punch line which is prepared in this way is: *dice Tarzan (–) Jane Jane,(–) accendi le tue luci il mio serpente s=è fa eh/(—) s=è perso nella tua giungl nella tua bo:sco* 'so Tarzan says – Jane, Jane, – light your lanterns my my serpent has go/ – is lost in your jungle: in your wood'. Thus, obscene words are avoided by the teller in her joke. Yet, the very fact that innocent code names are introduced instead of available obscene terms orients to the taboo that forbids the use of the first.

After Daniela has performed the first step in the coding sequence, Angela provides feedback; using the sequential format of a transformation, she introduces a direct (although non-obscene) referential item: *le mammelle* 'the breasts'. By re-transforming the coded expression into what it 'really' stands for, Angela proves that she has understood. However, in our case, the naming of the critical item violates the very taboo Daniela has made relevant by the coding; it presupposes the *luci* and *mammelle* are exchangeable, even though Daniela has put any direct reference 'off limits' by telling the joke as she has told it. Thus, it is Angela's explication of what must not be explicated which turns the situation into an 'embarrassing' one (for Daniela). All three participants try to defuse this embarrassment with the subsequent laughter (lines 17, 18, 19), which is initiated by Daniela, and joined in last by Angela. At the same time, this laughing ratifies the critical character of the interaction at that point. In addition to laughing, Daniela shows another reaction: she briefly switches into German.

In Extract 7, the conversation develops quite similarly, again between Angela and Daniela. This time, the critical topic is not sex, but boyfriends (*fidanzati*). Again, the topic is not critical in it, but is turned into a critical one, on an initiative by the adult. Angela does the trick by turning the girl's system of evaluation upside down. This system has 'having a boyfriend' as a positive, and 'not having a boyfriend' as a negative value (cf. her *peccate* 'it's a pity' after learning from Angela that she does not have a boyfriend). So there is disagreement in the first place (probably from line 06 on). In this delicate (and face threatening) situation, Angela can very easily cause Daniela's embarrassment. In our case, it is the register in which her answer to Daniela's question why she does not want a boyfriend is formulated. The mi *hanno rotto le scatole* 'they get on my nerves' is not a vulgar, but a rather colloquial expression. It is marked in this conversation where such a style is otherwise avoided. Again, Daniela switches into German, and also indicates her embarrassment by laughing (line 14).

Code-switching in either case has something to do with the precarious situation that has evolved. More precisely, it is one of the indicators that show to co-participants as well as to external observers that Daniela perceives Angela's preceding utterance as embarrassing. As such, the switching is discourse-related. But how is such a discourse-related interpretation possible? Here, matters of language preference come in. In this episode, Daniela displays a preference for German, although she usually adapts to Beate's and even more to Angela's preference for Italian. Given these preferences, it is evident that Daniela's response to an activity by Angela which is embarrassing to her, and which thus threatens her face, is to switch into the language, which she has agreed to avoid for Angela's benefit, but which is her own preferred language. Daniela 'retreats' on 'her' language. Given Angela's preference for Italian, this is tantamount to a ('symbolic') retreat from the interaction – one of its agreed upon features is dissolved. The discourse-related effect of this type of switching is an effect of one participant's rejecting the language of interaction. As it is this participant who is 'on the defensive', we will speak of *defensive* code-switching here.

The short duration of the other-language passage is in line with this analysis. The speaker on the defensive retreats from the interaction to compose himself or herself. The language of interaction is abandoned only as long as is necessary for this purpose.

Between Insertion and Alternation

Prototypical insertional code-switching does not have any impact on subsequent language choice, concerns a well-defined unit and is (a consequence of the latter) relatively short. Prototypical alternational code-switching implies a re-negotiation of the language of interaction, concerns a point in interaction and does not allow predicting return into the first language. Thus, the two distinguishing questions are (a) is it a unit or a point that is concerned? and (b) does language alternation relate to language negotiation? Both criteria can lead into polyvalent interpretations if they cannot be applied with unequivocal results.

One-word TCUs

The first case we want to consider is the diffusion of the boundary between units and points. In simple cases, such diffusion occurs in turns, which consist of just one well-defined unit (for example, a word):

Extract 8: Interview by Manuele with Clemente (CL).

01	M:	che lavoro fa papa,
		what job's your daddy in,
→02	CL:	DACHDECKER
		roofer
03	M:	aha (–) e mamma che lavoro fa,
		I see and mum what job is she in

→04   CL: VERKÄUFERIN;
                     saleswoman

Extract 9: Interview by Manuele with Camillo (CM).

01   M: quando i genitori (mi davano) (– –) un po di soldi no,
                     when my parents (gave me)   *a little money you know,*
02   andavo subito al cinema.
                     I immediately went to the cinema.
03   eh:: fai anche tu così oppure: (.)
                     eh do you also do like that or
→04   CM: SPARE
                     save
05   M: DU DUSCH SPAREN h h hn tu risparmi hẽh ?
                     you save it   *you save it right ?*

Both are taken from formal interviews with Clemente and Camillo, respectively. Due to this general setting, the 'interviewees' are quite taciturn; they laconically respond to the 'interviewer's' questions with one-word answers (*Dachdecker* 'roofer' and *Verkäuferin* 'saleswoman' in Extract 8, *spare* 'to save' in Extract 9). These turns are ambiguous between insertions and alternations. The recipient's behaviour does not provide us with clues as to how he interpreted the language alternation either. In one case, Manuele continues in Italian, that is, he does not orient to matters of language negotiation, in the other he uses German for his subsequent turn, that is, he seems to take up the boy's language choice. However, this evidence is not very conclusive in either case. For in Extract 8, the use of Italian by Manuele may just as well be analysed as his next step in all language negotiation sequence, that is, as his insisting on the preferred language, and in Extract 9, it seems that the adult's 'expansion' of Clemente's *spare* 'save' also changes 'key' of the interaction – at least, Manuele's laughter points to an attempt on his part to reinterpret a rather 'stiff' situation as a humorous one. In addition, Manuele quickly switches back into Italian in the same turn. I consider the diffusion of the clear borderline between a unit and a point in interaction in Clemente's and Camillo's turns not just as an analyst's problem. Our difficulties in arriving at a clear interpretation only mirror those of the participants.

However, it would be certainly wrong to imagine that co-participants are particularly puzzled by such instances of code-switching. They are polyvalent in the sense of being compatible with either 'insertion or 'alternation'. That is to say, the dichotomy just ceases to be important. Consequently, code-switching will be less readily interpretable and acquire interactional function in these cases than in those that can be mapped onto one of the prototypes.

Frequent Turn-Internal Code-Switching

The second criterion to tell code-switching from transfer is the impact that the alternation of language has on subsequent language choice. In addition to the existence of such an impact (alternation) and to its absence (insertion), we observe cases of frequent turn-internal language juxtaposition, which fall between these extremes, or more precisely, which are more or less neutral with respect to the language of interaction. Nevertheless, the distinction between points-in-interaction versus units-of-interaction remains an applicable criterion for classifying these cases as instances of (non-prototypical) code-switching for contrastive functions.

Consider the following contribution by Alfredo, in which Italian dialect and German play a role:

Extract 10: Conversation between Alfredo (AL), Camillo (CM), Clemente (CL) and Agostino (AG) and Manuele (M).

```
01   AL:   no: (–)       quandë=a casa nostra mbë- (–) a tedeschë (–)
           you know   when at our house (...)          the German (woman)
02         quilla NACHBARIN; (–) quando=nui=facimm da mangià o ange
           this      neighbour;      when we do the cooking          or also
03         (–) <<pressed>OH DA STINKTS WIEDER NACH DEM ZIGEUNERESSE
           UND SO>
                oh again it's stinking from this gipsy food and so on
04         [(si mett=a crapì)
           (she goes to open)
05   AG:   [ming=ië cë darisë nu scuppolo:ne a chill [che!
           if it was me I'd give her a kick to this one
06   AL:                                              [a fënestrë=
                                                       the window
07         =e=s mettë=a (–) mna u:: (–) SPRITZ SPRITZ DA PARFÜM
           and starts to (take) the          splash splash there perfume
08         [ma
           But
09   M:    [°ma ma verame[nte°
           but but really
10   AL:               [<<p>na=vo:t (–) si:: na: [vo:t=i: (–) ë: e;>
                        once           yes  once      I
11   AG:                                          [<<f, agitated> è qua-
                                                   is (she) there
12         u-   è quella [là (..........)>
           the  is it this one there (........)
13   AL:                 [<<mf>tornatë da scolë   I HAB GEDACHT KOMM JETZT
                          came home from school I thought I am stepping into
```

10		IN E PUFF NEI (–) SO HART=S GSTUNKE NACH DEM ZEUG;> (–)
		brothel that's how it was stinking from that stuff
11	AG:	e:: è [quellë che ci=ha i capelli::
		is it this one who's got the hair
12	AL:	[<<p>DES HAT DA GSTUNKEN>
		it was stinking there
13	AG:	m- a [chillë vecchjë zaganonë
		but this old (... ... ...)
14	AL:	[DA DIE MÖ:BEL:
		the furniture there!

(follows second story by Alfredo about the German neighbour))

For the purpose of this discussion, it is useful to look at a de-interactionalized version of the report and narrative:

quandë a casa nostra mbë/
a tedeschë
quilla NACHBARIN;
quando=nuj=facimm da mangià
o ange
OH DA STINKTS=WIEDER NACH ZIGEUNERESSE UND SO
(si mette a crapì) a fënestrë=
e=si mettë=a – m=na u: SPRITZ SPRITZ DA PARFÜM
na vo:t
na=vo:t ië e tornatë da scolë
I HAB GEDACHT KOMM JETZT IN E PUFF NEI
SO HAT=S GSTUNKE NACH DEM ZEUG;
DES HAT DA GSTUNKN

Although there is an overall tendency of the speaker to 'glide' from a more dialectal (Italian) beginning of the turn into (regional) German, such that the turn terminates more or less in that language, it is difficult to tell whether the contribution as a whole should be considered to be German or Italian dialect. A number of turn-internal switches contribute to the 'neutral' character of the contribution. Some of them are familiar patterns known from the literature on discourse-related code-switching. For instance, we notice that the voice of another person (the racist neighbour's speech) is rendered in another language (German). Other switches contribute to the internal organization of Alfredo's report and the subsequent narrative. *Spritz spritz da Parfüm* 'splash splash there perfume' is the climax or upshot of the teller's report of what the neighbour does when the Italian family cook their meals and therefore marks a step in its internal build-up; at the same time, it sets off the antagonist's action from that of the surrounding description of the scene. Switching into German after *ië e tornatë da scolë* 'I came home from school' marks the protagonist's internal thoughts (his voice). We are not at the level of language mixing yet: the individual juxtapositions of the two languages create meaning and have a structuring function. On the other hand, frequent turn-internal switching of this type is responsible for the neutrality of Alfredo's contribution with respect to the negotiation of the language of interaction. In fact, as documented in the original version of the transcript, other participants intervene in both languages: Agostino in Italian and Clemente in German. Becoming a habitualized form of talk, frequent turn-internal switching of this type is also the beginning of a development which may eventually lead into abolishing the preference for same language talk.

Conclusion

I have presented a model that accounts for the interactive meaning of one of the most prominent forms of bilingual behaviour here, that is, the juxtaposition of two languages during an interactive episode. The model is built on some basic assumptions which can be summarized as follows:

- The approach is essentially sequential, not 'semantic' in nature. This is to say that the interactional function of code-switching is not derived from decontextualized 'meaning' of the two languages established on other grounds, but as being embedded into the sequential development of the conversation. This sequential development constitutes its primary and most important context.
- The model presented here is procedural instead of classificatory. Two basic procedures relevant for the interactionally meaningful production and interpretation of code-switching were introduced and used to account for local instances of the juxtaposition of two 'codes': that between discourse- and participant-related code-switching, and that between alternational and insertional code-switching. In addition to defining four prototypical instances of code-switching, these two dichotomous procedures of the model also enable us to describe non-prototypical instances.
- In this sense, the model is both context sensitive and context independent (cf. Sacks et al. 1974/1978 for the same argument with respect to turn-taking). In order to take part in bilingual interaction, members deploy rather general procedural knowledge shared by all participants. This knowledge is flexible enough though to be applied to the needs of any new occasion. Thus, discourse-related code-switching may suggest redefining the participant constellation, separate the setting from the events in a

narrative or mark the different voices in story-telling. It is this procedural knowledge plus the local context of their application that jointly provide participants with the resources necessary to decide on the function of a particular instance of code-switching.

NOTE

This article is a slightly updated and terminologically adapted summary of some main arguments from my 1984 book with the same title, based on research with Italian/German bilingual children and adolescents of Italian family background in Germany. No references to later work by myself or in a similar spirit have been included in the text, but the reader is referred to Auer (1995, 1998 and 1999) for some recent developments as well as to Auer (forthcoming) for an overview.

REFERENCES

Auer, Peter. 1995. The pragmatics of code-switching: a sequential approach. In Lesley Milroy and Pieter Muysken (eds.) *One Speaker – Two Languages*. Cambridge: University Press. 115–135. [Reprinted in: Li Wei (ed.) 2007. *The Bilingualism Reader*. 2nd edition. London: Routledge.]

Auer, Peter (ed.). 1998. *Code-Switching in Conversation*. London: Routledge.

Auer, Peter. 1999. From code-switching via language mixing to fused lects: Toward a dynamic typology of bilingual speech. *International Journal of Bilingualism* 3: 309–332.

Auer, Peter. forthcoming. *Bilingual Talk*. Cambridge: Cambridge University Press.

Goffman, Erving. 1979. Footing. *Semiotica* 25: 1–29.

Gumperz, John. 1982. *Discourse Strategies*. Cambridge: Cambridge University Press.

Sacks, Harvey. 1992. *Harvey Sacks – Lectures on Conversation*. Edited by Gail Jefferson. Oxford: Blackwell.

Sacks, Harvey, Emanuel Schegloff and Gail Jefferson. 1974, A simplest systematics for the organization of turn-taking for conversation. *Language* 50: 696–735. [Enlarged version in John Schenkein (ed.). 1978. *Studies in the Organization of Conversational Interaction*. New York: Academic Press. 7–55.]

CHAPTER 35

Linguistic and Educational Aspects of Tok Pisin

JEFF SIEGEL

Tok Pisin (or New Guinea Pidgin) is the dialect of Melanesian Pidgin spoken in Papua New Guinea (PNG). It serves as the main language of wider communication in a country where over 800 separate indigenous languages are spoken by a population of approximately 4.5 million. The two other dialects of Melanesian Pidgin are Pijin, spoken in Solomon Islands (with over 80 indigenous languages and a population of around 390,000), and Bislama spoken in Vanuatu (over 100 languages, population 190,000). Torres Strait Creole (also known as Yumpla Tok) – spoken by approximately 10,000 people around the northern tip of eastern Australia – is closely related to Melanesian Pidgin but usually considered to be a separate language.

Melanesian Pidgin is an example of a contact language – a new language that has developed in a situation where speakers of different languages need to communicate but do not share common language. Most of the forms for the vocabulary come from one language, called the lexifier (English in the case of Melanesian Pidgin), but the words often have different functions or meanings (see Vocabulary, below). Furthermore, the phonology (sound system) and grammatical rules of a contact language are quite distinct from those of the lexifier (see Sounds, and Grammar). Such a contact language is called a 'pidgin' when it continues to be used primarily as a second language for intergroup communication, and a 'creole' if it becomes the mother tongue or native language of a particular community of speakers (for example, Jamaican Creole). But as will be seen below, there is some controversy about whether Tok Pisin (and Melanesian Pidgin in general) is actually a pidgin or a creole.

History

The first stage of the development of Melanesian Pidgin dates from the early 1800s when Melanesians began to have frequent contact with Europeans (including Australians and Americans). This was the result of whaling in the region, followed by trading in sandalwood and bêche-de-mer (the sea slug, which is widely believed to be an aphrodisiac). Since Melanesia is one of the most linguistically diverse areas of the world, it was impossible for Europeans to learn the local languages for trading (as they did in other areas of the Pacific). So in order to communicate, they tried to use simplified English or existing contact languages such as South Seas Jargon and various forms of Aboriginal Pidgin English from Australia. As a result of these limited encounters, many Melanesians picked up some vocabulary and phrases from English and the existing contact languages.

The second stage came with the beginning of the Pacific labour trade in 1863. Melanesians were recruited (and in some cases kidnapped) to become labourers on plantations in Queensland (Australia). Melanesians from diverse areas found themselves literally in the same boat, and their only common language was what they had acquired from earlier contacts with Europeans. So they used this to communicate with each other on the ships and later on the plantations. With continued use, new features were added, norms gradually emerged and a stable pidgin language began to develop – early Melanesian Pidgin. This had a small vocabulary, mainly based on English, no grammatical inflections, and only a few grammatical rules.

The earliest Queensland labourers were mainly from the New Hebrides (now Vanuatu) and the Solomon Islands. Some labourers from German New Guinea also went to Queensland in 1883 and 1884, but many more went to plantations in Samoa, from 1879 to 1912. Labourers from the other countries as well started going to German-controlled Samoa in 1878, and many of these had already worked in Queensland. So early Melanesian Pidgin was transported to Samoa. However, after 1885, labourers from the New Hebrides or Solomons were no longer recruited for Samoa, and early Melanesian Pidgin began to diverge into two slightly different varieties – one spoken in Queensland and one in Samoa.

The third stage of development began when the labourers' contracts finished and they returned to their home islands, bringing the developing pidgin with them. Previously, these islands had no lingua franca (common language), but the pidgin served this function well and spread like wildfire. It was also used by the large-scale internal labour force which worked on the plantations of German New Guinea, the New Hebrides and Solomon Islands after the external labour trade had ended at the turn of the century. In each of these countries, early Melanesian Pidgin further stabilized and changed under the influence of the local indigenous languages. Today, the three dialects differ mainly in vocabulary and a few grammatical rules (see below).

After Tok Pisin had stabilized and spread through the islands, it began to be used for new functions, such as religion. It was developed into a written language by missionaries in the 1930s, and later used in newspapers and radio broadcasting. As its use was extended into new areas, it changed linguistically to become more complex – for example acquiring more vocabulary and more grammatical rules and some inflections. (The same process occurred with Bislama and Pijin.) Thus, in both function and structure, Tok Pisin (and Melanesian Pidgin as a whole) became what is called an 'expanded pidgin'.

Finally, in recent years, especially in urban areas of Papua New Guinea, such as Port Moresby and Lae, many people have been marrying outside their traditional language groups. So often the common language of the parents is Tok Pisin and this is what their children acquire as their first language. Because of this nativization (the process of a pidgin becoming a native language), some linguists apply the term creole to Tok Pisin (and Melanesian Pidgin in general), emphasizing that it has thousands of native speakers and has the functions and grammatical features found in typical creoles. Those who say it is still a pidgin point out that more than 90 per cent of its speakers still use their ancestral language and learn Tok Pisin as a second rather than a first language. In contrast, creole-speaking populations generally have shifted from their ancestral languages and are monolingual in the creole. (For further information on the development of Tok Pisin, see Smith 2002.)

Linguistic Features

Vocabulary

Since English is the lexifier language of Tok Pisin, most of the words come from English. But they are often pronounced in a different way (see Sounds), and some have different meanings. For example: *spak* (from *spark*) means 'drunk' and *baksait* (from *backside*) refers to someone's back, not to their butt.

Many Tok Pisin words have a meaning much wider than that of the English word they came from. For example, *kilim* (from *kill*) can mean 'hit' or 'beat' as well as 'kill'; *pisin* (from *pigeon*) means 'bird' in general and *gras* (from *grass*) means not only 'grass' but also 'hair', 'fur' and 'feathers'. Also, some combinations of words have different meanings: for example *bel hevi* (from *belly heavy*) means 'sad'.

Tok Pisin also includes words from other languages. Here are some examples:

Origin	Tok Pisin word	Meaning
New Guinea Islands languages (such as Tolai)	*lapun* *kumul* *muruk* *palai* *kiau*	'old' 'bird of paradise' 'cassowary' 'lizard, gecko' 'egg'
Samoan	*malolo* *laplap*	rest loin cloth, sarong
Malay	*binatang* *lombo* *sayor*	'insect' 'chilli' 'leafy vegetable'
German	*gumi* *beten* *raus* *bros*	'rubber, tube' 'pray' 'get out!' 'chest'
Portuguese	*pikinini* save (pronounced *sah-vay*)	'child' 'know'

Sounds

Like other pidgins and creoles, Tok Pisin has its own individual system of sounds, or phonology, distinct from that of the lexifier. Also Tok Pisin has its own special writing system, which is being used here.

There aren't as many phonemes (sounds used to distinguish meaning) in Tok Pisin as there are in English. The consonant sounds that most speakers of Tok Pisin use are: *b, d, g, h, k, l, m, n, p, r, s, t, v, w* and *y*. The *sh* sound in English is replaced by the *s* sound in Tok Pisin, so the English word *shell* has become *sel* in Tok Pisin. Also the *f* sound is generally replaced by the *p* sound, so the English word *fish* has become *pis*. Like many dialects of English, Tok Pisin does not have the *r* sound following a vowel, so for example, the English word *work* has become *wok* in Tok Pisin. Also, Tok Pisin has a rule that consonants at the end of a word or a syllable must be devoiced – for example, *g* becomes *k* and *d* becomes *t*. So the word for 'pig' is *pik* and the word for 'road' is *rot*.

Tok Pisin vowels are *a, e, i, o* and *u*. In English, the letter for a vowel might have many different pronunciations – for example, compare the sound of the *u* in *rule*, *put*, *but*, and *fuse*. But in Tok Pisin, each vowel has only one pronunciation, much like the 'pure vowels' in languages such as Spanish:

a is pronounced similar to the *a* in the English word *father*
e is pronounced similar to the *e* in *vein*

i is pronounced similar to the *i* in *machine*

o is pronounced similar to the *o* in *boat*

u is pronounced similar to the *u* in *rule*

Because Tok Pisin doesn't have some of the sounds that English has, and because of the sound changes just mentioned, what are different words in English may be the same word in Tok Pisin. For example, *hat* means 'hat', 'hot', 'heart', and 'hard'.

Grammar

At first glance, Tok Pisin grammar seems to be a kind of simplified English. For example, you don't have to add an *-s* onto words to show plural:

wanpela pik	'one pig'
tripela pik	'three pigs'

You don't have to add *-ing* or *-ed* to show tense or aspect:

Mi wok nau.	'I'm working now.'
Mi wok asde.	'I worked yesterday.'

With regard to pronouns, Tok Pisin seems simpler than English because the same word *em* can mean 'he', 'him' 'she', 'her' and 'it'. For example, the following sentences can have three different meanings, depending on the context:

Em i stap long haus.	'He's in the house'; 'She's in the house'; or 'It's in the house.'
Em i lukim mi.	'He/she/it saw me.'
Mi lukim em.	'I saw him/her/it.'

But Tok Pisin has its own grammatical rules that are different from those of English. First of all, look at the following sentences:

Mi wok.	'I worked.'
Yu wok.	'You worked.'
Em i wok.	'He/she worked.'
Tom i wok.	'Tom worked.'

Note that the last two sentences have the particle *i* before the verb. (Remember that in Tok Pisin, *i* is pronounced something like the *i* in *machine*.) This particle is most often called a 'predicate marker', and it normally occurs in a sentence when the subject is the pronoun *em,* or a noun or noun phrase (like *Tom* or *the bicycle*).

Although plural does not have to be indicated, as we saw above, there is an optional way of doing so: by putting *ol* before the word (instead of *-s* at the end):

Mi lukim dok.   'I saw the dog.'
Mi lukim ol dok.   'I saw the dogs.'

To be more specific about tense or aspect, or about other things like ability, the language uses other short words. Some occur before the verb and some occur after. Here are some examples:

*Ben i **bin** wok asde.*   'Ben worked yesterday.'
*Ben **bai** i wok tumora.*   'Ben will work tomorrow.'
*Ben i wok **i stap** nau.*   'Ben is working now.'
*Ben i wok **pinis**.*   'Ben is finished working.'
*Ben i **save** wok long Sarere.* 'Ben works on Saturday.'
*Ben i **ken** wok.*   'Ben can work (he is allowed to).'
*Ben **inap** wok.*   'Ben can work (he has the ability).'

Although Tok Pisin seems simpler than English because pronoun *em* does not distinguish between male and female or animate and inanimate, this is not the full story. The pronoun system of Tok Pisin makes other distinctions that are not made in English. For example, while standard English has only one pronoun, *you*, for referring to either singular or plural, Tok Pisin has four different pronouns: *yu* 'you', *yutupela* 'you two', *yutripela* 'you three' and *yupela* 'you all'. So Tok Pisin pronouns make a four-way distinction in number – singular, dual, trial and plural – while English pronouns sometimes make no distinction, as with *you*, or at the most only a two-way singular-plural distinction, as with *I* versus *we*.

Tok Pisin pronouns also make another distinction not found in English. It has two sets of non-singular first person pronouns, 'inclusive' versus 'exclusive', all corresponding to English *we* or *us*. To understand this distinction, let's look at the following English sentence:

The girls said to Miriam, 'Fred invited us to the party!'

It would not be clear to Miriam from the statement 'Fred invited us to the party' whether she was included in the invitation or not. In other words, it could have two possible meanings:

1. Fred invited us (including you) to the party.
2. Fred invited us (but not you) to the party.

In Tok Pisin there would be no such confusion. There is an inclusive plural pronoun *yumi* ('we or us, including you') and an exclusive plural pronoun *mipela* ('we or us, not including you'). So the two possible meanings would be expressed in Tok Pisin in different ways:

1. *Fred i bin singautim yumi long pati.*
2. *Fred i bin singautim mipela long pati.*

You have just seen that in Tok Pisin the suffix *-pela* is attached to pronouns to show plural – for example, *yu* versus *yupela*. This suffix also has another function. It is attached to some adjectives and numbers:

bikpela haus	'big house'
strongpela man	'strong man'
blakpela pik	'black pig'
tripela dok	'three dogs'

Tok Pisin has another word ending with a function unlike anything in English. This is the suffix *-im* which is attached to some verbs. To see how it works, look at the following sentences:

Em i rit.	*'He is reading.'*
Em i ritim buk.	*'He's reading a book.'*
Wara i boil pinis.	*'The water has boiled.'*
Meri i boilim wara pinis.	*'The woman has boiled the water.*
Bai mi rait.	*'I'll write.'*
Bai mi raitim pas	*'I'll write a letter.'*
Kanu i kapsait.	'The canoe capsized.'
Ol i kapsaitim kanu.	'They capsized the canoe.'

You can see that the suffix *-im* is attached to the verb when it is followed by an object. So, for example, if you say 'he's reading', there's no need for *-im* on the verb *rit* 'read'. But if you say 'he's reading something', then you do need to add the *-im* suffix.

These examples illustrate that Tok Pisin has its own grammatical rules which are very different from the rules of English. Therefore, the answer to the question 'Is Tok Pisin simplified English?' is clearly NO!

Dialectal Differences

Tok Pisin differs from the other two Melanesian Pidgin dialects because most of the returned labourers had worked in German-controlled Samoa rather than Queensland. In addition, nearly all of the New Guinea labourers were from New Britain and New Ireland and the neighbouring small islands, where the internal German-owned plantations were also located. So Tok Pisin has many words from the languages of these islands (especially Tolai), as well as some from Samoan and German, whereas the other two dialects do not.

In contrast, Bislama has many words derived from the languages of central Vanuatu – for example *nakamal* 'meeting house' and *nabanga* 'banyan tree'. Bislama also differs from both Tok Pisin and Solomons Pijin in having many words derived from French. (Both France and Britain were the former colonial powers in the New Hebrides.) Some examples are *bonane* 'New Year's celebration', *pima* 'chilli pepper' and *lafet* 'holiday'. Solomon Pijin differs from the other two dialects in having very few words derived from local languages or any language other than English.

An example of a grammatical difference between the three dialects is in the ways they indicate progressive aspect (marked with *-ing* in English). Tok Pisin most often uses the locative or existential verb *stap* 'stay, exist' following the verb (with an intervening *i*); Bislama also uses *stap* but preceding the verb; and Pijin sometimes uses initial consonant-vowel reduplication (but often does not mark progressive aspect). For instance, 'I'm drinking' would be the following in the three dialects: *Mi dring i stap* (Tok Pisin); *Mi stap dring* (Bislama); and *Mi didring* (Pijin).

Current Use and Attitudes

Today Tok Pisin is the lingua franca of the entire country of PNG, known by an estimated three quarters of the country's four and a half million inhabitants. It is the most widely used language of urban areas. Despite this fact, English is the main language used in radio and television broadcasting; Tok Pisin only has limited use in interviews and news reports. (However, it is used in Radio Australia's Tok Pisin broadcasts <http://www.abc.net.au/ra/tokpisin>.) The two daily newspapers in the country are in English, but there is a weekly newspaper in Tok Pisin (*Wantok*) that has a readership of over 10,000. Many government publications are also in Tok Pisin. One of the widest uses of the language outside daily interactions is in religion, and there is a Tok Pisin translation of the New Testament of the Bible. With regard to government, much of the debate in Parliament is in Tok Pisin. However, English is more widely used for official government business. And until very recently, English was the official language of education and used from Grade 1 as the language of instruction and initial literacy in all government schools.

Tok Pisin and Education

In 1955 W.C. Groves, the Director of Education in the then Australia-administered Territory of Papua and New Guinea, wrote a report entitled: *The Problem of Language: Paper no 1: 'Pidgin'*, referring to New Guinea Pidgin (Tok Pisin). Here are some quotations from the summary of the report (pp. i–ii):

> Pidgin is a language in its own right ... Practically any concept that can be expressed in English can in fact be expressed fully and without ambiguity in Pidgin ...

> As to Education, experience has shown that Pidgin is not only a useful, but also an adequate means of instruction in most fields ...

> The use of Pidgin for formal instruction in organized teaching institutions enables instruction to be given through that medium immediately, since the language is known to the students as a starting point.

> I believe that, if Pidgin were officially and openly adopted for educational and other communication purposes in the Territory ... the result in accelerated development of the Native people would be inestimable.

Although Groves' recommendations certainly seem to have been sensible, they were never implemented, and until very recently, Tok Pisin was not used officially in government schools. In fact, throughout the world, pidgins and creoles rarely have any official role in formal education (Siegel 2002).

One of the reasons that pidgins and creoles such as Tok Pisin are not officially used in formal education is because of persisting negative attitudes towards these languages. First, they are still considered 'corrupted' or 'degenerate' languages by many educators, and even by their own speakers. This is mainly because of their superficial resemblance to the standard form of their lexifier languages. Rickford and Traugott (1985: 255) point out: 'One common charge is that the creole is not a real or legitimate language, this claim deriving from the erroneous but frequently asserted claim that it has no grammar or is merely a mangled version of the Standard'. For example, in reporting arguments against the use of Torres Strait Creole as a medium of education, Shnukal (1992: 4) notes that it is 'stigmatized as an inferior type of English, a "rubbish language"'. Similar reactions have occurred in PNG – for example, in 1970s when there was a national debate about a suggestion that Tok Pisin be used in education. Here is a comment from a letter to the editor written by a Tok Pisin speaker: 'Pidgin is such a rough and tough language, I can find no place for it, say, in a teaching situation' (Noah Warkia, *Post-Courier*, 13 June 1979: 14).

A second negative attitude towards pidgins and creoles is that they cannot be used to express abstract or complex concepts. For example, the letter writer above continues:

> [I]t is not a language in which it is easy to express concepts. There is very little chance we could effectively teach people in Pidgin about political development, abstract ideas, technical knowledge and new knowledge in other fields.

One of the most extreme examples is given by Kephart (1992: 68) with reference to educators' attitudes towards a creole spoken in the Caribbean:

> [They say] you can't express yourself precisely or accurately in Creole; children should be taken away from their creole speaking parents at birth and placed in standard-English speaking homes, because if they spend their whole lives speaking creole, their brain cells will deteriorate!

Another reason is that it is considered a waste of time to use a pidgin or creole in education because in countries where they are spoken, the educational goal is to learn the standard variety, and, indeed, knowing the standard is considered to be the key to success in education and employment. Therefore, it seems to follow that time should not be taken away from learning the standard. For example, Shnukal (1992: 4) notes that in the Torres Strait, people are 'reluctant to accept the use of creole as a formal medium of instruction in their schools, seeing it as a method of depriving them of instruction in the kind of English that white people use, and thus condemning them to permanent under-class status'. Another letter writer in PNG (a member of Parliament from Papua) had this to say:

> Pidgin English is absolutely no use in Papua, where it is a social disease of colonialism which prevents the less priviledged people from becoming fluent in our international language, which is English. (J. M Abaijah, *Post-Courier*, 25 June 1976: 2)

In a report on a survey of teachers' attitudes towards the use of Tok Pisin as a medium of instruction in PNG, Nidue (1988: 216) writes:

> The PNG elite have developed prejudiced attitudes towards TP [Tok Pisin] from the colonial administration including such groups as expatriate teachers and academics. As a result of this pro-English indoctrination, many of the indigenous elite, as well as many unsophisticated Papua New Guineans, believe there is no real education unless they learn how to read, write and speak English. To these people, Tok Pisin is not not *real* education...

Nidue's study reveals that teachers generally agree that using Tok Pisin would facilitate teacher-student communication, improve students' understanding of subject matter, enable parents to participate in their children's education and promote traditional cultural activities in the schools. Yet over 90 per cent of the teachers surveyed were strongly in favour of English-only medium schools.

Another reason for pidgins and creoles not being used as educational languages is the belief that such a use would be detrimental to students' subsequent acquisition of the standard because of negative transfer or interference. This is thought to be especially true because of the apparently close relationship between pidgins and creoles and the standard form of their lexifier languages. For example, with regard to Bislama, Thomas (1990: 245) notes:

> One of the most common fears concerning the introduction of Bislama as a language of education is that, owing to lexical similarities, negative transfer occurs when pupils subsequently learn English.

And according to Charpentier (1997: 236), using Bislama along with English in education in Vanuatu would 'lead to a social, psychological and pedagogical blockage, seriously compromising any passage to literacy'.

However, earlier in this reading, we have seen that Tok Pisin is not merely a degenerate version of its lexifier, English, but has its own grammatical rules. The same is true for other pidgins and creoles. Furthermore, many studies show the educational advantages of teaching initial literacy in a language students already know. For example, research shows that literacy skills can readily be transferred from one language to another. When time is taken away for learning literacy in a familiar language, it actually has a positive effect on eventual achievement in the mainstream educational language (see Cummins 2001; Thomas and Collier 2002).

On the other hand, the fear of negative transfer or interference is more difficult to argue against. Studies have shown that there are two ways that a first language (L1, in this case a pidgin or creole) can have a negative effect on learning a second language (L2, here the standard form of the lexifier language). First, it can bring about 'transfer errors' – the use of L1 features inappropriately in the L2 – or, second, it can delay passage through a normal developmental sequence. This is more likely when the L1 and the L2 are similar. To illustrate potential transfer, we will use this example from Tok Pisin:

Em i bin pait-im ol pik. 'She hit the pigs.'

The Tok Pisin words are derived from English, but most of them have different pronunciations, meanings or functions, as we have seen earlier: *em* comes from *him* but can mean 'he', 'him', 'she', 'her', 'it'; *bin* is from *been* but acts as a past tense marker; *pait-* is from *fight* but means 'hit' as well; *-im* is from *him* but is a transitive suffix; and *ol* is from *all* but acts as a plural marker, without the meaning 'all'. It is easy to see how the apparent similarity of Tok Pisin to English forms could possibly lead to different kinds of transfer errors. These could be of a phonological nature, such as saying *pight* for 'fight', of a lexical nature, such as *She fought* [meaning 'hit'] *the pigs*, or of a grammatical nature, such as *She been fight her brother*. Thus, it is theoretically feasible that when a pidgin or creole is the L1 and its lexifier language is the L2, there could be negative transfer. Empirical evidence is needed to find out whether this is really the case, and whether using pidgins and creoles as languages of formal education is actually a help or a hindrance to subsequently learning the standard form of the lexifier language.

I conducted research in PNG (Siegel 1997) to test educators' views about the use of Tok Pisin in education being detrimental to the acquisition of English because of interference. This was an evaluation over six years (1989–1995) of the Tok Pisin Prep-School program in the Ambunti district of Papua New Guinea. This community-run preschool program taught children initial literacy and numeracy through the medium of Tok Pisin before they began formal education in the English-medium primary schools.

The evaluation involved interviews with primary school teachers, village committee members and parents about the program and the progress in formal education of the students who had completed it. Formal comparative research was also carried out in the primary school at the district centre of Ambunti (St Joseph's Community School) with three cohorts of students, based on the year they started primary school (1988, 1989 and 1990). It involved comparing the educational achievement, based on term test results, of those who had gone through the prep-school program and those who had not. These tests are normally held at the end of each of the four terms in the school year, and are in three subject areas: English, Mathematics and General Subjects (health, social science, etc.). Results were examined in upper as well as lower grades for each cohort.

The interviews revealed overwhelming satisfaction with the programme. This can also be seen in the rapid growth of the programme; it started in 1985 with two schools and 150 students and by 1996 it had expanded to 45 schools and 1245 students. With regard to the acquisition of English, the teachers reported that there were no special problems of interference. In fact, the students who had learned initial literacy in Tok Pisin were said to learn English more easily than the other students.

The statistical analysis of the data on academic achievement showed that children who had been involved in the prep-school program scored significantly higher in term tests than those who had not been involved. These results included English, where those who learned initial literacy in Tok Pisin actually scored higher, not lower, than those students who learned literacy only in English. Furthermore, on the basis of the test scores, the prep-school children showed significantly higher academic achievement in English across time (that is, in upper grades as well). This study clearly refutes arguments that using an English-lexified pidgin language in formal education will adversely affect students' subsequent acquisition of standard English.

Recent Developments

A total reform of the nationwide education system in PNG began in the 1990s. This changed the six years of primary schooling in the medium of English to three years of Elementary School followed by six years of Primary School. The language of instruction and initial literacy in Elementary School is now chosen by the community; English is introduced in the second or third year of Elementary School and becomes the medium of instruction in Primary School. Although exact figures are not available, many communities, especially in urban areas, have chosen Tok Pisin for their schools. Also, in at least one rural area (in the Sepik Province where the Tok Pisin Prep-school programme was running), there are at least 26 Elementary Schools using Tok Pisin (Siegel 2005). Furthermore, in PNG's current National Literacy Policy, Tok Pisin and Hiri Motu (another pidgin language, though not so widely spoken as Tok Pisin) are recognized as the two national languages in addition to the official language, English. One of the National Goals of the policy (Papua New Guinea Department of Education 2000) is: 'All Papua New Guineans must be encouraged to become print literate in their own language and one of the two national languages.'

Although many people still feel that Tok Pisin is inferior to English, most accept it as a separate language, and an important language of Papua New Guinean identity. However, more and more people are now realizing that it can also be a useful medium of formal education.

REFERENCES

Charpentier, Jean-Michel. 1997. Literacy in a pidgin vernacular. In Andrée Tabouret-Keller, Robert B. LePage, Penelope Gardner-Chloros and Gabrielle Varro (eds.) *Vernacular Literacy: A Re-evaluation.* Oxford: Clarendon Press. 222–245.
Cummins, Jim. 2001. *Language, Power and Pedagogy: Bilingual Children in the Crossfire.* Clevedon: Multilingual Matters.

Kephart, Ronald F. 1992. Reading creole English does not destroy your brain cells! In Jeff Siegel (ed.) *Pidgins, Creoles and Nonstandard Dialects in Education*. Melbourne: Applied Linguistics Association of Australia (Occasional Paper no. 12). 67–86.

Papua New Guinea Department of Education. 2000. *National Literacy Policy of Papua New Guinea*. Port Moresby: Papua New Guinea Department of Education.

Shnukal, Anna. 1992. The case against a transfer bilingual program of Torres Strait Creole to English in Torres Strait schools. In Jeff Siegel (ed.) *Pidgins, Creoles and Nonstandard Dialects in Education*. Melbourne: Applied Linguistics Association of Australia (Occasional Paper no. 12). 1–12.

Siegel, Jeff. 1997. Using a pidgin language in formal education: Help or hindrance? *Applied Linguistics* 18: 86–100.

Siegel, Jeff. 2002. Pidgins and Creoles. In Robert Kaplan (ed.) *Handbook of Applied Linguistics*. New York: Oxford University Press. 335–351.

Siegel, Jeff. 2005. Literacy in pidgin and creole languages. *Current Issues in Language Planning* 6: 143–163.

Thomas, Andrew. 1990. Language planning in Vanuatu. In Richard B. Baldauf and Allan Luke (eds.) *Language Planning and Education in Australia and the South Pacific*. Clevedon: Multilingual Matters. 234–258.

Thomas, Wayne P. and Virginia P. Collier. 2002. *A National Study of School Effectiveness for Language Minority Students' Long-term Academic Achievement*. Santa Cruz: Center for Research on Education, Diversity and Excellence.

CHAPTER 36

Language Rights

Stephen May

This chapter explores the development of language rights (LR) as a nascent academic paradigm, along with its key theoretical and contextual concerns. The growing presence of LR in the disciplines of Sociolinguistics, the Sociology of Language, and Language Policy can be attributed to four distinct, albeit closely interrelated, academic movements. All these movements (discussed further below) adopt the usual distinction between so-called 'minority' and 'majority' languages – a distinction that is based not on numerical size but on clearly observable differences among language varieties in relation to power, status and entitlement – while also paying particular attention to the rights of minority language speakers.

The first of these is the Language Ecology (LE) movement, charting the links between linguistics and ecology, and situating the current exponential loss of many of the world's languages within a wider ecological framework (see, for example, Mühlhäusler 1996; Nettle and Romaine 2000). A second is the linguistic human rights (LHR) movement that argues, often on the basis of LE premises, for the greater institutional protection and support of minority languages within both national and supranational contexts (see, for example, Kontra et al. 1999; Skutnabb-Kangas 2000). These arguments are also echoed in a third domain of academic legal discourse that has developed with respect to minority group rights generally, but with an increasing focus on the specific implementation of minority language rights (MLR) in national and international law (see, for example, de Varennes 1996; Henrard 2000). A fourth, increasingly influential, position has seen a deliberate move away from the biological/ecological analyses of LE, and some LHR arguments, to a more overtly critical sociohistorical/sociopolitical analysis of language rights (see, for example, Blommaert 1999; Patrick and Freeland 2004; May 2005a, 2007). This position continues to focus on the importance of minority language rights (MLR), while also addressing social constructivist and post-modernist understandings of language that highlight the constructedness of language(s) and the contingency of the language-identity link. The latter have too-often been ignored in other MLR accounts, leading to an overly essentialized view of languages and those who speak them (see May 2005b for a useful overview).

While these various positions are thus by no means uniform, there is sufficient overlap for them to constitute collectively an increasingly important field of academic enquiry and related advocacy about language rights – particularly, MLR – within Sociolinguistics. In line with the particular emphases of the respective movements discussed above, five key concerns can be identified as underpinning much of this work.

Language Shift and Loss

The first concern has to do with the exponential decline and loss of many of the world's languages. Indeed, of the estimated 6,800 languages spoken in the world today (Grimes 2000), it is predicted on present trends that between 20 per cent and 50 per cent will 'die' by the end of the twenty-first century (Krauss 1992). Language decline and loss occur most often in bilingual or multilingual contexts in which a majority language – that is, a language with greater political power, privilege and social prestige – comes to replace the range and functions of a minority language. The inevitable result is that speakers of the minority language 'shift' over time to speaking the majority language.

The process of language shift described here usually involves three broad stages. The first stage sees increasing pressure on minority language speakers to speak the majority language, particularly in formal language domains. This stage is often precipitated and facilitated by the introduction of education in the majority language. It leads to the eventual decrease in the functions of the minority language, with the public or official functions of that language being the first to be replaced by the majority language. The second stage sees a period of bilingualism, in which both languages continue to be spoken concurrently. However, this stage is usually characterized by a decreasing number of minority language speakers, especially among the younger generation, along with a decrease in the fluency of speakers as the minority language is spoken less, and employed in fewer and fewer language domains. The third and final stage – which may occur over the course of two or three generations, and sometimes less – sees the replacement of the minority language with the majority language. The minority language may be 'remembered' by a residual group of language speakers, but it is no longer spoken as a wider language of communication (see Dorian, Chapter 37).

Of course, such language loss and language shift have always occurred – languages have risen and fallen, become obsolete, died, or adapted to changing circumstances in order to survive, throughout the course of human history. But never to this extent, and never before at such an exponential rate. Some sociolinguistic commentators have even described it as a form of 'linguistic genocide' (Skutnabb-Kangas 2000). Such claims may seem overwrought and/or alarmist but they are supported by hard data. For example, a survey by the US-based Summer Institute of Linguistics, published in 1999, found that there were 51 languages with only one speaker left, 500 languages with fewer than 100 speakers, 1,500 languages with fewer than a 1,000 speakers, and more than 3,000 languages with fewer than 10,000 speakers. The survey went on to reveal that as many as 5,000 of the world's more than 6,000 languages were spoken by fewer than 100,000 speakers each. It concluded, even more starkly, that 96 per cent of the world's languages were spoken by only 4 per cent of its people (Crystal 1999).

These figures graphically reinforce an earlier suggestion made by Krauss (1992) that, in addition to the 50 per cent of languages that may die within the next century, a further 40 per cent of languages are 'threatened' or 'endangered'. Given the processes of language shift and decline just outlined, and the current parlous state of many minority languages, it is not hard to see why. Even some majority languages are no longer immune to such processes, not least because of the rise of English as a global language (Crystal 1997; Phillipson 2003). Thus, if Krauss is to be believed, as few as 600 languages (10 per cent) will survive in the longer term – perhaps, he suggests, even as few as 300.

The potential scale and rapidity of language loss predicted here also highlights the inevitable social, economic and political *consequences* for minority language speakers of such shift and loss. Language loss – or linguistic genocide, as Skutnabb-Kangas (2000) would have it – almost always forms part of a wider pattern of social, cultural and political displacement. We can see this clearly if we consider which groups are most affected by language loss – almost always minority groups which are (already) socially and politically marginalized and/or subordinated. These groups have been variously estimated at between 5,000 and 8,000 and include within them the 250–300 million members of the world's indigenous peoples (Tully 1995), perhaps the most marginalized of all people groups. As Crawford (1994) notes, language death seldom occurs in communities of wealth and privilege, but rather among the dispossessed and disempowered. Moreover, linguistic dislocation for a particular community of speakers seldom, if ever, occurs in isolation from sociocultural and socioeconomic dislocation as well.

Nationalism, Politics and the Minoritization of Languages

This brings us to the second principal concern that underlies the advocacy of MLR – why certain languages, and their speakers, have come to be 'minoritized' in the first place. Advocates of MLR argue that the establishment of majority/minority language hierarchies is neither a natural process nor primarily even a linguistic one. Rather, it is a historically, socially and politically *constructed* process (May 2005b, 2007), and one that is deeply imbued in wider (unequal) power relations. Following from this, if languages, and the status attached to them, are the product of wider historical, social and political forces, there is, in turn, nothing 'natural' about the status and prestige attributed to particular majority languages and, conversely, the stigma that is often attached to minority languages, or to dialects.

There are two specific points at issue here. The first concerns what actually distinguishes a majority language from a minority language or a dialect. This distinction is not as straightforward as many assume. For example, the same language may be regarded as both a majority *and* a minority language, depending on the context. Thus Spanish is a majority language in Spain and many Latin American states, but a minority language in the USA. Even the term 'language' itself indicates this process of construction, since what actually constitutes a language, as opposed to a dialect for example, remains controversial (see Mühlhäusler 1996; Romaine 2000). Certainly, we cannot always distinguish easily between a language and a dialect on *linguistic* grounds, since some languages are mutually intelligible, while some dialects of the same language are not. The example often employed here is that of Norwegian, since it was regarded as a dialect of Danish until the end of Danish rule in 1814. However, it was only with the advent of Norwegian independence from Sweden in 1905 that Norwegian actually acquired the status of a separate language, albeit one that has since remained mutually intelligible with both Danish and Swedish. Contemporary examples can be seen in the former Yugoslavia, where we are currently seeing the (re)development of separate Serbian, Croatian and Bosnian language varieties in place of Serbo-Croat, itself the artificial language product of the post Second World War Yugoslav Communist Federation under Tito.

What these latter examples clearly demonstrate is that languages are 'created' out of the politics of state-making, not – as we often assume – the other way around (Billig 1995). Independence for Norway and the break-up of the former Yugoslavia have precipitated linguistic change, creating separate languages where previously none existed. The pivotal role of political context, particularly as it is outworked at the level of the nation-state, might also help to explain the scale of the projected language loss discussed earlier. One only has to look at the number of nation-states in the world today, at approximately 200, and the perhaps 300 or so languages that are projected to survive long term, to make the connection.

And this brings us to the second key point at issue here: the central and ongoing influence of nation-state organization, and the politics of nationalism, to processes of national (and international) language formation and validation, along with the linguistic hierarchies attendant upon them. In this respect, the model of the linguistically homogeneous nation-state – which has become the normative sociopolitical, as well as sociolinguistic model (cf. Bourdieu 1982) – is actually only a relatively recent historical phenomenon, arising from the French Revolution of 1789 and the subsequent development of European nationalism. Previous forms of political organization had not required this degree of linguistic uniformity. For example, empires were quite happy for the most part to leave unmolested the plethora of cultures and languages subsumed within them – as long as taxes were paid, all was well. Nonetheless, in the subsequent politics of European nationalism – which, of course, was also to spread throughout the world – the idea of a single, common 'national' language (sometimes, albeit rarely, a number of national languages) quickly became the leitmotif of modern social and political organization.

How was this accomplished? Principally via the political machinery of these newly emergent European states, with mass education playing a central role (Anderson 1991; Gellner 1983). The process of selecting and establishing a common national language usually involved two key aspects: *legitimation* and *institutionalization* (May 2007; Nelde, Strubell and Williams 1996). Legitimation is understood to mean here the formal recognition accorded to the language by the nation-state – usually, via 'official' language status. Institutionalization, perhaps the more important dimension, refers to the process by which the language comes to be accepted, or 'taken for granted' in a wide range of social, cultural and linguistic domains or contexts, both formal and informal. Both elements, in combination, achieved not only the central requirement of nation-states – cultural and linguistic homogeneity – but also the allied and, seemingly, necessary banishment of 'minority' languages and dialects to the private domain.

If the establishment, often retrospectively, of chosen 'national' languages was therefore a deliberate, and deliberative political act, it follows that so too was the process by which other language varieties were subsequently 'minoritized' or 'dialectalized' by and within these same nation-states. These latter language varieties were, in effect, *positioned* by these newly formed states as languages of lesser political worth and value. Consequently, national languages came to be associated with modernity and progress, while their less fortunate counterparts were associated (conveniently) with tradition and obsolescence.

More often than not, the latter were also specifically constructed as *obstacles* to the political project of nation-building – as threats to the 'unity' of the state – thus providing the raison d'être for the consistent derogation, diminution and proscription of minority languages that have characterized the last three centuries of nationalism (see May 2007 for a full overview). As Dorian summarizes it: 'it is the concept of the nation-state coupled with its official standard language ... that has in modern times posed the keenest threat to both the identities and the languages of small [minority] communities' (1998: 18). Coulmas observes, even more succinctly, that 'the nation-state as it has evolved since the French Revolution is the natural enemy of minorities' (1998: 67).

Proponents of language rights for minority groups argue that the emphasis on cultural and linguistic homogeneity within nation-states, and the attendant hierarchizing of languages, are thus neither inevitable nor inviolate – particularly in light of the historical recency of nation-states, and the related, often arbitrary and contrived, processes by which particular languages have been accorded 'national' or 'minority' status respectively. These arguments about the historical and geopolitical situatedness of national languages also apply at the supranational level. In particular, a number of prominent sociolinguistic commentators have argued that the burgeoning reach and influence of English as the current world language, or lingua mundi, is the result of equally constructed historical and political processes, most notably via the initial geopolitical influence of Britain and, subsequently, the USA (see, for example, Pennycook 1994; Phillipson 1992, 2003).

As with the construction of national languages, the current ascendancy of English is also invariably linked with modernity and modernization, and the associated benefits which accrue to those who speak it. The result, MLR proponents argue, is to position other languages as having less 'value' and 'use' and, by extension, and more problematically, to delimit and delegitimize the social, cultural and linguistic capital ascribed to 'non-English speakers' – the phrase itself reflecting the normative ascendancy of English. The usual corollary to this position is that the social mobility of the minority language speaker will be further enhanced if they *dispense* with any other (minority) languages.

Language Replacement and Social Mobility

A third principal concern of language rights' proponents is to critique the principle of 'language replacement' that centrally underlies the social and political processes just outlined – that one should/must learn these languages *at the expense of* one's first language. Consequently, the promotion of cultural and linguistic homogeneity at the collective/public level has come to be associated with, and expressed by, individual monolingualism. This amounts to a form of linguistic social Darwinism and also helps to explain why language shift/loss/decline has become so prominent.

Central to these language replacement arguments is the idea that the individual social mobility of minority language speakers will be enhanced as a result. Relatedly, minority language advocates are consistently criticized for consigning, or ghettoizing, minority language communities within the confines of a language that does not have a wider use, thus actively constraining their social mobility (see, for example, Barry 2000; Huntingdon 2005). Little wonder, such critics observe, that many within the linguistic minority itself choose to ignore the pleas of minority language activists and instead 'exit' the linguistic group by learning another (invariably, more dominant) language. It is one thing, after all, to proclaim the merits of retaining a particular language for identity purposes, quite another to have to live a life delimited by it – foreclosing the opportunity for mobility in the process. We can broadly summarize the logic of this argument as follows:

- majority languages are lauded for their 'instrumental' value, while minority languages are accorded 'sentimental' value, but are broadly constructed as obstacles to social mobility and progress;
- learning a majority language will thus provide individuals with greater economic and social mobility;
- learning a minority language, while (possibly) important for reasons of cultural continuity, delimits an individual's mobility; in its strongest terms, this might amount to actual 'ghettoization';
- if minority language speakers are 'sensible' they will opt for mobility and modernity via the majority language;
- whatever decision is made, the choice between opting for a majority or minority language is constructed as oppositional, even mutually exclusive.

These arguments appear to be highly persuasive. In response, however, language rights' proponents argue that the presumptions and assumptions that equate linguistic mobility *solely* with majority languages are themselves extremely problematic. For a start, this position separates the instrumental and identity aspects of language. On this view, minority languages may be important for identity but have no instrumental value, while majority languages are construed as primarily instrumental with little or no identity value. We see this in the allied notions of majority languages as 'vehicles' of modernity, and minority languages as (merely) 'carriers' of identity. However, it is clear that *all* language(s) embody and accomplish both identity and instrumental functions for those who speak them. Where particular languages – especially majority/minority languages – differ is in the *degree* to which they can accomplish each of these functions, and this in turn is dependent on the social and political (not linguistic) constraints in which they operate (May 2003). Thus, in the case of minority languages, their instrumental value is often constrained by wider social and political processes that have resulted in the privileging of other language varieties in the public realm. Meanwhile, for majority languages, the identity characteristics of the language *are* clearly important for their speakers, but often become subsumed within and normalized by the instrumental functions that these languages fulfil. This is particularly apparent with respect to monolingual speakers of English, given the position of English as the current world language.

On this basis, advocates for MLR argue that the limited instrumentality of particular minority languages at any given time need not always remain so. Indeed, if the minority position of a language is the specific product of wider historical and contemporary social and political relationships, changing these wider relationships positively with respect to a minority language should bring about both enhanced instrumentality for the language in question, and increased mobility for its speakers. We can see this occurring currently, for example, in Wales and Catalonia, with the emergence of these formerly subjugated languages into the public domain – particularly via, but by no means limited to, education.

Likewise, when majority language speakers are made to realize that their own languages fulfil important identity functions for them, both as individuals and as a group, they may be slightly more reluctant to require minority language speakers to dispense with theirs. Or to put it another way, if majority languages do provide their speakers with particular and often significant individual and collective forms of linguistic identity, as they clearly do, it seems unjust to deny these same benefits, out of court, to minority language speakers.

And this brings us to the fourth principal concern of language rights' proponents – the legal protections that can potentially be developed in order to enhance the mobility of minority language speakers while at the same time protecting their right to continue to speak a minority language, *if they so choose*. It is here that the influence of the linguistic human rights (LHR) movement, championed by Tove Skutnabb-Kangas, is most prominent.

Linguistic Human Rights

The LHR research paradigm argues that minority languages, and their speakers, should be accorded at least some of the protections and institutional support that majority languages already enjoy (see, for example, Kontra et al. 1999; Skutnabb-Kangas 2000; Skutnabb-Kangas and Phillipson 1995).

These arguments are also echoed in much of the academic legal discourse that has developed in recent years with respect to minority group rights more broadly (see, for example, de Varennes 1996; Henrard 2000). A central distinction in both discourses is made between national minority groups and indigenous peoples on the one hand, and ethnic minority groups on the other. The former may be regarded as groups which are historically associated with a particular territory (that is, they have not migrated to the territory from elsewhere) but because of conquest, confederation or colonization are now regarded as minorities within that territory. The latter may be regarded as voluntary migrants and (involuntary) refugees living in a new national context (see Kymlicka 1995 for further discussion).

Three key tenets of international law can be applied to the further development of LHR in relation to these two broad minority groupings. The first principle, which is widely accepted, is that it is not unreasonable to expect from national members some knowledge of the common public language(s) of the state. This is, of course, the central tenet underpinning the current public linguistic homogeneity of modern nation-states. However, LHR advocates assert that it is also possible to argue, on this basis, for the legitimation and institutionalization of the languages of national minorities within nation-states, according to them at least some of the benefits that national languages currently enjoy. LHR proponents qualify this by making it clear that the advocacy of such minority language rights is *not* the language replacement ideology in reverse – of replacing a majority language with a minority one. Rather, it is about questioning and contesting why the promotion of a majority (national) language should necessarily be *at the expense* of all others. By this, they argue, the linguistic exclusivity attendant upon the nationalist principle of cultural and linguistic homogeneity can be effectively challenged and contested.

A second principle is that in order to avoid language discrimination, it is important that where there is a sufficient number of other language speakers, these speakers should be allowed to use that language as part of the exercise of their individual rights as citizens. That is, they should have the *opportunity* to use their first language if they so choose. As de Varennes argues, 'the respect of the language principles of individuals, *where appropriate and reasonable*, flows from a fundamental right and is not some special concession or privileged treatment. Simply put, it is the right to be treated equally without discrimination, to which everyone is entitled' (1996: 117; my emphasis). Again, this principle can clearly be applied to minority language speakers within particular nation-states.

The third principle arises directly from the previous one – how to determine exactly what is 'appropriate and reasonable' with regard to individual language preferences. Following the prominent political theorist, Will Kymlicka

(1995), May (2007) has argued, for example, that only national minorities can demand *as of right* formal inclusion of their languages and cultures in the civic realm. However, this need not and should not preclude other ethnic minorities from being allowed *at the very least* to cultivate and pursue unhindered their own historic cultural and linguistic practices in the private domain. In other words, distinguishing between the rights of national and ethnic minorities still affords the latter far greater linguistic protection than many such groups currently enjoy – that is, *active* linguistic protection by the state for the *unhindered* maintenance of their first languages. This protection is applicable at the very least in the private domain and, 'where numbers warrant', a principle again drawn from international law, potentially in the public domain as well.

Extending greater ethnolinguistic *democracy* to minority language groups, via LHR, does not thus amount to an argument for ethnolinguistic *equality* for all such groups. Similarly, a call for greater ethnolinguistic democracy clearly does not amount to asserting linguistic equivalence, in all domains, with dominant, majority languages. Majority languages will continue to dominate in most if not all language domains, since, as should be clear by now, that is the nature of their privileged sociohistorical, sociopolitical position(ing). Conversely, arguing that only national minorities can claim minority language rights, as of right, is *not* an argument for simply ignoring the claims of other ethnic groups (see May 2003, 2007 for an extended discussion).

Avoiding Essentialism

The final concern of the language rights paradigm – most prominent in more recent work in the area (see the collections by Patrick and Freeland 2004 and May 2005a) – addresses directly the question of how to recognize language rights, while at the same time avoid essentializing the languages, and their speakers, to which these rights might apply. This difficult balancing act necessarily involves rejecting the 'essentialist tendency', closely allied with an often-deterministic account of the links between language, identity and the wider ecological system, that is most evident in arguments for language ecology (LE), as well as in those linguistic human rights (LHR) arguments that are predicated on LE principles (for example, in the work of Skutnabb-Kangas). Such arguments assume – in their less sophisticated manifestations, explicitly, and even in their most sophisticated forms, at least implicitly – an almost ineluctable connection between language and (ethnic) identity. And yet, this, position stands in marked contrast to the widespread consensus in social and political theory, and increasingly in Sociolinguistics and critical

Applied Linguistics, that language is at most only a contingent factor of one's identity. In other words, language does not define us, and may not be an important feature, or indeed even a necessary one, in the construction of our identities, whether at the individual or collective levels (see, for example, Brutt-Griffler 2002; Edwards 1994). This perspective on the detachability of language is complemented by a wider constructivist consensus within social theory on the merits of hybridity – that our social, political and linguistic identities are inevitably plural, complex and contingent (see, for example, Makoni and Pennycook 2007).

Clearly then, an acceptance of the contingent nature of the language-identity link, and the wider principle of hybridity, is a necessary prerequisite before language rights can continue to develop further theoretically. However, all is also not quite as it seems, because what constructivist accounts fail to address adequately is the central question of why, *despite* the clear presence of hybrid linguistic identities, historically associated languages continue often to hold considerable purchase for members of particular cultural or ethnic groups in their identity claims. As Canagarajah (2005: 439) observes of this: 'Hybridity of identity doesn't change the fact that ethnicity and mother tongue have always been a potent force in community relations... Change doesn't mean irrelevance or irreverence. Attachments to ethnicity and mother tongue are resilient, despite their limited value in pragmatic and material terms.'

To say that language is not an inevitable feature of identity is thus *not* the same as saying it is unimportant. Yet many constructivist commentators in (rightly) assuming the former position have also (wrongly) assumed the latter. In other words, they assume that because language is merely a contingent factor of identity it cannot therefore (ever) be a *significant* or *constitutive* factor of identity. As a result, contingency is coalesced with unimportance or peripheralism – an additional move that is neither necessary nor warranted.

Indeed, this position is extremely problematic, not least because of the considerable evidence that suggests that while language may not be a *determining* feature of ethnic identity in many geo- and sociopolitical contexts in the world today, it remains nonetheless a *significant* one in many instances. Or to put it another way, it simply does not reflect adequately, let alone explain, the heightened saliency of language issues in many historical and contemporary political conflicts, particularly at the intrastate level (see, for example, Blommaert 1999; May 2007). In these conflicts, particular languages clearly *are* for many people an important and constitutive factor of their individual, and at times, collective identities. This is so, *even* when holding onto such languages has specific negative social and political consequences for their speakers, most often via active discrimination and/or oppression.

In theory then, language may well be just one of many markers of identity. In practice, it is often much more than that. Indeed, this should not surprise us since the link between language and identity encompasses both significant cultural and political dimensions. The cultural dimension is demonstrated by the fact that one's individual and social identities, and their complex interconnections, are inevitably mediated in and through particular languages. The political dimension is significant to the extent that those languages come to be formally (and informally) associated with particular ethnic and national identities. These interconnections also help to explain why, as Fishman (1997) argues, a 'detached' scientific view of the link between language and identity may fail to capture the degree to which language is *experienced* as vital by those who speak it. It may also significantly understate the role that language plays in social organization and mobilization.

As for the ongoing concern over essentialism, this too can be addressed directly. Advocacy of MLR does not *necessarily* entail an essentialized, static view of the language-identity link, or a homogenous conception of the wider linguistic group. As Kymlicka has argued in relation to minority rights more generally, advocates of such rights are rarely seeking to preserve their 'authentic' culture if that means returning to cultural practices long past. If it were, it would soon meet widespread opposition from individual members. Rather, it is the right 'to maintain one's membership in a distinct culture, and to continue developing that culture in the same (impure) way that the members of majority cultures are able to develop theirs' (1995: 105). Cultural change, adaptation and interaction are entirely consistent with such a position. The crucial difference, however, is that members of the minority are themselves able to retain a significant degree of control over the process – something which until now has largely been the preserve of majority group members. The key issue for minority language speakers thus becomes one of cultural and linguistic *autonomy* rather than one of retrenchment, isolationism or stasis.

Conclusion

It should be clearly apparent from this brief overview that many challenges to the emergent paradigm of language rights still remain. Nonetheless, the development of arguments in support of language rights, particularly for minority groups, has provided a major impetus for rethinking processes of linguistic modernization, via the ascendancy of majority languages, as inevitable, apolitical and unproblematic. In contrast, arguments for minority language rights highlight centrally and critically the wider social and political conditions – and, crucially, their historical antecedents – that have *invariably* framed and shaped these processes of linguistic modernization, particularly with respect to the privileging and normalizing of majority languages within existing social and political contexts – often at the specific *expense* of minority languages. As Blommaert argues, a sociolinguistic approach that fails to take cognisance of these wider sociopolitical and sociohistorical factors takes no account of human agency, political intervention, power and authority in the formation of particular (national) language ideologies. Nor, by definition, is it able to identify the establishment and maintenance of majority languages as a specific 'form of practice, historically contingent and socially embedded' (1999: 7). And yet, as language rights' advocates quite clearly highlight, it is exactly these contingent, socially embedded, and often highly unequal practices, that have so disadvantaged minority languages, and their speakers, in the first place.

Moreover, if one can hold onto one fact that the language rights paradigm has so usefully highlighted – that processes of linguistic change are often, if not always, the result of wider social and political processes – then this provides a useful basis from which to mount an effective political challenge on behalf of minority languages and their speakers. From this, one can also question and critique the apparently ineluctable link between majority languages, mobility and 'progress', and in turn look to ways in which minority languages may be reconstituted not simply as 'carriers' of identity but also as instrumentally useful.

And finally, the issue of greater autonomy for minority language speakers that emerges from language rights arguments also highlights the need for greater reciprocity and accountability among majority language speakers – extending to minority language speakers the linguistic privileges that they themselves take for granted. After all, if members of dominant ethnolinguistic groups typically value their own cultural and linguistic membership(s), as they clearly do, it is demonstrably unfair to prevent minority groups from continuing to value theirs.

REFERENCES

Anderson, B. 1991. *Imagined Communities: Reflections on the Origin and Spread of Nationalism.* Revised edition. London: Verso.

Barry, B. 2000. *Culture and Equality: An Egalitarian Critique of Multiculturalism.* Cambridge Massachusetts: Harvard University Press.

Billig, M. 1995. *Banal Nationalism.* London: Sage.

Blommaert, J. (ed.) 1999. *Language Ideological Debates.* Berlin: Mouton de Gruyter.

Bourdieu, P. 1982. *Ce Que Parler Veut Dire: l'économie des échanges linguistiques.* Paris: Arthème Fayard.

Brutt-Griffler, J. 2002. Class, ethnicity and language rights: An analysis of British colonial policy in Lesotho and Sri Lanka and some implications for language policy. *Journal of Language, Identity and Education* 1: 207–234.

Canagarajah, S. 2005. Dilemmas in planning English/vernacular relations in post-colonial communities. *Journal of Sociolinguistics* 9: 418–447.

Coulmas, F. 1998. Language rights: Interests of states, language groups and the individual. *Language Sciences* 20: 63–72.

Crawford, J. 1994. Endangered Native American languages: What is to be done and why? *Journal of Navajo Education* 11: 3–11.

Crystal, D. 1997. *English as a Global Language*. Cambridge: Cambridge University Press.

Crystal, D. 1999. The death of language. *Prospect*, November 1999: 56–59.

de Varennes, F. 1996. *Language, Minorities and Human Rights*. The Hague: Kluwer Law International.

Dorian, N. 1998. Western language ideologies and small-language prospects. In L. Grenoble and L. Whaley (eds.) *Endangered Languages: Language Loss and Community Response*. Cambridge: Cambridge University Press. 3–21.

Edwards, J. 1994. *Multilingualism*. London: Routledge.

Fishman, J. 1997. Language and ethnicity: The view from within. In F. Coulmas (ed.) *The Handbook of Sociolinguistics*. London: Blackwell. 327–343.

Gellner, E. 1983. *Nations and Nationalism: New Perspectives on the Past*. Oxford: Basil Blackwell.

Grimes, B. (ed.). 2000. *Ethnologue: Languages of the World*. 14th edition. Dallas, Texas: SIL.

Henrard, K. 2000. *Devising an Adequate System of Minority Protection*. The Hague: Kluwer Law.

Huntingdon, S. 2005. *Who Are We? America's Great Debate*. New York: Free Press.

Kontra, M., T. Skutnabb-Kangas, R. Phillipson and T. Várady (eds.). 1999. *Language: A Right and a Resource: Approaches to Linguistic Human Rights*. Budapest: Central European University Press.

Krauss, M. 1992. The world's languages in crisis. *Language* 68: 4–10.

Kymlicka, W. 1995. *Multicultural Citizenship: A Liberal Theory of Minority Rights*. Oxford: Clarendon Press.

Makoni, S. and A. Pennycook (eds.). 2007. *Disinventing and Reconstituting Languages*. Clevedon: Multilingual Matters.

May, S. 2003. Rearticulating the case for minority language rights. *Current Issues in Language Planning* 4: 95–125.

May, S. (ed.) 2005a. Debating Language Rights. *Special issue of the Journal of Sociolinguistics* 9/3.

May, S. 2005b. Language rights: Moving the debate forward. *Journal of Sociolinguistics* 9: 319–347.

May, S. 2007. *Language and Minority Rights: Ethnicity, Nationalism and the Politics of Language*. New York: Routledge.

Mühlhäusler, P. 1996.. *Linguistic Ecology: Language Change and Linguistic Imperialism in the Pacific Region*. London: Routledge.

Nelde, P., M. Strubell and G. Williams. 1996. *Euromosaic: The Production and Reproduction of the Minority Language Groups in the European Union*. Luxembourg: Office for Official Publications of the European Communities.

Nettle, D. and S. Romaine. 2000. *Vanishing Voices: The Extinction of the World's Languages*. Oxford: Oxford University Press.

Patrick, D. and J. Freeland (eds.). 2004. *Language Rights and Language 'Survival': A Sociolinguistic Exploration*. Manchester: St Jerome Publishing.

Pennycook, A. 1994. *The Cultural Politics of English as an International Language*. London: Longman.

Phillipson, R. 1992. *Linguistic Imperialism*. Oxford: Oxford University Press.

Phillipson, R. 2003. *English-Only Europe: Challenging Language Policy*. London: Routledge.

Romaine, S. 2000. *Language in Society: An Introduction to Sociolinguistics*. 2nd edition. Oxford: Oxford University Press.

Skutnabb-Kangas, T. 2000. *Linguistic Genocide in Education – or Worldwide Diversity and Human Rights?* Mahwah, New Jersey: Lawrence Erlbaum.

Skutnabb-Kangas, T. and R. Phillipson. 1995. Linguistic human rights, past and present. In T. Skutnabb-Kangas and R. Phillipson (eds.) *Linguistic Human Rights: Overcoming Linguistic Discrimination*. Berlin: Mouton de Gruyter. 71–110.

Tully, J. 1995. *Strange Multiplicity: Constitutionalism in an Age of Diversity*. Cambridge: Cambridge University Press.

CHAPTER 37

Sociolinguistic Dimensions of Language Death

NANCY C. DORIAN

Introduction

Extinction is a common enough phenomenon in the history of the world's languages. Within the relatively well-studied and well-documented Indo-European family one or two cases leap to mind: Gothic and Hittite have deeply engaged the attention of historical linguists because of the availability of fairly extensive written materials from an early period, yet they have no modern descendants. In spite of the historical importance of these languages, it is probably the still-continuing loss of North and South American aboriginal languages that comes most forcibly to mind when extinction is under discussion. The title of James Fenimore Cooper's novel *The Last of the Mohicans* has become a metaphor for the lonely, and temporary, persistence of any isolated relic individual or group, and reports of Amerindian languages extinct or on the brink of extinction are still frequent. Grubb (1975: 2), for example, writes of the toll taken in a single Canadian province:

> Five of the languages known to have existed in the Province before the arrival of Europeans are now extinct, and of the remaining twenty-seven only four are considered viable: the remainder are deemed to be two generations or less away from total disappearance.

Linguistic extinction, or 'language death', to give it a simpler and more metaphorical name, is to be found under way currently in virtually every part of the world.

In recent years attention has turned to dying languages within several sub-disciplines of Linguistics and Anthropology. Linguists of various persuasions

Source: *Language Death: The Life Cycle of a Scottish Gaelic Dialect*, by Dorian, N. C. (1981) (Philadelphia, PA: University of Pennsylvania Press) pp. 1–8, 98–113.

have begun to look into what dying languages may reveal about simplification processes, whether phonological (Dressler 1972), morphophonological
(Dorian 1977), morphological (Dorian 1978; Dressler 1977), or syntactic
(Dorian 1973; Hill 1973). Because of the reductive aspects of language death,
comparisons with pidginization (Dorian 1978; Trudgill 1976–1977) and
with language acquisition (Voegelin and Voegelin 1977) have quite naturally
emerged. Sociologists of language have developed an interest in questions of
what Fishman (1964) dubbed 'language maintenance and language shift',
and language shift frequently leaves a dying language in its wake. Such a
shift is an aspect of sociocultural change, intimately linked to phenomena
like urbanization, industrialization, and secularization, though – interestingly – not predictable from any of them. Increasingly, studies of linguistic
persistence or replacement have focused on contexts of modernization and
nationalization (Cole 1975; Denison 1971; Timm 1973). Historical linguists,
for their part, look to current studies of language death for insights into earlier
extinctions: 'many languages of which we know are now extinct; the steps to
their extinction may be understood more clearly if we have thorough descriptions of languages now on the way to extinction' (Lehmann 1962: 111).

East Sutherland Gaelic (ESG) can make several claims to particular
interest and utility for the study of extinction. Its displacement has been fairly
gradual, encompassing a number of phases, which allows for a relatively long
historical and sociolinguistic perspective. Its competitor, English, is a language
of ever wider currency, and one which plays the replacive role in a great many
other extinction cases. Studies are available of other languages and dialects
of the same linguistic family which are also faced with extinction or probable
extinction (e.g., Breatnach 1964; Dressler and Leodolter 1973; Timm 1973);
in fact, one observer (Adler 1977) expects that this entire language family,
in all its branches, faces likely extinction. Further, two branches of the family –
Cornish and Manx – have already died relatively well-documented deaths
and are the focus of revival movements.

But perhaps the most useful feature of ESG for the purposes of a study of
linguistic extinction was the presence, during the period of study, of a fairly
broad range of speakers: a continuum of speakers of differing proficiency in
Gaelic and English. The oldest speakers included some who were noticeably
more at home in Gaelic than in English, while the youngest included many
who were considerably more adept at English than at Gaelic. This proficiency
continuum can be plumbed not only for differences in actual Gaelic usage,
but also for differences in personal linguistic history and in language attitudes
and habits.

Because ESG has become cut off from all other varieties of Gaelic and because
it is succumbing to English rather than to some more prestigious variety of
Gaelic, it seems proper to speak in this case of *language* death. What is dying here
is actually a particular local dialect of the Scottish Gaelic language, and what

it is yielding to is – equally – a particular local dialect of the English language, 'East Sutherland English'. But as the competition is between two quite different languages, so that the question is always one of which language, and not what dialect, a person chooses to speak, I take this to be a case of *language* shift. Scottish Gaelic will not become extinct with the loss of East Sutherland Gaelic, but where there were two distinct languages spoken in eastern Sutherland, only one will remain. In the regional context, then, a language will have died.

East Sutherland Bilingualism

Active East Sutherland bilingualism involves, almost exclusively on the current scene, only three of the speech varieties within the verbal repertoire: ESG and Gaelic-influenced East Sutherland English and/or Gaelic-influenced standard Highland English. Twenty years ago or more another variety of Gaelic – church Gaelic – would also have been involved, but although church Gaelic can be said to remain a part of most people's passive bilingualism, it belongs to the active bilingualism of very few. At the time when church Gaelic was still fairly widely used, it would clearly have been incorrect to suggest any diglossic relationship between Gaelic and English among the fisherfolk such that English served as the 'high' language and Gaelic as the 'low' language (as in Fishman's 1967 adaptation of Ferguson 1959), since a 'higher' use of language than the religious use could scarcely be found for this group. To my way of thinking, this adapted diglossic model does not apply well even today, when this extremely 'high' use of Gaelic has almost vanished from active use. Despite the tendencies toward language compartmentalization noted above, there is still not the 'high'/'low' specialization by language which would warrant comparison with the classic diglossic specialization by function sketched out by Ferguson as typical of the four linguistic communities he described (Chapter 31). Until less than ten years ago, for example, Gaelic was still used for sermons in one local church. News broadcasts are currently made in Gaelic (although not, to be sure, in ESG) as well as in English. Folk literature (including, for example, local-patriotic songs and obscene songs) exists in *both* ESG and East Sutherland English. Instructions to workmen can be given in both local speech forms, depending only on the linguistic capabilities of the receiver, not on the functional prestige of the speech form. In both ESG and East Sutherland English, a formal style of speech can be mustered for circumstances where it is appropriate, say in expressing condolences; this would seem to merit the 'high' label. That is to say, both languages have 'high' uses and 'low' uses, whether seen from the community perspective or from the point of view of a single bilingual's verbal behavior. It strikes me that the diglossia model is often much too readily invoked in descriptions of bilingual communities, and this is certainly the case in studies of communities where Scottish Gaelic is in use.

Seen from the society-wide point of view, present-day East Sutherland bilingualism is transitional, or unstable. It is only the last stage of a general transition from nearly universal monolingualism in Gaelic to nearly universal monolingualism in English. Preceding the transition period were at least three centuries of stable stratified societal bilingualism in eastern Sutherland. During those centuries the mass of the people were monolingual in Gaelic; the aristocracy (and probably some of its associates) monolingual in English; and the clergy and some functionaries of one kind or another formed a small bilingual bridge within the local society. On the basis of evidence from the two *Statistical Accounts,* it can be assumed that the transition period began during the first half of the nineteenth century. It will close with the death of ESG in the early decades of the twenty-first century, when (assuming healthy life expectancies) even the youngest of today's semi-speakers will be disappearing from the scene. The stable period of societal bilingualism was characterized by two groups each monolingual in a different language, with only a small number of people actually bilingual. East Sutherland has at no time in at least its post-Viking history espoused widespread individual bilingualism, nor is this the case now. Within the local society there are no rewards for Gaelic-English bilingualism, either in economic terms or in terms of social approval; in fact the reverse is the case. The expectation has been, from the time of the new *Statistical Account* onward, that those who learned English would give up Gaelic, or that their children would. The operative model has always been replacive, rather than additive, bilingualism.

In this context, bilingual skills are not, on the whole, a matter of pride or satisfaction. Indeed, within the fishing communities one hears more about flaws in verbal performance arising from bilingualism than one hears about proficiency in bilingual attainments, despite the fact that those attainments are considerable. Among them are conspicuous excellence in spontaneous Gaelic-English translation for the benefit of English monolinguals, and equal excellence in English-Gaelic translation for the benefit of Gaelic-dominant audiences; ability to understand, and in some cases to use, the conservative, rather archaic religious speech variety of both linguistic traditions; control of two partially overlapping traditions of verbal performance, including, for instance, a small repertory of both serious and comic song and a rich repertory of proverbial lore, jokes, insults and curses, and by-naming, all in both languages; and, among some members of the bilingual population, the ability to read both languages.

The four linguistic skills of understanding, speaking, reading, and writing Gaelic were represented to very different extents among the Gaelic-English bilinguals of East Sutherland in the period between 1963 and 1978. The number of people who *understood* ESG in addition to English was fairly large, perhaps almost double the number who spoke it; I make that estimate on the basis of both self-reports and my own experience with the families of active bilinguals. The number of those who read Gaelic was very much smaller than the number who spoke it (though larger than the number who professed to be able to read, thanks to some quasi-literacy through experience with the Bible and psalm singing). ESG is never written, and therefore any approach to literacy was over the hurdle of a largely unfamiliar form of Gaelic. Reading the Bible was possible for many because of familiarity, whereas reading a newspaper column in Gaelic was almost impossible because of the unfamiliar lexicon and grammar. The ability to read and write English was universal, of course. The ability to write a connected paragraph or an entire letter in Gaelic was limited to a very few, though most of those who could read could also write isolated words or phrases with greater or lesser accuracy.

Code-switching and Interference

Within the bilingual communities themselves there is considerable self-criticism of Gaelic speech performance (and, to a much lesser degree, of English speech performance) on grounds of code-switching and interference. A few individuals are notorious for their mix of codes; they are said to speak *dàrn' leth Gàidhlig, dàrn' leth Beurl'* ['half Gaelic, half English'], and are strongly criticized for failure to finish a sentence in the language in which they began it. In my own interactions with East Sutherland bilinguals, I have observed relatively little code-switching – nothing remotely approaching the single-sentence switches which are reported for some Spanish-English bilinguals in the United States, for example (Ma and Herasimchuk 1971: 359; Timm 1975: 482). Most of the switches made without a change in interlocutors, in my experience, have consisted of the insertion in a Gaelic sentence of a stock phrase like 'very good', or 'that's right', often followed immediately by the equivalent phrase (usually a calque) in Gaelic. In conversations with me, a mistake in Gaelic on my part, or some other verbal or nonverbal behavior, sometimes apparently reminded a bilingual that he or she was conversing with an English-dominant interlocutor and precipitated a switch. And sometimes a switch depended on the nature of the material being discussed; for example, when reference is made to the activities of English monolinguals in the family of a bilingual, a brief switch to English may occur. Switching is less a general community-wide behavior, however, than a characteristic of certain individuals who acquire a reputation for it:

> There's a woman down there at the end of the street, she starts off with the Gaelic, I answer her back; but in the middle of it, then she starts the English, so English then I've got to answer back. (Brora bilingual, 1972)

Interesting here is the degree to which the speaker feels constrained by her interlocutor's code switching; she switches herself in response to every change on the part of her conversation partner. A number of people say that they will speak as they are spoken to, even if it involves switching in mid-stream. Others, of course, will march on in the language in which the conversation was begun and will resist a switch tentatively initiated by the conversation partner. When Gaelic is the language that is persevered in, the reasons may range from a desire to keep the conversation private (that is, unintelligible to nearby English speakers) to a resistance to a suspected language disloyalty on the part of the conversation partner (see the next section of this chapter).

Far and away the greatest part of all code switching in the verbal performance of ESG speakers is the result of a change in interlocutors. A conversation begun in Gaelic will instantly be switched to English if a monolingual joins the group. A conversation begun in English may change to Gaelic if an older person with whom each of two younger bilinguals habitually speaks Gaelic joins the group, even though the two younger bilinguals may seldom speak Gaelic to each other. Under these circumstances the switch may even take place in mid-sentence. One Gaelic speaker who had spent years in domestic service in a house where Gaelic was not acceptable for public use could switch in the twinkling of an eye if an English monolingual approached.

In earlier days code switching might occur by reason of inadequate English. A struggling 'bilingual' might start off bravely in English but switch back to Gaelic whenever he struck a word or phrase which he did not know in English:

> One old lady, ... she was from Embo, and she had very, very poor English. And she was selling cockles, and this lady asked her, 'How do you cook them?' 'Well, you put them first in a *bùrn maoth bhlàth,* and then they'll *sgeith* out all the *gainmheach.*'[1] (Golspie bilingual, 1976)

This kind of switching is not really distinguishable from lexical 'interference', of which there is a great deal in present-day East Sutherland linguistic behavior. Now, however, most of the lexical movement runs from English into Gaelic, rather than the other way around; there is certainly some Gaelic-to-English movement, too, but the commoner phenomenon is English words used in Gaelic speech. When English words appear in Gaelic, they may be dealt with in either of two ways. They may be retained as strictly English words, with English morphology and morphophonology; or they may be adapted to Gaelic morphology and morphophonology in such a way that they are treated as if they were Gaelic words. The second of these two strategies is much the commoner overall, and it is hard to say at times whether an

English word should simply be considered a bona fide loanword in Gaelic or an instance of interference. Although such a classic treatment of lexical interference as Weinreich's (1964: 47–62) simply discusses loanwords as one of several types of lexical interference (along with, for example, loan translations or creations, hybrid compounds and semantic extension), the question arises of how long after its introduction a loanword remains an instance of interference. Some English words are so thoroughly ingrained in ESG that the bilingual has no apparent sense of using a loanword: /ənkəl/ 'uncle', /anti/ 'aunt', /kʰəsin/ 'cousin', and /stoːri/ 'story' are examples. Other words are consciously borrowed, either for want of an equivalent word in Gaelic or for their especially good fit and effect. Quite often these conscious borrowings are preceded by lead-in phrases which serve to announce their use:

Agus bhris a' ghloine, anns' anothri chaoban, no b' urrain dhomh chantuinn 'smithereens' ['And the glass broke, into several pieces, or I could say "smithereens" ']. (Golspie bilingual, 1968)

Here the English word is carefully introduced, and its English plural morphology is retained, as well as the very un-Gaelic stress on the ultimate syllable. But in the same story, a minute or two later, the speaker used the word *poilioschan* [ˈpʰɔlisxən] 'police', and in that case there was no lead-in, the plural allomorph is Gaelic *-chan,* and the stress is on the first syllable in conformity with Gaelic stress rules. It is clear that the first case is one of interference, but in the second case one might argue that the word was borrowed from English long since and has been so thoroughly re-formed that it no longer constitutes interference, any more than the use of the word *jaunty* constitutes French interference in English. The great majority of English loanwords in Gaelic, whether loanwords of very long standing or loans that are used on the spur of the moment by an individual bilingual, are well integrated into Gaelic in terms not only of phonology (though not phonotactics) but also of morphophonology, of derivational and grammatical morphology, and of syntax. In a particularly striking example, a Gaelic speaker said to her sister, /waˈčkʰə dɔstʰ, yiːn/ 'Watch the toast, Jean.' English *watch* picked up a verb-making derivational morpheme; the initial /tʰ/ of /tʰɔstʰ/ 'toast' was voiced in the presence of the preceding definite article as required by Gaelic syntax and morphophonology; and although the English form of the sister's name was used, /ʄiːn/, it was subjected to initial consonant mutation as required in the Gaelic vocative. Despite the fact that this short sentence contains only one entirely Gaelic word (the definite article), it is a thoroughly Gaelic performance. If English lexical items treated according to well-established patterns of phonological and morphological integration are discounted, then interference from English is minimal in ESG, although it varies from person to person and from setting to setting. On the other hand, in the broader sense of the sheer appearance of words of recognizably English origin, interference in present-day ESG is vast. English idiom is also carried over into Gaelic, although it is not rampant.

The use of recognizably English loanwords in Gaelic is currently a touchy matter in East Sutherland. English monolinguals, rather than giving credit to the bilinguals for command of two languages, frequently mock the bilinguals' Gaelic because of the English loanwords which they can perceive embedded in it. Remarks like 'What sort of Gaelic is that?' or 'I could speak that Gaelic myself!' are common. The bilinguals are self-conscious about the matter of loanwords and frequently check each other for the use of an English word, as when one Embo bilingual corrected his wife's borrowing of *tiun* 'tune' to *port,* the Gaelic equivalent. Precisely because everyone uses such loanwords, and because there is considerable self-consciousness about it, the number of loanwords in a verbal performance seems to have become a marker of degree of formality in ESG. In a relaxed and casual performance, the number of lexical borrowings will rise (most of them, as usual, well integrated into the Gaelic framework). On the other hand, the more formal the performance – for example, established narrative routines reproduced for tape recording – the lower the number of lexical borrowings and the greater the likelihood that some of those which appear will be accompanied by lead-in phrases like 'as we would say'. In one such tape-recorded narrative, a speaker even replaced the usual ESG [ˈpʰɔlis] or [ˈpʰɔlisxən] by *luchd an lagh* 'law people', elegant Gaelic but otherwise foreign to the lips of any East Sutherlander of my acquaintance.

In dealing with the phenomenon of Gaelic interference in East Sutherland forms of English, it must be remembered that both the local East Sutherland English and standard Highland English show a strong Gaelic substratum effect, though East Sutherland English is also heavily influenced by Scots. The idiomatic use of 'in it' (Gaelic *ann*) is a case in point (for example, 'There was no radio or television in it in my young days'), and so is 'it's' plus pronoun and relative clause introduced by 'that' (for example, 'It's you that should be thankful you weren't caught'). Consequently the interference of ESG in bilinguals' English is primarily noticeable in the form of a Gaelic accent and in lexical interference (Gaelic loanwords, and for some speakers a good many Gaelic interjections). Some occasional loan translation occurs (for example, to 'put' potatoes – Gaelic *cuir* – rather than to 'plant'), and some Gaelic idiom appears (to 'go on' fire rather than to 'catch' fire); syntactic influence can also be found: for example, the use of progressive forms of verbs like 'see' and 'believe', or the use of the demonstrative 'that' without inflection for number (for example, 'that cabbages'). As with English lexicon in Gaelic, there are accepted patterns for the integration of Gaelic loanwords in English. The

English sibilant plural is regularly applied to Gaelic nouns used in an English sentence, for example.

As in bilingual communities generally, the amount of English interference in a person's Gaelic, or Gaelic interference in a person's English, varies with the linguistic background of the interlocutor:

> In speaking to a unilingual, the bilingual often tends to limit interference and to eliminate even habitualized borrowings from his speech...But when the other interlocutor is also bilingual, the requirements of intelligibility and status assertion are drastically reduced. Under such circumstances, there is hardly any limit to interference.... (Weinreich 1964: 81)

Two Gaelic speakers engaged in conversation together, whether in Gaelic or in English, will show on the whole more interference from the other language than either will show in conversation with a monolingual.

Language Loyalty

Scotland has a long history of suppression (in the strongest form) and discouragement (in milder forms) of Gaelic. Anti-Gaelic attitudes in Sutherland go back at least to the time of Sir Robert Gordon's letter of advice to his nephew, the prospective thirteenth Earl of Sutherland, in the early seventeenth century. By the 1840s a newly 'opened' eastern Sutherland had begun so profound a flight from Gaelic that the extinction of the language in the area could be foreseen.

The fisherfolk were relatively slow to succumb to the pressures favoring a shift to English. Their separate work sphere reduced the economic pressure to master and adopt English, and their separate social sphere left them in a predominantly Gaelic subculture of their own. They were on the one hand 'protected' from English, and on the other hand 'prevented' from it, depending on the point of view. And of course there were people within the fishing communities who represented each of those points of view: those who were content to be left to their traditional ways, including the Gaelic language, and those who were eager for access to the wider society, which required English. In any language shift, some individuals will be in the vanguard, some will hold a middle ground, and some will lag behind. Where the subordinate language is associated with a stigmatized group, language choices are inevitably highly charged. Anyone who adopts the dominant language will be viewed as something of a traitor to his original group. A Norwegian investigator, working in an increasingly norwegianized Coast-Lappish area of Norway where Lapps are the stigmatized group, found that Lapps could enter into intimate relationships with resident Norwegian incomers, but at a cost:

> Within the local area, a Lapp might establish such a relation with a Norwegian. Those who have a perfect command of Norwegian, and a Norwegian physiognomy, have the best chances of doing this, especially *if they are willing to cut themselves off from intimate interaction with other Lapps.* (Eidheim 1969: 54; italics added)

Mobility out of the stigmatized group requires dissociation from that group. Adoption of the dominant language is one of the dissociative behaviors most obvious to the original group and consequently bitterly resented by them.

In eastern Sutherland the choice of English by a person of fisherfolk background is labeled 'pride', and the bitterest accusation one ESG speaker can level at another is that he is 'too proud' to speak Gaelic. The offense is greatest if the person is spoken to in Gaelic but replies in English. An elderly Golspie bilingual waxed indignant over the failure of fisher descendants a generation younger than she to answer in Gaelic when addressed in Gaelic, but in a rare burst of candor she recognized that she had been guilty of the same 'pride' when she was a young woman:

> Why aren't they speaking what I would call the Gaelic: 'the mother tongue'? Which they were born with. It's the first thing that went into their mouths, and why would they be so proud and not speak it? – I was a little proud myself, when I was younger. Because I wasn't going along with the fisherfolk west. I was always with the non-fishers, and Gaelic wasn't spoken. It was always the English. (Golspie bilingual 1968; translated from the Gaelic)

Bilinguals explicitly connect 'pride' with the local extinction of Gaelic: 'People today are too proud. Pride has a lot to do with it. That's how I'm saying it's a dying language' (Brora bilingual, 1972). This analysis recognizes the stigmatizing effect of Gaelic speech in East Sutherland, and the increasing tendency, in a local society which has allowed for much greater social mobility over the last sixty years, to opt for the widely favored language in one's repertoire.

On the whole, East Sutherland bilinguals are most critical of the language choices of the age groups closest to their own and are severely intolerant of linguistic disloyalty among their peers. Where some dislike exists between individuals, it is not uncommon for language disloyalty to be charged against the other person whether or not the speaker has any real knowledge of the other person's language habits. I have known two staunch language loyalists each to suggest that the other was guilty of a 'proud' abandonment of Gaelic. Willingness to use Gaelic, on the other hand, especially in public, is a sign of social solidarity among members of the former fishing communities and is vigorously approved of.

Coexisting with resentment of disloyalty to Gaelic among their own age group and others near in age, and with their own vein of language-loyal speech behavior, is a largely negative attitude where the transmission of Gaelic to the succeeding generation is concerned. It is *not* acceptable to behave as though one did not know Gaelic oneself, but it *is* acceptable to do nothing to see that one's children know it. No pride in being a Gaelic speaker was inculcated in the current bilinguals. They were not praised for their Gaelic or urged to speak it; it was simply something they automatically acquired through living in Gaelic-speaking homes in the 'fishertowns'. When they came to have children of their own, they adopted pragmatic attitudes. One woman who made no effort to teach her children Gaelic said: 'They couldn't get through the world with Gaelic. That's what we thou[ght] – took for granted. The Gaelic's no use to you through the world' (Brora bilingual, 1974). Another, taxed with raising monolingual children, said simply: 'It wouldn't be of any interest to them' (Brora bilingual, 1972). This last woman takes a realistic view of her modern-day surroundings and assesses the value of her two languages accordingly:

> See, when you go to the shops, here, or when you meet people on the road, and they don't understand, well, you've got to speak the language they understand and that's the English. There's more English in this parish now than there is of Gaelic, and before we were born it was more Gaelic than English. See, times have changed. People's changed with it.

A very common pattern consisted of parents speaking Gaelic between themselves but addressing their children in English. The result quite often was that the children were passively bilingual in varying degrees (some of them even perfect passive bilinguals) A few of the children clearly wished to dissociate themselves from their fisherfolk background and urged their parents not to speak Gaelic at all, but most merely ignored the second language in their environment and opted for English exclusively. Parents and children agreed on the positive value of English and the negative value of Gaelic for the rising generation.

The home is the last bastion of a subordinate language in competition with a dominant official language of wider currency. An impending shift has in effect arrived, even though a fairly sizable number of speakers may be left, if those speakers have failed to transmit the language to their children, so that no replacement generation is available when the parent generation dies away. The pattern of the shift is almost monotonously the same in diverse settings: the language of wider currency is recognized as the language of upward mobility, and as soon as the linguistic competence of the parents permits, it is introduced into the home.

Only where the decision to shift to English in the home was too early or too late, in terms of the norms for the particular fishing community where it occurred, did it attract sharp criticism. One woman who was frequently heard to tell her son not to speak Gaelic because it would spoil his English, at a time when all the children in that village were Gaelic speakers, was the object of much resentment. On the other hand, in the same village, a family which allowed its children to arrive at school without English, at a time when all the other children were bilingual at school age, was equally subject to criticism. Evidently neither language disloyalty nor language loyalty as such is regarded as the important issue, but conformity to the linguistic norm. Note that this is language loyalty with regard to the *transmission* of Gaelic; language loyalty with regard to the *use* of Gaelic by known bilinguals is regarded as a separate issue.

There is nothing surprising in the fact that some individuals in the fishing communities made an early decision in favor of English, or in the fact that most kept pace with their community as a whole in moving from Gaelic to English. Neither is there anything very surprising in the fact that many Gaelic-dominant bilinguals continued to choose to use mostly Gaelic themselves while they chose not to transmit Gaelic to their children; they were raised with Gaelic themselves, but recognized that times had changed and that their children would be operating in the open world of modern-day Britain rather than in the closed world of the fishing communities. But there is one group of individuals who do evoke surprise and require some explanation: the *semi-speakers*.

Unlike the older Gaelic-dominant bilinguals, the semi-speakers are not fully proficient in Gaelic. They speak it with varying degrees of less than full fluency, and their grammar (and usually also their phonology) is markedly aberrant in terms of the fluent-speaker norm. Semi-speakers may be distinguished from fully fluent speakers of any age by the presence of deviations in their Gaelic which are explicitly labeled 'mistakes' by the fully fluent speakers. That is, the speech community is aware of many (though not all) of the deficiencies in semi-speaker speech performance. Most semi-speakers are also relatively halting in delivery, or speak Gaelic in rather short bursts, or both; but it is not manner of delivery which distinguishes them, since semi-speakers of comparable grammatical ability may speak with very different degrees of confidence and 'fluency'. At the lower end of speaker skill, semi-speakers are distinguished from near-passive bilinguals by their ability to manipulate words in sentences. Near-passive bilinguals often know a good many words or phrases, but cannot build sentences with them or alter them productively. Semi-speakers can, although the resultant sentences may be morphologically or syntactically askew to a greater or lesser extent.

It seems perverse that a group of people whose control of ESG is imperfect, and whose agemates have for the most part opted for English only, should continue to use a stigmatized language of strictly local currency when they are fully proficient speakers of a language of wider currency. There are at least four identifiable factors which operate to produce the anomaly of the ESG semi-speaker. The simplest, because it involves least in the way of active choice, is late birth-order in a large, relatively language-loyal family. Quite often the last two or three children among a large group of siblings will emerge as semi-speakers. It is not so much that the parents alter their language practices with these last children (although that can happen, too), as that the number of older siblings who have received English-language schooling begins to affect the amount of Gaelic spoken in the home, especially among the children themselves.

Other factors presuppose more in the way of a conscious choosing of Gaelic among young potential speakers. The factor most frequently mentioned by semi-speakers themselves is a strong attachment to some kinsperson other than the parents in the first or – especially – second ascending generation. It may be older siblings or cousins or aunts or uncles of the parents who play the crucial role in this linguistic socialization, but more often than not it is the parents' parents. In one case, one daughter was frequently sent to stay for long periods with a grandmother who had very little English, while several of her siblings were sent to a far more bilingual grandmother; she became fluent as a child, and remains an exceedingly language-loyal semi-speaker, while the siblings who went to the other grandmother are not now Gaelic speakers. In another case, the younger of two daughters became a semi-speaker because of her greater attachment to the grandmother.

> I used to stay with my granny a lot, you see, this is the thing. And I – I suppose my granny and grandfather, they spoke Gaelic all the time More so, I suppose – I suppose I heard my granny and grandfather more than my mother and father, really...My sister's older, but funny enough, I think I – I probably knew more than she did. And I think it was because I lived with my granny so much. I was never out of my granny's. (Embo semi-speaker, 1974)

Thanks to the strong cross-generational ties outside the nuclear family which are characteristic of the fishing communities, a number of semi-speakers appeared even in households where the parents did not seek to pass Gaelic on to the children.

A third factor in the genesis of the semi-speaker is exile, temporary or even permanent. It seems that a period away from the home community, in the company of a few fellow exiles, can produce an allegiance to one's own community which may take the form of language loyalty:

> I remember when we were working away, when I was in Edinburgh and there were girls there from Brora, and we always went out and we spoke [Gaelic]

together. You know, the three of us. Because, you know, we just liked speaking. (Brora semi-speaker, 1974)

In permanent exile the emblematic value of the home language is even stronger. An Embo-born woman who has lived in London since she was seven years old clings tenaciously to her Highland fishing-village heritage:

> I think it's a privilege, really, to speak [Gaelic]...it's a connection with the Highlands. And I just – well, Scotland to me is *the* place...I just enjoy talking it. And I – the older I get, the more I want to keep it. You know, I don't want to lose it. I think the older I get, the more I speak it. (Embo semi-speaker, 1974)

This last semi-speaker is the most improbable example of language loyalty in my experience. London is an environment which can hardly be called favorable to Gaelic, and although her parents are active Gaelic speakers, they originally followed the pattern of speaking Gaelic to each other but not to the children. The daughter had extremely strong ties to one grandmother and lived in the grandmother's household until she was seven, but after that age she saw her grandmother only once or twice a year for brief periods. Aside from cross-generational linguistic socialization and exile, however, this woman exemplifies a fourth factor in the genesis of the semi-speaker: the inordinately inquisitive and gregarious personality. Outgoing and curious as a child, she insisted on being part of all linguistic interactions in her environment, Gaelic or English. Her parents, and even her beloved grandmother, tended to switch to English when speaking to her, but she demanded that they use Gaelic to her, too, so that she could learn both languages. Her goal was access to any verbal communication:

> *Investigator*: Now, did your parents want you to learn Gaelic, or didn't they?
> *Embo semi-speaker*: They didn't, they didn't pay any attention to what I was speaking...I was always saying to them, 'What's that you're saying?' It was my nose [that is, curiosity] (1974; translated from the Gaelic)

That this drive to be included linguistically is a characteristic of one individual's personality and not inherent in the situation is borne out by the fact that this semi-speaker's cousin of the same age, who lived in her grandmother's household in East Sutherland exactly as long as she did (and was also devoted to the grandmother) and then in London under exactly the same circumstances as she (Gaelic consistently spoken between the parents, adult visitors to the home likewise Gaelic speakers), neither speaks nor understands Gaelic today.

   There is no way to identify a semi-speaker except by testing. Some people who claim some Gaelic control prove to be excellent passive bilinguals but cannot make an intelligible sentence from the considerable number of isolated words which they know. One individual who actually *disclaimed* Gaelic control proved, on testing, to be a semi-speaker of the same proficiency as some others who speak freely and gladly and who *do* claim Gaelic control. The factors identified here are based on what is common to the backgrounds of both the 'claimers' and the 'disclaimer' who showed testable semi-speaker proficiency. The one 'disclaimer' in the sample makes little active use of her Gaelic but expresses great attachment to Gaelic and showed stable control of the language over a five-year testing period; that is, she is not losing the language at any observable rate. It should be noted that there is no *predictive* power to the factors identified here as important in the genesis of the semi-speaker. Exposure to a beloved Gaelic-speaking grandparent does not necessarily produce a semi-speaker, nor does exile from the community, although the more of the four factors that come into play the more likely it is that a semi-speaker will result.

Most semi-speakers seem to have rather fixed networks of Gaelic interaction, such that they use the language with a certain group of older bilinguals, mostly or wholly their own kin. They do not volunteer Gaelic with bilinguals outside this network, and to my suggestion that some of the older people might be delighted to discover that they could speak Gaelic they responded skeptically. They said that the older people outside their own networks would continue to speak English to them because English had become the older people's normal language of communication with people of the younger generation. In this they were most likely correct. A few semi-speakers attend Gaelic classes or sing in a Gaelic choir or both. These individuals tend to make wider use of their Gaelic; they will, for example, attempt to speak to Gaelic speakers from other parts of the Highlands. Two semi-speakers who live in a household where fluent speakers are still available as models have become noticeably better speakers of Gaelic during the five years over which they were tested. They say that having their Gaelic examined has roused their interest and curiosity, so that they now take note of what the fluent speakers are saying and how they say it.

Conclusion

The sociolinguistic perspective of this chapter has been dynamic where possible, static where necessary. Patterns of interaction between Gaelic and English, and the several varieties of each, have not been constant over the past seventy or eighty years but are ever-changing. In connection with some of the topics covered in this chapter, the patterns of change have been recoverable through observation and through in-depth interviewing of bilinguals and monolinguals of various ages. The movement of the linguistic domain of religion from wholly Gaelic to largely English is easily traced, for example, and patterns of language loyalty across various age groups are recoverable not only through interviewing but also by observing language behaviors over two and sometimes three generations of a family. On the other hand, self-reports of patterns of code switching fifty years previously are thoroughly unreliable, and it is impossible to get a realistic sense of whether some language behaviors have become more or less prevalent (for example, whether it is more true now than formerly that the presence of a single English interlocutor causes a Gaelic-speaking group to switch to English).

The only surprising thing about the sociolinguistic patterns treated here is that the triumph of English was not more rapid and more total. There are at least five aspects of linguistic behavior, in the areas described here, in which the dominance of English over Gaelic is less complete than might be anticipated.

First, despite the association of English with modernity and technology and the public spheres of life, no topic connected with these aspects of life forces a choice of English. If the setting and the interlocutor permit, any topic, no matter how sophisticated or remote from local life, can be discussed in Gaelic. Closely related to this aspect of resistance to English dominance is the thoroughgoing integration of English lexical borrowings into Gaelic; this integration makes possible the use of Gaelic for all topics. A third aspect of the resilience of Gaelic is the absence of a true diglossic relationship, in Fishman's (1967) extended sense, between Gaelic and English. Gaelic can be used for H purposes, and is; English can be used for L purposes, and is. English has not been allowed to usurp all of the higher-prestige functions in the local linguistic ecology, even though it is the higher-prestige language. Again, and fourth, code switching in East Sutherland has not become rampant, despite the fact that all Gaelic speakers also know English. Most of the code switching which occurs is the result of a change in interlocutors, rather than a change in topic or in the mood of the speaker. Finally, and most strikingly, a number of semi-speakers emerged from the very age groups in which Gaelic was largely abandoned, some of them acquiring their Gaelic very much by an act of will:

Brora semi-speaker: I was trying, myself, picking up words, and I was trying then – between my mother and my father, they were speaking Gaelic, I was trying what – to understand what they were saying. They were always speaking Gaelic...

Investigator [interrupting]: Didn't your parents want –

Brora semi-speaker [interrupting]: I don't think [so], I don't think they wanted [to teach us Gaelic]...They wanted to speak Gaelic so that we couldn't understand them. (1968; translated from the Gaelic)

This woman's elderly mother confirmed that she and her husband had not intended to transmit Gaelic to their children; it was a cousin of the father's who played the crucial linguistic socialization role in this semi-speaker's life. The power of the factors identified above as instrumental in producing semi-speakers can be measured by the perversity of the result: a group of fully proficient English speakers who choose to go on speaking, imperfectly, a language which links them to a stigmatized group.

Acknowledgements

Since my involvement with East Sutherland Gaelic spans a sixteen-year period, there are a great many people who have lent assistance to this project, in a great variety of forms, over the years.

Professor James Downer of the University of Michigan agreed to supervise a dissertation on an unlikely language, thereby enabling me to begin my study of Gaelic. Professor Eric Hamp of the University of Chicago ensured departmental approval of the project by agreeing to serve extramurally as a Celtic specialist. Professor Kenneth Jackson of the University of Edinburgh directed my attention to East Sutherland as an area of special linguistic interest. Eric Cregeen of the School of Scottish Studies provided limitless collegial support, ranging from bibliographic references to office space; he also made available to me the questionnaire he himself uses to investigate fisherfolk life in the British Isles. The School of Scottish Studies and the Gaelic Division of the Linguistic Survey of Scotland did me many professional courtesies during the entire period. David Clement of the Linguistic Survey of Scotland shared my interest in Sutherland and enthusiasm for its Gaelic. In East Sutherland the public library branch at Brora, where a collection of books of local interest is housed, was unfailingly helpful; unfortunately I can thank by name only the most recent of a series of kind staff members, Mrs. Dora MacLeod. Mr. Ian MacKay of the Golspie High School library also gave me free access to a large collection of books, journals, and papers of local interest and provided professional courtesies of several kinds. A great many old books and journals kept under lock and key in the Dornoch reading room were repeatedly made available to me through the good offices of a variety of public servants.

NOTE

1. *Bùrn maoth bhlàth* 'lukewarm water'; *sgeith* 'spew'; *gainmheach* 'sand'.

REFERENCES

Adler, Max K. 1977. *Welsh and the Other Dying Languages in Europe.* Hamburg: Helmut Buske Verlag.

Breatnach, R. B. 1964. Characteristics of Irish dialects in process of extinction. In *Communications et rapports du premier congres de dialectologie générale.* Louvain: Centre international de dialectologie générale. 141–145.

Cole, Roger L. 1975. Divergent and convergent attitudes towards the Alsatian dialect. *Anthropological Linguistics* 17: 293–304.

Denison, N. 1971. Some observations on language variety and plurilingualism. In Edwin Ardener (ed.) *Social Anthropology and Language.* London: Tavistock Publications. 157–183.

Dorian, Nancy C. 1973. Grammatical change in a dying dialect. *Language* 49: 414–438.

Dorian, Nancy C. 1977. A hierarchy of morphophonemic decay in Scottish Gaelic language death: The differential failure of lenition. *Word* 28: 96–109.

Dorian, Nancy C. 1978. The fate of morphological complexity in language death: Evidence from East Sutherland Gaelic. *Language* 54: 590–609.

Dressler, Wolfgang. 1972. On the phonology of language death. *Papers of the Chicago Linguistic Society* 8: 448–457.

Dressler, Wolfgang. 1977. Wortbildung bei Sprachverfall. In Herbert E. Brekle and Dieter Kastovsky (eds.) *Perspektiven der Wortbildungsforschung.* Bonn: Bouvier Verlag Herbert Grundmann. 62–69.

Dressler, Wolfgang and R. Leodolter. 1973. Sprachbewahrung und Sprachtod in der Bretagne. *Wiener linguistische Gazette* 3: 45–58.

Eidheim, Harald. 1969. When ethnic identity is a social stigma. In Fredrik Barth (ed.) *Ethnic Groups and Boundaries.* Boston: Little, Brown and Company. 39–57.

Ferguson, Charles A. 1959. Diglossia. *Word* 15: 325–340.

Fishman, Joshua A. 1964. Language maintenance and language shift as a field of inquiry. *Linguistics* 9: 32–70.

Fishman, Joshua A. 1967. Bilingualism with and without diglossia; diglossia with and without bilingualism. *Journal of Social Issues* 23: 29–38.

Grubb, David M. 1975. *Conference on American Indian Languages Clearinghouse Newsletter* 3: 2.

Hill, Jane H. 1973. Subordinate clause density and language function. In C. Corum, T. C. Smith-Stark and A. Weiser (eds.) *You Take the High Node and I'll Take the Low Node: Papers from the Comparative Syntax Festival.* Chicago: Chicago Linguistic Society. 33–52.

Lehmann, Winfred P. 1962. *Historical Linguistics: An Introduction.* New York: Holt, Rinehart, and Winston.

Ma, Roxana and Herasimchuk, Eleanor. 1971. The linguistic dimensions of a bilingual neighborhood. In Joshua A. Fishman, Robert L. Cooper, Roxana Ma, et al. (eds.) *Bilingualism in the Barrio,* Indiana University publications: *Language Science Monographs,* vol. 7. The Hague: Mouton. 347–464.

Timm, L. A. 1973. Modernization and language shift: The case of Brittany. *Anthropological Linguistics* 15: 281–298.

Timm, L. A. 1975. Spanish-English code-switching: Porque y how-not-to. *Romance Philology* 28: 473–482.

Trudgill, Peter. 1976–1977. Creolization in reverse: Reduction and simplification in the Albanian dialects of Greece. *Transactions of the Philological Society* 1976–1977: 32–50.

Voegelin, C. F. and Voegelin, F. M. 1977. Is Tübatulabal de-acquisition relevant to theories of language acquisition? *International Journal of American Linguistics* 43: 333–338.

Weinreich, Uriel. 1964. *Languages in Contact.* The Hague: Mouton.

CHAPTER 38

A Sociolinguistics of Globalization

JAN BLOMMAERT

Introduction

Johannes Fabian opens his *Anthropology with an Attitude* (2001) with an essay entitled 'With so much critique and reflection around, who needs theory?' Its title and the argument capture the spirit of our times: we live in an age in which *la pensée* and careful analysis have come under pressure from various sides, yet are more than ever necessary. Faced with deep transformations in society which demonstrate the failure of older paradigms, we need to unthink and reconstruct our paradigms, improve them and expand them (Wallerstein 2001). As announced by Nik Coupland (2003), when Sociolinguistics attempts to address globalization, it will need new theory. The first phase of the process is therefore the laborious and often unrewarding phase of trial-and-error: see what works, define topics, units and fields, and try some analysis. In what follows, I want to assemble some building blocks, useful for what I believe should be our ambition here: to start developing a Sociolinguistics of globalization. Second, I will add two suggestions for incorporating particular theoretical instruments in such an exercise: the notion of the *world system* and that of *second linguistic relativity*.

Necessary Building Blocks

A first, necessary building block for a Sociolinguistics of globalization is *scale*: the macro and the micro, the global and the local, the different levels at which 'language' can be said to exist and at which sociolinguistic processes operate (cf. Blommaert 2006): for instance, the relationship between a 'world language' – English – and local speech repertoires or speech communities, the different ways in which English permeates speech habits, propagates and organizes genres, or reorganizes functional hierarchies for languages. The scalar processes and phenomena are becoming less predictable and more chaotic and complicated, it seems, in the era of globalization; in many cases, we see how hard it becomes to separate and order 'small' versus 'large' processes. Machin and Van Leeuwen's (2003) discussion of different versions of *Cosmopolitan* shows that we are facing 'small' genres that are deeply connected to very specific audiences and forms of commodification. *Cosmopolitan* explicitly aspires to a global reach and uses similar modes of expression wherever it appears: it explicitly voices and identifies globalization as an identity issue for its readership by using the general recognizable template of the magazine all over the world, while adding adaptations to local customs and audience preferences (e.g. in showing or hiding female nudity). Thus, it is simultaneously oriented towards *national* elites and appeals to and emphatically flags 'national' (or 'national-cultural') characteristics. Ideals of female beauty and success are, thus, constructed on the basis of transnational templates (suggested to be universal patterns of femininity) to which local transformations have been added. Different scales seem to overlap and combine in one genre, and it is hard to determine which scale would hierarchically dominate the others.

Scale is definitely the keyword in any analysis of globalization. The term globalization itself suggests a process of lifting events from one level to a higher one, a global one, or vice versa, and a Sociolinguistics of globalization will definitely need to explain the various forms of interconnectedness between levels and scales of sociolinguistic phenomena. The complexity and simultaneity we are facing is a challenge, not a danger. But we need to be more precise, and I think two qualifications are in order.

First, we need to *move from Languages to language varieties and repertoires* (Hymes 1996: 67; Silverstein 1998). What is globalized is not an abstract Language, but specific speech forms, genres, styles, forms of literacy practice. And the way in which such globalized varieties enter into local environments is by a reordering or the locally available repertoires and the relative hierarchical relations between ingredients in the hierarchy. Sociolinguistic globalization results in a reorganization of the sociolinguistic stratigraphy – the layering of different hierarchically organized strata. This process does not necessarily lead to a new solid and lasting hierarchy but may best be seen as an ongoing, highly volatile process cross-cut, again, by matters of scale.

The point is made by Machin and Van Leeuwen (2003), who emphasize the domain-related spread of global registers rather than languages. What *Cosmopolitan* does sociolinguistically is to spread a *particular* discourse on femininity, success, beauty and sexuality. This particular discourse is globalized and it displays some degree of uniformity in each of the 40-plus local areas of circulation investigated by Machin and Van Leeuwen. But it is not a whole-sale import of a complete, new, set of ideologies of femininity – it is *niched*. Pennycook's (2003, this volume) Japanese rappers insert globalized slang into an idiosyncratic popular-cultural brew: a particular *niche*. The impact of such forms of speech is *niched* and restricted to particular groups (networks, com-munities of practice, etc.) in societies. Therefore, finding the particular niche on which the globalized flows eventually have an impact may be a crucial part of our sociolinguistic assignment: it would offer us a first clue about what glo-balized sociolinguistic phenomena mean to identifiable groups of people, and about what these people can actually do with it.

A second but closely related qualification is that we need to address the *language-ideological level* in these processes. In understanding the processes of 'globalized' insertion of varieties into newly stratified orders of indexicality, the key to an understanding is what such reorderings of repertoires actually mean and represent to people (Blommaert 2005). The globalized discourses on femininity in *Cosmopolitan*, for instance, reorder the discursive order on femininity in the countries where the magazine is sold, and so reorganize hierarchies of what is good and desirable in that domain: talk about femininity now proceeds within a new order of indexicality, words and images start meaning different things. There is ample evidence for the assumption that language ideologies affect language change, including forms of transformation now captured under the label 'globalized' (Blommaert 1999b; Gal and Woolard 2001; Kroskrity 2000; Schieffelin et al. 1998 and see chapters in Part IV). The ideological, metapragmatic and indexical aspects of language usage lead us to an understanding of meaning and function of 'new' ingredients in repertoires: they allow us to understand which functions people assign to such items, and why. Take both elements together: the fact that we have to deal with niched sociolinguistic phenomena related to the insertion of particular varieties of language in existing repertoires, and the language-ideological load both guid-ing the process and being one of its results. What we now see is how people create *semiotic opportunity* in globalization processes, framed in the larger picture of the new economies. People manage to assign specific new functions to sociolinguistic items (either 'global' items or 'local' ones), and accomplish specific, targeted (globalized) goals with them, often forms of identity work that could not be done without the potential offered by globalization. The Rip Slyme case discussed by Alastair Pennycook (2003, this volume) offers us good examples. We have here a Japanese hip-hop ensemble who use phonetically 'nativized' American English hip-hop slang in a peculiar blend with Japanese, thus constructing a genred semiotic product: rap lyrics. Furthermore, the packaging of indexicalities is firmly anchored in, and enabled by, globaliza-tion. The particular 'globalized' linguistic and cultural-stylistic blend allows the semiotization of unique indexicalities that point towards the local-global dynamics characterizing and contextualizing the cultural practice of hip-hop. It thus allows the construction of a particular commodified variety of language, a nicely globalized and globalizable language product.

Importantly, at this level of language usage, scale proves to be an issue again. We see no fundamental hierarchical difference between local and global indexicalities: they occur simultaneously. Metaphors such as the 'invasion' of English into Japanese, let alone linguistic and cultural 'imperialism' or worldwide linguacultural homogenization – 'McDonaldization' – are obviously inadequate for a description of this fantastic semiotic creativity *from below*, which allows language users opportunities to represent cultural, social and historical conditions of being.

It is an important accomplishment if we manage to see sociolinguistic globalization in these terms: as a matter of particular language varieties entering the repertoires of particular groups, creating new semiotic opportunities and commodities for members of such groups and indeed constructing them as groups. Some of these varieties come 'from above' through language policy or education regulations, others come 'from below' through informal markets for English such as popular culture and new globalized media. We can now move on and focus on *mobility* as a key feature of sign complexes in globalization: the fact that language varieties, texts, images travel across time and space, and that this is a journey across repertoires and sets of indexicalities attached to ingredients of repertoires. A Sociolinguistics of globalization is necessarily a Sociolinguistics of mobility.

The World System as Context

It is a regrettable feature of much discourse on globalization that it seems to present globalization as the creation of worldwide uniformity. Processes are often represented generically, as a universal shift in the nature of societies, semiosis or identities. Terms such as 'global flow' suggest a flow across *the whole of the globe*, a generalized spread of sociocultural and economic patterns, a new universalism. In our field of study, some work on discourse in the late modern world falls prey to this. Chouliaraki and Fairclough (1999), for instance, suggest that the conditions for the production and circulation of discourse (in general, without qualification) have changed in the present world. Both the nature of signs and discourses as well as their distribution, access and effects have undergone substantial transformations, and 'discourse' is now a different concept. I would suggest that this is a description of certain discourse genres in Late Modern Britain, but not a general theory of discourse in the world. What is seen as 'late modern discourse' is a new genre, spread across the globe *as* a specific genre, across specific groups of people in specific contexts. Like *Cosmopolitan* and Japanese hip-hop, discourses of the type discussed by

Chouliaraki and Fairclough thus need to be understood in relation to the rest of the semiotic landscape in which it enters and circulates.

We have to realize that the world is not a uniform space and that consequently, globalization processes need to be understood against the background of the world system. This world system, as Immanuel Wallerstein has extensively argued, is a system built on inequality, on particular, asymmetric divisions of labour between 'core regions' and 'peripheries', with 'semiperipheries' in between (e.g. Wallerstein 1983, 2001). Thus, the system is marked by both the existence of separate spaces (e.g. states) and deep interconnectedness of the different spaces, often, precisely, through the existence of worldwide elites and 'marginal' groups such as hip-hop fans. *Inequality, not uniformity, organizes the flows* across the 'globe'. Consequently, whenever sociolinguistic items travel across the globe, they travel across *structurally different* spaces, and will consequently be picked up differently in different places (see Calvet 2006; compare de Swaan 2001). The interconnectedness of the various parts of the system creates the previously mentioned issues of scales and levels of analysis: what occurs in a particular state can and must be explained by reference to state-level dynamics, but needs to be set simultaneously against the background of substate and superstate dynamics, and the hierarchical relations between the various levels is a matter of empirical exploration, not positing.

Globalization implies that developments at the 'top' or the core of the world system have a wide variety of effects at the 'bottom' or the periphery of that system. For instance, developments in the field of sophisticated, multimedia and multimodal communication have effects on other, less sophisticated forms of literacy. Important in all of this is that the different levels seem to operate at different speeds. Fernand Braudel's famous distinctions between slow time, intermediate time, and fast time may be a useful metaphor here (Braudel 1969 [1958]; see Blommaert 1999a for comments). Braudel first observes that historical developments are of different orders – a climate change (slow time) is something different from an economic conjuncture (intermediate time) or a battle (fast time) – but he adds that people usually only observe the fast and (parts of) the intermediate developments, and that historical processes are therefore not necessarily accessible in similar ways to the individual's awareness and agency. One may have degrees of consciousness about and agency over 'fast' and 'intermediate' processes, while the slow, macro processes are an invisible (yet very real) context, not open to individual agency.

A Sociolinguistics of globalization will need a holistic view in which local events are read locally as well as translocally, and in which *the world system with its structural inequalities is a necessary (but not self-explanatory) context* in which language occurs and operates. In my view, this is the main challenge of globalization to intellectual endeavours such as Sociolinguistics, which claims to contribute to an understanding of society through an understanding of language.[1] It is precisely the fragmented but interconnected nature of the world system that accounts for the *niched* character of sociolinguistic globalization: it occurs not everywhere, but in particular different but interconnected places and not in others, and this is a structural and systemic matter with deep historical roots, not a coincidental one. It is historical, and that means that we have to situate globalization processes in a wider picture of structural 'becoming', of processes of worldwide inequality that derive their systemic nature from the long history in which they fit. We are never investigating synchronicity, but always a particular stage in a historical process.

For a Sociolinguistics of globalization within a world systems perspective, I would suggest that emphasis is needed on the relative *value* of semiotic resources – value being often connected to translocally realizable functions, the capacity to perform adequately in and through language in a wide variety of social and geographical spaces and across linguistic economies. This capacity is the capacity for mobility, and this emphasis on value as a crucial aspect of function is due to the fact that globalization raises new issues of inequality, both locally and translocally, precisely with respect to the capacity for mobility of resources. Specifically, the 'weight' of social and cultural forms of capital *across* spaces (geographical as well as social) appears to vary enormously. What works in one place does not work elsewhere, and the kind of 'flows' usually associated with globalization processes involves important shifts in value and a reallocation of functions (Appadurai 1990; also Bourdieu 1990). When people move across physical as well as social space their repertoires undergo re-evaluation at every step of the trajectory and the functions of their repertoire are redefined. And conversely, movements *of others* (tourists or businesspeople) affect the value and function of local speech repertoires. This, to me, looks like a prime target for a Sociolinguistics of globalization, and the most adequate way to address it is by looking at the relative (and shiftable) value of linguistic practices as a component of their function. It is no longer a study of language per se, but of *what counts as language* (cf. Blommaert 2005).

Second Linguistic Relativity and Globalization

Let me now introduce a second concept, useful in my opinion for analyses of sociolinguistic globalization phenomena: Dell Hymes' notion of 'second linguistic relativity'. A central concern in Hymes' work is with *function*, and it is in this respect that he developed his notion of second relativity (Hymes 1966; also Hymes 1980, 1996). While indispensable to Hymes' view of language, Whorf's ('first') relativity of structure assumed stability in function: 'the inference of differential effect on world view assumed equivalent role in shaping world view' (Hymes 1966: 116). This is problematic, for

> the role of language may differ from community to community; ... in general the functions of language in society are a problem for investigation, not postulation ... If this is so, then the cognitive significance of a language depends not only on structure, but also on patterns of use. (ibid.)

And consequently:

> the type [of relativity] associated with Sapir and Whorf in any case is underlain by a more fundamental kind. The consequences of the relativity of the structure of language depend on the relativity of the function of language. Take, for example, the common case of multilingualism. Inferences as to the shaping effect of some one language on thought and the world must be qualified immediately in terms of the place of the speaker's languages in his biography and mode of life. Moreover, communities differ in the role they assign to language itself in socialization, acquisition of cultural knowledge and performance. ... This second type of linguistic relativity, concerned with the functions of languages, has more than a critical, cautionary import. As a sociolinguistic approach, it calls attention to the organization of linguistic features in social interaction. Work has begun to show that description of fashions of speaking can reveal basic cultural values and orientations. The worlds so revealed are not the ontological and epistemological worlds of physical relationships, of concern to Whorf, but worlds of social relationships. What are disclosed are not orientations toward space, time, vibratory phenomena, and the like, but orientations towards persons, roles, statuses, rights and duties, deference and demeanor .... (Hymes 1996: 44–45; also Hymes 1980: 38)

One will be reminded of the comments on indexicalities and language ideologies made above; we will return to this later. At this point, Hymes' emphasis on the *problematic* nature of language functions needs to be underscored: according to Hymes, such functions have been taken for granted by linguists while in fact they should be one of the foci of empirical investigation. Even if language forms are similar or identical, the way in which they get inserted in social actions may differ significantly and consequently there may be huge differences in what these (similar or identical) forms *do* in real societies. Hymes thus shifts the focus of attention away from 'linguistic systems' to 'sociolinguistic systems': systems that revolve around the concept of 'ways of speaking'. What we need to investigate is the way in which language actually *works* in societies, and function (ethnographically established!) is the key to this.

The impact of this relativity of function on sociolinguistic investigation is huge, as is its critical dimension. Social inequality partly depends on the incapacity of speakers to accurately perform certain discourse functions on the basis of available resources. Language functions and the ways in which they are performed by people are constantly assessed and evaluated: function and value are impossible to separate. Consequently, *differences* in the use of language are quickly, and quite systematically, translated into *inequalities* between speakers (the key argument of Hymes 1996; see also Blommaert 2001a, Maryns and Blommaert 2002 for illustrations). This observation holds for what language does in stratified societies and it is central to, for example, Bernstein's and Bourdieu's arguments on language; it accounts for almost any dynamics of prestige and stigma in language, and Sociolinguistics has built a remarkable track record of descriptions of such processes in single and synchronically viewed societies or speech communities. But there is more as soon as we start looking at globalization.

Globalization results in intensified forms of flow, causing forms of contact and difference perhaps not new in substance but perhaps new in scale and perception. Consequently, key sociolinguistic concepts such as speech community become more and more difficult to handle empirically (see Rampton 1998, and this volume Chapter 47, for an excellent survey and discussion). Even more disconcerting is the fact that the *presupposability of functions* for linguistic resources becomes ever more problematic, because the linguistic resources travel across time, space and different regimes of indexicalities and organizations of repertoires. The functions that particular ways of speaking will perform, and the functions of the particular linguistic resources needed for them, become less and less a matter of surface inspection, and some of the biggest errors (and injustices) may be committed by simply projecting locally valid functions onto the ways of speaking of people who are involved in transnational flows. Whenever discourses travel across the globe, what is carried with them is their shape, but their value, meaning or function do not always travel along. They are a matter of uptake, they have to be *granted* by others, on the basis of the dominant indexical frames and hierarchies.

The fact is that functions performed by particular ways of speaking and particular resources in one place can be altered in another place, and that in such instances the 'value' of these linguistic instruments is changed. The English acquired by urban Africans may offer them considerable prestige and access to middle-class identities in African towns. It may be an 'expensive' resource to them. But the same English, when spoken in London by the same Africans, may be an object of stigmatization and may qualify them as members of the lower strata of society. What is 'expensive' in Lusaka or Nairobi may be very 'cheap' in London or New York. What people can actually accomplish with these resources is likewise affected. 'Good' and status-carrying English in the periphery may be 'bad' and stigma-carrying English in the core of the world system. The opposite can, of course, also occur. Rampton's work on the delicate and complex reshuffling of linguistic and stylistic repertoires in contemporary multi-ethnic peer groups has brought us a long way in understanding the relativity (and the renegotiability) of associated 'values' to linguistic modes of conduct caused by diaspora or globalization flows in general (Harris, Leung and Rampton 2001; Rampton 1995). Social identities and the symbolic forms through which they are flagged become more and more deterritorialized – detached from conventional places – and transidiomatic – detached from 'ownership rights' over particular symbolic forms (Harris, Leung and Rampton 2001; Jacquemet 2000; Maryns and Blommaert 2001).

What this means for Sociolinguistics, I believe, is that we need to revisit our ways of addressing form–function relations, probably foregrounding them if we want to come to terms with globalization as a sociolinguistic phenomenon. And in doing so, it may be wise to keep in mind that globalization also results in global hierarchies in communication affecting existing local hierarchies and value-scales. As said above, developments at the top have effects at the bottom and vice versa. Consequently, a lot of what happens to linguistic resources in terms of value attribution is beyond the reach of individuals for it happens at macro-levels. It is *determined* in the Marxian sense of the term. In identifying form–function relationships, a concept such as determination probably deserves more attention than has hitherto been given to it for it may be indispensable for an accurate understanding of voice against the background of the world system. The 'limits of awareness' of language users (Silverstein 2001) may be precisely the take-off point for a Sociolinguistics of globalization, for it may be the point where societies come down on individuals' potential to decide and to act – to produce voice so as to be heard and read (Blommaert 2005). The more we look at this point, the more differences and inequalities will appear, and explanations of these will force Sociolinguistics to come to terms with, or even contribute to the construction of, theories of society in the world system.

Writing in/from the Margin (of the World System)

Instead of a conclusion I will offer a brief analytic vignette on a small sample of writing produced in sub-Saharan Africa – the periphery or margin of the world system – but lifted out of its context-of-production and moved into a transnational speech network involving the African author and an addressee from the core of the world system (the 'West'). The text is a handwritten letter addressed to me by a 16-year old girl from Dar es Salaam, Tanzania. The girl, Victoria (a pseudonym), is the daughter of a family I stayed with during field trips to Tanzania, and I first met her when she was two years old. Her father is an academic, and Victoria was in secondary school when she wrote the letter. Secondary education in Tanzania is done through the medium of English, while the majority of the pupils (and teachers) have either Kiswahili or other African languages as their mother tongue(s). In primary school, Kiswahili is the medium of instruction and pupils get English as a subject. Consequently, at the age of 16, Victoria would have had several years of 'deep' exposure to English. The girl is definitely a member of the local middle class, a class which uses proficiency in English as an emblem of class belonging (Blommaert 1999a). It is, in other words, an 'expensive' resource in Dar es Salaam.

Let us now take a look at what, and how, she writes. What follows is a transliteration of the handwritten version, in which line breaks and graphic organization are rendered as precisely as possible (all names are pseudonyms).

20/9/1999

    Dear !

        Uncle Jan

            How are you? I hope you
      The main aim of this letter is to tell
      you that, here in Tanzania, we have
      remember you so much. Dady, Mum, Uzuri
      Patrick, Furaha, and Victoria and other members
      like Kazili, Helena, Bahati, Fatima and
      and others. Other people forget to write for you
      a letter, geat all your family I don't
      have much to say. Sorry if you will
      came Tanzania we will go to beach

BYe BYe From VICTORIA MTANGULA

A few comments are in order. If we apply a punitive and mono-normative yardstick, the first thing that strikes us is the frequency of rather severe errors at the level of grammar ('we have remember you so much', 'to write for you', 'if you will came Tanzania'), as well as at the level of punctuation (absence of periods), orthography ('geat all your family', the alteration of upper and lower case symbols in the concluding line) and narrative style and control over literary conventions (the awkward list of names dominating the letter, the separation of 'dear!' and 'uncle Jan', the unfinished sentence 'I hope you'). Victoria struggles with English literacy, her control over the medium is incomplete. At the same time, her act of writing can best be seen as 'language display' in the sense of Eastman and Stein (1993), the mobilization of the best possible resources for a particular act of communication. Given the particular relationship I had with Victoria (and given the references to the other family members *not* writing to me), the act of writing is loaded with indexicalities, constructing a relational identity of a 'good girl', someone who behaves and performs well, is probably among the best pupils in her age-group, and is worthy of compliments from her European Uncle. Her letter also indexicalizes all kinds of things with regard to writing practices and the use of particular codes (English) within a local repertoire. In short, Victoria tries to exploit the semiotic opportunities offered by globalized sociolinguistic phenomena.

But she does so under world-systemic constraints. Victoria mobilizes the maximum status resources within her reach: the best possible (school) English, the language of status and upward social mobility in Tanzania. And it is in that respect that the errors become important: as soon as the document moves across the world system and gets transplanted from a repertoire in the periphery to a repertoire in the core of the world system, the resources used by Victoria fail to index elite status and prestige. The value of this variety of written English in Europe is deeply different from the value it has in Dar es Salaam. The indexicalities of success and prestige, consequently, only work within a local economy of signs, that of Tanzania, an economy in which even a little bit of English could pass as good, prestige-bearing English.

We are witnessing, in the process of intercultural/international transfer, a shift in indexical and referential aspects of signs from one 'placed' system to another. It is at this point that the critical rereading of Hymes' second relativity may be added to recent insights on indexicality and linguistic ideologies. The reallocation of functions for resources proceeds along indexical and referential lines: we allocate functions to resources on the basis of value systems in place – by interpreting and contextualizing indexical and referential meanings of signs. We also see huge discrepancies between what linguistic resources and ways of using them mean in local environments – that of grassroots literacy in Africa – and what they mean in other, transnational environments in which they get inserted. The kind of literacy shown here is, I believe, widespread in Africa, and it characterizes much of what exists in the way of literacy in the sub-elite strata of many African societies (Blommaert 1999b, 2001b, 2003a, 2003b; Blommaert et al. 2005). In these societies – the periphery of the world system – it may be quite sufficient to communicate adequately; in fact, it may even be an object of status and prestige. But lifted out of the periphery and placed into the order of indexicalities of the core of the world system, these forms of literacy lose their functions and receive new ones. From a rather high rank in the hierarchies of signs and communication practices, they tumble down to the lowest ranks of these hierarchies.

Consequently, we are facing '*placed resources*' here: resources that are functional in one particular place but become dysfunctional as soon as they are moved into other places. The process of mobility creates difference in value, for the resources are being reallocated different functions. The indexical links between signs and modes of communication on the one hand, and social value-scales on the other, allowing for example identity construction, status attribution and so forth – these indexical links are severed and new ones are projected onto the signs and practices. Particular linguistic resources, often those of people in the peripheries of the world system, do not travel well. (In another paper, we called this phenomenon 'pretextual gaps': gaps that originate when the resources people have fail to match the criteria of expected resources, cf. Maryns and Blommaert 2002.)

I would argue that such reallocation processes are central to the kinds of mobility that characterizes globalization: they define how mobile resources are or can become, how much opportunity particular resources will offer their users in various places across the world. Consequently, a Sociolinguistics of globalization should look carefully into such processes of reallocation, the remapping of forms over function, for it may be central to the various forms of inequality that also characterize globalization processes. For this we need careful ethnographic work, sustained by a social theory which takes the world system as the highest level of contextualization.

NOTE

1. I am surprised by the often myopic nature of social-theoretical reflections in our field. Scholars enthusiastically refer to social theorists such as Habermas and Giddens – theorists of the structure and development of First World societies – but hardly ever to theory that addresses the world system, (under)development and dependency issues. Wallerstein has already been mentioned, but one could also think of, for example Samir Amin, André Gunder Frank, Giovanni Arrighi and others, scholars whose work consistently emphasizes the interconnectedness of processes across different parts of the world, the effects of developments in one part on other parts, and the structural differences in value of resources from different parts of the world system. It is social theory that addresses the world, not just one part of it.

REFERENCES

Appadurai, Arjun. 1990. Disjuncture and difference in the global cultural economy. *Theory, Culture and Society* 7: 295–310.
Blommaert, Jan. 1999a. The debate is open. In Jan Blommaert (ed.) *Language Ideological Debates*. Berlin: Mouton de Gruyter: 1–38.
Blommaert, Jan (ed.). 1999b. *Language Ideological Debates*. Berlin: Mouton de Gruyter.
Blommaert, Jan. 2001a. Investigating narrative inequality: African asylum seekers' stories in Belgium. *Discourse and Society* 12: 413–449.

Blommaert, Jan. 2001b. The other side of history: Grassroots literacy and auto-biography in Shaba, Congo. *General Linguistics* 38: 133–155.

Blommaert, Jan. 2003a. Orthopraxy, writing and identity: Shaping lives through borrowed genres in Congo. *Pragmatics* 13: 33–48.

Blommaert, Jan. 2003b. Situating language rights: English and Swahili in Tanzania revisited. Paper presented at the African Studies Workshop, University of Chicago, Illinois. March.

Blommaert, Jan. 2005. *Discourse: A Critical Introduction.* Cambridge: Cambridge University Press.

Blommaert, Jan. 2006. Sociolinguistic scales. *Working Papers in Urban Languages and Literacies* 37. London: King's College.

Blommaert, Jan, Nathalie Muyllaert, Marieke Huysmans and Charlyn Dyers. 2005. Peripheral normativity: Literacy and the production of locality in a South African township school. *Linguistics and Education* 16: 378–403.

Bourdieu, Pierre. 1990. *Language and Symbolic Power.* Cambridge: Polity Press.

Braudel, Fernand. 1969 [1958]. Histoire et sciences sociales: La longue durée. In *Ecrits sur l'Histoire.* Paris: Flammarion: 41–83.

Calvet, Louis-Jean. 2006. *Towards an Ecology of World Languages.* Cambridge: Polity.

Chouliaraki, Lilie and Norman Fairclough. 1999. *Discourse in Late Modernity: Rethinking Critical Discourse Analysis.* Edinburgh: Edinburgh University Press.

Coupland, Nikolas. 2003. Introduction: Sociolinguistics and globalisation. *Journal of Sociolinguistics* 7: 465–472.

De Swaan, Abram. 2001. *Words of the World: The Global Language System.* Cambridge: Polity.

Eastman, Carol M. and Roberta F. Stein. 1993. Language display: authenticating claims to social identity. *Journal of Multilingual and Multicultural Development* 14 (3):187–202.

Fabian, Johannes. 2001. *Anthropology with an Attitude.* Stanford, California: Stanford University Press.

Gal, Susan and Kathryn Woolard (eds.). 2001. *Languages and Publics: Authority and Representation.* Manchester: St Jerome.

Harris, Roxy, Constant Leung and Ben Rampton. 2001. Globalisation, diaspora and language education in England. *Working Papers in Urban Languages and Literacies 17.* London: King's College.

Hymes, Dell. 1966. Two types of linguistic relativity (with examples from Amerindian ethnography). In William Bright (ed.) *Sociolinguistics: Proceedings of the UCLA Sociolinguistics Conference, 1964.* The Hague: Mouton: 114–167.

Hymes, Dell. 1980. *Language in Education: Ethnolinguistic Essays.* Washington D.C.: Center for Applied Linguistics.

Hymes, Dell. 1996. *Ethnography, Linguistics, Narrative Inequality: Toward an Understanding of Voice.* London: Taylor and Francis.

Jacquemet, Marco. 2000. Beyond the speech community. Paper, 7th International Pragmatics Conference, Budapest.

Kroskrity, Paul (ed.). 2000. *Regimes of Language.* Santa Fe, New Mexico: SAR Press.

Machin, David and Theo van Leeuwen. 2003. Global schemas and local discourses in *Cosmopolitan. Journal of Sociolinguistics* 7: 493–512.

Maryns, Katrijn and Jan Blommaert. 2001. Stylistic and thematic shifting as a narrative resource: Assessing asylum seekers' repertoires. *Multilingua* 20: 61–84.

Maryns, Katrijn and Jan Blommaert. 2002. Pretextuality and pretextual gaps: On de/refining linguistic inequality. *Pragmatics* 12: 11–30.

Pennycook, Alastair. 2003. Global Englishes, Rip Slyme, and performativity. *Journal of Sociolinguistics* 7: 513–533.

Rampton, Ben. 1995. *Crossing: Language and Ethnicity among Adolescents* London: Longman.

Rampton, Ben. 1998. Speech Community. In Jef Verschueren, Jan-Ola Östman, Jan Blommaert and Chris Bulcaen (eds.) *Handbook of Pragmatics 1998*. Amsterdam: John Benjamins: 1–30.

Schieffelin, Bambi, Kathryn Woolard and Paul Kroskrity (eds.). 1998. *Language Ideologies: Practice and Theory*. New York: Oxford University Press.

Silverstein, Michael. 1998. Contemporary transformations of local linguistic communities. *Annual Review of Anthropology* 27: 401–426.

Silverstein, Michael. 2001 [1981]. The limits of awareness. In Alessandro Duranti (ed.) *Linguistic Anthropology: A Reader*. London: Blackwell: 382–401.

Wallerstein, Immanuel. 1983. *Historical Capitalism*. London: Verso.

Wallerstein, Immanuel. 2001. *Unthinking Social Science*. 2nd edition. Philadelphia, Pennsylvania: Temple University Press.

PART VI

LANGUAGE, CULTURE AND

INTERACTION

Editors' Introduction to Part VI

Dell Hymes has been the seminal figure in developing the branch of Sociolinguistics which, from the inception of Sociolinguistics, has been known as the *Ethnography of Communication*, with its distinctive anthropological perspective. The opening chapter (39) in this part is one of Hymes's key texts in this regard. Hymes is concerned here with identifying different cultures in terms of different *ways of speaking*, understood as the diverse means available to people to express more or less the same meanings and to perform similar communicative functions across communities. Early work in American Anthropology, dating back to the beginning of the twentieth century (associated with Alfred Kroeber, Franz Boas, Edward Sapir and Benjamin Lee Whorf), focused on patterns of language and culture in Native American ('Indian') communities. It allowed us to appreciate the diversity and distinctiveness of Native American cultures, especially in contrast to the dominant, colonizing forces of white, Anglo-European languages and ideologies. While emphasizing the need for an ethnographic approach to language and culture (studying communities from an *emic* perspective, as an 'insider' or as a 'participant-observer', see the general Introduction), Hymes also proposed that researchers need to achieve *observational adequacy*. One useful summary device to help ensure that an adequate descriptive account was given was Hymes's *SPEAKING* mnemonic. Under this heading Hymes pointed to a possibly universal set of descriptive terms and categories. Each letter of 'SPEAKING' stands for a set of specific *components of speech events*: Setting; Participants; Ends (Goals); Act Sequence (Message Form and Content); Key (Tenor); Instrumentalities (Channels and Forms of Speech); Norms (of Interaction and Interpretation); Genre.

Hymes's work has directed Sociolinguistics away from the unidimensional formalism of theoretical and descriptive linguistics. Instead of treating language as a general competence, located in the mind of an individual and

575

expressed as a set of grammatical rules in pursuit of universalizing principles, Hymes drew attention to the enormous diversity and complexity that language expressed. The main locus of language for Hymes is the *speech community*, where people share a *repertoire* of different *ways of speaking* regulated by *relations of appropriateness*. These ways of speaking are made up of different *speech styles* embedded in and related to their *contexts of discourse* or *context of situation*. 'Speech' is here understood as a surrogate term for a wide-ranging set of different communicative modalities: speaking, writing, song, speech-based whistling, drumming, and other nonverbal codes. Most of these concepts have become staples of sociolinguistic analysis, and we have seen how they have been taken up and put to use in so many different aspects of the discipline. In some cases we have seen lively debate around the viability of specific concepts. One instance is speech community, and it would be useful to review the relationship between this idea and the newer idea of *community of practice* that is central to many contemporary analyses (see Chapters 10, 13, 15, 23, 28 and 43). This comparison is central to the critical discussion offered by Ben Rampton in Chapter 47.

As we argued in our general Introduction, the 'linguistic' and 'social' components of Sociolinguistics cannot be easily separated (see also Blommaert's Chapter 38, in Part V). Indeed, it was Hymes's early theoretical perspective – still highly influential in Sociolinguistics – that insists on *not* distinguishing conceptually between language and society in any clear-cut way. Particular forms and functions of language use are part of the normative organization of social life. They are constitutive of cultural distinctiveness. For Hymes, Sociolinguistics needs to be more than just a fusion of linguistic and sociological insights. He introduced the suggestive phrase *socially constituted linguistics*, to set an objective for the discipline – studying language and social interaction as the means by which we come to experience and structure our social lives. Seen in this way, Sociolinguistics is as much the study of social and cultural processes and practices as the study of language.

Hymes's chapter takes us back to some of the founding motivations for Sociolinguistics. The functional study of social life through language required Hymes to look beyond decontextualized sentences as his objects of analysis, as has been the case in much structural linguistics. Therefore, he developed a number of concepts with the aim to provide new *units of analysis*. *Speech event* is a culturally recognized, language-based communicative type or activity, such as a buying/selling exchange, a political speech, an exchange of social pleasantries, or a legal exchange in court. Every speech event is associated with a particular set of communicative *norms*, a generalized set of expectations about who should speak, when and how, and to what effect. Some speech events have particularly tightly specified linguistic and social norms, and this is when we can begin to think of sociolinguistic *rituals*, like those that often accompany and symbolize important moments of transition, such as young people reaching maturity, a couple getting married, or a funeral ceremony. Speech events often foreground the *performance* element of situated language use, when speakers use language in focused ways, to particular creative or aesthetic ends. Hymes and others have used the term *poetics* to refer to the sociolinguistic study of performance events, but it is increasingly recognized (as we saw especially in relation to chapters in Part III) that even those forms of talk that we consider to be 'ordinary', 'unexceptional' or 'mundane' can have an important performance dimension. For example, conversational narratives often show patterns and contrasts of the sort we more commonly associate with works of literary creativity (see, for example, Justine Coupland's Chapter 42, on narrative episodes in small talk).

A close confederate of Hymes was John Gumperz, who shared Hymes's emphasis on how cultural meaning is created and sustained in interaction. But Gumperz's contribution (Chapter 40) is different in emphasis. He recognized that social meaning can derive from listeners' interpretations of linguistic and nonverbal cues that 'contextualize' a speaker's talk. Gumperz calls them *contextualization cues*, which can include code choice (see Auer, Chapter 34), intonation patterns, the presence of particular discourse markers (such as 'well'), and many others. An important feature of contextualization cues is that they are *reflexive*. That is, they are constrained by particular contexts of interaction but they also provide information to co-participants about what *communicative frames* they are engaged in at a particular point in interaction. A related, important term that we owe to Gumperz is *conversational inferencing*, which refers to the cognitive processes by which social meaning is attributed to speakers on the basis of how they use language. Subtle details of a speaker's intonation or pronunciation may be enough to set in motion a chain of inferences that invoke ethnic or other sorts of stereotypes, leading to social division or systematic misunderstanding.

These seminal anthropological and interactional contributions to Sociolinguistics retain their original force and vigour, and many of the most important recent theoretical developments in the field are direct continuations of Hymes and Gumperz's orientations. In their chapter (41) Richard Bauman and Charles L. Briggs rework the notions of *performance* and *contextualization* that we have just associated with Hymes and Gumperz, and review their relevance to our understanding of *culture* – it is difficult to think of concepts that are more central to Sociolinguistics, old and new. Bauman and Briggs argue that we come to appreciate cultural differences largely through our observation of, or participation in, cultural performances (see Coupland's chapter in Part III). But performance is not in any simple sense the recycling of cultural forms; it inevitably involves a fresh component, a *recontextualization* of cultural material, respecting its own local conditions of enactment.

What's more, many cultural performances are 'packaged up' in ways that allow us to treat them as relatively free-standing, transportable, iconic (see Irvine and Gal in Chapter 26) representations. They can be *decontextualized* and *recontextualized* again elsewhere. Sociolinguistic analysis therefore needs to be sensitive to both what is familiar (and culturally continuous) in performance events, but also to what is new. And it is in the tension between given and new that cultural change can take place.

Although we have encountered William Labov's research so far in the Reader in connection with his ground-breaking studies of language variation and change (see Part I), his contribution has spanned the whole range of sociolinguistic themes and indeed methods that we have encountered in the book. Chapter 42 presents Labov's classic interactional study of Afro-American adolescents in Harlem. Like most other chapters in this Part of the Reader, it is a study which combines Discourse Analysis and ethnography. The analysis focuses on sequencing and poetic patterns in the competitive exchange of *ritual insults* (also referred to as *sounding* or *playing the dirty dozens*). Very much as Bauman and Briggs suggest, Labov shows how the structured routines that are involved in 'playing the dozens' require strong awareness of, and not a little skill in using, linguistic and cultural knowledge. These ritual practices are, from one point of view, a recycling of Black street culture. But crucially, they are a resource for making new social meanings at the level of social relationships. A speaker's verbal performance can be favorably evaluated by his peers only if he uses conventionally sanctioned, structurally and aesthetically effective ways of speaking. Rhythm, rhyme, alliteration, smart, timely and appropriate responses are needed for the performer to maintain his reputation – for a speaker to 'cut it'. A tacit semantic rule states that the speaker mustn't cross a fine line between ritual and personal insults, which morally regulates the speech events, despite their overt use of obscenity and taboo language. 'Playing the dozens' is clearly a transportable routine – one that can be picked up and used in different appropriate settings. But it is also subject to close ingroup scrutiny and monitoring. It is a reflexive cultural practice that allows its participants to rework their identities and change their social positions.

We then encounter a huge shift of focus, moving into Chapter 43 with Janet Holmes's analysis of interaction in corporate, governmental and other workplace settings in New Zealand. Holmes reveals that one of the rich resources used by co-workers to relate to one another, manage their interpersonal relations, and indeed to create the workplace culture is *humour*. Studying humour is not without its problems, including problems in identifying situations as 'humorous' in the first place. The 'funniness' of talk is one possible criterion, but not all people share the same sense of humour. Therefore, Holmes and her colleagues, just like their participants in the study, must rely on specific contextualization cues (Gumperz, Chapter 40), that is, paralinguistic, prosodic, and discursive clues, suggesting that a turn is intended to be, or is perceived to be, humorous. This may be signaled by the speaker's tone of voice or facial expression, or by the audience's response (most obviously, laughter). Finally, humour serves many different functions, beyond the obvious one of 'amusing'. It may also create a sense of solidarity, mitigate an instruction, or defuse tension or anger. It may also convey aggressive or jocular abuse (see also Labov, Chapter 42).

The discursive realization of humour is not homogeneous. Holmes shows that different workplace *communities of practice* employ different styles of humour. They construct distinct types of working environment, for example 'collegial' environments, through supportive and cooperative humour, or more challenging environments, through contestive and competitive humour. Interestingly, Holmes associates these two styles of 'doing humour' with 'feminine' and 'masculine' communicative styles, respectively. Although not always uniformly mapping onto the female and male sex of the speakers, these *styles of humour* may contribute to the *perceptions* of workplaces as gendered.

Holmes points out that even brief instances of humorous talk may momentarily *reframe* a dominant speech event (for example, a 'business meeting') into a passing 'time out episode' (for example, see her Extract 1a). In Chapter 44, Justine Coupland tackles related issues of 'doing sociability' through *small talk* and *gossip*. Although small talk, and Bronislaw Malinowski's related concept of *phatic communion*, is sometimes relegated to the category of 'trivial talk', occupying 'marginal', transitional, or *liminal* moments of interaction, Coupland clearly demonstrates that its role in managing interpersonal relations cannot be underestimated. Any breaches of social expectations concerning small talk, including the choice of a 'wrong' formula, violating the accepted sequence of routine exchanges, or simply avoidance of small talk where it is expected, are met with social censure. Extended episodes of small talk, for example in time-out talk among friends, chatting about mundane matters, swapping stories of personal experience, or gossiping create social cohesion of the group, construct identities for members of the group, and help police boundaries of acceptable behavior. While it is not surprising that 'sociable' talk takes place and is seen to be cooperatively constructed by co-interactants in time-out talk, it is also in predominantly transactional interactions (for example, medical interviews) that extended stretches of talk are reframed as small talk foregrounding relational goals (see, for example Extract 1 in Coupland's chapter).

Coupland draws our attention to the poetic and performative aspects of small talk (see Bauman and Briggs's Chapter 41). For example, the narrative in her Extract 3 is introduced by a 'special' phrase (*d'you know something?*), which not only signals the newsworthiness of the story but also frames it as a performance. The following chapter (45) by Adam Jaworski is also concerned with verbal performances of small talk. Jaworski examines greeting exchanges in tourist–host interactions. However, although greetings are typically regarded as phatic acts, their recontextualization and enactment as part of guided tours and staged shows, reconfigures their primary function from 'access rituals' (safe openings of interactional episodes) to tourists' displays of fleeting, often playful identities masquerading as 'locals', and hosts' commodified displays of their ethnic and linguistic identities. They create an exotic but easily accessible *linguascape* of the tourist destination. Tourist spaces, being typical *liminal* spaces, invert the rules of everyday behavior, which also affects the expected patterns of sequence and structure of the greetings. Marked by frequent instances of code-crossing (Rampton, Chapter 20), special paralinguistic features (high pitch, laughter), and a great deal of self-awareness and reflexivity, these greeting exchanges become performative acts at different levels of significance (see again Bauman and Briggs, Chapter 41, and chapters in Part III). They also offer opportunities for hosts to contest the dominant ideologies and power relations of global tourism.

Rachel Sutton-Spence (Chapter 44) provides us with an insight into *Deaflore*, 'the collective knowledge of individual Deaf communities and the shared World Deaf community' (p. 681). Her overview of interdisciplinary perspectives on sign language literature and performance opens our eyes to the structural, stylistic, and cultural aspects of cultural continuity but also *creativity* in British and American Deaf communities, different narrative genres, poetry, word play, and other poetic uses of handshapes and fingerspelling (one can think here of similarly creative uses of typography and layout in writing). As in other cultures, storytelling acts as a means of cultural transmission of tradition and community values, socialization, and identity building. It also provides Deaf people with opportunities to assert their rights by resisting the hegemony and oppression of hearing people. Deaf research has a long tradition in Sociolinguistics, and it is salutary to note that the range of contexts, perspectives, approaches to analysis, and critical sensitivities that we have been dealing with through the book are precisely those that are required to understand the politics and practices of Deaf communication.

One trend that will become more important in the future of Sociolinguistics is one we have regrettably, been unable to give much exposure to in the volume – the need to integrate the social analysis of spoken language into wider *multi-modal* perspectives. If we acknowledge the need to view language as social practice, and to understand many aspects of language use in terms of cultural performance, and so on, it will become increasingly untenable to draw a clear dividing line between linguistic and other (especially visual) modalities. In Deaf Sociolinguistics we already have a fund of knowledge and sensitivities that can carry this project forward.

We conclude this section with Ben Rampton's critical review of the concept of *speech community*. The word 'beyond' in Rampton's chapter title (47), however, provides a significant clue to why we have chosen this place to end the volume. Rampton's discussion moves freely between insights from different strands of Sociolinguistics, but also between insights from anthropology, ethnography, critical sociology, 'and beyond'. It looks back to the origins of the variationist paradigm (see the early chapters in Part I of the Reader), where the term 'speech community' was first used productively. This allows Rampton to reflect on the relationship between variationist and ethnographic perspectives in Sociolinguistics, and this is a comparison we have tried to keep in mind throughout our own editorial contributions to the book. But Rampton also introduces an explicitly *temporal* dimension into the debate, not so much in contrasting 'older' and 'newer' sociolinguistic studies, but in trying to assess what ambitions and problems Sociolinguistics itself has confronted across the very different social worlds of the 1960s (when Sociolinguistics was coming together as a distinctive discipline) and now, in the early twenty-first century. Although Rampton is careful not to present this as a simple dichotomy, he uses the terms *modernity* and *late-modernity* to identify at least some of the social, cultural, and intellectual differences that this history has spanned.

In this way Rampton helps us to appreciate why a *linguistics of community* perspective in Sociolinguistics, apposite to its earliest period, has tended to give way to a general approach he refers to as investigating 'the discourses of late/post-modernity'. His comments on this second approach take in many of the themes we have singled out as central to contemporary sociolinguistic approaches, including *communities of practice* and *language ideologies*. There are opportunities here, by reviewing relevant earlier sections of the Reader in relation to Rampton's own interpretations, to take stock of where Sociolinguistics stands on these topics, and what it is delivering in relation to them in terms of insights about the language/society interface.

CHAPTER 39

Models of the Interaction of Language and Social Life

DELL HYMES

Toward a Descriptive Theory

The primary concern now must be with descriptive analyses from a variety of communities. Only in relation to actual analysis will it be possible to conduct arguments analogous to those now possible in the study of grammar as to the adequacy, necessity, generality, etc., of concepts and terms. Yet some initial heuristic schema are needed if the descriptive task is to proceed. What is presented here is quite preliminary – if English and its grammarians permitted, one might call it 'toward toward a theory'. Some of it may survive the empirical and analytical work of the decade ahead.

Only a specific, explicit mode of description can guarantee the maintenance and success of the current interest in Sociolinguistics. Such interest is prompted more by practical and theoretical needs, perhaps, than by accomplishment. It was the development of a specific mode of description that ensured the success of linguistics as an autonomous discipline in the United States in the twentieth century, and the lack of it (for motif and tale types are a form of indexing, distributional inference a procedure common to the human sciences) that led to the until recently peripheral status of folklore, although both had started from a similar base, the converging interest of anthropologists, and English scholars, in language and in verbal tradition.

The goal of sociolinguistic description can be put in terms of the disciplines whose interests converge in Sociolinguistics. Whatever his questions about language, it is clear to a linguist that there is an enterprise, description of

Source: 'Models of the interaction of language and life', by Hymes, D. in Gumperz, J. J. and Hymes, D. (eds) *Directions in Sociolinguistics: The Ethnography of Communication* (1986) (Oxford: Blackwell Publishing) pp. 35–71.

languages, which is central and known. Whatever his questions about society and culture, it is clear to a sociologist or an anthropologist that there is a form of inquiry (survey or ethnography) on which the answers depend. In both cases, one understands what it means to describe a language, the social relations, or culture of a community. We need to be able to say the same thing about the sociolinguistic system of a community.

Such a goal is of concern to practical work as well as to scientific theory. In a study of bilingual education, e.g., certain components of speaking will be taken into account, and the choice will presuppose a model, implicit if not explicit, of the interaction of language with social life. The significance attached to what is found will depend on understanding what is possible, what universal, what rare, what linked, in comparative perspective. What survey researchers need to know linguistically about a community, in selecting a language variety, and in conducting interviews, is in effect an application of the community's sociolinguistic description (see Hymes 1969). In turn, practical work, if undertaken with its relevance to theory in mind, can make a contribution, for it must deal directly with the interaction of language and social life, and so provides a testing ground and source of new insight.

Sociolinguistic systems may be treated at the level of national states, and indeed, of an emerging world society. My concern here is with the level of individual communities and groups. The interaction of language with social life is viewed as first of all a matter of human action, based on a knowledge, sometimes conscious, often unconscious, that enables persons to use language. Speech events and larger systems indeed have properties not reducible to those of the speaking competence of persons. Such competence, however, underlies communicative conduct, not only within communities but also in encounters between them. The speaking competence of persons may be seen as entering into a series of systems of encounter at levels of different scope.

An adequate descriptive theory would provide for the analysis of individual communities by specifying technical concepts required for such analysis, and by characterizing the forms that analysis should take. Those forms would, as much as possible, be formal, i.e., explicit, general (in the sense of observing general constraints and conventions as to content, order, interrelationship, etc.), economical, and congruent with linguistic modes of statement. Only a good deal of empirical work and experimentation will show what forms of description are required, and of those, which preferable. As with grammar, approximation to a theory for the explicit, standard analysis of individual systems will also be an approximation to part of a theory of explanation.

Among the notions with which such a theory must deal are those of speech community, speech situation, speech event, speech act, fluent speaker, components of speech events, functions of speech, etc.

Social Units

One must first consider the social unit of analysis. For this I adopt the common expression *speech community*.

Speech Community. Speech is here taken as a surrogate for all forms of language, including writing, song and speech-derived whistling, drumming, horn calling, and the like. Speech community is a necessary, primary term in that it postulates the basis of description as a social, rather than a linguistic, entity. One starts with a social group and considers all the linguistic varieties present in it, rather than starting with any one variety.

Bloomfield (1933) and some others have in the past reduced the notion of speech community to the notion of language (or linguistic variety). Those speaking the same language (or same first language, or standard language) were defined as members of the same speech community. This confusion still persists, associated with a quantitative measure of frequency of interaction as a way of describing (in principle) internal variation and change, as speculatively postulated by Bloomfield. The present approach requires a definition that is qualitative and expressed in terms *norms for the use* of language. It is clear from the work of Gumperz, Labov, Barth, and others that not frequency of interaction but rather definition of situations in which interaction occurs is decisive, particularly identification (or lack of it) with others. [Sociolinguistics here makes contact with the shift in rhetorical theory from expression and persuasion to identification as key concept (see Burke 1950: 19–37, 55–59).]

Tentatively, a *speech community* is defined as a community sharing rules for the conduct and interpretation of speech, and rules for the interpretation of at least one linguistic variety. Both conditions are necessary.

The sharing of grammatical (variety) rules is not sufficient. There may be persons whose English I can grammatically identify but whose messages escape me. I may be ignorant of what counts as a coherent sequence, request, statement requiring an answer, requisite or forbidden topic, marking of emphasis or irony, normal duration of silence, normal level of voice, etc., and have no metacommunitative means or opportunity for discovering such things. The difference between knowledge of a variety and knowledge of speaking does not usually become apparent within a single community, where the two are normally acquired together. Communities indeed often mingle what a linguist would distinguish as grammatically and as socially or culturally acceptable. Among the Cochiti of New Mexico J. R. Fox was unable to elicit the first person singular possessive form of 'wings', on the grounds that the speaker, not being a bird, could not say 'my wings' – only to become the only person in Cochiti able to say it on the grounds that 'your name is Robin.'

The nonidentity of the two kinds of rules (or norms) is more likely to be noticed when a shared variety is a second language for one or both parties. Sentences that translate each other grammatically may be mistakenly taken as having the same functions in speech, just as words that translate each other may be taken as having the same semantic function. There may be substratum influence or interference (Weinreich 1953) in the one as in the other. The Czech linguist J. Neustupny has coined the term *Sprechbund* 'speech area' (parallel to *Sprachbund* 'language area') for the phenomenon of speaking rules being shared among contiguous languages. Thus, Czechoslovakia, Hungary, Austria, and southern Germany may be found to share norms as to greetings, acceptable topics, what is said next in a conversation, etc.

Sharing of speaking rules is not sufficient. A Czech who knows no German may belong to the same *Sprechbund,* but not the same speech community, as an Austrian.

The *language field* and *speech field* (akin to the notion of social field) can be defined as the total range of communities within which a person's knowledge of varieties and speaking rules potentially enables him to move communicatively. Within the speech field must be distinguished the *speech network,* the specific linkages of persons through shared varieties and speaking rules across communities. Thus in northern Queensland, Australia, different speakers of the same language (e.g., Yir Yoront) may have quite different networks along geographically different circuits, based on clan membership, and involving different repertoires of mutilingualism. In Vitiaz Strait, New Guinea, the Bilibili islanders (a group of about 200–250 traders and potmakers in Astrolabe Bay) have collectively a knowledge of the languages of all the communities with which they have had economic relations, a few men knowing the language of each particular community in which they have had trading partners.

In sum, one's speech community may be, effectively, a single locality or portion of it; one's language field will be delimited by one's repertoire of varieties; one's speech field by one's repertoire of patterns of speaking. One's speech network is the effective union of these last two.

Part of the work of definition obviously is done here by the notion of community, whose difficulties are bypassed, as are the difficulties of defining boundaries between varieties and between patterns of speaking. Native conceptions of boundaries are but one factor in defining them, essential but sometimes partly misleading (a point stressed by Gumperz on the basis of his work in central India). Self-conceptions, values, role structures, contiguity, purposes of interaction, political history, all may be factors. Clearly, the same degree of linguistic difference may be associated with a boundary in one case and not in another, depending on social factors. The essential thing is that the object of description be an integral social unit. Probably, it will prove most useful to reserve the notion of speech community for the local unit most specifically characterized for a person by common locality and primary interaction (Gumperz 1962: 30–32). Here I have drawn distinctions of scale and of kind of linkage within what Gumperz has termed the *linguistic community* (any distinguishable intercommunicating group). Descriptions will make it possible to develop a useful typology and to discover the causes and consequences of the various types.

Speech Situation. Within a community one readily detects many situations associated with (or marked by the absence of) speech. Such contexts of situation will often be naturally described as ceremonies, fights, hunts, meals, lovemaking, and the like. It would not be profitable to convert such situations en masse into parts of a sociolinguistic description by the simple expedient of relabeling them in terms of speech. (Notice that the distinctions made with regard to speech community are not identical with the concepts of a general communicative approach, which must note the differential range of communication by speech, film, art object, music.) Such situations may enter as contexts into the statement of rules of speaking as aspects of setting (or of genre). In contrast to speech events, they are not in themselves governed by such rules, or one set of such rules throughout. A hunt, e.g., may comprise both verbal and nonverbal events, and the verbal events may be of more than one type.

In a sociolinguistic description, then, it is necessary to deal with activities which are in some recognizable way bounded or integral. From the standpoint of general social description they may be registered as ceremonies, fishing trips, and the like; from particular standpoints they may be regarded as political, esthetic, etc., situations, which serve as contexts for the manifestation of political, esthetic, etc., activity. From the sociolinguistic standpoint they may be regarded as speech situations.

Speech Event. The term *speech event* will be restricted to activities, or aspects of activities, that are directly governed by rules or norms for the use of speech. An event may consist of a single speech act, but will often comprise several. Just as an occurrence of a noun may at the same time be the whole of a noun phrase and the whole of a sentence (e.g., 'Fire!'), so a speech act may be the whole of a speech event, and of a speech situation (say, a rite consisting of a single prayer, itself a single invocation). More often, however, one will find a difference in magnitude: a party (speech situation), a conversation during the party (speech event), a joke within the conversation (speech act). It is of speech events and speech acts that one writes formal rules for their occurrence and characteristics. Notice that the same type of speech act may recur in different types of speech event, and the same type of speech event in different contexts of situation. Thus, a joke (speech act) may be embedded in a private conversation, a lecture, a formal introduction. A private conversation may occur in the context of a party, a memorial service, a pause in changing sides in a tennis match.

Speech Act. The *speech act* is the minimal term of the set just discussed, as the remarks on speech events have indicated. It represents a level distinct from the sentence, and not identifiable with any single portion of other levels of grammar, nor with segments of any particular size defined in terms of other levels of grammar. That an utterance has the status of a command may depend upon a conventional formula ('I hereby order you to leave this building'), intonation ('Go!' vs. 'Go?'), position in a conversational exchange ['Hello' as initiating greeting or as response (perhaps used when answering the telephone)], or the social relationship obtaining between the two parties (as when an utterance that is in the form of a polite question is in effect a command when made by a superior to a subordinate). The level of speech acts mediates immediately between the usual levels of grammar and the rest of a speech event or situation in that it implicates both linguistic form and social norms.

To some extent speech acts may be analyzable by extensions of syntactic and semantic structure. It seems certain, however, that much, if not most, of the knowledge that speakers share as to the status of utterances as acts is immediate and abstract, depending upon an autonomous system of signals from both the various levels of grammar and social settings. To attempt to depict speech acts entirely by postulating an additional segment of underlying grammatical structure (e.g., 'I hereby X you to ...') is cumbersome and counterintuitive. (Consider the case in which 'Do you think I might have that last bit of tea?' is to be taken as a command.)

An autonomous level of speech acts is in fact implicated by that logic of linguistic levels according to which the ambiguity of 'the shooting of the blacks was terrible' and the commonality of 'topping Erv is almost impossible' and 'it's almost impossible to top Erv' together requires a further level of structure at which the former has two different structures, the latter one. The relation between sentence forms and their status as speech acts is of the same kind. A sentence interrogative in form may be now a request, now a command, now a statement; a request may be manifested by a sentence that is now interrogative, now declarative, now imperative in form.

Discourse may be viewed in terms of acts both syntagmatically and paradigmatically; i.e., both as a sequence of speech acts and in terms of classes of speech acts among which choice has been made at given points.

Speech Styles. Style has often been approached as a matter of statistical frequency of elements already given in linguistic description, or as deviation from some norm given by such description. Statistics and deviations matter, but do not suffice. Styles also depend upon qualitative judgments of appropriateness, and must often be described in terms of selections that apply globally to a discourse, as in the case of honorific usage in Japanese (McCawley 1968: 136), i.e., there are consistent patternings of speaking that cut across the components of grammar (phonology, syntax, semantics), or that operate within one independently of the selectional restrictions normally described for it. Whorf adumbrated as much in his conception of 'fashions of speaking'; Joos has made and illustrated the point with regard to English; Pike (1967) has considered a wide variety of contextual styles as conditions on the manifestation of phonological and morphological units. Besides the existence of qualitatively defined styles, there are two other points essential to sociolinguistic description. One is that speech styles involve elements and relations that conventionally serve 'expressive' or, better, stylistic, as well as referential function (e.g., the contrast in force of aspiration that convention-ally signals emphasis in English). The second point is that speech styles are to be considered not only in terms of co-occurrence within each but also in terms of contrastive choice among them. Like speech acts, they have both syntagmatic and paradigmatic dimensions. The coherence, or cohesion, of discourse depends upon the syntagmatic relation of speech acts, and speech styles, as well as of semantic and syntactic features.

Ways of Speaking. Ways of speaking is used as the most general, indeed, as a primitive, term. The point of it is the regulative idea that the communicative behavior within a community is analyzable in terms of determinate ways of speaking, that the communicative competence of persons comprises in part a knowledge of determinate ways of speaking. Little more can be said until a certain number of ethnographic descriptions of communities in terms of ways of speaking are available. It is likely that communities differ widely in the fea-tures in terms of which their ways of speaking are primarily organized.

Components of Speech

A descriptive theory requires some schema of the components of speech acts. At present such a schema can be only an etic, heuristic input to descriptions. Later it may assume the status of a theory of universal features and dimensions.

Long traditional in our culture is the threefold division between speaker, hearer, and something spoken about. It has been elaborated in information theory, linguistics, semiotics, literary criticism, and sociology in various ways. In the hands of some investigators various of these models have proven pro-ductive, but their productivity has depended upon not taking them literally, let alone using them precisely. All such schemes, e.g., appear to agree either in taking the standpoint of an individual speaker or in postulating a dyad, speaker-hearer (or source-destination, sender-receiver, addressor-addressee).

Even if such a scheme is intended to be a model, for descriptive work it cannot be. Some rules of speaking require specification of *three* participants [addressor, addressee, hearer (audience), source, spokesman, addressees; etc.]; some of but *one*, indifferent as to role in the speech event; some of *two*, but of speaker and audience (e.g., a child); and so on. In short, serious ethnographic work shows that there is one general, or universal, dimension to be postulated, that of *participant*. The common dyadic model of speaker-hearer specifies sometimes too many, sometimes too few, sometimes the wrong participants. Further ethnographic work will enable us to state the range of actual types of participant relations and to see in differential occurrence something to be explained.

Ethnographic material so far investigated indicates that some sixteen or seventeen components have sometimes to be distinguished. No rule has been found that requires specification of all simultaneously. There are always redundancies, and sometimes a rule requires explicit mention of a relation between only two, message form and some other. (It is a general principle that all rules involve message form, if not by affecting its shape, then by governing its interpretation.) Since each of the components may sometimes be a factor, however, each has to be recognized in the general grid.

Psycholinguistic work has indicated that human memory works best with classifications of the magnitude of seven, plus or minus two (Miller 1956). To make the set of components mnemonically convenient, at least in English, the letters of the term SPEAKING can be used. The components can be grouped together in relation to the eight letters without great difficulty. Clearly, the use of SPEAKING as a mnemonic code word has nothing to do with the form of an eventual model and theory.

1. *Message form.* The form of the message is fundamental, as has just been indicated. The most common, and most serious, defect in most reports of speaking probably is that the message form, and, hence, the rules governing it, cannot be recaptured. A concern for the details of actual form strikes some as picayune, as removed from humanistic or scientific importance. Such a view betrays an impatience that is a disservice to both humanistic and scientific purposes. It is precisely the failure to unite form and content in the scope of a single focus of study that has retarded understanding of the human ability to speak, and that vitiates many attempts to analyse the significance of behavior. Content categories, interpretive categories, alone do not suffice. It is a truism, but one frequently ignored in research, that *how* something is said is part of *what* is said. Nor can one prescribe in advance the gross size of the signal that will be crucial to content and skill. The more a way of speaking has become shared and meaningful within a group, the more likely that crucial cues will be efficient, i.e., slight in scale. If one balks at such detail, perhaps

because it requires technical skills in linguistics, musicology, or the like that are hard to command, one should face the fact that the human meaning of one's object of study, and the scientific claims of one's field of inquiry, are not being taken seriously.

Especially when competence, the ability of persons, is of concern, one must recognize that shared ways of speaking acquire a partial autonomy, developing in part in terms of an inner logic of their means of expression. The means of expression condition and sometimes control content. For members of the community, then, 'freedom is the recognition of necessity'; mastery of the way of speaking is prerequisite to personal expression. Serious concern for both scientific analysis and human meaning requires one to go beyond content to the explicit statement of rules and features of form.

While such an approach may seem to apply first of all to genres conventionally recognized as esthetic, it also applies to conversation in daily life. Only painstaking analysis of message form – how things are said – of a sort that indeed parallels and can learn from the intensity of literary criticism can disclose the depth and adequacy of the elliptical art that is talk.

2. *Message content.* One context for distinguishing message form from message content would be: 'He prayed, saying "..."' (quoting message form) vs. 'He prayed that he would get well' (reporting content only).

Content enters analysis first of all perhaps as a question of *topic* and of change of topic. Members of a group know what is being talked about and when what is talked about has changed, and manage maintenance and change of topic. These abilities are parts of their communicative competence of particular importance to study of the coherence of discourse.

Message form and message content are central to the speech act and the focus of its 'syntactic structure'; they are also tightly interdependent. Thus they can be dubbed jointly as components of 'act sequence' (mnemonically, A).

3. *Setting.* Setting refers to the time and place of a speech act and, in general, to the physical circumstances.

4. *Scene.* Scene, which is distinct from setting, designates the 'psychological setting', or the cultural definition of an occasion as a certain type of scene. Within a play on the same stage with the same stage set the dramatic time may shift: 'ten years later', In daily life the same persons in the same setting may redefine their interaction as a changed type of scene, say, from formal to informal, serious to festive, or the like. Speech acts frequently are used to define scenes, and also frequently judged as appropriate or inappropriate in relation to scenes. Settings and scenes themselves, of course, may be judged as appropriate and inappropriate, happy or unhappy, in relation to each other, from the level of complaint about the weather to that of dramatic irony.

Setting and scene may be linked as components of act situation (mnemonically, S). Since scene implies always an analysis of cultural definitions, setting probably is to be preferred as the informal, unmarked term for the two.

5. *Speaker,* or *sender.*

6. *Addressor.*

7. *Hearer,* or *receiver,* or *audience.*

8. *Addressee.*

These four components were discussed in introducing the subject of components of speech. Here are a few illustrations. Among the Abipon of Argentina -*in* is added to the end of each word if any participant (whatever his role) is a member of the Hocheri (warrior class). Among the Wishram Chinook, formal scenes are defined by the relationship between a source (e.g., a chief, or sponsor of a ceremony), a spokesman who repeats the source's words, and others who constitute an audience or public. The source whose words are repeated sometimes is not present; the addressees sometimes are spirits of the surrounding environment. In the presence of a child, adults in Germany often use the term of address which would be appropriate for the child. Sometimes rules for participants are internal to a genre and independent of the participants in the embedding event. Thus male and female actors in Yana myths use the appropriate men's and women's forms of speech, respectively, irrespective of the sex of the narrator. Use of men's speech itself is required when both addressor and addressee are both adult and male, 'women's' speech otherwise. Groups differ in their definitions of the participants in speech events in revealing ways, particularly in defining absence (e.g., children, maids) and presence (e.g., supernaturals) of participation. Much of religious conduct can be interpreted as part of a native theory of communication. The various components may be grouped together as participants (mnemonically, P).

9. *Purposes – outcomes.* Conventionally recognized and expected outcomes often enter into the definition of speech events, as among the Waiwai of Venezuela, where the central speech event of the society, the *oho-chant,* has several varieties, according to whether the purpose to be accomplished is a marriage contract, a trade, a communal work task, an invitation to a feast, or a composing of social peace after a death. The rules for participants and settings vary accordingly (Fock 1965). A taxonomy of speech events among the Yakan of the Philippines (analysed by Charles Frake is differentiated into levels according jointly to topic (any topic, an issue, a disagreement, a dispute) and outcome (no particular outcome, a decision, a settlement, a legal ruling).

10. *Purposes – goals.* The purpose of an event from a community standpoint, of course, need not be identical to the purposes of those engaged in it. Presumably, both sides to a Yakan litigation wish to win. In a negotiation the purpose of some may be to obtain a favorable settlement, of others simply that there be a settlement. Among the Waiwai the prospective father-in-law and son-in-law have opposing goals in arriving at a marriage contract. The strategies of participants are an essential determinant of the form of speech events, indeed, to their being performed at all.

With respect both to outcomes and goals, the conventionally expected or ascribed must be distinguished from the purely situational or personal, and from the latent and unintended. The interactions of a particular speech event may determine its particular quality and whether or not the expected outcome is reached. The actual motives, or some portion of them, of participants may be quite varied. In the first instance, descriptions of speech events seek to describe customary or culturally appropriate behavior. Such description is essential and prerequisite to understanding events in all their individual richness; but the two kinds of account should not be confused (see Sapir 1949: 534, 543).

Many approaches to communication and the analysis of speech have not provided a place for either kind of purpose, perhaps because of a conscious or unconsciously lingering behaviorism. [Kenneth Burke's (1945) approach is a notable exception.] Yet communication itself must be differentiated from interaction as a whole in terms of purposiveness (see Hymes 1964). The two aspects of purpose can be grouped together by exploiting an English homonymy, *ends* in view (goals) and *ends* as outcomes (mnemonically, E).

11. *Key.* Key is introduced to provide for the tone, manner, or spirit in which an act is done. It corresponds roughly to modality among grammatical categories. Acts otherwise the same as regards setting, participants, message form, and the like may differ in key, as, e.g., between *mock: serious* or *perfunctory: painstaking.*

Key is often conventionally ascribed to an instance of some other component as its attribute; seriousness, for example, may be the expected concomitant of a scene, participant, act, code, or genre (say, a church, a judge, a vow, use of Latin, obsequies). Yet there is always the possibility that there is a conventionally understood way of substituting an alternative key. (This possibility corresponds to the general possibility of choosing one speech style or register as against another.) In this respect, ritual remains always informative. Knowing what should happen next, one still can attend to the way in which it happens. (Consider, for example, critics reviewing performances of the classical repertoire for the piano.)

The significance of key is underlined by the fact that, when it is in conflict with the overt content of an act, it often overrides the latter (as in sarcasm). The signaling of key may be nonverbal, as with a wink, gesture, posture, style of dress, musical accompaniment, but it also commonly involves conventional units of speech too often disregarded in ordinary linguistic analysis, such as English aspiration and vowel length to signal emphasis. Such features are often termed *expressive,* but are better dubbed *stylistic* since they need not at all depend on the mood of their user. Revill (1966: 251) reports, for instance, that 'some forms have been found which *cannot* [emphasis mine] be described as reflecting feelings on the part of the speaker, but they will be used in certain social situations' (for emphasis, clarity, politeness).

12. *Channels.* By choice of channel is understood choice of oral, written, telegraphic, semaphore, or other medium of transmission of speech. With regard to channels, one must further distinguish modes of use. The oral channel, e.g., may be used to sing, hum, whistle, or chant features of speech as well as to speak them. Two important goals of description are accounts of the interdependence of channels in interaction and the relative hierarchy among them.

13. *Forms of speech.* A major theoretical and empirical problem is to distinguish the verbal resources of a community. Obviously, it is superficial, indeed misleading, to speak of the language of a community (Ferguson and Gumperz 1960). Even where there is but a single 'language' present in a community (no cases are known in the contemporary world), that language will be organized into various forms of speech. Three criteria seem to require recognition at the present time: the historical provenience of the language resources; presence or absence of mutual intelligibility; and specialization in use. The criteria often do not coincide. *Language* and *dialect* are suggested for the first; *codes* for the second; and *varieties* and *registers* for the third. One speaks normally of the English language, and of dialects of English, wherever forms of speech are found whose content is historically derived from the line of linguistic tradition we call 'English', The different dialects are not always mutually intelligible (see Yorkshire and Indian English), and their social functions vary considerably around the world, from childhood vernacular to bureaucratic lingua franca. 'Code' suggests decoding and the question of intelligibility. Unintelligibility may result when speech is in a language historically unrelated to one's own, but also from use of a simple transformation of one's own speech, e.g., Pig Latin, or 'op' talk. In short, some forms of speech derive from others by addition, deletion, substitution, and permutation in various combinations. Finally, forms of speech are commonly specialized to uses of various sorts. *Register* has become familiar in English linguistic usage for reference to specific situations; varieties, or 'functional varieties', has been

used in American linguistics in relation to broad domains (e.g., vernacular vs. standard).

For Sociolinguistics, *varieties* has priority as a standpoint from which to view the forms of speech of a community. The criteria of provenience and intelligibility have to do with sources and characteristics of the criterion of use with the functional organization, of the forms of speech. Channels and forms of speech can be joined together as means or agencies of speaking and labeled, partly for the sake of the code word, partly with an eye on the use of the term *instrumental* in grammar, as *instrumentalities* (mnemonically, I).

14. *Norms of interaction.* All rules governing speaking, of course, have a normative character. What is intended here are the specific behaviors and proprieties that attach to speaking – that one must not interrupt, for example, or that one may freely do so; that normal voice should not be used except when scheduled in a church service (whisper otherwise); that turns in speaking are to be allocated in a certain way. Norms of interaction obviously implicate analysis of social structure, and social relationships generally, in a community. An illustration follows:

The next morning during tea with Jikjitsu, a college professor who rents rooms in one of the Sodo buildings came in and talked of koans. 'When you understand Zen, you know that the tree is really *there*.' – The only time anyone said anything of Zen philosophy or experience the whole week. Zenbos never discuss koans or sanzen experience with each other (Snyder 1969: 52).

15. *Norms of interpretation.* An account of norms of interaction may still leave open the interpretation to be placed upon them, especially when members of different communities are in communication. Thus it is clear that Arabic and American students differ on a series of interactional norms: Arabs confront each other more directly (face to face) when conversing, sit closer to each other, are more likely to touch each other, look each other more squarely in the eye, and converse more loudly (Watson and Graves 1966: 976–977). The investigators who report these findings themselves leave open the meanings of these norms to the participants (984).

The problem of norms of interpretation is familiar from the assessment of communications from other governments and national leaders. One often looks for friendliness in lessened degree of overt hostility. Relations between groups within a country are often affected by misunderstandings on this score. For white middle-class Americans, for example, normal hesitation behavior involves 'fillers' at the point of hesitation ('uh', etc.). For many blacks, a normal pattern is to recycle to the beginning of the utterance (perhaps more than once). This black form may be interpreted by whites not as a different norm but as a defect. (I owe this example to David Dalby.)

Norms of interpretation implicate the belief system of a community. The classic precedent in the ethnographic analysis of a language is Malinowski's (1935) treatment of Trobriand magical formulas and ritual under the heading of *dogmatic context*. (Malinowski's other rubrics are roughly related to these presented here in the following way: His *sociological context* and *ritual context* subsume information as to setting, participants, ends in view and outcome, norms of interaction, and higher level aspects of genre; *structure* reports salient patterning of the verbal form of the act or event; *mode of recitation* reports salient characteristics of the vocal aspect of channel use and message form.)

The processes of interpretation discussed by Harold Garfinkel, including 'ad hocing' generally, would belong in this category. These two kinds of norms may be grouped together (mnemonically, N).

16. *Genres.* By genres are meant categories such as poem, myth, tale, proverb, riddle, curse, prayer, oration, lecture, commercial, form letter, editorial, etc. From one standpoint the analysis of speech into acts is an analysis of speech into instances of genres. The notion of genre implies the possibility of identifying formal characteristics traditionally recognized. It is heuristically important to proceed as though all speech has formal characteristics of some sort as manifestation of genres; and it may well be true (on genres, see Ben-Amos 1969). The common notion of 'casual' or unmarked speech, however, points up the fact that there is a great range among genres in the number of and explicitness of formal markers. At least there is a great range in the ease with which such markers have been identified. It remains that 'unmarked' casual speech can be recognized as such in a context where it is not expected or where it is being exploited for particular effect. Its lesser visibility may be a function of our own orientations and use of it; its profile may be as sharp as any other, once we succeed in seeing it as strange.

Genres often coincide with speech events, but must be treated as analytically independent of them. They may occur in (or as) different events. The sermon as a genre is typically identical with a certain place in a church service, but its properties may be invoked, for serious or humorous effect, in other situations. Often enough a genre recurs in several events, such as a genre of chanting employed by women in Bihar state in India; it is the prescribed form for a related set of acts, recurring in weddings, family visits, and complaints to one's husband (K. M. Tiwary, personal communication). A great deal of empirical work will be needed to clarify the interrelations of genres, events, acts, and other components (mnemonically, G).

As has been shown, the sixteen components can be grouped together under the letters of the code word SPEAKING: settings, participants, ends, act sequences, keys, instrumentalities, norms, genres. That the code word is not wholly ethnocentric appears from the possibility of relabeling and regrouping the necessary components in terms of the French PARLANT: *participants, actes, raison (resultat), locale, agents* (instrumentalities), *normes, ton* (key), *types* (genres).

REFERENCES

Ben-Amos, Dan. 1969. Analytical categories and ethnic genres. *Genre* 2: 275–301.

Bloomfield, Leonard. 1933. *Language*. New York: Holt, Rinehart and Winston, Inc.

Burke, Kenneth. 1945. *A Grammar of Motives*. Englewood Cliffs, New Jersey: Prentice-Hall. (Republished by Berkeley, California: University of California Press, 1969.)

Burke, Kenneth. 1950. *A Rhetoric of Motives*. Englewood Cliffs, New Jersey: Prentice-Hall. (Republished by Berkeley, California: University of California Press, 1969.)

Ferguson, Charles A. and John J. Gumperz. 1960. Linguistic diversity in South Asia: Studies in regional, social, and functional variation. Research Center in Anthropology, Folklore, and Linguistics, Publication 13 (*International Journal of American Linguistics* 26, 3, Part III).

Fock, Niels. 1965. Cultural aspects of the 'oho' institution among the Waiwai. Proceedings of the International Congress of Americanists. 136–140.

Gumperz, John J. 1962. Types of linguistic communities. *Anthropological Linguistics* 4: 28–40.

Hymes, Dell. 1964. Introduction: Toward ethnographies of communication. In John J. Gumperz and Dell Hymes (eds.) The ethnography of communication. *American Anthropologist* 66: 1–34.

Hymes, Dell. 1969. Linguistic aspects of comparative political research. In Robert T. Holt and John Turner (eds.) *Methodology of Comparative Research*. New York: Free Press.

McCawley, James. 1968. The role of semantics in grammar. In Emmon Bach and Robert Harms (eds.) *Universals in Linguistic Theory*. New York: Holt, Rinehart and Winston, Inc. 125–170.

Malinowski, Bronislaw. 1935. *Coral Gardens and Their Magic*, vol. II. London: Allen and Unwin.

Miller, G. A. 1956. The magical number seven, plus or minus two: Some limits on our capacity for processing information. *The Psychological Review* 63: 81–97.

Pike, Kenneth L. 1967. *Language in Relation to the Unified Theory of the Structure of Human Behavior*. (2nd Rev. Ed.). The Hague: Mouton.

Revill, P. M. 1966. Preliminary report on paralinguistics in Mbembe (Eastern Nigeria). Tagmemic and matrix linguistics applied to selected African languages, by K. L. Pike, 245–254, appendix VIII. Final report, contract no. OE-5-14-065. Washington, D.C., U.S. Department of Health, Education and Welfare, Office of Education, Bureau of Research.

Sapir, Edward. 1949. Speech as a personality trait. In David Mandelbaum (ed.) *Selected Writings of Edward Sapir*. Berkeley, California: University of California Press. 533–543. (Reprinted from *American Journal of Sociology* 32 (1927): 892–905.)

Snyder, Gary. 1969. *Earth Household: Technical Notes and Queries to Fellow Dharma Revolutionaries*. New York: New Directions.

Watson, O. Michael and T. D. Graves. 1966. Quantitative research in proxemic behavior. *American Anthropologist* 68: 971–985.

Weinreich, Uriel. 1953. *Languages in Contact*. Linguistic Circle of New York.

CHAPTER 40

Contextualization
Conventions

JOHN J. GUMPERZ

Linguistic diversity serves as a communicative resource in everyday life in that conversationalists rely on their knowledge and their stereotypes about variant ways of speaking to categorize events, infer intent and derive expectations about what is likely to ensue. All this information is crucial to the maintenance of conversational involvement and to the success of persuasive strategies. By posing the issue in this way, one can avoid the dilemma inherent in traditional approaches to Sociolinguistics, where social phenomena are seen as generalizations about groups previously isolated by nonlinguistic criteria such as residence, class, occupation, ethnicity and the like, and are then used to explain individual behavior. We hope to be able to find a way of dealing with what are ordinarily called sociolinguistic phenomena which builds on empirical evidence of conversational cooperation and does not rely on a priori identification of social categories, by extending the traditional linguistic methods of in-depth and recursive hypothesis testing with key informants to the analysis of the interactive processes by which participants negotiate interpretations.

Initially we approach the problem of the symbolic significance of linguistic variables by discovering how they contribute to the interpretation of what is being done in the communicative exchange. The hypothesis is that any utterance can be understood in numerous ways, and that people make decisions about how to interpret a given utterance based on their definition of what is happening at the time of interaction. In other words, they define the interaction in terms of a frame or schema which is identifiable and familiar (Goffman 1974). I will refer to the basic socially significant unit of interaction in terms of which meaning is assessed as the *activity type* or *activity* (Levinson 1978). The term is used to emphasize that, although

Source: 'Contextualization conventions' in Gumperz, J. J. *Discourse Strategies* (1982) (Cambridge: Cambridge University Press) pp. 130–52.

we are dealing with a structured ordering of message elements that represents the speakers' expectations about what will happen next, yet it is not a static structure, but rather it reflects a dynamic process which develops and changes as the participants interact. Moreover, its basis in meaning reflects something being *done*, some purpose or goal being pursued, much as Bartlett (1932), who originated the concept of 'schema' as an organizing principle in interpreting events, stated that he preferred the term 'active developing patterns'. Thus the activity type does not determine meaning but simply constrains interpretations by channelling inferences so as to *foreground* or make relevant certain aspects of background knowledge and to underplay others.

Contextualization Cues

A basic assumption is that this channelling of interpretation is effected by conversational implicatures based on conventionalized co-occurrence expectations between content and surface style. That is, constellations of surface features of message form are the means by which speakers signal and listeners interpret what the activity is, how semantic content is to be understood and *how* each sentence relates to what precedes or follows. These features are referred to as *contextualization cues*. For the most part they are habitually used and perceived but rarely consciously noted and almost never talked about directly. Therefore they must be studied in process and in context rather than in the abstract.

Roughly speaking, a contextualization cue is any feature of linguistic form that contributes to the signalling of contextual presuppositions. Such cues may have a number of such linguistic realizations depending on the historically given linguistic repertoire of the participants. The code, dialect and style switching processes, some of the prosodic phenomena we have discussed as well as choice among lexical and syntactic options, formulaic expressions, conversational openings, closings and sequencing strategies can all have similar contextualizing functions. Although such cues carry information, meanings are conveyed as part of the interactive process. Unlike words that can be discussed out of context, the meanings of contextualization cues are implicit. They are not usually talked about out of context. Their signalling value depends on the participants' tacit awareness of their meaningfulness. When all participants understand and notice the relevant cues, interpretive processes are then taken for granted and tend to go unnoticed. However, when a listener does not react to a cue or is unaware of its function, interpretations may differ and misunderstanding may occur. It is important to note that when this happens and when a difference in interpretation is brought to a participant's attention, it tends to be seen in attitudinal terms. A speaker is said to be unfriendly, impertinent, rude, uncooperative, or to fail to understand. Interactants do not ordinarily notice that the listener may have failed to perceive a shift in rhythm or a change in pronunciation. Miscommunication of this type, in other words, is regarded as a social faux pas and leads to misjudgements of the speaker's intent; it is not likely to be identified as a mere linguistic error.

The cues involved here are basically gradual or scalar; they do not take the form of discrete qualitative contrasts. What is involved is a departure from normal in one or another direction. But while the signalling potential of semantic directionality is, in large part, universal, the situated interpretation of the meaning of any one such shift in context is always a matter of social convention. Conversationalists, for example, have conventional expectations about what count as normal and what count as marked kinds of rhythm, loudness, intonation and speech style. By signalling a speech activity, a speaker also signals the social presuppositions in terms of which a message is to be interpreted. Notions of normality differ within what, on other grounds, counts as a single speech community. When this is the case, and especially when participants think they understand each others' words, miscommunication resulting in mutual frustration can occur.

The conversational analyses described in this chapter extend the methodological principle of comparing ungrammatical and grammatical sentences, by which linguists derive generalizations about grammatical rules, to the analysis of contextualization phenomena that underlie the situated judgements conversationalists make of each other. Naturally occurring instances of miscommunication are compared with functionally similar passages of successful communication in the same encounter or findings from other situations to derive generalizations about subculturally and situationally specific aspects of inferential processes.

The following example illustrates the type of miscommunication phenomena we look for and shows how we begin to isolate possible linguistic sources of misunderstanding. The incident is taken from an oral report by a graduate student in educational psychology who served as an interviewer in a survey.

(1) The graduate student has been sent to interview a black housewife in a low income, inner city neighborhood. The contact has been made over the phone by someone in the office. The student arrives, rings the bell, and is met by the husband, who opens the door, smiles, and steps towards him:

> Husband: So y're gonna check out ma ol lady, hah?
> Interviewer: Ah, no. I only came to get some information. They called from the office.

(Husband, dropping his smile, disappears without a word and calls his wife.)

The student reports that the interview that followed was stiff and quite unsatisfactory. Being black himself, he knew that he had 'blown it' by failing to recognize the significance of the husband's speech style in this particular case. The style is that of a formulaic opening gambit used to 'check out' strangers, to see whether or not they can come up with the appropriate formulaic reply. Intent on following the instructions he had received in his methodological training and doing well in what he saw as a formal interview, the interviewer failed to notice the husband's stylistic cues. Reflecting on the incident, he himself states that, in order to show that he was on the husband's wavelength, he should have replied with a typically black response like 'Yea, I'ma git some info' (I'm going to get some information) to prove his familiarity with and his ability to understand local verbal etiquette and values. Instead, his Standard English reply was taken by the husband as an indication that the interviewer was not one of them and, perhaps, not to be trusted.

The opener 'So y're gonna check out ma ol lady' is a formulaic phrase identifiable through co-occurrent selections of phonological, prosodic, morphological and lexical options. Linguists have come to recognize that, as Fillmore (1976) puts it, 'an enormous amount of natural language is formulaic, automatic and rehearsed, rather than propositional, creative or freely generated'. But it must be emphasized that although such formulas have some of the characteristics of common idioms like *kick the bucket* and *spill the beans,* their meaning cannot be adequately described by lexical glosses. They occur as part of routinized interactive exchanges, such as Goffman describes as 'replies and responses' (1981). Their use signals both expectations about what is to be accomplished and about the form that replies must take. They are similar in function to code switching strategies. Like the latter they are learned by interacting with others in institutionally defined networks of relationships. Where these relationships are ethnically specific they are often regarded as markers of ethnic background. But, as our example shows, their use in actual encounters is ultimately determined by activity specific presuppositions so that failure to react is not in itself a clear sign of ethnic identity. Basically, these formulaic phrases reflect indirect conversational strategies that make conditions favorable to establishing personal contact and negotiating shared interpretations.

Because of the indirect ways in which they function, and the variety of surface forms they can take, empirical analysis of contextualization strategies presents a major problem. New kinds of discovery methods are needed to identify differences in the perception of cues. The procedures we have begun to work out rely either on verbatim description of remembered happenings or on passages isolated from tape recorded or videotaped naturalistic encounters by methods patterned on those described in Erickson and Schultz (1982). The passages in question may vary in length, but a basic requirement is that they constitute self-contained episodes, for which we have either internal or ethnographic evidence of what the goals are in terms of which participants evaluate component utterances. These passages are then transcribed literally bringing in as much phonetic, prosodic and interactional detail as necessary, described in terms of the surface content and ethnographic background necessary to understand what is going on and, finally, analysed interpretively both in terms of what is intended and what is perceived.

In what follows we present additional examples illustrating interpretive differences. These will be analysed and elicitation strategies will be discussed that are capable of making explicit the unverbalized perceptions and presuppositions that underlie interpretation.

(2)   A husband sitting in his living room is addressing his wife. The husband is of middle class American background, the wife is British.

      They have been married and living in the United States for a number of years:

          Husband: Do you know where today's paper is?
          Wife: *I'll* get it for you.
          Husband: That's O.K. Just tell me where it is. *I'll* get it.
          Wife: No, *I'll* get it.

The husband is using a question which literally interpreted inquires after the location of the paper. The wife does not reply directly but offers to get the paper. Her 'I'll' is accented and this could be interpreted as 'I will if you don't.' The husband countersuggests that he had intended to ask for information, not to make a request. He also stresses 'I'll'. The wife then reiterates her statement, to emphasize that she intends to get it. The 'I'll' is now highly stressed to suggest increasing annoyance.

(3)   A mother is talking to her eleven year old son who is about to go out in the rain:

          Mother: Where are your boots?
          Son: In the closet.
          Mother: I want you to put them on *right* now.

The mother asks a question which literally interpreted concerns the location of the son's boots. When he responds with a statement about their location, the mother retorts with a direct request. Her stress on 'right now' suggests that she is annoyed at her son for not responding to her initial question as a request in the first place.

It would seem at first glance that what is at issue here is listeners' failure to respond appropriately to an indirect speech act (Searle 1975). But directness is often itself a matter of socio-cultural convention. Few Americans would claim for example that 'Have you got the time?' is not a direct request. Although it would be premature to make definitive claims on the basis of these two examples, interpretive differences of this type have been found to be patterned in accordance with differences in gender and ethnic origin.

(4) Telephone conversation between a college instructor and a student. The individuals know each other well since the student, who is black, had previously worked as an office helper in the white instructor's office for several years. The telephone rings:

> Instructor: Hello.
> Student: How's the family?
>   (pause)
> Instructor: Fine.
> Student: I'll get back to you next month about that thing.
> Instructor: That's O.K. I can wait.
> Student: I'm finished with that paper. It's being typed.
> Instructor: Come to the office and we'll talk about it.

The student answers the instructor's hello with what sounds like a polite inquiry about the instructor's family. The fact that he fails to identify himself can perhaps be explained by assuming that he would be recognized by his voice. But he also fails to give the customary greeting. More than the normal interval elapses before the instructor responds with a hesitant 'Fine'. He seems unsure as to what is wanted. The instructor has less difficulty with the student's next statement which makes indirect reference to the fact that the student has borrowed some money which he was promising to return soon. The topic then shifts to a paper which has not yet been turned in. When the instructor later refused to give the student a grade without seeing the finished paper, the student seemed annoyed. He claimed that the telephone call had led him to hope he would be given special consideration.

(5) Conversation in the office between a black undergraduate employed as a research assistant, who is busy writing at his desk, and a faculty member, his supervisor, who is passing by at some distance. The two are on first name terms:

> Student: John, help me with this. I'm putting it all down.
> Supervisor: What is it?
> Student: I'm almost done. 1 just need to fix it up a little.
> Supervisor: What do you want me to do?

> Student: I'm writing down everything just the way you said.
> Supervisor: I don't have the time right now.

The student opens with what sounds like a request for help. But the supervisor's request for more information is answered with further factual statements about what the student is doing. The second, more insistent question also fails to elicit an adequate reply. It seems as if the student, having asked for help, then refuses to say what he wants done.

Passages such as the above were played to sets of listeners including some who did and others who did not share participants' backgrounds. Each incident was first heard in its entirety and then repeated more slowly with frequent pauses. Initial questions tended to yield very general replies about what was ultimately intended, what listeners thought, how they felt, how well they did, and what they did wrong. Subsequent questioning attempted to induce respondents to relate their judgements more closely to what they actually heard. The aim here is to test the analyst's hypotheses about more immediate communicative goals, illocutionary force of particular utterances, and about the way listeners interpret speakers' moves. We therefore focus on particular exchanges such as question–answer pairs rather than on single utterances or on an entire passage. Respondents' answers are followed up with elicitation techniques patterned on those developed by linguistic anthropologists (Frake 1969) to recover native speakers' perceptual and inferential processes. For example, if a respondent states that the speaker, A, is making a request, we may then ask a series of questions such as the following: (a) What is it about the way A speaks that makes you think?; (b) Can you repeat it just about the way he said it?; (c) What is another way of saying it?; (d) Is it possible that he merely wanted to ask a question?; (e) How would he have said it if he?; (f) How did the answerer interpret what A said?; (g) How can you tell that the answerer interpreted it that way? These elicitation procedures yield hypotheses about the actual cues processed and the paradigmatic range of alternatives in terms of which evaluations are made. The analyst can then use this to reanalyse the passage at hand, deal with additional data and develop more specific elicitation procedures for particular types of situations. The main goal of all these procedures is to relate interpretations to identifiable features of message form, to identify chains of inferences, not to judge the absolute truth value of particular assessments.

Examination of our examples in these terms reveals significant differences in interpretation. Some judges identify the first utterance in (2) as a factual question, others as a request, others again suggest that it is ambiguous. The mother's remark in (3) is seen by some as an order to put on boots; others feel it could be a request for information. In (5) a number of judges note the student's failure to state clearly what he is doing and what he wants the supervisor to help him with. These same judges also note the student's failure to say hello in the telephone conversation of (4) and suggest that this omission seems rude. Others, however, instead of mentioning the student's vagueness in (5) claim that the supervisor's insistence on asking what is wanted is out of place. A common comment was: 'Why didn't the supervisor say that he doesn't have any time in the first place?'

At first glance, these evaluations seem to reflect individual interpretations of what are essentially inherent ambiguities or differences in degree. Although some trends begin to emerge, it would be premature to claim that they relate to cultural background. But when we examine choice of alternative expressions and sequencing strategies, more systematic relationships begin to emerge.

Judges who identify the husband's opener in (2) as a request also state that the wife's annoyance is justified since, if he did not want her to get the paper, he would not have used that expression. They argue he would have said something like 'I wonder where the paper is.' These same judges also claim that the child's answer to the mother's order in (3) is impertinent, and that this justified the mother's annoyance. They say that to justify himself the child should have answered indirectness with indirectness and replied with something like 'Why, is it raining?' Thus there seems to be an empirically recoverable implicational ordering to evaluations such that assessment at the speech act level of illocutionary force forms the basis for more specific interpretations.

Everyone listening to (2) and (3) recognized the opening utterances as meaningful strategies. The situation is different however with (4). Here judges point to the caller's failure (a) to identify himself and (b) to open with a greeting, such as 'Hi'. They argue that the participants know each other and can be presumed to recognize each other's voices, and that self-identification is not necessary, but the lack of a greeting evokes different responses. Some judges merely see it as a failure to say something that should have been said, an inappropriate strategy that seems odd, or perhaps rude. Others, however, recognize it as part of a meaningful gambit, an indirect way of suggesting that the speaker wants something. When pressed further they illustrate their comments with anecdotes from their own experience, listing other expressions that exemplify similar verbal strategies. These same judges point to the speaker's failure to state what he wants in (5) as a similar instance of indirectness. The strategy underlying both examples seems to be something like this: Do not verbalize explicitly what the conversation is about, rely on the listener's ability to use his background knowledge. If he is a friend, he will guess what is wanted and will cooperate, so that if he enters into this type of interaction and responds at all he can be presumed to understand.

The failure to say something that is normally expected is thus interpreted in attitudinal terms by some listeners, while others see it as having identifiable signalling value. For the latter group it counts as a contextualization strategy which is meaningful in the same sense that the idiomatic opener in example (1) and metaphorical switching are meaningful. Since the signalling mechanisms involved are covert, highly context bound and learned only through intensive formal contact under conditions allowing maximum feedback, such as we find in home and peer settings, they tend to reflect commonality of family or ethnic background. Therefore, whenever one set of listeners (a) identifies such features as conventionalized and (b) agrees on their interpretation and on appropriate sequencing strategies, while another group does not see such cues as meaningful, we have fairly good evidence that the interpretive differences also reflect significant variations in socio-cultural background. In fact judges who see meaningful indirectness in (4) and (5) are either black or familiar with black rhetoric. We might therefore tentatively identify the features in question as reflecting black style. The evidence for differences in cultural background is somewhat weaker in the case of examples (2) and (3), but it is of interest that the mother and wife are English and that other English judges tend to favor the request interpretation, while Americans tend toward the question interpretation.

REFERENCES

Bartlett, F. C. 1932. *Remembering.* Oxford: Oxford University Press.
Fillmore, C. 1976. The need for a frame semantics in linguistics. In *Statistical Methods in Linguistics.* Stockholm: Skriptor.
Frake, C. 1969. The ethnographic study of cognitive systems. In S. A. Tyler (ed.) *Cognitive Anthropology.* New York: Holt, Rinehart and Winston.
Goffman, E. 1974. *Frame Analysis.* New York: Harper and Row.
Goffman, E. 1981. *Forms of Talk.* Philadelphia, Pennsylvania: University of Pennsylvania Press.
Kendon, A., R. M. Harris and M. R. Key (eds.) 1975. *Organization of Behavior in Face-to-Face Interaction.* The Hague: Mouton.
Levinson, S. C. 1978. Activity types and language. *Pragmatics Microfiche* 3: 3–3 D1–G5.
Searle, J. R. 1975. Indirect speech acts. In P. Cole and J. Morgan (ed.) *Syntax and Semantics,* vol. 3. New York: Academic Press.

CHAPTER 41

Poetics and Performance as Critical Perspectives on Language and Social Life

RICHARD BAUMAN AND CHARLES L. BRIGGS

As many authors have stressed, performances are not simply artful uses of language that stand apart both from day-to-day life and from larger questions of meaning. Performance rather provides a frame that invites critical reflection on communicative processes. A given performance is tied to a number of speech events that precede and succeed it (past performances, readings of texts, negotiations, rehearsals, gossip, reports, critiques, challenges, subsequent performances, and the like). An adequate analysis of a single performance thus requires sensitive ethnographic study of how its form and meaning index a broad range of discourse types, some of which are not framed as performance. Performance-based research can yield insights into diverse facets of language use and their interrelations. Because contrastive theories of speech and associated metaphysical assumptions embrace more than these discourse events alone, studying performance can open up a wider range of vantage points on how language can be structured and what roles it can play in social life.

Much performance-oriented research on contextualization has focused on the grounding of performance in situational contexts. An alternative perspective has begun to emerge from performance studies and other areas that approaches some of the basic problems in linguistic anthropology from a contrary set of assumptions.

Consider for a moment why researchers have had to make such an issue of contextualization, to devote so much effort to establishing that the form, function, and meaning of verbal art cannot be understood apart from context. The reason is precisely that verbal art forms are so susceptible to treatment as

Source: 'Poetics and performance as critical perspectives on language and social life', by Bauman, R. and Briggs, C. L. in *Annual Review of Anthropology*, 19 (1990) (*Annual Reviews*) pp. 60–1, 72–78.

self-contained, bounded objects separable from their social and cultural contexts of production and reception. Taking the practice of decontextualization as the focus of investigation, we ask what makes it possible, how it is accomplished in formal and functional terms, for what ends, by whom, under what circumstances, and so on. We are currently far from having conclusive answers to these questions, but the inquiry can open up some productive new approaches.[1]

The past work of most investigators of contextualization has thus tended to take the opposite tack from the one on which we will now embark. It has established how performance is *anchored* in and inseparable from its context of use. Such work – on the ties of performance to the competence, expressive agenda, rhetorical strategy, and functional goals of the performer; on the phatic ties of the performer to the audience; on the indexical ties of the performed discourse to its situational surround, the participants, or other dimensions of the performance event; on the structure of the performed text as emergent in performance, and so on – served to establish how and why verbal art should be resistant to decentering, to extraction from context. We will contrastively ask what it is that makes verbal art decenterable despite all these anchoring counterforces. What makes it susceptible to decontextualization? What factors loosen the ties between performed discourse and its context?

One starting point for these inquiries is a distinction between discourse and text. At the heart of the process of decentering discourse is the more fundamental process – *entextualization*. In simple terms, though it is far from simple, it is the process of rendering discourse extractable, of making a stretch of linguistic production into a unit – a *text* – that can be lifted out of its interactional setting. A text, then, from this vantage point, is discourse rendered decontextualizable. Entextualization may well incorporate aspects of context, such that the resultant text carries elements of its history of use within it.

Basic to the process of entextualization is the reflexive capacity of discourse, the capacity it shares with all systems of signification 'to turn or bend back upon itself, to become an object to itself, to refer to itself'. In Jakobsonian terms, with regard to language, this reflexive capacity is manifested most directly in the metalingual and poetic functions. The metalingual (or metadiscursive) function objectifies discourse by making discourse its own topic; the poetic function manipulates the formal features of the discourse to call attention to the formal structures by which the discourse is organized.

Performance, the enactment of the poetic function, is a highly reflexive mode of communication. As the concept of performance has been developed in linguistic anthropology, performance is seen as a specially marked, artful way of speaking that sets up or represents a special interpretive frame within which the act of speaking is to be understood. Performance puts the act of speaking on display – objectifies it, lifts it to a degree from its interactional setting and opens it to scrutiny by an audience. Performance heightens awareness of the act of speaking and licenses the audience to evaluate the skill and effectiveness of the performer's accomplishment. By its very nature, then, performance potentiates decontextualization.

We may approach the process of entextualization in performance in formal and functional terms by exploring the means available to participants in performance situations to render stretches of discourse discontinuous with their discursive surround, thus making them into coherent, effective, and memorable texts. What discursive resources might serve this end? From a formal perspective, this line of inquiry takes us into familiar territory: the formal organization of texts, the devices of cohesion, and so forth. Here, the close formal analysis advanced in recent years under the stimulus of ethnopoetics, the comparative analysis of parallelism, and the analysis of folklore genres, has expanded our understanding of the textuality of verbal art forms. The means and devices outlined as 'keys to performance' by Bauman (1977) may be seen as indices of entextualization. Conversational analysis, and language-oriented studies of disputing and conflict offer vantage points on the formal analysis of discourse and entextualization and illuminate how the prepared-for detachability of texts may be interactively accomplished. They remind us that participants themselves may be directly and strongly concerned with the social management of entextualization, decontextualization, and recontextualization.

Beyond formal features, frame analysis, the phenomenological investigation of the 'worlds' created in performance, studies of the interaction of verbal performance and accompanying media such as music, dance, and material objects, analysis of composition process, and a range of other lines of inquiry illuminate the process of entextualization in performance. The task is to discover empirically what means are available in a given social setting, to whom they may be available, under what circumstances, for making discourse into a text.

Performance is clearly not the only mechanism of entextualization. Our claim, rather, is that performance as a frame intensifies entextualization. It is also important to recall that performance is a variable quality; its salience among the multiple functions and framings of a communicative act may vary along a continuum from sustained, full performance to a fleeting breakthrough into performance (Bauman 1984). Likewise, entextualization is a matter of degree across the speech genres of a community. Full performance seems to be associated with the most marked entextualization, but such correlation is far from perfect; a rigorously entextualized stretch of discourse may be reported, or translated, or rendered in a frame other than performance. This is an area that will reward further investigation.

The foregoing brief survey of entextualization must suffice here in establishing that discourse may be fashioned for ease of detachment from situational context. Processes that anchor discourse in contexts of use may be opposed by others that potentiate its detachability. If we now consider what becomes of text once decontextualized, we recognize that decontextualization from one social context involves recontextualization in another. For present purposes, we consider the decontextualization and recontextualization of texts to be two aspects of the same process, though time and other factors may mediate between the two phases. Because the process is transformational, we must now determine what the recontextualized text brings with it from its earlier context(s) and what emergent form, function, and meaning it is given as it is recentered.

At this stage, we can only suggest schematically and programmatically what some of the dimensions of the transformation may be. It helps, of course, if one has good data on successive points in the process, but examination even of apparently isolated texts may be productive precisely because a text may carry some of its history with it. Moreover, a succession of recenterings may be encompassed within a single event.

For example, in performing a treasure tale popular among Spanish-speakers in northern New Mexico, Melaquias Romero provides a summary of the tale, a performance of his parents' version, and several retellings based on other versions of the narrative. Such recenterings may also be simultaneous rather than serial. Mr. Romero thus presents a key scene in the treasure tale, a dialog between a sheepherder and his boss, as it was retold by the boss to another sheepherder, who in turn recounted it to two friends; Mr. Romero then recounts the way these two individuals presented the narrative to him (see Briggs 1990).

In mapping the dimensions of transformation one could employ any one of the following elements while keeping in mind the crucial task of examining their interrelations.

1. *Framing* – that is, the metacommunicative management of the recontextualized text. In Goffman's terms (1981: 124–159), what is the footing adopted toward the text in the text in the process of recontextualizing it? Is it linked to prior renderings as a repetition or quotation? Here, the recent growth of interest in reported speech and metapragmatics will be of special importance, as will developing research on blended genres, in which performed texts of one generic shape are embedded in texts of different generic shape. The differential framing of texts as they are rendered in rehearsal as opposed to performance is also worthy of further research.

2. *Form* – including formal means and structures from phonology, to grammar, to speech style, to larger structures of discourse such as generic packaging principles. Focus on this dimension of formal transformation from one

context to another affords insights into the evolution of genres. One especially interesting formal transformation is the recentering of text by metonymic substitution: mentioning the place where a narrated event happened, or a key portion of the plot, for example, to evoke the whole in the hearers' minds.

3. *Function* – manifest, latent, and performative (perlocutionary and illocutionary force; see above). A primarily ritual text, for example, may be used in entertainment, practice, or pedagogy.

4. *Indexical grounding,* including deictic markers of person, spatial location, time, etc. The analysis of 'metanarration' represents one productive vantage point on this problem.

5. *Translation,* including both interlingual and intersemiotic translation. At issue here are the different semiotic capacities of different languages and different media. What happens if a text is transferred from Zuni to English or from oral narration to print? These issues have been central to the enterprise of ethnopoetics and to the problematics of transcription. They thus afford an important critical and reflexive vantage point on our own scholarly practice as linguistic anthropologists.

6. The *emergent structure* of the new context, as shaped by the process of recontextualization. Texts both shape and are shaped by the situational contexts in which they are produced.

To this point, we have sketched a framework for the investigation of decentering and recentering largely in formal terms. But just as the formal analysis of the processes and practices of contextualization is a means of investigating larger social and cultural problems, so too the analysis of decontextualization and recontextualization will stand or fall as an anthropological enterprise by the degree to which it illuminates problems of broader concern. Let us suggest, then, some problem areas in which such an investigation might be productive.

The decontextualization and recontextualization of performed discourse bear upon the political economy of texts (Gal 1989; Irvine 1989), texts and power. Performance is a mode of social production; specific products include texts, decentered discourse. To decontextualize and recontextualize a text is thus an act of control, and in regard to the differential exercise of such control the issue of social power arises. More specifically, we may recognize differential access to texts, differential legitimacy in claims to and use of texts, differential competence in the use of texts, and differential values attaching to various types of texts. All of these elements, let us emphasize, are culturally constructed, socially constituted, and sustained by ideologies, and they accordingly may vary cross-culturally. None of these factors is a social or cultural given, for each may be subject to negotiation as part of the process of entextualization, decentering, and recentering.

1. Access depends upon institutional structures, social definitions of eligibility, and other mechanisms and standards of inclusion and exclusion (even such practical matters as getting to where the texts are to be found).

2. The issue of legitimacy is one of being accorded the authority to appropriate a text such that your recentering of it counts as legitimate. Cultural property rights, such as copyright, academic standards of plagiarism, and their counterparts in other cultures all regulate the exercise of legitimate power over performed discourse, as do such social mechanisms as ordination, initiation, or apprenticeship. Not only do institutional structures and mechanisms confer legitimate authority to control texts, but the reverse potential also exists: Contra Bourdieu (1977: 649), the appropriation and use of particular forms of discourse may be the basis of institutional power.

3. Competence, the knowledge and ability to carry out the decontextualization and recontextualization of performed discourse successfully and appropriately, may be locally conceived of as innate human capacity, learned skill, special gift, a correlate of one's position in the life cycle, and so on (e.g. Briggs 1988; Fox 1988: 13–16).

4. Finally, values organize the relative status of texts and their uses into a hierarchy of preference. Texts may be valued because of what you can use them for, what you can get for them, or for their indexical reference to desired qualities or states – Bourdieu's cultural capital (1984).

All of these factors – access, legitimacy, competence, and values – bear centrally on the construction and assumption of authority. From Hymes's early formulation (1975), in which performance consisted in the authoritative display of communicative competence, authority has held a central place in performance-oriented analysis. Hymes's definition highlights the assumption of an authoritative voice by the performer, which is grounded at least in part in the knowledge, ability, and right to control the recentering of valued texts. Control over decentering and recentering is part of the social framework and as such is one of the processes by which texts are endowed with authority, which in turn places formal and functional constraints on how they may be further recentered: An authoritative text, by definition, is one that is maximally protected from compromising transformation.

While the implications of the decentering and recentering of discourse for the construction and exercise of power may be approached from a variety of vantage points, including cultural conceptions of the nature and uses of performance, institutional structures, or ideology, the situated practice of decontextualization and recontextualization is an essential and foundational frame of reference. In this sense the investigation of decontextualization and recontextualization continues the program of the ethnography of speaking, adding a conceptual framework, centered on discursive practice itself, that links separate situational contexts in terms of the pragmatics of textuality. Moreover, the chain of linkages may be extended without temporal limit, for texts may be continuously decentered and recentered. At one level, this illuminates the process of traditionalization (Bauman 1990), the telling and retelling of a tale, the citing and reciting of a proverb as these recenterings are part of the symbolic construction of discursive continuity with a meaningful past. Attention to such processes locates performances, texts, and contexts in systems of historical relationship. At another level, the tracing of chains of decentering and recentering offers a unified frame of reference for the analysis of control over discourse that extends from the small-scale and local to the global. A given folktale performance, for example, may be traced through connected processes of decentering and recentering in local oral tradition, in the nationalization of culture as it is appropriated by learned elites in the service of nationalist ideology, or in the internationalization of culture as it is held up to view as part of world literature

Our approach to the decontextualization and recontextualization of texts also contributes operational and substantive specificity to Bakhtin's more abstract notion of dialogism (1981), increasingly influential in linguistic anthropology and folklore. If indeed, as Bakhtin tells us, our mouths are filled with the words of others, the program we have outlined here is designed to elucidate how these dialogical relations are accomplished, and in ways that take full account of form-function interrelationships and the sociology and political economy of Bakhtinian dialogue.

A further significant payoff offered by the investigation of the decontextualization and recontextualization of texts is a critical and reflexive perspective from which to examine our own scholarly practice. Much of what we do as linguistic anthropologists amounts to the decontextualization and recontextualization of others' discourse, which means as well that we exercise power along the lines outlined above. To be sure, the exercise of such power need not be entirely one-sided; our interlocutors may attempt to control how their discourse will be entextualized and recontextualized. These processes have significant implications for the methods, goals, and not least, ethics, of our profession.

NOTE

1. The problem of decontextualization (and recontextualization, of which more below) has been the principal focus of a seminar at the Center for Psychosocial Studies, chiefly

under the rubrics of the *decentering* and *recentering* of discourse. These terms draw on poststructuralist usage in the process of offering a critique of the perspectives in which that usage is rooted (Bauman 1987). Through the work of the group's members, these terms have begun to gain wider currency in linguistic anthropology (e.g. Hanks 1989; Parmentier 1989). We employ 'centering', 'decentering', and 'recentering' here, interchangeably with 'contextualization', 'decontextualization', and 'recontextualization'.

REFERENCES

Bakhtin, M. M. 1981. *The Dialogic Imagination.* Translated By C. Emerson, M. Holquist, edited by M. Holquist. Austin, Texas: University Texas Press.

Bauman, R. 1977. *Verbal Art as Performance.* Prospect Heights, Illinois: Waveland.

Bauman, R. 1984. Disclaimers of performance. Paper presented at 83rd Annual Meeting American Anthropological Association. Denver, Colorado.

Bauman, R. 1987. The decentering of discourse. Paper presented at 86th Annual Meeting American Anthropological Association. Chicago, Illinois.

Bauman, R. 1990. Contextualization, tradition, and the dialogue of genres. In C. Goodwin, A. Duranti (eds.) *Rethinking Context.* Cambridge: Cambridge University Press. In press

Bourdieu, P. 1977. The economics of linguistic exchanges. *Social Science Information* 16: 645–668.

Bourdieu, P. 1984. *Distinction: A Social Critique of the Judgement of Taste.* Cambridge, Massachusetts: Harvard University Press.

Briggs, C. L. 1988. *Competence in Performance: The Creativity of Tradition in Mexicano Verbal Art.* Philadelphia, Pennsylvania: University Pennsylvania Press.

Briggs, C. L. 1990. History, poetics, and interpretation in the tale. In C. L. Briggs, J. J. Vigil (eds.) *The Lost Gold Mine of Juan Mondragon: A Legend from New Mexico Performed by Melaquias Romero.* Tucson, Arizona: University Arizona Press. 165–240.

Fox, J. J. (ed.) 1988. *To Speak in Pairs: Essays on the Ritual Language of Eastern Indonesia.* Cambridge: Cambridge University Press.

Gal, S. 1989. Language and political economy. *Annual Review Anthropology* 18: 345–367.

Goffman, E. 1981. *Forms of Talk.* Philadelphia, Pennsylvania: University Pennsylvania Press.

Hanks, W. F. 1989. Text and textuality. *Annual Review Anthropology* 18: 95–127.

Hymes, D. H. 1975. Breakthrough into performance. In D. Ben-Amos, K. S. Goldstein (eds.) *Folklore: Performance and Communication.* The Hague: Mouton. 11–74.

Irvine, J. T. 1989. When talk isn't cheap: Language and political economy. *American Ethnologist* 16: 248–267.

Parmentier, R. 1989. The semiotics of ritual performativity. Paper presented at 88th Annual Meeting American Anthropological Association Washington, D.C.

CHAPTER 42

Rules for Ritual Insults

WILLIAM LABOV

Terms for the Speech Event

A great variety of terms describe this activity[1]: *the dozens, sounding,* and *signifying* are three of the most common. The activity itself is remarkably similar throughout the various black communities, both in the form and content of the insults themselves and in the rules of verbal interaction which operate. In this section we will refer to the institution by the most common term in Harlem – sounding.

Sounding, or playing the dozens, has been described briefly in a number of other sources, particularly Dollard (1939) and Abrahams (1962). Kochman (1970) has dealt with sounding in Chicago in his general treatment of speech events in the black community. The oldest term for the game of exchanging ritualized insults is the dozens. Various possibilities for the origin of this term are given in Abrahams (1962: fn. 1), but none are very persuasive. One speaks of *the dozens, playing the dozens,* or *putting someone in the dozens.* The term *sounding* is by far the most common in New York and is reported as the favored term in Philadelphia by Abrahams. *Woofing* is common in Philadelphia and elsewhere, *joining* in Washington, *signifying* in Chicago, *screaming* in Harrisburg, and on the West Coast, such general terms as *cutting, capping,* or *chopping.* The great number of terms available suggests that there will be inevitably some specialization and shift of meaning in a particular area. Kochman suggests that *sounding* is used in Chicago for the initial exchanges, *signifying* for personal insults, and *the*

Source: 'Rules for Ritual Insults', by Labov, W. in Sudnow, D. (ed.) *Studies in Social Interaction* (1972) (Oxford and New York: Blackwell and The Free Press), reprinted in Labov, W. (1972) Language in the Inner City: Studies in the Black English Vernacular (Philadelphia, PA and Oxford: Pennsylvania Press and Blackwell) pp. 297–353.

dozens for insults on relatives. In New York, *the dozens* seems to be even more specialized, referring to rhymed couplets of the form.

> I don't play the dozens, the dozens ain't my game
> But the way I fucked your mama is a god damn shame.

But *playing the dozens* also refers to any ritualized insult directed against a relative. *Sounding* is also used to include such insults and includes personal insults of a simpler form. Somebody can 'sound on' somebody else by referring to a ritualized attribute of that person.

It seems to be the case everywhere that the superordinate terms which describe a verbal activity are quite variable and take on a wide range of meanings, while the verbal behavior itself does not change very much from place to place. People talk much more than they talk about talk, and as a result there is more agreement in the activity than in the ways of describing it. A member of the Black English Vernacular subculture may have idiosyncratic notions about the general terms for sounding and the dozens without realizing it. He can be an expert on sounds and be quite untrustworthy on 'sounding'.

The Shape of Sounds

As noted above, some of the most elaborate and traditional sounds are dozens in the form of rhymed couplets. A typical opening dozen is cited above. Another favorite opening is:

> I hate to talk about your mother, she's a good old soul
> She got a ten-ton pussy and a rubber asshole.

Both of these initiating dozens have 'disclaiming' or retiring first lines, with second lines which contradict them. They are in this sense typical of the usage of young adults, who often back away from the dozens, saying 'I don't play that game', or quoting the proverb, 'I laugh, joke and smoke, but I don't play' (Abrahams 1962: 210). There is a general impression that sounding is gradually moving down in the age range – it is now primarily an adolescent and preadolescent activity and not practiced as much by young men 20 to 30 years old; but we have no exact information to support this notion. The rhymed dozens were used by adolescents in New York City 20 years ago. In any case, most young adolescents do not know many of the older rhymed dozens and are very much impressed by them. To show the general style, we can cite a few others which have impressed the Jets and Cobras (and were not included in the 20 examples given by Abrahams):

> I fucked your mother on top of the piano
> When she came out she was singin' the Star Spangled Banner.

> Fucked your mother in the ear,
> And when I came out she said, 'Buy me a beer.'

The couplet which had the greatest effect was probably

> Iron is iron, and steel don't rust,
> But your momma got a pussy like a Greyhound Bus.

The winner in a contest of this sort is the man with the largest store of couplets on hand, the best memory, and perhaps the best delivery. But there is no question of improvisation, or creativity when playing, or judgement in fitting one dozens into another. These couplets can follow each other in any succession: one is as appropriate as the other. The originators certainly show great skill, and C. Robins remembers long hours spent by his group in the 1940s trying to invent new rhymes, but no one is expected to manufacture them in the heat of the contest. The Jets know a few rhymed dozens, such as 'Fucked his mother on a red-hot heater/I missed her cunt 'n' burned my peter', but most of the traditional rhymes are no longer well known. One must be quite careful in using the rhymed dozens with younger boys: if they cannot top them, they feel beaten from the start, and the verbal flow is choked off. To initiate sounding in a single interview, or a group session, we used instead such primitive sequences as 'What would you say if someone said to you, 'Your momma drink pee?' The answer is well known to most peer-group members: 'Your father eat shit.' This standard reply allows the exchange to begin along conventional lines, with room for elaboration and invention.

For our present purposes, the basic formulas can be described in terms of the types of syntactic structures, especially with an eye to the mode of sentence embedding. I will draw most of the examples from two extended sounding sessions in which sounds were *used* rather than simply *quoted*. One was on a return trip from an outing with the Jets: 13 members were crowded in a microbus; 180 sounds were deciphered from the recording made in a 35-minute ride. The other was a group of session with five Thunderbirds in which Boot, Money, David, and Roger sounded against each other at great length. For those 60 sounds the record is complete and exact identification is possible.

There are of course many other sessions where sounds are cited or used; included in the examples given below are some from a trip with the Cobras where 35 sounds were deciphered from one short section of a recording. Where the quotations are actual sequences, speakers are indicated by names or initials.

a. *Your mother is (like)* ———. Perhaps the simplest of all sounds is the comparison or identification of the mother with something old, ugly, or bizarre: a simple equative prediction. The Jets use great numbers of such simple sounds:

> Your mother look like Flipper... Like *Hoppity* Hooper... Your mother's a Milk Dud... A Holloway Black Cow... a rubber dick... They say your mother was a Gravy Train... Your mother's a bookworm... a ass, period. Your mother James Bond, K.C.... Your mother Pussy Galore.

The Cobras use a number of sounds of this type:

> Your mama's a weight-lifter... a butcher... a peanut man... a iceman... a Boston Indian. Your mother look like Crooked-Mile Hank!... like that piece called King Kong!... Quahab's mother look like who did it and don't want to do it no more!

Note that the mass media and commercial culture provide a rich body of images. Such sounds were particularly appropriate on the Jet outing because every odd or old person that passed on the way would be a stimulus for another sound.

> Your mother look like that taxi driver... Your mother a applejack-eater... a flea-bag... the Abominable Snowman... Your mother is a Phil D. Basket (calypso accent)... Your mother's a diesel... a taxicab driver....

b. *Your mother got* ———. Equally simple, from a syntactic point of view, is the series of sounds with the form *Your mother got so and so*. The Thunderbirds use long sequences of this type.

> *Boot:*   Your mother got a putty chest.
> *Boot:*   Your mother got hair growin' out her dunkie hole.
> *Roger:*   Your mother got a 45 in her left titty.
> *Money:*   Your mother got a 45-degree titty.
> *Boot:*   Your mother got titties behind her neck.

The Jets use simple sounds of this sort as well. (The first statement here is not a sound: it simply provides the base on which the sound is built, in this case the verb *got*.)

> *J1:* You got the nerve to talk.
> *J2:* Your mother got funky drawers.
> *J3:* Your mother got braces between her legs....

The Cobra sounds on clothes gradually drift away from the basic sounding pattern to a more complex structure that plays on the names of New York City Department stores:

> Your momma got shit on...
> Bel's mother bought her clothes from Ohrbach's. All front and no back.
> You got your suit from Woolworth! All wool but it ain't worth shit!
> You get your shoes from Buster Brown – brown on the top and all busted on the bottom!...

c. *Your mother so* ——— *she* ———. More complex comparisons are done with a quantifier, an adjective, and an embedded sentence of the type *b* or other predication.

> *David*: Your mother so old she got spider webs under her arms.
> *Boot*:   Your mother so old she can stretch her head and lick out her ass.

Such sounds can be made freely against a member of the group.

> *Roger*:   Hey Davy, you so fat you could slide down the razor blade without gettin' cut.
>   ...an' he so thin that he can dodge rain drops....

Other Jet similes show a wide range of attributes sounded on:

> Bell grandmother so-so-so ugly, her rag is showin'.
> Bell mother was so small, she bust her lip on the curve (curb).
> Your mother so white she hafta use Mighty White.
> Your mother so skinny, she ice-skate on a razor blade.
> ...so skinny she can reach under the doorknob...
> ...so low she c'play Chinese handball on the curve.
> ...so low, got to look down to look up.
> ...so black, she sweat chocolate.
> ...so black that she hafta steal to get her clothes.
> ...so black that she has to suck my dick to get home.

The syntax of these similes can become very complex and involve a second subordination: 'your mother is so ——— that when she ——— she can ———.' It is not easy to get all of this into one proposition in the heat of the moment.

> Your mother's so small, you play hide-and-go-seek, y'all c'slip under a penny....

d. *Your mother eat* ———. We now return to a different type of sound which does not involve similes or metaphors, but portrays direct action with simple verbs. The power of these sounds seems to reside in the incongruity or absurdity of the elements juxtaposed – which may be only another way of saying that we do not really understand them.

> *Boot*:   I heard your mother eat rice crispies without any milk.
> *Roger*:   Eat 'em raw!
> *Boot*:   Money eat shit without puttin' any cornflakes on.

The Jets use such constructions freely as well.

> His mother eat Dog Yummies.
> They say your mother eat Gainesburgers.
> Your mother eat coke-a-roaches.
> Your mother eat rat heads.
> Your mother eat Bosco.
> Your mother a applejack-eater.

One obvious recipe for constructing sounds of this type is to mention something disgusting to eat. Yet most of the items mentioned here are not in that class, and as we will see below, less than half of the examples we have could actually be considered obscene. Dog Yummies are not disgusting (they are edible but not palatable) but it is plainly 'low' to eat dog food. Elegance in sounds of this type can also involve syntactic complexity. *Your mother a applejack-eater* seems to be a more effective sound then *Your mother eat applejack*. (Applejack, a new breakfast cereal at that time, may be favored because it suggests applejack whiskey). If so, it is a further piece of evidence that syntactic complexity is a positive feature of sounds.

e. *Your mother raised you on* ———. This is a specific pattern with fairly simple syntax, particularly effective in striking at both the opponent and his mother. In one Thunderbirds' session, we triggered a series of these sounds:

> *WL*:   Your mother raised you on ugly milk.
> *Boot*:   Your mother raised you on raw corn.
> *David*:   Your mother raised you on big lips.
> *Boot*:   Your mother gave you milk out of a cave.
> *Boot*:   Your mother gave you milk out of her ass.
>   ... when you just born, she say 'Take a shot.'

f. *I went to your house* ... A numerous and important series are sounds directed against the household and the state of poverty that exists there. Some of these are complex rhymes, quite parallel to the rhymed dozens:

> *Boot*: I went to your house to ask for a piece of cheese.
> The rat jumped up and say 'Heggies, please'.

(*Heggies* is the claiming word parallel to *dibbs, halfsies, allies, checks,* etc. which was standard in New York City some twenty years ago. Today *heggies* is a minor variant, though it is still recognized, having given way to *thumbs up*.)

Most sounds of this type are in prose and are disguised as anecdotes. Cockroaches are a favorite theme:

> *Boot*: Hey! I went up Money house and I walked in Money house, I say, I wanted to sit down, and then, you know a roach jumped up and said, 'Sorry, this seat is taken.'
> *Roger*: I went to David house, I saw the roaches walkin' round in *combat boots*.

Several sounds from a session with the Aces may be quoted here in which the members noted where they had learned various sounds.

> *Tony*: A boy named Richard learned me this one: When I came across your house, a rat gave me a jay-walkin' ticket.
> *Renard*: When I came to your house, seven roaches jumped me and one search me.
> *Ted*: And I made this one up: I was come in your house; I got hit on the back of my head with a Yoohoo bottle.

Ted's original sound seems weak; it leans upon the humor of the Yoohoo bottle but it departs from the rats-and-roaches theme without connecting up with any of the major topics of sounding.

Remarks about somebody's house are apt to become quite personal as we will see below. The Jets did not produce many of these sounds, but the following occurred in quick succession:

> *J1*: I went in Junior house 'n' sat in a chair that caved in.
> *J2*: You's a damn liar, 'n' you was eatin' in my house, right?
> *J3*: I went to Bell's house 'n' a Chinese roach said, 'Come and git it.'
> *J1*: I brought my uncle – I brought my uncle up Junior house – I didn't trust them guys.

The tendency to take 'house' sounds personally shows up in the second line of this series. As we will see below, the charge that 'You was eatin' in my house' returns the accusation of hunger against the originator, and this can have a solid basis in real life.

g. *Other anecdotal forms.* There are many other anecdotal sounds which do not fall into a single mold. Some are quite long and include the kind of extra detail which can give the illusion, at the outset, that an actual story is being told. From the Jets' session we find:

> I ran over Park Avenue – you know, I was ridin' on my bike – and – uh – I seen somebody fightin'; I said lemme get on this now. I ran up there and Bell and his mother, fallin' all over: I was there first x x x gettin' it – gettin' that Welfare food x x

The incoherent sections are filled with slurping noises which are an important part of such food sounds – indicating that those involved were so desperately hungry and so uncivilized that they behaved like animals.

One can also deliver an anecdote with the same theme as the rhymed dozens quoted above:

> *Boot:* I'm not gonna say who it was, boy. But I fucked somebody's mother on this bridge one night. Whooh! That shit was so good, she jumped overboard in the river.

There are any number of miscellaneous sounds that can be disguised as pseudoanecdotes.

> *Roger:* One day, Money's mother's ass was stuck up and she called Roto-Rooter.

On the other hand, there are anecdotes which take the form of rhymes:

> *Boot:* I went down south to buy a piece of butter
>   I saw yo' mother layin' in the gutter.
>   I took a piece of glass and stuck it up her ass
>   I never saw a motherfucker run so fas'.

Such narratives typically use the simplest type of syntax, with minimal subjects and preterit verb heads. The anecdotal type of sound appears to be most effective when it is delivered with hesitations and false starts, rather than with the smooth delivery of the other type of sounds. The technique is therefore closely associated with certain types of narrative styles in which the point is delayed to the final clause, where the evaluation is fused with result and coda, as in a joke. It is generally true that all sounds have this structure: the evaluative point must be at the very end.

h. *Portraits.* Just as narrative calls for simple syntax, sounds which present elaborate portraits demand syntactic complexity. The most common are those which place someone's mother on the street as a whore.

> *J1*: Willie mother stink; she be over here on 128 St. between Seventh 'n' Eighth, waving her white handkerchief: [falsetto] 'C'mon, baby, only a nickel.'
> *J2*: Hey Willie mother be up there, standin' the corner, be pullin' up her-her dress, be runnin' her ass over 'n' see those skinny, little legs.

i. *Absurd and bizarre forms.* The formal typology of sounds presented so far actually covers the great majority of sounds used. But there are a number of striking examples which are not part of any obvious pattern, sounds which locate some profoundly absurd or memorable point by a mechanism not easy to analyse. There is the darkly poetic sound used by Eddie of the Cobras:

> Your mother play dice with the midnight mice.

Rhyme also plays an essential part in this uncommon sound:

> Ricky got shot with his own fart.

We might also cite the following exchange; which develops its own deep complication:

> *J1*: Your mother take a swim in the gutter.
> *J2*: Your mother live in a garbage can.
> *J1*: Least I don't live on 1122 Boogie Woogie Avenue, two garbage cans to the right.

The attraction of trade names like *Right Guard* or *Applejacks* may be their bizarre and whimsical character. In charging somebody's mother with unfeminine behavior we can also observe comical effects:

> *J1*: Willie mother make a living' playin' basketball.
> *J2*: I saw Tommy mother wearing' high-heel sneakers to church.

j. *Response forms: puns and metaphors.* Sounds are usually answered by other sounds, and the ways in which they follow each other will be discussed below.

But there is one formal feature of a sound which is essentially made for responses: 'At least my mother ain't...' Although these forms cannot be used to initiate sounding, several can succeed each other, as in these sequences from the Aces session:

> *A1*: At least I don't wear bubblegum drawers.
> *A2*: At least his drawers ain't bubblegum, it's not sticky like yours.
> *A1*: At least my mother don't work in the sewer.
> *A2*: At least my mother don't live in the water-crack, like yours. ...

Attributes and Persons Sounded On

A review of the content of the sounds given above under *a–j* will show that a wide but fairly well-defined range of attributes is sounded on. A mother (grandmother, etc.) may be cited for her age, weight (fat or skinny), ugliness, blackness, smell, the food she eats, the clothes she wears, her poverty, and of course her sexual activity. As far as persons are concerned, sounding is always thought of as talking about someone's mother. But other relatives are also mentioned – as part of the speech for variety in switching, or for their particular attributes. In order of importance, one can list the opponent's relatives as: mother, father, uncle, grandmother, aunt. As far as number of sounds is concerned, the opponent himself might be included as second most important to his mother, but proverbially sounds are thought of as primarily against relatives.

One of the long epic poems of the BEV community called 'Signifying Monkey' gives us some insight into the ordering of relatives. Signifying Monkey stirs up trouble ('signifies') by telling the lion that the elephant had sounded on him:

> 'Mr. Lion, Mr. Lion, there's a big burly motherfucker comin' your way,
> Talks shit about you from day to day.'

The monkey successively reports that the elephant had talked about the lion's sister, brother, father and mother, wife, and grandmother.

> The monkey said, 'Wait a minute, Mr. Lion', 'That ain't all,
> he said your grandmother, said she was a lady playin' in the old backyard.
> Said ever'time he seen her, made his dick get on the hard.'

Even more relatives are brought in, which brings the monkey to the inevitable conclusion:

> He said, 'Yeah he talked about your aunt, your uncle, and your cousins,
> Right then and there I knew the bad motherfucker was playin' the dozens.'

What is said about someone's mother's age, weight, or clothes can be a general or traditional insult, or it can be local and particular. The presence of commercial trade names in the sounds is very striking; Bosco, Applejacks, Wonder Bread, Dog Yummies, Gainesburgers, Gravy Train, as well as the names of the popular figures in the mass media: James Bond, Pussy Galore, Flipper. The street culture is highly local, and local humor is a very large part of the sounds. As noted before, one of the best ways to start a loud discussion is to associate someone with a local character who is an 'ultra-rich' source of humor. Trade names have this local character – and part of the effect is the superimposing of this overspecific label on the general, impersonal figure of 'your mother' as in 'Your mother look like Flipper.' Local humor is omnipresent and overpowering in every peer group – it is difficult to explain in any case, but its importance cannot be ignored.

The odd or whimsical use of particular names can be illustrated by a sequence that occurred when John Lewis left the microbus at an early stop. As a parting shot, he leaned back in the window and shouted genially 'Faggots! Motherfuckers!' This set up a chain of responses including a simple 'Your mother!' from Rel, 'You razorblade bastard!' from someone else, and finally an anonymous 'Winnie the Pooh!'

Obscenity does not play as large a part as one would expect from the character of the original dozens. Many sounds *are* obscene in the full sense of the word. The speaker uses as many 'bad' words and images as possible – that is, subject to taboo and moral reprimand in adult middle-class society. The originator will search for images that would be considered as disgusting as possible: 'Your mother eat fried dick-heads.' With long familiarity the vividness of this image disappears, and one might say that it is *not* disgusting or obscene to the sounders. But the meaning of the sound and the activity would be entirely lost without reference to these middle-class norms. Many sounds are 'good' because they are 'bad' – because the speakers know that they would arouse disgust and revulsion among those committed to the 'good' standards of middle-class society. Like the toasts, sounds derive their meaning from the opposition between two major sets of values: *their* way of being 'good' and *our* way of being 'bad'.

The rhymed dozens are all uniformly sexual in character, they aim at the sexual degradation of the object sounded on. But the body of sounds cited above depart widely from this model: less than half of them could be considered obscene, in any sense. At one point in the Jet session, there is a sequence of three sounds concerning fried dick-heads; this is immediately followed by

J1: Your mother eat rat heads.
J2: Your mother eat Bosco.
J3: Your mother look that taxi driver.

J4: Your mother stinks.

J5: Hey Willie got a talkin' hat.

J4: Your mother a applejack-eater.

J5: Willie got on a talkin' hat.

J4: So, Bell, your mother stink like a bear.

J5: Willie mother... she walk like a penguin.

This sequence of nine remarks contains no sexual references; the strongest word is *stink*. Many sounds depend upon the whimsical juxtaposition of a variety of images, upon original and unpredictable humor which is for the moment quite beyond our analysis. But it can be noted that the content has departed very far from the original model of uniform sexual insult.

Only someone very unfamiliar with the BEV subculture could think that the current generation is 'nicer' and less concerned with sex than previous generations. The cry of 'Winnie the Pooh!' does not mean that the Jets are absorbing refined, middle-class wit and culture. Its significance can only be understood by a deeper study of the nature of this ritual activity.

Evaluation of Sounds

One of the most important differences between sounding and other speech events is that most sounds are evaluated overtly and immediately by the audience. In well-structured situations, like the Thunderbird sounding session, this is true of every sound. In wilder sessions with a great many participants, like the Jet session in the microbus, a certain number of sounds will follow each other rapidly without each one being evaluated.

The primary mark of positive evaluation is laughter. We can rate the effectiveness of a sound in a group session by the number of members of the audience who laugh. In the Thunderbird session, there are five members; if one sounded against the other successfully, the other three would laugh; a less successful sound would show only one or two laughs. (The value of having a separate recording track for each speaker is very great.)

A really successful sound will be evaluated by overt comments: in the Jet session the most common forms are: 'Oh!', 'Oh shit!' 'God damn!', or 'Oh lord!' By far the most common is 'Oh shit!' The intonation is important; when approval is to be signalled the vowel of each word is quite long, with a high sustained initial pitch, and a slow-falling pitch contour. The same words can be used to express negative reaction, or disgust, but then the pitch is low and sustained. The implication of the positive exclamations is 'That is too much' or 'That leaves me helpless.'

Another, even more forceful mode of approving sounds is to repeat the striking part of the sound oneself.

John L: Who father wear raggedy drawers?
Willie: Yeh the ones with so many holes in them when-a-you walk they whistle?
Others: Oh...shi-it! When you walk they whistle! Oh shit!

Negative reactions to sounds are common and equally overt. The most frequent is 'Tha's phony!' or 'Phony shit!', but sounds are also disapproved as *corny, weak,* or *lame.* Stanley elaborates his negative comments quite freely:

Junior: Aww, Nigger Bell, you smell like B.O. Plenty.
Bell: Aww, nigger, you look like – you look like Jimmy Durante's grandfather.
Stan: Aw, tha's phony [bullshit]...Eh, you woke me up with that phony one, man...
Bell: Junior look like Howdy Doody.
Stan: That's phony too, Bell. Daag, boy!...Tonight ain't your night, Bell.

At another point, Stanley denounces a sound with a more complicated technique: 'Don't tell 'im those phony jokes, they're so phony, you *got* to laugh.'

The difference between these negative terms is not clear. For our present purposes, we may consider them equivalent, although they are probably used in slightly different ways by different speakers. The Cobras do not use the same negative terms as the Jets. They will say 'You fake!' 'Take that shit outa here!' or most often, 'That ain't where it's at.'

These evaluative remarks are ways of responding to the overall effect of a sound. There is also considerable explicit discussion of sounds themselves. In the case of a traditional sound, like a rhymed dozen, one can object to an imperfect rendition. For example, Stevie answers one of our versions with 'Tha's wrong! You said it wrong! Mistake!' Members are also very clear on who the best sounders are. Among the Thunderbirds, it is generally recognized that 'Boot one of the best sounders...he's one of the best sounders of all.' This very reputation will interfere with the chances of getting other members to initiate sounding – they know in advance that they will be outdone. In general, sounding is an activity very much in the forefront of social consciousness: members talk a great deal about it, try to make up new sounds themselves, and talk about each other's success. Sounding practices are open to intuitive inspection. It is possible to ask a good sounder, 'What would you say if somebody said to you...' and he will be glad to construct an answer.

Members will also make metacomments on the course of a sounding session: 'Now he's sounding on you, Money!' or announce their intentions, as Roger does: 'Aw, tha's all right. Now I'm gonna sound on you pitiful.'

Furthermore, members take very sharp notice of the end result of a sounding contest, as noted below. In a sounding session, everything is public – nothing significant happens without drawing comment. The rules and patterning of this particular speech event are therefore open for our inspection.

The Rules for Ritual Sounding

In the presentation of sounding so far, we have seen that this speech event has a well-articulated structure. These rules can be broken: it is possible to hurl personal insults and it is possible to join in a mass attack on one person.

But there is always a cost in stepping out of the expected pattern; in the kind of uncontrolled and angry response which occurs or in the confusion as to who is doing what to who.

As we examine these examples of sounding, the fundamental opposition between ritual insults and personal insults emerges. The appropriate responses are quite different: a personal insult is answered by a denial, excuse, or mitigation, whereas a sound or ritual insult is answered by longer sequences, since a sound and its response are essentially the same kind of thing, and a response calls for a further response.

The following general formulation of the interactional structure of sounding is based upon the suggestions of Erving Goffman, in response to an earlier presentation of this analysis. Goffman's framework isolates four basic properties of *ritual* sounding, as opposed to other types of insult behavior:

1. A sound opens a *field*, which is meant to be sustained. A sound is presented with the expectation that another sound will be offered in response, and that this second sound may be built formally upon it. The player who presents an initial sound is thus offering others the opportunity to display their ingenuity at his expense.
2. Besides the initial two players, a third-person role is necessary.
3. Any third-person can become a player, especially if there is a failure by one of the two players then engaged.
4. Considerable symbolic distance is maintained and serves to insulate the event from other kinds of verbal interaction.

These properties, illustrated in the previous sections, are the means by which the process of insult becomes socialized and adapted for play. They may eventually be formalized in higher level rules of verbal interaction. In the following discussion, we will see in greater detail how the first principle operates in ritual sounding.

When a sound becomes too ordinary – too possible – we can then observe a sudden switch in the pattern of response to that appropriate for a personal insult. This can happen by accident, when a sound is particularly weak. For example, in the Jet session:

A: I went in Junior house 'n' sat in a chair that caved in.

B: You's a damn liar; 'n' you was eatin' in my house, right?

This is the only instance in the Jet sounding session where a statement is denied, and it is plainly due to the fact that the proposition P is not appropriate for ritual insult. Its untruth is not at all a matter of general knowledge – it is quite possible that a chair in somebody's house would cave in, and that the chair in Junior's house *did* cave in. First Junior denies the charge; second, he hits back with another proposition that is again a personal, not a ritual insult: 'You come over to my house to eat (since there was no food in your own), and so what right have you to complain?' Of course, the second part implicitly contradicts the first – if no chair caved in, how does Junior know what occasion is being talked about?

Sounds are directed as targets very close to the opponent (or at himself) but by social convention it is accepted that they do not denote attributes which persons actually possess: in Goffman's formulation, symbolic distance maintained serves to insulate this exchange from further consequences. The rules given above for sounding, and the development of sounds in bizarre and whimsical direction, all have the effect of preserving this ritual status. As we have seen, the ritual convention can break down with younger speakers or in strange situations – and the dangers of such a collapse of ritual safeguards are very great. Rituals are sanctuaries; in ritual we are freed from personal responsibility for the acts we are engaged in. Thus when someone makes a request for action in other subcultures, and he is challenged on the fourth precondition, 'What right have you to tell me that?' his reply may follow the same strategy:

It's not my idea – I just have to get the work done.

I'm just doing my job.

I didn't pick on you – somebody has to do it.

Any of these moves to depersonalize the situation may succeed in removing the dangers of a face-to-face confrontation and defiance of authority. Ritual insults are used in the same way to manage challenges within the peer group, and an understanding of ritual behavior must therefore be an important element in constructing a general theory of discourse.

NOTE

1. I am particularly indebted to Benji Wald for suggestions incorporated in the present version of the analysis of sounding.

REFERENCES

Abrahams, R. 1962. Playing the dozens. *Journal of American Folklore* 75: 209–218.
Dollard, J. 1939. The dozens: The dialect of insult. *American Image* 1: 3–24.
Kochman, T. 1970. Towards an ethnography of Black speech behaviour. in
    N. E. Whitten, Jr and J. F. Szwed (eds.) *Afro-American Anthology*. New York:
    Free Press.

CHAPTER 43

Humour, Power and Gender in the Workplace

JANET HOLMES

Introduction

Most people consider workplace interaction to be a serious business, focussed on completing tasks, making decisions, and achieving objectives. But our research in New Zealand workplaces tells a different story. Humour turns out to be an important ingredient in the meetings and conversations in many workplaces, indicating how people relate to one another in terms of power and politeness, and providing some interesting insights into the way the workplace 'ticks'.

This chapter first describes how we collected our workplace data and how we analysed humour in workplace interaction, with an illustration of some of the complex ways in which humour conveys messages about power and solidarity relationships at work. The main focus of the chapter is on the ways in which humour may contribute to the construction of workplace culture. An analysis of workplace humour can help explain why people feel more comfortable in some workplaces than others: different workplaces tend to have different amounts of humour and are often characterised by different styles of humour.

The notion of workplace culture is closely associated with the notion of the 'gendered' workplace and the role of humour in constructing a more 'feminine' or more 'masculine' workplace is also explored in this chapter. The analysis of workplace humour demonstrates that women and men draw on a range of styles of humour in their everyday workplace interactions, and that particular instances of humour may contribute to, or contest, the perception of a workplace as normatively feminine or stereotypically masculine. First, however, some methodological issues.

Collecting Workplace Data

The data used to analyse workplace humour in the various studies undertaken by the Wellington Language in the Workplace Project (LWP) team has been collected from a very wide range of New Zealand workplaces, including government departments, commercial companies, small businesses, factories and a hospital ward. Our ethnographic methodology was designed to give participants maximum control over the data collection process, whilst also allowing workplace interactions to be recorded as unobtrusively as possible (Holmes and Stubbe 2003a). Typically, after a period of participant observation by one of our research assistants to establish how the workplace operates, a group of volunteers from the workplace record a range of their everyday work interactions over a period of two to three weeks. Some keep the mini-disk recorder and microphone on their desks, while others carry the equipment round with them. In addition, where possible, a series of regular workplace meetings is video-recorded.

Over the recording period we find that people increasingly ignore the microphones and the video cameras (which are relatively small and fixed in place). They simply come to be regarded as a part of the standard furniture, like a hat-stand, and there are often comments indicating people have completely forgotten about the recording equipment. As a result, we have collected some excellent examples of workplace interaction which are as close to 'natural' as one could hope for. This database provides a rich resource for analysing humour in the workplace.

Defining and Quantifying Humour

Humour is notoriously difficult to define. Even if we focus exclusively on verbal humour, and exclude practical jokes and nonverbal humour in the workplace, defining humour is not straightforward. It is relatively easy to identify a witty quip as an instance of humour, as illustrated in Extract 1a (see Appendix for transcription conventions).

> **Extract 1a**: Meeting of a large group in a government department. Something falls past the tenth floor window of the meeting room.
>
> Will: whoops someone fell off the roof top
>   [laughter]

This seems clearly intended to amuse, and it is evidently interpreted as humorous, since at least some of the participants respond with laughter. But what if there was no laughter and no perceptible smiles? And when a second participant adds another witty line, as in Extract 1b, does this count as a new instance of humour, or should it be counted as part of the same instance?

Extract 1b

Viv: it's the CEO things must be worse than we thought
       [laughter]

These are some of the issues which must be resolved if any kind of quantitative or comparative analysis is to be undertaken. For our purposes, humorous utterances have been defined as those identified by the analyst, on the basis of paralinguistic, prosodic and discoursal clues, as intended to be amusing by the speaker(s), and perceived to be amusing by at least some participants (see Holmes 2000 for a fuller discussion of this issue). Clearly, a wide range of linguistic as well as contextual clues are relevant to identifying instances of humour, including the speaker's tone of voice and the audience's auditory and discoursal responses. Laughter, and, where video recording is available, facial expression, including smiles, are also very helpful clues. And when more than one person contributes to humour on a single topic, as in Extracts 1a and 1b, we generally treat this as one collaborative sequence of humour, that is one instance of humour for the purposes of the quantitative, comparative analysis.

This approach enabled us to compare meetings in different workplaces in terms of how much humour occurred in each, with very diverse results. So, for instance, using an index based on the proportion of humour per 100 minutes, Figure 43.1 summarises the results from four very different workplace teams. The diagram indicates that there is a great deal of humour in the factory meetings (FAC) and in the meetings at the private commercial sector organisation (PRI), while the meetings at the public sector government department (GOV) and the semi-public organisation (SPU) involved considerably less humour. Indeed, participants in one of the factory meetings averaged more than one instance of humour per minute, while, at the other extreme, in one government department meeting, people produced humorous remarks only every seven minutes or so, on average.

This is one measure, then, of what distinguishes different workplaces, and it is one that participants are very aware of, since we found that people frequently commented on how much humour and laughter there was around their workplace. Another subject of comment was the *kind* of humour which characterised the interactions of different workplace teams. Before discussing how different styles of humour distinguish different workplaces, however, it is useful to illustrate the complex and subtle ways in which humour may contribute to the construction of workplace relationships.

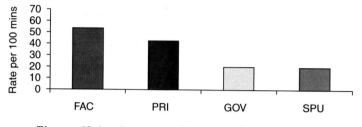

Figure 43.1   Amount of humour by workplace

The Role of Humour in Constructing Workplace Relationships

Humour is used to construct and enact many different types of relationships in the workplace (for example, friendly leader, office joker, mischievous secretary, friendly colleague, cheeky employee), and to express many different layers of meaning. At some level, humour is always intended to amuse, but it may also strengthen collegiality or bonds of friendship, soften an instruction, and release tension or defuse anger. It can provide a camouflage for an astringent, disparaging comment, or even take the form of direct face attack and insult; barbed humour and jocular abuse are frequent in some workplace contexts. Typically, a single humorous exchange is multi-functional, negotiating workplace relationships, and expressing a range of multifaceted meanings.

Extract 2: Meeting of communications team in a small commercial company. Gretel is the team manager. Gretel is referring in lines 1–3 to a procedure the team has developed for dealing with a particular communication issue.

```
1 Gret:    okay that's cool as long we've got something
2          so that when we need to go back and do this again
3          we've got [quietly]: it somewhere:
4 Zara:    yep
5 Gretel:  that's cool [high pitched]: sweet:
6 Zara:    and that is me and I'm getting a really sore throat too +
7 Gret:    well you just haven't got time this week for a sore throat
           [general laughter and smiles]
8 Zara:    no ++ alright + yeah no I'll have to look in my diary
9          and see if I can [laughs]: roster it for late next week instead:
           [laughs]
           [general laughter and smiles]
```

This humorous excerpt, which is a small section from a longer collaborative humour episode, begins as Zara finishes her weekly report to the team. Gretel responds approvingly (lines 1–3, 5) to the reassurance that they are keeping records of a particular transaction. Then Zara announces as she signs off (*that is me*) that she is *getting a really sore throat too* (line 6). Gretel responds with a multi-layered comment in a humorously threatening tone of voice *well you just haven't got time this week for a sore throat* (line 7). At one level this conveys a warning or instruction that they have too much work on to allow people to have time off. But on the other hand if someone is sick then taking time off is not a matter of choice. Hence Gretel's comment functions at another level to provoke laughter since it suggests – bizarrely – that people have a choice about when to be sick. Gretel here manages simultaneously to 'do power', using repressive humour, whilst also amusing her team, and thus softening or hedging the somewhat threatening message that her comment conveys. Zara smiles and after a pause she responds in kind, maintaining the humorous tone and treating Gretel's comment as rational: *I'll have to look in my diary and see if I can [laughs]: roster it for late next week instead* (lines 8–9). Her subversively humorous comment takes the offensive, as she wittily maintains the fiction that people can plan when to be sick, thus skilfully parrying Gretel's power play.

In this short exchange, then, we see humour used to amuse others, to soften a repressive message from a manager to an employee and to challenge or contest the power-play in a socially acceptable way. In what follows, the focus is on particular aspects of meaning for illustration purposes, and on how humour contributes to the construction of particular interactional styles, but, as this example illustrates, discourse in context is typically complex and multi-functional – there is always a great deal going on at different levels of meaning.

Humour and Workplace Culture

Humour is undoubtedly a component in the construction of a distinctive workplace culture. Most researchers agree that culture defines for its members 'what to pay attention to, what things mean, how to react emotionally to what is going on, and what actions to take in various kinds of situations' (Schein 1992: 22). The more specific concept, the community of practice, is particularly useful in distinguishing the different attitudes and values of working groups or teams within larger organisations. The distinctive culture of a community of practice is constantly being instantiated in ongoing talk and action, continually modified by large and small acts in regular social interaction within ongoing exchanges. Humour can play an important part in this process.

Styles of Humour

Different communities of practice develop different attitudes to and tolerance of humour, and particular recurring sources or topics of amusement. They establish distinctive verbal humour routines, and develop different styles of humour and ways of doing collegiality through humour. I will illustrate two contrasting styles of humour which characterised different workplaces in our data, namely a supportive and collaborative style of humour on the one hand, and a contestive and competitive style of humour on the other. It should be noted, however, that I have here conflated supportive and cooperative humour into one category, and competitive and contestive humour into another category. The various elements can be further teased apart, as explained in Holmes and Marra (2002) since, for example, a competitively performed utterance may contain supportive content, and challenging or contestive content may be delivered in a collaborative style.

Supportive and Cooperative Humour

Supportive and cooperative humour expressed in collaboratively constructed humour sequences is one obvious means by which people 'do collegiality' at work. Adopting this style, participants tend to agree with and support each other's propositions, and they may also discursively integrate their contributions tightly, using devices such as echoing, mirroring or completing another's utterance, as illustrated in Extract 3, where three women describe features of a hypothetical Ministry suit, comprising a formal skirt and jacket for anyone who needs to appear before the Minister looking respectable.

Extract 3: Three professional women in a government organisation discuss the problems which arise when someone is unexpectedly summoned to see the Minister.

```
 1 Eve:  I think we need a ministry suit just hanging up
 2       in the cupboard /[laughs]\
 3 Lei:  /you can just\ imagine the problems with the length
 4       /[laughs]\
 5 Eve:  /it would have\ it would have to have an elastic waist
 6          so /that we [laughs]\ could just be yeah
 7 Lei:  /[laughs] yes that's right [laughs]\
 8 Eve:  bunched in for some and [laughs] let it out
 9 Lei:  /laughs\
10 Eve:  /out for others\
11 Les:  and the jacket would have to be
12       /long to cover all the bulges\
```

```
13 Lei:   /no I'm quite taken with this\
14 Les:   /so\
15 Eve:   /[laughs]\
16 Lei:   /now that\ that is very nice
```

The three colleagues collaboratively construct a humorous fantasy sequence, an imaginary scenario describing an all-purpose suit which could be used by anyone unexpectedly summoned to see the Minister. This is very supportive humour constructing collegiality and solidarity with each woman explicitly agreeing with the others in terms of the overall content of the excerpt. In addition to positive feedback explicitly endorsing the humorous ideas proffered, such as *yeah* (line 6), *yes that's right* (line 7), *I'm quite taken with this* (line 13), *that is very nice* (line 16), the content of each humorous suggestion constructively adds to, expands and elaborates the initial fantasy humour idea (lines 3, 5, 8, 11–12). This is one frequent function of humour, then, to create and maintain collegial relationships, constructing and maintaining shared values and attitudes, and strengthening solidarity. There is laughter and supportive feedback throughout: for example, Leila's supportive comments *yes that's right* (line 7), *I'm quite taken with this* (line 13), *that is very nice* (line 16). And each of the women's contributions are supportive and collaborative: for example, Lesley seamlessly links her contribution to Eve's *let it out out for others* (line 10) with a coordinating conjunction, *and the jacket would have to be long* (lines 11–12). The effect is one of high energy, good humoured interaction, with all the features of cooperative and collaborative 'all-together now' talk, as defined by Coates (1996) in her analyses of the talk of women friends. It could also be analysed as instantiating 'positive politeness' using a term from Brown and Levinson's Politeness Theory (1987), that is, the sequence expresses friendliness and shared attitudes and values.

Extract 4 is another example of supportive humour (each contribution reinforces and expands previous propositions), expressed through the construction of a highly collaborative floor, using the semantic and syntactic cohesive devices of paraphrase and repetition. The participants' contributions overlap, and there is laughter throughout, as they jointly construct the humorous sequence.

Extract 4: Regular meeting of a project team in a large commercial organisation.

```
1 Jacob:   oh is this THE FINAL?
2 Barry:   this is THE FINAL /+ final steering\ committee
3 Jacob:   /[laughs]\
4 Barry:   oh Pete most probably enjoyed doing that /[laughs]\
5 Marco:   /(.............\)
```

```
 6 Dudley:  /he even sent\ me an e-mail to reinforce it with you
 7            [General laughter]
 8 Barry:    this
 9            [General laughter]
10 Barry:    this is THE final
11 Dudley:   THE final
12 Barry:    [laughs]
13 Dudley:   I'm switching out the lights and I'm leaving now
14 Barry:    [laughs] I'm switching out the lights and leaving
```

The words *the final*, first uttered with stress by Jacob (line 1) in the form of a request for confirmation, are repeated by Barry twice, first in response to Jacob's query (line 2), and then again with stress just on *the* to emphasise the point (line 10). Dudley echoes Barry's repetition (line 11), and paraphrases it with a humorous metaphor, *I'm switching off the lights and I'm leaving* (line 13), which Barry repeats (line 14). In between these repetitions, Dudley's comment, *he even sent me an e-mail to reinforce it with you* (line 6), further expands and emphasises the point. The whole sequence elicits much laughter (lines 3, 4, 7, 9, 12, 14), and exemplifies well a humorous sequence which is collaboratively constructed using strategies of repetition and paraphrase for cohesion and emphasis. It clearly serves to enhance collegiality between the men in this team, just as the exchange in Extract 3 did for the Ministry women.

Challenging and Competitive Humour

At the other end of the style continuum is challenging and competitive humour. This style of humour is often expressed through an extended sequence of humorous utterances involving a series of loosely semantically linked one-off quips or witty one-liners. These often have a 'competitive' edge, and may involve 'one-at-a-time' style of talk (Coates 1988: 120), with few overlaps between speaker turns.

Extract 5 illustrates contestive humour delivered in a competitive style. In this example, from a meeting of a group whose interactive style is typically contestive and challenging, Eric makes Callum the target of a jocular insult.

Extract 5: Regular meeting of a project team in a large commercial organisation. Callum has failed to update a header leading Barry to think he's got the wrong document.

```
1 Callum:   I definitely sent you the right one
2 Barry:    [laughs]
3 Eric:     yep Callum did fail his office management [laugh] word
4           processing lesson
```

5 Callum: [bright, cheery ironic tone] I find it really hard being perfect
6   at everything

Callum asserts that the document Barry has received is the correct document (line1), despite the fact that, as it emerges, he has failed to update the header. Barry, realising the reason for his confusion, laughs. Eric then humorously contests Callum's claim that it is the 'right' document with his comment *Callum did fail his office management [laugh] word processing lesson* (lines 3–4). Callum responds by challenging Eric's claim with his own ironic, mock-modest claim (lines 5–6). The interactive style is pragmatically contestive, with each contribution undermining or challenging the proposition or implied claim of the previous speaker, using a confrontational and competitive delivery style.

Extract 6 is another illustration of contestive humour delivered in a competitive style.

Extract 6: Ten women from a government department in a regular reporting and forward planning meeting.

1 Ellen: Grace you're gonna chair next week
2 Ruth: it must be my turn soon
3 Ellen: and Kaye can scribe
4 XF: so it's at three /(isn't it)\
5 Sally: /I must\ be due for a turn at chairing too +
6   and I'll put in my apologies now
7   [general laughter]
8 Kaye: no you're not you're not at all sorry [laughs]

Sally makes a humorous comment (line 6) saying she will put in an apology in advance for any meeting when it is her turn to chair. Kaye responds, extending the humour by challenging the sincerity of Sally's 'apology'. While the contributions are clearly semantically linked, they are minimally collaborative compared to many examples in the database. The contributions are independently constructed, with no cooperative overlapping or syntactically integrated structures. In this example, then contestive humour serves to mitigate Kaye's reproof to Sally for her attitude to chairing.

Because it is so useful as a means of mitigating of 'bad news', humour is often used to negotiate power relations in the workplace. Extract 2 illustrated how humour may attenuate a message which could be considered unwelcome or 'face-threatening' in some way, such as a directive, a complaint or a criticism. Strategies for ameliorating such messages have been analysed within Politeness Theory as instances of 'negative politeness', ways of indicating respect for a person's need for autonomy (Brown and Levinson 1987).

But humour can also be subversive, and thus a useful strategy in interactions with superiors, especially when employees do not agree with their managers or bosses, or when they do not like the tasks assigned to them. Contesting a superior is a risky business and humour can attenuate a critical comment, as in Extract 7, where the boss Harry is late for a meeting.

Extract 7: Regular meeting in a commercial organisation. Five people are waiting and talking as the manager Harry arrives.

1 Har: sorry I'm late
2 Jon: no problems we've been enjoying some quiet character
3   assassination while we waited
4   [*general laughter*]

One of the team members, Jonathan, here teases Harry by implying they have been making negative comments about him before his arrival. The humour here can be interpreted as contestive discourse, attenuating and thus concealing what could be considered the effrontery of a critical speech act in this context. It is delivered in the competitive, 'one-at-a-time' style associated with challenging discourse. Such comments are always slightly risky, and, however jocular, there is an underlying 'dark side' to the message (an aspect of humour which is not adequately analysed within the Politeness Theory framework). Clearly humour may subvert as well as construct and contribute to collegial relationships; and subversive humour can potentially undermine a leader's power, standing or influence.

As a component of discursive practice, humour can thus provide insights into one dimension of the distinctive cultures which develop in different workplaces or communities of practice. Moreover, the patterns identified were generally confirmed by detailed observations from our ethnographic data, providing another layer to support the overall characterisations of the distinctive workplace cultures described. An analysis of the amount of humour and the patterning of the different styles of humour which occur in interactions in different workplaces can thus suggest interesting differences in this dimension of workplace communication.

I turn now to the interaction between gender and humour in relation to the concept of the gendered workplace.

Gendered Workplaces and Humour

Gender is one particular type of meaning or social identity conveyed by particular linguistic choices, which may also concurrently convey other meanings as well. So, for example, a compliment such as *nice jacket* conveys positive affect, but may also communicate an admiring or a patronising stance, depending on who says it to whom and when. And it may also (indirectly) convey femininity in communities where compliments on appearance are much more strongly associated with women than with men. Ways of talking are associated with particular roles, stances (for example, authoritative, consultative, deferential, polite), activities, or behaviours, and to the extent that these are 'culturally coded as gendered … the ways of speaking associated with them become indices of gender' (Cameron and Kulick 2003: 57).

Assigning a label such as 'masculine' or 'feminine' to a workplace is overall a matter of how the dominant values and attitudes are perceived and enacted, a cultural, perceptual and structural issue and a matter of interactional style (rather than a reflection of the sex of those who work there). But styles of humour may contribute to such perceptions. Many decades of research by scholars working in the area of language and gender have established that certain styles of interaction (typically supportive, cooperative and collaborative) are widely regarded as normatively 'feminine', while others (typically challenging, contestive and competitive) are regarded as more 'masculine'. It will be apparent from the examples in the previous section that these styles do not equate with the gender of actual speakers in authentic interaction. Men use supportive and collaborative styles of humour (for example, Extract 4) when appropriate, and women use competitive styles (for example, Extract 6). But the accumulation of instances of these different styles may contribute to the perception of specific workplaces as gendered in particular ways. Hence, more 'feminine' workplaces are typically characterised by supportive social relationships, by more democratic and non-hierarchical structures, and by an 'orientation towards collaborative styles and processes of interaction, together with a high level of attention to the interpersonal dimension' (Holmes and Stubbe 2003b: 587–588). Supportive and collaborative humour can obviously contribute to such a construction. More 'masculine' workplaces tend to be characterised by competition, a stress on individuality, and more contestive interactional styles. Humour which is challenging and competitively expressed clearly contributes to the construction of such workplace cultures.

Of course, different workplaces can be characterised as more or less 'feminine', and more or less 'masculine' in different respects, and different contexts. So, in a particular workplace, meeting structures and interactional processes may conform to more masculine styles of interaction, while the way humour is expressed and its frequency may fit more conventionally feminine styles. Furthermore, individuals may, of course, behave in ways indexing masculine or feminine ways of speaking at different points within the same interaction. What I am drawing attention to here, however, is that humour is a relevant component in the interactional mix, since it may contribute to or challenge the perception of a workplace culture or community of practice as normatively feminine or masculine in interactional style.

Extract 3 above is an extreme example of a humorous and clearly gendered interaction. Concerned with clothes and appearance – topics stereotypically associated with women, it contributes to reinforcing feminine stereotypes as well as enacting femininity at work. Since other aspects of this workplace also indicate that it can be regarded as a very 'feminine' community of practice, with a 'feminine' workplace culture, this instance of humour reinforces this construction. By contrast, in another very 'masculine' workplace, with a very macho workplace culture, small talk was explicitly derided. Extract 8 illustrates this other end of the gendered humour spectrum with a group of men teasing one of their members for unmanly, voluntarily 'communicative' behaviour.

Extract 8: Regular meeting of a project team in a large commercial organisation. Callum's colleagues pretend to be horrified that he has actually talked face-to-face with clients

```
 1 Barr:   but we can we can kill this /particular=
 2 Marc:   /well yep\
 3 Barr:   =action\ point
 4 Marc:   you can kill this particular action point
 5 Barr:   and you /guys\
 6 Call:   /are\ you sure +++ I took the opportunity
 7        of talking with some of the users
 8 Barr:   what again? [laughs] /[laughs]\
 9 Marc:     /not again what are you doing talking to them\
10 Barr:   [laughs]: go on /Callum come on\
11 XM:     /[laughs]\
```

Barry and Marco suggest a particular proposed action be *killed*, that is, dropped. Callum protests, pointing out that the proposed action emerged from his discussions with users. Barry and Marco then proceed to make fun of Callum's complaint, ridiculing the notion that he should actually talk, that is, verbally communicate face-to-face, with clients. They use a 'one-at-a-time' floor in classic, competitive, 'top the previous speaker's contribution' discourse style. (The verbal contributions overlap laughter, not other people's contributions.) Extract 8 is thus a paradigmatic example of (stereo-)typically masculine conjoint humour. It is contestive in its pragmatic focus, involves a competitive, minimally collaborative floor, and its propositional content implicitly reinforces masculine conceptions of acceptable communicative strategies. Such examples reinforce traditional stereotypes of the way men interact in the workplace.

Needless to say, there are also many examples where a feminine style of interaction contests the interactional style of a predominantly masculine or 'masculinist' (Baxter 2003) workplace (especially associated in our data with the IT industry), as when a couple of women joke about the features of their 'girlie office' (see Holmes and Schnurr 2005). There are also instances where contestive and challenging humour disturbs the equilibrium of predominantly feminine workplaces. Often, these instances gain force and dramatic effect by contrast with the predominant interactional style of the workplace culture within which they occur. So, while it is undoubtedly true that in many industries, the 'male-as-norm' model of interaction still predominates (some of our participants explicitly referred to 'the boy's club' for instance), the analysis of ways in which these norms are adhered to, exploited or flouted from moment to moment in specific interactions can provide invaluable insights into the ways in which people communicate at work. Humour is one avenue for such investigation.

Conclusion

This chapter has illustrated ways in which the analysis of workplace humour can contribute to our understanding of what is going on at work. Our large database of authentic data, collected by participants themselves, and supported by ethnographic interviews and observations, makes it clear that humour is a usefully diagnostic feature of workplace interaction.

The analysis in this chapter also indicated that humour contributes in a range of subtle ways to the complex interaction of power and politeness in the workplace, and that the analysis of humour provides a means of distinguishing different types of workplaces. Different amounts of humour, and different styles of humour tend to characterise different communities of practice. Identifying the particular mix of supportive versus challenging styles of humour which distinguish a particular workplace can provide interesting insights into the ways in which people relate to each other. Such an approach can also contribute to the identification of the features which people associate with differently gendered workplaces. Humour can play an interesting role in both contributing to and contesting the perception of a workplace as normatively feminine or as stereotypically masculine. Humour is clearly a multifaceted discursive resource, and its analysis provides a rich source of information about the ways people communicate at work.

NOTE

The work reported in this chapter draws on a number of papers written by members of the Wellington Language in the Workplace Project, of which I am the Director, but especially

Holmes and Marra (2002). Extract 3 is from Holmes and Stubbe (2003a: chapter 6). The section headed 'Gendered workplaces and humour' draws on Holmes (2006) and Holmes and Stubbe (2003b). Details of the publications can be found on the website: www.vuw.ac.nz/lals/lwp.

Transcription conventions

All names used in the extracts are pseudonyms.

[laughs] : :	Paralinguistic features in square brackets, colons indicate start/finish
+	Pause of up to one second
... /......\ ... ... /........\ ...	Simultaneous speech
CAPS	Emphasis or loud delivery
(hello)	Transcriber's best guess at an unclear utterance
?	Rising or question intonation
-	Incomplete or cut-off utterance
... ...	Section of transcript omitted
XM/XF	Unidentified Male/Female voice
=	Continued speech

REFERENCES

Baxter, Judith. 2003. *Positioning Gender in Discourse: A Feminist Methodology.* Basingstoke: Palgrave Macmillan.

Brown, Penelope and Stephen C. Levinson. 1987. *Politeness: Some Universals in Language Usage.* Cambridge: Cambridge University Press.

Cameron, Deborah and Don Kulick. 2003. *Language and Sexuality.* Cambridge: Cambridge University Press.

Coates, Jennifer. 1988. Gossip revisited: Language in all-female groups. In Jennifer Coates and Deborah Cameron (eds.) *Women in their Speech Communities.* London: Longman. 94–121.

Coates, Jennifer. 1996. *Women Talk.* Oxford: Blackwell.

Holmes, Janet. 2000. Politeness, power and provocation: How humour functions in the workplace. *Discourse Studies* 2, 2: 159–185.

Holmes, Janet. 2006. English in the workplace – The real story: Handling disagreements and refusals at work. In Azirah Hashim and Norizah Hassan (eds.) *English in Southeast Asia: Prospects, Perspectives and Possibilities.* Kuala Lumpur: University of Malaya Press. 49–78.

Holmes, Janet and Meredith Marra. 2002. Having a laugh at work: How humour contributes to workplace culture. *Journal of Pragmatics* 34: 1683–1710.

Holmes, Janet and Maria Stubbe. 2003a. *Power and Politeness in the Workplace.* London: Pearson.

Holmes, Janet and Maria Stubbe. 2003b. 'Feminine' workplaces: Stereotype and reality. In Janet Holmes and Miriam Meyerhoff. (eds.) *The Handbook of Language and Gender*. Oxford: Blackwell. 573–599.

Holmes, Janet and Stephanie Schnurr. 2005. Politeness, humor and gender in the workplace: Negotiating norms and identifying contestation. *Journal of Politeness Research* 1, 1: 121–149.

Schein, Edgar. 1992. *Organizational Culture and Leadership*. 2nd edition. San Francisco, California: Jossey-Bass.

CHAPTER 44

Social Functions of Small Talk and Gossip

JUSTINE COUPLAND

On a greetings card currently on sale in the United Kingdom, a cartoon sequence shows Tarzan swinging from jungle vines and rehearsing various polite, conventionalised ways of introducing himself to Jane. 'How do you do. My name is Tarzan and I believe you are known as Jane'; 'Allow me to introduce myself...I am Tarzan, Lord of the Jungle...And you?'; 'You must be Jane...I am Tarzan. It's a pleasure to meet you.' Face-to-face with Jane, he blurts out 'Me Tarzan! You Jane!' In the cartoon's final frame, Jane sneers in disdain, while Tarzan covers his face with his hands, apparently in remorse. Both seem to be reacting to his social incompetence. His carefully prepared, ritualised conversational opening is replaced in the highly charged atmosphere of the moment by 'blunt talk' – extreme in this case – of the sort that more generally is unlikely to meet social demands. As humans (Tarzan included), we have significant emotional investment in the impressions others gain of us (Goffman 1972), so our social presence and competence, as displayed through our use of 'small talk', are not trivial matters.

Small Talk as a Genre

So can we identify a type of talk we can call 'small'? Small talk might be the overshadowed antithesis of 'real' or 'full' or 'serious' or 'useful' or 'powerful' or 'blunt' talk – talk that 'gets stuff done', talk that attends to task goals more than relational goals. From this perspective, sociality itself is marginalised as a 'small' concern, secondary to people's concerns with transacting business and other commercial or institutional instrumentalities. Of course, it is widely acknowledged that *all* talk carries social and affective meaning, along with its representational or task-focused aspects, as in Michael Halliday's (1985) model of language as simultaneously realising three functions, the *ideational* (the expression of content or the referential aspect of meaning), the *textual* (realising meanings via the structure and organisation of the message itself) and the *interpersonal* (how the message expresses the social relationships between the relevant interlocutors). If small talk is a genre of talk, then it is so because it involves specific 'orienting frameworks, interpretive procedures, and sets of expectations by which actors relate to and use language' (Bauman 1992: 100). Thus, in the widely cited case of making a comment on the weather to an acquaintance at the train station (for example, *lovely day today* or *what rain!*) it is not that there is no ideational meaning in the message. Rather, for the purpose of the exchange, *in that context and at that moment*, the focus on interpersonal goals is paramount. Sociality is prioritised, partly through the rather formulaic textual design of such messages, over the speaker's ostensible interest in the weather.

Naturally, all talk must be 'about something' and therefore have an ideational function, and all 'big talk' must carry interpersonal messages. To illustrate this, we might consider Stephen Levinson's (1992: 69) paradigm examples of 'activity types' within talk: teaching, a job interview, a legal interrogation, a football game, a task in a workshop, a dinner party. Small talk is more or less likely to occur in a sustained way in these different kinds of speech events. People have strong intuitions about what kinds of constraints there are within such activities, perhaps with the legal interrogation at one end of a cline (small talk being an unlikely and inappropriate format) and the dinner party at the other (small talk being likely and appropriate). This is not to say that the conversationalists at the dinner party cannot or will not, for example, do work-related talk. Levinson mentions 'business transactions conducted at a cocktail party' as an example of 'one kind of activity embedded in another' (99). But as he puts it, 'there are strong expectations about the functions that any utterance in a certain part of the proceedings can be fulfilling' (79).

Small Talk, Phatic Communion and the Performance of Sociality

Bronislaw Malinowski (1923) used the term *phatic communion* to describe a type of talk where speakers take up predictable 'safe' topic, such as the weather, the here and now of an event in progress, or other aspects of the locally shared environment. Phatic communion is talk joined in by strangers, acquaintances or indeed friends/intimates at transitional or liminal moments (Laver 1981), such as at the beginnings and ends of conversations or filling gaps between more focused activities. Such talk marks co-presence, perhaps between people standing together in a lift or colleagues passing in the corridor at work or strangers sitting in adjacent seats on an aeroplane. Phatic communion tends to be characterised by people maintaining a neutral-to-positive and solidary relational tenor, and by the use of conventionalised polite expressions like *good morning, how do you do, here we all are again then, warm in here, isn't it, nice to have met you again, we mustn't leave it so long next time.* The predictability of these small talk exchanges – what Malinowski described as purposeless expressions of preference or aversions, accounts of irrelevant happenings, comments on what is perfectly obvious – is functional in itself. We expect these small talk tokens to be present and we know how to respond to them.

We may feel that there is a semantic emptiness in such expressions, but they must be seen as meaningful at least in terms of what speakers could have chosen to say instead. So *good morning* contrasts with *hey dude!* which signals a different quality of relationship (see Kiesling 2004). The choice to speak at all rather than to remain silent is certainly meaningful. If comments about the weather, or noticings of the local environment, suggest that speakers have rather limited involvement in these topics of talk, this can still be described as being in the service of 'communion' itself, with talk for talk's sake legitimately overriding the significance of what is being talked about. By 'just talking' we might avoid the discomfort and face threat of silence, and potential attributions of interpersonal disinterest or even dislike. Koenraad Kuiper (2000) says that we have an 'inventory of formulae' to call on at such moments, precisely to avoid such problems. Sometimes small talk allows people to connect interactionally while they 'work up to' or 'down from' more transactional business, for example, in formal, hierarchical gatherings such as job interviews, where small talk serves to break the ice. Sometimes, as in some service encounters, small talk may fill out the whole of the verbal track, with non-verbal actions constituting the task goals of giving and getting service. All the same, there are many contexts where relational goals *are*, in a sense, the task goals for interacting – when relationships between people are what talk is principally for, in expressions of intimacy or love and their antitheses. So there is no necessary link between 'relational talk' and 'small talk'. Small talk can only be defined relative to the overall configuration of communicative functions and purposes that define particular speech events.

Research Perspectives

Not surprisingly, therefore, research on small talk has emphasised different tendencies in its social functioning (Coupland 2000, 2003). As we have already seen, small talk can construct social cohesion and reduce the inherent threat-value of social encounters, but it also helps to structure social interaction (Brown and Levinson 1987; Eggins and Slade 1997; Laver 1981). Small talk can allow people to avoid, retreat from or delay talk which is more serious, challenging or power-ridden. Small talk will sometimes be defined partly by its tone or key. Verbal play and humour, as in light-hearted 'banter', often allows people to develop a shared relational orientation to topics – sometimes weighty topics – in a way that protects them from dealing fully with those topics there and then. Small talk can therefore function in the identity dimension of discourse in different ways. It allows us not only to be 'nice', but also to be playful, ironic and sometimes subversive.

Suzanne Eggins and Diana Slade (1997) claim that the fact that 'nothing happens' is the central paradox of (what they call) 'casual conversation'. But even if we interpret this to mean 'nothing happening in the transactional dimension', 'doing nothing' can nevertheless be highly functional in other ways. Orienting to relational or face issues in discourse, concurrently with or adjacent to dealing with instrumental and task-related issues, and doing this in a more or less sustained and strategic way, is characteristic of a wide range of social contexts and activity-types. In medical consultations, for example, conventionalised formulae such as *nice to see you*, or even the apparently bland opening *how are you?* can be shown to be delicate structural moves towards broaching medical business.

Extract 1 is taken from the opening phase of a medical consultation in a geriatric clinic and involves a male consultant, an elderly male patient and the patient's wife. The patient has suffered several strokes. He presents with severe body aches and weight loss. He has been attending the clinic regularly for the past seven years. (Single brackets enclose brief interpretive comments on how talk is proceeding, and double brackets enclose partially audible speech. Square brackets show points of overlapping speech. Timed pauses are shown in seconds and (.) marks an untimed pause. Underlined syllables have heavy stress and upper-case text indicates a loud delivery. Names of participants and places have been changed to preserve anonymity.)

Extract 1

```
1 Patient:   (very quietly) ((morning))
2 Doctor:    morning
3 Wife:      good morning (door closes)
4 Doctor:    morning
             [
5 Wife:      you enjoy your holidays?
6 Doctor:    yes thank you
7 Wife:      that's good
8 Patient:   ((very nice)) (1.0)
```

 9 Doctor: come and sit down (wife helps patient, who sits down with some
            discomfort) (17.0)
10 Wife: I've got the chair here
11 Doctor: (to patient, teasing voice) oh! (1.0) you're not getting old
12   are you?
13 Patient: yes
14 Doctor: you are?
15   [
16 Wife: (laughs at length)
17 Doctor: (chuckles) (2.0)
18 Wife: old age doesn't come alone (.) does it Doctor (Name)?
                [
19 Doctor: no
20 Patient: oh no
21 Doctor: what's the problem?

Given the institutional context and the activity type (a medical interaction
in a geriatric care setting), the task goals and topical agenda are fairly clear
to participants before the interaction begins: the consultation is to review the
patient's medical condition. But characteristically of the opening phases of a
range of similar activity types, participants' initial talk is at least apparently
oriented to relational goals, framed through small talk/phatic communion,
serving to establish or re-establish a social consensus for talk. Small talk is
realized conventionally enough in the extract, through the shared greetings
(lines 1–4), talk about holidays (lines 5–8, instigated by the patient's wife on
this occasion rather than the doctor) and dispositional talk (talk oriented to
getting the patient comfortably seated, in lines 9 and 10). These participants'
familiarity with each other is also acknowledged in the playful talk initiated
by the doctor in the teasing sequence (lines 11–20). The utterance *you're not
getting old are you?* is at one level markedly out of place/out of genre in a geriatric consultation. It constructs a frame around age experience that resonates
with everyday, lay (non-medical) stereotypes about old age. Indeed it triggers
a *yes* response from the patient that is initially playful but blends back into
a more medical and serious account of the patient's well-being. It is only at
line 21 that the doctor finally broaches the medical business directly, by making a more explicitly health problem-focused enquiry, *what's the problem?*

Elsewhere in the same corpus of data we find similar transitions and frame
shifts, when ritualistic-sounding small talk expressions are developed into
institutionally relevant concerns. The conventionalised small talk token *how
are you?* when produced by a doctor in the very early phases of an encounter
is likely to be treated as phatic and responded to with an utterance of the
sort *fine thanks*, irrespective of the truth value of the response. There is a
pattern of doctors tending to make second formulations of *how are you?* after

an initial phatic exchange, sometimes with contrastive stress (*how <u>are</u> you today?*), but sometimes marked only by the utterance being a second formulation in the sequence (*how have you been getting along?*). This refocuses attention onto more medically based assessments of present health or well-being. So these reformulations serve as (re)framing moves or (re)contextualisation cues 'by which speakers signal and listeners interpret what the activity is, how semantic content is to be understood and how each sentence relates to what precedes or follows' (Gumperz 1982: 131). In institutional contexts, talk that masquerades as 'small' can function to address quite serious, task-related goals, when – to take another brief example – a nurse seeks to distract a patient during an unpleasant medical procedure by saying *is it still sunny outside?* In this case, what matters is not what is talked about but the sheer humanising force of communion achieved through talk. But of course, communion in the context of medical care is not at all irrelevant to the delivery of care itself.

In more obviously socially focused encounters, where talk is joined mainly for the purposes of communion or recreation, relational work is often much more sustained, for example through attention to the details of people's lives, interests and actions. Exploring and developing relationships, viewpoints and experiences becomes the primary business of talk, and, as suggested earlier, on these occasions participants would presumably not deem this talk to be 'small'. In the following extract, four young women, Cerys, Abby, Sian and Nia, are sitting together eating lunch. Abby has just been talking about her plans to make fishcakes with chilli sauce for dinner that evening.

Extract 2

1	Cerys:	how you gonna make chilli sauce?
2	Abby:	just got a recipe in my Ainsley Harriot book (.) my prawn
3		chilli cakes
4	Sian:	special event? or just for ((2 syllables))
5	Abby:	chilli chilli cakes (.) cos just looking through my low fat
6		recipe book thinking 'hm what could I make this month?' (.)
7		mm- and I chose recipes I liked the look of and bought
8		ingredients and ((2 syllables)) cos I spent the last two weeks
9		(.) not eating anything other than cereals and bread because I
10		haven't been able to afford anything else so
11	Nia:	((oh bad))
12	Abby:	should <u>eat</u> properly
13	Sian:	mm (3.0) when we did our shopping yesterday night we
14		didn't even go near the fruit section
15	Abby:	no

This is a fragment of 'time-out talk' where people are clearly at ease with each other. Here the participants are 'eating lunch together' – an activity that might be distinguished relationally, for example, from 'having a working lunch'. The friends talk about apparently mundane matters of choosing and cooking food as part of the minutiae of their everyday lives (Tannen 1989). It's a good example of 'nothing much happening' in conversation, and Abby twice uses the word *just* in minimising her account of her own motivations. Yet there seems to be social functionality in how the talk is *not* subject to pre-planning or apparent strategic operations, just as Abby's decision to make chilli cakes is ad hoc and relatively unmotivated. But as the conversation evolves, shared interests and experiences (interest in cookery, lack of money, failed good intentions to eat healthily, and so on) progressively emerge. Time may be being passed uneventfully and pleasantly, but it is reasonable to argue that opportunities to build the social cohesion of the group of friends also evolve.

Stories in Small Talk

Neal Norrick (2000: 2) and Deborah Tannen (1989) both describe storytelling as promoting communion and creating involvement in ways that enable conversationalists to achieve and to display alignment. This brings stories clearly into the functional remit of small talk. Conversationalists often entertain each other by telling newsworthy events, responding consensually, matching new stories to just-told stories, co-telling stories, negotiating and refining details, and so on. In Extract 3, two young men, Sam and Rob, are sitting in Rob's flat, drinking tea, eating chocolate and joining in talk. Sam settles into a story.

Extract 3

```
 1 Sam:   d'you know something? I saw something really strange coming
 2         here the Clover Road lights Clover Road Meadow Road isn't it?
(They discuss the precise location of Sam's 'noticing' over a few turns)
 3 Sam:   it's coming up to dusk I'm sitting there at the traffic lights uh
 4         (1.0) cranked up the radio right and I can see in the gloom this
 5         fellow on the other side of the lights with a Flymo strapped on
 6         his back in a sort of like a sort of canvas sack (.) can see the
 7         handle big curving handle come out ((of this))
 8 Rob:   huh!
 9 Sam:   a Flymo strapped to his back on a push-bike (.) I thought 'what
10         a lunatic' and I- they were
11 Rob:   huh
```

12	Sam:	cast my mind back to a time when (.) I've often done stupid
13		things since and I've- never quite as sort of spectacular like
14		coming back from Bigger Sounds with a brand new ((mobile))
		[ ]
15	Rob:	(laughs)
16	Sam:	tape deck balanced on my handlebars down Scott Road
		[ ]
17	Rob:	oh <u>no</u>
18	Sam:	a car pulling out in the like the Friday afternoon rush hour
		[ ]
19	Rob:	mm (laughs)
20	Sam:	had to slam on me brakes and the whole thing just sliding
21		between me fingers until I'm just gripping into the edge of the
22		box dangling off my handlebars yanking it back on and I'm
23		waving my fist at the (.) works van as it's driving away with a
24		passenger getting off (.) I thought this guy's <u>men</u>tal and I just
		[ ]
25	Rob:	mm
26	Sam:	sort of chuckled and I thought 'you know' and then as the
27		lights changed and I started moving across and he was turning
28		right into Field Street I recognized the guy he was a guy called
29		Charlie he used to rent a room off me in my house ...

At line 1, Sam marks his upcoming story as newsworthy and listenable. The event to be storied is not the here and now of an event in progress, which is often the focus of phatic communion, but it is certainly something Sam has 'noticed' in a 'past environment' that is made relevant to the moment of storytelling. From line 3, Sam works at the narrative's scene-setting. There are clear focusing and sharpening devices in Sam's story that present Rob with a visually striking account of the fellow on a push-bike with the Flymo (a hover-type lawn mover) strapped to his back. Sam gives an account of the visual/auditory/experiential context (*it's coming up to dusk...cranked up the radio...I can see in the gloom ...*) and paints the scene in some of its quirky detail (*big curving handle*). The tellability of the tale hinges on Sam's assessment *what a lunatic*, which he expresses as 'quoted' thought in lines 9–10 – Sam's evaluative reaction to the protagonist in the bizarre scene. Then, between lines 12 and 25, Sam embeds another story, a reminiscence of how in the past he has himself been a *stupid* protagonist, in an event that strongly parallels the lawn mower carrier. Although Sam says he was *never quite as sort of spectacular like* (line 13), he also performed the role of 'carrier of an object in an incongruous fashion' (lines 14–16). Rob continues to produce verbal signals of high involvement (Norrick 2000) in the narrative, including laughter (lines 15 and 19) and exclamations of surprise or disbelief (lines 8, 11, 17).

We might ask why stories like this matter, and what they achieve for inter-actants? Mutual entertainment and communion in the sharing of experience are certainly part of the answer, and some quite specific footings for mutuality are established in this particular story. Sam and Rob come to share a perspective on what it means to behave 'stupidly' or 'in lunatic fashion', which is something they appear to respect and enjoy as well as disparage. They revel in how the extraordinary (what Sam refers to as the *spectacular*) is there to be found in the detail of ordinary life on the street. Aesthetic and poetic dimensions of the telling of the story add relational value to the recounted events themselves. Sam and Rob can take pleasure in the collaborative recreation of these *stupid* events as well as in the events themselves. Their intersubjective orientation to the events is an achievement of the narrative process. The speech genre might be classified (including by the speakers) as 'trivial', 'playful' or 'inconsequential', but once again we can see how quite fundamental dimensions of social life – the making of individual and social identities and the articulation of social stances – are activated and engaged in small talk narratives.

Small Talk Backstage

Deborah Tannen (1995: 223–224) reminds us how, in the course of a working day, workers' talk tends to shift continually between work and social topics, and she argues that these shifts can reflect and negotiate status relations. Indeed, Janet Holmes' (2000) research on workplace interaction finds small talk more often controlled (instigated or closed down) by higher rather than lower ranking conversationalists, as the demands of work subside and rise. Generally, Tannen suggests that small talk is 'the grease that keeps the gears running' in working environments. Extract 4 illustrates the rapid shifts of participation frameworks (especially addressees), topics, styles and keys that can feature in workplaces, as the immediate demands of ongoing work ebb and flow. In a leisure centre, two assistants at a reception desk, Jenny and Iris, sustain a conversation about a third colleague, Susan, and how she has been treated by her managers. This talk on a relational theme is punctuated by the assistants dealing with customers, first face-to-face and later on the telephone.

Extract 4

1 Jenny: um (1.0) apparently while I was down there last week ((it was
2 Sean)) I was talking to Sean and he tells me the ins and outs

3		of a cat's arse cos I used to go down there a lot (.) well he was
4		telling me that they (4.0) had a meeting the other day and
5		Susan came out very <u>red</u> <u>faced</u> so you could say (.) she's had
6		quite a few jobs taken off her and she wasn't amused with the
7		fact that she had like and um they gave job descriptions like
8		[　　　　]
9	Iris:	yeah yeah
10	Jenny:	right 'Joe Bloggs you gotta do this and this' and um (1.0) Peter
11		Williams ((2 syllables)) said 'Susan your jobs for this month' or
12		whatever (.) 'are the the swimming pool and Craig Pool'
13	Child:	[　　　　] MAMMY
14	Iris:	(to the customer standing at the glass screen) <u>hi</u>ya!
15	Parent:	could I have two adult swims?
		[　　　　]
16	Iris:	((ok to pay for them)) then that's four pounds forty please
17	Parent:	have you had any certificates in?
18	Iris:	no sorry (1.0) well I don't think so (to Jenny) Jen baby first
19		swim certificates?
20	Jenny:	no we <u>did</u> have them but the last one we had was in the
21		cupboard about two weeks ago so I know they are all gone
22	Parent:	(sounding annoyed) well they said they would have them in!
23	Jenny:	no well we had one two weeks ago filled in mind ah um Derek
24		Rees or someone but ah the last one I seen was two weeks ago
25		(1.0) none since (.) ALRIGHT? (customer leaves) (3.0)
26		(to Iris) so he said to me 'she was very red faced' 'what do you
27		mean red faced' I said 'put it this way' he said um (2.0) she went
28		to the meeting and ah (1.0) Peter was giving out the job
29		descriptions and he said ((to her)) 'and I want you to take over
30		((1 syllable)) Craig Pool' he said (1.0) and ah 'Nina I want you
31		to do um' (1.0) oh what else 'right Sean you got the Sports
32		Centre the beach two parks' (.) basically he'd had something like
33		seven jobs to Susan's two so she was not very amused
34		(the phone starts to ring) and the fact that they weren't half and
35		ah he'd had more stuff than her like
		[　　]
36	Iris:	mm
37	Jenny:	(answers the phone) good morning Newtown Leisure Centre
38		Jenny speaking (3.0) for the pool or the gym? gym is ah
39		(to Iris) what time's the gym shut Ire nine o'clock?
40	Iris:	ah half past eight
41	Jenny:	(to the person on the phone) half past <u>eight</u> (.) alright? tara (1.0)

42 Iris: you got to tell them that to get em out (1.0)
43 Jenny   <u>oh</u> I <u>see</u>! (laughs)

Jenny and Iris need to manage the impressions they create with members of the visiting or calling public, and their small talk is, from that point of view, done 'backstage' (Goffman 1971). Jenny is some way through telling the story about Susan that she has heard from another colleague, Sean, when a customer and child appear at the glass screen of the reception area (at around line 13). Shifting to frontstage talk, Iris and Jenny work together to deal with both routine matters (lines 15–16) and more problematic institutional matters – the issuing of a certificate for a baby's first swim (lines 17–25) – with a customer. Iris' opening greeting, *hiya* (line 14), and Jenny's final high volume checking move, *ALRIGHT?* (line 25), mark off the boundaries around this service sequence. The ensuing three-second pause is followed by Jenny's marked drop in volume and the discourse marker *so*, as she resumes the story about Susan being *very red faced*, a phrase repeated from line 5. Although the customer has left, Jenny marks her story as being confidential and backstage.

Apart from the satisfaction which might be gained from sharing information about the misfortunes of others (of which, more later), Iris's and Jenny's talk about Susan may well be enabling them to negotiate their workplace culture and mores, and it certainly offers similar possibilities for mutuality to those we saw in Extracts 2 and 3. But in this case the relativities of back- versus frontstage allow Iris and Jenny to align themselves in sharply differentiated ways to the world of work. On the frontstage they live out their institutional roles, receiving payment, negotiating the handing out of certificates and (later in the extract) giving out information. In the backstage, not only do they expose and criticise the institutional procedures that position them into their roles (for example, Susan's rough treatment in the distribution of work roles), but they also give voice to some of the strategies and devices that allow them to exert control over customers. At line 42, having hung up the phone to a customer who had asked what time the gym shuts, Iris suggests to Jenny that *you got to tell them that to get em out*. This comment about how to manipulate customers by creatively shaping what they believe about closing time hints at a covert regime of talk and authority 'behind the scenes' of institutional practice.

Gossip

We have seen that small talk is a broad and differentiated genre, and genre labels are often contentious. Gossip is a genre commonly associated with small talk, and it is not unreasonable to see gossip as one of its sub-genres. Gossip is newsworthy, disclosive and critical talk about others (usually absent third parties). In the past, though not so much nowadays, it has been associated with 'women's talk'. Unlike small talk more generally, gossip is usually seen as a form of talk that is basically information-giving, with much of the disclosed information being confidential or personal. Some of the backstage talk in Extract 4 might qualify as gossip, at least in its secretive dimension. Jenny says that her informant, Sean, tells her *the ins and outs of a cat's arse*, which is an evocative metaphor for passing on detailed, grubby information that is not meant to be told. But gossip usually involves pejorative evaluation of social behaviours, appearance, or other qualities of a person, and in Extract 4 Susan is not imaged that way. Gossip has potential for *Schadenfreude*, taking pleasure from the misfortunes of others, so gossipers must monitor their interlocutors carefully, and perform 'dangerous' gossip only with 'safe' recipients, and often those who signal their willingness to partake. This ambivalence perhaps explains people's fascination with gossip, which is also linked to information control – being party to 'all the latest gossip'. For many people gossiping is recognised to be dishonourable ('talking behind someone's back'), but enjoyable.

As the themes of gossip are relationally risky, gossip potentially builds relational allegiances through who is included in the circle of disclosure and discussion ('co-gossipers') and relational conflicts with those who are excluded or those who are gossiped about ('gossipees'). Gossip is often realised through storytelling, but invariably involves explicit elements of appraisal or evaluation. Prototypical instances are therefore talking judgementally about what someone looks like or has done, against a template of assumptions of what the gossipers take to be desirable or acceptable. In Extract 5, two young women are collaborating to produce a negative evaluation of the new girlfriend of a male friend of theirs who they have recently met for the first time.

Extract 5

```
 1 Karen:   I would say that Andy's out of her league
 2 Becky:   I think so as well
 3 Karen:   you put people in leagues you do automatically and I would say
 4          he could be going out with some you know six foot blonde
 5 Becky:   well exactly
 6 Karen:   you'd think she would be thin and blonde and surf
 7 Becky:   I know yeah like a surfer exactly yeah
 8 Karen:   and all tanned you know that's what you'd think
 9 Becky:   I think she was making a bit of an attempt by wearing a hooch
10          top
11 Karen:   (laughs) trying to be a little bit alternative (laughs)
```

Eggins and Slade (1997: 276) suggest that 'in gossip texts people classify the world in terms of what people *should* or *should not* be doing'. Certainly, in Extract 5, Karen is explicit about processes of person classification (*you put people in leagues you do automatically*, line 3), and Becky agrees. These gossipers 'other' the unnamed gossipee by comparing her unfavourably with a fictional representation of the girl they envisage as a suitable partner for Andy (lines 6 and 8). The gossip indicates a high level of competitiveness in the dating marketplace, measured against particular stereotypes of female attractiveness, and it may well reflect Karen's and Becky's need to establish their own places in the dating pecking order. Such talk nicely illustrates the claim that gossip might help us to learn how to deal with, and in some cases compete with, strangers. More particularly it is in line with Marjorie Harness Goodwin's (1990) observation that gossip can be used to control aspiring individuals. This is gossip functioning as a social sanctioning mechanism and a form of 'moral policing' whereby speakers can construct and assert collective values and establish normative boundaries of acceptable behaviour. Group markers and group boundaries therefore surface in gossip (Karen's *leagues* and Becky's *surfer* type). Gossip negotiates the possible inclusion or exclusion of others, and thereby increases group cohesion (Gluckmann 1963; Goodwin 1990), giving us a sense of 'where we draw the line'.

Themes in gossip have varying degrees of value, linked to their newsworthiness and their ability to shock, entertain or outrage. Gossip disclosure, for example new information about the doings of others, can therefore be exchanged for other resources – reciprocal information, social status or even friendship. When gossip has this exchange value, it gives us rapid access to a larger amount of social information than we could achieve on our own. This is very much the case in Extract 6, where the gossipers are young men – Matt, Jon, Dave, Jeff and Sam – friends playing snooker in a snooker hall.

Extract 6

```
1 Matt:   hey J hey Jeff (.) you know Gareth Morgan yeah?
2 Jon:    yeah (laughs)
3 Matt:   (laughs) you remember him yeah? he won the lottery (laughs)
4 Dave:   no!
5 Jon:    GARETH MORGAN
6 Matt:   Gareth's mum and dad (.) Jane Morgan (.) their family have
7         won the lottery
                              [
8 Jon:                       I don't believe it
```

		[ ]
9	Dave:	no! (.) no!

10 Matt: honestly (.) he's dri- Gareth Morgan is driving around town in
11   some like thirty grand Toyota Corrolla (.) cruisin' around
12   Bridgetown acting real suave
13 Dave: no
14 Matt: I swear to God honestly
15 Jon: d'you know what (.) h he says hello to me and that (.) in the
16   street
17 Dave: it's not fair if you ask (.) someone like that (.) just can't
                                                   [
18 Matt: they're not they're not
19   going to appreciate it are they (.) they're just gonna like ((4
20   syllables)) I dunno what they're gonna spend it on
(Dave drops the scoreboard)
21 Dave: shit
22 Sam: oh you complete <u>arse</u>

(Some talk follows about recovering the score which was muddled when the board was dropped.)

23 Jon: maybe he'll be able to go to the doctor's now and get rid of that
24   cold he's had for years
25 Matt: yeah (laughs)
26 Jon: yeah (.) they might be blankin' you in the streets now instead
27   of you blankin' them
28 Matt: (laughs) good shot Dave (.) apparently right (.) Marriotts (.) the
29   pe- people who sell the winning ticket yeah (.) get like ten
30   percent

It is Matt who holds the gossip-worthy information that Gareth Morgan has won the lottery, and the particular value of this information lies in the judgement that Gareth (and his family) are unworthy winners. Matt opens this episode by establishing his target, *you know Gareth Morgan yeah? ... you remember him yeah?* (lines 1 and 3) before making the disclosure *he won the lottery (laughs)*. Dave's and Jon's repeated responses of performed disbelief (lines 4, 5, 8, 9 and 13) and Matt's repeat and confirmation of the veracity of the news (lines 6–7, and line 14, *I swear to God honestly*) clearly indicate that the whole group shares the judgement that this is 'good gossip' – surprising and somewhat scandalous, in their view. It is the fact that *this person* has won the lottery that carries weight, which explains Matt's self-correction in line 10 from *he* to *Gareth Morgan*, to emphasise a particular identity. Matt provides some narrative evidence that his story is true over lines 10–12 – what Eggins and Slade (1997) call 'authenticating detail'. Then at line 17, Dave is first to broaden the news into a category-based event, in his view that it's unfair that *someone like that* should win the lottery, othering and outgrouping Gareth and his family and introducing social comparisons between the gossipees and the gossipers. Jon's *they might be blankin' you now instead of you blankin' them* at lines 26–27 is overt reference to social in-and out-grouping (*blanking* means 'not acknowledging someone's presence').

So once again we see gossip's power to police both social and moral boundaries. This is a very particular and strong 'communing' function of talk, far removed from Malinowski's 'purposeless' and 'empty' language, filling social spaces with predictable formulae. But it is talk as communion that lies at the heart of all sub-genres of what we are referring to here as small talk. The irony within the term is that 'small talk' ultimately refers to what it is in interaction that builds our sense of groupness, and for Sociolinguistics, there can hardly be a more foundational function of language.

Acknowledgement

With thanks to students in my *Discourse* and *Social Interaction* classes for permission to use extracts from their data.

REFERENCES

Baumann, Richard. 1992. *Folklore, Cultural Performances, and Popular Entertainments.* Oxford: Oxford University Press.

Brown, Penelope and Stephen Levinson. 1987. *Politeness: Some Universals in Language Usage.* Cambridge: Cambridge University Press.

Coupland, Justine. 2000. (ed.) *Small Talk.* London: Longman/Pearson Education.

Coupland, Justine. 2003. (ed.) *Small Talk: Social Functions. Special Issue of Research on Language and Social Interaction* 36, 1.

Eggins, Susanne and Diana Slade. 1997. *Analysing Casual Conversation.* London: Cassell.

Gluckmann, Max. 1963. Gossip and scandal. *Current Anthropology* 4: 307–316.

Goffman, Erving. 1971. *The Presentation of Self in Everyday Life.* Harmondsworth: Penguin.

Goffman, Erving. 1972 [1955]. On face-work: An analysis of ritual elements in social interaction. In John Laver and Sandy Hutcheson (eds.) *Communication in Face-to-Face Interaction.* Harmondsworth: Penguin. 319–345.

Goodwin, Marjorie Harness. 1990. *He-Said-She-Said: Talk as Social Organisation Among Black Children.* Bloomington, Indiana: Indiana University Press.

Gumperz, John J. 1982. *Discourse Strategies*. Cambridge: Cambridge University Press.

Halliday, Michael. 1985. *An Introduction to Functional Grammar*. London: Edward Arnold.

Holmes, Janet. 2000. Doing collegiality and keeping control at work: Small talk in government departments. In Justine Coupland (ed.) *Small Talk*. London: Longman/Pearson Education: 32–61.

Kiesling, Scott F. 2004. Dude. *American Speech* 79: 306–316.

Kuiper, Koenraad. 2000. Social rituals, formulaic speech and small talk at the supermarket checkout. In Justine Coupland (ed.) *Small Talk*. London: Longman/Pearson Education. 183–207.

Laver, John. 1981. Linguistic routines and politeness in greeting and parting. In Florian Coulmas (ed.) *Conversational Routine*. The Hague: Mouton. 289–304.

Levinson, Stephen. 1992. Activity types and language. In Paul Drew and John Heritage (eds.) *Talk at Work: Interaction in Institutional Settings*. Cambridge: Cambridge University Press. 66–100.

Malinowski, Bronislaw. 1923. The problem of meaning in primitive languages. In C. K. Ogden and I. A. Richards (eds.) *The Meaning of Meaning*. London: Routledge and Kegan Paul. 146–152.

Norrick, Neal R. 2000. *Conversational Narrative: Storytelling in Everyday Talk*. Amsterdam/Philadelphia: John Benjamins.

Tannen, Deborah. 1989. *Talking Voices: Repetition, Dialogue and Imagery in Conversational Discourse*. Cambridge: Cambridge University Press.

Tannen, Deborah. 1995. *Talking from 9 to 5: How Women's and Men's Conversational Styles Affect who Gets Heard, who Gets Credit, and what Gets Done at Work*. London: Virago.

CHAPTER 45

Greetings in Tourist–Host Encounters

ADAM JAWORSKI

SAY HELLO
– Laurie Anderson

The Greeting

In his study of greetings in Western Samoa, Alessandro Duranti (1997) proposes six 'universal' criteria for identifying greetings cross-linguistically and cross-culturally:

1. near-boundary occurrence;
2. establishment of a shared perceptual field;
3. adjacency pair format;
4. relative predictability of form and content;
5. implicit establishment of a spatio-temporal unit of interaction; and
6. identification of the interlocutor as a distinct being worth recognizing. (Duranti 1997: 67)

In elaborating the above criteria, however, Duranti himself departs from their rigid application in describing greeting exchanges. On the one hand, they provide a useful 'etic' grid for the identification and description of greetings, while on the other they suggest a need for a more nuanced 'emic' analysis of empirical data. What follows is my own brief exposition of Duranti's criteria (1997: 68–71) for identifying greetings across languages:

1. Greetings tend to occur close to the beginning of a social encounter, though they are not necessarily the first words uttered. For example, they

may follow a summons and, as in the case of complex, ceremonial greetings, they may be delayed and preceded by short and informal greetings and other forms of talk (for example, an exchange of jokes).

2. Greetings are constitutive of the interactants' mutual recognition of one another in a shared visual or auditory space, or follow soon after such recognition is established by other means (for example, if a ceremonial greeting is preceded by an exchange of some preliminary remarks). Although greetings are often used by participants to acknowledge one another (cf. Bach and Harnish 1979), for Duranti, this is not a universal feature. For example, ceremonial greetings (more akin to welcomings) may follow other types of exchanges such as jokes or question and answer sequences, with the delayed greetings recognizing that participants have moved to a new physical or symbolic space.

3. Most greetings are organized as one or more sets of adjacency pairs (cf. Schegloff and Sacks 1973), with some communities, for example, in West Africa (cf. Irvine 1974), organizing their greetings in several adjacency pairs. The joint production of greetings by the participants allows them to test their relationships and relative position vis-à-vis one another and provide a basis for mutual recognition and mutual understanding. As Duranti observes, the not uncommon one-pair-part greetings are perceived as 'defective' or in need of an explanation.

4. In English, greetings are frequently accomplished via a small set of relatively predictable linguistic formulae such as 'hi', 'hello', 'good morning', or 'how are you?' They are typically associated with low denotative or ideational value although they do index important social information. However, Duranti also notes that greetings are not always completely predictable and they may involve exchange of relevant new information (for example, as illustrated by Duranti in the 'Where are you going?' type of Samoan greeting, also found in other languages).

5. An exchange of greetings may occur on its own as a 'minimal proper conversation' (Sacks 1975), or it may mark the beginning of a new temporal unit or a subsequent shared activity (for example, two colleagues may greet each other at the start of a new working day, and they may greet each other again at the start of a meeting later that same day).

6. The decision to greet someone (or not), the choice of a particular greeting and of other accompanying forms (for example, terms of address) identifies interlocutors as specific types of people. Thus,

> the use of greetings can distinguish between Us and Them, insiders and outsiders, friends and foes, valuable and nonvaluable interactants. For example, in many societies children and servants are not greeted. The absence of greetings then marks these individuals not only as nonproper conversationalists or strangers but also as not worthy of the attention implied by the use of greetings (71).

In this chapter, I build on Duranti's work in an attempt to demonstrate how the greeting should be recognized as a central but distinctive speech act constitutive of tourist–host encounters. Based on data collected at different tourist sites, I will argue that, other things being equal, by engaging in greeting exchanges, hosts and tourists enact their respective roles as 'hosts' and 'tourists', the former being largely motivated commercially, the latter creating a sense of involvement with hosts and/or playfully and fleetingly assuming the cultural identity of their host community. I also discuss how the pragmatic and metapragmatic practices surrounding greeting exchanges in tourist encounters are indicative of general ideological positions underlying contemporary global tourism.

As has been indicated above, the notion of the greeting cannot be simply reduced to exchanges of a small set of formulaic expressions. However, due to the relatively limited linguistic repertoires from which greeting exchanges are constituted in my data in this chapter, I examine primarily greetings as defined by a fairly narrow range of formulae commonly used in what Goffman (1971) has referred to as 'access rituals', for example, 'hi', 'hello', 'how are you?' and 'welcome'. What I intend to demonstrate, however, is that the use of these relatively few linguistic formulae in tourist discourse goes beyond their typically expected remit of what Malinowski and Laver (see J. Coupland, this volume Chapter 44, for references) would refer to as *phatic communion*, or 'expressive' speech acts devoid of propositional meaning with the function of 'a courteous indication of recognition, with the presupposition that the speaker has just encountered the hearer' (Searle and Vanderveken 1985: 216).

Phatic communion is a mode of talk that aims to establish and maintain good interpersonal relations between participants, mark their willingness to communicate with one another and to keep channels of communication open. Traditionally, phatic communion, or small talk, has been located in the *marginal* stages of conversation. For example, Laver (1981: 301) defines phatic communion as largely confined to the opening and closing phases of conversation with the aim to 'defuse the potential hostility of silence in situations where speech is conventionally anticipated'.

To some extent, Duranti's criteria for identifying greetings, most notably near-boundary occurrence and the highly predictable form, orient to their phatic properties. However, Duranti emphasizes that the narrow view of greetings as phatic communion is unnecessarily limiting and inadequate. By examining specific socio-historical circumstances in which greetings occur, he demonstrates how they can be adapted to create new contexts beyond the narrow definition of 'marginal' small talk. His approach is consistent with the more functional approach adopted by J. Coupland, N. Coupland

and Robinson (1992) in which they focus on interactional goals of talk, whereby

> phatic communion would cease to be associated *uniquely* with fringes of encounters (Laver) or extended chatting... and we should expect to find instances where a relationally designed and perhaps phatic mode of talk surfaces whenever relational goals become salient – even *within* sequences of transactional, instrumental, or task-oriented talk. (J. Coupland et al. 1992: 213)

Consequently, I shall examine a range of instances in which greetings are recontextualized from supposedly phatic (or expressive) to performative acts, while at the same time providing new contexts for the fleeting, cross-cultural encounters characteristic of tourist–host interaction. In undertaking this task I make two general assumptions: (1) Being socially *constituted* and socially *constitutive*, discourse is a site and vehicle for ideological *work* between social actors (for example, Fairclough and Wodak 1997; see chapters in Part IV); (2) Following Goffman's (1959) theatrical metaphor of interpersonal relations, the experiences and interactions in tourism are best conceived of as performances of social roles and identities (for example, MacCannell 1999).

Greetings in Tourist–Host Interaction

The greeting speech act dominates the tourist linguistic landscape. For example, the most common formulae listed in foreign language phrasebooks accompanying almost all guidebooks are greetings and other forms of 'sociable' talk. 'G'day Australia', 'Un saluto da Bologna', 'Ciao Sicilia', 'Greetings from Florida' and so on, are among the most common taglines found on the most ubiquitous of the tourist genres – the postcard. 'Welcome to ...' signs front most tourist destinations, from the smallest tourist attractions to whole regions and countries (see Thurlow and Jaworski 2009; Jaworski et al. 2009 for more detailed discussion of these data types). Greetings are also frequently used in face-to-face interactions between tourists and hosts. I will discuss four such data extracts recorded in a range of different settings and tourist sites. They will further demonstrate the centrality of greeting exchanges in tourist–host encounters for the management of the fleeting relationships between tourists and hosts.

Greetings and Linguistic Crossing

Having studied their phrasebooks and having learnt some basic expressions in a local language, some tourists are likely to 'try them out' on unsuspecting hosts. In Extract 1, a Polish tourist in Greece (Ania) puts her guidebook Greek to the test in approaching a taverna owner whom she has known for the past three weeks of her stay in a small village on the southern coast of Crete.

Extract 1: 'Kalispera'

On the last day of their holiday, a family of Polish tourists visit a taverna, where they have become friendly with the owners. Before sitting at a table, they go into the bar/kitchen area to greet one of the owners who is working in the kitchen. (Data example collected by A. J., August 1999 [family video])

Personnel:

Adam	= me
Ania	= my wife
Maja	= our daughter (not amused by her dad's videotaping, she remains silent)
Voula	= taverna owner
Kitchen Assistant	

1 ADAM: to idziemy do pani się przywitać najpierw?
            (trans: shall we first go and say hello to the lady?)
2 ANIA: tak
            (trans: yes)
3   (7; they walk towards the taverna)
4 ANIA: (on approach waves to Voula) good evening how are you?
5 VOULA: (waves back to Ania; unclear talk to assistant)
6 ANIA: (loud voice) kalispera
            (trans: good evening)
7 VOULA: (to assistant; jocular tone) Pir' ena potiri kai m'evreske
8   kalispera
            (trans: He got a glass and threw water on me, good evening)
9 ANIA: (slight laughter) kalispera
10 VOULA: (faces Ania, head nod, exaggerated formal tone) kalispe:ra
11 ANIA: how are you?
12 VOULA: good? and you?
13 ANIA: have you got anything special tonight? (laughs)

Following Duranti's Criterion 3, the above greeting exchanges follow a clear adjacency pair format involving verbal and nonverbal elements:

lines 4–5:	hand wave, *good evening how are you?*
	hand wave
lines 6–8:	*kalispera*
	kalispera

lines 9–10:   *kalispera*
             kalispera
lines 11–12: *how are you?*
             good? and you?

The occurrence of four adjacency pairs in one greeting sequence may appear somewhat odd. Ania initiates the greeting sequence ratified by Voula from the distance of about 15 meters, which creates the necessity to keep the interaction alive until she reaches the counter marking the boundary of the kitchen. The exchanges between lines 4–12 last approximately ten seconds, even though the initial exchange between lines 4–5 would have satisfied all the six greeting criteria mentioned above. The moment of the approach then becomes a speech event in its own right, a small talk or chatting sequence (cf. above), preceding more instrumentally oriented talk about food. Ania and Voula do not share a lingua franca with which they are both comfortable and fluent enough to converse freely, so their 'extended' greeting sequence allows them both to prolong the act of sociability initiated by Ania and ratified by Voula. However, there is more than just asserting the mutual sociability of both interactants here. In line 6, in an act of code-crossing (Rampton, this volume, Chapter 20), Ania switches to Greek articulating an expression learned from a tourist phrasebook. As this is not part of Ania's 'normal' linguistic repertoire, 'kalispera' is here a playful if courteous attempt to greet Voula. As in other examples of code-crossing, the formula becomes then less of a greeting and more of a *performance of a* greeting with the increased attention to the code itself marked, for example, by 'special' paralinguistic features such as laughter, high pitch, louder than normal voice and, arguably, the somewhat redundant repetition of 'kalispera' in line 9 (cf. chapters by Rampton (20); Cutler (21); N. Coupland (22); Bauman and Briggs (41)).

What we see here is probably a fairly typical example of the tourist ideology displaying an 'integrationist' ethos towards her hosts by appropriating their language code, albeit briefly, playfully and with a very limited repertoire. The repetition of the local greeting seems to make the exchange more 'busy'. That this part of the greeting is largely symbolic (using the local language to enact fleetingly a new ethnolinguistic identity), rather than being a proper preamble for the ensuing conversation (about food), is indicated by Ania's 'sandwiching' the Greek greeting sequences between English greeting sequences in lines 4–5 and 11–12. This allows her to extend the speech event of 'saying hello to the lady' (cf. line 1); also it appears that it is the English greeting which achieves the perlocutionary effect of accomplishing *access* to Voula (in the sense of Duranti's Criterion 5). While the exchange of the relatively new and unfamiliar Greek greeting gives Ania the pleasure of 'going native', and reassurance to Voula that her guests are keen on linguistically accommodating to her, it is the familiar English greeting phrase that takes over the usual job of giving interactants a way into the next step in the conversation (talking about food).

Greetings and Language Display

In the next example, 'Cesar', the local guide in Chiapas, Mexico, brings up the apparent exoticity of the local language (Tzotzil) to the attention of the tourists, and engages actively in linguascaping the site (Jaworski et al. 2003), which involves encouraging the tourists to repeat Tzotzil words and phrases after him. The following extract from an ongoing guided tour is the beginning of a longer sequence, in which the guide 'teaches' tourists different Tzotzil words and phrases such as colour terms, words for 'mother', 'father', 'the sun', 'moon', the phrase 'I don't have any money' and so on. However, he starts, quite predictably, with the Tzotzil greeting formula.

Extract 2: Cesar's Greetings

A group of international tourists follow a guided tour in Chamula (Chiapas) Mexico.
(Data example collected by Sarah Lawson, autumn 2002.)

Personnel:
    Cesar   = the guide
    T   = Tourists

```
1  CESAR:  the people here in Chamula? (1) you hear the the children
2          they are speaking (.) a different language (.) do you
3          understand? (1) no? er: the language is spoken here is not
4          er Spanish (.) is er Tzotzil (.) er is completely different to
5          Spanish (.) so if you want to say good morning? you can
6          say leeoté (.) leeoté=
                   [
7  T:      (quiet voices) leeoté (.) leeoté=
8  CESAR:  =leeoté means good morning
```

Extract 2 offers another example of tourists' crossing into a host language. Encouraged to do so by the guide (himself not a first language Tzotzil speaker), however, theirs is not *use* of the greeting but *mention*, rote repetition of the citation form. Here, even more so than in Extract 1, the performance of the greeting becomes a representation of the greeting. When Cesar says 'you can say leeoté' (lines 5–6), he elicits the repetition of the formula rather than initiates a greeting exchange with the tourists. The recontextualized greeting loses its phatic, interpersonal function in place of the textual, metalinguistic one, orienting to and illustrating the code itself and indexing Chamula as ethnolinguistically distinct area from other parts of Mexico. Although it is possible for Cesar to use any other word or phrase for this purpose (which he does later, perhaps to display and legitimate his own linguistic expertise), he starts with a greeting formula as the most typical candidate for creating the Tzotzil linguascape.

The tourists' own articulation of 'leeoté' (line 7) is marked by tentative, soft and 'latched' articulation. The form of the greeting is not highly predictable and familiar to all. On the contrary, the contiguous speech across lines 6–8 and Cesar's repeated explanation of the 'meaning' of 'leeoté' are reminiscent of a 'language learning' second situation displaying metalingual rather than interpersonal orientation to the greeting.

Tourists as Performers

As has been mentioned above, tourist interactions are typically associated with performances of cultural, ethnic and national identities. However, it is not only the prerogative of hosts to do this. Tourists are equally likely to act out a variety of roles associated with their home (for example, national) or visitor (for example, 'dumb foreigner') identities for the benefit of hosts or fellow tourists. In the next example, recorded at *pheZulu* in KwaZulu-Natal, the cultural village that presents *amaZulu* (or Zulus) of South Africa, the ethnic/national identity of tourists becomes a focal point of conversation and subsequent linguistic display.

Extract 3: 'Say Hello in Polish'
A guide (Patrick) and a group of international tourists are waiting inside a hut for a performer to come and demonstrate traditional ways of cooking maize. While waiting for the performer to arrive, the guide starts asking the tourists sitting around the edges of the hut to state their place of origin. Once the round is completed and silence falls, one of the tourists from KwaZulu suggests to Patrick that the Polish tourists in the group 'should say hello in Polish'. (Data example collected by Crispin Thurlow, spring 2003)

Personnel:

Patrick	= guide
T1, T2	= tourists from KwaZulu
T3	= tourist from Poland (T4's mother)
T4	= tourist from Poland (male, approximately 8 years old)
T5	= tourist from Poland (T4's father)
T6	= unidentified tourist

	CT	= tourist/researcher
1	T1:	they should say hello in Po:lish
2		[
3	T2:	in Po:lish
4	PATRICK:	that's just what I'm looking for
5	T1, T2:	(laugh)
6	PATRICK:	(to T3 and T4) how do you say hello in Polish? (2)
7	T3:	(quietly to T4) no powiedz (.) pan się (unclear) chce żebyś
8		powiedział cześć po polsku powiedz cześć=
		(trans: well say it (.) the gentleman (unclear)
		wants you to say hello in Polish say hello)
9		(T4 turns towards his mother and hides his face)
10	PATRICK:	= how do you say hello in your language?=
11	T3:	(to Patrick, softly) cześć
		(trans: hello)
12	PATRICK:	sorry?
13	T3:	cześć
14	PATRICK:	(looks at other tourists, smiles) I can't say it
15		(general laughter)
16	T5:	nothing ((for)) easy
17		(general laughter)
18	CT:	cześć
19	PATRICK:	(to CT) can you say it?
20	CT:	cześć
21	T6:	cześć
22	T3:	cześć
23	PATRICK:	(surprised tone) have you heard it before?
24		[
25	CT:	cześć I have a friend who is Polish I know
26		dziekuję 'thank you' but that's it
		(trans: thank you)
26	T3:	(nods and smiles, outburst of general laughter)

In an instance of 'reverse' crossing, Polish tourists demonstrate one of the Polish greeting formulae to the guide and other tourists. This situation is a mirror image of that in Extract 2, where it was the guide 'teaching' the tourists how to use local greetings. The initial move to ethnotype the Polish tourists as 'Polish' by T1 is premised on her request to hear a sample of the Polish language and a greeting formula is chosen as a token Polish expression. The request appears to be unexpected and does not trigger immediate compliance. There is a pause of two seconds followed by the boy's mother encouraging him to say *cześć*, 'hello', in Polish (lines 7–8), rather than spontaneously offering to demonstrate it herself. The elicitation of the Polish greeting by T1 and T2 seems like a childish game – it is reminiscent more of requesting a small, pre-literate child at a family gathering to recite a poem, spell his or her name or 'count to 100' rather that requesting expert advice on the use of a second language (which is not known to T1 and T2) (see also next extract on the game show-like features of such performances).

The embarrassed boy struggles *not* to have to perform (line 9), and finally, his mother says the first, soft instance of 'cześć' (line 11). Patrick does not quite grasp the pronunciation of the word and asks for repetition (line 12) but even after he hears it again (line 13) he still appears confused and uncertain as to how to pronounce the greeting. Two participants try to rescue Patrick from his embarrassment. The father declares the Polish greeting is rather hard to pronounce (line 16), possibly in the hope of closing off further attempts for anyone to say it, followed by CT's demonstration of his ability to do so (line 18). This triggers four more repetitions of 'cześć' by CT, T6 (a non-Polish tourist) and T3.

Most of Duranti's conditions for a successful greeting are violated here. The greeting crops up as part of an ongoing (though faltering) interaction; the perceptual field among the participants is already established; there is no adjacency pair format; the form and content are not predictable to non-Polish language speakers (except CT); it does not mark a start of a new unit of interaction; and it is not necessary to identify any of the participants as 'worth recognising'. This is why the resulting sequence does not constitute a greeting in terms of Duranti's criteria – a fact seemingly recognized and acted on by the boy through his refusal to articulate it.

However, I suggest that the function of the string of Polish 'hellos' here is an example of a recontextualized greeting, whereby the primary function is that of (dis-)play through which the national/ethnic identity of the Polish tourists is elicited and enacted. The greeting, as in so many other contexts (for example, commercial, social, etc.), becomes a 'ticket' (Youssouf, Grimshaw and Bird, 1976, after Sacks 1972), that is, a reason for initiating and interacting with strangers. In the fleeting context of tourism, the greeting – or its performance, representation, learning, repetition and metapragmatic commentary – may constitute the focal and exclusive orientation of talk, as is the case among the tourists in the PheZulu hut.

The Commodified Greeting

The processes of commodification and appropriation of language in the new economic order of flexible accumulation and time–space compression (Harvey 1990) has in the past decade become an object of considerable interest among sociolinguists (for example, Cameron 2000; Fairclough 1999; Heller 2003). The new economy of signs (Lash and Urry 1994) has privileged the symbolic and cultural cachet of consumer goods over their material and utilitarian worth. The tourist industry has led to the intensified production and consumption of iconic and indexical displays of culture, ethnicity, the nation, and so on. As Culler observes: 'the tourist is interested in everything as a sign of itself...All over the world the unsung armies of semioticians, the tourists, are fanning out in search of the signs of Frenchness, typical Italian behaviour, exemplary, Oriental scenes, typical American thruways, traditional English pubs' (Culler 1981: 127; cited in Urry 2002: 3). In the context of New Zealand, for example, one of the key resources for packaging Maori heritage has been the commodification of the Maori greeting, the *hongi*, which involves two people pressing their noses against one another.

For example, in Tamaki Maori Village in Rotorua, tourists can have a picture taken of themselves doing a hongi with an actor against a photographic backdrop of idyllic rural scenery and a wooden carved totem pole. Images of Maori people performing a hongi can be bought on postcards and posters. However, despite what the tourist guides and websites may suggest, it is virtually impossible for a tourist to perform a hongi with a Maori person other than in the context of a paid performance.

My final example is in fact an instance of a commodified greeting exchange (involving a hongi) between a Maori guide/coach driver and an American tourist en route for a night's entertainment at Tamaki Maori Village at Rotorua, New Zealand. The tourists are collected by several coaches from hotels in the area. Once all the tourists are on board their designated bus (*waka*, 'boat', 'vessel'), the guide/driver welcomes everyone and announces that the tourists will not only experience Maori song, dance, food and so on, but will also 'become' Maori for the night. Each busload of tourists is branded as a 'tribe' (*iwi*) with a 'chief' (*rangatira*) ('elected' from among the tourists; the chief usually ends up being white, male, American), and the driver offers to 'teach' the tourists some Maori language – typically just one phrase/greeting formula *Kia Ora*, 'Hello/ Good Luck/Good Health/Thank You' to be repeated in unison by the tourists following a prompt from the guides and other performers. The 'chiefs' become privileged participants in representing their 'tribes' in the Village Welcome, 'gift' presentation, various speeches throughout the night, and so on. One of such privileges includes a performance of a hongi with the guide/driver. The following extract presents such a sequence on the coach before its departure for Tamaki Maori Village, some 12 kilometres away from town.

Extract 4: The Maori Greeting

A group of international tourists on the way to Tamaki Maori Village, Rotorua, New Zealand. After the group elected Kenny, an American, middle-aged white male, as its 'chief' and before the coach departs, the driver demonstrates the hongi instructing Kenny what to do. (Data example collected by A.J., 5 April 2003)

Personnel:

> Guide (Driver)
> Kenny = tourist
> T = Unidentified tourists

1	GUIDE:	for you people from different tribes? (.) this is how we the
2		Maori people will usually greet each other (.) grab my right
3		hand Kenny? (.) (off mike) stand up stand up
4		(Kenny stands; he towers over the driver)
5	T:	(light laughter) (1)
6	GUIDE:	now go down on the step (Kenny goes one step down)
7	T:	(laughter) (2)
8	GUIDE:	ok we- (.) put your left hand on my shoulder Kenny (1) ok?
9		(.) now what we do, we press our noses together twice (.)
10		and then we say kia ora ok? nice and gentle (.) don't go
11		(thrusts his head forward quickly towards Kenny's face;
12		Kenny tilts his head backwards in a reflex)
13	T:	(light laughter) (2)
14	GUIDE:	and whatever you do:? <u>don't</u> <u>kiss</u> me.
		[
15	KENNY:	(inaudible speech to Guide)
16	T:	(continued laughter) (2)
17		(Guide and Kenny perform a hongi, cameras flash)
18	GUIDE:	kia ora: didn't he do well (.) how-bout a big round=
19	T:	(applause 4; loud female voice) yeeeahh
20	GUIDE:	=of applause for Kenny (.) my people interpret the hongi
21		like this when the two noses come together (.) it's the
22		sharing of common breath creating a legion of friendship
23		(1) as a point of interest for you, we the Maori tribe here in
24		Te Arawa are familiar to all this area of Rotorua and Bay of
25		Plenty (.) we are the only Maori tribe in New Zealand that
26		hongi <u>twice</u> (.) all other tribes do it <u>once</u> (.) that's our
27		trademark. (.) we're now gonna pull out rangatira our big
28		kahuna the big chief Ken here, to the entrance way (.) I'll

29   make the official welcome the challenge, you're gonna
30   have a <u>won</u>derful evening (.) <u>kia ora</u>.
31   T: (loud voices) kia ora

Although the hongi is framed as a typical Maori greeting (lines 1–2) and as a way of establishing 'a legion of friendship' (line 22) between two people, the guide's display and 'lesson' in Maori etiquette has an undercurrent of cultural subversion and resistance to dominant ideologies of tourism. The guide does not unambiguously adopt a stance of a friendly, deferential and subservient host. Under the guise of humour reminiscent of genres where mock-aggression and mild humiliation are part of the participation ritual (for example, TV quiz-shows), he positions Kenny, the archetypal powerful and wealthy Westerner about to be exposed to 'Pre-European lifestyle experience of customs and traditions' (http://www.maoriculture.co.nz/ Maori%20Village/Home), as a relatively powerless and ignorant 'foreigner'. To 'teach' Kenny the hongi ritual, the guide instructs him to adopt appropriate body posture. When Kenny comes to the front of the coach and faces the guide, the guide unceremoniously orders Kenny to go one step down, to reduce the difference in their height: having their faces at the same level is more amenable to hongi and symbolically maintains a proxemic equilibrium between the two men. The driver uses unmitigated directives, 'stand up stand up' (line 3), 'now go down on the step' (line 6), reminiscent of an adult disciplining a child, and this 'bossing' Kenny around elicits outbursts of laughter from the onlookers on the coach.

In lines 10–11, the guide teases Kenny, implying that he is likely to hongi inappropriately – 'nice and gentle (.) don't go (thrusts his head forward ...)'. The guide's hyperbolic headbutt is clearly an exaggeration for comic effect as he cannot realistically expect Kenny to act in such a foolish manner. The guide also seems to intentionally frighten Kenny with his mock headbutt only to elicit a reaction of slight panic from Kenny and more laughter from the other tourists. Another ridiculing turn at Kenny's expense is the guide's teasing, homophobic joke, 'and whatever you do:? don't kiss me' (line 14). The guide then proceeds with the hongi (line 17) and again positions Kenny as a child-like figure who deserves a 'round of applause' as a reward for his performance (another game show-like feature). The guide appears in total control of the situation, a knowledgeable expert, as well as a mocking director-choreographer of the scene, blatantly 'othering' Kenny by adopting the key of teasing and ridicule.

The Performativity of Greetings

Tourists taking part in local rituals, festivals and dance routines access new cultures through a complex process of cultural production that MacCannell

(1999) terms as 'staged authenticity'. Yet the cultural, including sociolinguistic, resources available to hosts and tourists in co-constructing the staged events of heritage, ethnic, regional or national identity as *authentic* lend themselves in various ways to making cultures 'more vital and more accessible' (N. Coupland, Garrett and Bishop 2005: 216). I do not want to eulogise tourists' reliance on their phrasebook knowledge of host languages in their encounters with hosts (cf. Thurlow and Jaworski 2009, Chapter 6), but it's clear that tourists will cling to any linguistic resources available to them in attempting to enact their identity as 'tourists'. In this sense, I see the use of greetings and greeting sequences demonstrated in the above extracts as performative of tourist and host identities.

The heightened intensity of the greetings and greeting sequences in the examples above makes them performances in the sense of Bauman and Briggs (this volume, Chapter 41). Their contextual and formal features are also consistent with several dimensions of what Coupland (2007: 147–148; this volume) refers to as 'high performance'. Thus,

- Participants orient to the formal properties of code (pronunciation, kinesic sequence of *hongi*).
- Although the greetings' propositional content is of relatively little significance, their social meaning is explicitly oriented to through accompanying metapragmatic comments, translation and labelling (for example, Extracts 2 and 4).
- Participants are not simply co-present but 'gathered' with clearly pre-assigned roles (Extracts 2, 3, 4).
- Performers hold a 'stage' even if only created *ad hoc* (for example, on the steps of a coach, Extract 4) and perform *for* (rather than *to*) audiences (who may be other tourists, for example, Extract 4, and/or hosts, for example, Extract 3).
- Greetings are produced to specific norms and demands; they are treated as achievement and are subject to scrutiny and evaluation – praise (for example, Extract 4), or admission of failure and embarrassment (cf. the young Polish boy's shy refusal to say *cześć*, and Patrick's inability to repeat *cześć* after the boy's mother and other tourists).
- Greetings are also produced with sensitivity to the speakers' own repertoires available to them in the context of tourist exchanges. As examples of code-crossing, speaking languages that they cannot claim 'belong' to them (Rampton, this volume, Chapter 20), tourists' performances are highly styled – accompanied by exaggerated high pitch and loudness (for example, Extract 1), softness (for example, Extract 2), laughter (for example, Extracts 1, 3, 4), overlapping talk or speaking in unison (for example, Extracts 2, 3, 4). In fact, Extracts 2, 3 and 4 are reminiscent of second language learning situations or rehearsals with instructors providing model variants and explanations of usage followed by the ritualized practice.

What is especially salient here is the ideological work of the greetings through which speakers undertake the linguistics of differentiation (Irvine and Gal, this volume, Chapter 26). In other words, greetings act as indexes (Ochs, this volume, Chapter 29) of social, cultural, ethnic, tribal and national difference, for example, separating the Tzotzil from other Mexicans (Extract 2); Maoris from other New Zealanders and tourists (cf. 'you people from different tribes', Extract 4, line 1); and Polish tourists from other tourists and hosts in South Africa (Extract 3). The commodified greeting is both an act of appropriation of hosts' cultural identity (for example, Extract 1), as well as a means of policing cultural boundaries between hosts and tourists and controlling access to local culture through the use of local knowledge (Shaw and Williams 2004) (for example, Extract 4). These are the boundaries which tourists may attempt to breach in a bid to become likeable, if not fully accepted, fleeting members of the host community (Extract 1).

Finally, the performance of the tourist greeting, as is the case with any performative speech acts (Austin 1962) and performative discourse more broadly (Butler 1990), may be a site of ideological work in another sense – undermining the authority of the context from which it originates (cf. Coupland 2007: 101). In Extract 3, the (Polish) tourists are put on the spot in a spontaneous role reversal which defies their safe and privileged status and turns them from 'spectators' to 'performers'. In Extract 4, the subversive work of the guide positions the wealthy and powerful American tourist as a somewhat inept and ludicrous figure, totally dominated by the guide exercising a degree of vernacular authority through his display of expert, local knowledge, and control of the unfolding performance.

It may be argued that the speech act of the greeting is quite incidental as a sociolinguistic resource for the production of cultural identities and ideologies of tourism. Clearly, other speech forms and semiotic codes may achieve similar effects. For example, Senft (1999) demonstrates how in their untranslated songs performed in Kilivila for unsuspecting (German) tourists on the beach or inside a village, contemporary Trobriand Islanders engage in acts of ridicule and mockery (for example, through performing a cricket team song mocking the opponents, or an explicitly erotic, pornographic song) sending the applauding tourists away from the islands as humiliated and defeated opponents. However, I believe that the centrality of the greeting in tourist–host encounters cannot be challenged, on the grounds of its sheer ubiquity. And its study in the tourist context provides an interesting test-case for the universality of Duranti's criteria for defining greetings, with which I started this chapter. Far from attempting to invalidate them here, I want to suggest that, as much of the social practice of tourism is premised on the notion of departure from the ordinary into the extraordinary experiences of the liminal zone (cf. Urry 2002), the expected conditions for performing greetings (and other forms of talk) may be inverted.

Let us revisit briefly Duranti's criteria in view of the data presented above:

1. *near-boundary occurrence*: rather than occupying a marginal position in conversation, the tourist greeting may become the central focus of interaction and metapragmatic scrutiny (Extracts 2, 3, 4);
2. *establishment of a shared perceptual field*: maintenance of a shared perceptual field (Extract 3);
3. *adjacency pair format*: relative asymmetry, frequent lack of second pair part, repetition (often in unison by a group) (Extracts 2, 3, 4);
4. *relative predictability of form and content*: relative unpredictability – novelty, second language learning, code-crossing (Extracts 1, 2, 3, 4);
5. *implicit establishment of a spatio-temporal unit of interaction*: ongoing/rolling interaction (Extracts 2, 3, 4);
6. *identification of the interlocutor as a distinct being worth recognizing*: commodification, tokenism, synthetic personalization (Extracts 3, 4).

Acknowledgements

The research for this chapter was in part supported by funding from the Leverhulme Trust (Grant No. F/00 407/D) to the Centre for Language and Communication Research, Cardiff University, for a larger project on Language and Global Communication (2001–2006). I am grateful to Georgia Eglezou and Gerard O'Grady for their help with Greek.

Transcription Conventions

[	=	start of overlapping talk
(word)	=	nonverbal, paralinguistic and other contextual information
((word))	=	best approximation of talk
<u>word</u>	=	perceptible additional emphasis
wo:rd	=	perceptible lengthening
wo-	=	truncated word
(.)	=	pause shorter than one second
(1)	=	length of pause in seconds
?	=	rising intonation, possibly a question
=	=	contiguous, latched talk

REFERENCES

Austin, J. L. 1962. *How to Do Things with Words*. Oxford: Oxford University Press.

Bach, Kent and Robert M. Harnish. 1979. *Linguistic Communication and Speech Acts*. Cambridge, Massachusetts: MIT Press.

Butler, Judith. 1990. *Gender Trouble: Feminism and the Subversion of Identity*. New York: Routledge.

Cameron, Deborah. 2000. Styling the worker: Gender and the commodification of language in the globalized service economy. *Journal of Sociolinguistics* 4: 323–347.

Coupland, Justine, Nikolas Coupland and Jeffrey D. Robinson. 1992. 'How are you?': Negotiating phatic communion. *Language in Society* 21: 207–230.

Coupland, Nikolas. 2007. *Style: Language Variation and Identity*. Cambridge: Cambridge University Press.

Coupland, Nikolas, Peter Garrett and Hywel Bishop. 2005. Wales underground: Discursive frames and authenticities in Welsh mining heritage tourism events. In Adam Jaworski and Annette Pritchard (eds.) *Discourse, Communication and Tourism*. Clevedon: Channel View. 199–222.

Culler, Jonathan. 1981. Semiotics of tourism. *American Journal of Semiotics* 1: 127–140.

Duranti, Alessandro. 1997. Universal and culture-specific properties of greetings. *Journal of Linguistic Anthropology* 7: 63–97.

Fairclough, Norman. 1999. Global capitalism and critical awareness of language. *Language Awareness* 8: 71–83.

Fairclough, Norman and Ruth Wodak. 1997. Critical discourse analysis. In Teun A. Van Dijk. (ed.) *Discourse Studies: A Multidisciplinary Introduction. Volume 2: Discourse as Social Interaction*. London: Sage. 258–284.

Goffman, Erving. 1959. *The Presentation of Self in Everyday Life*. New York: Doubleday Anchor.

Goffman, Erving. 1971. *Relations in Public: Microstudies of the Public Order*. New York: Basic Books.

Harvey, David. 1990. *The Condition of Postmodernity: An Enquiry into the Origins of Cultural Change*. Oxford: Blackwell.

Heller, Monica. 2003. Globalization, the new economy and the commodification of language and identity. *Journal of Sociolinguistics* 7: 473–498.

Irvine, Judith. 1974. Strategies of status manipulation in Wolof greetings. In Richard Bauman and Joel Sherzer (eds.) *Explorations in the Ethnography of Speaking*. Cambridge: Cambridge University Press. 167–191.

Jaworski, Adam, Crispin Thurlow, Sarah Lawson and Virpi Ylänne-McEwen. 2003. The uses and representations of host languages in tourist destinations: A view from British TV holiday programmes. *Language Awareness* 12, 1: 5–29.

Jaworski, Adam, Crispin Thrlow, Virpi Ylanne and Sarah Lawson. In press. *Language, Tourism, Globalisation: The Sociolinguistics of Fleeting Relationships*. London: Routledge. (in press)

Lash, Scott and John Urry. 1994. *Economies of Signs and Spaces*. London: Sage.

Laver, John. 1981. Linguistic routines and politeness in greeting and parting. In Florian Coulmas (ed.) *Conversational Routine*. The Hague: Mouton. 289–304.

MacCannell, Dean. 1999. *The Tourist: A New Theory of the Leisure Class*. Berkeley, California: University of California Press.

Sacks, Harvey 1972. On the analyzability of stories by children. In John J. Gumperz and Dell H. Hymes (eds.) *Directions in Sociolinguistics: The Ethnography of Communication*. New York: Holt, Rinehart and Winston. 325–345.

Sacks, Harvey. 1975. Everyone has to lie. In Mary Sanches and Ben G. Blount (eds.) *Sociocultural Dimensions of Language Use*. New York: Academic Press. 57–80.

Schegloff, Emanuel A. and Harvey Sacks. 1973. Opening up closings. *Semiotica* 8: 289–329.

Searle, John R. 1969. *Speech Acts: An Essay in the Philosophy of Language*. Cambridge: Cambridge University Press.

Searle, John, and Daniel Vanderveken. 1985. *Foundations of Illocutionary Logic*. Cambridge: Cambridge University Press.

Senft, Gunter. 1999. The presentation of self in touristic encounters: A case study from the Trobriand Islands. *Anthropos* 94: 21–33.

Shaw, Gareth and Allan M. Williams. 2004. *Tourism and Tourist Spaces*. London: Sage.

Thurlow, Crispin and Adam Jaworski. 2009. *Tourism Discourse: The Language of Global Mobility*. Basingstoke: Palgrave Macmillan.

Urry, John. 2002. *The Tourist Gaze*. 2nd edition. London: Sage. [First published in 1990.]

Youssouf, Ibrahim J., Allen D. Grimshaw and Charles S. Bird. 1976. Greetings in the desert. *American Ethnologist* 3: 797–824.

CHAPTER 46

Creativity in Sign Languages

RACHEL SUTTON-SPENCE

Sign Language Literature

Sign languages are the key identifying feature of Deaf culture in Deaf communities. Although there are many Deaf communities and many different sign languages, their use of creative language in their literature shares many similarities. Within sign language literature, we can consider both Deaf Folklore (the traditional narratives, jokes and language games of a Deaf community) and Performance Art (especially sign language poems). Deaf storytellers and poets use creative sign language for entertainment and enjoyment, and Deaf audiences celebrate and respect good storytellers in their communities, where stories, skits and performances are regularly seen at formal and informal gatherings.

Analytical interest in creative sign language is recent and it is becoming clear that creative sign language crosses conventional boundaries of our understanding of art forms. Although linguists were the first to write in depth about sign creativity (for example, Klima and Bellugi 1979), literary critics, performance artists, theatre practitioners and art historians are also now discovering how this visual linguistic art form can inform and challenge ideas in their own disciplines. The visual imagery allows art historians to consider the relationship between signed art and other visual arts, while the strong performance element of any signed art invites comparisons with dance and other theatrical work (Bauman, Nelson and Rose 2006). Although this chapter will focus primarily on the language and cultural issues surrounding creative signing, there are many other ways to view the art form.

The importance of sign language literature can be understood within the frameworks of Deaflore (for example, Rutherford 1993) and Deafhood (Ladd

2003). Deaflore is the collective knowledge of individual Deaf communities and the shared World Deaf community. At a language level, it refers to the language knowledge that is seen as the cultural heritage of these Deaf communities. Deafhood is the process through which Deaf people discover and develop their Deaf identity as members of a visual collective community. Whereas 'Deafness' is a state of being, determined audiologically, Deafhood is an active process of belonging to a linguistic and cultural group. In 'doing' Deaflore (including storytelling and poetry), Deaf people are 'doing' Deafhood.

Sign language literature is not only a major source of entertainment and amusement but it is also vital for education, as it serves to transmit the community's culture down the generations. The themes and the language used in creative signing also empower Deaf people, by showing their cultural identity in a positive way as 'visual people' with a strong collective community identity. Every performance of a sign language art form is an act of empowerment for Deaf people, and an expression of pride in the language that has been historically oppressed. For a long time, Deaf people were taught that 'deaf signing' was less good than spoken language. The result was that many members of Deaf communities did not value their creative language art forms and believed that 'literature' was not possible for sign language. This has changed since the emergence of 'Deaf Pride' in the 1970s, with the increasing recognition of sign languages as 'real' languages, and the work of pioneering sign language advocates and artists in many countries. Sign literature is frequently optimistic and shows Deaf people controlling their own destiny. It does not deny problems faced by Deaf people, and some of the best sign literature identifies the role that hearing people have played in oppressing Deaf people, but the signed stories and poems create a sense of community unity that inspires members to resist that oppression.

Because sign languages are traditionally unwritten, their literature is similar in some ways to 'oral literature', in that distribution, composition and performance do not rely on the written or printed word (Finnegan 1977; Peters 2000). Rather than use the term 'oral literature' for an art form that does not use speech, however, Bahan (2006) has proposed the term 'face-to-face tradition' to capture the live and embodied nature of the genre. In sign language literature, the stories may be totally memorised or their approximate form can be memorised while the signer makes up the rest during performance. As in oral literature, even if the stories or poems are memorised, sign language performers will often create variations upon a basic theme to best match the audience and context of the performance.

Video recording has had a tremendous impact on the previously ephemeral 'face-to-face' literature of sign language. Until the 1970s sign language literature existed entirely in its live performance but it is now frequently filmed and transmitted using video and digitally stored material. Filming allows an even closer record of the story or poem than we see in a written version because it also contains the details of the performance and the performer, blurring traditional distinctions between 'text' and 'performance'. Heidi Rose (1992) has observed that the present canon of signed literature could not exist without video. Ben Bahan (2006) has also noted the importance of video for creative sign language art forms in America, claiming that signed literature was traditionally borrowed from spoken language literature, and the impetus to create literature in sign languages came from video. Filming sign language literature makes texts static so stories become 'fixed' in a particular form, but it also frees texts from constraints of time and place, helping performances reach mass audiences. Video recording naturally distances performers from their audiences, losing the immediacy of face-to-face interaction, but there is also increased recognition of some Deaf artists, as they become better known through video distribution. The commercialisation of signed literature is finally possible, as recordings and live performances work together, further increasing the popularity of the art form and enabling some artists to make a living from it. Finally, the fact that video permits multiple reviews of the same text or performance has allowed artists to become more experimental with their work and has made audiences more analytical (Krentz 2006).

The Cultural Importance of Sign Language Narratives

The mainstay of Deaf literature is the narrative. In any community – literate or with face-to-face traditions – stories are the way to store, organise and pass on tradition and culture (Peters 2000). The function of signed language narratives is described by Ladd (2003), Lane, Hoffmeister and Bahan (1996), and Padden and Humphries (1988). The studies repeatedly find that stories are the means of supporting, nurturing, developing and perpetuating Deaf culture and the language, customs and morals of the Deaf community. Stories are also often seen as opportunities to show prowess in signed language.

To appreciate the fundamental importance of signed stories to the Deaf community, it is necessary to understand the way that most Deaf people come to learn their sign language and join the Deaf community (see Ladd 2003; and Lane et al. 1996 for detailed explanations of this). In some countries, a few deaf children (perhaps as many as 5 per cent) are born to Deaf parents and have wider Deaf families, creating an environment where sign languages and Deaf culture are passed directly from parents to children. However, the majority of deaf children have hearing families with no knowledge of sign language or the Deaf community. These deaf children have traditionally learned their signing from other deaf children at residential Deaf schools.

Many schools worldwide have failed to provide education for children in sign language – either through explicit rejection and proscription of sign languages in favour of spoken and written languages (in the educational philosophy of oralism), or through hearing teachers' inadequate sign language skills. However, the children at these schools have taught themselves and each other to sign, and have frequently used this signing to help educate each other. In many Deaf schools, the telling of stories helped children learn sign language and to learn about life, both generally and as a Deaf person – in other words, they developed their Deafhood through stories. Since the 1980s, however, increased inclusion of deaf children into mainstream education has threatened this source of linguistic and cultural development. Concerned adults in Deaf communities are trying to redress this loss by providing sign language performance events and video materials of creative sign language for deaf children in mainstream education.

Rutherford (1993) has described how storytelling developed early in residential schools for deaf children, when children used sign language to describe the idiosyncratic mannerisms of hearing teachers. Children who went to the cinema would tell stories to the other children based on films they had seen. Children with Deaf parents or access to Deaf clubs and adult Deaf society were often the sources of national and local news – of both deaf and hearing life. They would use the narrative form to tell the other children what they had learned. Ladd (2003) also described how children who were punished in school would then make up stories about their punishment. These stories did not need to be true and could be 'embellished' to make the story more interesting. With frequent repetition, the facts became less important, while the social importance and the language itself became the focus. Like Padden and Humphries (1988), Peters (2000) argues that *how* something is communicated in signed language storytelling has more cultural importance than *what* is communicated, and, given its history of oppression, that signed language is used for literary purposes at all is a cultural asset to deaf people.

As Deaf storytelling has traditionally begun in residential Deaf schools, with children signing stories to each other in their free time, many stories were generated by the children and frequently developed with no adult input at all. Some children were noted to have 'the knack' (Rutherford 1993) or be 'smooth signers' (Bahan 2006) and they attracted the largest and most loyal audiences. These children began to be identified as storytellers, carrying this role into adulthood. Although signers from Deaf families have the greatest access to sign languages at an early age, cultural leaders in storytelling are frequently deaf people from hearing families, who have developed a highly creative visual style of signing. Acknowledged British Deaf storytellers such as Dot Miles, Richard Hanifin, Richard Carter and Clive Mason all come from hearing families but are widely considered to have 'the knack'.

Signed Narrative Types

Signed narratives may be original narratives from the Deaf heritage, or may be translated from other written languages but signed in an especially creative way (Ryan 1993). In some narratives, such as traditional fairy tales told to deaf children, aspects of the plot or characters may be altered to become more Deaf-focussed. For example, in *The Pied Piper*, the child left behind is not lame but Deaf and in *Red Riding Hood* all the characters are Deaf except for the hearing wolf. For Peters (2000), these represent examples of the Deaf storyteller as 'trickster' who mixes elements of deaf and hearing culture, and signed and spoken language traditions. It is worth noting that, while the adaptation of traditional narratives to make them more culturally relevant to Deaf audiences is long standing in America, it is very recent in Britain, where signers previously believed it was inappropriate to change a story that came from the language of the powerful hearing social majority. More recently, increased community confidence and pride in sign language has allowed British Deaf people to adapt traditional narratives to great effect.

'Traditional' deaf stories include those that Ladd (2003) has classified under the 'lamppost trope', referring to often-repeated stories of Deaf people standing around under lampposts to continue to sign in their light after the Deaf club closed for the night. Rutherford gives several examples of 'traditional' American sign language (ASL) stories. Much of the sign literature used to develop and maintain cultural identity focuses on identifying not just the 'self' but also the 'other'. In Deaf communities, 'others' might be hearing people, hard-of-hearing people or oral deaf people who do not sign and so do not belong to Deaf communities. In the stories of 'Deaf Can', the Deaf person succeeds in a challenging situation when 'others' might expect them to fail because they are Deaf, or succeeds where 'others' fail. Ladd has called these the stories of '1001 victories'. Each victory is only a small one, but they boost the Deaf sense of pride. There are also anecdotes showing deaf ingenuity, like mechanical clocks rigged with weights that fall at the appointed hour and awaken deaf owners with vibrations.

The traditional stories are frequently very funny and often use imitation and caricature. Rutherford notes that imitations are traditional pastimes of children at residential Deaf schools but are also seen in skits or entertainments by Deaf adults. Although imitation is often directed at 'others', Rutherford notes that character flaws such as pompousness are targeted, so Deaf people are not immune. Imitation results from careful studying of the targeted people. It often occurs in stories told about schooldays because lessons were often conducted in spoken languages that the Deaf children could not understand and the children were bored in class so had nothing better to do than study the mannerisms of the teachers. It is affirming for a child to be good at imitation and be appreciated by other children for their language skills.

Bahan has drawn attention to the narratives of personal experience, which are central to the storytelling of many Deaf communities. These stories recount things that happened to the signer (or someone like the signer). Bahan has identified three main themes that arise repeatedly: (1) communication, language and values; (2) social prejudice and ignorance; (3) sensory worlds. Exploring these themes allows storytellers and their audiences to understand their cultural heritage through their language heritage, providing insight to the Deaf experience and discovery of Deafhood.

Bahan has also noted that characters may frequently be divided broadly into 'deaf' and 'hearing'. Deaf characters are generally portrayed as Visual-tactile people, signers and 'Us'. The sensory experience of Deaf people occurs repeatedly in stories through references to vision and touch. Deaf people's speaking skills may also be mentioned. Unsuccessful attempts to speak to hearing people can create conflict (for example, getting the wrong drink at a bar) but successful 'deaf' speech can also scare hearing people (for example, a bus driver ignores hearing passengers shouting 'stop!' but comes to a rapid halt when he hears the unusual voice of a Deaf person shouting). There are also many stories referring to the Deaf person's lack of hearing. This can lead to some sort of conflict (such as Deaf youth trying to be cool, cruising round town with their car radio turned up loud believing they are playing hip-hop music, only to be told by a hearing friend that it is a gospel preacher's station) but other stories show the benefits to not being able to hear.

Hearing people in Deaf narratives may be portrayed in a variety of less than flattering ways, and usually as 'Them' in direct contrast to the 'Us' of Deaf people. They are characterised as 'Know-nothings' or well meaning but patronising. They might be bullies who oppress or tease Deaf people, or idiots who never learn despite knowing Deaf people. The 'Hyper-hearing' who react nervously to sound (especially sound made by a Deaf person) are frequent butts of Deaf narratives. The signing skills of hearing people are also lampooned. Hearing people who are 'allies' in Deaf communities tend not to appear in narratives because they do not contribute to the conflict needed to make a good story.

Narratives need not just be single-authored. Rutherford has described the idea of a group narrative in American Sign Language, which fulfils many of the functions of folkloric storytelling for Deaf people and especially Deaf children. It is a Deaf cultural strategy to build linguistic competence by giving the children opportunities to use language in a specific social context. They also learn cultural rules such as understanding and obeying rules of a game, negotiating, co-operating, turn-taking and fulfilment of roles. The storyteller can invite the audience to help create the story. Audience members can volunteer signs, and the storyteller picks and chooses from the suggestions so the audience work collectively to weave the story. This jointly constructed group narrative genre is seen on both sides of the Atlantic. Clive Mason has described a group narrative concerning a battle scene constructed when he was at school in Glasgow in the 1960s. Each night in the dormitories, the children would take turns to be the 'director' of the stories. The director would allocate roles to all the children and then invite them to contribute to his story as he controlled it.

Another widespread genre in some countries is the legend of origins. The Deaf story of the Abbé de l'Epée and the foundation of deaf education have been told many times in Europe and North America. The same is true of the meeting between Thomas Gallaudet and the little deaf girl Alice Cogswell, and how it led to the establishment of deaf education in North America. British Deaf people may be aware of these stories because they have learned about American Deaf history, but they have no direct relevance for British signers. In British sign language (BSL), legends of origin are more likely to be personal narratives of discovery of the individual signer's Deaf identity as they meet other deaf people for the first time, learn sign language and become part of the Deaf community.

Allegorical stories told in sign language may reflect the experience of many Deaf people, while not necessarily referring to deafness. Some of these stories are adapted from traditional stories in hearing society, and some are specific to Deaf communities. There are many BSL versions of *The Ugly Duckling*, in which the duckling is deaf. In some versions (such as Philip Green's moving story), the duckling is explicitly highlighted as being deaf. In other versions, however, (such as the narrative poem by Dorothy Miles) there is no mention of the duckling's deafness, but the implications are so clear that audiences often believe that there is direct reference to it. The duckling's outsider status, combined with its suffering for being different and its final vindication as something beautiful provides a powerful metaphor for Deaf people who grew up feeling outsiders in the hearing world before they found their identity as Deaf. Ben Bahan's *Bird of a Different Feather* is an original ASL composition that has been performed in many other sign languages (with additional specific national characteristics appropriate to each country). In this story, a songbird hatches in a family of eagles. The eagles, finding that the chick cannot be 'cured', try to bring it up as an eagle but it cannot hunt or fly like an eagle. It meets other songbirds, and learns to sing and eat fruit but returns to its eagle family. Eventually it undergoes a cosmetic operation to make its beak more like an eagle's beak, but it is still not an eagle. Additionally, it finds it can no longer sing or eat fruit, and eventually flies away to make its own life. As with so many Deaf allegories, there is no overt mention that the songbird is deaf but audiences immediately understand it to be the case.

Stories may be based on word play, as in the well-known ABC stories created in North America. In ABC stories, the storyteller needs to create a story (or retell a classic) in which each successive sign uses the handshape of letters from the manual alphabet, running from A to Z. In ASL, the letter 'A' is made with a closed fist, the letter 'B' with all the fingers open but together to make a flat hand and 'C' is made with all the fingers curved making a 'C' shape, so the first sign of the story should have a fist handshape, the second sign has a flat handshape and the third has a curved handshape. Bahan (2006) explains how the rules of the stories include:

- Succession (appropriate alphabetical order; consistent rhythm; transition between letters; combination of letters);
- Minimal Deviation (not changing the manual letter to fit the sign or changing the sign to fit the manual letter);
- Use of cohesive devices (role shift; space; gaze; pacing; pausing and phrasing);
- Integrity of story line (make sense; flow; have a plot with conflict; conclusion).

Rutherford (1993) has described other ABC games. In 'fingerspelled/ASL word characterisations' signers make signs with each handshape related to the meaning to show the character of the word spelled. For example, for the word 'golf', the handshape for the letter -g- is used in the sign for a golf tee, the -o- is the handshape showing the golf ball in the tee, the -l- is the swinging golf club that strikes the ball and the -f- shows the ball flying out of sight.

'Fingerspelled/Iconic representation' uses the fingerspelling sequence of handshapes in a way that shows the meaning of the word. For example, l-e-a-f-f-a-l-l-i-n-g has the movement that echoes a falling leaf, the hands bounce while spelling out b-o-u-n-c-i-n-g-b-a-l-l, and r-e-f-l-e-c-t-i-o-n is spelled out by using both hands placed symmetrically against each other to reflect.

These fingerspelling word games are an important part of American Deaf culture and have been adopted in some other countries with one-handed manual alphabets, including Brazil. However, there is no such tradition in other countries, including Britain. Partly, this arises because Britain uses a two-handed manual alphabet that does not lend itself so readily to the games as the one-handed manual alphabets do. However, it also shows cultural differences, so that even countries that do use a one-handed manual alphabet (such as Ireland) have no tradition of these ABC stories.

Form in Creative Sign Language

Signers using creative language to tell stories or perform poems will modify their language in specific ways. Signed narratives are valued for being especially highly visual, so that signers not only say what they are talking about but also actively show it. The language is used to create unusually strong visual images, often through productive signs, using what may be termed 'Highly Iconic Structures' (for example, Sallandre 2006). In these signs, the signer may directly transfer the situation and movement of referents or the form or size of the referent by creating productive signs in which the handshape and movement directly show the appearance of the referents. They may also show transfer of person, in which the signer becomes the directly embodied entity of the character through 'role shift'. In this role shift, the gaze, facial expression, body movements and hand configurations and movements of the signer directly represent those of the character described. Highly Iconic Structures are especially common in narratives. Sallandre reports that highly iconic signs make up only 30 per cent of a prescriptive text such as a recipe but account for 70 per cent of a narrative. Within this construction of the highly iconic structures, there is great scope for exaggeration and caricature, as gaze and facial expression are frequently used to great comic effect.

A further important feature is the use of personification, in which the signer shows the appearance and behaviour of non-humans, as though they were human. Most importantly for sign language narratives, the personification creates Deaf human characteristics for these non-humans. Descriptions of how they use their faces and eyes (central to the Deaf experience), and how they sign are common. June Smith's *Tree* uses facial expression and body movement to show directly how trees feel in all weathers and explains how they communicate through sign language using their branches and twigs as hands and fingers. Richard Carter has shown how the (Deaf) reindeer that pulls the sleigh of the (Deaf) Father Christmas might sign with his antlers, and how a (Deaf) bird on a wire would use its wings to sign to a (Deaf) farmer. Even objects that have no eyes are given them in creative signing. In Dorothy Miles' poem *Autumn*, leaves watch people passing by. John Wilson's untitled signed haiku shows a lift that opens its doors to find that nobody wants to get in. In this very short poem, in which the hands simply function to indicate that the subject is a lift, the face and eyes show the lift looking around eagerly for the people and being deeply disappointed to find nobody there. Each of these examples shows sign language narratives 'doing Deafhood' by showing Deaf audiences what the world would be like if everyone – and everything – was Deaf. Such a vision is strongly empowering to a language and cultural minority.

Sign Language Poetry

It is difficult, and perhaps unnecessary, to draw a clear dividing line between narrative and poetry in any language. Many of the themes and the highly creative linguistic forms may be seen in poetry as they may in narratives. Within poetry, though, the language used is even more clearly the focus of the utterance than it is in narratives, and this is seen in sign languages as much as it is in spoken language. For this reason, sign language poetry can be treated rather more as performance art than as folklore. Sign language poets deliberately manipulate their language, either by unusually regular use of existing features in the language or by creating new signs, so that the language becomes strongly obtrusive (Leech 1969).

As in a lot of other poetry, repetition of elements is a key feature of sign language poems. This repetition may be in the timing and stress of the signs, for example choosing signs of the same length and strength of articulation, or alternating fast and slow movements to create strongly rhythmic signing. Additionally, similar formational features of signs can be selected to create repetitive patterns. Each sign is made of a specific handshape, location, palm and finger orientation and movement path. Poets may select signs that share any of these parameters but it is especially common for poems to contain signs with shared handshapes. For example, in the poem *Five Senses* by Paul Scott, the open flat handshape is used in several signs referring to touch, the closed fist is repeatedly used during the section referring to taste and the open hand with pinched thumb and forefinger is used when describing smell (see Figure 46.1). The patterning of handshapes serves to create feelings of 'stanzas' within the poem.

In Dot Miles' poem *Trio*, however, repetition also carries extra symbolic meaning. This poem, divided into 'Morning', 'Afternoon' and 'Evening', uses the widespread conceptual metaphor *a lifetime is a day* to show the passage of life for a Deaf person. In the stanza 'Morning', the handshapes of the signs are repeatedly open and the signs move outwards; in 'Evening' the handshapes are frequently clawed at the knuckles and the signs move inwards. In BSL, there is a strong correlation between open handshapes and signs having 'positive' implications (for example, 'happy', 'calm' and 'love' all have open handshapes), and also between 'clawed' handshapes and signs with negative implications (for example, 'angry', 'jealous' and 'mean' are all 'clawed'). The poem exploits these symbolic handshape meanings to reflect the positive feelings of happiness and freshness in 'Morning' (and youth) and the more negative feelings of fear and the world closing in on us in 'Evening' (and old age) (see Figure 46.2).

Signs in BSL may be made using one hand or two, and of those signs that are two-handed, both hands frequently have the same handshape and movement. Sign poets will frequently select two-handed signs or create signs that are highly symmetrical, because symmetry brings with it connotations

Open handshapes in Touch

Closed fist handshapes in Taste

'Pinched' handshape
in Smell

**Figure 46.1   Paul Scott signing 'Five Senses', showing different hand-
shapes for each sense**

of beauty, balance and harmony. However, this signed symmetry is usually set across the vertical plane because the arrangements of the arms and hands on the human body make vertically symmetrical signs fairly straightforward to articulate. We have hands and arms on the left and right side of our bodies, so signs can be made that are symmetrical left to right across a vertical plane. It is physically possible to articulate signs across other planes – front to back, diagonal or horizontal, for example – but less physically convenient (Sutton-Spence 2005; Sutton-Spence and Kaneko 2007). In *Trio*, many signs are symmetrical across the vertical plane, creating a highly aesthetic image. The creation of the horizontally symmetrical sign 'twin-trees' in *Morning*, however, very marked and highly noticeable, brings the language to the foreground (see Figure 46.3).

WIND and WIND-DIES using open
handshapes, located off the body

EVENING and OLD using 'clawed'
handshapes located on the body

**Figure 46.2 Dorothy Miles signing 'Trio', using contrasting handshapes
and locations of the signs in 'Morning' and 'Evening'**

TWIN-TREES showing
horizontal symmetry

THREE-OF-US-DOZE
showing vertical
symmetry

**Figure 46.3 Dorothy Miles signing 'Trio', creating highly marked
symmetrical signs**

Sign language poetry is a relatively recent genre that is developing rapidly. Reviewing the styles of poetry of the sign language poetry pioneers (such as Dot Miles, Paul Scott and John Wilson for BSL, and Dot Miles, Clayton Valli and Ella Mae Lentz for ASL) show their forms of poetry changed quite radically over the past few decades. New poets are experimenting with new language techniques, pushing the boundaries of sign languages in novel ways and challenging conventional understandings of what constitutes a sign language poem.

Conclusion

Creativity in sign languages extends through a wide range of signed genres. While the exact form and function of the creativity will vary among different communities, there are many similarities. Creative signing draws heavily on the highly visual aspects of sign languages, emphasising the strong relationship between sign languages and the visual sensory experience of members of Deaf communities. This highly visual language, used skilfully by community members, is entertaining and very enjoyable. It also empowers performers and audiences by educating new members of the community about the cultural rules and realities of their society and by celebrating the world of a collective visual people, enabling them to resist the oppression of the more powerful hearing majority. It also challenges hearing people, with preconceived ideas about what constitutes a language art form, to reassess the potential for language creativity.

Acknowledgements

I am grateful to Paul Scott, Don Read and the BBC for permission to reproduce the images here.

REFERENCES

Bahan, Ben. 2006. Face-to-Face tradition in the American Deaf Community: Dynamics of the teller, the tale and the audience. In H-Driksen Bauman, Jennifer L. Nelson and Heidi M. Rose (eds.) *Signing the Body Poetic*. Berkeley, California: University of California Press. 21–50.

Bauman H-Dirksen, Jennifer L. Nelson and Heidi M. Rose (eds.). 2006. *Signing the Body Poetic*. Berkeley, California: University of California Press.

Finnegan, Ruth. 1977. *Oral Poetry*. Cambridge: Cambridge University Press.

Klima, Edward and Ursula Bellugi. 1979. *Signs of Language*. Cambridge, Massachusetts: Harvard University Press.

Krentz, Christopher. 2006. The camera as printing press: How film has influenced ASL Literature. In H-Diksen Bauman, Jennifer L. Nelson and Heidi M. Rose (eds.) *Signing the Body Poetic*. Berkeley: University of California Press. 51–70.

Ladd, Paddy. 2003. *Understanding Deaf Culture: In Search of Deafhood*. Clevedon: Multilingual Matters.

Lane, Harlan, Robert Hoffmeister and Ben Bahan. 1996. *A Journey into the DEAF-WORLD*. San Diego, California: Dawn Sign Press.

Leech, Geoffrey. 1969. *A Linguistic Guide to English Poetry*. London: Longman.

Padden, Carol and Tom Humphries. 1988. *Deaf in America*. Cambridge, Massachusetts: Harvard University Press.

Peters, Cynthia. 2000. *Deaf American Literature: From Carnival to the Canon*. Washington, D.C.: Gallaudet University Press.

Rose, Heidi M. 1992. A semiotic analysis of artistic American Sign Language and a performance of poetry. *Text and Performance Quarterly* 12: 146–159.

Rutherford, Susan. 1993. *A Study of American Deaf Folklore*. Silver Spring, Maryland: Linstok Press.

Ryan, Stephen. 1993. Let's tell an ASL story. In *Gallaudet University College for Continuing Education: Conference Proceedings, April 22–25, 1993*. Washington, D.C.: Gallaudet University Press. 145–150.

Sallandre, Marie-Anne. 2006. Iconicity and space in French Sign Language. In Maya Hickman and Stephane Robert (eds.) *Space in Languages: Linguistic Systems and Cognitive Categories*. Amsterdam: John Benjamins.

Sutton-Spence, Rachel. 2005. *Analysing Sign Language Poetry*. Basingstoke: Palgrave Macmillan.

Sutton-Spence Rachel and Michiko Kaneko. 2007. Symmetry in Sign Language poetry. *Sign Language Studies* 7: 284–318.

CHAPTER 47

Speech Community
and Beyond

BEN RAMPTON

'Speech community' has been a troubled term, caught in a number of methodological and political cross-currents, and in this chapter I will try to trace some of the most important shifts in meaning since the 1960s. Some of this movement has occurred within the arena of Sociolinguistics itself, but Sociolinguistics has always been more than just a technical activity, and 'speech community' has been especially hard to isolate from the much larger debates that affect our understanding of community as a concept in everyday language and in social science more generally.

   Prior to these changes in conceptualisation, there was a strong tendency to treat people's actions as a mere reflection of their belonging to 'big' communities that pre-existed them, but now there is much more emphasis on the part that here-and-now social action plays in the production of 'small' but new communities, and rather than just concentrating on behaviour at the core, there has been a burst of interest in the flow of people, texts, objects and ideas across local and global networks, as well as in the interaction with 'strangers' inside, outside and at the boundaries of specific groups and institutions. In comparison, scholarship itself is no longer regarded as simply reporting on communities – it also helps to create them, destroy and prevent their inception. To give a clearer idea of these more general changes in perspective and focus, I will suggest that during the 1960s and 1970s (and often much later), treatments of 'speech community' were dominated by a preoccupation with the encounter

Source: The chapter draws on Ben Rampton (1998). Speech community, by Rampton, B., in Verschueren, J., Östman, J., Blommaert, J. and Bulcaen, C. (eds.) *Handbook of Pragmatics* (1998) (Amsterdam/Philadelphia: John Benjamins). A longer version can also be found in *Working Papers in Urban Language and Literacies* at www.kcl.ac.uk/education/wpull.html.

between 'tradition' and 'modernity', while we can make better sense of more recent developments if we refer to the discourses of late/post-modernity.

From the start of sociolinguistic discussion of speech community, the aim has been to show that social organisation and language use are profoundly interwoven, and so when our sense of speech community alters, there are often consequences for the kinds of language use that we attend to. In line with this, I also try to describe important changes in linguistic focus, covering expansions of interest from, for example, competence to ignorance and reflexivity, from use to representation and artful performance, and from regularity to spectacle. I will begin, though, with a comparison of how speech community figured in classic (modernist) research in ethnographic and variationist Sociolinguistics from the 1960s.

'Speech community' in ethnographic and variationist Sociolinguistics from the 1960s

Right from their inception in the 1960s, 'speech community' was a significant concept in both the ethnography of speaking (Gumperz 1962, 1968; Hymes 1972, this volume, Chapter 39) and in variationist Sociolinguistics (Labov 1972).

In the ethnography of speaking, which was rooted in anthropology, membership of a particular speech community was postulated *in the background* as the origin of the social norms that determined the appropriacy of speech, producing social meaning beyond referential intelligibility (Hymes 1972; this volume, Chapter 39; Gumperz 1968: 381). With the emphasis on the complexity of communicative action, on acts and events in their ecology, the ethnography of speaking entailed quite substantial immersion in the fieldwork setting, as well as analysis which treated language as just one among a great many resources for the creation of meaning (Bauman and Sherzer 1974: 89). The practicalities of data elicitation and analysis generally required deep involvement with a relatively small number of informants, and the outcome was likely to be the detailed portrait of an internally differentiated but coherent group, outlining the cultural integrity of distinctive speech practices, as well, sometimes, as the ways in which they were transmitted intergenerationally. Claims about the extent to which the particular group being studied was representative of a larger population tended to be weak (Irvine 1987: 18), and the demands of fieldwork and analysis in this approach generally inhibited any empirical specification of limits to the demographic spread of a particular practice. In line with this, studies in this tradition moved rapidly beyond any technical notion to more intuitive everyday uses of 'community' to describe the settings where their fieldwork was located.

In striking contrast, variationist Sociolinguistics treated 'speech community' as the empirical territory spanned by the patterned variability of a linguistic structure. The multi-layered complexity of communicative action was subordinated to an interest in the social and historical spread, change and maintenance of specific linguistic variables, and survey methods elicited comparative data from quite large numbers of speakers, who often formed a systematic sample from larger populations (Labov 1981; Hudson 1996: 28; Trudgill 1974). The outcome of this was a map of the speech community which could point to its outer boundaries, and which claimed to be able to identify inauthentic members (Labov 1980). At the same time, however, it might only be a handful of linguistic variables that provided the empirical basis for this map (J. Milroy 1992: 61), and this meant that the definition of speech community was very vulnerable to revision by researchers looking at more or other language variables (Kerswill 1994: 26–27). As it became clear that different variables actually had different social distributions, with people in different regions sharing some linguistic features but not others, the meaning of speech community became increasingly item-specific and therefore technical, amounting to not much more than (some aspect of) the socio-linguistic patterning encompassed within the spread of a particular variable and/or its evaluation.

It would be a mistake to try to allocate sociolinguists unambiguously to either of these two approaches, but the logics of ethnographic and variationist enquiry led in different directions, and this has tended to undermine attempts to achieve a unified overall definition of 'speech community' available for use by sociolinguists generally (Hudson 1996: 24–30; Wardhaugh 1986: Chapter 5). Seen at a more abstract level, however, both approaches shared a common orientation to the problematic interface between 'tradition' and 'modernity', and below, I shall try to show that this distinguishes them from recent work.

Frames for Understanding 'Speech Community' – 'Tradition', 'Modernity', and 'Late/Post-Modernity'

The interface between 'tradition' and 'modernity' has been enormously formative for the social sciences, and according to Giddens:

> [S]ociology has its origins in the coming of modernity – in the dissolution of the traditional world and the consolidation of the modern. Exactly what 'traditional' and 'modern' should be taken to mean is a matter of chronic debate. But this much is plain. With the arrival of industrialism, the transfer of millions of people from rural communities to cities, the progressive development of mass democracy, and other quite fundamental

institutional changes, the new world was savagely wrenched away from the old. (1990: 15–16)

In definitions of speech community in the 1960s and 1970s, the encounter between 'tradition' and 'modernity' was often mentioned, and one of the central missions of Sociolinguistics was to make *modern* institutions – especially schools – more hospitable to the diverse and often supposedly *non*-modern populations that they served. In the process, debates about the relationship between children and schools generated a large variety of binary dichotomies, many of which resonated with arguments about the philosophical underpinnings of liberal modernity.[1] These dichotomies ranged across:

modes of expression: vernacular versus standard, oral versus literate, concrete versus abstract, implicit versus explicit, narrative versus argument, metaphorical versus rational, contextualised versus decontextualised, particularistic versus universalistic, grounded in high versus low shared knowledge;

types of social organisation: home versus school, close versus open networks, homogeneous versus heterogeneous, solidarity- versus status-based;

social categories: migrant versus host, minority versus majority, female versus male, working versus middle class.

Sociolinguists often devoted considerable energy to contesting these polarities and the collocational chains that they tended to form (for example, vernacular + oral + narrative + particularistic + close networks + working class + traditional *versus* standard + literate + argument + universalistic + open networks + middle class + modern). Efforts were made to complicate, uncouple and refute these associations, to negate or reverse their valuation as better versus worse (Bauman and Sherzer 1989: xvii; Heath 1982; Hymes 1980: 129–130; Labov 1969; Street 1984), and when tradition and modernity figured in their discussions of 'speech community', Gumperz, Hymes, Fishman and others made deliberate efforts to prevent it from being primarily associated with the 'tradition' side of the 'tradition–modernity' dichotomy. 'Speech community', it was proposed, was a neutral *superordinate* concept, capable of embracing all types of society, from small face-to-face bands to modern nations, the differences between societies could be analysed with lower level concepts like network and role repertoire, and there was resistance to the more ordinary associations of 'community' with notions of mutuality, fellowship or locally based interactive *Gemeinschaft* (Tönnies 1963; Yeo and Yeo 1988). Nevertheless, it was difficult to stop 'speech community' from becoming the framework within which modernity's 'others' were studied, especially when it coalesced with more everyday uses of community.

In research that focuses exclusively on the functioning of modern bureaucratic institutions, community is an unnecessary term, since 'formal organisational criteria can be counted upon to identify and separate the personnel within which relationships, behaviour and attitude are to be studied' (Arensberg 1961: 247) – it is enough to talk of 'middle managers', 'research officers', 'clients', 'patients', 'pupils', and so forth. But where (a) the focus turns to people and groups who don't conform to the expectations of modern institutions, and where (b) there is drive to conceptualise their performance in terms of difference rather than deficit – that is, not just as 'awkward patients', 'dim pupils' – it is difficult to find any term other than community to encompass the diversity of the alternative organisational forms within which these non-standard abilities are held to develop and be well-adapted. In the end, this makes it very hard to hold to the technical/neutral definition of speech community that the early theorists intended, and for a number of reasons (including the fact that it was actually subordinate groups that sociolinguists tended to study), community often came to be associated with the second element in the binary dichotomies above (vernacular, oral modes of expression; close, solitary, home-based networks; minority and working class groups).

At the same time, Sociolinguistics participated in a current of romanticism about the 'other' that ran deep in the social sciences, and along with a 'celebration of everyday oral language' and a suspicion of 'official socialisers' like teachers (Bernstein 1996: Chapter 7),[2] it also often treated community belonging as the prerequisite for *any* valid language use, emphasising shared norms and consensus – key community characteristics – as the condition in which people developed their communicative competence. The existence of internal differentiation was obviously an article of faith, but the assumption was that this was a describable sort of structure (Bauman and Sherzer 1974: 8, 89), and the aim was to describe system-in-grammar and coherence-in-discourse in ways that *accommodated* diversity within the community. In the process, system and coherence retained their position (a) as the most highly prized attributes that analysis could recover, (b) as principal arguments in public advocacy of non-standard varieties, and (c) more generally, as cornerstone modernist values themselves (see Note 2). Pratt calls this cluster of assumptions about system, coherence and socialisation-to-consensual norms the 'linguistics of community' (1987; Barrett 1997; also LePage 1980), and she argues that 'when social division and hierarchy *[were]* studied, the linguist's choice [was] often to imagine separate speech communities with their own boundaries, sovereignty, fraternity and authenticity ... [This gave] rise to a linguistics that [sought] to capture identity, but not the relationality of social differentiation', a linguistics that looked within but not across the 'lines of social differentiation, of class, race, gender, age' (1987: 56, 59, 61). Conflict and misunderstanding were certainly recognised, but they were thought to occur *in the gap* between integrated cultural and linguistic systems. The gap itself was seen as (merely) the place for educational interventions designed to help the proponents of different systems to understand each other and adjust, not as a site where people improvised practices and relationships that deserved sociolinguistic study in themselves.

The *development* of alternatives to the 'linguistics of community' can be linked to the discourses of late/post-modernity,[3] and among these, 'social constructionism' has been particularly influential. Instead of arguing that our worlds are the product of forces that few of us either control or comprehend, social constructionism takes the view that human reality is extensively reproduced, contested and created anew in the socially and historically specific activities of everyday life (Berger and Luckmann 1966; Giddens 1984),[4] and this facilitates the development of two more recent approaches to the analysis of community. The first of these – the 'communities of practice' perspective – entails a close-up analysis of face-to-face interaction in relatively focussed settings and consolidated social relationships where feedback tends to draw conduct into close conformity with dominant expectations. The second – the 'language ideologies' approach – looks at how a sense of community itself gets constructed, focusing on the way it develops and operates as an ideological product and a semiotic sign.[5] These two perspectives are broadly compatible, but in the work on language ideologies, there is a more insistent sense of 'otherness' and of life *without* 'community'. This has opened the door, first to recognition of the inherent bias towards rather well-focussed situations in a number of major sociolinguistic concepts themselves, and second, to attempts to develop conceptual tools better suited to analysis of movement in diffuse, indeterminate and border territories. I shall take each of these perspectives in turn and then outline their complementarity, before concluding with an overview of the challenge to modernist concepts in Sociolinguistics.

Communities of practice (CofP)

Right from the outset, the adoption of a communities of practice perspective in Sociolinguistics has been linked to a rejection of the tendency in variationist survey research to treat speakers as if they are 'assembled out of independent modules: [for example] part European American, part female, part middle-aged, part feminist, part intellectual' (Eckert and McGonnell-Ginet 1992: 471; 1999: 190–191). Rather than seeing the identities of men and women – or 'ethnics' and 'mainstreamers' – as being defined and determined by biological or cultural inheritance, CofP research is concerned with the way in which these and other identities take shape within activities where constraints and opportunities are unequally distributed, positioning the participants differently within environments that are nevertheless still shared quite extensively. Rather than being just an aggregation of 'tickbox' social variables, speakers are regarded as 'embodied, situated and social' (New London Group 1996: 82), and there is an interest in how their notionally multiple memberships and identities are constructed and integrated in social practice.

In the formal definition of a community of practice (Holmes and Meyerhoff 1999; Wenger 1998), there is mutual engagement among the participants, a joint negotiated enterprise, and a shared repertoire of negotiable resources accumulated over time, and this covers a wide range of social relationships of varying duration – for example, unions, trades, boards of directors, marriages, bowling teams, classrooms (cf. Lave and Wenger 1991: 98; Eckert and McGonnell-Ginet 1992). In fact, there are a number of ways in which CofP research retains links with the ethnography of speaking as outlined above in ethnographic and variationist Sociolinguistics from the 1960s, although the shift of focus from 'speech' to 'practice' is significant, since speech loses some of its centrality and empirical research quite often attends more intensively to situated activity as a multi-modal process involving visual, gestural and proxemic channels as well as the physical environment, material artefacts and other objects (Goodwin 1981; Hanks 1996: Chapter 11; McDermott, Gospodinoff and Aron 1978). This dovetails with the development of micro-ethnography as an alternative to traditional anthropological ethnography – itself extensively problematised in late modernity (Clifford 1983; Trueba and Wright 1981) – and more generally, at times when there is a feeling that social totality has been 'dissipated into a series of randomly emerging, shifting and evanescent islands of order' (Z. Bauman 1992: 189), the move to 'communities of practice' as a key unit of analysis tunes well with late modern uncertainty about grand theoretical totalisations (Z. Bauman 1992: 65). There are firmer limits than before on the level of abstraction to which the analyst can take the term 'community', and an orientation to the lived texture of situated experience prohibits its extension to cover to all forms of social organisation, as intended in the formulations of 'speech community' by Gumperz and Fishman. 'Community' as a concept is also much less likely to slip towards the folk/vernacular side of the tradition–modernity divide, and in fact notions from the discourse of 'communities of practice' (and 'situated learning') are not only used to analyse workplace interaction but also have currency in 'fast capitalist' management theory (Barton and Tusting 2005; Gee et al. 1996: 65 et passim).

However, even though the ongoing production of community involves the partial coordination of heterogeneous strategies and resources, as well as an unending process of improvisation within micro-contexts that are continuously shifting (Hanks 1991: 16, 20), there is a temptation in CofP research to prioritise relations *within* groups rather than *between* or *across*. If one steps back from the micro-scopic flow, 'community' puts principal emphasis on the repetitive affirmation of relatively durable social ties in practical activity, rather than their collapse, rupture or irrelevance. Although there is nothing that makes them mutually exclusive (see for example, Bucholtz 1999, this volume, Chapter 15), attention tends more to be given to movement inside the horizons of a particular type of institutional activity (Lave and Wenger 1991: 98), to its evolving reproduction, to the local use of resources, and to the socialisation, 'prime' and 'eventide' of its *members*, than to commodity exchange between communities, their plans for territorial expansion, their treatment of intruders and the construction, policing or invasion of their boundaries. The relationship between different communities of practice is certainly identified as an important issue, and there is extensive recognition that particular communities of practice are affected by larger social and historical processes (Eckert and McConnell-Ginet 1992, 1999; Goodwin 1994; Lave and Wenger 1991: 70, 92, 122). Even so, of itself the CofP perspective says relatively little about how language and social life are influenced by, for example, a fear of outsiders, a longing for elsewhere, or more generally by the profile that particular groups and communities might have when seen from outside or far off (Bergvall 1999). Putting it a little differently, 'community' can't only be seen as co-participation in locally embedded practice – analysis also has to extend to the way in which 'community' (and other notionally collective entities) serves as a symbol and sign itself, and at this point it is worth referring to the work on language ideologies.

Language Ideologies

There has been a steadily growing recognition in linguistic anthropology that the tools of face-to-face analysis are limited when it comes to

> the ways in which linguistic practices contribute to the reproduction and legitimation of hierarchy in larger social institutions such as the state, or about the ways in which speech communities are linked to broader political economic structures ... Similarly, within this framework it has been difficult to analyze adequately the processes of mass-mediated communication that often connect disparate communities and that are increasingly of interest in social theory. (Gal and Woolard 1995: 134–135)

This is a view that has fed into the development of research on language ideologies (see Blommaert 1999; Gal and Irvine 1995: 987; Kroskrity 2004; Schieffelin, Woolard and Kroskrity 1998; Woolard and Schieffelin 1994), and one of the main aims here is to examine the ways in which a spread of people gets constituted as a 'community' in the first place, how 'linguistic units come to be linked with social units', languages with peoples (Gal and Irvine 1995: 970).

Anderson's (1983) work on the role that mass-produced print genres played in the 'imagining' and production of nation-states as communities has been a major inspiration, and in this way, late modern sensitivity in Sociolinguistics to the problems of 'totalising' over-generalisation about communities and social groups take an important step further than the CofP perspective. In the CofP perspective, presuppositions about the reality and force of generalised categories like 'man', 'woman' or 'society' are treated as a source of contamination to avoid in rigorous empirical analysis, but in the work on language ideologies, totalising ideas are actually treated as focal objects of analysis themselves, and there are accounts of the social, political and discursive processes involved in both the historical and contemporary institutionalisation of 'communal' entities like nation-states and autonomous languages.

Within this, the political history and dynamics of language scholarship itself are a major interest. The role that language scholarship and its 'philological incendiaries' (Anderson 1983: 81) played in the development of the nineteenth-century European nation-state has been long and widely recognised, as has the important role that it has played in the expansion and organisation of empires (Anderson 1983; Blommaert 1999; Collins 1998: 5, 60; Gal and Irvine 1995; Hymes 1980; Pratt 1987; Robins 1979: Chapters 6 and 7; Said 1978). Within these processes of language and identity construction, research and politics – knowledge and power – have often been mutually endorsing. The idea of autonomous languages free from agency and individual intervention meshed with the nineteenth century differentiation of peoples in terms of spiritual essences (Gal and Irvine 1995; Taylor 1990), while much more recently, the post-war British and American commodification and export of English has been aided by models which treat language (a) as an isolable structural entity that is much more aligned with the universals of mind than anchored in the specifics of culture, but that is nevertheless (b) guaranteed authentic only in and by 'native speakers' (cf. Phillipson 1992; Pennycook 1994).

Although the processes and settings addressed in language ideology research are typically more macro – larger, slower, longer or more wide-reaching – than those studied within the CofP framework, both seek to provide accounts of activity that are properly situated, and in this regard, they are clearly compatible. Furthermore, ideology isn't just confined to policies, media texts and public documents and so on – it also lives and breathes in everyday activity (Rampton 1995: Chapter 12; Vološinov 1973: Part II Chapter 3; Williams 1977). So it is worth considering the ways in which these perspectives come together.

Language Ideology in Everyday Practice

Beyond the sketch of it provided above, language ideology research differs from the CofP approach in emphasising boundaries of exclusion and the ways in which representations of the 'other' contribute to the ideological construction of 'us'. Some of the stereotyped 'others' portrayed or implied in discourse, or evoked, for example, through stylised code-switching, may be constructed as objects of fear, contempt and/or charity (Blommaert and Verschueren 1998; Hinnenkamp 1987), while others may be produced as objects of desire, fashion accoutrements and/or marketised life-style options, with 'authenticity' becoming as much an issue of commodity branding as a matter of ethnic roots (Hill 1993, 1995; K. Hall 1995: 201–203, this volume, Chapter 16; Urciuoli 1996). Indeed, pushing this a little further, as well as 'them for you', discourse can also construct 'us for you', as revealed in critical discourse analyses of conversationalisation in advertising and official communications (Fairclough 1995). But this kind of interest in the (more and less) explicit ideological *representation* of identities, ingroups and outgroups need not exclude attention to the (more and less) tacit interactional *enactment* of identities and groups emphasised in CofP, and indeed, among other lines of work (for example, Barton and Tusting 2005), this combination of perspectives is often entailed in the research on code-switching just alluded to above.

Studies of code-switching have shown that when someone switches to a different language in everyday interaction, they often conjure a different group identity or persona, altering their relationship with the other participants. These shifts are inextricably bound into the interactional enactment of specific activities and social relations, but at the same time, the symbolism of the change of code often works ideologically, 'serv[ing] as the rallying point for interest group sharing', 'act[ing] as [a] powerful instrument...of persuasion in everyday communicative situations for participants who share [the] values [of the group that is thereby indexed]' (Gumperz and Cook-Gumperz 1982). Traditionally, research on code-switching has looked at how bilingual speakers move between the different language-marked identities that they bring to the interaction from their prior experience growing up in minority communities amidst dominant institutions, but if we follow the logic of social constructionism, the interplay between practice and representation in code choice may carry further, challenging or reshaping inherited perceptions of community and developing new forms of solidarity, temporarily at least. This can be seen in research on 'language crossing' (Rampton this volume), which is centrally concerned with the manner and extent to which prevailing ideologies of language, ethnicity and race do or don't get contested when members of the dominant group switch into minority speech varieties in interaction (Cutler 1999, this volume; Hewitt 1986; Rampton 1995, 1999, this volume). In fact, this interest in communicative practice destabilising traditional/established perceptions of belonging coincides with some rather general experiences of transnational globalisation:

> everywhere, cultural identities are emerging which are not fixed, but poised, *in transition* between different positions; which draw on different cultural traditions at the same time; and which are the product of those complicated crossovers and cultural mixes which are increasingly common in a globalised world ... [People with experience of living in two places] are not and will never be *unified* in the old sense, because they are irrevocably the product of several interlocking histories and cultures, belong at one and the same time to several 'homes' (and to no one particular 'home'). People belonging to such *cultures of hybridity* have had to renounce the dream or ambition of rediscovering any kind of 'lost' cultural purity, or ethnic absolutism. They are irrevocably *translated...'*. (Hall 1992: 310)

From the 'Linguistics of Community' to the 'Linguistics of Contact'

So neither contemporary social experience nor contemporary social theory provide a warrant for the overwhelming priority that linguistics has traditionally accorded to the idea of a speech community as a group of people – 'native speakers' indeed – producing systematic language and coherent discourse as a result of their early socialisation into consensual norms. Even though linguistics can itself be said to have emerged through the experience of contact with other groups and languages (Hymes 1980: 55; Robins 1979; Vološinov 1973: Part II, Chapter 2; Williams 1977), disorderly hybridity and mixing have been overwhelmingly repressed, either regularised and idealised out (as in Chomskyan approaches), or analysed in ways that discovered system and rationality beneath the surface (modernist Sociolinguistics). Recent research, however, interrogates these ideas about community: in the CofP approach, a real but relatively limited concept of 'community' is empirically instantiated in fairly small-scale, local activities; in language ideology research, 'community' is analysed as a political construct; and the two come together in sociolinguistic studies of how the symbolic connotations (or 'indexical' meanings) of the language that people use in everyday interaction do and don't connect with prevailing assumptions about social identities, positions, groups, hierarchies and so on.

This problematisation of the traditional notion of speech community certainly doesn't signal a loss of empirical interest in the larger social, historical and geographical arenas in which language circulates (see Blommaert 2004; Scollon and Scollon 2004). But for this, 'speech community' drops from its traditional position as the most general entity in sociolinguistic description, replaced by a more differentiating vocabulary which includes 'institutions', 'media' and 'networks', this latter term being a particularly flexible concept capable of describing the social links involved in, for example, quite tightly clustered activities of the CofP-type, much more widely dispersed transnational diaspora, and the very varied paths through which language, texts and practices circulate.

In fact, the conceptual re-tooling now required in Sociolinguistics stretches much further than the replacement of 'speech community' with 'networks' and 'institutions'. As already noted, although they are certainly not the 'whole story', randomness and disorder have become much more important in recent social theory, and instead of trying to define the core features of any social group or institution, there is major interest now in the experience of being in transition between places, institutions and groups, in the flows of people, knowledge, texts and objects across social and geographical space, in the boundaries of inclusion and exclusion, in fragmentation, indeterminacy and ambivalence (Clifford 1992; Hannerz 1990). In fact, following Pratt (1987), we could describe the reorientation that this demands as a move from the 'linguistics of community' to a 'linguistics of contact'.[6]

So, for example, with the experience of anomalous social difference now treated as a central rather than subsidiary characteristic of contemporary life, there are grounds for questioning the significance of 'negotiation' as the central principle in interaction. In Barth's view, for instance,

> '[n]egotiation' suggests a degree of conflict of interests ... within a framework of shared understandings[, but ... t]he disorder entailed in ... religious, social, ethnic, class and cultural pluralism [sometimes ...] goes far beyond what can be retrieved as ambiguities of interest, relevance, and identity resolved through negotiation. (1992: 27)

Therefore, instead of treating shared knowledge and common ground as something that interactants simply fall back in moments of difficulty, the initial identification of any common ground available as a starting point itself needs to be seen as a major task (Barrett 1997: 188–191; Gee 1999: 15ff). In line with this, the traditional priority given to 'competence' looks over-optimistic, and instead, ignorance itself becomes a substantive issue for theory and description, not just a technical problem contracted out to the applied linguistics of language teaching. The salience of *non*-shared knowledge increases the significance of 'knowing one's own ignorance, knowing that others know something else, knowing whom to believe, developing a notion of the potentially knowable' (Hannerz 1992: 45; Rampton 1997), and as well as not being able to take cooperation and mutual understanding for granted, winning and holding attention – having 'a voice' – also needs to be seen as a challenge.

When hegemonic assumptions about smooth cooperative negotiation being the normal condition for interaction are disrupted in this way, attention necessarily also turns to the different ways in which people reflect meta-linguistically and meta-culturally on the shape of their own discourse and its reception by others (Bauman and Briggs 1990, this volume, Chapter 41; Gal and Irvine 1995: 973; Urciuoli 1996; Hannerz 1992: 44). In fact, linguistic reflexivity (or 'metapragmatic awareness') is increasingly seen as a crucial feature in all language use, and an interest in *stylised* and *artful performance,* where there is heightened awareness of both the act of expression and the performer (Bauman and Briggs 1990, this volume, Chapter 41; Rampton 1999) is now moving from the margins to the centre of Sociolinguistics. In the process, tacit, *unself-conscious* language use is unseated from the throne it has occupied in Sociolinguistics for the past 30 years,[7] and the premium that variationist Sociolinguistics has always put on the unconscious and the repetitive looks rather 'Fordist'.[8] In fact, Zygmunt Bauman suggests that in late modernity, '[s]ignificance and numbers have parted ways... statistically insignificant phenomena may prove to be decisive' (1992: 192), and if he is correct, then our focus needs to extend beyond regularity, consistency and system to the unusual and *spectacular.* To analyse this, we need a conceptualisation of language in psychological and social process that is rather different from, for example, Labov's, but in fact there are resources quite close at hand, first in the linguistics of practice rather than in the linguistics of system, and second in the shift from 'variation' to 'transposition' as a way of envisaging linguistic movement across settings, time and space.

The linguistics of practice has a considerable pedigree (Hanks 1996; Verschueren 1999), but the key point here lies in the priority given to situated action in the relationship between language and language use. Instead of seeing language use simply as system output, *language* as a set of social conventions or mental structures is reduced to being just one among a number of semiotic resources available for local text production and interpretation. Instead of the system itself being viewed as the main carrier of meaning, meaning is analysed as a process of here-and-now inferencing, ranging across all kinds of percept, sign and knowledge. By definition, spectacular texts rupture expectations of regularity and co-occurrence, but since we are always plugging holes with whatever we can gather from the contingent links between different semiotic modes and levels anyway, that is obviously not fatal.

Once one treats language as playing only a subsidiary part in meaning, and once one says that local and historical context play a constitutive rather than ancillary role in communication, then it is also difficult to see *variation* as an adequate frame for analysing communicative processes across social space and time. Modernist sociolinguists have taken the systematicity of language for granted, and seen it as their task to describe the parts and properties of the system that adjust to different situations. But if you're interested in situated meaning and you see people as getting to this through immersion in all the contingent particularities of a given context, then the first thing you have to do if you want to understand communication across time and space is to try to work out how people construct semiotic objects that will hold together long enough to carry over from one context to the next, going on after that to look at what people make of it the other end. The key words here are <u>entex</u>tualisation, *trans*position and *re*contextualisation (Bauman and Briggs 1990, this volume, Chapter 41; Silverstein and Urban 1996), and again, these are concepts that one can usefully use to study the spectacular. If a spectacular practice or event is actually significant, then obviously it can't be just done once and forgotten, and there has to be some record or memory of it which gets circulated over time and space. With transposition rather than variation as a conceptual framework, one looks beyond the producer's communicative competence and their flexible-but-durable underlying disposition to (a) the multiple people and processes involved in the design or selection of textual 'projectiles' which have some hope of travelling across settings, (b) to the alteration and revaluation of texts in 'transportation', and (c) to their embedding in new contexts. Overall, there is a major expansion of sociolinguistic interest here, from the *production* of language and text *within* specific settings to the *projection* of language and text *across* settings or from the 'use-value' to the 'exchange-value' of language practices.

As flourishing interest in 'communities of practice' clearly demonstrates, late modern Sociolinguistics certainly hasn't abandoned the interest in the kind of regular and consensual phenomena and processes that were brought together under the banner of 'speech community' and that preoccupied its modernist forebears. But these can no longer be taken for granted or prioritised, neglecting the potential sociolinguistic significance of what's hybrid, disorientating, uncertain, unusual or in transition, and Sociolinguistics is now engaged in developing concepts, topics and methods that can do justice to both the expected *and* the exceptional. In doing so, Sociolinguistics is upgrading its capacity to understand the dynamics of language and communication in contemporary culture, and holding open the door for further distinctive contributions to wider debate in the humanities and social sciences.

NOTES

1. The liberal tradition is complex and contested, but among other things, it can be characterised as involving:
   a. a strong sense of reason as impartiality, with the reasoner standing 'apart from his own emotions, desires and interests ... abstracting ... away from the concrete situation' (Frazer and Lacey 1993: 48);
   b. a belief that public and private realms should be clearly separated, with state activity limited to the public sphere and human diversity and difference regarded as private (Frazer and Lacey 1993: 47);
   c. an a-historical and 'disembodied' view of the individual, seen as having a 'moral primacy ... against the claims of any social collectivity' (Gray 1986: x) and grounded in the 'presocial or transcendent features of human beings' (Frazer and Lacey 1993: 45);
   d. an insistence that the legitimacy of the state be based on consent and on a public and universal conception of law committed to rationality (Frazer and Lacey 1993: 49–50);
   e. a conviction that social reality is knowable, and that social policy and technology might be used to ameliorate poverty, unhappiness and other ills (Frazer and Lacey 1993: 50).
   Within Sociolinguistics, these values have been at issue in the debates about concrete vs. abstract etc. modes of expression, in disputes about the extent to which school and other institutions should recognise different home cultures, in the argument with Chomsky, in the prioritisation of system and coherence, and lastly, in sociolinguistics' commitment to social intervention. (For fuller discussions of liberal modernity relevant to Sociolinguistics, cf. Scollon and Scollon 1995: Chapter 6; Collins 1998; Heller 1999; Rampton 2006).
2. In an account of Sociolinguistics and other social sciences, Bernstein discusses the influence of ideas about 'competence', which he characterises as follows:
   The social logic of the concept competence may reveal:
   1. an announcement of the universal democracy of acquisition. All are inherently competent. There is no deficit.
   2. the individual as *active* and *creative* in the construction of a *valid* world of meaning and practice. There can only be *differences* between such worlds, meanings and practices
   3. a celebration of everyday, oral language use and a suspicion of specialised languages
   4. official socialisers are suspect, for acquisition is a tacit, invisible act, not subject to public regulation or, perhaps, not primarily acquired through such regulation
   5. a critique of hierarchical relations, where domination is replaced by facilitation and imposition by accommodation. (1996: 150)
3. Late/post-modernity is generally interpreted in at least two ways (cf. Frazer and Lacey 1993; Rampton 2006: Chapter 1). One line argues for the emergence of a *new perspective*, abandoning the liberal project of rationality together with the hope that social science can understand and harness the laws of social life – the values of individuality, freedom and equality are themselves regarded as biased in the interests of powerful groups, and 'grand theories' which make claims to 'truth' are either treated sceptically or seen as repressive

instruments of power. The other perspective proposes that Western societies are actually *in a new globalised era*, profoundly affected, for example, by information technologies, by cheap travel and migration, by a decline in traditional political institutions, by the rise of new social movements.

4. There is a strong case that this actually has rather deep roots in Sociolinguistics (Bauman and Sherzer 1974: 8, 1989: xvii–xix; Halliday 1978: 169–70; Sapir [1931] 1949:104), though it is only relatively recently that agent- and practice-centred perspectives have become mainstream orthodoxy.

5. Although they did not become central to Sociolinguistics at the time, precedents for both of these conceptions of community can be found in the 1960s and 1970s – on the former, see for example, Hymes (1972: 54), this volume, Chapter 39; Fishman (1972: 23), and on the latter, see for example, Gumperz (1962: 34); Fishman (1972: 23).

6. See also the paradigm-shifting work of LePage and Tabouret-Keller (1985).

7. In Bakhtin's terms, 'direct unmediated discourse, directed exclusively towards its referential object, as an expression of the speaker's ultimate semantic authority', loses its supremacy, making way instead for 'doublevoicing', where there is an uneasiness in speech produced by its penetration by other people's talk (1984).

8. Gee et al. characterise Fordism as follows: '[w]orkers, hired from the head down had only to follow directions and mechanically carry out a rather meaningless piece of a process they did not need to understand as a whole, and certainly did not control' (1996: 26).

REFERENCES

Anderson, B. 1983. *Imagined Communities: Reflections on the Origin and Spread of Nationalism*. London: Verso.

Arensberg, C. 1961. The community as object and sample. *American Anthropologist* 63: 241–264.

Bakhtin, M. 1984. *Problems in Dostoevsky's Poetics*. Minneapolis, Minnesota: University of Minnesota Press.

Barrett, R. 1997. The 'Homo-genius' speech community. In A. Livia and Kira Hall (eds.) *Queerly Phrased: Language, Gender and Sexuality*. Oxford: Oxford University Press. 181–201.

Barth, F. 1992. Towards greater naturalism in conceptualising societies. In A. Kuper (ed.) *Conceptualising Society*. London: Routledge. 17–33.

Barton, D. and K. Tusting (eds.). 2005. *Beyond Communities of Practice*. Cambridge: Cambridge University Press.

Bauman, R. and C. L. Briggs. 1990. Poetics and performance as critical perspectives on language and social life. *Annual Review of Anthropology*. 19: 59–88.

Bauman, R. and J. Sherzer (eds.). 1974. *Explorations in the Ethnography of Speaking*. Cambridge: Cambridge University Press.

Bauman, R. and J. Sherzer. 1989. Introduction to the second edition. In R. Bauman and J. Sherzer (eds.) *Explorations in the Ethnography of Speaking*. 2nd edition. Cambridge: Cambridge University Press. ix–xxvii.

Bauman, Z. 1992. *Intimations of Post-modernity*. London: Routledge.

Berger, P. and T. Luckmann. 1966. *The Social Construction of Reality*. Harmondsworth: Penguin.

Bergvall, V. 1999. Toward a comprehensive theory of language and gender. *Language in Society* 28: 273–294.

Bernstein, B. 1996. Sociolinguistics: A personal view. In *Pedagogy, Symbolic Control and Identity*. London: Taylor & Francis. 147–156.

Blommaert, J. (ed.). 1999. *Language Ideological Debates*. Berlin: Mouton de Gruyter.

Blommaert, J. 2004. *Discourse: A Critical Introduction*. Cambridge: Cambridge University Press.

Blommaert, J. and J. Verschueren. 1998. *Debating Diversity: Analysing the Discourse of Tolerance*. London: Routledge.

Bucholtz, M. 1999. 'Why be normal?': Language and identity practice in a community of nerd girls. *Language in Society* 28: 203–223.

Clifford, J. 1983. On ethnographic authority. *Representations* 1:118–46.

Clifford, J. 1992. Travelling cultures. In L. Grossberg, C. Nelson, P. Treichler (eds.) *Cultural Studies*. London: Routledge. 96–116.

Collins J. 1998. *Understanding Tolowa Histories: Western Hegemonies and Native American Responses*. London: Routledge.

Cutler, C. 1999. Yorkville crossing: White teens, hip hop and African American English. *Journal of Sociolinguistics* 3: 428–442. [Reprinted in R. Harris and B. Rampton (eds.). 2003. *The Language, Ethnicity and Race Reader*. London: Routledge. 314–327.]

Eckert, P. and S. McConnell-Ginet. 1992. Think practically and look locally: Language and gender as community-based practice. *Annual Review of Anthropology*. 21: 461–490.

Eckert, P. and S. McConnell-Ginet. 1999. New generalisations and explanations in language and gender research. *Language in Society*. 28: 185–201.

Fairclough, N. 1995. *Critical Discourse Analysis*. London: Longman.

Fishman, J. 1972. *The Sociology of Language*. Rowley, Massachusetts: Newbury House.

Frazer, E. and N. Lacey. 1993. *The Politics of Community*. Hemel Hempstead: Harvester Wheatsheaf..

Gal, S. and J. Irvine. 1995. The boundaries of languages and disciplines: How ideologies construct difference. *Social Research* 62: 967–1001.

Gal, S. and K. Woolard. 1995. Constructing languages and publics: Authority and representation. *Pragmatics* 5: 129–138.

Gee, J. 1999. *An Introduction to Discourse Analysis*. London: Routledge.

Gee, J., G. Hull and C. Lankshear. 1996. *The New Work Order: Behind the Language of the New Capitalism*. Sydney: Westview Press.

Giddens, A. 1984. *The Constitution of Society*. Cambridge: Polity.

Giddens, A. 1990. *Social Theory and Modern Sociology*. Cambridge: Polity.

Goodwin, C. 1981. *Conversational Organisation: Interaction between Speakers and Hearers*. New York: Academic Press.

Goodwin, C. 1994. Professional vision. *American Anthropologist*. 96: 606–633.

Gray, J. 1986. *Liberalism*. Milton Keynes: Open University Press.

Gumperz, J. J. 1962. Types of linguistic community. *Anthropological Linguistics* 4: 28–40.

Gumperz, J. J. 1968. The speech community. In *International Encyclopedia of the Social Sciences*. London: Macmillan. 381–386.

Gumperz, J. J. and J. Cook-Gumperz 1982. Introduction: Language and the communication of social identity. In J. J. Gumperz (ed.) *Language and Social Identity*. Cambridge: Cambridge University Press. 1–21.

Hall, K. 1995. Lip service on the fantasy lines. In K. Hall and M. Bucholtz (eds.) *Gender Articulated*. London: Routledge. 183–216.

Hall, S. 1992. The question of cultural identity. In S. Hall, D. Held and T. McGrew (eds.) *Modernity and its Futures*. Cambridge: Polity. 274–316.

Halliday, M.A. K. 1978. *Language as Social Semiotic*. London: Edward Arnold.

Hanks, W. 1991. Foreword. In J. Lave and E. Wenger. *Situated Learning: Legitimate Peripheral Participation*. Cambridge: CUP. 13–24.

Hanks, W. 1996. *Language and Communicative Practices*. Boulder, Colorado: Westview Press.

Hannerz, U. 1990. Cosmopolitans and locals in world culture. *Theory, Culture and Society* 7: 237–251.

Hannerz, U. 1992. *Cultural Complexity: Studies in the Social Organisation of Meaning*. New York: Columbia University Press.

Heath, S. 1982. What no bedtime story means. *Language in Society* 11: 49–76.

Heller, M. 1999. *Linguistic Minorities and Modernity: A Sociolinguistic Ethnography*. London: Longman.

Hewitt, R. 1986. *White Talk Black Talk*. Cambridge: Cambridge University Press.

Hill, J. 1993. Hasta la vista, baby: Anglo Spanish in the American Southwest. *Critique of Anthropology* 13: 145–176.

Hill, J. 1995. Junk Spanish, covert racism, and the (leaky) boundary between public and private spheres. *Pragmatics* 5: 197–212.

Hinnenkamp, V. 1987. Foreigner talk, code-switching and the concept of trouble. In K. Knapp, W. Enninger and A. Knapp-Potthoff (eds.) *Analysing Intercultural Communication*. Amsterdam: Mouton de Gruyter. 137–180.

Holmes, J. and M. Myerhoff. 1999. The community of practice: Theories and methodologies in language and gender research. *Language in Society* 28: 173–183

Hudson, R.A. 1996. *Sociolinguistics*. 2nd edition. Cambridge: Cambridge University Press.

Hymes, D. 1972. Models of the interaction of language and social life. In J.J. Gumperz and D. Hymes (eds.) *Directions in Sociolinguistics*. Oxford: Blackwell. 35–71.

Hymes, D. 1980. *Language in Education: Ethnolinguistic Essays*. Washington, D.C.: Centre for Applied Linguistics.

Irvine, J. 1987. Domains of description in the ethnography of speaking: A retrospective on the 'speech community'. Working Papers and Proceedings of the Centre of Psychosocial Studies 11. Illinois: University of Chicago. 13–24.

Kerswill, P. 1994. *Dialects Converging: Rural Speech in Urban Norway*. Oxford: Clarendon Press.

Kroskrity, P. V. 2004. Language ideologies. In A. Duranti (ed.) *A Companion to Linguistic Anthropology*. Oxford: Blackwell. 496–517.

Labov, W. 1969. The logic of non-standard English. *Georgetown Monographs on Language and Linguistics* 22: 134–155.

Labov, W. 1972. The reflection of social processes in linguistic structures. In *Sociolinguistic Patterns*. Oxford: Blackwell. 110–121.

Labov, W. 1980. Is there a creole speech community? In A. Valdman and A Highfield (eds.) *Theoretical Orientations in Creole Studies*. New York: Academic Press. 389–424.

Labov, W. 1981. Field methods used by the project on linguistic change and variation. Sociolinguistic Working Paper 81. Austin: South Western Educational Development Laboratory.

Lave, J. and E. Wenger. 1991. *Situated Learning: Legitimate Peripheral Participation*. Cambridge: Cambridge University Press.

LePage, R. 1980. Projection, focusing and diffusion. York Papers in Linguistics 9.

LePage, R. and A. Tabouret-Keller. 1985. *Acts of Identity*. Cambridge: Cambridge University Press.

McDermott, R., K. Gospodinoff and J. Aron. 1978. Criteria for an ethnographically adequate description of concerted activities and their contexts. *Semiotica*. 24: 245–275.

Milroy, J. 1992. *Linguistic Variation and Change*. Oxford: Blackwell.

New London Group. 1996. A pedagogy of multiliteracies: Designing social futures. *Harvard Educational Review*. 66: 60–92.

Pennycook, A. 1994. *The Cultural Politics of English as an International Language*. London: Longman.

Phillipson, R. 1992. *Linguistic Imperialism*. Oxford: Oxford University Press.

Pratt, M. L. 1987. Linguistic utopias. In N. Fabb, D. Attridge, A. Durant and C. MacCabe (eds.) *The Linguistics of Writing*. Manchester: Manchester University Press. 48–66.

Rampton, B. 1995. Crossing: Language and Ethnicity among Adolescents. London: Longman. [2nd edition 2005. Manchester: St Jerome Press.]

Rampton, B. 1997. A sociolinguistic perspective on L2 communication strategies. In G. Kasper and E. Kellerman (eds.) *Communication Strategies: Psycholinguistic and Sociolinguistic Perspectives*. London: Longman. 279–303.

Rampton, B. (ed.). 1999. Styling the Other. *Special issue of Journal of Sociolinguistics* 3(4).

Rampton, B. 2006. *Language in Late Modernity: Interaction in an Urban School*. Cambridge: Cambridge University Press.

Robins, R. H. 1979. *A Short History of Linguistics*. London: Longman.

Said, E. 1978. *Orientalism*. Harmondsworth: Penguin.

Sapir, E. 1949 [1931]. Communication. In D. Mandelbaum (ed.) *Edward Sapir: Selected Writings in Language, Culture and Personality*. Berkeley, California: California University Press. 104–109.

Scollon R. and S. Scollon. 1995. *Intercultural Communication*. Oxford: Blackwell.

Scollon, R. and S. Scollon. 2004. *Nexus Analysis*. London: Routledge.

Schieffelin, B., K. Woolard and P. Kroskrity (eds.). 1998. *Language Ideologies: Practice and Theory*. Oxford: Oxford University Press.

Silverstein, M. and G. Urban (eds.). 1996. *Natural Histories of Discourse*. Cambridge: Cambridge University Press.

Street, B. 1984. *Literacy in Theory and Practice*. Cambridge: Cambridge University Press.

Taylor, T. 1990. Which is to be master? The institutionalisation of authority in the science of language. In J. Joseph and T. Taylor (eds.) *Ideologies of Language*. London: Routledge. 9–26.

Tönnies, F. 1963. *Community and Society: Gemeinschaft und Gesellschaft*. New York: Harper Row.

Trudgill, P. 1974. *The Social Differentiation of English in Norwich*. Cambridge: Cambridge University Press.

Trueba, H. and P. Wright. 1981. Ethnographic researchers in bilingual settings. *Journal of Multilingual and Multicultural Development* 2: 243–257.

Urciuoli, B. 1996. *Exposing Prejudice: Puerto Rican Experiences of Language, Race and Class*. New York: Westview Press.

Verschueren, J. 1999. *Understanding Pragmatics*. London: Edward Arnold.

Vološinov, V. 1973. *Marxism and the Philosophy of Language*. Seminar Press.

Wardhaugh, R. 1986. *Introduction to Sociolinguistics*. Oxford: Blackwell.

Wenger, E. 1998. *Communities of Practice*. Cambridge: Cambridge University Press.

Williams, R. 1977. *Marxism and Literature*. Oxford: Oxford University Press.

Woolard, K. and B. Schieffelin. 1994. Language ideology. *Annual Review of Anthropology* 23: 55–82.

Yeo, E. and S. Yeo. 1988. On the uses of 'community': From Owenism to the present. In S. Yeo (ed.) *New Views of Cooperation*. London: Routledge. 229–258.

Other Resources for Studying Sociolinguistics

Sociolinguistics is very well served by textbooks written at various levels, from basic to more advanced. There are also several important international journals that report the most up-to-date research. In preparing this Reader we have made the assumption that it is necessary for students and researchers to engage directly with texts written by the most influential authors in the field. The following lists, obviously to be used very selectively, should supplement the core texts we have included here.

Introductory Textbooks

Aitchison, Jean. 2000. *Language Change: Progress or Decay.* 3rd edition. Cambridge: Cambridge University Press.

Cameron, Deborah. 2001. *Working with Spoken Discourse.* London: Sage.

Coulmas, Florian. 2005. *Sociolinguistics: The Study of Speakers' Choices.* Cambridge: Cambridge University Press.

Holmes, Janet. 2008. *An Introduction to Sociolinguistics.* 3rd edition. London: Longman.

Hutchby, Ian and Robin Wooffitt. 2008. *Conversation Analysis.* 2nd edition. Cambridge: Polity Press.

Meyerhoff, Miriam. 2006. *Introducing Sociolinguistics.* London and New York: Routledge.

Montgomery, Martin. 2008. *An Introduction to Language and Society.* 3rd edition. London and New York: Routledge.

Romaine, Suzanne. 2000. *Language in Society: An Introduction to Sociolinguistics.* 2nd edition. Oxford: Oxford University Press.

Salzmann, Zdenek. 2004. *Language, Culture, and Society: An Introduction to Linguistic Anthropology.* 3rd edition. Boulder, Colorado: Westview Press.

Stockwell, Peter. 2007. *Sociolinguistics: A Resource Book for Students.* 2nd edition. London and New York: Routledge.

Spolsky, Bernard. 1998. *Sociolinguistics.* Oxford: Oxford University Press.

Thomas, Linda and Shân Wareing. 1999. *Language, Society and Power: An Introduction.* London and New York: Routledge.

Trudgill, Peter. 2000. *Sociolinguistics: An Introduction to Language and Society.* 4th edition. Harmondsworth: Penguin.

Wardhaugh, Ronald. 2006. *An Introduction to* Sociolinguistics. 5th edition. Oxford: Blackwell Publishing.

Intermediate/Advanced Level Textbooks

Blommaert, Jan. 2005. *Discourse: A Critical Introduction*. Cambridge: Cambridge University Press.

Downes, William. 1988. *Language and Society*. 2nd edition. Cambridge: Cambridge University Press.

Duranti, Alessandro. 1997. *Linguistic Anthropology*. Cambridge: Cambridge University Press.

Fasold, Ralph. 1984. *The Sociolinguistics of Society*. Oxford: Blackwell.

Fasold, Ralph. 1990. *The Sociolinguistics of Language*. Oxford: Blackwell.

Fishman, Joshua A. 1971. *Sociolinguistics: A Brief Introduction*. Rowley, Massachusetts: Newbury House.

Foley, William A. 1997. *Anthropological Linguistics: An Introduction*. Oxford: Blackwell.

Giles, Howard and Nikolas Coupland. 1991. *Language: Contexts and Consequences*. Milton Keynes: Open University Press.

Goodwin, Charles. 1981. *Conversational Organisation: Interaction between Speakers and Hearers*. New York: Academic Press.

Hudson, R. A. 1996. *Sociolinguistics*. 2nd edition. Cambridge: Cambridge University Press.

Johnstone, Barbara. 2000. *Qualitative Methods in Sociolinguistics*. New York: Oxford University Press.

Johnstone, Barbara. 2007. *Discourse Analysis*. 2nd edition. Oxford: Blackwell Publishing.

Leith, Dick. 1997. *A Social History of English*. 2nd edition. London and New York: Routledge.

Mesthrie, Rajend, Joan Swann, Andrea Deumert and William L. Leap. 2000. *Introducing Sociolinguistics*. Edinburgh: Edinburgh University Press.

Potter, Jonathan and Margaret Wetherell. 1987. *Discourse and Social Psychology: Beyond Attitudes and Behaviour*. London: Sage.

Saville-Troike, Muriel. 2006. *The Ethnography of Communication: An Introduction* 3rd edition. Oxford: Blackwell Publishing.

Other Readers and Collections

Bauman, Richard and Joel Sherzer (eds.). 1989. *Explorations in the Ethnography of Speaking*. 2nd edition. Cambridge: Cambridge University Press.

Cameron, Deborah (ed.). 1998. *The Feminist Critique of Language: A Reader*. London and New York: Routledge.

Cameron, Deborah and Don Kulick (eds.). 2006. *The Language and Sexuality Reader*. London and New York: Routledge.

Chambers, J. K., Peter Trudgill and Natalie Schilling-Estes (eds.). 2002. *The Handbook of Language Variation and Change*. Malden, Massachusetts: Blackwell Publishing.

Cheshire, Jenny (ed.). 1991. *English Around the World: Sociolinguistic Perspectives*. Cambridge: Cambridge University Press.

Coates, Jennifer (ed.). 1988. *Language and Gender: A Reader*. Oxford: Blackwell.

Coulmas, Florian (ed.). 1997. *The Handbook of Sociolinguistics*. Oxford: Blackwell.

Coupland, Nikolas and Adam Jaworski (eds.). 2009. *Sociolinguistics: Critical Concepts in Linguistics. Volumes 1–6*. London and New York: Routledge.

Duranti, Alessandro (ed.). 2001a. *Linguistic Anthropology: A Reader*. Malden, Massachusetts: Blackwell Publishing.

Duranti, Alessandro (ed.). 2001b. *Key Terms in Language and Culture*. Malden, Massachusetts: Blackwell Publishing.

Duranti, Alessandro (ed.). 2004. *A Companion to Linguistic Anthropology*. Malden, Massachusetts: Blackwell Publishing.

Giglioli, Pier Paolo (ed.). 1972. *Language and Social Context*. Harmondsworth: Penguin.

Harris, Roxy and Ben Rampton (eds.). 2003. *The Language, Ethnicity and Race Reader*. London and New York: Routledge.

Holmes, Janet and Miriam Myerhoff (eds.). 2005. The Handbook of Language and Gender. Oxford: Blackwell Publishing.

Hymes, Dell. (ed.) 1964. *Language in Culture and Society. A Reader in Linguistics and Anthropology*. New York: Harper & Row.

Jaworski, Adam and Nikolas Coupland (eds.). 2006. *The Discourse Reader*. 2nd edition. London and New York: Routledge.

Kiesling, Scott, F. and Christina Bratt Paulston (eds.). 2005. *Intercultural Discourse and Communication*. Malden, Massachusetts: Blackwell Publishing.

Laver, John and Sandy Hutcheson (eds.). 1972. *Communication in Face to Face Interaction*. Harmondsworth: Penguin.

Llamas, Carmen, Louise Mullany and Peter Stockwell (eds.). 2007. *The Routledge Companion to Sociolinguistics*. Abingdon: Routledge.

Li Wei (ed.). 2006. *The Bilingualism Reader*. 2nd edition. London and New York: Routledge.

Long, Daniel and Dennis, R. Preston (eds.). 2002. *Handbook of Perceptual Dialectology. Volume 2*. Amsterdam/Philadelphia: John Benjamins.

Monaghan, Leila and Jane E. Goodman (eds.). 2007. *A Cultural Approach to Interpersonal Communication: Essential Readings*. Oxford: Blackwell Publishing.

Nussbaum, Jon F. and Justine Coupland (eds.). 2004. *Handbook of Communication and Aging*. 2nd edition. Mahwah, New Jersey: Lawrence Erlbaum.

Paulston, Christina Bratt and G. Richard Tucker (eds.). 2003. *Sociolinguistics: The Essential Readings*. Malden, Massachusetts: Blackwell Publishing.

Preston, Dennis R. (ed.). 1999. *Handbook of Perceptual Dialectology. Volume 1*. Amsterdam/Philadelphia: John Benjamins.

Pride, John B. and Janet Holmes (ed.). 1972. *Sociolinguistics*. Harmondsworth: Penguin.

Robinson, W. Peter and Howard Giles (eds.). 2001. *The New Handbook of Language and Social Psychology*. Chichester: Wiley.

Schiffrin, Deborah, Deborah Tannen and Heidi H. Hamilton (eds.). 2001. *The Handbook of Discourse Analysis*. Oxford: Blackwell Publishing.

Swann, Joan, Ana Deumert, Theresa Lillis and Rajend Mesthrie. 2004. *A Dictionary of Sociolinguistics*. Edinburgh: Edinburgh University Press.

Academic Journals in Sociolinguistics

The following is a list of journals publishing research in Sociolinguistics, broadly defined.

American Speech (Duke University Press). Publishes research on all aspects of English in the Western Hemisphere.

Annual Review of Anthropology (Annual Reviews). Publishes position / state-of-the art analytic reviews in all aspects of Anthropology including Anthropological Linguistics.

Applied Linguistics (Oxford University Press). Publishes an eclectic range of papers in many areas, such as language contact; computer-mediated communication; conversation and discourse analysis; deaf linguistics; pragmatics; first and additional language learning, teaching, and use; literacies; multimodal communication, and others.

Communication and Medicine (Mouton de Gruyter). Specialises in discourse-based approaches to healthcare.

Current Issues in Language Planning (Routledge). Publishes research on language policy and language planning in various areas around the world.

Discourse and Communication (Sage). An inter-disciplinary journal aiming to introduce the qualitative, discourse analytical approach to issues in communication studies.

Discourse Studies (Sage). Open to all traditions of Discourse Analysis.

Discourse and Society (Sage). Specialises in Critical Discourse Analysis.

Discourse Processes (Routledge). Subtitled 'a multidisciplinary journal', publishes articles in Sociolinguistics, ethnomethodology, sociology, educational psychology, computer science, descriptive linguistic and cognitive as well as interpretive studies of discourse.

English World-Wide (John Benjamins). Deals with all aspects of dialectology and Sociolinguistics of the English-speaking communities.

Ethnography (Sage). Publishes qualitative research in Sociology and Anthropology including interdisciplinary, discourse-oriented approaches.

Gender and Language (Equinox Press). Publishes on all aspects of language in relation to femininities and masculinities, on sexuality and identities, gender performativity, perceptions and representations of gender, and gender ideologies.

Humor – International Journal of Humor Research (Mouton de Gruyter). Publishes interdisciplinary research on linguistic, visual and other aspects of humour. No laughing matter.

International Journal of Applied Linguistics (Wiley-Blackwell). Very broad-based, includes articles in applied linguistics, Sociolinguistics and some discourse studies.

International Journal of Bilingual Education and Bilingualism (Routledge). Focuses on issues of multilingualism in education internationally with a special focus on the USA.

International Journal of Multilingualism (Routledge). Specialises in psycholinguistic and sociolinguistic aspects of multilingual acquisition and multilingualism.

International Journal of Sociology of Language (Mouton de Gruyter). A long-standing journal dealing with all aspects of the Sociology of Language, especially multilingualism, language planning and minority/ lesser used languages.

Journal of Asian Pacific Communication (John Benjamins). Focuses on language and communication issues of the people in Asian Pacific regions and their Diaspora immigrant communities worldwide.

Journal of Pidgin and Creole Languages (John Benjamins). Focuses on the theory and description of pidgin and creole languages, language planning, education, and social reform in creole-speaking societies.

Journal of Language and Social Psychology (Sage). Covers quantitative and experimental research, but is increasingly open to qualitative discourse research on themes relevant to social psychology, especially attitudinal research.

Journal of Linguistic Anthropology (Wiley-Blackwell). Specialises in the anthropological study of language, including analysis of discourse, language in society, language and cognition, and language acquisition of socialization.

Journal of Multicultural Discourses (Routledge). Promotes research on language, communication and culture with a particular focus on non-Western and marginalised communities.

Journal of Multilingual and Multicultural Development (Routledge). Publishes primarily quantitative and qualitative research on inter-cultural communication and language and ethnicity.

Journal of Politeness Research (Mouton de Gruyter). Specialist journal dealing with linguistic and non-linguistic research on politeness phenomena.

Journal of Pragmatics (Elsevier). Focuses mainly on linguistic aspects of pragmatics and discourse, but increasingly open to socially and culturally inclined studies.

Journal of Sociolinguistics (Wiley-Blackwell). Covers the whole interdisciplinary field of Sociolinguistics and discourse studies and is open to innovative approaches.

Language Awareness (Routledge). Promotes varied approaches, including critical and applied approaches to language and discourse.

Language and Communication (Elsevier). Another very broad-based journal, publishing theoretical as well as empirical studies.

Language and Education (Routledge). Specialises in linguistic aspects of the theory and practice in education including classroom interaction.

Language and Intercultural Communication (Routledge). Publishes interdisciplinary, critical research on all aspects of language and culture broadly defined.

Language in Society (Cambridge University Press). A long-established Sociolinguistics journal, open to discourse analytic research with a strong anthropological/ethnographic bias.

Language Problems and Language Planning (John Benjamins). Covers political, sociological, and economic aspects of language contact and language use.

Language Sciences (Elsevier). Publishes a wide-ranging mix of research including social, cognitive and anthropological approaches to language.

Language Variation and Change (Cambridge University Press). Publishes research on all aspects of linguistic variation: synchronic, diachronic (historical), social, cultural, and interactional.

Multilingua (Mouton de Gruyter). Originally exploring the interface between language, culture and second language acquisition, now open to all current research in Sociolinguistics and discourse analysis.

Narrative Inquiry (John Benjamins). Provides an interdisciplinary forum for the study of narratives.

Pragmatics (International Pragmatics Association). Wide-ranging, includes culturally-focused, linguistic and critical approaches to discourse.

Research on Language and Social Interaction (Routledge). Specialises in talk-in-interaction/conversation analytic research.

Semiotica (Mouton de Gruyter). Interdisciplinary and orientated towards the analysis of different semiotic systems and multimodality; notable for many review articles of books in all areas of semiotic research occasionally publishing conversation and discourse analytic research.

Sign Language and Linguistics (John Benjamins). This e-format journal is concerned with the social, cultural and educational issues concerning sign languages.

Sign Language Studies (Gallaudet University Press). Deals with all aspects of signed languages and their communities.

Talk and Text (Mouton de Gruyter). Subtitled 'an interdisciplinary journal for the study of discourse', this is another broad-based, established journal, open to all traditions of discourse analysis.

Visual Communication (Sage). Major journal for visual communication and multimodal discourse research strongly associated with Social Semiotics and Hallidayan Systemic-Functional Linguistics.

World Englishes (Wiley-Blackwell). Publishes research on methodological and empirical study of English in global, social, cultural and linguistic contexts.

Further Reading: Part I – Language Variation

Auer, Peter, Frans Hinskens and Paul Kerswill (eds.). *Dialect Change: Convergence and Divergence in European Languages*. Cambridge: Cambridge University Press.

Bayley, Robert and Ceil Lucas (eds.). 2007. *Sociolinguistic Variation: Theories, Methods, and Applications*. Cambridge: Cambridge University Press.

Chambers, J. K. 2002. *Sociolinguistic Theory*. 2nd edition. Oxford: Blackwell.

Cheshire, Jenny. 1982. *Variation in an English Dialect*. Cambridge: Cambridge University Press.

Eckert, Penelope. 1989. *Jocks and Burnouts: Social Categories and Identity in the High School*. New York: Teachers College Press.

Eckert, Penelope. 2000. *Linguistic Variation as Social Practice*. Malden, Massachusetts: Blackwell Publishing.

Finegan, Edward and John R. Rickford (eds.). 2004. *Language in the USA: Themes for the Twenty-First Century*. Cambridge: Cambridge University Press.

Fought, Carmen (ed.). 2004. *Sociolinguistic Variation: Critical Reflections*. New York: Oxford University Press..

Foulkes, Paul and Gerard Docherty (eds.). 1999. *Urban Voices: Accent Studies in the British Isles*. London: Arnold.

Labov, William. 1972. *Sociolinguistic Patterns*. Philadelphia, Pennsylvania: University of Pennsylvania Press.

Labov, William. 1994. *Principles of Linguistic Change. Volume 1: Internal Factors*. Oxford: Blackwell.

Labov, William. 2001 *Principles of Linguistic Change. Volume 2: Social Factors*. Oxford: Blackwell.

Labov, William. 2006. *The Social Stratification of English in New York City*. 2nd edition. Cambridge: Cambridge University Press. [First edition published in 1966, Washington, D.C.: Center for Applied Linguistics.]

Macaulay, Ronald K. S. 2005. *Talk that Counts: Age, Gender, and Social Class Differences in Discourse*. New York: Oxford University Press.

Milroy, James. 1992. *Language Variation and Change*. Oxford: Blackwell.

Milroy, Lesley. 1987. *Language and Social Networks*. 2nd edition. Oxford: Blackwell. [First published 1980].

Romaine, Suzanne. 1982. *Socio-Historical Linguistics: Its Status and Methodology*. Cambridge: Cambridge University Press.

Tagliamonte, Sali. 2006. *Analysing Sociolinguistic Variation*. Cambridge: Cambridge University Press.

Wolfram, Walt and Ben Ward (eds.). 2005. *American Voices: How Dialects Differ from Coast to Coast*. Malden, Massachusetts: Blackwell Publishing.

Trudgill, Peter. 1974. *The Social Differentiation of English in Norwich*. Cambridge: Cambridge University Press.

Trudgill, Peter. 1978. *Sociolinguistic Patterns in British English*. London: Edward Arnold.

Trudgill, Peter. 1983. *On Dialect: Social and Geographic Factors*. Oxford: Blackwell.

Trudgill, Peter. 1986. *Dialects in Contact*. Oxford: Blackwell.

Trudgill, Peter. 2002. *Sociolinguistic Variation and Change*. Edinburgh: Edinburgh University Press.

Trudgill, Peter. 2004. *New-Dialect Formation: The Inevitability of Colonial Englishes*. Edinburgh: Edinburgh University Press.

Wolfram, Walt and Natalie Schilling-Estes. 2006. *American English: Dialects and Variation*. 2nd edition. Oxford: Blackwell Publishing.

Further Reading: Part II – Language, Gender and Sexuality

Baron, Dennis. 1986. *Grammar and Gender*. New Haven, Connecticut: Yale University Press.

Cameron, Deborah. 2006. *On Language and Sexual Politics*. London and New York: Routledge.

Cameron, Deborah and Don Kulick. 2003. *Language and Sexuality*. Cambridge: Cambridge University Press.

Coates, Jennifer. 1996. *Women Talk. Conversation Between Women Friends*. Oxford: Blackwell.

Coates, Jennifer. 2004. *Women, Men and Language*. 3rd edition. London: Longman.

Coates, Jennifer. 2003. *Men Talk: Stories in the Making of Masculinities*. Oxford: Blackwell Publishing.

Coates, Jennifer and Deborah Cameron (eds.). 1989. *Women in their Speech Communities*. London: Longman.

Eckert, Penelope and Sally McConnell-Ginet. 2003. *Language and Gender*. Cambridge: Cambridge University Press.

Goddard, Angela and Lindsey M. Patterson. 2000. *Language and Gender*. London: Routledge.

Goodwin, Marjorie H.. 1990. *He-Said-She-Said: Talk as Social Organisation among Black Children*. Bloomington, Indiana: Indiana University Press.

Goodwin, Marjorie H. 2006. *The Hidden Life of Girls: Games of Stance, Status, and Exclusion*. Malden, Massachusetts: Blackwell Publishing.

Graddol, David and Joan Swann (eds.). 1989. *Gender Voices*. Oxford: Basil Blackwell.

Hall, Kira and Mary Bucholtz (eds.). 1995. *Gender Articulated: Language and the Socially Constructed Self*. London and New York: Routledge.

Henley, Nancy. 1977. *Body Politics: Power, Sex, and Nonverbal Communication*. Englewood Cliffs, New Jersey: Prentice-Hall.

Hill, A. O. 1986. *Mother Tongue, Father Time: A Decade of Linguistic Revolt*. Bloomington, Indiana: Indiana University Press.

Holmes, Janet. 1995. *Women, Men and Politeness*. London: Longman.

Holmes, Janet. 2006 *Gendered Talk at Work: Constructing Social Identity through Workplace Interaction*. Oxford: Blackwell Publishing.

Key, Mary Ritchie. 1975. *Male/female language*. Metuchen, New Jersey: Scarecrow Press.

Kotthoff, Helga and Ruth Wodak (eds.). 1997. *Communicating Gender in Context*. Amsterdam/Philadelphia: John Benjamins

Kramarae, Cheris. 1981. *Women and Men Speaking: Frameworks for Analysis*. Rowley, Massachusetts: Newbury House.

Lakoff, Robin. 1975. *Language and Woman's Place*. New York: Harper and Row.

Leap, William L. (ed.). 1995. *Beyond the Lavender Lexicon: Authenticity, Imagination and Appropriation in Gay and Lesbian Languages*. New York: Gordon & Breach.

Leap, William L. Tom Bollstroff (eds.). 2004. *Speaking in Queer Tongues: Globalization and Gay and Lesbian Languages*. Urbana, Illinois: University of Illinois Press.

Livia, Anna and Kira Hall (eds.). 1997. *Queerly Phrased: Language, Gender, and Sexuality*. New York: Oxford University Press.

Litosseliti, Lia. 2006. *Gender and Language: Theory and Practice*. London: Hodder Arnold.

McConnell-Ginet, Sally, Ruth Borker and Nelly Furman (eds.). 1980. *Women and Language in Literature and Society*. New York: Preager.

Miller, Casey and Kate Swift. 1975. *The Handbook of Non-sexist Writing for Writers, Editors and Speakers*. London: The Women's Press.

Miller, Casey and Kate Swift. 1981. *Words and Women*. Garden City, New York: Doubleday.

Mills, Sara. 1995. *Feminist Stylistics*. London and New York: Routledge.

Mills, Sara. 2003. *Gender and Politeness*. Cambridge: Cambridge University Press.

Romaine, Suzanne. 1999. *Communicating Gender*. Mahwah, New Jersey: Lawrence Erlbaum.

Smith, Philip M. 1985. *Language, the Sexes and Society*. Oxford: Blackwell.

Spender, Dale. 1980. *Man Made Language*. London: Routledge and Kegan Paul.

Sunderland, Jane. 2006. *Language and Gender: An Advanced Resource Book*. London: Routledge.

Swann, Joan. 1992. *Girls, Boys and Language*. Oxford: Blackwell.

Talbot, Mary M. 1998. *Language and Gender: An Introduction*. Cambridge: Polity.

Tannen, Deborah. (ed.). 1993. *Gender and Conversational Interaction*. New York: Oxford University Press.

Tannen, Deborah. 1994. *Gender and Discourse*. Oxford: Oxford University Press.

Thorne, Barrie and Nancy Henley (eds.). 1975. *Language and Sex: Difference and Dominance*. Rowley, Massachusetts: Newbury House.

Thorne, Barrie, Cheris Kramarae and Nancy Henley (eds.). 1983. *Language, Gender and Society*. Rowley, Massachusetts: Newbury House.

Further Reading: Part III – Style, Stylization and Identity

Auer, Peter (ed.). 2007. *Social Identities and Communicative Style*. Berlin: Mouton de Gruyter.

Bakhtin, Mikhail. M. 1981. *The Dialogic Imagination: Four Essays*, Edited by Michael Holquist. Translated by Vern W. McGee. Austin, Texas: University of Texas Press.

Bakhtin, Mikhail M. 1986. *Speech Genres and Other Late Essays.* Translated by Vern W. McGee. Austin, Texas: University of Texas Press.

Bell, Allan. 1991. *The Language of the News Media.* Oxford: Blackwell.

Coupland, Nikolas. 2007. *Style: Language Variation and Identity.* Cambridge: Cambridge University Press.

Eckert, Penelope and John R. Rickford (eds.). 2001. *Style and Sociolinguistic Variation.* Cambridge: Cambridge University Press.

Hebdige, Dick. 1988. *Subculture: The Meaning of Style.* London and New York: Routledge.

Hewitt, Roger. 1986. *White Talk Black Talk.* Cambridge: Cambridge University Press.

Johnstone, Barbara. 1996. *The Linguistic Individual: Self-Expression in Language and Linguistics.* New York: Oxford University Press.

LePage, R. B. and Andrée Tabouret-Keller. 1985. *Acts of Identity: Creole-Based Approaches to Language and Ethnicity.* Cambridge: Cambridge University Press.

Rampton, Ben. 1995. *Crossing: Language and Ethnicity Among Adolescents.* London: Longman.

Rampton, Ben. 2006. *Language in Late Modernity: Interaction in an Urban School.* Cambridge: Cambridge University Press.

Reyes, Angela. 2007. *Language, Identity, and Stereotype among Southeast Asian American Youth: The Other Asian.* Mahwah, New Jersey: Lawrence Erlbaum.

Tannen, Deborah. 2005. *Conversational Style: Analyzing Talk among Friends.* New edition. New York: Oxford University Press.

Wortham, Stanton. 2006. *Learning Identity: The Joint Emergence of Social Identification and Academic Learning.* Cambridge: Cambridge University Press.

Further Reading: Part IV – Language Attitudes, Ideologies and Stances

Andersson, Lars G. and Peter Trudgill. 1990. *Bad Language.* Oxford: Basil Blackwell.

Bauer, Laurie and Peter Trudgill (eds.). 1998. *Language Myths.* Harmondsworth: Penguin.

Baugh, John. 2000. *Beyond Ebonics: Linguistic Pride and Racial Prejudice.* Oxford: Oxford University Press.

Bauman, Richard and Charles Briggs. 2003. *Voices of Modernity: Language Ideologies and the Politics of Inequality.* Cambridge: Cambridge University Press.

Bex, Tony and Richard J. Watts (eds.). 1999. *Standard English: The Widening Debate.* London and New York: Routledge.

Blommaert, Jan. (ed.). 1999. *Language Ideological Debates.* Berlin: Mouton de Gruyter.

Bourdieu, Pierre. 1991. *Language and Symbolic Power.* Edited and Introduced by John B. Thompson. Translated by Gino Raymond and Matthew Adamson. Cambridge: Polity.

Cameron, Deborah. 1995. *Verbal Hygiene.* London and New York: Routledge.

Cameron, Deborah. 2000. *Good to Talk? Living and Working in a Communication Culture.* London: Sage.

Cameron, Deborah, Elizabeth Frazer, Penelope Harvey, M. B. H. Rampton and Kay Richardson. 1992. *Researching Language: Issues of Power and Method.* London and New York: Routledge.

Coupland, Nikolas, Srikant Sarangi and Christopher N. Candlin (eds.). 2001. *Sociolinguistics and Social Theory.* London: Longman.

Crowley, Tony. 1989. *The Politics of Discourse.* London: Macmillan.

Duchêne, Alexandre and Monica Heller (eds.). 2007. *Discourse of Endangerment*. London: Continuum.

Englebreston, Robert (ed.). 2007. *Stancetaking in Discourse*. Amsterdam/Philadelphia: John Benjamins.

Fairclough, Norman. 1992. *Discourse and Social Change*. Cambridge: Polity.

Fairclough, Norman. 2006. *Language and Globalization*. London and New York: Routledge.

Gal, Susan and Kathryn A. Woolard (eds.). 2001. *Languages and Publics: The Making of Authority*. Manchester: St. Jerome.

Garrett, Peter, Nikolas Coupland and Angie Williams. 2003. *Investigating Language Attitudes: Social Meanings of Dialect, Ethnicity and Performance*. Cardiff: University of Wales Press.

Giles, Howard and Peter Powesland. 1975. *Speech Style and Social Evaluation*. London: Academic Press.

Hodge, Robert and Gunther Kress. 1988. *Social Semiotics*. Cambridge: Polity.

Jaffe, Alexandra. 1999. *Ideologies in Action: Language Politics on Corsica*. Berlin: Mouton De Gruyter.

Jaffe, Alexandra. 2009. *The Sociolinguistics of Stance*. New York: Oxford University Press.

Jaworski, Adam, Nikolas Coupland, Dariusz Galasiński (eds.). 2004. *Metalanguage: Social and Ideological Perspectives*. Berlin: Mouton de Gruyter.

Johnson, Sally. 2005. *Spelling Trouble? Language, Ideology and the Reform of German Orthography*. Clevedon: Multilingual Matters.

Johnson, Sally and Astrid Ensslin (eds.). 2007. *Language in the Media: Representations, Identities, Ideologies*. London and New York: Continuum.

Joseph, John E. and Talbot J. Taylor (eds.). 1990. *Ideologies of Language*. London and New York: Routledge.

Kress, Gunther and Robert Hodge. 1979. *Language as Ideology*. London: Routledge.

Kroskrity, Paul V. (ed.). 2000. *Regimes of Language: Ideologies, Polities and Identities*. Santa Fe: School of American Research Press.

Lippi-Green, Rosina. 1997. *English with an Accent: Language, Ideology and Discrimination in the United States*. London and New York: Routledge.

Lucy, John A. (ed.). 1993. *Reflexive Language: Reported Speech and Metapragmatics*. Cambridge: Cambridge University Press.

Milroy, James and Lesley Milroy. 1999. *Authority in Language: Investigating Standard English*. 3rd edition. London: Routledge.

Mugglestone, Lynda. 2003. *Talking Proper: The Rise of Accent as Social Symbol*. Oxford: Oxford University Press.

Niedzielski, Nancy and Dennis R. Preston. 2000. *Folk Linguistics*. Berlin: Mouton de Gruyter.

Schieffelin, Bambi B., Kathryn A. Woolard, and Paul V. Kroskrity (eds.). 1998. *Language Ideologies: Practice and Theory*. New York: Oxford University Press.

Watts, Richard and Peter Trudgill (eds.). 2002. *Alternative Histories of English*. London and New York: Routledge.

Further Reading: Part V – Multilingualism, Code-switching and Diglossia

Auer, Peter. 1994. *Bilingual Conversation*. Amsterdam/Philadelphia: John Benjamins.

Auer, Peter (ed.). 1998. *Code-Switching in Conversation: Language, Interaction and Identity*. London and New York: Routledge.

Bickerton, Derek. 1981. *Roots of Language*. Ann Arbor, Michigan: Karoma Press.

Blackledge, Adrian. 2005. *Discourse and Power in a Multilingual World*. Amsterdam/Philadelphia: John Benjamins.

Block, David. 2006. *Multilingual Identities in a Global City: London Stories*. Basingstoke: Palgrave Macmillan.

De Swaan, Abram. 2001. *Words of the World*. Cambridge: Polity Press.

Dorian, Nancy C. 1981. *Language Death: The Life Cycle of a Scottish Gaelic Dialect*. Philadelphia, Pennsylvania: University of Pennsylvania Press.

Dorian, Nancy C. (ed.). 1989. *Investigating Obsolescence*. Cambridge: Cambridge University Press.

Edwards, Viv. 2004. *Multilingualism in the English-Speaking World*. Oxford: Blackwell Publishing.

Fishman, Joshua A. 1991. *Reversing Language Shift: Theoretical and Empirical Assistance to Threatened Languages*. Clevedon: Multilingual Matters.

Gardner-Chloros, Penelope. 1991. *Language Selection and Switching in Strasbourg*. Oxford: Clarendon.

Grenoble, Lenore A. and Lindsay J. Whaley (eds.). 1998. *Endangered Languages: Language Loss and Community Response*. Cambridge: Cambridge University Press.

Heller, Monica (ed.). 1988. *Codeswitching: Anthropological and Sociolinguistic Perspectives*. Berlin: Mouton de Gruyter.

Heller, Monica. 2006. *Linguistic Minorities and Modernity*. London: Continuum.

Heller, Monica (ed.). 2007. *Bilingualism: A Social Approach*. Basingstoke: Palgrave Macmillan.

Hymes, Dell (ed.) 1971. *Pidginization and Creolization of Languages*. Cambridge: Cambridge University Press.

Kelly-Holmes, Helen. 2005. *Advertising as Multilingual Communication*. Basingstoke: Palgrave Macmillan.

King, Kendall A., Natalie Schilling-Estes, Lyn Fogle, Jia Lackie Lou and Barbara Soukup (eds.). 2008. *Sustaining Linguistic Diversity: Endangered and Minority Languages and Language Varieties*. Washington, D.C.: Georgetown University Press.

Kontra, Miklós, Robert Phillipson, Tove Skutnabb-Kangas and Tibor Várady (eds.). 1999. *Language: A Right and a Resource. Approaches to Linguistic Human Rights*. Budapest: Central European University Press.

Köpke, Barbara, Monika S. Schmid, Merel Keijzer, Susan Dostert (eds.). 2007. *Language Attrition: Theoretical Perspectives*. Amsterdam/Philadelphia: John Benjamins.

Kulick, Don. 1992. *Language Shift and Cultural Reproduction: Socialization, Self, and Syncretism in a Papua New Guinean Village*. Cambridge: Cambridge University Press.

Mac Giolla Chríost, Diarmait. 2007. *Language and the City*. Basingstoke: Palgrave Macmillan.

May, Stephen. 2001. *Language and Minority Rights: Ethnicity, Nationalism and the Politics of Language*. Harlow: Pearson Education.

Milroy, Lesley and Pieter Muysken (eds.). 1995. *One Speaker, Two Languages*. Cambridge: Cambridge University Press.

Muysken, Pieter. 2000. *Bilingual Speech: A Typology of Code-Mixing*. Cambridge: Cambridge University Press.

Mühlhäusler, Peter. 1997. *Pidgin and Creole Linguistics*. 2nd edition. London: University of Westminster Press.

Myers-Scotton, Carol. 1997. *Duelling Languages*. 2nd edition. Oxford: Oxford University Press.

Myers-Scotton, Carol (ed.). 1998. *Codes and Consequences: Choosing Linguistic Varieties.* New York: Oxford University Press.

Nettle, David. 1999. *Linguistic Diversity.* New York: Oxford University Press.

Nettle, Daniel and Suzanne Romaine. 2000. *Vanishing Voices: The Extinction of the World's Languages.* Oxford: Oxford University Press.

Norton, Bonny. 2000. *Identity and Language Learning: Gender, Ethnicity and Educational Change.* Harlow: Pearson Education.

Pavlenko, Aneta. 2005. *Emotions and Multilingualism.* Cambridge: Cambridge University Press.

Pavlenko, Aneta (ed.). 2006. *Bilingual Minds: Emotional Experience, Expression and Representation.* Clevedon: Multilingual Matters.

Pennycook, Alastair. 1994. *The Cultural Politics of English as an International Language.* London: Longman.

Pennycook, Alastair. 2007. *Global Englishes and Transcultural Flows.* London: Routledge.

Phillipson, Robert. 1992. *Linguistic Imperialism.* Oxford: Oxford University Press.

Piller, Ingrid. 2002. *Bilingual Couples Talk: The Discursive Construction of Hybridity.* Amsterdam/Philadelphia: John Benjamins.

Poplack, Shana. 1980. Sometimes I'll start a sentence in SpanishY TERMINO EN ESPAÑOL: Toward a typology of code-switching. *Linguistics* 18: 581–618.

Rassool, Naz. 2007. *Global Issues in Language, Education and Development Perspectives from Postcolonial Countries.* Clevedon : Multilingual Matters.

Ricento, Thomas (ed.). 2005. *An Introduction to Language Policy: Theory and Method.* Oxford: Blackwell Publishing.

Rickford, John R. 1987. *Dimensions of a Creole Continuum.* Stanford, California: Stanford University Press.

Romaine, Suzanne. 1988. *Pidgin and Creole Languages.* London: Longman.

Romaine, Suzanne. 1995. *Bilingualism.* 2nd edition. Oxford: Blackwell.

Rubdy, Rani and Mario Saraceni (eds.). 2006. *English in the World: Global Rules, Global Roles.* London: Continuum.

Siegel, Jeff. 2008. *The Emergence of Pidgin and Creole Languages.* New York: Oxford University Press.

Skutnabb-Kangas, Tove. 2000. *Linguistic Genocide in Education – or Worldwide Diversity and Human Rights?* Mahwah: New Jersey: Lawrence Erlbaum.

Thomason, Sarah G. and Terrence Kaufman. 1998. *Language Contact, Creolization, and Genetic Linguistics.* Berkeley, California: University of California Press.

Williams, Colin H. 2008. *Linguistic Minorities in Democratic Context.* Basingstoke: Palgrave Macmillan.

Woolard, Kathryn A. 1989. *Double Talk: Bilingualism and the Politics of Ethnicity in Catalonia.* Stanford, California: Stanford University Press.

Zentella, Ana Celia. 1997. *Growing up Bilingual: Puerto Rican Children In New York.* Oxford: Blackwell.

Further Reading: Part VI – Language, Culture and Interaction

Bauman, Richard. 1977. *Verbal Art as Performance.* Prospect Heights, Illinois: Waveland Press.

Bauman, Richard (ed.). 1992. *Folklore, Cultural Performances, and Popular Entertainments: A Communications-centered Handbook*. New York: Oxford University Press.

Bauman, Richard. 2004. A World of Others' Words: Cross-Cultural Perspectives on Intertextuality. Malden, Massachusetts: Blackwell Publishing.

Bethan Benwell and Elizabeth Stokoe. 2006. *Discourse and Identity*. Edinburgh: Edinburgh University Press.

Brown, Penelope and Stephen C. Levinson. 1987. *Politeness: Some Universals in Language Usage*. Cambridge: Cambridge University Press. [Originally published in 1978.]

Coupland, Justine. 2000. (ed.) *Small Talk*. London: Longman/Pearson Education.

Drew, Paul and John Heritage, J. (eds.). 1992. *Talk at Work: Interaction in Institutional Settings*. Cambridge: Cambridge University Press.

Goffman, Erving. 1959. *The Presentation of Self in Everyday Life*. New York: Doubleday Anchor.

Goffman, Erving. 1967. *Interaction Ritual: Essays on Face-to-Face Behavior*. New York: Doubleday Anchor.

Goffman, Erving. 1971. *Relations in Public*. London: Allen Lane.

Goffman, Erving. 1974. *Frame Analysis: An Essay on the Organization of Experience*. New York: Harper and Row.

Goffman, Erving. 1981. Footing. In Erving Goffman *Forms of Talk*. Philadelphia, Pennsylvania: University of Pennsylvania Press. 124–159. [Originally published in *Semiotica* 25, 1979: 1–29.)

Goffman, Erving. 1983. The interaction order. *American Sociological Review* 48: 1–17.

Gumperz, John J. 1982a. *Discourse Strategies*. Cambridge: Cambridge University Press.

Gumperz, John J. (ed.). 1982b. *Language and Social Identity*. Cambridge: Cambridge University Press.

Gumperz, John J. and Dell Hymes (eds.). 1986. *Directions in Sociolinguistics: The Ethnography of Communication*. Oxford: Blackwell. [Originally published in 1972, New York: Holt, Rinehart and Winston.]

Gumperz, John J. and Stephen C. Levinson (eds.). 1996. *Rethinking Linguistic Relativity*. Cambridge: Cambridge University Press

Jaworski, Adam and Annette Pritchard (eds.). 2005. *Discourse, Communication and Tourism*. Clevedon: Channel View Publications.

Kress, Gunther (ed.). 1998. *Communication and Culture*. Victoria, Australia: New South Wales University Press.

Labov, William and David Fanshel. 1977. *Therapeutic Discourse*. New York: Academic Press.

Lucas, Ceil (ed.). 2001. *The Sociolinguistics of Sign Languages*. Cambridge: Cambridge University Press.

Lucy, John. 1992. *Language Diversity and Thought: A Reformulation of the Linguistic Relativity Hypothesis*. Cambridge: Cambridge University Press.

Myers, Greg. 2004. *Matters of Opinion: Talking about Public Issues*. Cambridge: Cambridge University Press.

Niloofar Haeri. 2003. *Sacred Language, Ordinary People: Dilemmas of Culture and Politics in Egypt*. London: Palgrave Macmillan.

Norrick, Neal R. 2000. *Conversational Narrative*. Amsterdam/Philadelphia: John Benjamins.

Ochs, Elinor. 1988 *Culture and Language Development: Language Acquisition and Language Socialization in a Samoan Village*. Cambridge: Cambridge University Press.

Ochs, Elinor, Emanuel A. Schegloff and Sandra A. Thompson (eds.). 1996. *Interaction and Grammar*. Cambridge: Cambridge University Press.

Schieffelin, Bambi B. 1990. *The Give and Take of Everyday Life: Language Socialization of Kaluli Children*. Cambridge: Cambridge University Press.

Scollon, Ron. 2001. *Mediated Discourse: The Nexus of Practice*. London and New York: Routledge.

Scollon, Ron and Suzie Wong Scollon. 2004. *Nexus Analysis: Discourse and the Emerging Internet*. London and New York: Routledge.

Sherzer, Joel. 2002. *Speech Play and Verbal Art*. Austin, Texas: University of Texas Press.

Silverstein, Michael and Greg Urban (eds.). 1996. *Natural Histories of Discourse*. Chicago: University of Chicago Press.

Thornborrow, Joanna and Coates, Jennifer. (eds.). 2005. *The Sociolinguistics of Narrative*. Amsterdam/Philadelphia: John Benjamins.

Thurlow, Crispin and Adam Jaworski. 2009. *Tourism Discourse*. Basingstoke: Palgrave Macmillan.

Watts, Richard J. 2003. *Politeness*. Cambridge: Cambridge University Press.

Whorf, Benjamin L. 1956. *Language, Thought and Reality: Selected Writings of Benjamin Lee Whorf*. Edited by J. B. Carroll. Cambridge MA: MIT Press.

Index

AAVE (African American Vernacular English), 5, 24–5, 43–5, 70, 89, 133, 157, 241, 250–6, 262, 277, 284, 298n, 299–309, 328–33, 356, 370, 418, 429, 595, 600–1, 603, 606, 615–30

accent, 2, 4, 6, 18, 23–5, 28–30, 35, 42, 54, 56–7, 59n, 61, 67, 104, 156, 160, 217, 241, 243, 251, 260, 266, 273, 277–8, 283, 300, 303, 305, 311–24, 333, 341–2, 344, 349, 358–9, 369, 444, 451, 495, 515, 522, 548, 577, 600, 602, 671, 675

accommodation theory, 14, 32, 126, 259–61, 270–1, 276–85, 428–9, 476

activity type, 155, 189–92, 496, 598–9, 647, 649–50, 696

Afro-Caribbean English, 288, 292, 297n, 381

age, 4, 6, 10, 13, 17, 23, 27–8, 32, 41–4, 66–74, 75–90, 97, 101–4, 110–11, 119–34, 136–51, 171, 193–5, 216–17, 237, 240, 246–7, 277–9, 282–3, 350, 407, 428, 432, 457, 460–70, 481, 542–6

agency, 8, 15–16, 19, 115–16, 226, 299, 476, 538, 564, 702

American Sign Language, 580, 680–92

anthropology, 2, 93, 159, 221, 236, 343, 373–7, 381, 390, 405–20, 436, 441, 443–4, 475, 541, 560, 575, 577, 581, 583–97, 604, 695, 700–1

audience design, 259–61, 265–74, 428, 476

audience roles, 271–2

authenticity, 294, 301–2, 309, 320–4, 437, 440–3, 537, 641, 660, 675, 696, 698, 702–3

awareness, *see* reflexivity

backstage–frontstage talk, 654–7

bilingual education, 394–403, 426, 444, 584, 703

bilingualism and multilingualism, 7–8, 94, 270–3, 283–8, 333, 335, 337, 345–6, 390–403, 425–33, 444, 447–56, 457–71, 473–87, 490–511, 527, 543–57

bricolage, 318, 337n

British Sign Language, 580, 680–92

burnouts, *see* jocks and burnouts

children and adolescents, 16, 27, 32, 66–74, 75–90, 119–34, 136–51, 168–84, 201–13, 215–27, 278, 283, 287–98, 299–309, 342–3, 349–55, 378, 395–401, 405–20, 438–41, 451, 460, 470, 475, 490–511, 514, 523–4, 544–7, 568–70, 592, 605, 615–30, 663, 682–6, 697

Cockney, *see* posh, and Cockney

code-switching, 94, 287–97, 425–33, 457–71, 473–87, 490–511, 545–9, 599, 601

community of practice, 9, 11–12, 33, 579, 581, 635, 699–705, 707

competence
  bilingual, 427–8
  communicative, 10, 282, 584, 589, 591, 608, 611–12, 698, 707
  cultural, 291, 409
  linguistic, 291, 335, 357, 477, 551, 575, 695, 705, 708n
  pragmatic, 477

contextualization and contextualization cues, 430, 476, 495, 577, 598–606, 607–8

conversation analysis, 8, 12, 201, 211, 405, 429, 479–83, 490–511

covert prestige, 24, 29, 46, 187, 350, 354

creativity, 7, 10, 17, 211, 233, 236, 245–6, 248, 262–4, 273, 314, 336, 401, 420n, 425, 440–1, 443, 476, 478, 481, 563, 577, 580, 617, 656, 680–92, 708

critical realism, 17
cultural capital, 155, 612
culture
    and language rights, 529–37
    as performance, 311–24, 326–37,
        577–81, 607–14
    as socialization process, 346, 411
    as ways of speaking, 575

Deaf culture, 680–92
decentering, 608, 611–14
decontextualization, 608–14
dialect, 2, 4–6, 11, 15, 23–35, 35–47,
    66, 69, 94, 97, 124, 189, 260, 271,
    273, 277, 283–4, 299–300, 305, 307,
    311–24, 328, 341–3, 349–55, 356–72,
    374, 402, 411, 428–9, 432, 447–8,
    451–2, 454–5, 459, 471, 474–5, 492,
    508–9, 512–24, 529–30, 542–3, 594,
    599
dialectology, 4, 23, 35–47
dialogism, 613
diglossia, 345, 392–5, 401, 425–33,
    447–56, 543, 556
discourse analysis, 2, 8, 109, 211, 261,
    429, 483, 578
discourse markers, 32, 577
discursive psychology, 201–12
double-voicing, *see* multiple voicing
drag queens, 157, 250–6, 265, 429

education, 37, 53, 82, 99, 117, 138, 144–5,
    203, 280, 307, 378–88, 394–5, 405,
    430, 445, 451, 454, 455n, 475, 481,
    512–24, 527, 530, 533, 563, 569,
    681, 683, 686, 692, *see also* bilingual
    education
emic and etic analysis, 7, 10, 575, 662
entextualization, 608–14, 707
erasure, 344, 375–7, 392
essentialism, 10, 426, 535–7
ethnicity, 13, 17, 23, 27, 35–6, 41, 43,
    53, 101, 103–4, 108, 110, 151, 157,
    188, 226, 241, 243, 261–3, 276–7,
    281, 283–5, 287–98, 299–309, 314,
    318, 381, 405, 425–6, 431, 435–45,
    457, 534–7, 568, 577, 580, 598, 601,
    603, 606, 669, 671–2, 675, 676, 699,
    703–5

ethnography of communication and
    speaking, 2, 13, 19, 26, 31–3, 41–2,
    92, 109, 136–51, 156, 160, 189, 203,
    217–18, 225, 259, 261, 266, 297n,
    358–60, 374–5, 395, 429, 566, 571,
    575–81, 583–97, 602, 607, 613, 632,
    640, 643, 695–6, 700
ethnomethodology, 405
ethno-semantics, 412

facework, 113, 176, 220–1, 223, 505, 506,
    639, 648–9, *see also* politeness
femininity, 64, 156–7, 187, 197–9, 201–2,
    215–27, 232–3, 239–47, 250, 252,
    283, 349–55, 561–2, 579, 631, 641–3
feminism, 31, 114–15, 155, 196, 203, 205,
    211, 230, 236–7, 699
folk linguistics, 25, 117, 343, 356–72
folklore, 583, 609, 613, 680, 689
footing, 420n, 430, 476, 495–8, 610
form–function, 7–8, 568, 610–11, 613
forms of address, 114, 167n, 168, 266,
    305, 307, 592, 663
formulaic language, *see* ritual and routine
fractal recursivity, 145, 344, 375–6, 391,
    393, 402
fraternity community, 155, 187–99
friendship, 32–3, 103, 120, 124, 127, 140,
    142, 146, 149–50, 156, 181–2, 188,
    210, 215, 217–24, 287, 405, 634, 658

gay men, 250–6
gender, 4, 6, 10, 13, 16–17, 27, 30, 41,
    44, 70–2, 102–3, 108, 110, 114,
    116, 119–20, 130–4, 137–51, 153–7,
    174, 176, 181, 188, 196–9, 201, 211,
    216–18, 225–7, 230, 234, 236, 239,
    241, 243, 246, 247, 250–6, 277, 321,
    326, 336, 341–2, 347, 376, 381, 405,
    412, 419, 481, 579, 603, 631–44, 698
gesturing, *see* nonverbal communication
global and local, 14, 297, 613, 694
globalization, 14, 156, 263, 326–37, 342,
    384, 426, 431–2, 475, 528, 560–73,
    580, 664, 704, 709n
Goldvarb, *see* research methods,
    quantitative
gossip, 579, 656–60
grammaticalization, 79, 89

greetings, 12, 580, 603–5, 662–77
grotesque, 315
Guttman scale, 121

habitus, 247, 315, 394, 403
hegemony, 25, 155–7, 197, 201–4, 212,
    217–18, 226, 231, 243, 256, 311–17,
    322, 337n, 380–1, 391, 431, 443, 483,
    580, 706
heterosexism, 197–8
hip-hop, 14, 24, 299–309, 326–37, 562–3
humour, 9–10, 578–9, 631–44, 649

icons and iconization, 145, 188, 323, 344,
    375–6, 391–4, 402, 578, 672, 687, 688
identity, 8, 10–11, 32–3, 41–2, 98, 108,
    111, 113, 116, 120, 140, 151, 155–7,
    193, 196, 201–12, 215–27, 229–48,
    250–6, 259–64, 269, 273–4, 279,
    284–5, 287–98, 299–309, 311–24,
    326–37, 345–7, 376–7, 391, 401,
    405–20, 425–6, 458, 461–3, 467, 470,
    476, 480–2, 524, 527, 532–3, 535–8,
    561–2, 570–1, 580, 586, 601, 640,
    649, 659, 664, 667, 669, 671, 675–6,
    681, 684, 696, 698, 702–3, 705
ideologies of language, see language
    ideology
ideology, 6, 9, 13–14, 31, 33, 70, 156, 190,
    195–6, 217, 226, 314, 316–17, 328,
    341–7, 425–6, 580, 612–13, 676, see
    also language ideology
imagined communities, 702
implicational scale, 427, 461–5
in-betweens (neither jocks nor burnouts),
    71–2, 141, 144, 148–50
indexicality, 11–12, 24–5, 195, 197–8,
    211, 216–17, 224, 251–3, 256, 311,
    317, 320–1, 323–4, 326, 328, 332–3,
    344, 346, 375–6, 383, 386–7, 390–1,
    394, 397, 398–402, 405–20, 428–9,
    477, 482, 562–3, 566–7, 570–1, 583,
    607–9, 611–12, 641, 663, 669, 672,
    676, 703–4
indirectness, 154, 174–6, 220, 230, 251,
    305, 346, 370, 401, 410, 414, 601,
    603, 605–6, 641
inference, 4, 67, 279, 293, 321, 479–80,
    483, 565, 577, 599–600, 604, 706

interactional sociolinguistics, 2, 8, 10, 18,
    261, 297n, 312, 577, 628
inter-ethnic communication, 101, 262,
    287–97
intergroup theory, 276–85
interpretive frames, 598, 609–10, 650
intonation, see prosody

jocks and burnouts, 32–3, 136–51, 215–27

language
    as behaviour, 15
    as code, 4–5
    as constructing social reality, 2, 13,
        15–17, 19–20, 31, 41, 155–7, 202,
        260, 299, 312, 323, 381, 411, 699
    as an organism, 30, 114, 117
    post-modern conceptions of, 17, 695–9
    as reflection of society, 4, 13–14, 27,
        30–1, 42, 50, 53, 61, 65, 103,
        106–17, 122, 126, 142, 144, 160,
        167, 225, 241, 253, 273–4, 279,
        308, 331–2, 351, 375, 383–4, 536,
        641, 654, 686
    as social action, see social action
    as social practice, see social practice
language attitudes, 15, 19, 57, 78, 108,
    113, 116, 341–7, 357–72, 394, 406,
    449, 474, 519–21, 542, 549, 551, 599,
    605, see also subjective orientation
language commodification, 156, 300, 328,
    561, 563, 580, 671–4, 702
language contact, 326–7, 430, 432, 475,
    484, 487, 512–13, 704–7
language crossing, 287–97, 299–309, 326,
    368, 580, 665–8, 703–4
language death, 432, 541–57
language ecology, 431, 526, 535
language functions, 7, 9, 448–9, 584, 647
language ideology, 6, 8, 25, 326, 343–4,
    374–7, 378–88, 390–403, 426, 428,
    430–2, 581, 701–4
language majority and minority, 14, 97,
    342, 393, 426, 431, 526–38, 684,
    688, 692, 697–8, 703–4
language planning, 345–6, 386, 394, 425,
    444, 476
language play, 156, 224, 317, 329, 337n,
    399, 401, 403, 649

language repertoires, 31, 271, 405, 430, 475, 482, 561–8, 586, 664, 675
language rights, 5, 342, 431, 440, 526–38, 580, 612
language shift, 394, 425, 427, 431–2, 457–71, 527–8, 532, 541–57
language variation and change, 2–4, 6–7, 12, 23–33, 35–47, 49–59, 60–5, 66–74, 75–90, 92–105, 107–16, 119–34, 136–51, 155, 159–60, 163–4, 166–7, 187–99, 217, 229, 246, 250–6, 259–60, 265–6, 269–71, 273–4, 277, 293, 305, 307, 311–24, 329, 344, 352, 359, 375–6, 384, 388, 392, 399, 402, 405–7, 415, 426, 428, 451–2, 457–71, 491, 578, 581, 585, 598, 606, 609, 616, 621, 675, 681, 695–6, 699–700, 706–7
  from above, 65, 563
  in apparent time, 28, 82, 89, 464
  from below, 65, 73, 563
  transmission of, 27, 66–74, 89, 551–2
lexical variation, 36, 67–8, 102–3, 156, 160, 216, 217, 229, 239, 265, 302, 305, 307–8, 369, 430, 452, 457, 523, 545–8, 599, 601
liminality, 292, 442, 579–80, 647, 676
lingua franca, 513, 519, 594, 667
linguascape, 580
linguistic landscapes, 285, 564, 665
linguistic marketplace, 33, 70, 143–5, 230, 247, 313, 329, 563, 658
linguistic relativity, 414, 560, 565–70, *see also* Sapir–Whorf Hypothesis
linguistic strategies, 129–30, 133–4, 156–7, 168–84, 196, 198, 201–12, 225, 233, 247, 271, 277, 279, 281–2, 315, 323, 327, 345, 363, 370, 458–9, 470, 478, 481, 483, 495–6, 499–500, 546, 593, 598–9, 601–2, 605–6, 608, 629, 638–40, 642, 649, 652, 656, 685, 700

markedness model, 429, 477–83
masculinity, 64, 155, 187–99, 201–12, 252, 262, 302, 349–55, 579, 631, 641–3, *see also* gender
mass media, 14, 45, 268, 278, 296, 302, 307, 327–8, 379, 381, 391, 398, 430, 563, 564, 609, 618, 652, 701–2, 705

Melanesian Pidgin, 430–1, 512–24
metalinguistics, 6, 116–17, 314, 343, 345, 390–1, 608, 668–9, 706
metapragmatics, 314, 345, 562, 610, 664, 671, 675, 677, 706
monolingualism, 270–2, 328, 335, 426, 428, 432, 459–60, 470, 473, 485–6, 500, 514, 532–3, 548–9, 551, 563, 570–1
morphological variation, 32, 66, 114, 119–21, 127, 308, 369, 408, 410, 430, 452, 542, 546–7, 552, 589, 601
multiple voicing, 155, 262–3, 294–5, 314–15, 709n

narrative, 579–80, 652–4, 682–8
nation and nationalism, 437–40, 561, 613
nerds, 215–27
non-standard language, *see* standard–non-standard language
nonverbal communication, 18, 165, 174, 278, 280, 284, 299–300, 409–10, 545, 576–7, 587, 594, 632, 648, 666
NORMS (non-mobile, old, rural, male speakers), 23
Northern Cities Shift (NCS), 24, 28, 46, 70–2, 74n, 147, 216, 359, 369

orthography, 344–5, 378–88

pantomime, 262–3, 318–24
performance, 8, 311–24, 326–37, 577–8, 579–80, 607–14, 665–77, 680–92, 694, 706
performative acts, 580, 676
performativity, 154, 157, 196, 202, 251–2, 263, 335–7, 674–7
phatic communion, 579, 647–8, 650, 664–5, 668
phonological variation, 2, 36, 38–40, 46, 50, 60–1, 65, 87, 103, 119, 136, 156, 189–90, 216–17, 302–3, 307, 321, 333, 407, 410, 453, 455, 458, 523, 542, 547, 589, 601, *see also* Northern Cities Shift
pidgins and creoles, 430–1, 512–24, *see also* Melanesian Pidgin
poetics, 607–14
poetry, 689–92

politeness, 113, 171, 271, 449, 594, 631, 637, 639–40, 643, *see also* facework

posh (accent), 27, 263, 317, 320–4, 369 and Cockney, 13, *see also* Received Pronunciation; standard–non-standard language

positivism, 15–16, 20, 26

power and solidarity, 13, 168–84, 197–8, 612

pragmatic variation, 87, 129–31, 369, 457

pragmatics, 405

prejudice, 13, 117, 341, 364, 366, 521, 685

prestige, 24, 45–6, 50–1, 53, 58n, 65n, 74n, 79, 98–9, 109–10, 117, 120, 187, 267, 273, 281, 300, 313, 349–50, 367, 449–50, 455, 458, 460, 468, 527, 529, 543, 556, 567, 570

presupposition, 408, 420n, 599–602

principle of accountability, 76–80

pronunciation, *see* accent

prosody, 18, 160–1, 165, 239–40, 253, 305, 408, 410, 495, 499, 577, 579, 588, 599–602, 626, 633

punning, *see* language play

quotative expressions, 28, 75–90, 262

race, 13, 54, 188, 237, 240–1, 243, 247, 252, 296, 297n, 445n, 698, 703

racism, 157, 241, 252, 255–6, 301–2, 307, 425–6, 442–5, 509

rap, *see* hip-hop

Received Pronunciation (RP), 273, 277, 317, 320–2, *see also* posh (accent); standard–non-standard language

recentering, 610–14

recontextualization, 608–14, 668, 671, 707

reflexivity, 6, 15, 25, 28, 43, 46–7, 62–4, 65n, 156, 211, 225, 246, 260, 295, 303–4, 314–16, 320, 324, 341, 343, 349–50, 356–72, 481, 552, 564, 568, 577–8, 580, 599, 608–9, 611, 613, 633, 695, 706

register, 4, 6, 160, 217, 225–6, 299, 327, 333, 337, 410, 429, 474, 505, 561, 593–4

research methods, 3, 7, 9, 15, 18–20, 24–6, 29–33, 36–7, 49, 53–5, 60–1, 120, 137, 150–1, 153–4, 203, 218, 225, 259, 261, 278, 297n, 327, 341–3, 351–2, 360, 428–9, 483, 490, 500, 578, 598, 601–2, 613, 632, 694, 696, 707

and data elicitation, 18–19, 36, 55, 359, 367, 602, 604, 695

empirical, 18, 26–7, 50, 92–3, 99, 140, 202, 296, 343, 479, 481–3, 523, 564, 566–7, 583–4, 594, 598, 601, 605, 609, 662, 695–6, 700, 702, 704–5

experimental, 15, 18, 26, 151, 160, 261, 342, 367, 395, 476, 584

and idealization, 6, 92–5, 107–8, 428

and interviews, 18, 25–7, 36–7, 49, 50, 53–5, 59n, 69, 82, 85, 111, 128, 137, 150–1, 156, 189–92, 205, 236–7, 266–8, 295, 297n, 302, 395, 486, 523, 555–6, 584, 600–1, 617, 643

and objectivity, 15, 20, 26, 31, 37, 51, 53, 110, 190, 283, 314, 393, 439

observation as, 9, 18–19, 33, 49–55, 67, 69, 120, 139–40, 151, 161, 197, 297n, 308, 341, 343, 359, 374, 380, 382, 395, 461, 483, 555–6, 575, 632, 640, 643

qualitative, 7, 15, 19–20, 97, 202, 227, 261, 341, 585, 588–600

quantitative, 7, 15, 19–20, 25–6, 29–30, 44, 61, 69, 76–7, 81–6, 88, 93, 103, 107–14, 117, 147, 166, 227, 259, 261, 270–2, 311–12, 341, 360, 371, 428, 478, 482, 484, 523, 544, 585, 588, 633, 706

questionnaires as, 18, 61, 151, 395, 461, 557

and sampling, 20, 27, 43, 50, 53, 90n, 137, 139, 149–50, 189, 342, 369, 464–5, 467, 696

surveys as, 15, 19, 23, 29, 36, 51, 53, 58n, 112, 136–7, 150–1, 259, 313, 342, 371, 380, 398, 474, 521–2, 528, 557, 567, 584, 600, 609, 696, 699

ritual and routine, 576, 579–80, 599, 601, 631–44, 662–77

ritual insults, 578–9, 615–30

Sapir–Whorf hypothesis, 410, 412, 565–6, 589, *see also* linguistic relativity

second language learning, 66, 278, 302, 307, 343, 372, 449, 522–3, 531–2, 544, 665, 668–9, 675, 677

semi-speaker, 544, 552–7

sex, 23, 27, 32–3, 41, 44, 54, 60, 63–5, 66–74, 75–82, 86–9, 102–4, 153–7, 159–69, 203, 229–30, 235–8, 242, 248, 250, 342, 349–55, 457–71, 579, 592, 641

sexism, 31, 114–16, 154, 445

sexuality, 153–7, 159–67, 187–99, 201–12, 229–48, 250–6, 302, 445, 561

shibboleth, 35

small talk, 4, 579–80, 646–60, 664–5

social action, 2, 8–10, 15, 27, 31, 323, 390, 411, 566, 694

social actors, 8–10, 32, 111, 115, 157, 202, 218, 380–2, 384–5, 430, 665

social class, 4, 6, 10, 13, 17, 23–7, 29–30, 39–46, 49–59, 60–5, 70–3, 92–105, 108, 110–11, 119–34, 136–51, 154–5, 157, 165, 179, 187, 188–9, 190, 196, 201–2, 212, 215, 217, 225–6, 237, 243, 246, 250–6, 311–24, 349–55, 386, 412–13, 439, 457–8, 567, 569, 595, 598, 602, 625–6, 697–8, 705

social constructionism, 2, 11, 13, 15–17, 19–20, 31, 41, 44, 106–17, 136–51, 155–7, 201–12, 215–27, 229–48, 250–6, 260–1, 264, 299–309, 311–24, 326–37, 341, 344, 346, 375–6, 380–3, 386, 411, 413–15, 426, 443, 480, 527, 529, 531, 536, 561, 563, 570–1, 579, 611, 601–14, 631, 633–42, 648, 650, 658, 675, 686, 699–704, 707–8

social context, 1–2, 4, 7–8, 12, 20, 29, 32–3, 36–7, 40–1, 46, 49, 55, 57, 60, 62–3, 72, 76–7, 79, 110–11, 141, 154, 159, 161, 171, 174, 176–7, 188–9, 201, 203, 211–12, 225, 227, 248, 251, 252–3, 256, 261–3, 268, 273, 276–9, 284–5, 291, 293, 305, 312–15, 320–1, 323, 327, 331, 337n, 342–6, 359, 384, 393, 409, 413, 416, 429–32, 481–3, 485, 487, 495, 498, 510–11, 516, 526–7, 529–30, 534, 536, 538, 542–3, 563–5, 568, 576–7, 578–80, 587–8, 591, 596, 599–600, 606–13, 634–5, 641, 647–51, 653–5, 671–2, 675–6, 681, 685, 700, 707

social meaning, 7, 9, 24, 37–8, 42, 111, 115, 134, 147, 149, 151, 192, 198, 218, 225, 251, 259, 265, 271, 429, 470, 481–3, 577–8, 675, 695

social practice, 3, 9, 13, 31, 33, 115, 137, 141, 149–50, 156, 196–7, 203, 216–17, 226–7, 311, 346, 580, 676, 700

social reality, 15–17, 31, 41, 44, 274, 294, 708

social networks, 11, 27–30, 33, 41–2, 69, 82, 92–105, 112, 123, 142, 149–50, 428, 461, 463, 464–7, 470

social order, 13, 16, 141, 144, 226, 287, 291, 316, 409, 411

social psychology of language, 260, 278, 342, 357–8, 363

social status, 5, 8, 12, 23–5, 29, 43, 45–7, 50–1, 58n, 63–4, 70–1, 73, 110, 114, 136, 138, 144–5, 147, 151, 154–5, 165–7, 171, 176, 189, 203, 205, 224, 226, 229, 267, 277, 281, 341, 345–6, 353, 355n, 359–60, 366–7, 383, 386, 388, 394, 397–8, 401–2, 410, 413, 420, 427, 431, 433, 449, 458, 460, 464, 469, 500, 521, 526, 529–31, 549, 566–71, 583, 654, 658, 676, 697, *see also* prestige; social stratification; stigmatization

social stratification, 17, 25–6, 44–7, 49–59, 60–5, 70, 73, 93, 136, 138, 150, 311, 544, 561–7

social structure, 8, 11, 15, 17, 36–7, 42, 63, 69–70, 108, 226–7, 274, 298, 411, 480, 595

social theory, 30, 108, 110, 113, 226, 380, 435–8, 445, 536, 571, 701, 704–5

socialization, 9, 16, 405–20, 698

sociolinguistics
 and anti-realist stance, 17, 263
 as social science, 1, 15–16, 109–10, 698, 707, 708n
 as socially constituted linguistics, 9–14, 106–17, 576
 and sociology, 8, 93, 108–9, 112–13, 116, 187, 215, 292, 435–6, 445n, 576, 581, 584, 589, 613

sociology of language, 1, 109, 410, 425–6, 436, 526, 542

sounding, 615–30

SPEAKING (Hymes's components of speech), 575, 584, 589–97

speech act, 584, 588, 603, 662–77

speech community, 12, 567, 581, 585–7, 600, 694–709

speech event, 50, 53–5, 188, 189, 313–14, 317, 429, 577–9, 584, 587–8, 590, 592–3, 596, 607, 615, 626, 628, 647–8, 667, see also SPEAKING

speech situation, 272, 475, 584, 587

speech style, see style of speech

stance, 192–6, 341–7, 405–20

standardization, 45, 116, 345, 379, 382, 385–6, 387–8, 447–8, 451

standard–non-standard language, 5–6, 14, 24–9, 44–6, 55–7, 104, 111, 116–17, 119–27, 136, 143–7, 149, 156, 196, 217, 252, 255, 266–7, 273, 279, 292, 305, 309, 312–14, 317, 320–1, 329, 342, 345, 350, 353–4, 359, 363, 368, 369, 379, 381–8, 397, 401–2, 427–8, 431, 447–55, 459–60, 474, 517, 520–4, 531, 543, 548, 585, 595, 601, 612, 621, 625, 697–8, see also posh (accent); Received Pronunciation

stereotypes, 24–5, 27, 42–4, 46–7, 71, 144, 153, 157, 217, 229, 240–1, 246, 248, 252–4, 256, 283, 291, 301, 322, 326, 344, 350–1, 354, 412, 577, 598, 631, 642–3, 650, 658, 703

stigmatization, 5, 24, 45–6, 297, 317, 341, 363, 520, 529, 549–50, 553, 557–8

street culture, 24, 301, 307, 578, 625

structuration theory, 17

style of speech, 8, 13, 24, 33, 136–51, 259–64, 265–74, 311–24, 588–9, 600

style-shifting, 13, 19, 32, 68, 124–7, 225, 242, 246, 260, 264–74, 278, 283, 321–4, 401, 429, 474, 594, 599, 600–1, 654–6

styling, 8, 32–3, 261, 263, 309, 312, 314–15, 326–7, 381

stylistic stratification, 50, 60–3, 68, 73, 124–7, 259, 269, 271, 274, 312

stylization, 8, 155, 259–64, 273, 287–97, 299–309, 311–24, 326, 706

subjective orientation, 2, 11–12, 20, 27, 37, 94, 283, 343, 345, 349–55, 409, 439, 478, 482, 654

symbolic capital, 24, 217, 220

syntactic variation, 2, 119–34, 156, 216–17, 223–4, 251, 265, 303–4, 308, 333, 369, 430, 452, 457, 461, 542, 548, 552, 588–9, 599

taboo, 145, 505, 578, 625

Tok Pisin, see Melanesian Pidgin

transnationalism, 262, 328, 561, 567–8, 570, 704–5

use variation, see register

user variation, see dialect

variationism, 2, 12, 23–33, 35–47, 49–59, 60–5, 75–90, 92–105
  correlational fallacy in, 30
  critiqued, 106–17, 696
  external and internal factors, 24, 38–47
  organic fallacy in, 31

verbal art, 607–9

verbal hygiene, 31, 116

verbal repertoire, see language repertoires

Verlan, see language play

vernacular, 5, 8, 24, 26, 29–30, 32–3, 38, 44, 46, 49, 66, 92–3, 98, 103, 112, 119–34, 138, 157, 252, 262–3, 284, 290, 295, 297, 298n, 299–301, 307, 313, 320–4, 341, 455, 594–5, 616, 676, 697–700

vernacular culture index, 32, 120–3

voice (as self), 210, 262, 273, 283, 291, 294–5, 313, 315, 317, 320–4, 398, 400, 476, 483, 509–11, 568, 612, 706

voicing, see stylization

ways of speaking, 432, 575–6, 589

women's language
  features of (Lakoff hypothesis), 153–4, 157, 160, 175, 229–30, 240, 252; as perfect woman stereotype, 229–48; as white woman style, 250–6
  vs. men's language, 7, 154, 229
  vs. powerless language, 2, 159–69

workplace communication, 631–44

world system, as context, 560–71

Printed and bound in the United States of America